THE MAMMOTH BOOK OF

Combat

Edited by Jon E. Lewis

ROBINSON   RUNNING PRESS
PHILADELPHIA · LONDON

Constable & Robinson Ltd

respondents
, 2001

ok of Combat

of this
he

dition

A copy of the British Library Cataloguing in
Publication Data is available from the British Library

ISBN: 978-1-78033-917-7 (paperback)
ISBN: 978-1-78033-918-4 (ebook)

First published in the United States in 2013 as *The Mammoth Book of Combat*
by Running Press Book Publishers, a Member of the Perseus Books Group

Books published by Running Press are available at special discounts for bulk purchases
in the United States by corporations, institutions, and other organizations. For
more information, please contact the Special Markets Department at the Perseus
Books Group, 2300 Chestnut Street, Suite 200, Philadelphia, PA 19103, or call
(800) 810-4145, ext. 5000, or e-mail special.markets@perseusbooks.com.

US ISBN: 978-0-7624-4812-8
US Library of Congress Control Number: 2012942536

9   8   7   6   5   4   3   2   1
Digit on the right indicates the number of this printing

Running Press Book Publishers
2300 Chestnut Street
Philadelphia, PA 19103-4371

Visit us on the web!
www.runningpress.com

Printed and bound in the UK

Contents

PART II

The Era of Total War, 1914–1946

PART III

The Savage Little Wars of Peace, 1950–2006

Contents

Foreword

Honest war reporters have never had it easy. From the earliest days of their trade to the present, cheerleaders rather than skeptics have been the most successful. The London *Times*' William Howard Russell, who covered the Crimea War to great acclaim, would discover just five years later how picking the wrong side could backfire when his predictions of a Union victory in the American Civil War scandalized his readers and led to his resignation. He was not, as he claimed, the "first and greatest" of war correspondents but he was indeed one of the "miserable" parents of a "luckless tribe" that has dared to ask the wrong questions of the odds-on favourites and paid for their insolence ever since, often with their lives.

The Civil War was perhaps the first war whose horror was revealed in heart-rending detail by at least some correspondents, for what could be glorious about a fratricide in which more Americans died than in WWII? Samuel Wilkeson of the *New York Times*, for example, reported on the slaughter at Gettysburg with great power and poignancy, delivering his dispatch having just learned that his own son had died.

It was the first great celebrity reporter, Richard Harding Davis, working for William Randolph Hearst's "yellow press", who delivered perhaps the most impactful newspaper report in history, in the run up to the Spanish-American War in 1898. "The Death of Rodriguez", the story of the public execution of a rebel, whom Davis watched die, "the blood from his breast sinking into the soil he had tried to free," changed public opinion in America like no other report before or since. Desperate to increase circulation, Hearst was delighted with Davis's breath-less propaganda. Davis was not a flat-out liar, however, and lesser figures had to be employed to guarantee Hearst the circu-lation-boosting conflict he so desired.

Davis was again in the thick of the action during the Russo-Japanese War in 1904, the first time a Western power was humiliated by an Asian nation. The Japanese were so strict in their censorship that Davis's celebrity grew not through his der-ring-do on the battlefield but because he managed to save Jack London, a fellow correspondent and world famous author of *The Call of the Wild*, from incarceration. London had struck a Japanese in frustration, having stewed with the rest of the press corps in Tokyo, barred from the front.

"The first casualty, when war comes, is truth." So declared American Senator Hiram Johnson at the height of the first great bloodbath of the last century: a war to end all wars in which the best and brightest in Europe were mowed down in Flanders for four long years. Throughout the First World War, censorship was even stricter than that suffered by Jack London at the hands of the Japanese. Even jingoists like Rudyard Kipling – "There are human beings and Germans" – con-fronted a military whose leaders feared and therefore despised war correspondence.

Britain's Secretary of State for War, Lord Kitchener, was chief among the detractors, describing the press as "drunken swabs". Rare was the sober report throughout the war, even when young men were falling in the tens of thousands each week on the Somme and at Verdun for just a few yards of barbed wire and mud. It is doubtful that America's entry into the con-flict, shamefully managed throughout with horrendous and callous loss of life, would have occurred had it not been for the hysterical reporting of much of the American press.

The truth of war was still hard to find between the two world wars, whether in Russia or Spain, where ideologies violently divided nations. As Europe teetered on the brink yet again, George Orwell wrote from the Spanish Civil War, trying to warn of the horrors of fascism. Yet he left the conflict disillusioned by all sides, disgusted by the bias of left and right: "I saw newspa-per reports which did not bear any relation to the facts, not even the relationship which is implied in an ordinary lie."

The Second World War was, by contrast, perhaps a golden age of frontline prose, starring such humanistic scribblers as Ernie Pyle whose sparse and heart-felt reports on ordinary GIs were adored by his subjects and readers alike. To this day, historians of that conflict – a "crazy hysterical mess" as John Steinbeck called it – swoon over Pyle's elegiac account of the death of a captain called Waskow in Italy. Unlike Hemingway's self-regarding reports, Pyle's beautifully crafted story of young men mourning their young leader still evokes the immense sadness of a war in which Pyle saw many "swell kids having their heads blown off".

Pyle was in fact so nauseated by what he had seen that he eventually "lost track of the whole point of the war". But it did have a point. Although it entailed the death in Europe of over 130,000 mostly working-class Americans, with a final butcher's bill of over fifty million lives around the globe, the fighting in WWII was without doubt necessary if barbarism was to be defeated. The concentration camps visited by Richard Dimbleby and others in 1945 were all the evidence one needed of why the sacrifice was so important, if no less palatable. Tragically, Pyle was one of 53 US-accredited reporters to lose their lives covering the war, killed just a few months from the end of the war by a Japanese machine gunner.

During the Korean War in the early 1950s, reporting restrictions continued but a more critical tone began to emerge in the press as a whole. It was also marked by the extraordinary bravery of Marguerite Higgins, ambitious, blonde, the first woman to enter Dachau in 1945, and the first to win a Pulitzer Prize for foreign reporting thanks to her work in Korea. She did not plan to marry, she quipped, until she found a man who was as exciting as war. For all her bravado, however, she had to fight sexist generals as much as she did the elements and censorship in order to get her stories from the battlefront.

The impact of the military-industrial complex that President Eisenhower warned of in 1961, which has since embroiled America in seemingly endless combat around the globe, has imbued war reporting since Korea with a far darker, nihilistic tinge. As the next major war dragged on in Vietnam, for more and more reporters so much of what they were witnessing no longer had any moral foundation. The sacrifice was seemingly in vain, as was the gross expenditure and the destruction.

At the height of the Vietnam War, half of Americans had no idea what the war was about. Today, far more still don't. What would become "the longest running front-page story in history", wreaking untold environmental damage and killing at least half a million Vietnamese civilians, began in earnest in 1962 and lasted more than a decade. For year after year, the war escalated with hundreds of reporters noting the daily body counts. Only when Walter Cronkite raised doubts from a US television studio in 1968, thousands of miles from Saigon and Khe Sanh, did many Americans first begin to wonder if all the blood and sacrifice was worth it.

The war couldn't last long enough for some of those actually covering it. To many of the male correspondents, noted the perceptive Nora Ephron, "the war is not hell. It is fun." Perhaps the most skilled of the stalwarts was New Zealander Peter Arnett, who spent more time covering the war than any other reporter. "As hard-boiled as a Chinese thousand-year-old egg," according to another astute female observer, Marina Warner, Arnett was notable for his emotional detachment, at least in his reporting. Many others were far less objective, providing visceral, unforgettable images of the Green Machine sinking further into the South East Asian quagmire of hubris and bullshit that led to the US's humiliating withdrawal in 1975. Amid all the madness and hallucinatory scenes, young writers such as Michael Herr managed to transcend the confines and clichés of deadline reporting, producing prose of lasting eloquence about young Americans performing for nightly news broadcasts, "doing little guts and glory Leatherneck dances under fire, getting their pimples shot off for the networks".

The Vietnam War was, on reflection, arguably covered better than any in history, certainly by more journalists from more countries for longer than any other conflict. "But that is not saying a lot," the Australian journalist Phillip Knightley has observed in his classic book, *The First Casualty*, an eviscerating examination of the war correspondent as "hero and myth maker". "With a million-dollar corps of correspondents in Vietnam the war in Cambodia was kept hidden for a year."

Barely a generation later, determined not to allow the press to lose them another war, the politicians who planned the invasion of Iraq in 2003 made sure things would be done right. They had their usual way with the eager to please military, which proudly introduced to primetime audiences "Shock and Awe"'s most potent weapon, far more effective than a SCUD missile – the "embedded reporter". Every hack knew the only option was to get in bed with the military's public relations corps in the hope of a ride with a bunch of grunts. The resulting exclusives usually entailed sweating in a flack jacket in a Bradley fighting vehicle while dodging IEDs. Other than the reporters' egos, little was revealed. The fog of war got only thicker the closer most got to the grunts they were covering.

August sections of the media had built the case for the war in Iraq. Short and victorious conflicts are always great for circulation and ratings. It was expected to be both. And indeed much of the coverage in the first heady weeks after invasion was predictably gung-ho, the kind of "yellow journalism" that would have made Hearst proud. The Lebanese-American reporter Anthony Shadid was one exception. His March 2003 report on the burial of Iraqi civilians – the first collateral damage of the war – raised questions that few cared to answer back in Washington where post 9-11 hysteria had been shamelessly whipped up to aggrandize men who had ducked out of service in Vietnam: "If the Americans are intent on liberation, why are innocent people dying? If they want to attack the government, why do bombs fall on civilians? How can they have such formidable technology and make such tragic mistakes?"

Ten years later, Shadid is sadly no longer with us, dead on assignment covering Assad's atrocities in Syria. But the question civilians ask – how they, not the men in uniform, do most of the dying – is still a familiar lament as drones, not Hueys or B-52s, strike suspected militants, terrorists as well as innocents, on an almost daily basis. Indeed, there is no end in sight to the suffering in Iraq and Afghanistan despite a decade of countless reporters' questions.

It is not the reporters' fault that so few lessons have been learnt from so many conflicts. The fact is we are a destructive species. To pretend otherwise is to be ignorant of history or in denial. War gives men meaning. It is addictive – to combatants, megalomaniacs and journalists, male and female as the reporting in recent years of Janine di Giovianni and Christina Lamb, to name but two women, has shown.

Any writer worth their salt will tell you little comes close to the adrenaline high of bullets cracking over one's head as you fumble for a notebook. As many of the brave reporters included in this compelling anthology would attest, there's nothing quite as effective as a stiff shot of combat when it comes to sharpening your prose. Thankfully, at least every war produces its fair share of great writing, even when censorship is at its most stringent and suffocating.

Alex Kershaw

Introduction

*"Those newly invented curse to armies who eat all the rations of
the fighting man and do no work at all."*

So famously wrote Sir Garnet Wolseley in *The Soldier's Pocket
Book* of 1869. The "curse", of course, were the war correspondents who gathered to observe and report the military endeavours
of Victorian Britain. And sometimes find those endeavours
wanting, hence the spleen in Wolseley's words.

War correspondents, though, weren't quite a Victorian invention. One Henry Crabb Robinson was employed by *The Times*
to report on Napoleon's campaign along the Elbe in 1807. But
by the time Robinson's dispatch "from the seat of war" had
wended its leisurely postal way to London three weeks later it
wasn't news. It was olds.

Real war journalism needed something else. It needed technology, some means of instantly communicating the story back
to the paper. This came with the invention of the telegraph in
the 1840s, first used for reports of war by William Howard Russell of *The Times* in the Crimea in 1854. Moreover, whereas
Robinson had written up his accounts from very second-hand
sources – he didn't actually deign to visit Napoleon's front line
– Russell was "eyewitness" to the war in the Crimea, living and
marching with the troops (and, yes, eating their rations). With
combat *reportage* plus instant communication, the era of the war
correspondent had arrived, fathered in by the bearded Irishman
Russell. It is difficult to underestimate Russell's impact on his
times or the business of reporting war. His dispatches highlight-
ing military bungling and the lack of proper food and clothing

afforded the British troops resulted in public outrage and eventually in reform. Sales of *The Times* shot up and soon every major newspaper in the Western world had a combat correspondent aboard to satisfy the readers' seemingly insatiable appetite for news of war. After all, war is the ultimate press story – human interest plus the destiny of nations. Nothing compares to it.

Successful as Russell was, he was also bedevilled by the dilemmas that would face all who walked in his bootsteps. There were vociferous charges that his dispatches provided the enemy with information and undermined public and military morale. Stung by the criticisms of succouring the enemy, Russell offered his reports up for vetting. This was refused, but the problems of Truth v National Security would always henceforth haunt the war correspondent, as Russell himself found a decade later when he was chased out of America for writing – accurately – of Union soldiers running away at Bull Run. Meanwhile, his prophecy that the Confederacy would lose the struggle angered the readers of the pro-South *Times*. Abused on all sides, Russell handed in his resignation and began his own newspaper, the *Army and Navy Gazette*.

Of course, not a few war correspondents when the bullets have started flying have forsaken objectivity for propaganda, spinning lies for political causes and masters. More still have found the reporting of war hampered by censorship and a tight-lipped military. These are the occupational hazards of war journalism. Some wars, though, have been "freer" than others. Censorship in the First World War was gargantuan. At first Kitchener branded war correspondents "outlaws" and barred them from the front line, before cleverly integrating them into the war machine as semi-official mouthpieces. The slaughters on the Western Front went almost unknown on the Home Front because war journalists would not or could not report them. The years 1914–18 were the dog days of the craft. To get a good story one American journalist, Floyd Gibbons, resorted himself to going "over the top" at Belleau Wood in 1917 and losing an eye in the process.

Fast-forward fifty years to Vietnam, arguably the freest war to report. Sure, there were the heavy-handed official briefings in Saigon known – by the typewriter boys and girls – as "The Five

O'Clock Follies", but MACV (Military Assistance Command Vietnam) did little to put obstacles in the correspondents' way. Hell, MACV even flew "warcos" to the front line. Turn up and climb aboard, no questions asked. For journalists, Vietnam was the Good War. Of course when the USA lost the match v Ho Chi Minh's pyjama-clad warriors, the warcos got the blame. Their vivid, painful reports, went the military's let-out, had plunged a pen into America's back and bled her of the morale needed to fight the "gooks".

Russell would have recognized the brass's complaint.

For the most part, the 101 war dispatches collected here are by those journalists who were fearless of death and bureaucracy and brought the truth home. There are a few curiosities – a Red Army correspondent's high-patriotic account of the Battle of Berlin, George Warrington Steevens's imperial pomp at the re-interring of Gordon's bones in the Sudan, the *New York Post*'s politic editorial on the 1940 draft – but the remainder tell us of the world's wars over 150 years in words as full of authenticity as they are of understanding, imagery and feeling. War journalism is reportage, is poetry, is the first draft of military history. They say that a picture can paint a thousand words, but a thousand words by Michael Herr, by Richard Harding Davis, by John Reed, by Ernie Pyle, will tell you everything, everything you ever wanted to know about a certain historical situation. Plus the nature of war itself. And what a nature. War is hell, but it is also a prodigality of other things. Death, life, suffering, nobility, depravity, courage, torture – small wonder that the craft of war correspondence has not only attracted the best journalists but some of the best writers period, drawn to war like moths to a flame. Those authors who have done their tour of duty as a warco include Ernest Hemingway, John Steinbeck, John Dos Passos, Rudyard Kipling – to name but four heavyweights.

Of course, sometimes the flames burn. Reporting the wars has cost the lives of a small legion of correspondents, among them Ernie Pyle and Nick Tomalin, both of whom are represented on the following pages.

War correspondence is a dangerous job, but someone has got to do it.

The readers demand it. Need it. Warfare has changed much since Russell's day, so has the technology of war journalism, from telegraph to sat phone, and live commentary as you watch war-u-like on the tube. (The dispatches in this book are arranged in chronological order, to catch and reflect these developments.) The readers' hunger for war news has changed too. It's even greater. In the Information Age the one information you can't do without is Mars's latest havoc.

Somewhere, a war correspondent is dying to give it to you.

Part I

The Age of Empire and Emancipation, 1854–1913

The Crimean War

WILLIAM HOWARD RUSSELL

The Battle of Balaclava

An Irishman who fell into journalism by accident, Russell was employed by the London *Times* to accompany the British army on its 1854 mission to Crimea. The job appeared a pleasant jaunt – the army believed it had only to rattle its sabres to deter Russia from spreading southwards – but turned into a two-year tour of grinding journalistic duty, during which Russell's accurate and clear dispatches made him the most famous war reporter of the Victorian era. His criticisms of the army's system of command, its unsuitable clothing and its poor food, led to sweeping reform. After the Crimean War, Russell reported the Indian Mutiny, the American Civil War (where his candid account of Union cowardice at Bull Run obliged him to leave the country), the Franco-Prussian War and the Zulu War. He was knighted for his services to journalism.

Russell pioneered the use of the telegraph, although many of his pieces were written as long descriptive letters, including his celebrated account of the Battle of Balaclava, 25 October 1854. This proved the major engagement of the Crimean War, and is forever remembered for its melancholic "Charge of the Light Brigade".

The Times, 14 November 1854

If the exhibition of the most brilliant valour, of the excess of courage, and of a daring which would have reflected lustre on the best days of chivalry can afford full consolation for the disaster of today, we can have no reason to regret the melancholy loss which we sustained in a contest with a savage and barbarian enemy.

I shall proceed to describe, to the best of my power, what occurred under my own eyes, and to state the facts which I have heard from men whose veracity is unimpeachable, reserving to myself the exercise of the right of private judgement in making public and in suppressing the details of what occurred on this memorable day . . .

It will be remembered that in a letter sent by last mail from this place it was mentioned that eleven battalions of Russian infantry had crossed the Tchernaya, and that they threatened the rear of our position and our communication with Balaclava. Their bands could be heard playing at night by travellers along the Balaclava road to the camp, but they "showed" but little during the day and kept up among the gorges and mountain passes through which the roads to Inkermann, Simpheropol, and the south-east of the Crimea wind towards the interior. It will be recollected also that the position we occupied in reference to Balaclava was supposed by most people to be very strong – even impregnable. Our lines were formed by natural mountain slopes in the rear, along which the French had made very formidable intrenchments. Below those intrenchments, and very nearly in a right line across the valley beneath, are four conical hillocks, one rising above the other as they recede from our lines . . . On the top of each of these hills the Turks had thrown up earthen redoubts, defended by 250 men each, and armed with two or three guns – some heavy ship guns – lent by us to them, with one artilleryman in each redoubt to look after them. These hills cross the valley of Balaclava at the distance of about two and a half miles from the town. Supposing the spectator then to take his stand on one of the heights forming the rear of our camp before Sebastopol, he would see the town of Balaclava, with its scanty shipping, its narrow strip of water, and its old forts on his right hand; immediately below he would behold the valley and plain of coarse meadowland, occupied by our cavalry tents, and stretching from the base of the ridge on which he stood to the foot of the formidable heights on the other side; he would see the French trenches lined with Zouaves a few feet beneath, and distant from him, on the slope of the hill; a

Turkish redoubt lower down, then another in the valley, then in a line with it some angular earthworks, then, in succession, the other two redoubts up Canrobert's Hill.

At the distance of two or two and a half miles across the valley there is an abrupt rocky mountain range of most irregular and picturesque formation, covered with scanty brushwood here and there, or rising into barren pinnacles and plateaux of rock. In outline and appearance, this position of the landscape is wonderfully like the Trossachs. A patch of blue sea is caught in between the overhanging cliffs of Balaclava as they close in the entrance to the harbour on the right. The camp of the Marines pitched on the hillsides more than one thousand feet above the level of the sea is opposite to you as your back is turned to Sebastopol and your right side towards Balaclava. On the road leading up the valley, close to the entrance of the town and beneath these hills, is the encampment of the 93rd Highlanders.

The cavalry lines are nearer to you below, and are some way in advance of the Highlanders, and nearer to the town than the Turkish redoubts. The valley is crossed here and there by small waves of land. On your left the hills and rocky mountain ranges gradually close in toward the course of the Tchernaya, till at three or four miles' distance from Balaclava the valley is swallowed up in a mountain gorge and deep ravines, above which rise tier after tier of desolate whitish rock garnished now and then by bits of scanty herbage, and spreading away towards the east and south, where they attain the alpine dimensions of Tschatir Dagh. It is very easy for an enemy at the Belbek, or in command of the road of Mackenzie's Farm, Inkermann, Simpheropol, or Bakhchisarai, to debouch through these gorges at any time upon this plain from the neck of the valley, or to march from Sebastopol by the Tchernaya and to advance along it towards Balaclava, till checked by the Turkish redoubts on the southern side or by the fire from the French works on the northern side, i.e., the side which in relation to the valley of Balaclava forms the rear of our position.

At half past seven o'clock this morning an orderly came galloping in to the headquarters camp from Balaclava, with the news that at dawn a strong corps of Russian horse supported by guns and battalions of infantry had marched into the valley, and had already nearly dispossessed the Turks of the redoubt No. 1 (that on Canrobert's Hill, which is farthest from our lines) and that they were opening fire on the redoubts Nos. 2, 3 and 4, which would speedily be in their hands unless the Turks offered a stouter resistance than they had done already.

Orders were dispatched to Sir George Cathcart and to HRH the Duke of Cambridge to put their respective divisions, the 4th and 1st, in motion for the scene of action, and intelligence of the advance of the Russians was also furnished to General Canrobert. Immediately on receipt of the news the General commanded General Bosquet to get the Third Division under arms, and sent a strong body of artillery and some 200 Chasseurs d'Afrique to assist us in holding the valley. Sir Colin Campbell, who was in command of Balaclava, had drawn up the 93rd Highlanders a little in front of the road to the town at the first news of the advance of the enemy. The Marines on the heights got under arms; the seamen's batteries and Marines' batteries on the heights close to the town were manned, and the French artillerymen and the Zouaves prepared for action along their lines. Lord Lucan's little camp was the scene of great excitement. The men had not had time to water their horses; they had not broken their fast from the evening of the day before, and had barely saddled at the first blast of the trumpet, when they were drawn up on the slope behind the redoubts in front of the camp to operate on the enemy's squadrons. It was soon evident that no reliance was to be placed on the Turkish infantrymen or artillerymen. All the stories we had heard about their bravery behind stone walls and earthworks proved how differently the same or similar people fight under different circumstances. When the Russians advanced the Turks fired a few rounds at them, got frightened at the distance of their supports in the rear, looked round, received a few shots and shell, and then "bolted", and fled with an agility quite at variance with the commonplace notions of oriental deportment on the battlefield. But Turks on the Danube are very different beings from Turks in the Crimea, as it appears that the Russians of Sebastopol are not at all like the Russians of Silistria.

Soon after eight Lord Raglan and his staff turned out and cantered towards the rear of our position. The booming of artillery, the spattering roll of musketry, were heard rising from the valley, drowning the roar of the siege guns in front before Sebastopol. As I rode in the direction of the firing over the thistles and large stones which cover the undulating plain which stretches away towards Balaclava, on a level with the summit of the ridges above it, I observed a French light infantry regiment (the 27th, I think) advancing with admirable care and celerity from our right towards the ridge near the telegraph house, which was already lined with companies of French infantry, while mounted officers scampered along its broken outline in every direction.

General Bosquet, a stout soldierlike-looking man, who reminds one of the old *genre* of French generals as depicted at Versailles, followed, with his staff and small escort of Hussars, at a gallop. Faint white clouds rose here and there above the hill from the cannonade below. Never did the painter's eye rest upon a more beautiful scene than I beheld from the ridge. The fleecy vapours still hung around the mountain tops and mingled with the ascending volumes of smoke; the patch of sea sparkled freshly in the rays of the morning sun, but its light was eclipsed by the flashes which gleamed from the masses of armed men below.

Looking to the left towards the gorge we beheld six compact masses of Russian infantry which had just debouched from the mountain passes near the Tchernaya, and were slowly advancing with solemn stateliness up the valley. Immediately in their front was a regular line of artillery, of at least twenty pieces strong. Two batteries of light guns were already a mile in advance of them, and were playing with energy on the redoubts, from which feeble puffs of smoke came at long intervals. Behind the guns, in front of the infantry, were enormous bodies of cavalry. They were in six compact squares, three on each flank, moving down *en échelon* towards us, and the valley was lit up with the blaze of their sabres and lance points and gay accoutrements. In their front, and extending along the intervals between each battery of guns, were clouds of mounted skirmishers, wheeling and whirling in the front of their march like autumn leaves tossed by the wind. The Zouaves close to us were lying like tigers at the spring, with ready rifles in hand, hidden chin deep by the earthworks which run along the line of these ridges on our rear, but the quick-eyed Russians were manoeuvring on the other side of the valley, and did not expose their columns to attack. Below the

Zouaves we could see the Turkish gunners in the redoubts, all in confusion as the shells burst over them. Just as I came up the Russians had carried No. 1 redoubt, the farthest and most elevated of all, and their horsemen were chasing the Turks across the interval which lay between it and redoubt No. 2. At that moment the cavalry, under Lord Lucan, were formed in glittering masses – the Light Brigade, under Lord Cardigan, in advance of the Heavy Brigade, under Brigadier-General Scarlett, in reserve. They were drawn up just in front of their encampment, and were concealed from the view of the enemy by a slight "wave" in the plain. Considerably to the rear of their right, the 93rd Highlanders were drawn up in line, in front of the approach to Balaclava. Above and behind them on the heights, the Marines were visible through the glass, drawn up under arms, and the gunners could be seen ready in the earthworks, in which were placed the heavy ships' guns. The 93rd had originally been advanced somewhat more into the plain, but the instant the Russians got possession of the first redoubt they opened fire on them from our own guns, which inflicted some injury, and Sir Colin Campbell "retired" his men to a better position. Meantime the enemy advanced his cavalry rapidly. To our inexpressible disgust we saw the Turks in redoubt No. 2 fly at their approach. They ran in scattered groups across towards redoubt No. 3, and towards Balaclava, but the horse-hoof of the Cossacks was too quick for them, and sword and lance were busily plied among the retreating band. The yells of the pursuers and pursued were plainly audible. As the Lancers and Light Cavalry of the Russians advanced they gathered up their skirmishers with great speed and in excellent order – the shifting trails of men, which played all over the valley like moonlight on water, contracted, gathered up, and the little *peloton* in a few moments became a solid column. Then up came their guns, in rushed their gunners to the abandoned redoubt, and the guns of No. 2 redoubt soon played with deadly effect upon the dispirited defenders of No. 3 redoubt. Two or three shots in return from the earthworks, and all is silent. The Turks swarm over the earthworks and run in confusion towards the town, firing their muskets at the enemy as they run. Again the solid column of cavalry opens like a fan, and resolves itself into the "long spray" of skirmishers. It laps the flying Turks, steel flashes in the air, and down go the poor Muslim quivering on the plain, split through fez and musket-guard to the chin and breast-belt. There is no support for them. It is evident the Russians have been too quick for us. The Turks have been too quick also, for they have not held their redoubts long enough to enable us to bring them help. In vain the naval guns on the heights fire on the Russian cavalry; the distance is too great for shot or shell to reach. In vain the Turkish gunners in the earthen batteries which are placed along the French intrenchments strive to protect their flying countrymen; their shots fly wide and short of the swarming masses. The Turks betake themselves towards the Highlanders, where they check their flight and form into companies on the flanks of the Highlanders.

As the Russian cavalry on the left of their line crown the hill, across the valley they perceive the Highlanders drawn up at the distance of some half-mile, calmly awaiting their approach. They halt, and squadron after squadron flies up from the rear, till they have a body of some 1500 men along the ridge – Lancers and Dragoons and Hussars. Then they move *en échelon* in two bodies, with another in reserve. The cavalry who have been pursuing the Turks on the right are coming up the ridge beneath us, which conceals our cavalry from view. The heavy brigade in advance is drawn up in two columns. The first column consists of the Scots Greys and of their old companions in glory, the Enniskillens; the second of the 4th Royal Irish, of the 5th Dragoon Guards, and of the 1st Royal Dragoons. The Light Cavalry Brigade is on their left in two lines also. The silence is oppressive; between the cannon bursts, one can hear the champing of bits and the clink of sabres in the valley below. The Russians on their left drew breath for a moment, and then in one grand line dashed at the Highlanders. The ground flies beneath their horses' feet – gathering speed at every stride they dash on towards that thin red streak topped with a line of steel. The Turks fire a volley at 800 yards, and run. As the Russians come within 600 yards, down goes that line of steel in front, and out rings a rolling volley of Minié musketry. The distance is too great. The Russians are not checked, but still sweep onwards with the whole force of horse and man, through the smoke, here and there knocked over by the shot of our batteries above. With breathless suspense everyone awaits the bursting of the wave upon the line of Gaelic rock; but ere they came within 150 yards, another deadly volley flashes from the levelled rifles, and carries death and terror into the Russians. They wheel about, open files right and left, and fly back faster than they came.

"Bravo Highlanders! Well done!" shout the excited spectators; but events thicken. The Highlanders and their splendid front are soon forgotten. Men scarcely have a moment to think of this fact that the 93rd never altered their formation to receive that tide of horsemen.

"No," said Sir Colin Campbell, "I did not think it worth while to form them even four deep!"

The ordinary British line, two deep, was quite sufficient to repel the attack of these Muscovite chevaliers. Our eyes were, however, turned in a moment on our own cavalry. We saw Brigadier-General Scarlett ride along in front of his massive squadrons. The Russians – evidently *corps d'élite* – their light-blue jackets embroidered with silver lace, were advancing on their left at an easy gallop, towards the brow of the hill. A forest of lances glistened in their rear, and several squadrons of grey-coated dragoons moved up quickly to support them as they reached the summit. The instant they came in sight the trumpets of our cavalry gave out the warning blast which told us all that in another moment we would see the shock of battle beneath our very eyes. Lord Raglan, all his staff and escort, and groups of officers, the Zouaves, the French generals and officers, and bodies of French infantry on the height, were spectators of the scene as though they were looking on the stage from the boxes of a theatre. Nearly everyone dismounted and sat down, and not a word was said.

The Russians advanced down the hill at a slow canter, which they changed to a trot and at last nearly halted. The first line was at least double the length of ours – it was three times as deep. Behind them was a similar line, equally strong and compact. They evidently despised their insignificant-looking enemy, but their time was come.

The trumpets rang out through the valley, and the Greys and Enniskillens went right at the centre of the Russian cavalry. The space between them was only a few hundred yards; it was scarce enough to let the horses "gather way", nor had the men quite space sufficient for the full play of their sword arms. The

Russian line brings forward each wing as our cavalry advance and threaten to annihilate them as they pass on. Turning a little to their left, so as to meet the Russians' right, the Greys rush on with a cheer that thrills to every heart – the wild shout of the Enniskillens rises through the air at the same moment. As lightning flashes through a cloud the Greys and Enniskillens pierced through the dark masses of the Russians. The shock was but for a moment. There was a clash of steel and a light play of sword blades in the air, and then the Greys and the redcoats disappear in the midst of the shaken and quivering columns. In another moment we see them merging and dashing on with diminished numbers, and in broken order, against the second line, which is advancing against them to retrieve the fortune of the charge.

It was a terrible moment. "God help them! They are lost!" was the exclamation of more than one man, and the thought of many. With unabated fire the noble hearts dashed at their enemy – it was a fight of heroes. The first line of Russians which had been smashed utterly by our charge, and had fled off at one flank and towards the centre, were coming back to swallow up our handful of men. By sheer steel and sheer courage Enniskillen and Scot were winning their desperate way right through the enemy's squadrons, and already grey horses and redcoats had appeared right at the rear of the second mass, when, with irresistible force, like one bolt from a bow, the 1st Royals, the 4th Dragoon Guards, and the 5th Dragoon Guards rushed at the remnants of the first line of the enemy, went through it as though it were made of pasteboard, and dashing on the second body of Russians, as they were still disordered by the terrible assault of the Greys and their companions, put them to utter rout. This Russian horse in less than five minutes after it met our dragoons was flying with all its speed before a force certainly not half its strength.

A cheer burst from every lip – in the enthusiasm officers and men took off their caps and shouted with delight, and thus keeping up the scenic character of their position, they clapped their hands again and again . . .

And now occurred the melancholy catastrophe which fills us all with sorrow. It appears that the Quartermaster General, Brigadier Airey, thinking that the Light Cavalry had not gone far enough in front when the enemy's horse had fled, gave an order in writing to Captain Nolan, 15th Hussars, to take to Lord Lucan, directing His Lordship "to advance" his cavalry nearer to the enemy. A braver soldier than Captain Nolan the army did not possess. He was known to all his arm of the service for his entire devotion to his profession, and his name must be familiar to all who take interest in our cavalry for his excellent work published a year ago on our drill and system of remount and breaking horses. I had the pleasure of his acquaintance, and I know he entertained the most exalted opinions respecting the capabilities of the English horse soldier. Properly led, the British Hussar and Dragoon could in his mind break square, take batteries, ride over columns of infantry, and pierce any other cavalry in the world, as if they were made of straw. He thought they had not had the opportunity of doing all that was in their power, and that they had missed even such chances as they had offered to them – that, in fact, they were in some measure disgraced. A matchless rider and a first-rate swordsman, he held in contempt, I am afraid, even grape and canister. He rode off with his orders to Lord Lucan. He is now dead and gone.

God forbid I should cast a shade on the brightness of his honour, but I am bound to state what I am told occurred when he reached His Lordship. I should premise that, as the Russian cavalry retired, their infantry fell back towards the head of the valley, leaving men in three of the redoubts they had taken and abandoning the fourth. They had also placed some guns on the heights over their position, on the left of the gorge. Their cavalry joined the reserves, and drew up in six solid divisions, in an oblique line, across the entrance to the gorge. Six battalions of infantry were placed behind them, and about thirty guns were drawn up along their line, while masses of infantry were also collected on the hills behind the redoubts on our right. Our cavalry had moved up to the ridge across the valley, on our left, as the ground was broken in front, and had halted in the order I have already mentioned.

When Lord Lucan received the order from Captain Nolan and had read it, he asked, we are told, "Where are we to advance to?"

Captain Nolan pointed with his finger to the line of the Russians, and said, "There are the enemy, and there are the guns, sir, before them. It is your duty to take them," or words to that effect, according to the statements made since his death.

Lord Lucan with reluctance gave the order to Lord Cardigan to advance upon the guns, conceiving that his orders compelled him to do so. The noble Earl, though he did not shrink, also saw the fearful odds against him. Don Quixote in his tilt against the windmill was not near so rash and reckless as the gallant fellows who prepared without a thought to rush on almost certain death.

It is a maxim of war that "cavalry never act without support", that "infantry should be close at hand when cavalry carry guns, as the effect is only instantaneous", and that it is necessary to have on the flank of a line of cavalry some squadrons in column, the attack on the flank being most dangerous. The only support our Light Cavalry had was the reserve of Heavy Cavalry at a great distance behind them – the infantry and guns being far in the rear. There were no squadrons in column at all, and there was a plain to charge over before the enemy's guns were reached of a mile and a half in length.

At ten past eleven our Light Cavalry Brigade rushed to the front. They numbered as follows, as well as I could ascertain:

	MEN
4th Light Dragoons	118
8th Irish Hussars	104
11th Prince Albert's Hussars	110
13th Light Dragoons	130
17th Lancers	145
	Total 607 sabres

The whole brigade scarcely made one effective regiment, according to the numbers of continental armies; and yet it was more than we could spare. As they passed towards the front, the Russians opened on them from the guns in the redoubts on the right, with volleys of musketry and rifles.

They swept proudly past, glittering in the morning sun in all the pride and splendour of war. We could hardly believe the evidence of our senses! Surely that handful of men were not going to charge an army in position? Alas! it was but too true – their desperate valour knew no bounds, and far indeed was it removed from its so-called better part – discretion. They advanced in two lines, quickening their pace as they closed towards the enemy. A more fearful spectacle was never witnessed than by those who, without the power to aid, beheld their heroic countrymen rushing to the arms of death. At the distance of 1200 yards the whole line of the enemy belched forth, from thirty iron mouths, a flood of smoke and flame, through which hissed the deadly balls. Their flight was marked by instant gaps in our ranks, by dead men and horses, by steeds flying wounded or riderless across the plain. The first line was broken – it was joined by the second, they never halted or checked their speed an instant. With diminished ranks, thinned by those thirty guns, which the Russians had laid with the most deadly accuracy, with a halo of flashing steel above their heads, and with a cheer which was many a noble fellow's death cry, they flew into the smoke of the batteries; but ere they were lost from view, the plain was strewed with their bodies and with the carcasses of horses. They were exposed to an oblique fire from the batteries on the hills on both sides, as well as to a direct fire of musketry.

Through the clouds of smoke we could see their sabres flashing as they rode up to the guns and dashed between them, cutting down the gunners as they stood. The blaze of their steel, as an officer standing near me said, was "like the turn of a shoal of mackerel". We saw them riding through the guns, as I have said; to our delight we saw them returning, after breaking through a column of Russian infantry, and scattering them like chaff, when the flank fire of the battery on the hill swept them down, scattered and broken as they were. Wounded men and dismounted troopers flying towards us told the sad tale – demigods could not have done what they had failed to do. At the very moment when they were about to retreat, an enormous mass of lancers was hurled upon their flank. Colonel Shewell, of the 8th Hussars, saw the danger, and rode his few men straight at them, cutting his way through with fearful loss. The other regiments turned and engaged in a desperate encounter. With courage too great almost for credence, they were breaking their way through the columns which enveloped them, when there took place an act of atrocity without parallel in the modern warfare of civilized nations. The Russian gunners, when the storm of cavalry passed, returned to their guns. They saw their own cavalry mingled with the troopers who had just ridden over them, and to the eternal disgrace of the Russian name the miscreants poured a murderous volley of grape and canister on the mass of struggling men and horses, mingling friend and foe in one common ruin. It was as much as our Heavy Cavalry Brigade could do to cover the retreat of the miserable remnants of that band of heroes as they returned to the place they had so lately quitted in all the pride of life.

At twenty-five to twelve not a British soldier, except the dead and dying, was left in front of these bloody Muscovite guns. Our loss, as far as it could be ascertained in killed, wounded, and missing at two o'clock today, was as follows:

	Went into Action Strong	Returned from Action	Loss
4th Light Dragoons	118	39	79
8th Hussars	104	38	66
11th Hussars	110	25	85
13th Light Dragoons	130	61	69
17th Lancers	145	35	110
	607	198	409

The American Civil War

B.S. OSBON

The Ball is Opened, War is Inaugurated

The American Civil War, occasioned by the secession of Southern states to preserve slavery, opened with an attack by
Confederate forces on Fort Sumter, South Carolina, on 12 April
1861. Bradley Sillick Osbon's dispatches were among the first to
announce the commencement of hostilities.

New York *World*, 13 April 1861

The batteries of Sullivan's Island, Morris Island, and other
points were opened on Fort Sumter at four o'clock this morning. Fort Sumter has returned the fire, and a brisk cannonading
has been kept up.

The military are under arms, and the whole of our population are on the streets. Every available space facing the harbor is
filled with anxious spectators.

The firing has continued all day without intermission.

Two of Fort Sumter's guns have been silenced, and it is
reported that a breach has been made in the southeast wall.

The answer to General Beauregard's demand by Major
Anderson was that he would surrender when his supplies were
exhausted; that is, if he was not reinforced.

CIVIL WAR HAS AT LAST BEGUN. A terrible fight is at this
moment going on between Fort Sumter and the fortifications by
which it is surrounded. The issue was submitted to Major

Anderson of surrendering as soon as his supplies were exhausted, or of having fire opened on him within a certain time. He refused to surrender, and accordingly at twenty-seven minutes past four o'clock this morning Fort Moultrie began the bombardment by firing two guns.

Major Anderson has the greater part of the day been directing his fire principally against Fort Moultrie, the Stevens and floating battery, these and Fort Johnson being the only ones operating against him. The remainder of the batteries are held in reserve.

The Stevens battery is eminently successful and does terrible execution on Fort Sumter. Breaches, to all appearances, are being made in the several sides exposed to fire. Portions of the parapet have been destroyed, and several of the guns there mounted have been shot away.

The excitement in the community is indescribable. With the first boom of the gun, thousands rushed from their beds to the harbor front, and all day every available place has been thronged by ladies and gentlemen, viewing the solemn spectacle through their glasses. Most of these have relatives in the several fortifications, and many a tearful eye attested the anxious affection of the mother, wife, and sister, but not a murmur came from a single individual.

Business is entirely suspended. Only those stores are open necessary to supply articles required by the army.

Troops are pouring into the town by hundreds, but are held in reserve for the present, the force already on the islands being ample. The thunder of the artillery can be heard for fifty miles around, and the scene is magnificently terrible.

The American Civil War

GEORGE W. SMALLEY

The Contest in Maryland

The battle fought at Antietam Creek on 17 September 1862 was the bloodiest single-day engagement of the US Civil War. Although the casualties were near evenly split at 12,000 each for the North and the South, the battle crucially stemmed Robert E. Lee's invasion of the Union states. George Washburn Smalley, a Harvard attorney turned war correspondent, witnessed the contest at Antietam by posing as an aide-de-camp to General Hooker (correspondents, in 1862, were forbidden to accompany units in the field), a piece of cleverness he turned to even greater effect by being the first person to bring news of Antietam out of Maryland, sending a brief telegraphic report – intercepted by an anxious War Department in Washington DC – to the New York *Tribune* at 7 a.m. on the 18th, enabling it to be the only paper in the world to carry the story. His inspiration and determination not deserting him, Smalley then made a headlong dash for New York by train, writing a longer account of Antietam by the swinging oil lamp of the railroad coach, which the *Tribune* carried on the morning of Sunday, 19 September in a special edition. It was the journalistic feat of the nineteenth century. Most of his peers either missed the bloody game or were still becalmed in Maryland.

New York *Tribune*, 19 September 1862

Fierce and desperate battle between 200,000 men has raged since daylight, yet night closes on an uncertain field. It is the greatest battle since Waterloo – all over the field contested with an obstinacy equal even to Waterloo. If not wholly a victory to-night, I believe it is the prelude to victory to-morrow. But what can be foretold of the future of a fight in which from five in the morning till seven at night the best troops of the continent have fought without decisive result?

I have no time for speculation – no time even to gather detail of the battle – only time to state its broadest features – then mount and spur for New York.

After the brilliant victory near Middletown, Gen. McClellan pushed forward his army rapidly, and reached Keedysville with three corps on Monday night. That march has already been described. On the day following the two armies faced each other idly, until night. Artillery was busy at intervals; once in the morning with spirit, and continuing for half an hour, with vigor, till the Rebel battery, as usual, was silenced.

McClellan was on the hill where Benjamin's battery was stationed and found himself suddenly under rather heavy fire. It was still uncertain whether the Rebels were retreating or re-enforcing – their batteries would remain in position in either case, and as they had withdrawn nearly all their troops from view, there was only the doubtful indication of columns of dust to the rear.

On the evening of Tuesday, Hooker was ordered to cross Antietam Creek with his corps, and feeling the left of the enemy, to be ready to attack next morning. During the day of apparent inactivity, McClellan had been maturing his plan of battle, of which Hooker's movement was one development.

The position on either side was peculiar. When Richardson advanced on Monday he found the enemy deployed and displayed in force on a crescent-shaped ridge, the outline of which followed more or less exactly the course of Antietam Creek. Their lines were then forming, and the revelation of force in front of the ground which they really intended to hold, was probably meant to delay our attack until their arrangements to receive it were complete.

During that day they kept their troops exposed and did not move them even to avoid the artillery fire, which must have been occasionally annoying. Next morning the lines and columns which had darkened cornfields and hill crests, had been withdrawn. Broken and wooded ground behind the sheltering hills concealed the Rebel masses. What from our front looked like only a narrow summit fringed with woods was a broad table-land of forest and ravine cover for troops everywhere, nowhere easy access for an enemy. The smoothly sloping surface in front and the sweeping crescent of slowly mingling lines was only a delusion. It was all a Rebel stronghold beyond.

Under the base of those hills runs the deep stream called Antietam Creek, fordable only at distant points. Three bridges cross it, one on the Hagerstown road, one on the Sharpsburg pike, one to the left in a deep recess of steeply falling hills. Hooker passed the first to reach the ford by which he crossed, and it was held by Pleasanton with a reserve of cavalry during the battle. The second was close under the Rebel center, and no way important to yesterday's fight. At the third, Burnside attacked and finally crossed. Between the first and third lay most of the battle lines. They stretched four miles from right to left.

Unaided attack in front was impossible. McClellan's forces lay behind low, disconnected ridges, in front of the Rebel summits, all or nearly all unwooded. They gave some cover for artillery, and guns were therefore massed on the center. The enemy had the Shepherdstown road and the Hagerstown and Williamsport road open to him in the rear for retreat. Along one or the other, if beaten, he must fly. This, among other reasons, determined, perhaps, the plan of battle which McClellan finally resolved on.

The plan was generally as follows: Hooker was to cross on the right, establish himself on the enemy's left if possible, flanking his position, and to open the fight. Sumner, Franklin and Mansfield were to send their forces also to the right, co-operating with and sustaining Hooker's attack while advancing also nearer the center. The heavy work in the center was left mostly to the batteries, Porter massing his infantry supports in the hollows. On the left Burnside was to carry the bridge already referred, advancing then by a road which enters the pike at Sharpsburg, turning at once the Rebel left flank and destroying his line of retreat. Porter and Sykes were held in reserve. It is obvious that the complete success of a plan contemplating widely divergent movements of separate corps, must largely depend on accurate timing, that the attacks should be simultaneous and not successive.

Hooker moved on Tuesday afternoon at four, crossing the creek at a ford above the bridge and well to the right, without opposition. Fronting south-west his line advanced not quite on the Rebel flank but over-lapping and threatening it. Turning off from the road after passing the stream, he sent forward cavalry skirmishers straight into the woods and over the fields beyond. Rebel pickets withdrew slowly before them, firing scattering and harmless shots. Turning again to the left, the cavalry went down on the Rebel flank, coming suddenly close to a battery which met them with unexpected grape shot. It being the nature of cavalry to retire before batteries, this company loyally followed the law of its being, and came swiftly back without pursuit.

Artillery was sent to the front, infantry was rapidly deployed, and skirmishers went out in front and on either flank. The corps moved forward compactly, Hooker as usual reconnoitering in person. They came at last to an open grass-sown field inclosed on two sides with woods, protected on the right by a hill, and entered through a cornfield in the rear. Skirmishers entering these woods were instantly met by Rebel shots, but held their ground, and as soon as supported advanced and cleared the timber. Beyond, on the left and in front, volleys of musketry opened heavily, and a battle seemed to have begun a little sooner than it was expected.

General Hooker formed his lines with precision and without hesitation. Rickett's Division went into the woods on the left in force. Meade, with the Pennsylvania Reserves, formed in the center. Doubleday was sent out on the right, planting his batteries on the hill, and opening at once on a Rebel battery that began to enfilade the central line. It was already dark, and the Rebel position could only be discovered by the flashes of their guns. They pushed forward boldly on the right, after losing ground on the other flank, but made no attempt to regain their first hold on the woods. The fight flashed; and glimmered, and faded, and finally went out in the dark.

Hooker had found out what he wanted to know. When the firing ceased the hostile lines lay close to each other – their pickets so near that six Rebels were captured during the night. It was inevitable that the fight should commence at daylight. Neither side had suffered considerable loss; it was a skirmish, not a battle. "We are through for to-night, gentlemen," remarked the

General, "but to-morrow we fight the battle that will decide the fate of the Republic."

Not long after the firing ceased, it sprang up again on the left. General Hooker, who had taken up his headquarters in a barn, which had been nearly the focus of the Rebel artillery, was out at once. First came rapid and unusually frequent picket shots, then several heavy volleys. The General listened a moment and smiled grimly. "We have no troops there. The Rebels are shooting each other. It is Fair Oaks over again." So everybody lay down again, but all the night through there were frequent alarms.

McClellan had been informed of the night's work, and of the certainties awaiting the dawn. Sumner was ordered to move his corps at once, and was expected to be on the ground at daylight. From the extent of the Rebel lines developed in the evening, it was plain that they had gathered their whole army behind the heights and were waiting for the shock.

The battle began with the dawn. Morning found both armies just as they had slept, almost close enough to look into each other's eyes. The left of Meade's reserves and the right of Rickett's line became engaged at nearly the same moment, one with artillery, the other with infantry. A battery was almost immediately pushed forward beyond the central woods, over a plowed field, near the top of the slope where the cornfield began. On this open field, in the corn beyond, and in the woods which stretched forward into the broad-fields, like a promontory into the ocean, were the hardest and deadliest struggles of the day.

For half an hour after the battle had grown to its full strength, the line of fire swayed neither way. Hooker's men were fully up to their work. They saw their General everywhere in front, never away from the fire, and all the troops believed in their commander, and fought with a will. Two-thirds of them were the same men who under McDowall had broken at Manassas.

The half hour passed, the Rebels began to give way a little, only a little, but at the first indication of a receding fire, Forward, was the word, and on went the line with a cheer and a rush. Back across the cornfield, leaving dead and wounded behind them, over the fence, and across the road, and then back again into the dark woods, which closed around them, went the retreating Rebels.

Meade and his Pennsylvanians followed hard and fast – followed till they came within easy range of the woods, among which they saw their beaten enemy disappearing – followed still, with another cheer, and flung themselves against the cover.

But out of those gloomy woods came suddenly and heavily terrible volleys – volleys which smote, and bent, and broke in a moment that eager front, and hurled them swiftly back for half the distance they had won. Not swiftly, nor in panic, any further. Closing up their shattered lines, they came slowly away – a regiment where a brigade had been, hardly a brigade where a whole division had been victorious. They had met from the woods the first volleys of musketry from fresh troops – had met them and returned them till their line had yielded and gone down before the might of fire, and till their ammunition was exhausted.

In ten minutes the fortune of the day seemed to have changed – it was the Rebels now who were advancing, pouring out of the woods in endless lines, sweeping through the cornfield from which their comrades had just fled. Hooker sent in his nearest brigade to meet them, but it could not do the work. He called for another. There was nothing close enough unless he took it from his right. His right might be in danger if it was weakened, but his center was already threatened with annihilation. Not hesitating one moment, he sent to Doubleday: "Give me your best brigade instantly."

The best brigade came down the hill on the run, went through the timber in front through a storm of shot and bursting shell and crashing limbs, over the open field beyond, and straight into the cornfield, passing as they went the fragments of three brigades shattered by the Rebel fire, and streaming to the rear. They passed by Hooker, whose eyes lighted as he saw these veteran troops led by a soldier whom he knew he could trust. "I think they will hold it," he said.

General Hartsuff took his troops very steadily, but now they they were under fire, not hurriedly, up the hill from which the cornfield begins to descend, and formed them on the crest. Not a man who was not in full view – not one who bent before the storm. Firing at first in volleys, they fired them at will with wonderful rapidity and effect. The whole line crowned the hill and stood out darkly against the sky, but lighted and shrouded ever in flame and smoke. There were the 12th and 18th Massachusetts and another regiment which I cannot remember – old troops all of them.

There for half an hour they held the ridge unyielding in purpose, exhaustless in courage. There were gaps in the line, but it nowhere quailed. Their General was wounded badly early in the fight, but they fought on. Their supports did not come – they were determined to win without them. They began to go down the hill and into the corn, they did not stop to think their ammunition was nearly gone; they were there to win the field and they won it. The Rebel line for the second time fled through the corn into the woods. I cannot tell how few of Hartsuff's brigade were left when the work was done, but it was done. There was no more gallant, determined heroic fighting in all this desperate day. General Hartsuff is very severely wounded, but I do not believe he counts his success too dearly purchased.

The crisis of the fight at this point had arrived: Rickett's division, vainly endeavoring to advance and exhausted by the effort had fallen back. Part of Mansfield's corps was ordered into their relief but Mansfield's troops came back again, and their General was mortally wounded. The left nevertheless was too extended to be turned, and too strong to be broken. Rickett sent word he could not advance, but could hold his ground. Doubleday had kept his guns at work on the right, and had finally silenced a Rebel battery that for half an hour had poured in a galling enfilading fire along Hooker's central line.

There were woods in front of Doubleday's hill which the Rebels held, but so long as those guns pointed that way they did not care to attack. With his left then able to take care of itself, with his right impregnable with two brigades of Mansfield still fresh and coming rapidly up, and with his center a second time victorious, General Hooker determined to advance. Orders were given to Crawford and Gordon – the two Mansfield brigades – to move directly forward at once, the batteries in the center were ordered on, the whole line was called on, and the General himself went forward.

To the right of the cornfield and beyond it was a point of woods. Once carried and firmly held, it was the key of the position. Hooker determined to take it. He rode out in front of his furthest troops on a hill to examine the ground for a battery. At the top he dismounted and went forward on foot, completed his reconnaissance, returned and remounted. The musketry fire from the point of woods was all the while extremely hot. As he put his foot in the stirrup a fresh volley of rifle bullets came whizzing by. The tall soldierly figure of the General, the white horse which he rode, the elevated place where he was – all made him a most dangerously conspicuous mark. So he had been all day, riding often without a staff officer or an orderly near him – all sent off on urgent duty – visible everywhere on the field. The Rebel bullets had followed him all day, but they had not hit him, and he would not regard them. Remounting on this hill he had not ridden five steps when he was struck in the foot by a ball.

Three men were shot down at the same moment by his side. The air was alive with bullets. He kept on his horse for a few moments, though the wound was severe and excessively painful, and he would not dismount till he had given his last order to advance. He was himself in the very front. Swaying unsteadily on his horse, he turned in his seat to look about him. "There is a regiment to the right. Order it forward! Crawford and Gordon are coming up. Tell them to carry these woods and hold them – and it is our fight!"

It was found that the bullet had passed completely through his foot. The surgeon who examined it on the spot could give no opinion whether bones were broken, but it was afterward ascertained that though grazed they were not fractured. Of course the severity of the wound made it impossible for him to keep the field which he believed already won, so far as it belonged to him to win it. It was nine o'clock. The fight had been furious since five. A large part of his command was broken, but with his right still untouched and with Crawford's and Gordon's brigades just up, above all, with the advance of the whole central line which the men had heard ordered, with a regiment already on the edge of the woods he wanted, he might well leave the field, thinking the battle won – that *his* battle was won, for I am writing, of course, only about the attack on the Rebel left.

I see no reason why I should disguise my admiration of General Hooker's bravery and soldierly ability. Remaining nearly all the morning on the right, I could not help seeing the sagacity and promptness of his maneuvers, how completely his troops were kept in hand, how devotedly they trusted to him, how keen was his insight into the battle; how every opportunity was seized and every reverse was checked and turned into another success. I say this the more unreservedly, because I have no personal relation whatever with him, never saw him till the day before the fight, and don't like his politics or opinions in general. But what are politics in such a battle?

Sumner arrived just as Hooker was leaving, and assumed command. Crawford and Gordon had gone into the woods, and were holding them stoutly against heavy odds. As I rode over toward the left I met Sumner at the head of his column advancing rapidly through the timber, opposite the point where Crawford was fighting. The veteran General was riding alone in the forest far ahead of his leading brigade, his hat off, his gray hair and beard contrasting strangely with the fire in his eyes and his martial air, as he hurried on to where the bullets were thickest.

Sedgwick's division was in advance, moving forward to support Crawford and Gordon. Rebel re-enforcements were approaching also, and the struggle for the roads was again to be renewed. Sumner sent forward two divisions, Richardson and French, on the left. Sedgwick moving in column of divisions through the woods in the rear, deployed and advanced in line over the cornfield. There was a broad interval between him and the nearest division, and he saw that if the Rebel line was complete his own division was in immediate danger of being flanked. But his orders were to advance, and those are the orders which a soldier – and Sedgwick is every inch a soldier – loves best to hear. To extend his own front as far as possible, he ordered the 34th New York to move by the left flank. The maneuver was attempted under a fire of the greatest intensity, and the regiment broke. At the same moment the enemy, perceiving their advantage, came round on that flank. Crawford was obliged to give on the right, and his troops pouring in confusion through the ranks of Sedgwick's advance brigade, threw it into disorder and back on the second and third lines. The enemy advanced, their fire increasing.

General Sedgwick was three times wounded, in the shoulder, leg and wrist, but he persisted in remaining on the field so long as there was a chance of saving it. His Adjutant-General, Major Sedgwick, bravely rallying and trying to reform the troops, was shot through the body, the bullet lodging in the spine, and fell from his horse. Severe as the wound is it is probably not mortal. Lieutenant Howe of General Sedgwick's staff endeavored vainly to rally the 34th New York. They were badly cut up and would not stand. Half their officers were killed or wounded, their colors shot to pieces, the Colour-Sergeant killed, everyone of the color-guard wounded. Only thirty-two were afterward got together.

The 15th Massachusetts went into action with 17 officers and nearly 600 men. Nine officers were killed or wounded, and some of the latter are prisoners. Captain Simons, Captain Saunders of the Sharpshooters, Lieutenant Derby and Lieutenant Berry are killed. Captain Bartlett and Captain Jocelyn, Lieutenant Sourr, Lieutenant Gale and Lieutenant Bradley are wounded. One hundred and thirty-four men were the only remnant that could be collected of this splendid regiment.

General Dans was wounded. General Howard, who took command of the division after General Sedgwick was disabled, exerted himself to restore order, but it could not be done there. General Sumner ordered the line to be reformed under fire. The test was too severe for volunteer troops under such fire. Sumner himself attempted to arrest the disorder, but to little purpose. Lieutenant-Colonel Revere and Captain Andenried of his staff were wounded severely, but not dangerously. It was impossible to hold the position. General Sumner withdrew the division to the rear, and once more the cornfield was abandoned to the enemy.

French sent word he would hold his ground. Richardson, while gallantly leading a regiment under heavy fire, was severely wounded in the shoulder. General Meagher was wounded at the head of his brigade. The loss in general officers was becoming frightful.

At one o'clock affairs on the right had a gloomy look. Hooker's troop were greatly exhausted, and their General away from the field. Mansfield's were no better. Sumner's command had lost heavily, but two of his divisions were still comparatively fresh. Artillery was yet playing vigorously in front, though the ammunition of many of the batteries was entirely exhausted, and they had been compelled to retire.

Doubleday held the right inflexibly. Sumner's headquarters were now in the narrow field where the night before, Hooker had begun the fight. All that had been gained in front had been lost! The enemy's batteries, which if advanced and served vigorously might have made sad work with the closely massed troops, were fortunately either partially disabled or short of ammunition. Sumner was confident that he could hold his own; but another advance was out of the question. The enemy, on the other hand, seemed to be too much exhausted to attack.

At this crisis Franklin came up with fresh troops and formed on the left. Slocum, commanding one division of the corps, was sent forward along the slopes lying under the first range of rebel hills, while Smith, commanding the other division, was ordered to retake the cornfields and woods which all day had been so hotly contested. It was done in the handsomest style. His Maine and Vermont regiments and the rest went forward on the run, and cheering as they went, swept like an avalanche through the cornfields, fell upon the woods, cleared them in ten minutes, and held them. They were not again retaken.

The field and its ghastly harvest which the reaper had gathered in those fatal hours remained finally with us. Four times it had been lost and won. The dead are strewn so thickly that as you ride over it you cannot guide your horse's steps too carefully. Pale and bloody faces are everywhere upturned. They are sad and terrible, but there is nothing which makes one's heart beat so quickly as the imploring look of sorely wounded men who beckon wearily for help which you cannot stay to give.

General Smith's attack was so sudden that his success was accomplished with no great loss. He had gained a point, however, which compelled him to expect every moment an attack, and to hold which, if the enemy again brought up reserves, would take his best energies and best troops. But the long strife, the heavy losses, incessant fighting over the same ground repeatedly lost and won inch by inch, and more than all, perhaps, the fear of Burnside on the left and Porter in front, held the enemy in check. For two or three hours there was a lull even in the cannonade on the right which hitherto had been incessant. McClellan had been over on the field after Sumner's repulse, but had speedily returned to his headquarters. Sumner again sent word that he was able to hold his position, but could not advance with his own corps.

Meanwhile where was Burnside, and what was he doing? On the right where I had spent the day until two o'clock, little was known of the general fortunes of the field. We had heard Porter's guns in the center, but nothing from Burnside on the left. The distance was too great to distinguish the sound of his artillery from Porter's left. There was no immediate prospect of more fighting on the right, and I left the field which all day long had seen the most obstinate contest of the war, and rode over to

McClellan's headquarters. The different battle-fields were shut out from each other's view, but all partially visible from the central hill which General McClellan had occupied during the day. But I was more than ever impressed on returning with the completely deceitful appearance of the ground the Rebels had chosen when viewed from the front.

Hooker's and Sumner's struggle had been carried on over an uneven and wooded surface, their own line of battle extending in a semicircle not less than a mile and a half. Perhaps a better notion of their position can be got by considering their right, center and left as forming three sides of a square. So long therefore as either wing was driven back, the centre became exposed to a dangerous enfilading fire, and the further the center was advanced the worse off it was, unless the lines on its side and rear were firmly held. This formation resulted originally from the efforts of the enemy to turn both flanks. Hooker at the very outset threw his column so far into the center of the Rebel lines that they were compelled to threaten him on the flank to secure their own center.

Nothing of all this was perceptible from the hills in front. Some directions of the Rebel lines had been disclosed by the smoke of their guns, but the whole interior formation of the country beyond the hills was completely concealed. When McClellan arranged his order of battle, it must have been upon information, or have been left to his corps and division commander to discover for themselves. Up to three o'clock Burnside had made little progress. His attack on the bridge had been successful, but the delay had been so great that to the observer it appeared as if McClellan's plans must have been seriously disarranged. It is impossible not to suppose that the attacks on the right and left were meant in a measure to correspond, for otherwise the enemy had only to repel Hooker on the one hand, then transfer his troops, and hurl them against Burnside.

Finally, at four o'clock, McClellan sent simultaneous orders to Burnside and Franklin; to the former to carry the batteries in his front at all hazards and at any cost; to the latter to carry the woods next in front of him to the right, which the Rebels still held. The order to Franklin, however, was practically countermanded in consequence of a message from General Sumner that if Franklin went on and was repulsed, his own corps was not yet sufficiently reorganized to be depended on as a reserve.

Franklin, thereon, was directed to run no risk of losing his present position, and, instead of sending his infantry into the woods, contented himself with advancing his batteries over the breadth of the fields in front, supporting them with heavy columns of infantry, and attacking with energy the Rebel batteries immediately opposed to him. His movement was a success so far as it went, the batteries maintaining their new ground and sensibly affecting the steadiness of the Rebel fire. That being accomplished, and all hazard of the right being again forced back having been dispelled, the movement of Burnside became at once the turning point of success and the fate of the day depended on him.

How extraordinary the situation was may be judged from a moment's consideration of the facts. It is understood that from the outset Burnside's attack was expected to be decisive; it certainly must have been if things went well elsewhere, and if he succeeded in establishing himself on the Sharpsburg road in the Rebel rear.

Yet Hooker, and Sumner, and Franklin, and Mansfield were all sent to the right three miles away while Porter seems to have done double duty with his single corps in front, both supporting the batteries and holding himself in reserve. With all this immense force on the right, but 16,000 then were given to Burnside for the decisive movement of the day.

Still more unfortunate in its results was the total failure of these separate attacks on the right and left to sustain, or in any manner co-operate with each other. Burnside hesitated for hours in front of the bridge which should have been carried at once by a *coup de main*. Meantime, Hooker had been fighting for four hours with various fortune, but final success. Sumner had come up too late to join in the decisive attack which his earlier arrival would probably have converted into a complete success; and Franklin reached the scene only when Sumner had been repulsed. Probably before his arrival the Rebels had transferred a considerable number of troops to their right to meet the attack of Burnside, the direction of which was then suspected or developed.

Attacking first with one regiment, then with two, and delaying both for artillery, Burnside was not over the bridge before two o'clock – perhaps not till three. He advanced slowly up the slope in his front, his batteries in rear covering, to some extent, the movements of the infantry. A desperate fight was going on in a deep ravine on his right, the Rebel batteries were in full play and, apparently, very annoying and destructive, while heavy columns of Rebel troops were plainly visible, advancing as if careless of concealment, along the road and over the hills in the direction of Burnside's forces. It was at this point of time that McClellan sent him the order above given.

Burnside obeyed it most gallantly. Getting his troops well in hand, and sending a portion of his artillery to the front, he advanced them with rapidity and the most determined vigor, straight up the hill in front, on top of which the Rebels had maintained their most dangerous battery. The movement was in plain view of McClellan's position, and as Franklin, on the other side, sent his batteries into the field about the same time, the battle seemed to open in all directions with greater severity than ever.

The fight in the ravine was in full progress, the batteries which Porter supported were firing with new vigor. Franklin was blaring away on the right, and every hill-top ridge and woods along the whole line was crested and vailed with clouds of smoke. All day had been clear and bright since the early cloudy morning, and now this whole magnificent, unequalled scene shone with the splendor of an afternoon September sun. Four miles of battle, its glory all visible, its horrors all veiled, the fate of the Republic hanging on the hour – could anyone be insensible of its grandeur.

There are two hills on the left of the road, the further the lower. The Rebels have batteries on both. Burnside is ordered to carry the nearer to him, which is the furthest from the road. His guns opening first from this new position in front, soon entirely controlled and silenced the enemy's artillery. The infantry came on at once, moving rapidly and steadily up long dark lines, and broad, dark masses, being plainly visible without a glass as they moved over the green hill-side.

The next moment the road in which the Rebel battery was planted was canopied with clouds of dust swiftly descending into the valley. Underneath was a tumult of wagons, guns, horses, and men flying at speed down the road. Blue flashes of smoke burst now and then among them, a horse or a man or half a dozen went down, and then the whirlwind swept on.

The hill was carried, but could it be held? The Rebel columns, before seen moving to the left, increased their pace. The guns, on the hill above, sent an angry tempest of shell down among Burnside's guns and men. He had formed his columns apparently in the near angles of two fields bordering the road – high ground about them everywhere except in the rear.

In another moment a Rebel battle-line appears on the brow of the ridge above them, moves swiftly down in the most perfect order, and though met by incessant discharge of musketry, of which we plainly see the flashes, does not fire a gun. White spaces show where men are falling, but they close up instantly, and still the line advances. The brigades of Burnside are in heavy column; they will not give way before a bayonet charge in line. The Rebels think twice before they dash into those hostile masses.

There is a halt, the Rebel left gives way and scatters over the field, the rest stand fast and fire. More infantry comes up, Burnside is outnumbered; flanked, compelled to yield the hill he took so bravely. His position is no longer one of attack; he defends himself with unfaltering firmness, but he sends to McClellan for help. McClellan's glass for the last hour has seldom been turned away from the left.

He sees clearly enough that Burnside is pressed – he needs no messengers to tell him that. His face grows darker with anxious thought. Looking down into the valley where 15,000 troops are lying, he turns a half-questioning eye on Fitz John Porter, who stands by his side, gravely scanning the field. They are Porter's troops below, are fresh and only impatient to share in this fight. But Porter slowly shakes his head, and one may believe that the same thought is passing through the minds of both Generals: "They are the only reserves of the army; they cannot be spared."

McClellan remounts his horse, and with Porter and a dozen officers of his staff rides away to the left in Burnside's direction. Sykes meets them on the road – a good soldier, whose opinion is worth taking. The three Generals talk briefly together. It is easy to see that the moment has come when everything may turn on one order given or withheld, when the history of the battle is only to be written in thoughts and purposes and words of the General.

Burnside's messenger rides up. His message is "I want troops and guns. If you do not send them I cannot hold my position for half an hour." McClellan's only answer for the moment is a glance at the western sky. Then he turns and speaks very slowly, "Tell General Burnside that this is the battle of the war. He must hold his ground till dark at any cost. I will send him Miller's battery. I can do nothing more. I have no infantry." Then as the messenger was riding away he called him back. "Tell him if he *cannot* hold his ground, then the bridge, to the last man! – always the bridge! If the bridge is lost, all is lost."

The sun is already down; not half an hour of daylight is left. Till Burnside's message came, it had seemed plain to everyone that the battle could not be finished today. None suspected how near was the peril of defeat; of sudden attack on exhausted forces – how vital to the safety of the army and the nation were those 15,000 waiting troops of Fitz John Porter in the hollow. But the Rebels halted instead of pushing on, their vindictive cannonade died away as the light faded. Before it was quite dark, the battle was over. Only a solitary gun of Burnside's thundered against the enemy, and presently this also ceased, and the field was still.

The peril came very near, but it has passed, and in spite of the peril, at the close the day was partly a success – not a victory, but an advantage had been gained. Hooker, Sumner, and Franklin held all the ground they had gained, and Burnside still held the bridge and his position beyond. Everything was favorable for a renewal of the fight in the morning. If the plan of the battle is sound, there is every reason why McClellan should win it. He may choose to postpone the battle to await his reinforcements.

The Rebels may choose to retire while it is still possible. Fatigue on both sides might delay the deciding battle, yet, if the enemy means to fight at all, he cannot afford to delay. His reenforcements may be coming, his losses are enormous. His troops have been massed in woods and hollows, where artillery has its most terrific effect. Ours have been deployed and scattered. From infantry fire there is less difference.

It is hard to estimate losses on a field of such extent, but I think ours cannot be less than 6000 killed and wounded – it may be much greater. Prisoners have been taken from the enemy – I hear of a regiment captured entire, but I doubt it. All the prisoners whom I saw agree in saying that their whole army is there.

The American Civil War

WALT WHITMAN

The Great Army of the Sick
Military Hospitals in Washington

The American poet volunteered as a nurse in Army hospitals
during the Civil War. The article was later collected in Whitman's
Memoranda During the Wars.

New York Times, 26 February 1863

The military hospitals, convalescent camps, & c. in Washington
and its neighborhood sometimes contain over fifty thousand sick
and wounded men. Every form of wound, (the mere sight of some
of them having been known to make a tolerably hardy visitor faint
away,) every kind of malady, like a long procession, with typhoid
fever and diarrhea at the head as leaders, are here in steady motion.
The soldier's hospital, how many sleepless nights, how many
woman's tears, how many long and aching hours and days of suspense, from every one of the Middle, Eastern and Western States,
have concentrated here! Our own New York, in the form of hundreds and thousands of her young men, may consider herself here
– Pennsylvania, Ohio, Indians and all the West and Northwest the
same – and all the New-England States the same.

Upon a few of these hospitals I have been almost daily calling
as a missionary, on my own account, for the sustenance and
consolation of some of the most needy cases of sick and dying
men, for the last two months. One has much to learn in order to
do good in these places. Great tact is required. These are not like

other hospitals. By far the greatest proportion (I should say five-sixths) of the patients are American young men, intelligent, of independent spirit, tender feelings, used to a hardy and healthy life; largely the farmers are represented by their sons – largely the mechanics and working men of the cities. Then they are *soldiers*. All these points must be borne in mind.

People through our Northern cities have little or no idea of the great and prominent feature which these military hospitals and convalescent camps make in and around Washington. There are not merely two or three or a dozen, but some fifty of them, of different degrees of capacity. Some have a thousand and more patients. The newspapers here find it necessary to print every day a directory of the hospitals; a long list, something like what a directory of the churches would be in New-York, Philadelphia or Boston.

BARRACKS ADOPTED BY GOVERNMENT

The Government, (which really tries, I think, to do the best and quickest it can for these sad necessities,) is gradually settling down to adopt the plan of placing the hospitals in clusters of one-story wooden barracks, with their accompanying tents and sheds for cooking and all needed purposes. Taking all things into consideration, no doubt these are best adapted to the purpose; better than using churches and large public buildings like the Patent Office. These sheds now adopted are long, one-story edifices, sometimes ranged along in a row, with their heads to the street, and numbered either alphabetically, Wards A, or B, C, D, and so on; or Wards 1, 2, 3, &c. The middle one will be marked by a flagstaff, and is the office of the establishment, with rooms for the Ward Surgeons, &c. One of these sheds or wards, will contain sixty cots – sometimes, on an emergency, they move them close together, and crowd in more. Some of the barracks are larger, with, of course, more inmates. Frequently, there are tents, more comfortable here than one might think, whatever they may be down in the army.

Each ward has a Ward-master, and generally a nurse for every ten or twelve men. A Ward Surgeon has, generally, two wards – although this varies. Some of the wards have a woman nurse – the Armory-square wards have some very good ones. The one in Ward E is one of the best.

THE PATENT OFFICE

A few weeks ago the vast area of the second story of that noblest of Washington buildings, the Patent Office, was crowded close with rows of sick, badly wounded and dying soldiers. They were placed in three very large apartments. I went there several times. It was a strange, solemn and, with all its features of suffering and death, a sort of fascinating sight. I went sometimes at night, to soothe and relieve particular cases; some, I found, needed a little cheering up and friendly consolation at that time, for they went to sleep better afterward. Two of the immense apartments are filled with high and ponderous glass cases, crowded with models in miniature of every kind of utensil, machine or invention, it ever entered into the mind of man to conceive; and with curiosities and foreign presents. Between these cases were lateral openings, perhaps eight feet wide, and quite deep, and in these were placed many of the sick; besides a great long double row of them up and down through the middle of the hall. Many of them were very bad cases, wounds and amputations. Then there was a gallery running above the hall, in which there were beds also. It was, indeed, a curious scene at night, when lit up. The glass cases, the beds, the sick, the gallery above and the marble pavement under foot – the suffering, and the fortitude to bear it in various degrees – occasionally, from some, the groan that could not be repressed – sometimes a poor fellow dying, with emaciated face and glassy eye, the nurse by his side, the doctor also there, but no friend, no relative – such were the sights but lately in the Patent Office. The wounded have since been removed from there, and it is now vacant again.

Of course, there are among these thousands of prostrated soldiers in hospital here, all sorts of individual cases. On recurring to my note-book, I am puzzled which cases to select to illustrate the average of these young men and their experiences. I may here say, too, in general terms, that I could not wish for more candor and manliness, among all their sufferings, than I find among them.

CASE OF J.A.H., OF COMPANY C., TWENTY-NINTH MASSACHUSETTS

Take this case in Ward 6, Campbell Hospital – a young man from Plymouth County, Massachusetts; a farmer's son, aged about 20 or 21, a soldierly American young fellow, but with sensitive and tender feelings. Most of December and January last, he lay very low, and for quite a while I never expected he would recover. He had become prostrated with an obstinate diarrhea; his stomach would hardly keep the least thing down, he was vomiting half the time. But that was hardly the worst of it. Let me tell his story – it is but one of thousands.

He had been some time sick with his regiment in the field, in front, but did his duty as long as he could – was in the battle of Fredericksburgh – soon after was put in the regimental hospital. He kept getting worse – could not eat anything they had there – the doctor told him nothing could be done for him there – the poor fellow had fever also – received (perhaps it could not be helped) little or no attention – lay on the ground getting worse. Toward the latter part of December, very much enfeebled, he was sent up from the front, from Falmouth Station, in an open platform car, (such as hogs are transported upon north,) and dumped with a crowd of others on the boat at Aquia Creek, falling down like a rag where they deposited him, too weak and sick to sit up or help himself at all. No one spoke to him, or assisted him – he had nothing to eat or drink – was used (amid the great crowds of sick) either with perfect indifference, or, as in two or three instances, with heartless brutality.

On the boat, when night came and the air grew chilly, he tried a long time to undo the blankets he had in his knapsack, but was too feeble. He asked one of the employees, who was moving around deck, for a moment's assistance, to get the blankets. The man asked him back if he could not get them himself. He answered no, he had been trying for more than half an hour, and found himself too weak. The man rejoined, he might then go without them, and walked off. So H. lay, chilled and damp, on deck all night, without anything under or over him, while two good blankets were within reach. It caused him a great injury – nearly cost him his life.

Arrived at Washington, he was brought ashore and again left on the wharf, or above it, amid the great crowds, as before, without any nourishment – not a drink for his parched mouth – no kind hand offered to cover his face from the forenoon sun. Conveyed at last some two miles by ambulance to the hospital, and assigned a bed, (bed 47, ward 6, Campbell Hospital, January and February, 1863,) he fell down exhausted upon the bed; but the Ward-master (he has since been changed) came to him with a growling order to get up – the rules, he said, permitted no man to lie down in that way with his old clothes on – he must sit up – must first go to the bath-room, be washed, and have his clothes completely changed. (A very good rule, properly applied.) He was taken to the bath-room and scrubbed well with cold water. The attendants, callous for a while, were soon alarmed, for suddenly the half-frozen and lifeless body fell limpsy in their hands, and they hurried it back to the cot, plainly insensible, perhaps dying.

Poor boy! the long train of exhaustion, deprivation, rudeness, no food, no friendly word or deed, but all kinds of upstart airs, and impudent, unfeeling speeches and deeds, from all kinds of small officials, (and some big ones,) cutting like razors into that sensitive heart, had at last done the job. He now lay, at times out of his head, but quite silent, asking nothing of anyone, for some days, with death getting a closer and surer grip upon him – he cared not, or rather he welcomed death. His heart was broken. He felt the struggle to keep up any longer to be useless. God, the world, humanity – all had abandoned him. It would feel so good to shut his eyes forever on the cruel things around him and toward him.

As luck would have it, at this time, I found him. I was passing down Ward No. 6 one day, about dusk (4th of January, I think,) and noticed his glassy eyes with a look of despair and hopelessness, sunk low in his thin pallid-brown young face. One learns to divine quickly in the hospital, and as I stopped by him and spoke some commonplace remark, (to which he made no reply,) I saw as I looked that it was a case for ministering to the affections first, and other nourishment and medicine afterward. I sat down by him without any fuss – talked a little – soon saw that it did him good – led him to talk a little himself – got him somewhat interested – wrote a letter for him to his folks in Massachusetts, (to L. H. CAMPBELL, Plymouth County,) – soothed him down as I saw he was getting a little too much agitated, and tears in his eyes – gave him some small gifts, and told him I should come again soon. (He has told me since that this little visit, at that hour, just saved him – a day more, and it would have been perhaps too late.)

Of course I did not forget him, for he was a young fellow to interest any one. He remained very sick – vomiting much every day, frequent diarrhea, and also something like bronchitis, the doctor said. For a while I visited him almost every day – cheered him up – took him some little gifts, and gave him small sums of money, (he relished a drink of new milk, when it was brought through the ward for sale). For a couple of weeks his condition was uncertain – sometimes I thought there was no chance for him at all. But of late he is doing better – is up and dressed, and goes around more and more (Feb. 21) every day. He will not die, but will recover.

The other evening, passing through the ward, he called me – he wanted to say a few words, particular. I sat down by his side on the cot, in the dimness of the long ward, with the wounded soldiers there in their beds, ranging up and down. He told me I had saved his life. He was in the deepest earnest about it. It was one of those things that repay a soldiers' hospital missionary a thousand-fold – one of the hours he never forgets.

THE FIELD IS LARGE, THE REAPERS FEW

A benevolent person with the right qualities and tact cannot perhaps make a better investment of himself, at present, any-where upon the varied surface of the whole of this big world, than in these same military hospitals, among such thousands of most interesting young men. The army is very young – and so much more American than I supposed. Reader, how can I describe to you the mute appealing look that rolls and moves from many a manly eye, from many a side cot, following you as you walk slowly down one of these wards? To see these, and to be incapable of responding to them, except in a few cases, (so very few compared to the whole of the suffering men,) is enough to make one's heart crack. I go through in some cases cheering up the men; distributing now and then little sums of money – and regularly, letter-paper and envelopes, oranges, tobacco, jellies, &c., &c.

OFFICIAL AIRS AND HARSHNESS

Many things invite comment, and some of them sharp criticism, in these hospitals. The Government, as I said, is anxious and liberal in its practice toward its sick, but the work has to be left, in its personal application to the men, to hundreds of officials of one grade or another about the hospitals, who are sometimes entirely lacking in the right qualities. There are tyrants and shysters in all positions, and especially those dressed in subordinate authority. Some of the ward doctors are careless, rude, capricious, needlessly strict. One I found who prohibited the men from all enlivening amusements. I found him sending them to the guard-house for the most trifling offence. In general, perhaps, the officials – especially the new ones, with their straps or badges – put on too many airs. Of all places in the world, the hospitals of American young men and soldiers, wounded in the volunteer service of their country, ought to be exempt from more conventional military airs and etiquette of shoulder-straps. But they are not exempt.

The American Civil War

SPECIAL CORRESPONDENT

Siege by Moonlight

General Ulysses S. Grant besieged Vicksburg from May to early July 1863, and his eventual victory brought the Mississippi under Union control.

Cleveland Herald, 30 May 1863

... Let us climb the parapet and see the siege by moonlight. In front of us, beyond the enemy's works, but hidden from us, lies the city of Vicksburg. Look carefully, and you can distinguish the spires of the courthouse and two or three churches. The rebels had a signal station on the former when we came, but our shells made it too warm for them, and they withdrew. The mortars are playing tonight, and they are well worth seeing. We watch a moment, and in the direction of Young's Point, beyond the city, suddenly up shoots a flash of light, and in a moment the ponderous shell, with its fuse glowing and sparkling, rises slowly from behind the bluffs; up, up, it goes, as though mounting to the zenith, over it comes towards us, down through its flight trajectory into the city, and explodes with a shock that jars the ground for miles. There are women and tender children where those shells fall, but war is war.

Sherman's eight-inch monsters are grumbling far away on the right. Nearer, McPherson's, too, are playing – we can even see the cannoneers beside them at each flash. Ours will open at midnight; then there will be music to your heart's content. Meanwhile, let us go to the front. A hundred yards to the right of where we now are we enter a deep trench. Following this, as it winds down around the hill, we reach the opening of a cave or mine. The air within is damp and close, like that of a vault. Candles are burning dimly at intervals, and we hear a hum of voices far within and out of sight. We proceed, and presently meet two men carrying a barrow of earth, for our boys are at work night and day. Finally, we reach the moonlight again, and emerge into a wide, deep trench, cut across the line of the covered way. This is open, and filled with troops, who protect the working party. A heavy parapet of cotton bales and earth is built on the side towards the enemy, and we must mount them to look over.

We are now within sociable distance of the chivalry. Those men lying on the ground, ten to thirty yards from us, are our boys, our advance pickets; but that grey fellow, with the bright musket, which glistens so, a few steps beyond, is a "reb.", long-haired and hot-blooded, one of Wall's famous Texas legion – a bulldog to fight, you may be sure.

Now jump down and enter the mouth of the other mine, which leads toward the salient of the enemy's work. Stumbling along, we reach the end where the men are digging. The candle burns very dimly – the air is almost stifling. Never mind, let us watch them. See that slender, bright-looking fellow swinging that pick. Great beaded drops of perspiration trickle down his face; there is not a dry thread in his coarse, grey shirt; but no matter, the pick swings, and each stroke slices down six inches of the tough subsoil of Mississippi. That fellow was "Jim", once a tender-handed, smooth-faced, nice young man, whose livery-stable, billiard and cigar bills were a sore trial to his worthy governor. Jim says that he used to wear gloves and "store-clothes", and that girls called him good-looking, but that's played out now; he is going for Uncle Sam.

But we return to the fresh air. Look over the parapet again towards the turret, where we saw the rebel picket. Do you see the little grey mounds which cover the hillside so thickly? – ten, twenty, thirty, you can count on a few square rods. Ah, my friend, this is sacred ground you are looking upon. There our boys charged; there they were slain in heaps; but they pressed on, and leaped into the ditch. They climbed the parapet, and rolled back into eternity. Others followed them; their flag was planted, and they sprang over, to meet their certain death. An hour passed, and *one* returned; the rest were dead.

The American Civil War

SAM WILKESON

Gettysburg: A Dispatch Written Beside the Body of my Dead Son

The Battle of Gettysburg was fought thirty-five miles south-west of Harrisburg, Pennsylvania, and resulted in the defeat of the invasionary Confederate force under General Robert E. Lee. It was the turning point of the Civil War. The battle was covered for the *New York Times* by Sam Wilkeson, who found his eldest son, Union artillery Lieutenant Bayard Wilkeson, among the 40,000 fallen.

New York Times, 4 July 1863

Who can write the history of a battle whose eyes are immovably fastened upon a central figure of transcendingly absorbing interest – the dead body of an oldest born, crushed by a shell in a position where a battery should never have been sent, and abandoned to death in a building where surgeons dared not to stay? . . .

For such details as I have the heart for. The battle commenced at daylight, on the side of the horseshoe position, exactly opposite to that which Ewell had sworn to crush through. Musketry preceded the rising of the sun. A thick wood veiled this fight, but out of the leafy darkness arose the smoke and the surging and swelling of the fire . . .

Suddenly, and about ten in the forenoon, the firing on the east side and everywhere about our lines ceased. A silence of deep sleep fell upon the field of battle. Our army cooked, ate and slumbered. The rebel army moved 120 guns to the west, and massed there, Longstreet's corps and Hill's corps to hurl them upon the really weakest point of our entire position.

Eleven o'clock – twelve o'clock – one o'clock. In the shadow cast by the tiny farmhouse, sixteen by twenty, where General Meade had made his headquarters, lay wearied staff officers and tired reporters. There was not wanting to the peacefulness of the scene the singing of a bird, which had a nest in a peach tree within the tiny yard of the whitewashed cottage. In the midst of its warbling a shell screamed over the house, instantly followed by another and another, and in a moment the air was full of the most complete artillery prelude to an infantry battle that was ever exhibited. Every size and form of shell known to British and to American gunnery shrieked, moaned, whirled, whistled, and wrathfully fluttered over our ground ... Through the midst of the storm of screaming and exploding shells an ambulance, driven by its frenzied conductor at full speed, presented to all of us the marvellous spectacle of a horse going rapidly on three legs. A hinder one had been shot off at the hock ... During this fire the houses at twenty and thirty feet distant were receiving their death, and soldiers in Federal blue were torn to pieces in the road and died with the peculiar yells that blend the extorted cry of pain with horror and despair. Not an orderly, not an ambulance, not a straggler was to be seen upon the plain swept by this tempest of orchestral death thirty minutes after it commenced.

The American Civil War

H.J. WINSER

Our Prisoners

Andersonville was the most notorious of the Confederate POW camps. H.J. Winser was the first to bring to the public attention the inhumane conditions in which Union prisoners were held there, and the *New York Times* gave over the entire front page to his report. After the war, Andersonville's commandant was hanged.

New York Times, 26 November 1864

The past few days have been fraught with a very painful interest to everybody who has been connected in any way whatever with the exchange of our sick and wounded prisoners now in progress on the Savannah River. Col. Mulford began to receive our poor fellows last Friday, and the delivery is to continue at the rate of from eight hundred to twelve hundred per day, until the aggregate number of the wretched suffering creatures, estimated at ten thousand, return to our welcome keeping. I shall attempt in this letter to give some idea of the outward appearance, physical condition, animating spirit and expression of opinion of these soldiers of the Republic who have escaped from unutterable misery, with the sole object of presenting facts to the country which must result in the release of their fifty thousand comrades who cannot survive the coming Winter, under the conditions in which they are kept through the unparalleled vindictiveness of the Southern authorities. This is a hard charge, but I make it deliberately. The irrefragable proof is lying before me not alone in the ex parte testimony and wasted hungry aspect of the sufferers, whose filth and squalor and skeleton frames appeal for justice to the God of justice, but in the official papers of the rebel surgeons at Andersonville and the records of the charnel-houses, miscalled hospitals, at that terrestrial hell – records never meant to pass the limits of the Confederacy, but which a merciful Providence has brought to light, that out of their own mouths these barbarians, with whom we are at war, should be convicted . . .

It is a distressing fact, but one of which I have found abundant proof in many conversations with the men so far brought back, that the prisoners very generally believe that they have been abandoned by our Government. This idea is sedulously inculcated by the rebel authorities. I am convinced that many a brave heart has succumbed under the cruel aspersion that the sympathies of the people are dead to their woes. Hunger, squalor, filth, nakedness and disease may be borne, but that hope deferred which results in heartsickness – that longing for home which superinduces mental depression, cannot long be survived. Nostalgia is the parent of physical ailments, and, under the terrible monotony and privations of the prison pens, it is more fatal than bullets on the field of battle. A very large proportion of these prisoners have been held as such for periods of from nine to sixteen months, and the exchange question between the two Governments as yet gives promise of a speedy settlement. The rebels assure the captives that they are prepared to yield all the points at issue, and have long since announced the fact to the United States Government, whose only reason for nonacceptance is one of simple expediency, viz: that by resuming the exchanges thousands of rugged, strong men would be sent into the armies of the South from the prison camps of the North and no equivalent would be received in the broken-down, emaciated wrecks of humanity that would be sent home from the pens at Andersonville, Columbus, Milan and Richmond. Is it a matter of marvel that under the innocence of this monstrous belief, hundreds of the disheartened soldiers endeavor to escape the horrors of the prisons by enlisting in the rebel service? Such is the fact and it behooves our Government to weigh it well. The exchanges are in abeyance on well-taken grounds, from which there can be no retraction without a sacrifice of national honor. But there are two sides to the question, and the national faith and honor are just as deeply plighted to the fifty thousand soldiers languishing and dying in captivity as it can possibly be in other quarters. Justice to the heroic men whom the fortune of war has placed in the hands of the enemy, demands that no effort should be relaxed to release them from a condition which will bring to the majority of them certain death during the fast approaching Winter. The resources of the North in men have scarcely been drawn upon as yet, in comparison with the resources of the South, and the question of expediency in releasing a few thousand Southern soldiers should not be entertained an instant, even if a draft in the Northern States were not able to put their equivalent in the field . . .

When the rebel boat moves off and the men are huddled together on the decks of our own vessels, all fully understand that the last link which bound them to rebeldom has been severed, then rises hearty shouting and cheering, which only can be given under these circumstances. There is the music of intense gratefulness in it. Three cheers and a tiger for the old flag; three more and a tiger for Col. Mulford; then comes a burst of song, most often the words being "Rally round the flag, boys, from near and from far, down with the traitor and up with the star," the rebels still within hearing, probably gnashing their teeth at the pointed personal allusion, but everybody else feeling that the bad taste of the happy fellow is excusable, even though exhibited under the sacred folds of a flag of truce. Then vermin-infested rags, till now highly prized as the only cover for nakedness, are rudely torn off and flung into the water or cast with glee into the flaming furnaces of the steamers, and new clothes are issued, and a general cleaning-time inaugurated. But the bathing has long been needed and scarcely comes soon enough. Many of the men, through illness or carelessness, are so begrimed with filth, that, were it not for the dead color of the blackened epidermis, they might be taken for the sons of Ham . . . It is a touching sight to see them, each with his quart can, file by the steaming coffee barrels, and receive the refreshing draught whose taste has long been unfamiliar. It seems scarcely possible that men should feel such childish joy as they express in once more receiving this common stimulant. And then, the eager, hungry glare which their glassy eyes cast upon the chunks of ham as they clutch and devour their allowance with a wolf-like avidity . . .

Such is the condition of the men whom we are now receiving out of chivalrous Dixie. These the sons, brothers, husbands and fathers of the North. Men reduced to living skeletons; men almost naked; shoeless men, shirtless men, hatless men; men with no other garment than an overcoat; men whose skins are blackened by dirt and hang on their protruding bones loosely as bark on a tree; men whose very presence is simply disgusting, exhaling an odor so fetid that it almost stops the breath of those unaccustomed to it, and causes an involuntary brushing of the garments if with them there is accidental contact. Imagine twenty-five thousand of such wretched creatures penned together in a space scarcely large enough to hold them, and compare their conditions with the most miserable condition that can be imagined. The suffering of the Revolutionary captives on the prison ships at Wallabout Bay will not stand the comparison, and the horrible sight in the Blackhole of Calcutta scarcely exceeds it in atrocity. Remember, too, that the men thus returned are the best specimens of the suffering. Only those are forwarded to us whom the rebel medical authorities decide to be strong enough to bear the fatigue of transportation. If those whose wretchedness I have vainly endeavored to portray are the best specimens of our sick and wounded, is it not awful to contemplate what must be the woe of the remainder? . . .

The stockade or pen in which the prisoners at Andersonville are confined, is an enclosure of fourteen acres, five of which were a morass. Here the men were without shelter, and in many instances almost naked, huddled together without room for exercise. During the hot Summer months there were scattered about in this pen an average of at least five hundred prisoners who were suffering from disease in almost every form incident to man, in a climate to which he is unaccustomed. Five acres of the surface of the ground were covered with human excrement, exhaling a morbidic influence which would prove fatal even to the rice plantation laborer, accustomed from infancy to breathing the malarious atmosphere of his native savannahs. Constantly drenched by rains, receiving bad food, always poorly prepared and often raw, in many instances naked and laboring under a mental depression verging upon melancholy, feeling that their days were numbered, the prisoners were kept in their dreadful prison.

The Franco-Prussian War

ARCHIBALD FORBES

The Battle and Surrender at Sedan

Unnerved by the rise of Prussia under Bismarck, France engineered a war with the burgeoning German state in July 1870. The French expectation, however, of seizing Berlin in days was rudely shattered when a French incursion into southern Germany was swatted aside, and a French army further north, under General Bazaine, encircled at Metz. An attempt to relieve Bazaine resulted in one of the great upsets of modern warfare, the utter rout of French forces under Napoleon III. Archibald Forbes, a jobbing journalist on military matters, made his way to the Franco-Prussian front line on his own initiative. There his letters caught the attention of Sir John Robinson, editor of the popular penny paper the *Daily News*, who duly put the Scottish ex-Dragoon on the staff payroll. Although Forbes, almost as famous a war reporter in his day as William Howard Russell, was the very master of the fast-written, fast-transmitted (by telegraph) dispatch, his account of the debâcle at Sedan was sent by post.

Daily News, 1 September 1870

Headquarters of the Crown Prince of Prussia,
Chemistry, near Sedan

The German arms have to-day been crowned with wonderful success. The greatest triumph of the war has been achieved in this battle of Sedan, and the Emperor of the French himself is among the prisoners. I have not time to tell of the clamour and rejoicing of the soldiery round about me. Before the post goes out there will not be time enough to describe the battle in its barest details. An army cut off and surrounded, an Emperor taken prisoner! Those are not common results. It is so overwhelming a catastrophe for France that one can excuse the tears in the old soldier's eyes, who dashes his crutch upon the floor, and will not even smoke his pipe. It is so overwhelming a catastrophe that one cannot but sigh over the evident pleasure of the ordinary villagers at seeing a hope of peace.

The French had got so near to Belgium that, as you might say of a ship, the least puff of wind would put them ashore. They had a chance of escaping on the morning of 31 August by leaving their baggage and most of their artillery in Sedan, and making a running fight of it with the whole army towards Mézíres and Laon. But they were too proud to run away, too slow in their movements to retreat with dignity, and were caught at a hopeless disadvantage.

The battle of Sedan was begun by the Bavarians. General von Der Tau, chief of the 1st Bavarian Corps, was ready in the grey twilight to open fire, and was only prevented from leading off the attack at 4 a.m. by the thick mist in the valley of the Meuse. When we came to the hill above Donchery, at about six o'clock, there was still a mist in the valley, but it had somewhat lifted, and the dull booming of cannon told that the Bavarians were at work.

Like some ship labouring in the trough of the sea, the beleaguered host of France is pitifully helpless. There was a time when a squadron of light horse, or even a travelling carriage at a brisk trot, might have got away to Belgium. The northern road was open when the battle began, but the French seemed to have no idea of flight. Crushed and hampered as they are, they fight like brave men. The battle is a mere *battue* by one o'clock, and the circle of white smoke puffs almost shuts in the French position. This is essentially an affair of artillery, and the German guns seem to be well served, besides being powerful. But there is a constant rattle of small-arms fire in the direction of Bazeilles, where flames and black smoke tell of a conflagration. If that slope be once cleared of Frenchmen, the only thing for the French to do will be to cut their way out through the Crown Prince of Saxony's army, or to retreat almost within the walls of the town. They cannot fight on their present line with Prussians in their rear.

There are other points carried by the Germans, and a closing in of the circle of white smoke round Sedan. Then a fresh attempt to break through, as though somebody of importance were to be cut out at any cost. We see numbers of Frenchmen making for the gates of the town, others wandering about as though not knowing what to do. There is a gradual cessation of the cannonade and, by about five o'clock, all is quiet, save for the dropping shots from the batteries near the King's position. There is a great outburst of flame and smoke in the town, as if some stores of combustibles had taken light, and there is a rumour that the white flag has been hoisted by the French. Then it is whispered that all these crowded troops – sixty, seventy, perhaps eighty thousand men – must surrender, for that they have no food. They surrender? Not only they, the Imperial soldiers, but the Emperor too. It is known that General Reille, an aide-de-camp of Napoleon, has come out to King William with a letter from the Emperor to his Prussian Majesty. The troops are wild with joy; they have caught him; then and there will be an end to the war.

3 September

When the firing had ceased on that terrible day before yesterday, and the great smoke cloud of the explosion in the town had slowly drifted away, there was as strange a scene of military disaster as could well be imagined. A large army was shut into the space which one division might have occupied. The fortress of Sedan had so many defenders as to make it indefensible. I have told, in a former letter, how General Reille, aide-de-camp to the Emperor, came out with a flag of truce, and was brought to King William on the hill above the Meuse. Napoleon wrote simply, as one soldier to another, proposing an armistice in which to treat of surrender. To have gone on fighting would have been madness, for the German troops held every approach to the town, and the French troops, shattered and discouraged, could not have hoped to cut their way through. They were reduced to so small a circle of outworks that whilst they attacked one German corps, they might have been cannonaded in rear by most of the others. In a word, their condition was desperate.

The Crown Prince was wildly cheered as he came back to his quarters at Chemery. Everyone was ordered to have lighted candles in their windows, and the soldiers made such a joyous din that there was a panic among the French inhabitants. Women screamed, and men retreated to their houses, not knowing what the hubbub might mean. My poor old landlady rushed at me for protection, and clung to my arm, saying "Ah, *monsieur*, you will save me, will you not? You can speak to them. You can tell them that I have given all the bread I had. There is none left; not even a morsel for my supper!" She trembled with terror as the shouts grew louder, and was only reassured by being told that this wild hurrahing meant "*Vive le Prince!*" The Emperor a prisoner – the army surrendered; what did villagers know about such great matters? She hoped there would be peace; she knew that, and so did they all. It was lucky that an illumination had been ordered, for otherwise somebody must have been run over in the noisy, crowded street.

Yesterday morning, quite early, a carriage containing four French officers drove out from Sedan and came into the German lines. The carriage was accompanied by three officers on horseback, but had no other escort, and when it had got among the Germans one of its occupants put out his head, and asked them, in their own language, where was Count Bismarck? We must see him at once. The Germans said that Donchery was the most likely spot in which to find the Count, though no one knew exactly his whereabouts. Forward, then, to Donchery. The carriage dashed away, and many a curious glance was cast after it. That short drive was known to be a great historic event. Count Bismarck might live all the years that a courteous Arab would wish him, and never have such another visitor in the early morning. They met at a small house outside the town, on the left bank of the Meuse, a house where, oddly enough, the inmates, being from Luxembourg, spoke both French and German. On his first arrival the Emperor went inside. But it was thought that they could sit more comfortably in the open air – it was a delightfully fine fresh morning – so chairs were placed for them, and there they sat talking for a couple of hours. The Emperor wore the undress uniform of a general, with but one decoration on his

breast, and with the usual *képi* of the French service. Count
Bismarck was in his white cuirassier uniform undress, with a flat
cap and long boots. If you picture them sitting outside the small
house, with the staff officers present lying on the patch of grass
not far off, and the tall poplar trees flanking the *chaussée* as far
as it can be seen, you will realize this striking episode. Napoleon
looked better in health than last year, but anxious and careworn.
He asked to see King William, and said that he placed himself at
his Majesty's disposition. As to politics, he avoided all show of
dealing in any way, whilst a prisoner, with the fate of France. He
surrendered with his army, but could not yield one jot, politi-
cally, on behalf of the French people or of the Government of
the Empress Regent. Count Bismarck, in his turn, placed before
Napoleon the fact that this surrender of Sedan must be complete – I had well-nigh said, must be "unconditional" – but that
would be going too far. It must be a complete surrender, because
the French were not in a position to ask better terms. The
Emperor much desired to see King William before the articles
of capitulation were signed. This, however, the King had thought
it better, both for himself and his illustrious prisoner, to refuse.
They could not so well arrange a hard bargain as could their
ministers and generals. In everything personal the King was
resolved to treat the Emperor with consideration. But as to the
question of the terms to be granted, that was another matter.

When Napoleon and Bismarck had chatted for a little while
more of indifferent things, this long-to-be-remembered interview beside the Meuse was brought to an end. The Count went
to prepare his own quarters in Donchery for the Emperor's
reception, but it was afterwards decided that a snug chateau
near Frenois would be more convenient, as Napoleon wished to
be as little seen by people as possible. Hither, then, he was
escorted by a detachment of the First Prussian Cuirassiers, and
here he remained whilst Generals de Wimpffen and Von Moltke
discussed the terms of the surrender of Sedan.

King William made a visit to the captive Emperor in the chateau of Frenois yesterday afternoon. Napoleon remained
perfectly calm at the beginning of the visit. He received his guest
of 1867, and his conqueror of to-day, with grave politeness,
spoke with him for a few moments in an outer room, and then
withdrew with the King into another room, where no one

followed them. The Crown Prince stepped to the door and closed it, and the French and German officers present remained some little time waiting before Napoleon and the King returned. What they had said to each other may have concerned the status of the captive Emperor. Certain it is that Napoleon was much affected by the courtesy of King William and that he expressed to the Crown Prince in warm terms his sense of the generous manner in which he had been treated.

To-day, 3 September, the Emperor has started for Aix-la-Chapelle on his way to his future residence in Germany.

I rode over the greater part of the battle-field yesterday morning – the morning after the fight. It was a shocking thing to see so many dead men and wounded men, and dead and wounded horses, crowded together in some places. It was a sight to cause reflections as the old Frenchman said who lived in the village where the fighting had been hottest. "*Ah! mon Dieu, Monsieur, c'est la guerre.*" He took a sombre view of *la guerre* for the scene was horrible. With two friends who were anxious to study the positions of the armies contending on 1 September I went round through Donchery and past the great bend of the Meuse, came towards the French lines as the 11th Prussian Corps had come, and pushing southward between the outposts of the hostile armies, traversed the railway bridge at Bazeilles, to return to headquarters. The first sign of active and immediate war was the block of prisoners at Donchery. There they were, of all arms of the service, the dark-faced Turco and the young, boyish conscript, collected in a mass, ready to be marched away. The plain beyond Donchery was covered with slightly wounded men wandering to the rear. French and German, friend and foe, it mattered not; they went amicably along, the common suffering making them friends. No one seemed to dream of further violence and further fighting. The battle was over, and they were glad to creep together to the rear, with little civilities exchanged in the way of pipe lights and sips of brandy, and with no more hostile feeling than two patients already in a hospital. We passed hundreds of them as we went round the bend of the stream and came upon the first signs of the conflict of the day before. There was a dead horse, a cuirass, a heap of broken weapons. In this cottage were several wounded Frenchmen taking some soup with a wounded Prussian, who seemed almost too much hurt to eat. Behind the garden wall was a dead cuirassier, his hands clutching the grass in the agony of death, his face stern and determined. No one noticed him, any more than if he were a dead horse. It is a curious thing to think that whole districts in quiet England will turn out to see a murdered family, and that here on a battle-field the same murdered family would be trampled in to the mud without being noticed. This meadow on the hill-side is full of mangled horses and dead cuirassiers. It was here that they made a frantic attempt to break through, and were mowed down by the Prussian fusillade. You must have been on several battle-fields to understand the signs of what has taken place by the look of the spot next morning. This group of dead horses, with a helmet or two and a dozen cuirasses with a broken trumpet and three dead cuirassiers, means serious work. The dark stains on the ground are where the wounded have lain and been removed. The little heap of swords under that hedge is where some dismounted troopers were forced to surrender. Then we come to Prussian helmets crushed and trampled. Some are marked by a shell or bullet, and have blood upon them. They tell of loss to the regiment to which they belonged. Others have no particular trace of violence, and may either be signs of wounded men, or of men who have simply thrown their helmets away in the heat of action, and put on their forage caps to march more lightly. These dark stains, surrounded by knapsack and rifle, by greatcoat and cooking tin, are where men have lain who have been badly wounded, or even killed, but whose friends have made them as comfortable as could be under the difficulties of the time. One has a little shelter of twigs and branches put to keep off the sun; another has had the blanket propped on two rifles, and his knapsack for a pillow. But he has died in the night, and is left with his cloak over his face until the burying party shall come round. See yonder drums and knapsacks, stains of blood and dead men lying on their faces. It is where a heavy blow has been struck at some infantry regiment. The men have fallen under a musketry fire, and the line of dead shows where the ground was held. Come a few steps further to the rear. You perceive a few more dead men, shot whilst in flight, and a number of bright, well-cleaned rifles scattered on the turf. This is where the regiment broke and fled, where some perished with their backs to the foe and others threw down their arms. We might gather the minutest details of the loss on either side if only human strength and energy sufficed to traverse this immense tract in a single morning. At one place there were horses as thick as they could lie. But this was a little further down the slope to the southward, where I had seen that gallant cavalry charge. The *Chasseurs à cheval* and the *Chasseurs d'Afrique* had dashed along the hill-side, half-hidden in the dust which they raised, and had been destroyed by a steady fusillade. Here lay the famous light horsemen, with their bright uniforms dabbled in blood, and their fiery little steeds crushed and mangled by Prussian shells. Most of the men and horses now on the ground were dead, but some few wounded men yet lingered in agony, with white rings tied to sticks that were planted beside them as a means of calling the surgeon's attention when he should have time to revisit them. The badly wounded horses, more fortunate for once in being brutes, had been killed to put them out of pain, and only a stray horse slightly wounded stood dismally here and there, wondering, perhaps, what it could all mean.

The Franco-Prussian War

HENRY LABOUCHERE

The Siege of Paris

A part-proprietor of the *Daily News*, Henry "Labby" Labouchere
became a war correspondent on a whim after finding himself "on
the spot" in Paris when the Prussians began their encircling of the
city after victory at Sedan. Although most of the city suffered deprivation as well as bombardment, Labouchere saw out the siege in
some comfort at the British Embassy, sustained by a resident flock
of sheep. Most of his dispatches were famously sent out by balloon
over Prussian lines, and resulted in a trebling of the *Daily News*'s
circulation.

Daily News, 30 December 1870

When the Fenians in the United States meditate a raid upon
Canada, they usually take very great care to allow their intentions to be known. Our sorties are much like these Hibernian
surprises. If the Prussians do not know when we are about to
attack, they cannot complain that it is our fault. The "*Après
vous, Monsieurs les Anglais*", still forms the chivalrous but
somewhat naif tactics of the Gauls. On Sunday, as a first step
to military operations, the gates of the city were closed to all
unprovided with passes. On Monday a Grand Council of generals and admirals took place at the Palais Royal. Yesterday and
all last night drums were beating, trumpets were blowing, and
troops were marching through the streets. The war battalions
of the National Guard, in their new uniforms, spick and span,
were greeted with shouts, to which they replied by singing a

song, the chorus of which is "*Vive la guerre Piff-Paff*", and which has replaced the "Marseillaise". As the ambulances had been ordered to be ready to start at six in the morning, I presumed that business would commence at an early hour, and I ordered myself to be called at 5.30. I was called, and got out of my bed, but, alas for noble resolutions! having done so, I got back again into it and remained between the sheets quietly enjoying that sleep which is derived from the possession of a good conscience, and a still better digestion, until the clock struck nine.

It was not until past eleven o'clock that I found myself on the outside of the gate of La Villette, advancing, as Grouchy should have done at Waterloo, in the direction of the sound of the cannon. From the gate a straight road runs to Le Bourget, having the Fort of Aubervilliers on the right, and St Denis on the left. Between the fort and the gate there were several hundred ambulance waggons, and above a thousand *brancardiers* stamping their feet and blowing on their fingers to keep themselves warm. In the fields on each side of the road there were numerous regiments of Mobiles drawn up ready to advance if required. The sailors, who are quartered here in great numbers, said that they had carried Le Bourget early in the morning, but that they had been obliged to fall back, with the loss of about a third of their number. Most of them had hatchets by their sides, and they attack a position much as if they were boarding a ship. About a hundred prisoners had been brought into the town in the morning, as well as two *frères Chrétiens*, who had been wounded, and for whom the greatest sympathy was expressed. Little seemed to be known of what was passing. "The Prussians will be here in an hour," shouted one man; "The Prussians are being exterminated," shouted another. At a farm yard close by Drancy I saw Ducrot with his staff. The General had his hood drawn over his head, and both he and his aide-de-camp looked so glum, that I thought it just as well not to congratulate him upon the operations of the day. In and behind Drancy there were a large number of troops, who I heard were to camp there during the night. None seemed exactly to know what had happened. The officers and soldiers were not in good spirits. On my return into Paris, however, I found the following proclamation of the Government posted on the walls: – "2 p.m. – The attack was commenced this morning by a great deployment from Mount Valerein to Nogent, the combat has commenced, and continues everywhere, with favourable chances for us. – Schmitz." The people on the Boulevards seem to imagine that a great victory has been gained. When one asks them where? they answer "everywhere". I can only answer myself for what occurred at Le Bourget. I hear that Vinoy has occupied Nogent, on the north of the Marne; the resistance he encountered could not, however, have been very great, as only seven wounded have been brought into this hotel and only one to the American ambulance. General Trouchu announced this morning that 100 battalions of the National Guard are outside the walls, and I shall be curious to learn how they conduct themselves under fire. Far be it from me to say that they will not fight like lions. If they do, however, it will surprise most of the military men with whom I have spoken on the subject. As yet all they have done has been to make frequent "pacts with death", to perform unauthorized strategical movements to the rear whenever they have been sent to the front, to consume much liquor, to pillage houses and – to put it poetically – toy with Amaryllis in the trench, or with the tangles of Nereas's hair. Their general, Clement Thomas, is doing his best to knock them into shape, but I am afraid that it is too late. There are cases in which, in defiance of the proverb, it is too late to mend.

In order to form an opinion with regard to the condition of the poorer classes, I went yesterday into some of the back slums in the neighbourhood of the Boulevard de Clichy. The distress is terrible. Women and children, half starved, were seated at their doorsteps, with hardly clothes to cover them decently. They said that, as they had neither firewood nor coke, they were warmer out-of-doors than in-doors. Many of the National Guards, instead of bringing their money home to their families, spend it in drink; and there are many families, composed entirely of women and children, who, in this land of bureaucracy, are apparently left to starve whilst it is decided to what category they belong. The Citizen Moltu, the ultra-Democratic Mayor, announced that in his *arrondissement* all left-handed marriages are to be regarded as valid, and the left-handed spouses of the National Guards are to receive the allowance which is granted to the legitimate wives of these warriors. But a new difficulty has arisen. Left-handed polygamy prevails to a great extent among the Citizen Moltu's admirers. Is a lady who has five husbands entitled to five rations, and is a lady who only owns the fifth of a National Guard to have only one-fifth of a ration? These are questions which the Citizen Moltu is now attempting to solve. A few lays ago Madame Hamelin was discovered dead in bed in a garret of Belleville, of cold and starvation. Her husband has been, under Louis Philippe, ambassador at Constantinople. I went to see yesterday what was going on in the house of a friend of mine in the Avenue de l'Impératrice, who has left Paris. The servant who was in charge told me that up there they had been unable to obtain bread for three days, and that the last time that he had presented his ration ticket he had been given about half an inch of cheese. "How do you live, then?" I asked. After looking mysteriously round to see that no one was watching us, he took me down into the cellar, and pointed to some meat in a barrel. "It is half a horse," he said, in the tone of a man who is showing someone the corpse of his murdered victim. "A neighbouring coachman killed him, and we salted him down and divided it." Then he opened a closet in which sat a huge cat. "I am fattening her up for Christmas-day," he observed.

The Franco-Prussian War

ARCHIBALD FORBES

The Suppression of the Paris Commune

In September 1870 the Third Republic of France was proclaimed, but surrender by its leaders in the Franco-Prussian War
led working-class Parisians to rise in the famed "Commune". On
21 May troops loyal to the Royalist government at Versailles
entered the French capital to suppress the rebellion. An estimated 20,000 Parisians lost their lives in the slaughter that
followed.

Daily News, 26 May 1871

Paris, Tuesday, 23 May, Five o'clock. The firing is furious and
confusing all round. At the Opera House it is especially strong.
I see troops and man after man skulking along the parapet of
its roof. They have packs on, so I think they are Versaillists; but
I cannot see their breeches and so cannot be certain. The *drapeau rouge* still waves from the statue on the summit of the
New Opera House. The Federals are massed now at the top of
the Rue Lafitte and firing down towards the boulevards. This
must mean that the Versaillists are on the boulevards now. On
account of the Versaillist fire the Federals cannot well come out
into the Rue de Provence, and everywhere they seem between
the devil and the deep sea. The people in the Porte Cochère
are crying bravo and clapping their hands, because they think
the Versaillists are winning.

Twenty minutes past five. They were Versaillists that I saw on the parapet of the New Opera. There is a cheer; the people rush out into the fire and clap their hands. The tricolor is waving on the hither end of the Opera House. I saw the man stick it up. The red flag still waves at the other end. A ladder is needed to remove it. Ha! you are a good plucky one, if all the rest were cowards. You deserve to give the army a good name. A little grig of a fellow in red breeches, he is one of the old French linesman breed. He scuttles forward to the corner of the Rue Halévy in the Boulevard Haussmann, takes up his post behind a tree, and fires along the Boulevard Haussmann towards the Rue Taitbout. When is a Frenchman not dramatic? He fires with an air; he loads with an air; he fires again with a flourish, and is greeted with cheering and clapping of hands. Then he beckons us back dramatically, for he meditates firing up the Rue de Lafayette, but changes his mind and blazes away again up Haussmann. Then he turns and waves on his fellows as if he were on the boards of a theatre, the Federal bullets cutting the bark and leaves all around him. He is down. The woman and I dart out from our corner and carry him in. He is dead, with a bullet through the forehead.

Twenty-five minutes to six. The scene is intensely dramatic. A Versaillist has got a ladder and is mounting the statue of Apollo on the front elevation of the New Opera House. He tears down the *drapeau rouge* just as the Versailles troops stream out of the Chaussée d'Antin across the Boulevard Haussmann, and down the Rue Meyerbeer and the continuation of the Chaussée d'Antin. The people rushed from their houses with bottles of wine; money was showered into the streets. The women fell on the necks of the sweaty, dusty men in red breeches, and hugged them amid shouts of *Vive la ligne*. The soldiers fraternized warmly; drank and pressed forward. Their discipline was admirable. They formed in companies behind the next barricade and obeyed the officer at once when he called them from conviviality. Now the wave of Versaillists is over us for good, and the red breeches are across the Great Boulevard and going at the Place Vendôme. Everybody seems wild with joy, and Communist cards of citizenship are being torn up wholesale. It is not *citoyen* now under pain of suspicion. You may say *monsieur* if you like.

Ten p.m. Much has been done since the hour at which I last dated. The Versaillist soldiers, pouring down in one continuous stream by the Chaussée d'Antin, horse, foot, and artillery, crossed the Great Boulevard, taking the insurgents in flank, not without considerable fighting and a good deal of loss, for the Federals fought like wildcats wherever they could get the ghost of a cover. Anxious to ascertain whether there was any prospect of an Embassy bag to Versailles, I started up the now quiet Boulevard Haussmann, and by tacks and dodges got down into the Rue de Miromesnil, which debouches in the faubourg opposite the Palace of the Elysée. Shells were bursting very freely in the neighbourhood, but the matter was urgent, and I pressed on up to the Rue du Faubourg Saint-Honoré, and looked round the corner for a second. Had I looked a second longer, I should not have been writing these lines. A shell splinter whizzed past me as I drew back, close enough to blow my beard aside. The street was a pneumatic tube for shellfire. Nothing could have lived in it. I fell back, thinking I might get over to the Embassy as the firing died away, and waited in the entry of an ambulance for an hour. There were not a few ambulances about this spot. I saw, for a quarter of an hour, one wounded man carried into the one I was near every minute, for I timed the stretchers by my watch. Looking into others, I could see the courtyards littered with mattresses and groaning men. A few but not many corpses, chiefly of National Guards, lay in the streets, behind the barricades, and in the gutters.

As I returned to the Hôtel de la Chaussée d'Antin, I had to cross the line of artillery pouring southward from the Church of the Trinity, and so down the Rue Halévy, towards the quarter where the sound indicated hot fighting was still going on. The artillerymen received a wild ovation from the inhabitants of the Chaussée d'Antin. The men gave them money, the women tendered them bottles of wine. All was *gaudeamus*. Where, I wonder, had the people secreted the tricolor all these days of the Commune? It now waved from every window, and flapped in the still night air, as the shouts of *Vive la ligne* gave it a lazy throb.

Wednesday. And so evening wore into night, and night became morning. Ah! this morning! Its pale flush of aurora bloom was darkest, most sombre night for the once proud, now stricken and humiliated, city. When the sun rose, what saw he? Not a fair fight – on that within the last year Sol has looked down more than once. But black clouds flouted his rays – clouds that rose from the Palladium of France. Great God! that men should be so mad as to strive to make universal ruin because their puny course of factiousness is run! The flames from the Palace of the Tuileries, kindled by damnable petroleum, insulted the soft light of the morning and cast lurid rays on the grimy recreant Frenchmen who skulked from their dastardly incendiarism to pot at countrymen from behind a barricade. How the place burned! The flames revelled in the historical palace, whipped up the rich furniture, burst out the plate-glass windows, brought down the fantastic roof. It was in the Prince Imperial's wing facing the Tuileries Gardens where the demon of fire first had his dismal sway. By eight o'clock the whole of the wing was nearly burned out. As I reached the end of the Rue Dauphine the red belches of flames were bursting out from the corner of the Tuileries facing the private gardens and the Rue de Rivoli: the rooms occupied by the King of Prussia and his suite on the visit to France the year of the Exhibition. There is a furious jet of flame pouring out of the window where Bismarck used to sit and smoke. Crash! Is it an explosion or a fall of flooring that causes this burst of black smoke and red sparks in our faces? God knows what fell devices may be within that burning pile; it were well surely to give it a wide berth.

And so eastward to the Place du Palais-Royal, which is still unsafe by reason of shot and shell from the neighbourhood of the Hôtel de Ville. And there is the great archway by which troops were wont to enter into the Place du Carrousel – is the fire there yet? Just there, and no more; could the archway be cut, the Louvre, with its artistic riches, might still be spared. But there are none to help. The troops are lounging supine in the rues; intent – and who shall blame weary, powder-grimed men? – on bread and wine. And so the devastator leaps from chimney to chimney, from window to window. He is over the archway now, and I would not give two hours' purchase for all the riches of the Louvre. In the name of modern vandalism, what means that burst of smoke and jet of fire? Alas for art; the Louvre is on fire independently. And so is the Palais-Royal and the Hôtel de Ville, where the rump of the Commune are cowering amidst their incendiarism; and the Ministry of Finance, and many another public and private building besides.

I turn from the spectacle sad and sick, to be sickened yet further by another spectacle. The Versaillist troops collected about the foot of the Rue Saint-Honoré were enjoying the fine game of Communist hunting. The Parisians of civil life are caitiffs to the last drop of their thin, sour, white blood. But yesterday they had cried *Vive la Commune!* and submitted to be governed by this said Commune. Today they rubbed their hands with livid currish joy to have it in their power to denounce a Communist and reveal his hiding place. Very eager at this work are the dear creatures of women. They know the rat-holes into which the poor devils have got, and they guide to them with a fiendish glee which is a phase of the many-sided sex. *Voilà!* the braves of France returned to a triumph after a shameful captivity! They have found him, the miserable! Yes, they drag him out from one of the purlieus which Haussmann had not time to sweep away, and a guard of six of them hem him round as they march him into the Rue Saint-Honoré. A tall, pale, hatless man, with something not ignoble in his carriage. His lower lip is trembling, but his brow is firm, and the eye of him has some pride and defiance in it. They yell – the crowd – "Shoot him; shoot him!" – the demon women most clamorous, of course. An arm goes into the air; there are on it the stripes of a non-commissioned officer, and there is a stick in the fist. The stick falls on the head of the pale man in black. Ha! the infection has caught; men club their rifles, and bring them down on that head, or clash them into splinters in their lust for murder. He is down; he is up again; he is down again; the thuds of the gunstocks on him sounding just as the sound when a man beats a cushion with a stick. A certain British impulse, stronger than consideration for self, prompts me to run forward. But it is useless. They are firing into the flaccid carcass now, thronging about it like blowflies on a piece of meat. His brains spurt on my boot and plash into the gutter, whither the carrion is bodily chucked, presently to be trodden on and rolled on by the feet of multitudes and wheels of gun carriages.

Womanhood, then, is not quite dead in that band of bedlamites who had clamoured "Shoot him." Here is one in hysterics; another, with wan, scared face, draws out of the press an embryo bedlamite, her offspring, and, let us hope, goes home. But surely all manhood is dead in the soldiery of France to do a deed like this. An officer – one with a bull throat and the eyes of Algiers – stood by and looked on at the sport, sucking a cigar meanwhile.

The merry game goes on. Denouncing becomes fashionable, and denouncing is followed in the French natural sequence by braining. Faugh! let us get away from the truculent cowards and the bloody gutters, and the yelling women, and the Algerian-eyed officers. Here is the Place Vendôme, held, as I learn on credible authority, by twenty-five Communists and a woman, against all that Versailles found it in its heart to do, for hours. In the shattered Central Place Versaillist sentries are stalking about the ruins of the column. They have accumulated, too, some forces in the rat-trap. There is one corpse in the gutter buffeted and besmirched – the corpse, as I learn, of the Communist captain of a barricade who held it for half an hour single-handed against the braves of France, and then shot himself. The braves have, seemingly, made sure of him by shooting him and the clay, which was once a man, over and over again.

And how about the chained wildcats in the Hôtel de Ville? Their backs are to the wall, and they are fighting now, not for life, but that they may do as much evil as they can before their hour comes – as come it will before the minute hand of my watch makes many more revolutions. The Versaillists do not dare to rush at the barricades around the Hôtel de Ville; they are at once afraid of their skins and explosions. But they are mining, circumventing, burrowing, and they will be inside the cordon soon. Meanwhile the holders of the Hôtel de Ville are pouring out death and destruction over Paris in miscellaneous wildness. Now it is a shell in the Champs-Elysées; now one in the already shattered Boulevard Haussmann; now one somewhere about the Avenue Reine Hortense. It is between the devil and the deep sea with the people in the Hôtel de Ville. One enemy with weapons in his hand is outside; another, fire, and fire kindled by themselves, is inside. Will they roast, or seek death on a bayonet point?

It is hard to breathe in an atmosphere mainly of petroleum smoke. There is a sun, but his heat is dominated by the heat of the conflagrations. His rays are obscured by the lurid, blue-black smoke that is rising with a greasy fatness everywhere into the air. Let us out of it, for goodness' sake. I take horse, and ride off by the river bank towards the Point-du-Jour, leaving at my back the still loud rattle of the firing and the smoke belches. I ride on to the Point-du-Jour through Dombrowski's "second line of defence" by the railway viaduct. Poor Dombrowski! a good servant to bad masters. I should like to know his fate for certain. Versaillists have told me that they saw him taken prisoner yesterday morning, dragged on to the Trocadéro, and there shot in cold blood in the face of day, looking dauntlessly into the muzzles of the chassepots. Others say he is wounded and a prisoner.

As I ride up the broad slope of the avenue between Viroflay and Versailles, I pass a very sorrowful and dejected company. In file after file of six each march the prisoners of the Commune – there are over two thousand of them together – patiently, and it seems to me with some consciousness of pride they march, linked closely arm in arm. Among them are many women, some of them the fierce barricade Hecates, others mere girls, soft and timid, who are here seemingly because a parent is here too. All are bareheaded and foul with dust, many powder-stained too, and the burning sun beats down on bald foreheads. Not the sun alone beats down, but the flats of sabres wielded by the dashing Chasseurs d'Afrique, who are the escort of these unfortunates. Their experiences might have taught them decency to the captives. No sabre blades had descended on their pates in that long, dreary march from Sedan to their German captivity; they were the prisoners of soldiers. But they are prisoners now no longer, as they caper on their wiry Arab stallions, and in their pride of cheap victory, they belabour unmercifully the miserable of the Commune. In front are three or four hundred prisoners, lashed together with ropes, and among these are not a few men in red breeches, deserters taken red-handed. I marvel that they are here at all, and not dead in the streets of Paris.

As I drive along the green margin of the placid Seine to Saint-Denis, the spectacle which the capital presents is one never to be forgotten. On its white houses the sun still smiles. But up through the sunbeams struggle and surge ghastly swart waves and folds and pillars of dense smoke; not one or two, but I reckon them on my fingers till I lose the count. Ha! there is a sharp crack, and then a dull thud on the air. No artillery that, surely some great explosion, which must have rocked Paris to its base. There rises a convolvulus-shaped volume of whiter smoke, with a jetlike spurt, such as men describe when Vesuvius bursts into eruption, and then it breaks into fleecy waves and eddies away to the horizon all round as the ripple of a stone thrown into a pool spreads to the margin of the water. The crowds of Germans who sit by the Seine, stolidly watching, are startled into a burst of excitement – the excitement might well be world-wide. "Paris the beautiful" is Paris the ghastly, Paris the battered, Paris the burning, Paris the blood-spattered, now. And this is the nineteenth century, and Europe professes civilization, and France boasts of culture, and Frenchmen are braining one another with the butt ends of muskets, and Paris is burning. We want but a Nero to fiddle.

The Bulgarian Revolt

JANUARIUS ALOYSIUS MACGAHAN

Massacre in Batak

The Bulgarian nationalist uprising of 1876 was ruthlessly repressed by the Turkish authorities, although when rumours of indiscriminate slaughters by Turkish Bashi-Bazouk irregulars surfaced in London these were denied by Istanbul. The London *Daily News* dispatched American correspondent Januarius Aloysius MacGahan to verify the reports; the horrific evidence found by MacGahan caused a sensation all over Europe, led Russian to declare war on Turkey, and so indirectly brought about Bulgarian independence in 1878.

The Turkish Atrocities in Bulgaria, 1876

Down in the bottom of one of these hollows we could make out a village, which our guide informed us it would still take us an hour and a half to reach, although it really seemed to be very near. This was the village of Batak, which we were in search of. The hillsides were covered with little fields of wheat and rye, that were golden with ripeness. But although the harvest was ripe, and over-ripe, although in many places the well-filled ears had broken down the fast-decaying straw that could no longer hold them aloft, and were now lying flat, there was no sign of reapers trying to save them. The fields were as deserted as the little valley, and the harvest was rotting in the soil. In an hour we had neared the village.

As we approached our attention was directed to some dogs on a slope overlooking the town. We turned aside from the road, and, passing over the debris of two or three walls, and through several gardens, urged our horses up the ascent towards the dogs. They barked at us in an angry manner, and then ran off into the adjoining fields. I observed nothing peculiar as we mounted, until my horse stumbled. When looking down I perceived he had stepped on a human skull partly hid among the grass. It was quite dry and hard, and might, to all appearances, have been there for two or three years, so well had the dogs done their work. A few steps further there was another, and beside it part of a skeleton, likewise white and dry. As we ascended, bones, skeletons, and skulls became more frequent, but here they had not been picked so clean, for there were fragments of half-dry, half-putrid flesh still clinging to them. At last we came to a kind of little plateau or shelf on the hillside, where the ground was nearly level, with the exception of a little indentation where the head of a hollow broke through. We rode towards this, with the intention of crossing it, but all suddenly drew rein with an exclamation of horror, for right before us, almost beneath our horses' feet, was a sight that made us shudder. It was a heap of skulls, intermingled with bones from all parts of the human body, skeletons, nearly entire, rotting clothing, human hair, and putrid flesh lying there in one foul heap, around which the grass was growing luxuriantly. It emitted a sickening odour, like that of a dead horse, and it was here the dogs had been seeking a hasty repast when our untimely approach interrupted them.

In the midst of this heap I could distinguish one slight skeleton form still enclosed in a chemise, the skull wrapped about with a coloured handkerchief, and the bony ankles encased in the embroidered footless stockings worn by the Bulgarian girls. We looked about us. The ground was strewed with bones in every direction, where the dogs had carried them off to gnaw them at their leisure. At the distance of a hundred yards beneath us lay the town. As seen from our standpoint, it reminded one somewhat of the ruins of Herculaneum or Pompeii.

There was not a roof left, not a whole wall standing; all was a mass of ruins, from which arose, as we listened, a low plaintive wail, like the "keening" of the Irish over their dead, that filled the little valley and gave it voice . . .

On the other side of the way were the skeletons of two children lying side by side, partly covered with stones, and with frightful sabre cuts in their little skulls. The number of children killed in these massacres is something enormous. They were often spitted on bayonets, and we have several stories from eye witnesses who saw little babies carried about the streets, both here and at Otluk-kui, on the point of bayonets. The reason is simple. When a Mahometan has killed a certain number of infidels, he is sure of Paradise, no matter what his sins may be. Mahomet probably intended that only armed men should count, but the ordinary Mussulman takes the precept in broader acceptation, and counts women and children as well. Here in Batak the Bashi-Bazouks, in order to swell the count, ripped open pregnant women, and killed the unborn infants. As we approached the middle of the town, bones, skeletons, and skulls became more numerous. There was not a house beneath the ruins of which we did not perceive human remains, and the street besides was strewn with them. Before many of the doorways women were walking up and down wailing their funeral chant. One of them caught me by the arm and led me inside of the walls, and there in one corner, half covered with stones and mortar, were the remains of another young girl, with her long hair flowing wildly about among the stones and dust. And the mother fairly shrieked with agony, and beat her head madly against the wall. I could only turn round and walk out sick at heart, leaving her alone with her skeleton. A few steps further on sat a woman on a doorstep, rocking herself to and fro, and uttering moans heartrending beyond anything I could have imagined. Her head was buried in her hands, while her fingers were unconsciously twisting and tearing her hair as she gazed into her lap, where lay three little skulls with the hair still clinging to them. How did the mother come to be saved, while the children were slaughtered? Who knows? Perhaps she was away from the village when the massacre occurred. Perhaps she had escaped with a babe in her arms, leaving these to be saved by the father; or perhaps, most fearful, most pitiful of all, she had been so terrorstricken that she had abandoned the three poor little ones to their fate and saved her own life by flight. If this be so, no wonder she is tearing her hair in that terribly unconscious way as she gazes at the three little heads lying in her lap . . .

The church was not a very large one, and it was surrounded by a low stone wall, enclosing a small churchyard about fifty yards wide by seventy-five long. At first we perceive nothing in particular, and the stench is so great that we scarcely care to look about us, but we see that the place is heaped up with stones and rubbish to the height of five or six feet above the level of the street, and upon inspection we discover that what appeared to be a mass of stones and rubbish is in reality an immense heap of human bodies covered over with a thin layer of stones. The whole of the little churchyard is heaped up with them to the depth of three or four feet, and it is from here that the fearful odour comes. Some weeks after the massacre, orders were sent to bury the dead. But the stench at that time had become so deadly that it was impossible to execute the order, or even to remain in the neighbourhood of the village. The men sent to perform the work contented themselves with burying a few bodies, throwing a little earth over others as they lay, and here in the churchyard they had tried to cover this immense heap of festering humanity by throwing in stones and rubbish over the walls, without daring to enter. They had only partially succeeded. The dogs had been at work there since, and now could be seen projecting from this monster grave, heads, arms, legs, feet, and hands, in horrid confusion. We were told there were three thousand people lying here in this little churchyard alone, and we could well believe it. It was a fearful sight – a sight to haunt one through life. There were little curly heads there in that festering mass, crushed down by heavy stones; little feet not as long as your finger on which the flesh was dried hard, by the ardent heat before it had time to decompose; little baby hands stretched out as if for help; babes that had died wondering at the bright gleam of sabres and the red hands of the fierce-eyed men who wielded them; children who had died shrinking with fright and terror; young girls who had died weeping and sobbing and begging for mercy; mothers who died trying to shield their little ones with their own weak bodies, all lying there together, festering in one horrid mass. They were silent enough now. There are no tears nor cries, no weeping, no shrieks of terror, nor prayers for mercy. The harvests are rotting in the fields, and the reapers are rotting here in the churchyard.

The Afghan War

PHILIP HENSMAN

The Storming of Takht-i-Shah Peak

Fear of Russian influence in central Asia led Britain to secure the
north-west frontier of its Indian Empire by invading Afghanistan.
After two years of war Britain installed a "friendly" monarch,
Abdurrahman Shah, on the country's throne. Philip Hensman
covered the conflict for the London *Times*.

The Afghan War of 1879–80, 1881

Sherpur, 12 December 1879, midnight
I left Mahomed Jan and his followers in possession of the hills
to the south of the Sherderwaza Heights, with a part of General Macpherson's brigade on the latter, ready to attack him.
To-day a party of 560 men, made up in nearly equal propor-
tions from the 67th Foot, 72nd Highlanders, 3rd Sikhs, and
5th Ghoorkas, aided by two guns of Morgan's mountain battery, have made that attack, and have established themselves
on a lower hill between the Sherderwaza Heights and the high
conical peak of Takht-i-Shah, whereon the enemy muster in
great force and have sixteen standards flying. This peak is the
highest of the clump of mountains south of Cabul and lying
between the city and Charasia, and was the point whence Captain Straton tried to heliograph to the Shutargardan in the
early days of our occupation. It is cone-shaped, looked at from
Sherpur, and on its southern side joins a ridge running southwards above the village of Indikee. The sides facing Cabul are
very steep, and covered with huge boulders polished by wind

and rain, and of a kind to check any storming party. Perfect cover is afforded to men holding it, and on the summit is a well-built sungar of great thickness, covering a natural cavity in the rocks which has been made bomb-proof by some Afghan engineer, who understood the strength of the point. Fifty men could lie in perfect security behind the sungar or in the hole below it, and could choose their own time for firing at an advancing enemy. Outside the sungar, and a little lower down, is a cave, wherein another strong body of men could hide themselves and act in a similar way, while their flank to the left would be guarded by a broken line of rocks extending down to the kotal, where the Bala Hissar Ridge meets them. Just between the two ranges is a low, dome-shaped hill, blocking up the otherwise open kotal; and round this a footpath winds, leading to the sungar, but so narrow as only to admit of men going up in Indian file. The enemy occupied this morning the Takht-i-Shah Peak and the line of rocks I have mentioned, and had also a few score of men on the lower hill in the kotal. Away on the south, hidden from our view, were some 5,000 or 6,000 men, waiting for an attack to develop, in order to reinforce the peak. At eight o'clock our guns opened fire from the picket on the ridge. There were then only seven standards on the peak, but during the day nine others were brought up; and the long ridge, stretching downwards to Beni Essar, was lined with men. These were, by the contour of the ground, safe from our shells, and they quietly watched the guns all day. From eight o'clock until evening Captain Morgan fired shell after shell into the sungar and the rocks below. The enemy were of quite a different order to those we have hitherto had to deal with. They stood up boldly to their flags, and waved their rifles and knives in derision at each shot. We could not spare more infantry for the attack, as we had to protect Sherpur, which, we learnt, was to be attacked by Kohistanis from over the Paen Minar Kotal, north of the lake. The city, too, was known to be in a ferment, and a demonstration might at any time be made from it against our cantonment. General Baker with his flying column was still absent, and our object was rather to hold the main body of Mahomed Jan's force in check, than try to disperse them with 560 men. At nine o'clock heliographic communication was opened with General Baker, then on the

Argandeh Kotal. He reported that his rear-guard had been harassed for the last two days, and that the hills in all directions were lined with tribesmen. He was ordered to march without delay to Sherpur, and it was hoped at first that he would arrive in time to assist General Macpherson in attacking the enemy's position. As he had to march fourteen miles with his rear-guard engaged from time to time, he did not reach Sherpur until evening, so his troops, foot-sore and tired, were not available.

After several hours' shelling of the Takht-i-Shah Peak, the 67th, the Highlanders, Sikhs, and Ghoorkas made their attack; and, in spite of the stubbornness with which the Afghans fought, established themselves on the low hill on the kotal. They tried to work upwards to the sungar; but the fire of the Afghans was so true and sustained, that the attempt had to be given up. Our men also ran short of ammunition, and they contented themselves finally with holding the position captured, so as to be able to co-operate on the morrow with any force sent out from Sherpur to attack by way of Beni Hissar on the enemy's flank. Our casualties included Major Cook, VC, 5th Ghoorkas, shot below the knee; Lieutenant Fasken, 3rd Sikhs, bullet wound in both thighs; and Lieutenant Fergusson, 72nd Highlanders, seriously wounded in the face. The enemy this evening still hold the Takht-i-Shah Peak in strength, and large reinforcements are said to have joined them from Logar, the Ghilzais from that district being up in arms. It has been decided to-night to send a brigade, under General Baker, to attack the peak from Beni Hissar village to-morrow at the same time that Colonel Money, of the 3rd Sikhs, moves up another force from the hill on the kotal.

13 December 1879, evening
To-day the Takht-i-Shah Peak has been carried, and a strong picket now holds it. The action has been a great success, but there are still large bodies of the enemy above Indikee; and as they may try to regain the position, General Macpherson has abandoned Dehmazung altogether, and posted his brigade on the Sherderwaza Heights. At eight o'clock this morning General Baker left cantonments with the following troops:

G-3, Royal Artillery, four guns;
No. 2 Mountain Battery, four guns;
92nd Highlanders (six companies);
Guides' Infantry (seven companies);
3rd Sikhs (wing of 300 men);
5th Punjab Cavalry.

General Baker took the road past the Bala Hissar, and, upon debouching into the plain north of Beni Hissar, found the enemy posted in force all along the ridge in front, leading down from the Takht-i-Shah Peak. Beni Hissar was also full of Afghans, and in the fields about it were detached parties. These, seeing our force advancing, began to stream towards the ridge, and the original plan of attack was so far modified that, instead of working round through Beni Hissar village, the Highlanders and Guides were sent straight across some marshy ground at the ridge. The object in view was to cut the enemy's line in two, and it was attained most successfully. Our eight guns opened fire at 1,400 yards upon the masses of Afghans on the ridge, and the shells kept under the musketry fire opened upon our infantry. The 3rd Sikhs protected General Baker's left flank, while the cavalry aided in keeping the scattered parties about Beni Hissar in check. Nothing could be finer than the advance of the 92nd and the Guides; they reached the slope of the hill, and opened fire upon the enemy, one continued roll of musketry being heard as they pushed upwards. They gained the crest, and the Afghan line was severed, about 2,000 being left about Beni Hissar while the assault was made upon the peak. The rapid fire from our breech-loaders swept away such of the enemy as stood firm, while the bayonet made short work of the ghazis who defended the standards. At some points twenty and thirty bodies were found lying piled together, shot through and through by Martini and Snider bullets, showing how well the volleys had told. In a very short time the majority opposed to the storming party had broken and fled. A few ghazis fought desperately, but upwards went the Highlanders in the same gallant style they had shown at Charasia, and under the same leader, Major White. The Guides, under Colonel Jenkins, were equally eager, this being their first chance in the campaign, and they shared with the 92nd the honour of scattering the defenders of the ridge. One

young Highland officer fell a victim to that uncalculating courage which becomes rashness when pushed to extremes.
Lieutenant Forbes, with only a few men, scaled the ridge, and
got detached from the regiment which was toiling up as fast as
the men with their heavy load of rifles and ammunition could
climb. He was left at last with only Colour-Sergeant Drum-
mond, an old twenty-one years man, and a band of ghazis
turned back and attacked him. The Sergeant was shot down,
and Lieutenant Forbes rushed forward to save his body from
mutilation. After cutting down a ghazi he was overpowered and
killed before the Highlanders could save him. Not a man of the
ghazis who had turned back escaped: they were shot and bayoneted on the rocks. As the attacking party neared the
Takht-i-Shah Peak the Afghans deserted it; and when a party of
the 72nd Highlanders and 5th Ghoorkas from the Bala Hissar
side reached the sungar, they found the flags still flying, but no
one guarding them. The position had been captured in about
two hours, and as the mid-day gun was fired in Sherpur, the
heliograph flashed from the sungar, and the peak was known to
be ours. Some of the enemy ventured too near the Chardeh
plain in their retreat, and a squadron of the 14th Bengal Lancers
charged among them, killing between twenty and thirty.

While the Highlanders and Guides were storming the ridge,
an attack had been attempted from Beni Hissar upon General
Baker's left flank, but the 3rd Sikhs drove back the enemy, who
began to move round towards Siah Sung, and eventually collected in force upon these hills. They were shelled by our guns,
and the 5th Punjab Cavalry were reinforced by two squadrons
of the 9th Lancers, a squadron of the 14th Bengal Lancers, and
the Guides' Cavalry. Wherever the ground was good, our sowars
and Lancers charged and did great execution. The Afghans
fought bravely, forming up to receive the cavalry with a steadiness that trained infantry would not have surpassed, and
reserving their fire until the horses were close upon them. One
brilliant charge by the 9th Lancers cost that regiment one officer
killed and two wounded, besides the loss of several troopers.
Captain Butson and Captain Chisholme, at the head of their
respective squadrons, swept down upon 500 or 600 men, taking
them on the right and left flank. Captain Butson turned in his
saddle as he faced the enemy, and cried out: "Now, men, at

them for the honour of the old 9th," and the next moment he fell dead, shot through the heart. He was in command of the regiment, the affair of the 11th having sadly thinned the ranks of the officers, and his death is universally regretted. Captain Chisholme was shot through the leg, the flash of the rifle burning his clothes, so steadily had the Afghan in front of him waited before discharging his piece. Lieutenant Trower was also slightly wounded, while the Sergeant-Major and three troopers were killed and seven wounded. The Lancers rode through and through the Afghans opposed to them, and scattered them all over the plain. The 5th Punjab Cavalry also made a successful charge; and the Guides twice got well among the fugitives. Their second charge was upon a body of Lehistanis, who had crossed the plain east of Bemaru and made for Siah Sung with the intention of joining Mahomed Jan. They were shelled from the eastern end of the Bemaru Heights; and, upon seeing General Baker's force engaged, halted irresolutely near Siah Sung. They tried to retrace their steps, but were suddenly charged down upon by the Guides, who had waited for them behind the northern slopes of Siah Sung. Sixty are said to have been killed in this charge alone, the Guides chasing them as far as the Logar river, where the swampy ground checked the cavalry. Altogether the day's fighting has been a wonderful success; and though our casualties are eleven killed and forty-three wounded, the enemy's loss in killed alone must have been between 200 and 300. One hundred and fifty of the 5th Punjab Infantry, sent out to reinforce General Baker, came upon a large party of Afghans marching down the Bala Hissar Road. They were at first mistaken for Highlanders; but when they fired a volley at the officer who rode up to speak to them, the mistake was soon apparent. The Punjabees at once extended themselves in skirmishing order among the willow plantations on each side of the road, and opened a rapid fire. The Afghans faced about and made for the Bala Hissar, but a company of the 5th cut off half their number, and in a hand-to-hand fight killed forty. These men, who are believed to have been from the city, were really run to earth, and were so exhausted that they could scarcely use their knives.

One feature of the day's fighting has been the attitude of the villagers about Cabul. A straggler from the 92nd Highlanders was found cut up between Sherpur and the Cabul river; officers riding alone have been fired at, and pelted with stones; and two villages on either side of the road to Beni Hissar opened a heavy fire upon our troops. General Baker halted on his way back to cantonments to burn these villages as a reward for their treachery. The lives of the men in one were spared on condition that they fired the other, the gates of which could not be forced open by our guns. The defenders were shot as they tried to escape from the ruins. From the Bala Hissar and near the city shots were fired, and the flanking parties of the 92nd, in their homeward march, came upon 200 or 300 men in the willow plantations, who fled towards the city walls. A convoy of wounded sent from the Sherderwaza Heights to Sherpur had also a narrow escape, the bravery of the non-commissioned officer in charge of the escort alone preventing a catastrophe on a small scale . . .

Sergeant Cox, with twenty men of the 72nd, was in charge of the dhoolies, and among the wounded were Major Cook, VC, 5th Ghoorkas; Lieutenant Fergusson, 72nd Highlanders; and Lieutenant Fasken, 3rd Sikhs. Upon arriving at the foot of the hill, the road leading under the southern wall of the Bala Hissar was followed, and it was soon seen that parties of armed men were lining the parapets. Sergeant Cox, fearing to draw the fire by striking across the fields towards Beni Hissar, where General Baker was shelling some villages, put on a bold face, and marched on steadily. This had the best effect, as not a shot was fired from the walls. Ten Highlanders were at the head of the dhoolies, and ten in rear. Just as the little party got near the Bala Hissar gate a large body of Afghans sprang out from among the willows lining either side of the road, and, drawing their knives, came straight upon the advance-guard. The road from Beni Hissar joins the road to Sherpur just at this point, and seeing that it would be impossible to cut through the enemy, or to retreat the way he had come (as in the latter case the men on the walls would probably open fire), Sergeant Cox pushed on, ordering his men to reserve their fire. His object was to get the dhoolies fairly on the Beni Hissar Road on his right, and then to fall back until help should come from that quarter. The manoeuvre succeeded admirably. Waiting until he was within twenty yards of the Afghans, he ordered the ten men with him to fire a volley. This was too much for the enemy, who broke and took cover in the trees. The dhoolie-bearers thought all was over, and those carrying Major Cook dropped their dhoolie in the middle of the road. They soon recovered courage, and while rapid volleys from the advance-guard kept the Afghans in check, all the dhoolies were got safely upon the Beni Hissar Road, and finally reached General Baker's force in safety. Sergeant Cox managed the whole business splendidly, and under such leadership the men were cool and collected, skirmishing and retiring without being touched by the scattered fire directed at them. After waiting an hour, the escort was strengthened by some cavalry, and the whole convoy of wounded reached cantonments in safety. The position in which Sergeant Cox was placed was a most dangerous one, as the least hesitation or want of decision would have been fatal: the Afghans were, indeed, so sure of success, that they did not fire at first, but trusted to cutting up the guard at close quarters with their knives. The three officers, whose lives were saved by Sergeant Cox's steadiness, reported the incident to Colonel Money, who had sent the dhoolies down the hill. Sergeant Cox was one of the men decorated with the distinguished service medal on December 8th for gallantry at the Peiwar Kotal. General Baker's force is now safely in quarters again. General Macpherson has sent back to Sherpur the 72nd Highlanders and the 3rd Sikhs, and, with the 67th Foot and the 5th Ghoorkas, holds the Bala Hissar Heights and the Takht-i-Shah Peak. The enemy are still in force above Indikee and at Dehmazung, which commands the Cabul gorge, and the road into the city has been abandoned. They may try to work round in that direction – that is, if to-day's defeat has not disheartened them. This evening a party of Kohistanis have come over the Surkh Kotal, and are bivouacking on a hill a mile and a half west of Sherpur. These are the reinforcements sent by Mir Butcha, who has no doubt heard of the success of Mahomed Jan on the 11th. The casualties to-day were eleven killed (two officers) and forty-three wounded. Of these the 92nd lost one officer and two men killed and nineteen wounded. The Guides had three killed and eight wounded.

The Transvaal Revolt

JOHN ALEXANDER CAMERON

The Fight on Majuba Hill

The Transvaal Revolt – or First Boer War – was occasioned by Britain's annexation of the Transvaal, a region of South Africa Boer settlers regarded as their own. On 10 December 1880 they hoisted their national flag and prepared for armed resistance. The British severely underestimated Boer resilience and guerrilla warfare expertise (learned fighting native Africans), and as a result the Boers achieved a fantastic rout at Majuba Hill when they appeared in the midst of a supposedly impregnable British position. The war correspondent for the *Illustrated London News* found himself in the centre of the action.

Illustrated London News, 24 April 1881

Major Fraser and myself were discussing the situation, when we were startled by a loud and sustained rattle of musketry, the bullets of which shrieked over our heads in a perfect hail. Lieutenant Wright, of the 92nd, rushed back, shouting out for immediate reinforcements. The General, assisted by his Staff, set about getting these forward, and then for the first time it dawned upon us that we might lose the hill, for the soldiers moved forward but slowly and hesitatingly. It was only too evident they did not like the work before them. By dint of some hard shouting and even pushing they were most of them got over the ridge, where they lay down, some distance behind Hamilton and his thin line of Highlanders, who, although opposed to about five hundred men at 120 yards, never budged an inch.

It seems that the advance of the enemy had been thoroughly checked, when one of our people – an officer, I believe – noticing the Boers for the first time, ejaculated, "Oh, there they are, quite close," and the words were hardly out of his lips ere every man of the newly arrived reinforcements bolted back panic-stricken. This was more than flesh and blood could stand, and the skirmishing line under Hamilton gave way also, the retreating troops being exposed, of course, to the Boer fire with disastrous effect.

I was on the left of the ridge when the men came back on us, and was a witness of the wild confusion which then prevailed. I saw McDonald, of the 92nd, revolver in hand, threaten to shoot any man who passed him; and, indeed, everybody was hard at work rallying the broken troops. Many, of course, got away and disappeared over the side of the hill next to the camp; but some hundred and fifty good men, mostly Highlanders, blue-jackets, and old soldiers of the 58th, remained to man the ridge for a final stand.

Some of the Boers appeared, and the fire that was interchanged was something awful. Three times they showed themselves, and three times they as quickly withdrew, our men, when that occurred, at once stopping their fire. I could hear the soldiers ejaculate, "We'll not budge from this. We'll give them the bayonet if they come closer," and so on, but all the time dropping fast, for Boer marksmen had apparently got to work in secure positions, and every shot told, the men falling back hit, mostly through the head.

It was a hot five minutes, but nevertheless I thought at the time we should hold our own. I expected every minute to hear the order given for a bayonet charge. That order unfortunately never came, although I am sure the men would have responded to it. But our flanks were exposed, and the enemy, checked in front, were stealing round them; across the hollow on the side of the hill facing the camp we had no one, and as the men were evidently anxious about that point, frequently looking over their shoulders, Colonel Stewart sent me over to see how matters were going on. There I reported all clear, and, indeed, if the enemy had attempted to storm the hill on that face he would have been decimated by the fire of his own people aimed from the other side.

We were most anxious about our right flank. It was evident that the enemy were stealing round it, so men were taken to prolong the position there. They were chiefly blue-jackets, led by a brave young officer, and, as I watched them follow him up, for the third time that day, the conviction flashed across me that we should lose the hill. There was a knoll on the threatened point, up which the reinforcements hesitated to climb. Some of them went back over the top of the plateau to the further ridge, others went round.

By-and-by there was confusion on the knoll itself. Some of the men on it stood up, and were at once shot down; and at last the whole of those who were holding it gave way. Helter skelter they were at once followed by the Boers, who were able then to pour a volley into our flank in the main line, from which instant the hill of Majuba was theirs. It was *sauve qui peut*. Major Hay, Captain Singleton, of the 92nd, and some other officers, were the last to leave, and these were immediately shot down and taken prisoners.

The General had turned round the last of all to walk after his retreating troops, when he also was shot dead, through the head. A minute or two previously Lieutenant Hamilton, requesting the General to excuse his presumption, had asked for a charge, as the men would not stand the fire much longer. Sir George Colley replied, "Wait until they come on, we will give them a volley and then charge," but before that moment arrived it was too late.

To move over about one hundred yards of ground under the fire of some five hundred rifles at close range is not a pleasant experience, but it is what all who remained of us on the hill that day had to go through. On every side, men were throwing up their arms, and with sharp cries of agony were pitching forward on the ground. At last we went over the side of the hill.

The Boers were instantly on the ridge above, and for about ten minutes kept up their terrible fire on our soldiers, who plunged down every path. Many, exhausted with the night's marching and the day's fighting, unable to go further, lay down behind rocks and bushes, and were afterwards taken prisoners: but of those who remained on the hill to the very last probably not one in six got clear away. The Boers were everywhere assisting our disabled men. Dr London, who, when the hill was abandoned by our panic-stricken troops, had steadily remained by his wounded, was lying on the ground with a shot through his chest. The Boers, as they rushed on the plateau, not seeing or not caring for the Geneva Cross, had fired into and knocked over both him and his hospital assistant; so there was only one, Dr Mahon, left to look after a great number of very bad cases.

The Spanish-American War

RICHARD HARDING DAVIS

The Death of Adolfo Rodriguez

A former short-story writer, Davis was one of the first reporters to cover the Cuban uprising against Iberian rule (which, after the sinking of the USS *Maine* by the Spanish in 1898, segued into the Spanish-American War). The assignment came courtesy of William Randolph Hearst's *New York Journal*, but when Hearst gave Davis's measured dispatches his trademark sensationalist spin, the correspondent decamped to *The Times* of London and the New York *Herald*. Davis's reports from Cuba not only made his own reputation, but that of a Rough Rider colonel named Theodore Roosevelt, later to become President of the USA.

A Year From a Reporter's Notebook, 1897

Adolfo Rodriguez was the only son of a Cuban farmer, who lived nine miles outside of Santa Clara, beyond the hills that surround that city to the north.

When the revolution in Cuba broke out young Rodriguez joined the insurgents, leaving his father and mother and two sisters at the farm. He was taken, in December of 1896, by a force of the Guardia Civile, the corp d'elite of the Spanish army, and defended himself when they tried to capture him, wounding three of them with his machete.

He was tried by the military court for bearing arms against the government, and sentenced to be shot by a fusillade some morning before sunrise.

Previous to execution he was confined in the military prison of Santa Clara with thirty other insurgents, all of whom were sentenced to be shot, one after the other, on mornings following the execution of Rodriguez.

His execution took place the morning of the 19th of January, 1897, at a place a half-mile distant from the city, on the great plain that stretches from the fort out to the hills, beyond which Rodriguez had lived for nineteen years. At the time of his death he was twenty years old.

I witnessed his execution, and what follows is an account of the way he went to his death. The young man's friends could not be present, for it was impossible for them to show themselves in that crowd and that place with wisdom or without distress, and I like to think that, although Rodriguez could not know it, there was one person present when he died who felt keenly for him, and who was a sympathetic though unwilling spectator.

There had been a full moon the night preceding the execution, and when the squad of soldiers marched from town it was still shining brightly through the mists. It lighted a plain two miles in extent, broken by ridges, and gullies and covered with thick, high grass, and with bunches of cactus and palmetto. In the hollow of the ridges the mist lay like broad lakes of water, and on one side of the plain stood the walls of the old town. On the other rose hills covered with royal palms that showed white in the moonlight, like hundreds of marble columns. A line of tiny camp-fires that the sentries had built during the night stretched between the forts at regular intervals and burned clearly.

But as the light grew stronger and the moonlight faded these were stamped out, and when the soldiers came in force the moon was a white ball in the sky, without radiance, the fires had sunk to ashes, and the sun had not yet risen.

So even when the men were formed into three sides of a hollow square, they were scarcely able to distinguish one another in the uncertain light of the morning.

There were about three hundred soldiers in the formation. They belonged to the volunteers, with their band playing a jaunty quickstep, while their officers galloped from one side to the other through the grass, seeking a suitable place for the execution. Outside the line the band still played merrily.

A few men and boys, who had been dragged out of their beds by the music, moved about the ridges behind the soldiers, half-clothed, unshaven, sleepy-eyed, yawning, stretching themselves nervously and shivering in the cool, damp air of the morning.

Either owing to discipline or on account of the nature of their errand, or because the men were still but half awake, there was no talking in the ranks, and soldiers stood motionless, leaning on their rifles, with their backs turned to the town, looking out across the plain to the hills.

The men in the crowd behind them were also grimly silent. They knew that whatever they might say would be twisted into a word of sympathy for the condemned man or a protest against the government. So no one spoke; even the officers gave their orders in gruff whispers, and the men in the crowd did not mix together, but looked suspiciously at one another and kept apart.

As the light increased a mass of people came hurrying from town with two black figures leading them, and the soldiers drew up at attention, and part of the double line fell back and left an opening in the square.

With us a condemned man walks only the short distance from his cell to the scaffold or the electric chair, shielded from sight by the prison walls, and it often occurs even then that the short journey is too much for his strength and courage.

But the Spaniards on this morning made the prisoner walk for over a half-mile across the broken surface of the fields. I expected to find the man, no matter what his strength at other times might be, stumbling and faltering on this cruel journey; but as he came nearer I saw that he led all the others, that the priests on either side of him were taking two steps to his one and that they were tripping on their gowns and stumbling over the hollows in their efforts to keep pace with him as he walked, erect and soldierly, at a quick step in advance of them.

He had a handsome, gentle face of the peasant type, a light, pointed beard, great wistful eyes, and a mass of curly black hair. He was shockingly young for such a sacrifice, and looked more like a Neapolitan than a Cuban. You could imagine him sitting on the quay at Naples or Genoa lolling in the sun and showing his white teeth when he laughed. Around his neck, hanging outside the linen blouse, he wore a new scapular.

It seems a petty thing to have been pleased with at such a time, but I confess to have felt a thrill of satisfaction when I saw, as the Cuban passed me, that he held a cigarette between his lips, not arrogantly nor with bravado, but with the nonchalance of a man who meets his punishment fearlessly, and who will let his enemies see that they can kill but not frighten him.

It was very quickly finished, with rough and, but for one frightful blunder, with merciful swiftness. The crowd fell back when it came to the square, and the condemned man, the priests, and the firing squad of six volunteers passed in and the line closed behind them.

The officer who had held the cord that bound the Cuban's arms behind him and passed across his breast, let it fall on the grass and drew his sword, and Rodriguez dropped his cigarette from his lips and bent and kissed the cross which the priests held up before him.

The elder of the priests moved to one side and prayed rapidly in a loud whisper, while the other, a younger man, walked behind the firing squad and covered his face with his hands. They had both spent the last twelve hours with Rodriguez in the chapel of the prison.

The Cuban walked to where the officer directed him to stand, and turning his back on the square, faced the hills and the road across them, which led to his father's farm.

As the officer gave the first command he straightened himself as far as the cords would allow, and held up his head and fixed his eyes immovably on the morning light, which had just begun to show above the hills.

He made a picture of such pathetic helplessness, but of such courage and dignity, that he reminded me on the instant of that statue of Nathan Hale which stands in the City Hall Park, above the roar of Broadway. The Cuban's arms were bound, as are those of the statue, and he stood firmly, with his weight resting on his heels like a soldier on parade, and with his face held up fearlessly, as is that of the statue. But there was this difference, that Rodriguez, while probably as willing to give six lives for his country as was the American rebel, being only a peasant, did not think to say so, and he will not, in consequence, live in bronze during the lives of many men, but will be remembered only as one of thirty Cubans, one of whom was shot at Santa Clara on each succeeding sunrise.

The officer had given the order, the men had raised their pieces, and the condemned man had heard the clicks of the triggers as they were pulled back, and he had not moved. And then happened one of the most cruelly refined, though unintentional acts of torture that one can very well imagine. As the officer slowly raised his sword, preparatory to giving the signal, one of the mounted officers rode up to him and pointed out silently that, as I had already observed with some satisfaction, the firing squad was so placed that when they fired they would shoot several of the soldiers stationed on the extreme end of the square.

Their captain motioned his men to lower their pieces, and then walked across the grass and laid his hand on the shoulder of the waiting prisoner.

It is not pleasant to think what that shock must have been. The man had steeled himself to receive a volley of bullets. He believed that in the next instant he would be in another world; he had heard the command given, had heard the click of the Mausers as the locks caught – and then, at the supreme moment, a human hand had been laid upon his shoulder and a voice spoke in his ear.

You would expect that any man, snatched back to life in such a fashion, would start and tremble at the reprieve, or would break down altogether, but this boy turned his head steadily, and followed with his eyes the direction of the officer's sword, then nodded gravely, and with his shoulders squared, took up the new position, straightened his back, and once more held himself erect.

As an exhibition of self-control this should surely rank above feats of heroism performed in battle, where there are thousands of comrades to give inspiration. This man was alone, in sight of the hills he knew, with only enemies about him, with no source to draw on for strength but that which lay in himself.

The officer of the firing squad, mortified by his blunder, hastily whipped up his sword, the men once more leveled their rifles, the sword rose, dropped, and the men fired. At the report the Cuban's head snapped back almost between his shoulders, but his body fell slowly, as though someone had pushed him gently forward from behind and he had stumbled.

He sank on his side in the wet grass without a struggle or a sound, and did not move again.

It was difficult to believe that he meant to lie there, that it could be ended without a word, that the man in the linen suit would not rise to his feet and continue to walk on over the hills, as he apparently had started to do, to his home; that there was not a mistake somewhere, or that at least someone would be sorry or say something or run and pick him up.

But, fortunately, he did not need help, and the priests returned – the younger one with tears running down his face – and donned their vestments and read a brief requiem for his soul, while the squad stood uncovered, and the men in the hollow square shook their accoutrements into place, and shifted their pieces and got ready for the order to march, and the band began again with the same quickstep which the fusillade had interrupted.

The figure still lay on the grass untouched, and no one seemed to remember that it had walked there of itself, or noticed that the cigarette still burned, a tiny ring of living fire, at the place where the figure had first stood.

The figure was a thing of the past, and the squad shook itself like a great snake, and then broke into little pieces and started off jauntily, stumbling in the high grass and striving to keep step to the music.

The officers led it past the figure in the linen suit, and so close to it that the file closers had to part with the column to avoid treading on it. Each soldier as he passed turned and looked down on it, some craning their necks curiously, others giving a careless glance, and some without any interest at all, as they would have looked at a house by the roadside, or a hole in the road.

One young soldier caught his foot in a trailing vine just opposite to it, and fell. He grew very red when his comrades giggled at him for his awkwardness. The crowd of sleepy spectators fell in on either side of the band. They, too, had forgotten it, and the priests put their vestments back in the bag and wrapped their heavy cloaks about them, and hurried off after the others.

Every man seemed to have forgotten it except two men, who came slowly towards it from the town, driving a bullockcart that bore an unplaned coffin, each with a cigarette between his lips, and with his throat wrapped in a shawl to keep out the morning mists.

At that moment the sun, which had shown some promise of its coming glow above the hills, shot up suddenly from behind them in all the splendor of the tropics, a fierce, red disk of heat, and filled the air with warmth and light.

The bayonets of the retreating column flashed in it, and at the sight a rooster in a farm-yard near by crowed vigorously, and a dozen bugles answered the challenge with the brisk, cheery notes of the reveille, and from all parts of the city the church bells jangled out the call for early mass, and the little world of Santa Clara seemed to stretch itself and to wake to welcome the day just begun.

But as I fell in at the rear of the procession and looked back, the figure of the young Cuban, who was no longer a part of the world of Santa Clara, was asleep in the wet grass, with his motionless arms still tightly bound behind him, with the scapular twisted awry across his face, and the blood from his breast sinking into the soil he had tried to free.

The War in the Sudan

GEORGE WARRINGTON STEEVENS

The Attack on the Atbara

The death of General Gordon at the hands of Pan-Islamic Mahdists at Khartoum in 1895 was viewed in Britain as an unmitigated national disgrace. Victorian pride and geo-politics (the threat posed to the Suez Canal, the Empire's trade lifeline to India and the East) required the suppression of the Mahdi uprising and the reconquest of vast and barren Sudan. This was accomplished by Major-General Horatio Kitchener, whose campaign was covered by no fewer than sixteen London correspondents, among them the tyro Winston Churchill, but which was caught most authentically by the twenty-eight-year-old *Daily Mail* correspondent, George Warrington Steevens, an imperial voice for an imperial newspaper in a time of imperialist endeavour. The action described below was part of Kitchener's drive on Omdurman and Khartoum.

Daily Mail, 29 April 1898

Fort Atbara, 10 April

As the first rays of sunrise glinted on the desert pebbles, the army rose up and saw that it was in front of the enemy. All night it had moved blindly, in faith. At six in the evening the four brigades were black squares on the rising desert outside the bushes of Umdabea Camp, and they set out to march. Hard gravel underfoot, full moon overhead, about them a coy horizon that seemed immeasurable, yet revealed nothing.

The squares tramped steadily for an hour. Then all lay down, so that the other brigades were swallowed up into the desert, and the faces of the British square were no more than shadows in the white moonbeams. The square was unlocked, and first the horses were taken down to water, then the men by half-battalions. We who had water ate some biscuits, put our heads on saddle-bags, rolled our bodies in blankets, and slept a little.

The next thing was a long rustle overhead; stealing in upon us, urgently whispering us to rise and mount and move. The moon had passed overhead. It was one o'clock. The square rustled into life and motion, bent forward, and started, half asleep. No man spoke, and no light showed, but the sand-muffled trampling and the moon-veiled figures forbade the fancy that it was all a dream. The shape of lines of men – now close, now broken, and closing up again as the ground broke or the direction changed – the mounted officers, and the hushed order, "Left shoulder forward," the scrambling Maxim mules, the lines of swaying camels, their pungent smell, and the rare neigh of a horse, the other three squares like it, which we knew of but could not see – it was just the same war machine as we had seen all these days on parade. Only this time it was in deadly earnest, moving stealthily but massively forward towards an event that none of us could quite certainly foretell.

We marched till something after four, then halted, and the men lay down again and slept. The rest walked up and down, talking to one and another, wondering in half-voices *were they there*, would they give us a fight or should we find their lines empty, how would the fight be fought, and, above all, how were we to get over their zariba. For Mahmud's zariba was pictured very high, and very thick and very prickly, which sounded awkward for the Cameron Highlanders, who were to assault it. Somebody had proposed burning it, either with war-rockets or paraffin and safety matches; somebody else suggested throwing blankets over it, though how you throw blankets over a ten by twenty feet hedge of camel-thorn, and what you do next when you have thrown them the inventor of the plan never explained; others favoured scaling ladders, apparently to take headers off on to the thorns and the enemy's spears, and even went so far as to make a few; most were for the simpler plan of just taking hold

of it and pulling it apart. But how many of the men who pulled
would ever get through the gap?

We could see their position quite well by now – the usual river
fringe of grey-green palms meeting the usual desert fringe of
yellow-grey mimosa. And the smoke-grey line in front of it all
must be their famous zariba. Before its right centre fluttered half
a dozen flags, white and pale blue, yellow and pale chocolate.
The line went on till it was not half a mile from the flags. Then
it halted.

Thud! went the first gun, and phutt! came faintly back, as its
shell burst on the zariba into a wreathed round cloud of just the
zariba's smoky grey. I looked at my watch, and it marked 6.20.
The battle that had now menaced, now evaded us for a month
– the battle had begun.

The bugle sang out the advance. The pipes screamed war,
and the line started forward, like a ruler drawn over the tussock-
broken sand. Up a low ridge they moved forward: when would
the dervishes fire? The Camerons were to open from the top of
the ridge, only 300 yards short of the zariba; up and up, forward
and forward: when would they fire? Now the line crested the
ridge; the men knelt down. "Volley-firing by sections" – and
crash it came. It came from both sides, too, almost the same
instant. Wht-t, wht-t, wht-t piped the bullets overhead: the line
knelt very firm, and aimed very steady, and crash, crash, crash,
they answered it.

Oh! A cry more of dismayed astonishment than of pain, and
a man was upon his feet and over on his back and the bearers
were dashing in from the rear. He was dead before they touched
him, but already they found another for the stretcher. Then
bugle again, and up and on: the bullets were swishing and lashing now like rain on the river. But the line of khaki and purple
tartan never bent nor swayed; it just went slowly forward like a
ruler. The officers at its head strode self-containedly; they might
have been on the hill after grouse; only from their locked faces
turned unswervingly towards the bullets could you see that they
knew and had despised the danger. And the unkempt, unshaven
Tammies, who in camp seemed little enough like covenanters or
Ironsides, were now quite transformed. It was not so difficult to
go on – the pipes picked you up and carried you on – but it was
difficult not to hurry: yet whether they aimed or advanced they

did it orderly, gravely, without speaking. The bullets had whispered to raw youngsters in one breath the secret of all the glories of the British Army.

Forward and forward, more swishing about them and more crashing from them. Now they were moving, always without hurry, down a gravelly incline. Three men went down without a cry at the very foot of the Union Jack, and only one got to his feet again; the flag shook itself and still blazed splendidly. Next, a supremely furious gust of bullets, and suddenly the line stood fast. Before it was a loose low hedge of dry camel-thorn – the zariba, the redoubtable zariba. That it? A second they stood in wonder, and then, "Pull it away," suggested somebody. Just half-a-dozen tugs; and the impossible zariba was a gap and a scattered heap of brushwood. Beyond is a low stockade and trenches, but what of that? Over and in! Hurrah, hurrah, hurrah!

Now fall in, and back to the desert outside. And unless you are congenitally amorous of horrors don't look too much about you. Black spindle-legs curled up to meet red-gimbleted black faces, donkeys headless and legless or sieves of shrapnel, camels with necks writhed back on to their humps, rotting already in pools of blood and bile-yellow water, heads without faces and faces without anything below, cobwebbed arms and legs, and black skins grilled to crackling on smouldering palm-leaf – don't look at it. Here is the Sirdar's white star and crescent on red; here is the Sirdar, who created this battle, this clean-jointed, well-oiled, smooth-running clockwork-perfect masterpiece of a battle. Not a flaw, not a check, not a jolt; and not a fleck on its shining success. Once more, hurrah, hurrah, hurrah.

The War in the Sudan

GEORGE WARRINGTON STEEVENS

We Buried Gordon After the Manner of His Race

After defeating the Mahdi at Omdurman on 2 September 1898, British forces once again entered Khartoum, where they disinterred the bones of the slain General Gordon and gave them a Christian burial. No sooner was the Sudan war over than Steevens, war correspondent of the *Daily Mail*, edited his dispatches into a bestselling campaign record, *With Kitchener to Khartum*.

With Kitchener to Khartum, 1898

The troops formed up before the palace in three sides of a rectangle – Egyptians to our left as we looked from the river, British to the right. The Sirdar, the generals of division and brigade, and the staff stood in the open space facing the palace. Then on the roof – almost on the very spot where Gordon fell, though the steps by which the butchers mounted have long since vanished – we were aware of two flagstaves. By the right-hand halliards stood Lieutenant Staveley, RN, and Captain Watson, KRR; by the left hand Bimbashi Mitford and his Excellency's Egyptian ADC.

The Sirdar raised his hand. A pull on the halliards: up ran, out flew, the Union Jack, tugging eagerly at his reins, dazzling gloriously in the sun, rejoicing in his strength and his freedom. "Bang!" went the "Melik's" 12½-pounder, and the boat quivered to her backbone. "God Save our Gracious Queen" hymned

the Guards' band – "bang!" from the "Melik" – and Sirdar and
private stood stiff – "bang!" – to attention, every hand at the
helmet peak in – "bang!" – salute. The Egyptian flag had gone
up at the same instant; and now, the same ear-smashing, soul-
uplifting bangs marking time, the band of the 11th Sudanese
was playing the Khedivial hymn. "Three cheers for the Queen!"
cried the Sirdar: helmets leaped in the air, and the melancholy
ruins woke to the first wholesome shout of all these years. Then
the same for the Khedive. The comrade flags stretched themselves lustily, enjoying their own again; the bands pealed forth
the pride of country; the twenty-one guns banged forth the
strength of war. Thus, white men and black, Christian and
Moslem, Anglo-Egypt set her seal once more, for ever, on
Khartum [Khartoum].

Before we had time to think such thoughts over to ourselves,
the Guards were playing the Dead March in "Saul". Then the
black band was playing the march from Handel's "Scipio",
which in England generally goes with "Toll for the Brave"; this
was in memory of those loyal men among the Khedive's subjects who could have saved themselves by treachery, but
preferred to die with Gordon. Next fell a deeper hush than ever,
except for the solemn minute guns that had followed the fierce
salute. Four chaplains – Catholic, Anglican, Presbyterian, and
Methodist – came slowly forward and ranged themselves, with
their backs to the palace, just before the Sirdar. The Presbyterian read the Fifteenth Psalm. The Anglican led the rustling
whisper of the Lord's Prayer. Snow-haired Father Brindle, best
beloved of priests, laid his helmet at his feet, and read a memorial prayer bareheaded in the sun. Then came forward the pipers
and wailed a dirge, and the Sudanese played "Abide with me".
Perhaps lips did twitch just a little to see the ebony heathens
fervently blowing out Gordon's favourite hymn; but the most
irrestible incongruity would hardly have made us laugh at that
moment. And there were those who said the cold Sirdar himself
could hardly speak or see, as General Hunter and the rest
stepped out according to their rank and shook his hand. What
wonder? He has trodden this road to Khartum for fourteen
years, and he stood at the goal at last.

Thus with Maxim-Nordenfeldt and Bible we buried Gordon
after the manner of his race. The parade was over, the troops

were dismissed, and for a short space we walked in Gordon's garden. Gordon has become a legend with his countrymen, and they all but deify him dead who would never have heard of him had he lived. But in this garden you somehow came to know Gordon the man, not the myth, and to feel near to him. Here was an Englishman doing his duty, alone and at the instant peril of his life; yet still he loved his garden. The garden was a yet more pathetic ruin than the palace. The palace accepted its doom mutely; the garden strove against it. Untrimmed, unwatered, the oranges and citrons still struggled to bear their little, hard, green knobs, as if they had been full ripe fruit. The pomegranates put out their vermilion star-flowers, but the fruit was small and woody and juiceless. The figs bore better, but they, too, were small and without vigour. Rankly overgrown with dhurra, a vine still trailed over a low roof its pale leaves and limp tendrils, but yielded not a sign of grapes. It was all green, and so far vivid and refreshing after Omdurman. But it was the green of nature, not of cultivation: leaves grew large and fruit grew small, and dwindled away. Reluctantly, despairingly, Gordon's garden was dropping back to wilderness. And in the middle of the defeated fruit-trees grew rankly the hateful Sodom apple, the poisonous herald of desolation.

The bugle broke in upon us; we went back to the boats. We were quicker steaming back than steaming up. We were not a whit less chastened, but every man felt lighter. We came with a sigh of shame: we went away with a sigh of relief. The long-delayed duty was done. The bones of our countrymen were shattered and scattered abroad, and no man knows their place; none the less Gordon had his due burial at last. So we steamed away to the roaring camp and left him alone again. Yet not one nor two looked back at the mouldering palace and the tangled garden with a new and a great contentment. We left Gordon alone again – but alone in majesty under the conquering ensign of his own people.

The Spanish-American War

STEPHEN CRANE

Stephen Crane at the Front for the *World*

Although Stephen Crane wrote his famous war novel, *The Red Badge of Courage* (1895), without any personal experience of combat, he made good his lack of education by reporting in quick succession the Greco-Turkish War and the Spanish-American conflict. Richard Harding Davies, the veteran war correspondent, thought Crane "the coolest man, whether army officer or civilian, that I saw under fire". Crane died in 1900, aged twenty-eight, of tuberculosis.

World, 24 June 1898

Siboney, June 24

And this is the end of the third day since the landing of the troops. Yesterday was a day of insurgent fighting. The Cubans were supposed to be fighting somewhere in the hills with the regiment of Santiago de Cuba, which had been quite cut off from its native city. No American soldiery were implicated in any way in the battle. But to-day is different. The mounted infantry – the First Volunteer Cavalry – Teddie's Terrors – Wood's Weary Walkers – have had their first engagement. It was a bitter hard first fight for new troops, but no man can ever question the bravery of this regiment.

As we landed from a despatch boat we saw the last troop of

the mounted infantry wending slowly over the top of a huge hill.
Three of us promptly posted after them upon hearing the statement that they had gone out with the avowed intention of finding
the Spaniards and mixing it up with them.

THROUGH THE THICKETS

They were far ahead of us by the time we reached the top of the
mountain, but we swung rapidly on the path through the dense
Cuban thickets and in time met and passed the hospital corps, a
vacant, unloaded hospital corps, going ahead on mules. Then
there was another long lonely march through the dry woods,
which seemed almost upon the point of crackling into a blaze
under the rays of the furious Cuban sun. We met nothing but
blankets, shelter-tents, coats and other impediments, which the
panting Rough Riders had flung behind them on their swift
march.

In time we came in touch with a few stragglers, men down
with the heat, prone and breathing heavily, and then we struck
the rear of the column. We were now about four miles out, with
no troops nearer than that by the road.

I know nothing about war, of course, and pretend nothing,
but I have been enabled from time to time to see brush fighting,
and I want to say here plainly that the behavior of these Rough
Riders while marching through the woods shook me with terror
as I have never before been shaken.

SUPERB COURAGE

It must now be perfectly understood throughout the length and
breadth of the United States that the Spaniards have learned a
great deal from the Cubans, and they are now going to use
against us the tactics which the Cubans have used so successfully against them. The marines at Guantanamo have learned it.
The Indian-fighting regulars know it anyhow, but this regiment
of volunteers knew nothing but their own superb courage. They
wound along this narrow winding path, babbling joyously, arguing, recounting, laughing; making more noise than a train going
through a tunnel.

Any one could tell from the conformation of the country

when we were liable to strike the enemy's outposts, but the clatter of tongues did not then cease. Also, those of us who knew heard going from hillock to hillock the beautiful coo of the Cuban wood-dove – ah, the wood-dove! the Spanish guerilla wood-dove which had presaged the death of gallant marines.

For my part, I declare that I was frightened almost into convulsions. Incidentally I mentioned the cooing of the doves to some of the men, but they said decisively that the Spaniards did not use this signal. I don't know how they knew.

SILENCE – ACTION

Well, after we had advanced well into the zone of the enemy's fire-mark that – well into the zone of Spanish fire – a loud order came along the line: "There's a Spanish outpost just ahead and the men must stop talking."

"Stop talkin', can't ye, —it," bawled a sergeant.

"Ah, say, can't ye stop talkin'?" howled another.

I was frightened before a shot was fired; frightened because I thought this silly brave force was wandering placidly into a great deal of trouble. They did. The firing began. Four little volleys were fired by members of a troop deployed to the rights. Then the Mauser began to pop – the familiar Mauser pop. A captain announced that this distinct Mauser sound was our own Krag-Jorgensen. O misery!

Then the woods became aglow with fighting. Our people advanced, deployed, reinforced, fought, fell – in the bushes, in the tall grass, under the lone palms – before a foe not even half seen. Mauser bullets came from three sides. Mauser bullets – not Krag-Jorgensen – although men began to cry that they were being fired into by their own people – whined in almost all directions. Three troops went forward in skirmish order and in five minutes they called for reinforcements. They were under a cruel fire; half of the men hardly knew whence it came; but their conduct, by any soldierly standard, was magnificent.

GREEN HEROES

Most persons with a fancy for military things suspect the value of an announcedly picked regiment. Better gather a simple collection of clerks from anywhere. But in this case the usual view changes. This regiment is as fine a body of men as were ever accumulated for war.

There was nothing to be seen but men straggling through the underbrush and firing at some part of the landscape. This was the scenic effect. Of course men said that they saw five hundred, one thousand, three thousand, fifteen thousand Spaniards, but – poof – in bush country of this kind it is almost impossible for one to see more than fifty men at a time. According to my opinion there were never more than five hundred men in the Spanish firing line. There might have been aplenty in touch with their center and flanks, but as to the firing there were never more than five hundred engaged. This is certain.

The Rough Riders advanced steadily and confidently under the Mauser bullets. They spread across some open ground – tall grass and palms – and there they began to fall, smothering and threshing down in the grass, marking man-shaped places among those luxurious blades. The action lasted about one-half hour. Then the Spaniards fled. They had never seen men fight them in this manner and they fled. The business was too serious.

Then the heroic rumor arose, soared, and screamed above the bush. Everybody was wounded. Everybody was dead. There was nobody. Gradually there was somebody. There was the wounded, the important wounded. And the dead.

MARSHALL'S COURAGE

Meanwhile a soldier passing near me said: "There's a correspondent all shot to hell."

He guided me to where Edward Marshall lay, shot through the body. The following conversation ensued:

"Hello, Crane!"

"Hello, Marshall! In hard luck, old man?"

"Yes, I'm done for."

"Nonsense! You're all right, old boy. What can I do for you?"

"Well, you might file my despatches. I don't mean file 'em ahead of your own, old man – but just file 'em if you find it handy."

I immediately decided that he was doomed. No man could be so sublime in detail concerning the trade of journalism and not die. There was the solemnity of a funeral song in these absurd and fine sentences about despatches. Six soldiers gathered him up on a tent and moved slowly off.

"Hello!" shouted a stern and menacing person, "who are you? And what are you doing here? Quick!"

"I am a correspondent, and we are merely carrying back another correspondent who we think is mortally wounded. Do you care?"

The Rough Rider, somewhat abashed, announced that he did not care.

NEW YORK TO THE FORE

And now the wounded soldiers began to crawl, walk and be carried back to where, in the middle of the path, the surgeons had established a little field hospital.

"Say, doctor, this ain't much of a wound. I reckon I can go now back to my troop," said Arizona.

"Thanks, awfully, doctor. Awfully kind of you. I dare say I shall be all right in a moment," said New York.

This hospital was a spectacle of heroism. The doctors, gentle and calm, moved among the men without the common-senseless bullying of the ordinary ward. It was a sort of fraternal game. They were all in it, and of it, helping each other.

In the mean time three troops of the Ninth Cavalry were swinging the woods, and a mile behind them the Seventy-first New York was moving forward eagerly to the rescue. But the day was done. The Rough Riders had bitten it off and chewed it up – chewed it up splendidly.

The Boer War

WINSTON S. CHURCHILL

Escape

Winston Churchill cut his teeth as a war correspondent during the Sudan campaign, where he employed family influence to wheedle a commission in the 21st Lancers, thus guaranteeing himself a front-seat view of the action at Omdurman. He used a similar ploy when war broke out between Britain and uppity Dutch settlers in South Africa in 1899, persuading the army to grant him a commission in the South Africa Light Horse – at the same time as he enjoyed his £250 monthly wage from the *Morning Post*. This duality of occupation, however, almost cost Churchill his life when he was captured by Boer horsemen. General Joubert was inclined to shoot him because he was caught bearing arms, but in the event Churchill escaped from captivity in Pretoria and made his way to safety in Lourenço Marques, a colourful escapade which made his name.

Morning Post, 24 January 1900

How unhappy is that poor man who loses his liberty! What can the wide world give him in exchange? No degree of material comfort, no consciousness of correct behaviour, can balance the hateful degradation of imprisonment. Before I had been an hour in captivity I resolved to escape. Many plans suggested themselves, were examined and rejected. For a month I thought of nothing else. But the peril and difficulty restrained action. I think that it was the news of the British defeat at Stormberg that clinched the matter. All the news we heard in Pretoria was derived from Boer sources, and was hideously exaggerated and distorted. Every day we read in the *Volksstem* – probably the most amazing tissue of lies ever presented to the public under the name of a newspaper – of Boer victories and of the huge slaughters and shameful flights of the British. However much one might doubt and discount these tales they made a deep impression. A month's feeding on such literary garbage weakens the constitution of the mind. We wretched prisoners lost heart. Perhaps Great Britain would not persevere; perhaps foreign powers would intervene; perhaps there would be another disgraceful, cowardly peace. At the best the war and our confinement would be prolonged for many months. I do not pretend that impatience at being locked up was not the foundation of my determination; but I should never have screwed up my courage to make the attempt without the earnest desire to do something, however small, to help the British cause. Of course, I am a man of peace. I do not fight. But swords are not the only weapons in the world. Something may be done with a pen. So I determined to take all hazards; and, indeed, the affair was one of very great danger and difficulty.

The State Model Schools, the building in which we were confined, is a brick structure standing in the midst of a gravel quadrangle and surrounded on two sides by an iron grille and on two by a corrugated iron fence about ten feet high. These boundaries offered little obstacle to anyone who possessed the activity of youth, but the fact that they were guarded on the inside by sentries armed with rifle and revolver fifty yards apart made them a well-nigh insuperable barrier. No walls are so hard to pierce as living walls. I thought of the penetrating power of gold, and the sentries were sounded. They were incorruptible. I seek not to deprive them of the credit, but the truth is that the bribery market in this country has been spoiled by the millionaires. I could not afford with my slender resources to insult them heavily enough. So nothing remained but to break out in spite of them. With another officer who may for the present – since he is still a prisoner – remain nameless I formed a scheme.

After anxious reflection and continual watching, it was discovered that when the sentries near the offices walked about on their beats they were at certain moments unable to see the top of a few yards of the wall. The electric lights in the middle of the quadrangle brilliantly lighted the whole place, but cut off the sentries beyond them from looking at the eastern wall. For behind the lights all seemed by contrast darkness. The first thing was therefore to pass the two sentries near the offices. It was necessary to hit off the exact moment when both their backs should be turned together. After the wall was scaled we should be in the garden of the villa next door. There our plan came to an end. Everything after this was vague and uncertain. How to get out of the garden, how to pass unnoticed through the streets, how to evade the patrols that surrounded the town and, above all, how to cover the two hundred and eighty miles to the Portuguese frontiers, were questions which would arise at a later stage. All attempts to communicate with friends outside had failed. We cherished the hope that with chocolate, a little Kaffir knowledge and a great deal of luck we might march the distance in a fortnight, buying mealies at the native kraals and lying hidden by day. But it did not look a very promising prospect.

We determined to try on the night of 11 December, making up our minds quite suddenly in the morning, for these things are best done on the spur of the moment. I passed the afternoon in positive terror. Nothing has ever disturbed me as much as this. There is something appalling in the idea of stealing secretly off in the night like a guilty thief. The fear of detection has a pang of its own. Besides, we knew quite well that on occasion, even on excuse, the sentries – they were armed police – would fire. Fifteen yards is a short range. And beyond the immediate danger lay a prospect of severe hardship and suffering, only faint hopes of success, and the probability at the best of five months in Pretoria Gaol.

The afternoon dragged tediously away. I tried to read Mr Lecky's *History of England*, but for the first time in my life that wise writer wearied me. I played chess and was hopelessly beaten. At last it grew dark. At seven o'clock the bell for dinner rang and the officers trooped off. Now was the time. But the sentries gave us no chance. They did not walk about. One of them stood exactly opposite the only practicable part of the wall. We waited for two hours, but the attempt was plainly impossible, and so with a most unsatisfactory feeling of relief to bed.

Tuesday, the 12th! Another day of fear, but fear crystallising more and more into desperation. Anything was better than further suspense. Night came again. Again the dinner bell sounded. Choosing my opportunity I strolled across the quadrangle and secreted myself in one of the offices. Through a chink I watched the sentries. For half an hour they remained stolid and obstructive. Then all of a sudden one turned and walked up to his comrade and they began to talk. Their backs were turned. Now or never. I darted out of my hiding-place and ran to the wall, seized the top with my hands and drew myself up. Twice I let myself down again in sickly hesitation, and then with a third resolve scrambled up. The top was flat. Lying on it I had one parting glimpse of the sentries, still talking, still with their backs turned; but, I repeat, fifteen yards away. Then I lowered myself silently down into the adjoining garden and crouched among the shrubs. I was free. The first step had been taken and it was irrevocable.

It now remained to await the arrival of my comrade. The bushes of the garden gave a good deal of cover, and in the moonlight their shadows lay black on the ground. Twenty yards away was the house, and I had not been five minutes in hiding before I perceived that it was full of people; the windows revealed brightly lighted rooms, and within I could see figures moving about. This was a fresh complication. We had always thought the house unoccupied. Presently – how long afterwards I do not know, for the ordinary measures of time, hours, minutes and seconds, are quite meaningless on such occasions – a man came out of the door and walked across the garden in my direction. Scarcely ten yards away he stopped and stood still, looking steadily towards me. I cannot describe the surge of panic which nearly overwhelmed me. I must be discovered. I dared not stir an inch. But amid a tumult of emotion, reason, seated firmly on her throne, whispered, "Trust to the dark background." I remained absolutely motionless. For a long time the man and I remained opposite each other, and every instant I expected him to spring forward. A vague idea crossed my mind that I might silence him. "Hush, I am a detective. We expect that an officer will break out here tonight. I am waiting to catch him." Reason – scornful this time – replied: "Surely a Transvaal detective would speak Dutch. Trust to the shadow." So I trusted, and after a spell another man came out of the house, lighted a cigar, and both he and the other walked off together. No sooner had they turned than a cat pursued by a dog rushed into the bushes and collided into me. The startled animal uttered a "miaul" of alarm and darted back again making a horrible rustling. Both men stopped at once. But it was only the cat, and they passed out of the garden gate into the town.

I looked at my watch. An hour had passed since I climbed the wall. Where was my comrade? Suddenly I heard a voice from within the quadrangle say quite loud "All up." I crawled back to the wall. Two officers were walking up and down the other side jabbering Latin words, laughing and talking all manner of non-sense – amid which I caught my name. I risked a cough. One of the officers immediately began to chatter alone. The other said slowly and clearly: ". . . cannot get out. The sentry suspects. It's all up. Can you get back again?" But now all my fears fell from me at once. To go back was impossible. I could not hope to climb the wall unnoticed. Fate pointed onwards. Besides, I said to myself, "Of course, I shall be recaptured, but I will at least have a run for my money." I said to the officers: "I shall go on alone."

Now, I was in the right mood for these undertakings – that is to say that, thinking failure almost certain, no odds against success affected me. All risks were less than the certainty. The gate which led into the road was only a few yards from another sentry. I said to myself, "*Toujours l'audace*": put my hat on my head, strode out into the middle of the garden, walked past the windows of the house without any attempt at concealment, and so went through the gate and turned to the left. I passed the sentry at less than five yards. Most of them knew me by sight. Whether he looked at me or not I do not know, for I never turned my head. But after walking a hundred yards I knew that the second obstacle had been surmounted. I was at large in Pretoria.

I walked on leisurely through the night humming a tune and choosing the middle of the road. The streets were full of burgh-ers, but they paid no attention to me. Gradually I reached the suburbs, and on a little bridge I sat down to reflect and consider. I was in the heart of the enemy's country. I knew no one to whom I could apply for succour. Nearly three hundred miles stretched between me and Delagoa Bay. My escape must be known at dawn. Pursuit would be immediate. Yet all exits were barred. The town was picketed, the country was patrolled, the trains were searched, the line was guarded. I had £75 in my pocket and four slabs of chocolate, but the compass and the map which might have guided me, the opium tablets and meat lozenges which should have sustained me, were in my friend's pockets in the State Model School. Worst of all, I could not speak a word of Dutch or Kaffir, and how was I to get food or direction?

But when hope had departed, fear had gone as well. I formed a plan. I would find the Delagoa Bay railway. Without map or compass I must follow that in spite of the pickets. I looked at the stars. Orion shone brightly. Scarcely a year ago he had guided me when lost in the desert to the bank of the Nile. He had given me water. Now he should lead me to freedom. I could not endure the want of either.

After walking south for half a mile I struck the railroad. Was it the line to Delagoa Bay or the Pietersburg branch? If it were the former it should run east. But as far as I could see this line ran northwards. Still, it might be only winding its way out among the hills. I resolved to follow it. The night was delicious. A cool breeze fanned my face and a wild feeling of exhilaration took hold of me. At any rate I was free, if only for an hour. That was something. The fascination of the adventure grew. Unless the stars in their courses fought for me I could not escape. Where was the need for caution? I marched briskly along the line. Here and there the lights of a picket fire gleamed. Every bridge had its watchers. But I passed them all, making very short detours at the dangerous places, and really taking scarcely any precautions.

As I walked I extended my plan. I could not march three hundred miles to the frontier. I would go by train. I would board a train in motion and hide under the seats, on the roof, on the couplings – anywhere. What train should I take? The first, of course. After walking for two hours I perceived the signal lights of a station. I left the line and, circling round it, hid in the ditch by the track about two hundred yards beyond it. I argued that the train would stop at the station and that it would not have got up too much speed by the time it reached me. An hour passed. I began to grow impatient. Suddenly I heard the whistle and the approaching rattle. Then the great yellow headlights of the engine flashed into view. The train waited five minutes at the station and started again with much noise and steaming. I crouched by the track. I rehearsed the act in my mind. I must wait until the engine had passed, otherwise I should be seen. Then I must make a dash for the carriages.

The train started slowly but gathered speed sooner than I had expected. The flaring lights drew swiftly near. The rattle grew into a roar. The dark mass hung for a second above me. The engine driver silhouetted against his furnace glow, the black profile of the engine, the clouds of steam rushed past. Then I hurled myself on the trucks, clutched at something, missed, clutched again, missed again, grasped some sort of handhold, was swung off my feet – my toes bumping on the line, and with a struggle seated myself on the couplings of the fifth truck from the front of the train. It was a goods train, and the trucks were full of sacks, soft sacks covered with coal dust. I crawled on top and burrowed in among them. In five minutes I was completely buried. The sacks were warm and comfortable. Perhaps the engine driver had seen me rush up to the train and would give the alarm at the next station; on the other hand, perhaps not. Where was the train going to? Where would it be unloaded? Would it be searched? Was it on the Delagoa Bay line? What should I do in the morning? Ah, never mind that. Sufficient for the day was the luck thereof. Fresh plans for fresh contingencies. I resolved to sleep, nor can I imagine a more pleasing lullaby than the clatter of the train that carries you at twenty miles an hour away from the enemy's capital.

How long I slept I do not know, but I woke up suddenly with all feelings of exhilaration gone, and only the consciousness of oppressive difficulties heavy on me. I must leave the train before daybreak, so that I could drink at a pool and find some hiding-place while it was still dark. Another night I would board another train. I crawled from my cosy hiding-place among the sacks and sat again on the couplings. The train was running at a fair speed, but I felt it was time to leave it. I took hold of the iron handle at the back of the truck, pulled strongly with my left hand, and sprang. My feet struck the ground in two gigantic strides, and the next instant I was sprawling in the ditch considerably shaken but unhurt. The train, my faithful ally of the night, hurried on its journey.

It was still dark. I was in the middle of a wide valley, surrounded by low hills and carpeted with high grass drenched in dew. I searched for water in the nearest gully and soon found a clear pool. I was very thirsty, but long after I had quenched my thirst I continued to drink that I might have sufficient for the whole day.

Presently the dawn began to break, and the sky to the east grew yellow and red, slashed across with heavy black clouds. I saw with relief that the railway ran steadily towards the sunrise. I had taken the right line after all.

Having drunk my fill, I set out for the hills, among which I hoped to find some hiding-place, and as it became broad daylight I entered a small group of trees which grew on the side of a deep ravine. Here I resolved to wait till dusk. I had one consolation: no one in the world knew where I was – I did not know myself. It was now four o'clock. Fourteen hours lay between me and the night. My impatience to proceed doubled their length. At first it was terribly cold, but by degrees the sun gained power, and by ten o'clock the heat was oppressive. My sole companion was a gigantic vulture, who manifested an extravagant interest in my condition, and made hideous and ominous gurglings from time to time. From my lofty position I commanded a view of the whole valley. A little tin-roofed town lay three miles to the westward. Scattered farmsteads, each with a clump of trees, relieved the monotony of the undulating ground. At the foot of the hill stood a Kaffir kraal, and the figures of its inhabitants dotted the patches of cultivation or surrounded the droves of goats and cows which fed on the pasture. The railway ran through the middle of the valley, and I could watch the passage of the various trains. I counted four passing each way, and from this I drew the conclusion that the same number would run at night. I marked a steep gradient up which they climbed very slowly, and determined at nightfall to make another attempt to board one of these. During the day I ate one slab of chocolate which, with the heat, produced a violent thirst. The pool was hardly half a mile away, but I dared not leave the shelter of the little wood, for I could see the figures of white men riding or walking occasionally across the valley, and once a Boer came and fired two shots at birds close to my hiding-place. But no one discovered me.

The elation and the excitement of the previous night had burned away, and a chilling reaction followed. I was very hungry, for I had had no dinner before starting, and chocolate though it sustains does not satisfy. I had scarcely slept, but yet my heart beat so fiercely and I was so nervous and perplexed about the future that I could not rest. I thought of all the chances that lay against me; I dreaded and detested more than words can express the prospect of being caught and dragged back to Pretoria. I do not mean that I would rather have died than have been retaken, but I have often feared death for much less. I found no comfort in any of the philosophical ideas that some men parade in their hours of ease and strength and safety. They seemed only fair weather friends. I realised with awful force that no exercise of my own feeble wit and strength could save me from my enemies, and that without the assistance of that High Power which interferes more often than we are always prone to admit in the eternal sequence of causes and effects, I could never succeed. I prayed long and earnestly for help and guidance. My prayer, as it seems to me, was swiftly and wonderfully answered. I cannot now relate the strange circumstances which followed, and which changed my nearly hopeless position into one of superior advantage. But after the war is over I shall hope to lengthen this account, and so remarkable will the addition be that I cannot believe the reader will complain.

The long day reached its close at last. The western clouds flushed into fire; the shadows of the hills stretched out across the valley. A ponderous Boer waggon, with its long team, crawled slowly along the track towards the town. The Kaffirs collected their herds and drew around their kraal. The daylight died, and soon it was quite dark. Then, and not till then, I set forth. I hurried to the railway line, pausing on my way to drink at a stream of sweet, cold water. I waited for some time at the top of the steep gradient in the hope of catching a train. But none came, and I gradually guessed, and I have since found out that I guessed right, that the train I had already travelled in was the only one that ran at night. At last I resolved to walk on and make, at any rate, twenty miles of my journey. I walked for about six hours. How far I travelled I do not know, but I do not expect it was very many miles in the direct line. Every bridge was guarded by armed men; every few miles were gangers' huts; at intervals there were stations with villages clustering round them. All the veldt was bathed in the bright rays of the full moon, and to avoid these dangerous places I had to make wide circuits and often to creep along the ground. Leaving the railroad I fell into bogs and swamps, and brushed through high grass dripping with dew, and so I was drenched to the waist. I had been able to take little exercise during my month's imprisonment, and I was soon tired out with walking, as well as from want of food and sleep. I felt very miserable when I looked around and saw here and there the lights of houses, and thought of the warmth and comfort within them, but knew that they only meant danger to me. After six or seven hours of walking I thought it unwise to go further lest I should exhaust myself, so I lay down in a ditch to sleep. I was nearly at the end of my tether. Nevertheless, by the will of God, I was enabled to sustain myself during the next few days, obtaining food at great risk here and there, resting in concealment by day and walking only at night. On the fifth day I was beyond Middleburg, as far as I could tell, for I dared not inquire nor as yet approach the stations near enough to read the names. In a secure hiding-place I waited for a suitable train, knowing that there is a through service between Middleburg and Lourenço Marques.

Meanwhile there had been excitement in the State Model Schools, temporarily converted into a military prison. Early on Wednesday morning – barely twelve hours after I had escaped – my absence was discovered – I think by Doctor Gunning, an amiable Hollander who used often to come and argue with me the rights and wrongs of the war. The alarm was given. Telegrams with my description at great length were despatched along all the railways. A warrant was issued for my immediate arrest. Every train was strictly searched. Everyone was on the watch. The newspapers made so much of the affair that my humble fortunes and my whereabouts were discussed in long columns of print, and even in the crash of the war I became to the Boers a topic all to myself. The rumours in part amused me. It was certain, said the *Standard and Digger's News*, that I had escaped disguised as a woman. The next day I was reported captured at Komati Poort dressed as a Transvaal policeman. There was great delight at this, which was only changed to doubt when other telegrams said that I had been arrested at

Bragsbank, at Middleburg and at Bronkerspruit. But the captives proved to be harmless people after all. Finally it was agreed that I had never left Pretoria. I had – it appeared – changed clothes with a waiter, and was now in hiding at the house of some British sympathiser in the capital. On the strength of this all the houses of suspected persons were searched from top to bottom, and these unfortunate people were, I fear, put to a great deal of inconvenience. A special commission was also appointed to investigate "stringently" (a most hateful adjective in such a connection) the causes "which had rendered it possible for the war correspondent of the *Morning Post* to escape".

The *Volksstem* noticed as a significant fact that I had recently become a subscriber to the State Library, and had selected Mill's essay *On Liberty*. It apparently desired to gravely deprecate prisoners having access to such inflammatory literature. The idea will, perhaps, amuse those who have read the work in question.

All these things may provoke a smile of indifference; perhaps even of triumph after the danger is past; but during the days when I was lying up in holes and corners waiting for a good chance to board a train, the causes that had led to them preyed more than I knew on my nerves. To be an outcast, to be hunted, to be under a warrant for arrest, to fear every man, to have imprisonment – not necessarily military confinement either – hanging overhead, to fly the light, to doubt the shadows – all these things ate into my soul and have left an impression that will not perhaps be easily effaced.

On the sixth day the chance I had patiently waited for came. I found a convenient train duly labelled to Lourenço Marques standing in a siding. I withdrew to a suitable spot for boarding it – for I dared not make the attempt in the station – and, filling a bottle with water to drink on the way, I prepared for the last stage of my journey.

The truck in which I ensconced myself was laden with great sacks of some soft merchandise, and I found among them holes and crevices by means of which I managed to work my way into the inmost recess. The hard floor of the truck was littered with gritty coal dust, and made a most uncomfortable bed. The heat was almost stifling. I was resolved, however, that nothing should lure or compel me from my hiding-place until I reached

Portuguese territory. I expected the journey to take thirty-six hours; it dragged out into two and a half days. I hardly dared sleep for fear of snoring.

I feared lest the trucks should be searched at Komati Poort, and my anxiety as the train approached this neighbourhood was very great. To prolong it we were shunted on to a siding for eighteen hours either at Komati Poort or the station beyond it. Once indeed they began to search my truck, but luckily did not search deep enough so that, providentially protected, I reached Delagoa Bay at last, and crawled forth from my place of refuge and of punishment, weary, dirty, hungry but free once more.

Thereafter everything smiled. I found my way to the British Consul, Mr Ross,* who at first mistook me for a fireman off one of the ships in the harbour, but soon welcomed me with enthusiasm. I bought clothes, I washed, I sat down to dinner with a real tablecloth and real glasses; and fortune, determined not to overlook the smallest detail, had arranged that the steamer *Induna* should leave that very night for Durban. It is from the cabin of this little vessel, as she coasts along the sandy shores of Africa, that I write these lines, and the reader who may persevere through this hurried account will perhaps understand why I write them with a feeling of triumph, and better than triumph, a feeling of pure joy.

---

* Alexander Carnegie Ross (1859–1940). Served as British Consul at Lourenço Marques 1898–1900. CB 1900.

The Boer War

RUDYARD KIPLING

Skirmish at Kari Siding

The skirmish at Kari Siding took place during Lord Roberts's 1900 mopping-up operation before he advanced on Kruger's base in the Transvaal. At the time of the incident Kipling, the famed writer of *Barrack Room Ballads* and the *Jungle Books*, was working for the *Friend*, a newspaper for British soldiers in the Boer War.

Something of Myself, 1937

So there had to be a battle, which was called the Battle of Kari Siding. All the staff of the Bloemfontein *Friend* attended. I was put in a Cape cart, with native driver, containing most of the drinks, and with me was a well-known war-correspondent. The enormous pale landscape swallowed up seven thousand troops without a sign, along a front of seven miles. On our way we passed a collection of neat, deep and empty trenches well under-cut for shelter on the shrapnel side. A young Guards officer, recently promoted to *Brevet-Major* – and rather sore with the paper that we had printed it *Branch* – studied them interestedly. They were the first dim lines of the dug-out, but his and our eyes were held. The Hun had designed them *secundum artem*, but the Boer had preferred the open within reach of his pony. At last we came to a lone farmhouse in a vale adorned with no less than five white flags. Beyond the ridge was a sputter of mus-ketry and now and then the whoop of a field-piece. "Here," said my guide and guardian, "we get out and walk. Our driver will wait for us at the farmhouse." But the driver loudly objected. "No, sar. They shoot. They shoot me." "But they are white flagged all over," we said. "Yess, sar. That *why*," was his answer, and he preferred to take his mules down into a decently remote donga and wait our return.

The farmhouse (you will see in a little why I am so detailed) held two men and, I think, two women, who received us disinterestedly. We went on into a vacant world full of sunshine and distances, where now and again a single bullet sang to himself. What I most objected to was the sensation of being under aimed fire – being, as it were, required as a head. "What are they doing this for?" I asked my friend. "Because they think we are the Something Light Horse. They ought to be just under this slope." I prayed that the particularly Something Light Horse would go elsewhere, which they presently did, for the aimed fire slackened and a wandering Colonial, bored to extinction, turned up with news from a far flank. "No; nothing doing and no one to see." Then more cracklings and a most cautious move forward to the lip of a large hollow where sheep were grazing. Some of them began to drop and kick. "That's both sides trying sighting-shots,' said my companion. "What range do you make it?" I asked. "Eight hundred, at the nearest. That's close quarters nowadays. You'll never see anything closer than this. Modern rifles make it impossible. We're hung up till something cracks somewhere." There was a decent lull for meals on both sides, interrupted now and again by sputters. Then one indubitable shell – ridiculously like a pipsqueak in that vastness but throwing up much dirt. "Krupp! Four- or six-pounder at extreme range," said the expert. "They still think we're the —Light Horse. They'll come to be fairly regular from now on." Sure enough, every twenty minutes or so, one judgmatic shell pitched on our slope. We waited, seeing nothing in the emptiness, and hearing only a faint murmur as of wind along gas-jets, running in and out of the unconcerned hills.

Then pom-poms opened. These were nasty little one-pounders, ten in a belt (which usually jammed about the sixth round). On soft ground they merely thudded. On rock-face the shell breaks up and yowls like a cat. My friend for the first time seemed interested. "If these are *their* pom-poms, it's Pretoria for us," was his diagnosis. I looked behind me – the whole length of

South Africa down to Cape Town – and it seemed very far. I felt
that I could have covered it in five minutes under fair conditions, but – *not* with those aimed shots up my back. The
pom-poms opened again at a bare rock-reef that gave the shells
full value. For about two minutes a file of racing ponies, their
tails and their riders' heads well down, showed and vanished
northward. "Our pom-poms," said the correspondent. "Le
Gallais, I expect. *Now* we shan't be long." All this time the
absurd Krupp was faithfully feeling for us, *vice* —Light Horse,
and, given a few more hours, might perhaps hit one of us. Then
to the left, almost under us, a small piece of hanging woodland
filled and fumed with our shrapnel much as a man's moustache
fills with cigarette-smoke. It was most impressive and lasted for
quite twenty minutes. Then silence; then a movement of men
and horses from our side up the slope, and the hangar our guns
had been hammering spat steady fire at them. More Boer ponies
on more skylines; a flurry of pom-poms on the right and a little
frieze of far-off meek-tailed ponies, already out of rifle range.

"*Maffeesh*," said the correspondent, and fell to writing on his
knee. "We've shifted 'em."

Leaving our infantry to follow men on ponyback towards the
Equator, we returned to the farmhouse. In the donga where he
was waiting someone squibbed off a rifle just after we took our
seats, and our driver flogged out over the rocks to the danger of
our sacred bottles.

Then Bloemfontein, and Gwynne storming in late with his
accounts complete – one hundred and twenty-five casualties,
and the general opinion that "French was a bit of a butcher" and
a tale of the General commanding the cavalry who absolutely
refused to break up his horses by galloping them across raw
rock – "not for any dam' Boer".

Months later, I got a cutting from an American paper, on
information from Geneva – then a pest-house of propaganda –
describing how I and some officers – names, date, and place
correct – had entered a farmhouse where we found two men
and three women. We had dragged the women from under the
bed where they had taken refuge (I assure you that no Tantie
Sannie of that day could bestow herself beneath any known
bed) and, giving them a hundred yards' start, had shot them
down as they ran.

Even then, the beastliness struck me as more comic than significant. But by that time I ought to have known that it was the Hun's reflection of his own face as he spied at our back-windows. He had thrown in the "hundred yards' start" touch as a tribute to our national sense of fair play.

From the business point of view the war was ridiculous. We charged ourselves step by step with the care and maintenance of all Boerdom – women and children included. Whence horrible tales of our atrocities in the concentration-camps.

One of the most widely exploited charges was our deliberate cruelty in making prisoners' tents and quarters open to the north. A Miss Hobhouse among others was loud in this matter, but she was to be excused.

We were showing off our newly built little "Woolsack" to a great lady on her way up-country, where a residence was being built for her. At the larder the wife pointed out that it faced south – that quarter being the coldest when one is south of the Equator. The great lady considered the heresy for a moment. Then, with the British sniff which abolishes the absurd, "Humm! I shan't allow *that* to make any difference to *me*."

Some Army and Navy Stores Lists were introduced into the prisoners' camps, and the women returned to civil life with a knowledge of corsets, stockings, toilet-cases, and other accessories frowned upon by their clergymen and their husbands. *Qua* women they were not very lovely, but they made their men fight, and they knew well how to fight on their own lines.

In the give-and-take of our work our troops got to gauge the merits of the commando-leaders they were facing. As I remember the scale, De Wet, with two hundred and fifty men, was to be taken seriously. With twice that number he was likely to fall over his own feet. Smuts (of Cambridge), warring, men assured me, in a black suit, trousers rucked to the knees, and a top-hat, could handle five hundred but, beyond that, got muddled. And so with the others. I had the felicity of meeting Smuts as a British General, at the Ritz during the Great War. Meditating on things seen and suffered, he said that being hunted about the veldt on a pony made a man think quickly, and that perhaps Mr Balfour (as he was then) would have been better for the same experience.

Each commando had its own reputation in the field, and the

grizzlier their beards the greater our respect. There was an elderly contingent from Wakkerstroom which demanded most cautious handling. They shot, as you might say, for the pot. The young men were not so good. And there were foreign contingents who insisted on fighting after the manner of Europe. These the Boers wisely put in the forefront of the battle and kept away from. In one affair the Zarps – the Transvaal Police – fought brilliantly and were nearly all killed. But they were Swedes for the most part, and we were sorry.

Occasionally foreign prisoners were gathered in. Among them I remember a Frenchman who had joined for pure logical hatred of England, but, being a professional, could not resist telling us how we ought to wage the war. He was quite sound but rather cantankerous.

The "war" became an unpleasing compost of "political considerations", social reform, and housing; maternity-work and variegated absurdities. It is possible, though I doubt it, that first and last we may have killed four thousand Boers. Our own casualties, mainly from preventable disease, must have been six times as many.

The junior officers agreed that the experience ought to be a "first-class dress-parade for Armageddon", but their practical conclusions were misleading. Long-range, aimed rifle-fire would do the work of the future: troops would never get nearer each other than half a mile, and Mounted Infantry would be vital. This was because, having found men on foot cannot overtake men on ponies, we created eighty thousand of as good Mounted Infantry as the world had seen. For these Western Europe had no use. Artillery preparation of wire-works, such as were not at Magersfontein, was rather overlooked in the reformers' schemes, on account of the difficulty of bringing up ammunition by horse-power. The pom-poms, and Lord Dundonald's galloping light gun-carriages, ate up their own weight in shell in three or four minutes.

In the ramshackle hotel at Bloemfontein, where the correspondents lived and the officers dropped in, one heard free and fierce debate as points came up, but – since no one dreamt of the internal-combustion engine that was to stand the world on its thick head, and since our wireless apparatus did not work in those landscapes – we were all beating the air.

Eventually the "war" petered out on political lines. Brother Boer – and all ranks called him that – would do everything except die. Our men did not see why they should perish chasing stray commandos, or festering in block-houses, and there followed a sort of demoralizing "handy-pandy" of alternate surrenders complicated by exchange of Army tobacco for Boer brandy which was bad for both sides.

At long last, we were left apologizing to a deeply indignant people, whom we had been nursing and doctoring for a year or two; and who now expected, and received, all manner of free gifts and appliances for the farming they had never practised. We put them in a position to uphold and expand their primitive lust for racial domination, and thanked God we were "rid of a knave".

The Russo-Japanese War

JACK LONDON

Beware the Monkey Cage

The Hearst newspaper group hired Jack London to be its chief correspondent during the Russo-Japanese War (1904–5). On arriving in Tokyo, London discovered that the Imperial military authorities were forbidding journalists to accompany the Japanese Army as it marched through Manchuria to engage the Russians. Undaunted, London took passage on tramp steamers, sleeping on the open deck in midwinter, hired a native junk, then a horse – to become the first war correspondent to reach the north of the war zone, from where he filed the following report.

Hearst Newspapers, 10 May 1904

Antung, Manchuria. May 10th, 1904 – The Japanese, following the German model, make every possible preparation, take every possible precaution, and then proceed to act, confident in the belief that nothing short of a miracle can prevent success. Opposed to their three divisions on the Yalu was a greatly inferior Russian force, but the Japanese had to cross the river under fire and attack an enemy lying in wait for them.

By the manipulation of their three divisions, and what of their ruses, they must have sadly befuddled the Russians. At the mouth of the Yalu the Japanese had two small gunboats, two torpedo boats and four small steamers armed with Hotchkiss-guns. Also they had fifty sampans loaded with bridge materials. These were intended for a permanent bridge at Wiju; but they served another purpose – first, farther down the stream. The presence of the small navy and the loaded sampans led the Russians to believe that right there was where the bridge was to be built. So right there they stationed some three thousand men to prevent the building of the bridge. Thus a handful of Japanese sailors kept 3,000 Russian soldiers occupied in doing nothing and reduced the effectiveness of the Russian strength that much.

Another ruse was the building of a bridge in front of Wiju. This was in plain view of the Russians on the conical hill opposite just east of Kieu-Liang-Cheng, and they consumed much time and powder in shelling it. This was precisely what the Japanese intended for the bridge. While it held the Russian attention, a little farther down the stream the Japanese were at work on another bridge screened by small willow trees on the intervening island, and which, when completed, had never had a shot fired at it.

Have you ever stood in front of a cage wherein there was a monkey gazing innocently and peaceably into your eyes – so innocent and peaceable the hands grasping the bars and wholly unbelligerent, the eyes that bent with friendly interest on yours, and all the while and unbeknown a foot sliding out to surprise your fancied security and set you shrieking with sudden fright? Beware the monkey cage! You have need of more than your eyes; and beware the Japanese. When he sits down stupidly to build a bridge with his two hands before your eyes, have a thought to the quiet place behind the willow-screen where another bridge is builded by his two feet. He works with his hands and his feet, he works night and day, and he never does one thing expected of him, and that is the unexpected thing.

The night of April 29th and the day of the 30th was an anxious time for the Japanese. Their army was cut in half, and it was no less than the Yalu that divided it. One-third of its force, the Z division, had crossed the river to the right and was in Manchuria. They had no very accurate knowledge of the Russian strength, and it was not beyond liability that the Russians might make a counter attack on the Z division and destroy it. So the X and Y divisions on the south bank were in momentary readiness to prevent this by delivering an attack upon the Russians straight across the river. But there was no need for this. The Russians were not in sufficient force to attack a single division, advancing as it was across mountainous country. This, in turn, the

Japanese did not know, but they prepared for the possibility as they prepare for everything.

The Ai-ho river flows out of Manchuria and enters the Yalu valley a mile or more above Kieu-Liang-Chen. It also flows past that village, close to the Manchurian shore, thus interposing an obstacle to the advance of the whole Japanese army (even the Z division), after it had crossed the Yalu proper. The crossing of the Ai-ho was seriously menaced by the sixteen guns of the Russian right on the conical hill. The day's work for April 30th was to put these sixteen guns out of business. The Japanese bent themselves to the task. It was an exposed position and a concentration of fire lasting twenty-five minutes and in which time sixty common shells were thrown, did the work. The Russian fire was silenced and the guns were withdrawn that night! Incidentally the Japanese bombed the Russian camp, carelessly situated where it was exposed from the Korean hills, and wrought great havoc.

On the night of April 30th the X and Y divisions crossed the main Yalu and rested on the sands, with the Ai-ho between them and the Russians. The X division forming the Japanese left, faced the Russian right on the conical hill, and the Y division was extended near the mouth of the Ai-ho; and up the Ai-ho, extended for several miles, lay the Z division. Opposing these three divisions was a Russian actual fighting force of about 4,000 men. The Russian line, extending some six or seven miles, was not intact. In fact, because of the lay of the land, the Russians really occupied two positions – one on and about the conical hill at Kieu-Leng-Cheng, the other at the Ai-ho, from its mouth several miles up.

Against these two positions, occupied by about 2,000 men, was hurled an army of three divisions (probably 25,000 men actually on the spot), backed by a powerful artillery of field guns and howitzers. Prevented by shell fire and shrapnel from doing their best to repel the general attack, and being flanked by an immensely superior force, the Russian left on the Ai-ho broke first and fled in the direction of the Hamatan. The Russian right on the conical hill fought, more tenaciously, the survivors in turn fleeing toward Hamatan.

The Japanese understand the utility of things. Reserves they consider should be used, not only to strengthen the line or protect the repulsed line, but in the moment of victory to clinch victory hard and fast. The reserves, fresh and chafing from inaction wild to take part in a glorious day, received the order for general pursuit. Right, left and center, they took after the Russians. The field guns, delayed by the Ai-ho, followed at a gallop.

The retreat became a rout. The Russian reserves, two regiments, had fled without firing a shot – at least the Japanese have no record of these two regiments. Hamatan is at the conjunction of three roads, six miles to the rear of the conical hill. Down these three roads the Russians ran, coming together and passing on to the main road – the Pekin or Mandarin road. And down these three roads, from left, right, and center, came the fresh reserves, and after them the artillery.

In the meantime, however, far from the Japanese right and outstripping the rest of the pursuit, arrived one company of men in time to cut off fifteen Russian guns and eight maxims. The remnants of the three battalions rallied around the guns. A hasty position was taken. The rest of the pursuing Japanese did not arrive. But one company of men stood between the Russians and the Pekin Road. And it stood. Its captain and three lieutenants were killed. One officer only remained alive. The last cartridge was fired. Those that survived fixed their bayonets ready to receive a charge. And in the moment, left, right, and center, their pursuing comrades arrived.

The Russians were assailed from three sides. The tables were turned but they fought with equal courage. The day was lost; they knew it; yet they fought on doggedly. Night was falling. As the Japanese grew closer the Russians turned loose their horses, destroyed or threw away the breechblocks of their guns, smashed the breeches of the maxims and then, as bayonet countered bayonet, drew white handkerchiefs from their pockets in token of surrender.

One other noteworthy thing occurred in the Japanese pursuit. Midway to Hamatan, flying on the heels of a rout, in the very heat and sweep of triumph, they dropped a line of reserves to receive and protect them should they be hurled back broken and crushed by Russian re-enforcements. Hand in hand with terrifying bravery goes this cold-blooded precaution. Verily, nothing short of the miracle can wreck a plan they have once started to put into execution. The men furnish the unfaltering bravery, confident in their knowledge that their officers have furnished the precaution.

Of course, the officers are as brave as the men. On the night of the 30th, when the army took up its position on the Ai-ho, it was not known whether that stream was fordable. Officers from each of the three divisions stripped and swam or waded the river at many different points, practically under the rifles of the Russians. "Men determined to die" is the way one Japanese officer characterized the volunteers who answer in large number to every call for dangerous work. Not knowing whether the Ai-ho was fordable, three plans were seriously considered. First, each soldier was to go into action May 1st dressed in cartridge belt and equipped with a rifle and a board, the latter to be used as a means for paddling across the Ai-ho. Second, same garb and equipment with a tub substituted for the board, and third, the strongest swimmers to cross over with ropes, along which, when once fast on the other side bank, the weaker swimmers and non-swimmers could make their way. In any case, had the river not proved fordable, Kipling's "Taking the Long-Tong-Pen" would have been repeated on a most formidable scale. Surely the Russians would have broken and fled perceptibly before so terrible a charge.

Every division, every battery was connected with headquarters by field telephone. When the divisions moved forward they dragged their wires after them like spiders drag the silk of their webs. Even the tiny navy at the mouth of the Yalu was in constant communication with headquarters. Thus, on a wide-stretching and largely invisible field, the commander-in-chief was in immediate control of everything. Inventions, weapons, systems (the navy modeled after the English, the army after the German), everything utilized by the Japanese has been supplied by the Western world; but the Japanese have shown themselves the only Eastern people capable of utilizing them.

The Balkan Wars

LEON TROTSKY

The Seamy Side of Victory

Leon Trotsky covered the conflict between the Balkan nations and Turkey for the Ukranian newspaper *Kievskaya Mysl*. He later reported the opening salvoes of the First World War in France. The experience gained proved to be of no small importance, for Trotsky used it to found the Red Army of the U.S.S.R. The dispatch below was written from the Bulgarian capital, Sofia.

Kievskaya Mysl, 19 October 1912

Hitherto the war has shown us only one of its aspects: it has taken the flower of the male population from the villages and towns, crammed them into trains, and sent them off to the scene of military operations. This process is still not at an end: the mobilization is completing its work, selection of recruits is going forward, the military trains continue to pump out the working population of the country. But another stream is already flowing back to meet them. During the last two days trains have not only been taking away but also bringing back. The great outflow is being to some extent compensated. I refer to the transports of wounded and prisoners that are now arriving here.

The arrival of the wounded has not yet set a sorrowful imprint upon the life of the city. In the first place, the wounded are still not numerous here – there are only two or three hundred of them – and secondly, they are not Sofia men, but all from remote places. The wounded from Sofia have been distributed between Philippopolis, Slivno, and other centers. In the Red Cross hospital there are still a lot of empty beds, the nurses still look fresh, unexhausted, unworried, the ladies of Sofia's moneyed circles bring flowers and the aroma of perfume into the hospital wards, and with their lovely, tender fingers pat the patients on their brows and cheeks, covered with cold sweat. There are still not many prisoners, and they are a curiosity. People take an interest in them, scrutinize them, and "interview" them. Yesterday 320 arrived from Mustafa-Pasha, among whom were twenty Bulgars (Orthodox), two Armenians, one Mountain Jew, and the rest Turks.

But there will be more of them – both wounded and prisoners. The beds will have to be placed closer together in Sofia's hospitals, the nurses will no longer be able to change their white aprons every time fresh blood spurts on them, their eyes will no longer look lively and welcoming, as now, but will be red with fatigue, and there will no longer be enough left in Sofia of those flowers with which the ladies are at present decorating the hospital wards . . .

Hardly had mobilization been proclaimed when journalists came rushing into the Balkans from all over the world. They filled all the hotels, cafés, and ministerial waiting rooms in Belgrade and Sofia. They cursed the ministers when they declined to be interviewed, they cursed the telegraph operators for working too slowly, they cursed the government and general staff because they kept military developments secret for too long. From time to time they were reminded that war is not, strictly speaking, carried on for the benefit of films and newspapers, and military activities are governed by preoccupations other than these. Soon after the start of hostilities, the journalists, with few exceptions, went off to GHQ, emptying the hotels and cafés. Their place has now been taken by medical orderlies – Russians, Germans, Austrians, Czechs. With Red Cross armbands and satchels over their shoulders, they roam the streets in groups, waiting for "assignments". Yesterday I met some Russian nurses who were making their way through the crowds in a state of perplexed curiosity.

"We're waiting to be sent somewhere. They say we'll be sent to . . . where did they say?"

"Lozevy, I think it was."

"Lozengrad, perhaps?"

"That's it," the nurse agreed, happily, "to Lozengrad . . . But is it true what they say, that the Bulgarians have given the Turks another beating?"

"Yes, it is: it happened before Lüle Burgas."

"That's good."

"Good?"

"Good!" says the nurse, confidently.

I have been twice to see the prisoners who are housed in the barracks of the 4th Regiment of fortress artillery. To do this it was necessary first of all to visit the commandant's office and arrange for permission.

Owing to the state of martial law, all the threads of the administration are now concentrated in the commandant's office. It is stuffy, crowded, smoke-filled, and noisy. The decor, the procedure, the words and gestures are in our own familiar Russian style. Here is an elderly man, a townsman to judge by his dress, asking for a permit to go to Philippopolis, where his wounded son is in the hospital. He is whispering about something with the deputy commandant.

"Well, all right then, go. Only don't tell anybody that I gave you permission, or they'll all be pestering me."

A German in civilian clothes, but with a military bearing, is silently holding out a piece of paper. The deputy cannot make out what he wants and has to call in an interpreter. It turns out that the German is a sergeant major from the German regiment that bears the name Ferdinand of Bulgaria; he has come here at his own expense to volunteer his services to the Bulgarian army, but for two days now has not been able to get any sense out of anyone . . .

"Please tell him to go and see the adjutant at the war ministry. If they give the authority, I'll issue him a travel permit and a free ticket to Stara Zagora."

"He's already been to the war ministry twice. They wouldn't let him see the adjutant, and sent him here. Perhaps you could telephone the ministry about the matter?"

"I shouldn't get through: the war ministry's line is busy all the time. But, anyway, what could he do in the army if he doesn't know our language: he's German, isn't he?"

"He says he'll manage all right. We Germans, he says, know what to do on the battlefield. The Bulgarian ambassador in Berlin promised him, he says, that he would be accepted into the active army here, and presented to the king, who is the colonel of his regiment."

My permit to visit the prisoners is ready, and I leave the ill-starred German sergeant major, who is ready to fight the Turks just because his regiment is named after King Ferdinand . . .

The home guard at the gate of the barracks started to prevent our entering. I showed him the paper I had been given. But he proved to be illiterate, and the paper made no impression on him at all. He called out the guard commander, however, and the difficulty was removed. In a huge rectangular courtyard, the front of which is occupied by the barracks, while the other three sides are stables, stand horses, groups of home guards, and recruits, and a score of prisoners are fetching manure out of the stables in wheelbarrows. We want to photograph this scene, but the NCO won't allow it.

"Is it necessary to have a special permit to take photographs?"

"Come tomorrow when they're having their midday meal – then you can photograph them. But what's the point of photographing them now? . . ."

I tried to discover what the problem was. It turned out that the authorities do not want the prisoners to be photographed at work: in Europe, apparently, people are saying that the Bulgarians are treating their prisoners badly, making them cart horsedung. So deep does concern about European public opinion run in this country.

The barracks commandant, a reserve officer, takes us to see the prisoners. He knocks on a door: an orderly opens it from inside, and we enter the first room. There are 150 men in it. Along the walls and in the midst of the room, in four rows, close together on the ground, lie palliasses with worn and dirty covers. Turkish prisoners are lying or sitting on these. As we enter, nearly all of them hastily jump up and stand at attention. They are all wearing sandals or down-at-the-heel shoes, with puttees carefully wound round their legs, and military breeches and jackets of a gray-green protective color, and fezzes of the same, except that some of the latter are red. Their faces . . . are human faces of various sorts. Some are good-natured or indifferent, others sullen or embittered. Some are quite young, some elderly. They were lying here on their straw-filled sacks, chatting, or remembering, or dozing. Our entry excited them. Some, apparently, thought that the officer had brought with him some high personage who would announce a change in their lot: they followed us closely and suspiciously with their eyes. About a dozen men demonstratively failed to stand up. Others pretended to be asleep. In one corner a prisoner was shaving another prisoner while a third waited his turn.

"They are very strict with themselves where shaving is concerned," says the officer. "In general, though, they are a dirty people."

In the second room we come to, the scene is the same. In the third there are no mattresses. The floor is covered with straw, already dirty and caked together. Here everything is even more cramped and unsightly than in the other two rooms. Only a few of the men get up when we enter.

"That's the lot, gentlemen," says the officer. "I've got 403 altogether: two are in hospital at present. Thirty to forty of them are Bulgars, Greeks, and Armenians, the rest Turks. They were taken at Skech and Mustafa-Pasha. For your photographs, come tomorrow at twelve, when they are having their meal. That's much more interesting, I assure you. They arrange themselves about the yard in very picturesque groups."

Today I went again to the artillery barracks. In the yard, outside a door with *gotvarnitsa* (cook-house) written on it, stood about fifty men carrying large tin bowls and pails – evidently the trusties of the different squads. "*Dur bakalam, dur bakalam!*" (Wait, wait!) said a reservist at the cookhouse door to the men who were showing too much impatience. Out here in the yard there was nothing prisoner-like about the Turks, who differed little from the Bulgarian recruits who were also waiting for their food. They ate in groups, sitting cross-legged around the bowls. They were given as much *chorba* (cabbage soup with meat in it) as they wanted, and then some sort of stew. The Turks ate in silence, intently, not hurrying to finish before the next man, but eating up everything, and then licking their spoons and their fingers; they ate honestly, like peasants.

"And how do they feel; aren't they depressed?" I ask a Bulgarian home guard who speaks Turkish.

"How could they not be? Yes, they're depressed. They are all great family men, and look forward to the day when it will all be over and they can go back to their families. They are all recruits, even the not-so-young ones. What happens with them is this: they buy themselves off from several levies, but then they've no more money left, and so, the next time, they are taken. They know nothing at all about soldiering. We captured them without a fight – they gave themselves up."

"And they're not frightened?"

"No, not now. In the evening they sing their songs. Hey, lads," he said, turning to the prisoners, "who wants some more? There's still some *chorba* left in the cookhouse . . ."

In the post office I saw three Russian volunteers. They did not rejoice my patriotic heart.

At the post office window a cleanshaven gentleman wearing mufti, but with a sword, was complaining to the postal officials about some breach of discipline. He spoke in Russian, decorated with a few Bulgarian words; his speech was not firm, and he gave off a strong smell of vodka. The post office clerks glanced at each other, but politely agreed with him: discipline is, indeed, a necessary thing . . .

"Pardon me," the gentleman with the sword was saying, "if that son-of-a-bitch isn't disciplined, my good sirs, he's (hic) going to impose on me . . ."

Two Russian volunteers, hardly more than boys, told me that they had made their way on foot, from wherever it was they came from, as far as Odessa, and from there had gone by steamboat to Ruschuk. There is something morbidly loudmouthed and insistent about both of them.

"We've heard how the Turks behave: they put up a white flag, and then, when they get close, they start shooting. That's bloody bad, eh? Don't you think so, eh?"

"Yes, that's bad."

"After all, it's not allowed – it's really disgraceful. How can we fight under conditions like that, eh?"

"But you, gentlemen, won't fire on the white flag."

"Still, we'll obviously have to provide against . . ."

"Well, gentlemen, all the best."

The Mexican Revolution

JOHN REED

The Coming of the Colorados

The Mexican Revolution began in 1910, with a popular uprising against the dictatorship of Porfirio Díaz led by the democratic politician Francisco Madero; although Madero succeeded Díaz as president, Madero's principal supporters, Francisco "Pancho" Villa and Emiliano Zapata, sought to turn the political revolution into a social and agrarian one. It took nine years and nearly a million lives before any kind of stable peace settled on Mexico.

The radical American journalist John Reed spent four months in 1913 riding with Pancho Villa's army, sending back dispatches for *Metropolitan Magazine*. The articles were reworked into *Insurgent Mexico*. Reed later covered the Russian Revolution; he died, of typhus, in the Soviet Union in 1920. He was immortalized by Warren Beatty in the movie *Reds*.

Insurgent Mexico, 1914

Before sunrise next morning, Fernando Silveyra, fully dressed, came into the room and said calmly to get up, that the *colorados* [pro-Díaz troops] were coming. Juan Vallejo laughed: "How many, Fernando?"

"About a thousand," he answered in a quiet voice, rummaging for his bandolier.

The patio was unusually full of shouting men saddling horses. I saw Don Petronilo, half dressed, at his door, his mistress buckling on his sword. Juan Santillanes was pulling at his trousers with furious haste. There was a steady rattle of clicks as cartridges slipped into rifles. A score of soldiers ran to and fro aimlessly, asking everyone where something was.

I don't think we any of us really believed it. The little square of quiet sky over the patio gave promise of another hot day. Roosters crowed. A cow that was being milked bellowed. I felt hungry.

"How near are they?" I asked.

"Near."

"But the outpost – the guard at the Puerta?"

"Asleep," Fernando said, as he strapped on his cartridge belt.

Pablo Arriola clanked in, crippled by his big spurs.

"A little bunch of twelve rode up. Our men thought it was only the daily reconnaissance. So after they drove them back, the Puerta guard sat down to breakfast. Then Argumedo himself and hundreds – hundreds—"

"But twenty-five could hold that pass against an army until the rest got there . . ."

"They're already past the Puerta," said Pablo, shouldering his saddle. He went out.

"The—!" swore Juan Santillanes, spinning the chambers of his revolver. "Wait till I get at them!"

"Now Meester's going to see some of those shots he wanted," cried Gil Tomas. "How about it, Meester? Feel scared?"

Somehow the whole business didn't seem real. I said to myself, "*You lucky devil, you're actually going to see a fight. That will round out the story.*" I loaded my camera and hurried out in front of the house.

There was nothing much to see there. A blinding sun rose right in the Puerta. Over the leagues and leagues of dark desert to the east nothing lived but the morning light. Not a movement. Not a sound. Yet somewhere out there a mere handful of men were desperately trying to hold off an army.

Thin smoke floated up in the breathless air from the houses of the peons. It was so still that the grinding of *tortilla* meal between two stones was distinctly audible – and the slow, minor song of some woman at her work way around the Casa Grande. Sheep were maaing to be let out of the corral. On the road to Santo Domingo, so far away that they were mere colored accents in the desert, the four peddlers sauntered behind their burros. Little knots of peons were gathered in front of the hacienda, pointing and looking east. And around the gate of the big enclosure where the soldiers were quartered a few troopers held their horses by the bridle. That was all.

Occasionally the door of the Casa Grande vomited mounted men – two or three at a time – who galloped down the Puerta road with their rifles in their hands. I could follow them as they rose and fell over the waves of the desert, growing smaller all the time, until they mounted the last roll – where the white dust they kicked up caught the fierce light of the sun, and the eye couldn't stand it. They had taken my horse, and Juan Vallejo didn't have one. He stood beside me, cocking and firing his empty rifle.

"Look!" he shouted suddenly. The western face of the mountains that flanked the Puerta was in shadow still. Along their base, to the north and to the south, too, wriggled little thin lines of dust. They lengthened out – oh so slowly. At first there was only one in each direction; then two others began, farther down, nearer, advancing relentlessly, like raveling in a stocking – like a crack in thin glass. The enemy, spreading wide around the battle, to take us in the flank!

Still the little knots of troopers poured from the Casa Grande, and spurred away. Pablo Arriola went, and Nicanor, waving to me brightly as they passed. Longinos Giiereca rocketed out on his great *tordillo* horse, yet only half broken. The big gray put down his head and buckjumped four times across the square.

"Tomorrow for the mines," yelled' Gino over his shoulder. "I'm very busy today – very rich – the lost mines of —" But he was too far away for me to hear. Martinez followed him, shouting to me with a grin that he felt scared to death. Then others. It made about thirty so far. I remember that most of them wore automobile goggles. Don Petronilo sat his horse, with field glasses to his eyes. I looked again at the lines of dust – they were curving slowly down, the sun glorifying them – like scimitars.

Don Tomas galloped past, Gil Tomas at his heels. But someone was coming. A little running horse appeared on the rise, headed our way, the rider outlined in a radiant dust. He was going at furious speed, dipping and rising over the rolling land . . . And as he spurred wildly up the little hill where we stood, we saw a horror. A fan-shaped cascade of blood poured from the front of him. The lower part of his mouth was quite shot away by a soft-nosed bullet. He reined up beside the colonel, and tried earnestly,

terribly, to tell him something; but nothing intelligible issued from
the ruin. Tears poured down the poor fellow's cheeks. He gave a
hoarse cry, and, driving his spurs deep in his horse, fled up the
Santo Domingo road. Others were coming, too, on the dead run
– those who had been the Puerta guard. Two or three passed right
through the hacienda without stopping. The rest threw themselves upon Don Petronilo, in a passion of rage. "More
ammunition!" they cried. "More cartridges!"

Don Petronilo looked away. "There isn't any!" The men went
mad, cursing and hurling their guns on the ground.

"Twenty-five more men at the Puerta," shouted the Colonel.
In a few minutes half of the new men galloped out of their cuartel and took the eastern road. The near ends of the dust lines
were now lost to view behind a swell of ground.

"Why don't you send them all, Don Petronilo?" I yelled.

"Because, my young friend, a whole company of *colorados* is
riding down that arroyo. You can't see them from there, but I
can."

He had no sooner spoken than a rider whirled around the
corner of the house, pointing back over his shoulder to the
south, whence he had come.

"They're coming that way, too," he cried. "Thousands!
Through the other pass! Redondo had only five men on guard!
They took them prisoner and got into the valley before he knew
it!"

"*Valgame Dios!*" muttered Don Petronilo.

We turned south. Above the umber rise of desert loomed a
mighty cloud of white dust, shining in the sun, like the biblical
pillar of smoke.

"The rest of you fellows get out there and hold them off!"
The last twenty-five leaped to their saddles and started southward.

Then suddenly the great gate of the walled square belched
men and horses – men without rifles. The disarmed *gente* of
Salazar! They milled around as if in a panic. "Give us our rifles!"
they shouted. "Where's our ammunition?"

"Your rifles are in the cuartel," answered the Colonel, "but
your cartridges are out there killing *colorados*!"

A great cry went up. "They've taken away our arms! They
want to murder us!"

"How can we fight, man? What can we do without rifles?" screamed one man in Don Petronilo's face.

"Come on, *compañeros*! Let's go out and strangle 'em with our hands, the – *colorados*!" yelled one. Five struck spurs into their horses, and sped furiously toward the Puerta – without arms, without hope. It was magnificent!

"We'll all get killed!" said another. "Come on!" And the other forty-five swept wildly out on the road to Santo Domingo. The twenty-five recruits that had been ordered to hold the southern side had ridden out about half a mile, and there stopped, seeming uncertain what to do. Now they caught sight of the disarmed fifty galloping for the mountains.

"The *compañeros* are fleeing! The *compañeros* are fleeing!"

For a moment there was a sharp exchange of cries. They looked at the dust cloud towering over them. They thought of the mighty army of merciless devils who made it. They hesitated, broke – and fled furiously through the chaparral toward the mountains.

I suddenly discovered that I had been hearing shooting for some time. It sounded immensely far away – like nothing so much as a clicking typewriter. Even while it held our attention it grew. The little trivial pricking of rifles deepened and became serious. Out in front now it was practically continuous – almost the roll of a snare drum.

Don Petronilo was a little white. He called Apolinario and told him to harness the mules to the coach.

"If anything happens that we get the worst of it," he said lightly to Juan Vallejo, "call my woman and you and Reed go with her in the coach. Come on, Fernando – Juanito!" Silveyra and Juan Santillanes spurred out; the three vanished toward the Puerta.

We could see them now, hundreds of little black figures riding everywhere through the chaparral; the desert swarmed with them. Savage Indian yells reached us. A spent bullet droned overhead, then another; then one unspent, and then a whole flock singing fiercely. Thud! went the adobe walls as bits of clay flew. Peons and their women rushed from house to house, distracted with fear. A trooper, his face black with powder and hateful with killing and terror, galloped past, shouting that all was lost ...

Apolinario hurried out the mules with their harness on their backs, and began to hitch them to the coach. His hands trembled. He dropped a trace, picked it up, and dropped it again. He shook all over. All at once he threw the harness to the ground and took to his heels. Juan and I rushed forward. Just then a stray bullet took the off mule in the rump. Nervous already, the animals plunged wildly. The wagon tongue snapped with the report of a rifle. The mules raced madly north into the desert.

And then came the rout, a wild huddle of troopers all together, lashing their terrified horses. They passed us without stopping, without noticing, all blood and sweat and blackness. Don Tomas, Pablo Arriola, and after them little Gil Tomas, his horse staggering and falling dead right in front of us. Bullets whipped the wall on all sides of us.

"Come on, Meester!" said Juan. "Let's go!" We began to run. As I panted up the steep opposite bank of the arroyo, I looked back. Gil Tomas was right behind me, with a red- and black-checked serape round his shoulders. Don Petronilo came in sight, shooting back over his shoulder, with Juan Santillanes at his side. In front raced Fernando Silveyra, bending low over his horse's neck. All around the hacienda was a ring of galloping, shooting, yelling men; and as far as the eye could reach, on every rise of the desert, came more.

Part II

The Era of Total War, 1914–1946

World War I

RICHARD HARDING DAVIS

Saw German Army Roll On Like Fog

After years of enmity and sabre-rattling, the powers of Europe went to war on 4 August 1914 in a conflict that became most famous for its trench warfare on the Western Front, but spread around the world as the combatants – principally Germany and Austria on the Axis side, and Britain, France and Russia in the Allied camp – mauled over their colonial possessions.

The very day war was declared, the veteran American correspondent Richard Harding Davis sailed for Europe. He reached the epicentre of the conflict, luckless would-be neutral Belgium, just as the Germany army advanced through it towards the Channel.

New York *Tribune*, 23 August 1914

Brussels, Friday, Aug. 21, 2 p.m.
The entrance of the German army into Brussels has lost the human quality. It was lost as soon as the three soldiers who led the army bicycled into the Boulevard du Regent and asked the way to the Gare du Nord. When they passed the human note passed with them.

What came after them, and twenty-four hours later is still coming, is not men marching, but a force of nature like a tidal wave, an avalanche or a river flooding its banks. At this moment it is rolling through Brussels as the swollen waters of the Conce-maugh Valley swept through Johnstown.

At the sight of the first few regiments of the enemy we were thrilled with interest. After three hours they had passed in one unbroken steel gray column [and] we were bored. But when hour after hour passed and there was no halt, no breathing time, no open spaces in the ranks, the thing became uncanny, inhuman. You returned to watch it, fascinated. It held the mystery and menace of fog rolling toward you across the sea.

The gray of the uniforms worn by both officers and men helped this air of mystery. Only the sharpest eye could detect among the thousands that passed the slightest difference. All moved under a cloak of invisibility. Only after the most numerous and severe tests at all distances, with all materials and combinations of colors that give forth no color could this gray have been discovered. That it was selected to clothe and disguise the German when he fights is typical of the German staff striving for efficiency to leave nothing to chance, to neglect no detail.

After you have seen this service uniform under conditions entirely opposite you are convinced that for the German soldier it is his strongest weapon. Even the most expert marksman cannot hit a target he cannot see. It is a gray green, not the blue gray of our Confederates. It is the gray of the hour just before daybreak, the gray of unpolished steel, of mist among green trees.

I saw it first in the Grand Place in front of the Hotel de Ville. It was impossible to tell if in that noble square there was a regiment or a brigade. You saw only a fog that melted into the stones, blended with the ancient house fronts, that shifted and drifted, but left you nothing at which you could point.

Later, as the army passed below my window, under the trees of the Botanical Park, it merged and was lost against the green leaves. It is no exaggeration to say that at a hundred yards you can see the horses on which the Uhlans ride, but cannot see the men who ride them.

If I appear to overemphasize this disguising uniform, it is because of all the details of the German outfit, it appealed to me as one of the most remarkable. The other day, when I was with the rear guard of the French Dragoons and Curassiers and they threw out pickets, we could distinguish them against the yellow wheat or green course at half a mile, while these men passing in the street, when they have reached the next crossing, become merged into the gray of the paving stones and the earth swallows them. In comparison the yellow khaki of our own American army is about as invisible as the flag of Spain.

Yesterday Major General von Jarotzky, the German Military Governor of Brussels, assured Burgomaster Max that the German army would not occupy the city, but would pass through it. It is still passing. I have followed in campaigns six armies, but, excepting not even our own, the Japanese or the British, I have not seen one so thoroughly equipped. I am not speaking of the fighting qualities of any army, only of the equipment and organization. The German army moved into this city as smoothly and as compactly as an Empire State Express. There were no halts, no open places, no stragglers.

This army has been on active service three weeks, and so far there is not apparently a chinstrap or a horseshoe missing. It came in with the smoke pouring from cookstoves on wheels, and in an hour had set up postoffice wagons, from which mounted messengers galloped along the line of column distributing letters and at which soldiers posted picture postcards.

The infantry came in in files of five, two hundred men to each company; the Lances in columns of four, with not a pennant missing. The quick fire guns and field pieces were one hour at a time in passing, each gun with its caisson and ammunition wagon taking twenty seconds in which to pass.

The men of the infantry sang "Fatherland, My Fatherland." Between each line of song they took three steps. At times two thousand men were singing together in absolute rhythm and beat. When the melody gave way the silence was broken only by the stamp of iron-shod boots, and then again the song rose. When the singing ceased the bands played marches. They were followed by the rumble of siege guns, the creaking of wheels and of chains clanking against the cobble stones and the sharp bell-like voices of the bugles.

For seven hours the army passed in such solid column that not once might a taxicab or trolley car pass through the city. Like a river of steel it flowed, gray and ghostlike. Then, as dusk came and as thousands of horses' hoofs and thousands of iron boots continued to tramp forward, they struck tiny sparks from the stones, but the horses and the men who beat out the sparks were invisible.

At midnight pack wagons and siege guns were still passing. At seven this morning I was awakened by the tramp of men and bands playing jauntily. Whether they marched all night or not I do not know; but now for twenty-six hours the gray army has rumbled by with the mystery of fog and the pertinacity of a steam roller.

World War I

ARTHUR MOORE

The Great Retreat

Moore's dispatch originally appeared unsigned in the Sunday edition of *The Times*, and was the first announcement of the British defeat at Mons. *The Times* was fiercely criticized for carrying it, particularly by the War Office which had carefully peddled the misinformation that the British Expeditionary Force was enjoying easy and continued successes on the Western Front.

The Times, 30 August 1914

Amiens, 29 August

I read this afternoon in Amiens this morning's Paris papers. To me, knowing some portion of the truth, it seemed incredible that a great people should be so kept in ignorance of the situation which it has to face. The papers read like children's prattle, gleanings from the war talk of their parents a week ago. Not a word of the fall of Namur (the English papers containing the news are not allowed in Paris, and the Paris *Daily Mail* was forced to publish a denial of the English Press Bureau's statement which it had published), and considerable talk about new successes on the Meuse.

This is not well. I would plead with the English censor to let my message pass. I guarantee him that as regards the situation of troops I have nothing to say that is not known and noted already by the German General Staff. There is no reason, either in strategy or tactics, why every word I write should not be published. And to get my information I have broken no promise and no obligation. I have moved far and fast in Northern France between Wednesday morning and the hour of writing. The car has been challenged and stopped perhaps above a hundred times. But the papers that we carried have passed us everywhere.

On the other hand, it is important that the nation should know and realize certain things. Bitter truths, but we can face them. We have to cut our losses, to take stock of the situation, to set our teeth.

First let it be said that our honour is bright. Amongst all the straggling units that I have seen, flotsam and jetsam of the fiercest fight in history, I saw fear in no man's face. It was a retreating and a broken army, but it was not an army of hunted men. Nor in all the plain tales of officers, non-commissioned officers, and men did a single story of the white feather reach me. No one could answer for every man, but every British regiment and every battery of which anyone had knowledge had done its duty. And never has duty been more terrible.

Since Monday morning last the German advance has been one of almost incredible rapidity. As I have already written you, the British Force fought a terrible fight – which may be called the action of Mons, though it covered a big front – on Sunday. The German attack was withstood to the utmost limit, and a whole division was flung into the fight at the end of a long march and had not even time to dig trenches. The French supports expected on the immediate right do not seem to have been in touch, though whether or not they were many hours late I cannot say.

Further to the right, along the Sambre and in the angle of the Sambre and the Meuse, the French, after days of long and gallant fighting, broke. Namur fell, and General Joffre was forced to order a retreat along the whole line. The Germans, fulfilling one of the best of all precepts in war, never gave the retreating army one single moment's rest. The pursuit was immediate, relentless, unresting. Aeroplanes, Zeppelins, armoured motors, and cavalry were loosed like an arrow from the bow, and served at once to harass the retiring columns and to keep the German Staff fully informed of the movements of the Allied Forces.

The British force fell back through Bavai on a front between

Valenciennes and Maubouge, then through Le Quesney, where desperate fighting took place, southwards continually. Regiments were grievously injured, and the broken army fought its way desperately with many stands, forced backwards and ever backwards by the sheer unconquerable mass of numbers of an enemy prepared to throw away three or four men for the life of every British soldier. Where it is at present it might not be well to say even if I knew, but I do not know, though I have seen to-day in different neighbourhoods some units of it. But there are some things which it is eminently right that I should say.

To-night I write to the sound of guns. All the afternoon the guns were going on the eastern roads. A German aeroplane flew over us, this morning, and was brought crashing down.

An RE chauffeur told me that the axle of his car was broken and he had to abandon it. He had no more than left it when it also was blown up. In scattered units with the enemy ever on its heels the Fourth Division, all that was left of 20,000 fine troops, streamed southward.

Our losses are very great. I have seen the broken bits of many regiments. Let me repeat that there is no failure in discipline, no panic, no throwing up the sponge. Everyone's temper is sweet, and nerves do not show. A group of men, it may be a dozen or less or more, arrives, under the command of whoever is entitled to command it. The men are battered with marching, and ought to be weak with hunger, for, of course, no commissariat could cope with such a case, but they are steady and cheerful, and whenever they arrive make straight for the proper authority, report themselves, and seek news of their regiment.

I saw two men give such reports, after saluting smartly. "Very badly cut up, Sir," was the phrase one used of his regiment. The other said, "Very heavy loss, I'm afraid, Sir," when asked if much was left.

Apparently every division was in action. Some have lost nearly all their officers. The regiments were broken to bits, and good discipline and fine spirit kept the fragments together, though they no longer knew what had become of the other parts with which they had once formed a splendid whole.

Certain things about the fighting seem clear. One is the colossal character of the German losses. I confess that when I read daily in official bulletins in Paris of how much greater the

German losses were than those of the Allies I was not much impressed. Much contemplation of eastern warfares, where each side claims to have annihilated the other, has made me over-sceptical in such matters. But three days among the combatants has convinced me of the truth of the story in this case.

It is clear that although the French General Staff knew that their eastern frontier defences had been so perfected as to force Germany to turn to the flank to find a weak spot, although they knew also that not for nothing did Germany antagonize England and outrage international opinion by violating the neutrality of Belgium, nevertheless they under-estimated the force of the German blow through Belgium. All estimates of the number of German army corps in Belgium will need revision, and behind the screen in Alsace and Lorraine there were probably far fewer than was supposed – else, perhaps, Mülhausen would not have had to be retaken twice.

The German commanders in the north advance their men as if they had an inexhaustible supply. Of the bravery of the men it is not necessary to speak. They advance in deep sections, so slightly extended as to be almost in close order, with little regard for cover, rushing forward as soon as their own artillery has opened fire behind them on our position. Our artillery mows long lanes down the centres of the sections, so that frequently there is nothing left of it but its outsides. But no sooner is this done than more men double up, rushing over the heaps of dead, and remake the section. Last week, so great was their superiority in numbers that they could no more be stopped than the waves of the sea. Their shrapnel is markedly bad, though their gunners are excellent at finding the range. On the other hand their machine-guns are of the most deadly efficacy, and are very numerous. Their rifle shooting is described as not first-class, but their numbers bring on the infantry till frequently they and the Allied troops meet finally in bayonet tussles. Superiority of numbers in men and guns, especially in machine-guns; a most successfully organized system of scouting by aeroplanes and Zeppelins; motors carrying machine-guns, cavalry; and extreme mobility are the elements of their present success.

To sum up, the first great German effort has succeeded. We have to face the fact that the British Expeditionary Force, which bore the great weight of the blow, has suffered terrible losses and requires immediate and immense reinforcement. The British Expeditionary Force has won indeed imperishable glory, but it needs men, men, and yet more men. The investment of Paris cannot be banished from the field of possibility. I saw the rolling stock being hurriedly moved to-day. *Proximus ardei Ucalegon*. We want reinforcements and we want them now. Whether the Chief of the German General Staff, after reckoning up his losses, will find that he has enough men left to attempt a further assault with any hope of success is more doubtful. His army has made a colossal effort and moved with extraordinary speed. It is possible that its limits have been reached.

World War I

PHILIP GIBBS

Heroic Incidents in the Advance

The Battle of the Somme opened on 1 July 1916, claiming 60,000 British casualties on that day alone. A week later Philip Gibbs, the war correspondent for the London *Daily Chronicle*, was among a small group of reporters allowed to interview surviving participants of that first day of fighting on the Somme.

Daily Chronicle, 10 July 1916

The officer who came round the village with me had a lonely look. After battle, such a battle as this, it is difficult to keep the sadness out of one's eye. So many good fellows have gone . . . But they were proud of their men. They found a joy in that.

The men had done gloriously. They had won their ground and held it, through frightful fire. "The men were topping."

There were a lot of Yorkshire men among them who fought at Fricourt, and it was those I saw to-day. They were the heroes, with other North Country lads, of one of the most splendid achievements of British arms ever written down in history.

Some of them were still shaken. When they spoke to me their words faltered now and then, and a queer look came into their eyes. But, on the whole they were astoundingly calm, and had not lost their sense of humour.

In the first advance over No Man's Land, which was 150 yards across to the enemy's front line trench, some of these men could remember nothing.

It was just a dreadful blank. "I was just mad at the time," said one of them. "The first thing I know is that I found myself scrambling over the German parapets with a bomb in my hand. The dead were lying all around me."

But a sergeant there remembered all. He kept his wits about him, strangely clear at such a time. He saw that his men were being swept with machine-gun fire, so that they all lay down to escape its deadly scythe.

But he saw also that the bullets were first washing the ground so that the prostrate men were being struck in great numbers. He stood up straight and called upon the others to stand, thinking it would be better to be hit in the feet than in the head. Then he walked on and came without a scratch to the German front line.

Here and in the lines behind there was a wreckage of earth from our bombardment, but several of the dug-outs had been untouched and in them during our gunfire men were sitting, thirty feet down, with machine-guns ready, and long periscopes, through which they could see our lines and first wave of advancing men.

Before the word reached them, those German machine-gunners had rushed upstairs and behind the cover of their wrecked trenches fired bursts of bullets at our men.

Each gun team had with them a rifleman who had a crack shot, and who obeyed his army orders to pick off English officers. So they sniped our young lieutenants with cool and cruel deliberation. Two of them who were dressed as privates escaped for this reason. Many of the others fell.

"With so many officers gone," said one of the Yorkshire lads, "it was every man for himself, and we carried on as best we could."

They carried on as far as the second and third lines, in a desperate fight with German soldiers who appeared out of the tumbled earth and flung bombs with a grim refusal of surrender.

"Well, if you're asking for it," said one of our men – and he hurled himself upon a great German and ran his bayonet through the man's body.

There was not much killing at that spot. When most of our men were within ten yards many of the Germans who had been flinging bombs lifted up their hands and cried "Mercy!" to those whom they had tried to blow to bits.

It was rather late to ask for mercy, but it was given to them. There was a search into the dug-outs – do you understand that all this was done under great shell fire? – and many Germans were found in hiding there.

"I surrender," said a German officer, putting his head out of a hole in the earth, "and I have a wounded man with me." "All right," said a Yorkshire sergeant, "fetch him up, and no monkey tricks."

But out of the hole came not one man, but forty, in a long file that seemed never to end, all of whom said "Kamerad!" to the sergeant, who answered, "Good day to you! – and how many more?"

They were a nuisance to him then. He wanted to get on and this was a waste of time. But he sent back forty-two prisoners with three lightly wounded fellows of his company – he could not spare more – and then advanced with his men beyond the German third line.

Bunches of men were straggling forward over the shell-broken ground towards the German line at Crucifix trench, to the left of Fricourt. They knew that this trench was important, that their lives were well given if they could capture it. And these Yorkshire boys from the hills and dales thought nothing of their lives so that they could take it.

They unslung their bombs, looked to the right and left, where German heavies were falling, cursed the chatter of machine-guns from Fricourt village, and said, "Come on, lads!" to the men about them. Not one man faltered or turned back, or lingered with the doubt that he had gone far enough.

They stumbled forward over the shell craters, over dead bodies, over indescribable things. Crucifix trench was reached. It was full of Germans who were hurling bombs from it, from that trench and the sunken road near by.

The Yorkshire boys went through a barrage of bombs, hurled their own, worried through the broken parapets and over masses of tumbled earth, and fought single fights with big Germans, like terrier dogs hunting rats and worrying them. Parties bombed their way down the sunken road.

Those who fell, struck by Germans bombs, shouted "Get on to 'em, lads" to others who came up. In bits of earthworks German heads looked up, white German faces, bearded, and covered with clay like dead men risen. They put up trembling hands and cried their words of comradeship to those enemy boys.

"Well, that's all right," said a Yorkshire captain. "We've got the Crucifix. And meanwhile our guns are giving us the devil." Our gunners did not know that Crucifix Trench was taken. Some of our shells were dropping very close.

"It's time for a red light," said the Yorkshire captain. He had a bullet in his ribs, and was suffering terribly, but he still commanded his men. A red rocket went up, high through the smoke over all the corners of the battlefield. Somewhere it was seen by watchful eyes, in some OP or by some flying fellow. Our guns lifted. The shells went forward, crashing into Shelter Wood beyond.

"Good old gunners!" said a sergeant. "By God, they're playing the same game to-day!"

But other men had seen the red rocket above Crucifix Trench. It stood in the sky like a red eye looking down upon the battlefield. The German gunners knew that the British were in Crucifix Trench. They lowered their guns a point or two, shortening their range, and German shells came crumping the earth, on either side, registering the ground.

"And where do we go next, captain?" asked a Yorkshire boy. It seemed he felt restless where he was. The captain thought Shelter Wood might be a good place to see. He chose ten men to see it with him, and they were very willing.

With a bullet in his ribs – it hurt him horribly – he climbed out of Crucifix Trench, and crawled forward, with his ten men to the wood beyond. It was full of Germans. At the south-west corner of it was a redoubt, with machine-guns and a bomb-store. The Germans bombers were already flinging their grenades across to the Crucifix.

The wounded captain said that ten men were not enough to take Shelter Wood – it would need a thousand men, perhaps, so he crawled back with the others.

They stayed all night in Crucifix Trench, and it was a dreadful night. At ten o'clock the enemy opened an intense bombardment of heavies and shrapnel, and maintained it full pitch until two o'clock next morning. There were 900 men up there and in the neighbourhood. When morning came there were not so many, but the others were eager to get out and get on.

The Yorkshire spirit was unbeaten. The grit of the North Country was still there in the morning after the first assault.

Queer adventures overtook men who played a lone hand in this darkness and confusion of battle. One man I met to-day – true Yorkshire, with steel in his eyes and a burr in his speech – it was strange to hear the Saxon words he used – rushed with some of his friends into Birch Tree Wood, which was not captured until two days later.

There were many Germans there, but not visible. Suddenly the Yorkshire lad found himself quite alone, his comrades having escaped from a death-trap, for the wood was being shelled – as I saw myself that day – with an intense fire from our guns.

The lonely boy, who was a machine-gunner without his gun, thought that things were "pretty thick", as, indeed, they were, but he described the risks of death as less if he stayed still than if he moved.

Presently, as he crouched low, he saw a German coming. He was crawling along on his hands and knees, and blood was oozing from him. As he crawled, a young Yorkshire soldier, also badly wounded, passed him at a little distance in the wood.

The German stared at him. Then he raised himself, though still on his knees, and fired at the boy with his revolver, so that he fell dead. The German went on his hands again to go on with his crawling, but another shot ripped through the tree, and he crawled no more.

It was fired by the man who had been left alone – the young man I saw today. "I killed the brute," he said, "and I'm glad of it."

Our shells were bursting very fiercely over the wood, slashing off branches and ploughing up the earth. The lonely boy searched about for a dug-out and found one. When he went down into it he saw three dead Germans there, and he sat with them for more than eight hours while our bombardment lasted.

There was another lad I met who was also a machine-gunner, and alone in the battle zone. He was alone when fourteen of his comrades had been knocked out. But single-handed he carried and served his gun, from one place to another, all through the day, and part of the next day, sniping odd parties of Germans with bursts of bullets.

Another sturdy fellow I met came face to face with a German, who called out to him in perfect English.

"Don't shoot. I was brought up in England and played footer for Bradford City . . . By Jove! I know your face, old man. Weren't you at the Victoria Hotel, Sheffield?"

It was a queer meeting on a battlefield. One of the grimmest things I have heard was told me by another Yorkshire boy. A German surrendered, and then suddenly, as this lad approached to make him prisoner, pulled the detonator of a bomb and raised it to throw.

"I put my bayonet right close to him so suddenly that he was terrified, and forgot to fling his bomb. Then a queer kind of look came into his eyes. He remembered that the blooming bomb was going off. It went off, and blew him to bits."

That is war. And the men who have told me these things are young men who do not like the things they have seen. But, because it is war, they go through to the last goal with a courage that does not equal.

The men of this division next day took Shelter Wood and Fricourt, and captured many prisoners.

World War I

LUIGI BARZINI

The Battle in the Snows

Barzini began his career at war covering the Boxer Rebellion (1898–1901) for Italy's most prestigious newspaper, *Corriere della Sera*, and remained with the paper until 1923 when he moved to the USA to edit the Italian-American *Corriere d'America*; a committed supporter of Mussolini, Barzini returned to Italy to become a Fascist senator. He continued, however, to work as a war correspondent and covered both the Spanish Civil War and Nazi invasion of Russia for the Blackshirt *Il Popolo d'Italia*.

During the Great War Barzini had been the official war reporter attached to the Italian army. Here "the king of Italian journalists" reports from the campaign in the Alps.

War Illustrated, 9 August 1916

We were encamped on the mountain side, in caverns dug into the ice-hardened snow, around us the rugged and angry peaks of Pal Piccolo, beneath us the Pass of Monte Croce. Here is one of the vital spots in the Italian line, for it commands the Freikofel approaches, and consequently the way into the Italian plains. Where the cluster of hills reaches its highest point two crests tower above all the others, to a height of about 6000 feet. They stand opposite to one another, running somewhat parallel along their summits, separated by a distance of about one hundred yards. One is in our hands, the other in those of the Austrians.

At half-past two in the morning, in the midst of a driving snowstorm, we were awakened by the incessant crackle of rifle fire. "There is a fight at Pal Piccolo," telephoned the sentry, "but it is a matter of no importance."

A few moments later the captain in command at Quota 1859 – which is the great military trenchwork guarding our position on the Pal – telephoned for reinforcements. The Austrians had come over the snow and had attacked him.

"Counter-attack immediately," was the order from the colonel. "I have done so already," replied the captain, "but I have lost a number of my men." Suddenly the telephone communications were broken off – a proof that he was already besieged and had his lines of communication destroyed.

White Phantoms in a Blizzard

The situation was extremely grave. One of our most important positions had suddenly fallen into Austrian hands. Over the intervening snow they had come, clad entirely in white. It was in the depth of night, with a blinding and bitter storm raging, so that the sentries could not have seen the moving mass. Generally on the darkest night a figure moving on the mountain, even though clad in the colour of the snow, throws a distinct reflection on the ice-encrusted ground; but on that night no eye could pierce the dense screen of the storm. Our men were shoveling the freshly fallen snow from their trenches when they were surprised by the phantom-like Austrians, who fell upon them in enormous masses. They bound the hands of the sentries with wire and smashed their skulls with rifles.

On they came, wave after wave in quick succession, flooding the main trenches and connecting galleries. From these galleries to the caves where our Alpini dwell a system of subterranean corridors run. The corridors are in the form of stairways whose steps are made of wood or hewn into the rock. Up to the openings of the corridors the Austrians came, destroying the stairways as far as possible and building barricades across the exits, so as to prevent any advance on the part of those who had retired to the refuges.

Having fought bravely and lost heavily, the garrison of Quota 1859 withdrew into its refuge, bringing as many of its wounded as possible, and decided to await reinforcements. Its position became surrounded and its communications entirely cut off. But the captain was determined not to surrender. Screened somewhat by the darkness and the blinding storm, his men rushed to and fro, bringing sand-bags, tables, and iron plates to block the mouths of their fortress. When the morning broke they peered out, only to see the phantom mass of howling enemies surrounding them. Jeeringly the Austrians shouted: "Down, Italians! We are your masters. To-day, Pal Piccolo; to-morrow, Pal Grande." They were but twenty yards distant, shouting hurrahs, hymns, and songs of victory. And they had reason to be confident of success; for their enterprise had been carefully planned and skilfully carried out. An enormous mass of defensive material was brought up – sand-bags, steel plates, searchlights, ammunition, and artillery – and the position consolidated. Should they succeed in holding their ground they would eventually control one of the main roads to Italy.

The Italian Counter-Attack

We realised the seriousness of it fully. One of the most important spots along our whole line, a vital spot, was in danger. "We must act immediately," ordered the general. "Each hour's delay may cost hundreds of lives."

A company of Bersaglieri at once received orders to attack the Austrians on the left. Forward they went, forging ahead in single file, tunnelling the newly fallen snow to afford themselves a passage. But they were soon swept by the rifle fire and artillery of the enemy. The commander, two leading officers, and several of the men fell. Further advance was impossible; so they wheeled to the left and sought protection under the lee of a towering snow-peak. In order to understand this form of warfare one must know something of the conditions under which it is waged.

On the mountain the distances are short but the journeys are long. In order to arrive at a point not more than two hundred yards away, one must follow a zigzag course, leading downwards over precipitous declines and again upwards, scaling angry crags and circumventing treacherous ravines. As one moves forward the path must be excavated, and this is absolutely necessary where fresh snow has fallen. The battlefield is small but the manoeuvring is on a colossal scale. The enemy is near at hand, but the movements necessary to come into touch with him lie through distances that are well-nigh infinite. The mountain takes part in the conflict, pushing forward gigantic obstacles which make every step a combat. It has thrown up its fortresses and delved its moats, and it must be conquered before the enemy can be attacked.

The attack of the Bersaglieri failed, and for the moment it appeared as if our line would be broken. So we hastily built new trenches and brought up reserves for the defence. Our artillery came into action, but the blanket of clouds rendered aim impossible. The sky was our target, the heavens themselves were now against us. The wounded were falling into the deep glacial ravines, their cries for help reverberating against the cruel walls, piteous and tragic.

Then another plan of attack was decided upon. The Alpini took the centre of the advance, with the infantry on the right and the Barsagheri on the left. To make progress possible, and escape the withering fire of the Austrian artillery, they had to tunnel the mountain, through the hard ice and snow. In subterranean corridors they moved forward. It was tedious work, and all the while the Austrian position on the crest was growing stronger. After hours and hours of anxious waiting we saw our men emerge from their tunnels. Little black specks they looked on the side of the great white mountain. They appeared in batches of three, calling out orders and cries of encouragement to one another. One could see hands lifted to the grasping hand above, pulling one another upward by means of axes, ropes, alpenstocks, and rifles.

Then we saw circles of white smoke floating over the Austrian position. Our machine-guns rent the air. The crackle of their shells against the steel-plate Austrian defences was re-echoed from the glacial walls of the surrounding peaks. Recognising the sound, our troops on the lower portions of the hill shouted, "Bravo, Carlino! Bravo, Carlino!" – the pet name given by the mountaineers to the little bronze machine-gun which is the watchdog of the trenches.

The Austrians sneeringly shouted, "Come on, Italians!" They were not more than one hundred yards away, but they occupied a crest which controlled every approach. The intervening ground consisted of a rugged steep, teeming with jagged crags and deep ravines, the whole terrain swept by the enemy's artillery. To advance in daytime was out of the question, so it was decided to wait for the cover of night.

Red Tracks Across the Snow

At nine o'clock the signal was given, and a riot of fire surrounded the crest. An Austrian searchlight swept the mountain side, the dark sky was lit up by an orange glow, and the whole zone became a palpitating mass of living flame. Our infantry swept around the shoulder of the crest, taking advantage of the shelter given them by the craggy banks of a mountain torrent. But our frontal attack could not proceed. There they stood, immobile and determined, but unable to advance, grappled together in groups, awaiting a more auspicious moment, annealed to the crags by the congealing snow and ice, insensible to cold and hunger, but determined not to yield an inch.

A little before midnight they sprang once more to the attack. Wounded again and again, lines of red marked their track across the snow, but still they went forward and upward. At midnight some sections had already arrived at a spot within six yards of the Austrians; other sections were within fifty yards. But the Austrian rain of hand-grenades was devastating. Our troops lost all their officers, and the attack had to be suspended once again. A damp snow was falling, freezing into a mailcoat of ice as it covered the bodies of the men.

At one in the morning a new order was given. Up from the shoulder of the hill came a detachment of Bersaglieri and Alpini. Some had rackets on their feet, tobogganing over mountains of snow, while others waded breast-deep through the newly-fallen drifts. Sometimes several hours were spent in covering only a few yards.

Then came the dawn – the dawn of the third day of struggle – ashen grey, cold and sad, filling one's soul with a sense of death. Because of the nearness of our troops to the Austrians our artillery could not come into action, but Carlino kept barking at the enemy, so that he was unable to show himself above the parapet. However, the Austrians were ready with a store of hand-grenades and rifles at the mouth of the gallery, just above the parapet. While they remained there, further attack was impossible.

Out of the unknown, like shades of the dead wandering on the mountain, came two Alpini, clad in white shirts. Nobody could divine whence they had come or whither they would go. They were utterly unarmed, simply carrying a harmless bread-basket. Soon they were at the mouth of the gallery, which towered above them like the balcony of a castle built of glistening ice. One was seen to stoop and lift the wooden ladder which the Austrians had thrown down. They placed it against the side of the wall and climbed upwards, while a shower of hand-grenades and rifle fire from the Austrians poured over their heads. Poising with the coolness of an athlete in the games, one launched his loaf of bread against the parapet. Another and another throw. Then the parapet leaped upwards. A wild cry of "Savoia!" rent the air; the breach had been made. From crag to crag, from crest to crest, the loud hurrahs were passed, until the whole mountain became vocal. Upwards rushed the infantry, Bersaglieri, and Alpini, from right and left and centre. It was a struggle of sublime terror, waged on towering cliffs in the midst of the clouds, on a winter island, cast into the skies from the tepid seas of spring. As the battle raged the fighting units became intermixed. As the officers fell, the sergeants and soldiers leapt forward to command, but, dominating all and directing all was the sublime faith and enthusiasm, which burned in each breast.

"Avanti, alia baionetta!"

"Up, up, Savoia!" rang the wild cry. Bersaglieri and Alpini pulled one another up the sides of the glistening crags, some holding the bare bayonet between their teeth.

"Up, up, Savoia!" Soon they were scaling the parapet. An Alpine colonel threw his feathered hat in the air, crying out, "Avanti, alia baionetta!" Then a heavy green cloud of poison gas was belched forth from the Austrians, but the wind blew it away from our men. Heaven was with us. "Avanti, Savoia!"

In a thousand echoes the mountains crashed back the cry. Soon the bayonets were at work in the trenches, and the ground became encumbered with heaps of Austrian dead. The struggle of the terrible three days was over. Pal Piccolo was ours once more.

We counted six hundred dead, but that was only a fraction of the enemy's losses. They fought well and bravely, but they could not master the bravery and skill of our men. And thus Pal Piccolo remains the most heroic and sublime struggle ever fought on the mountains. In the moment of victory the besieged garrison came forth gleamingly and shook the hands of their deliverers. "We knew you would come," they said.

World War I

RUDYARD KIPLING

The Battle of Jutland

The sea battle of Jutland, the major encounter between the British and German fleets in the First World War, was fought in the North Sea on 31 May 1916. It was described in a series of reports for the London *Daily Telegraph* by Nobel Laureate Rudyard Kipling, then fifty-one, and on his third turn as a war correspondent. For reasons of security, Kipling used fictitious names for the destroyers.

Daily Telegraph, 19–31 October 1916

When the German fleet ran for home, on the night of May 31, it seems to have scattered – "starred", I believe, is the word for the evolution – in a general *sauve qui peut*, while the Devil, lively represented by our destroyers, took the hindmost. Our flotillas were strung out far and wide on this job. One man compared it to hounds hunting half a hundred separate foxes.

I take the adventures of several couples of destroyers who, on the night of May 31, were nosing along somewhere towards the Schleswig-Holstein coast, ready to chop any Hun stuff coming back to earth by that particular road. The leader of one line was *Gehenna*, and the next two ships astern of her were *Eblis* and *Shaitan*, in the order given . . .

Towards midnight our destroyers were overtaken by several three- and four-funnel German ships (cruisers, they thought) hurrying home. At this stage of the game anybody might have been anybody – pursuer or pursued. The Germans took no

chances, but switched on their searchlights and opened fire on
Gehenna. Her Acting Sublieutenant reports: "A salvo hit us forward. I opened fire with the afterguns. A shell then struck us in
a steampipe, and I could see nothing but steam. But both starboard torpedoes were fired."

Eblis, *Gehenna*'s next astern, at once fired a torpedo at the
second ship in the German line, a four-funnelled cruiser, and hit
her between the second funnel and the mainmast, when "she
appeared to catch fire fore and aft simultaneously, heeled right
over to starboard, and undoubtedly sank." *Eblis* loosed off a
second torpedo and turned aside to reload, firing at the same
time to distract the enemy's attention from *Gehenna*, who was
now ablaze fore and aft. *Gehenna*'s Acting Sublieutenant (the
only executive officer who survived) says that by the time the
steam from the broken pipe cleared he found *Gehenna* stopped,
nearly everybody amidships killed or wounded, the cartridge
boxes round the guns exploding one after the other as the fires
took hold, and the enemy not to be seen. Three minutes or less
did all that damage.

Eblis had nearly finished reloading when a shot struck the
davit that was swinging her last torpedo into the tube and
wounded all hands concerned. Thereupon she dropped torpedo
work, fired at an enemy searchlight which winked and went out,
and was closing in to help *Gehenna*, when she found herself
under the noses of a couple of enemy cruisers . . . The enemy did
her best. She completely demolished the *Eblis*'s bridge and
searchlight platform, brought down the mast and the forefunnel,
ruined the whaler and the dinghy, split the foc's'le open above
water from the stern to the galley which is abaft the bridge, and
below water had opened it up from the stern to the second bulkhead. She further ripped off *Eblis*'s skin plating for an amazing
number of yards on one side of her, and fired a couple of large-
calibre shells into *Eblis* at point-blank range narrowly missing her
vitals. Even so, *Eblis* is as impartial as a prize court . . .

After all that *Eblis* picked herself up, and discovered that she
was still alive, with a dog's chance of getting to port. But she did
not bank on it. That grand slam had wrecked the bridge, pin-
ning the commander under the wreckage. By the time he had
extricated himself he "considered it advisable to throw overboard the steel chest and dispatch box of confidential and secret

books". [These] are never allowed to fall into strange hands, and their proper disposal is the last step but one in the ritual of the burial service of His Majesty's ships at sea. *Gehenna,* afire and sinking, out somewhere in the dark, was going through it on her own account. This is her Acting Sublieutenant's report: "The confidential books were got up. The First Lieutenant gave the order: 'Every man aft,' and the confidential books were thrown overboard. The ship soon afterwards heeled over to starboard and the bows went under. The First Lieutenant gave the order: 'Everybody for themselves.' The ship sank in about a minute, the stern going straight up into the air."

But it was not written in the Book of Fate that stripped and battered *Eblis* should die that night as *Gehenna* died. After the burial of the books it was found that the several fires on her were manageable, that she "was not making water aft of the damage", which meant two thirds of her were, more or less, in commission, and, best of all, that three boilers were usable in spite of the cruiser's shells. So she "shaped course and speed to make the least water and the most progress towards land".

On the way back the wind shifted eight points without warning – and, what with one thing and another, *Eblis* was unable to make any port till the scandalously later hour of noon June 2, "the mutual ramming having occurred about 11.40 p.m. on May 31". She says, this time without any legal reservation whatever, "I cannot speak too highly of the courage, discipline, and devotion of the officers and ship's company." . . .

In that flotilla alone there was every variety of fight, from the ordered attacks of squadrons under control, to single ship affairs, every turn of which depended on the second's decision of the men concerned; endurance to the hopeless end; bluff and cunning; reckless advance and redhot flight; clear vision and as much of blank bewilderment as the Senior Service permits its children to indulge in. That is not much. When a destroyer who has been dodging enemy torpedoes and gunfire in the dark realizes about midnight that she is "following a strange British flotilla, having lost sight of my own", she "decides to remain with them", and shares their fortunes and whatever language is going.

If lost hounds could speak when they cast up next day, after an unchecked night among the wild life of the dark, they would talk much as our destroyers do.

World War I

ARTHUR RANSOME

War and Revolution

Long before he penned *Swallows and Amazons*, Arthur Michell Ransome worked as a war correspondent, covering the Eastern Front and then the Russian Revolution for the radical *Daily News*, and later for the *Manchester Guardian* and the Sunday *Observer*. In his *Autobiography* (1976) Ransome recounted his first visit to the Russian front as correspondent:

Autobiography, 1976, telegrams, 1916–17,
Daily News, 16 March 1917

It was March 1916 before I was given my first limited permission to visit the Russian front as a war correspondent. We went to Kiev and thence to the South Western Army Headquarters at Berditchev, where we met for the first time General Brusilov, the smartest-uniformed and most elegant of all Russian generals, later to be famous for his break-through in the west, and for the disasters his armies suffered in retreat.

I remember interminable driving in vehicles of all kinds along roads that war had widened from narrow cart-tracks to broad highways half a mile wide. Drivers had moved out of the original road to ground on either side of it not yet churned to mud. As each new strip turned to a bog, the drivers steered just outside it, so that in many places two carts meeting each other going in opposite directions would be out of shouting distance.

On one occasion he visited the Eastern Front by air:

In August I had flown along the front in one of the old two-seated Voisin machines in which the passenger sat as if in an open canoe with a foot on each side of the pilot, in whose stupidity he had the utmost confidence. It was cold in the air and I well remember beating my hand against the outside of the canoe to get my fingers warm enough to take a photograph. Our real trouble, such as it was, began when just before dusk we flew black to the place from which we had started. We began to spiral down and instantly there appeared puff after puff of smoke from shells sent up to meet us. The pilot suddenly turned the nose of the machine up, pointing with a grin to a small new tear in one wing. Presently he spiralled down again and again was greeted with shells from below. Once more we sheered off, this time with curses, and on coming back yet again we were, at last, recognised as friends and allowed to land.

I dined that night with the battery that had done the shooting, and sat next to the officer in charge. I complained that I did not think he had given me a very hospitable reception.

"Perhaps not," he replied. "I'm very sorry, but really you ought to count yourself lucky, for usually when we fire at our own machine we hit it." He explained that the aeroplanes had been given to the Russian army because they were not good enough for the French. They were very slow and therefore easy targets.

Ransome was sympathetic to both the February and October Revolutions; unsurprisingly then, he was one of the Western journalists most favoured by the Bolsheviks and was frequently accorded an inner ringside seat at events. In 1924 Ransome married Evgenia Shelepina, Trotsky's secretary.

Telegrams from Ransome to *Daily News*, December 1916 – January 1917

26 December 1916

WITH RUSSIAN ARMY IN FIELD WINTER LATE THIS YEAR HAS AT LAST DESCENDED ON RUSSIAN FRONT

STOP BORDERS SNOW COVERED ICE EITHER SIDE
DVINA GRADUALLY SPREADING TOWARDS MIDDLE
RIVER WHERE LITTLE ICEBERGS FLOAT STEADY
PROCESSION STOP TEN DAYS OR LESS RIVER WILL BE
FROZEN OVER STOP SCOUTS ONCE MORE COVERED
THEMSELVES WHITE OVERALLS AS EVEN PALEST
COLOURS SHOWS UP DARK ON GLITTERING SNOW
UNDER LIGHT OF ROCKETS WHICH GERMANS SEND
UP CONSTANTLY CLEARLY AFRAID RUSSIAN
ACTIVITY STOP BESIDES RAPIDLY INCREASING
MOTOR TRANSPORT THERE IS HUGE VOLUME HORSE
TRAFFIC AND WHEELED CARTS ALREADY BEING
CHAINED FOR SLEDGES STOP EVERYWHERE ALONG
FRONT MET LONG TRAINS SLEDGES PULLED LITTLE
SHAGGY HORSES DRIVEN BY FURCAPPED MEN IN
SHEEPSKINS STOP PICTURESQUE SIGHT ON FRONT
GREAT BANDS KHIRGIZES TARTARS FROM
TASHKENT BROUGHT FROM FAR EAST FOR
ROADMAKING AND FORTIFICATION STOP RUSSIAN
ARMY SETTLING CHEERFULLY DOWN TO THIRD
WINTER CAMPAIGN BETTER EQUIPPED BETTER
ORGANISED STRONGER THAN EVER BEFORE AND
FULLY CONSCIOUS ITS STRENGTH STOP EMPERORS
PROCLAMATION WITH ITS INSISTENCE THAT PEACE
CANNOT BE THOUGHT OF UNTIL TASK OF ALLIES
COMPLETED PRODUCED GREAT ENTHUSIASM AT
FRONT STOP WHILE WE LOOKING ACROSS SNOW TO
GERMAN POSITIONS AND SHELL BATTERED
CHURCH ILLUKST RUSSIAN OFFICER SAID ME
QUOTE WE FEAR NOTHING EXCEPT PESSIMISM IN
REAR STOP NO PESSIMISM AT FRONT AND RUSSIAN
ARMY COULD NEVER CONSENT PEACE UNDER
PRESENT CONDITIONS UNQUOTE FEELING IN
GERMAN ARMY EXACTLY REVERSE STOP ALTHOUGH
IN MILITARY SENSE STILL STRONG GERMAN ARMY
WANTS PEACE AND FEARS NOT PESSIMISTS BUT
OPTIMISTS IN ITS REAR STOP GERMANS
FREQUENTLY MAKE WAY OVER TO RUSSIAN
TRENCHES TO SURRENDER THING UNHEARD OF
EARLIER STAGES WAR STOP GERMAN UNDER

OFFICER WHO CAME OVER THIS WAY SAID WE HAVE
ALWAYS PROMISED PEACE NEVER GETTING IT STOP
THEY HAVE PROMISED TOO OFTEN STOP HOW CAN
THEY EXPECT US FIGHT WHEN WE GET LITTLE AND
KNOW OUR FAMILIES GET LESS TO EAT STOP
GERMANS ON EASTERN FRONT GET FISH
OCCASIONALLY BUT NEVER SEE MEAT FOR MONTHS
AT TIME STOP RUSSIAN PRISONERS WHO ESCAPE
FROM GERMANS COME BACK WITH TEETH LOOSE IN
GUMS FROM LACK SOLID FOOD STOP THEY BRING
WITH THEM BITTERNESS AGAINST GERMANY AND
INCREASES COMRADES CONFIDENCE BY TELLING
WHAT ACTUALLY SEEN OF PLIGHT OF BESIEGED
EMPIRE STOP RETURNING FROM POSITIONS OTHER
DAY MET GROUP SOLDIERS ROUND FIELD KITCHEN
EACH MAN SQUATTING ON GROUND HIS STEAMING
PANNIKIN MELTING DARK HOLE IN SNOW STOP
THEY GAVE ME AN EXCELLENT PEA SOUP AND
OFFERED ME MEAT ONE OF THEM SAYING WITH
LAUGH QUOTE THEY DO NOT GET THIS OVER
YONDER STOP EVERYWHERE FOUND CLEAR
REALISATION ENGLANDS SHARE BRINGING THIS
ABOUT STOP GENERAL WHOSE NAME MUST NOT
MENTION SAID ME WE KNOW WELL IF ENGLAND
HAD NOT BEEN WITH US WAR WOULD HAVE ENDED
LONG AGO IN GERMAN VICTORY STOP HERE ON
FRONT AFTER TWO AND HALF YEARS WAR DURING
WHICH GERMANS TRIED EVERY MEANS SEPARATE
ALLIES FEELING OF RUSSIA FOR ENGLAND
STRONGE[R] MORE CORDIAL THAN EVER HAS BEEN
STOP NOT ONCE BUT MANY TIMES HEARD IT SAID
THAT ON ALLIANCE BETWEEN RUSSIA AND
ENGLAND DEPENDS FUTURE OF EUROPE
RANSOME

28 December 1916

WITH RUSSIAN ARMY IN FIELD STOP TALKED
TODAY WITH GENERAL H RUSZKY WHO EARNED
GRATITUDE ALL ALLIES EARLIER STAGES WAR AND

NOW RECOVERED FROM ILLNESS WHICH FOR TIME
FORCD HIM TO REST COMMANDS THE RUSSIAN
ARMIES ON NORTHERN FRONT STOP ASKED
GENERAL WHAT WAS IMPRESSION MADE BY
GERMAN PEACE OFFERS IN RUSSIAN ARMY STOP
ANSWERED QUOTE NONE UNQUOTE SURE I
SHOULD EVERYWHERE HERE AS IN ENGLAND FIRM
DETERMINATION NOT GIVE GERMANS ARMISTICE
THEY SO BADLY NEED BUT CARRY WAR STEADILY
ON TO ITS INEVITABLE VICTORIOUS CONCLUSION

22 January 1917

JUST RECEIVED DETAILS FIGHTING NORTHERN
FRONT FROM EYEWITNESS RETURNED FROM RIGA
STOP MOST IMPORTANT FIGHTING WAS SOUTH
WEST LAKE BABIT WHERE GERMANS HELD
CONSIDRABLE SALIENT WITH VERY STRONG
POSITION MACHINE GUN HILL PROJECTING
NORTHWARDS INTO RUSSIAN LINE ENABLING
THEM BOMBARD SHLOK AND THREATEN
COMMUNICATIONS RUSSIAN FORCES STEP BY STEP
PUSHING WESTWARDS BY KANGER AND KEMMERN
STOP ALTHOUGH OVER HUNDRED MACHINE GUNS
WERE CAPTURED ON HILL RUSSIANS TOOK IT
WITHOUT ARTILLERY PREPARATION BY FLANK
ATTACK AFTER ADVANCE TO EAST STOP RUSSIANS
SPENT FORTY EIGHT HOURS SLOW SECRET
ADVANCE THROUGH FOREST WHICH GERMANS HAD
MADE INTO GIGANTIC WIRE ENTANGLEMENT STOP
FINAL RUSH TOOK GERMANS BY SURPRISE STOP
ACTUAL BATTLE ALMOST ENTIRELY BAYONET
FIGHTING STOP COLD SO INTENSE THAT BODIES
FROZE AT ONCE ATTITUDE AS FELL AND GRIM
FROZEN GROUPS CORPSES INTERLOCKED IN
COMBAT REMAINED FOR SEVERAL DAYS BEHIND
ADVANCING RUSSIANS AS THESE PUSHED FORWARD
NEEDING EVERY AVAILABLE MAN THROW UP
DEFENCES ON HARD GROUND BEFORE FOREST
LINE TO WHICH GERMANS HAD THROWN BACK

SEVEN VERSTS BEHIND ORIGINAL POSITIONS STOP
RUSSIAN SOLDIERS CONSIDERED ACTUAL
TRENCHES OF GERMANS INFERIOR TO THEIR OWN
SAID QUOTE THESE MEN NOT KNOW HOW WORK
UNQUOTE BUT OFFICERS QUARTERS FAR BETTER
AND CONCRETE BLOCKHOUSES IMPREGNABLE BY
DIRECT ASSAULT AND FORMING INTERDEPENDENT
SERIES MADE RUSSIAN TASK EXTRAORDINARILY
DIFFICULT STOP THIS FIRST TIME SINCE 1915 THAT
GERMANS NOT AUSTRIANS SUSTAINED HEAVY
DEFEAT ON RUSSIAN SOIL STOP LIMITED
OBJECTIVE RADKO DIMITRIEV'S OFFENSIVE FULLY
ACHIEVED STOP GERMANS LOST ALL CHANCE
CUTTING OFF RUSSIAN RIGHT WING BY ADVANCE
ROUND CORNER LAKE BABIT STOP THEY
STUBBORNLY DEFENDED THREE LINES TRENCHES
IN VAIN HOPE SAVING GUNS WHICH TRUSTING
STRENGTH THEIR POSITIONS HAD BROUGHT
FORWARD STOP THEY LOST WHOLE THEIR HEAVY
ARTILLERY ON SECTIONS ATTACKED STOP THEIR
LINE FORCED RIGHT BACK AT ITS MOST
THREATENING POINT AND ADVANCE ON TUKKUS
MITTAU BROUGHT WITHIN IMMEDIATE
POSSIBILITIES NEXT RUSSIAN OFFENSIVE
   RANSOME

TROOPS KILL THEIR OFFICERS

The revolution, which began in disorders deliberately provoked
by the police and the old Ministry of the Interior, definitely
began on Sunday, when the first troops passed over to the side
of the people. By Monday four regiments were on the side of
the revolutionaries. Other regiments joined in one by one, in a
few cases killing their officers.

The first regiment to come in was the Litovsky, whose overcoats had been worn by the police on the previous day, with a
view of persuading the people that the soldiers were against
them. On Monday I tried to get to the Duma, but was held up
by the battle on the Liteini Prospect, one of the chief streets. I
saw soldiers going over and handing their rifles to the crowd.

The battle moved towards the river after the capture of the Arsenal, of the District Courts, and prison. The arrested Labour members were liberated.

The New Government

By Imperial ukase signed on Saturday, the Duma had been dissolved, but continued sitting in private, and formed a temporary Executive Committee composed of MM. Rodzianko (the President), Shidlovsky, Miliukov, Kerenesky (Labour), Shulgin (Left Nationalist), Dimitrioukov (Secretary of the Duma), Vladimir Lvov, Chkheidze (Social Democrat), Shingarev (Caset), Karaulov, Konovalov (Vice-President of the War Industrial Committee), Rjevsky, Nekrassov, and after the capitulation of the Peter and Paul Fortress, Colonel Engelhardt.

The battle for Petrograd proceeded in fairly orderly fashion. All the members of the old government were arrested. M. Protopopoff gave himself up to a student. As the regiments sent to restore order arrived at Petrograd they marched to the Duma and put themselves at the disposal of M. Rodzianko. The soldiers' attitude towards the officers was polite, firm, and not unfriendly.

Prison Ablaze

I witnessed the siege of the prison, which is still burning. On Monday might a party of 13 generals of the old regime got into the Admiralty with a number of police, and there were besieged. They were ordering the issue of notices to be printed telling the people to go home. However, the Admiralty was taken at four o'clock on Tuesday.

Red flags were hung out from the spire. Red flags also flew on the Peter and Paul fortress and on all public buildings. Motors were all commanded by the revolutionaries and dashed through the streets with armed soldiers or sailors lying with rifles ready on the mudguards of the front wheels. Each car flew the red flag. Lorries carried troops where needed.

Yesterday with difficulty I got to the Duma through dense crowds and fresh regiments of soldiers waiting to go there. I got in and found the main hall piled with ammunition, sacks of flour, and machine guns.

Soldiers, sailors, and officers are everywhere waiting for safe conduct from the Provisional Committee. The "Labour Marseillaise" is being played in the streets. I have been all over the town, and can say that order is being definitely restored. The Provisional Committee is strongly in favour of carrying the war to a successful end, and so are the great masses of the people.

World War I

FLOYD GIBBONS

The Sinking of the *Laconia*

Sent by the Chicago *Tribune* to cover the war in Europe, Gibbons secured his first story even before he reached the Continent; his liner, the British *Laconia*, was torpedoed in the Atlantic by a German U-boat. A year later Gibbons' left eye was shot out when he "went over the top" with American troops at Belleau Wood. The French elected him to the Legion of Honour for his heroism under fire.

Chicago *Tribune*, 25 February 1917

Queenstown, February 26 (via London) – I have serious doubts whether this is a real story. I am not entirely certain that it is not all a dream and that in a few minutes I will wake up back in stateroom B19 on the promenade deck of the Cunarder *Laconia* and hear my cockney steward informing me with an abundance of "and sirs" that it is a fine morning.

It is now a little over thirty hours since I stood on the slanting decks of the big liner, listened to the lowering of the lifeboats, heard the hiss of escaping steam and the roar of ascending rockets as they tore lurid rents in the black sky and cast their red glare over the roaring sea.

I am writing this within thirty minutes after stepping on the dock here in Queenstown from the British mine sweeper which picked up our lifeboat after an eventful six hours of drifting and darkness and bailing and pulling on the oars and of straining aching eyes toward the empty, meaningless horizon in search of help. But, dream or fact, here it is:

The Cunard liner *Laconia*, 18,000 tons' burden, carrying seventy-three passengers; men, women, and children, of whom six were American citizens, manned by a mixed crew of 216, bound from New York to Liverpool, and loaded with foodstuffs, cotton, and raw material, was torpedoed without warning by a German submarine last night off the Irish coast. The vessel sank in about forty minutes.

Two American citizens, mother and daughter, listed from Chicago and former residents there, are among the dead ...

The first cabin passengers were gathered in the lounge Sunday evening, with the exception of the bridge fiends in the smoke room.

"Poor Butterfly" was dying wearily on the talking machine, and several couples were dancing.

About the tables in the smoke room the conversation was limited to the announcement of bids and orders to the stewards. Before the fireplace was a little gathering which had been dubbed the Hyde Park corner – an allusion I don't quite fully understand. This group had about exhausted available discussion when I projected a new bone of contention.

"What do you say are our chances of being torpedoed?" I asked.

"Well," drawled the deliberative Mr Henry Chetham, a London solicitor, "I should say four thousand to one."

Lucien J. Jerome, of the British diplomatic service, returning with an Ecuadorian valet from South America, interjected: "Considering the zone and the class of this ship, I should put it down at two hundred and fifty to one that we don't meet a sub."

At this moment the ship gave a sudden lurch sideways and forward. There was a muffled noise like the slamming of some large door at a good distance away. The slightness of the shock and the meekness of the report compared with my imagination were disappointing. Every man in the room was on his feet in an instant.

"We're hit!" shouted Mr Chetham.

"That's what we've been waiting for," said Mr Jerome.

"What a lousy torpedo!" said Mr Kirby in typical New Yorkese. "It must have been a fizzer."

I looked at my watch. It was 10:30 p.m.

Then came the five blasts on the whistle. We rushed down the corridor leading from the smoke room at the stern to the lounge, which was amidship. We were running, but there was no panic. The occupants of the lounge were just leaving by the forward doors as we entered . . .

The torpedo had hit us well astern on the starboard side and had missed the engines and the dynamos. I had not noticed the deck lights before. Throughout the voyage our decks had remained dark at night and all cabin portholes were clamped down and all windows covered with opaque paint . . .

Steam began to hiss somewhere from the giant gray funnels that towered above. Suddenly there was a roaring swish as a rocket soared upward from the captain's bridge, leaving a comet's tail of fire. I watched it as it described a graceful arc in the black void overhead, and then, with an audible pop, it burst in a flare of brilliant colors.

There was a tilt to the deck. It was listing to starboard at just the angle that would make it necessary to reach for support to enable one to stand upright. In the meantime electric floodlights – large white enameled funnels containing clusters of bulbs – had been suspended from the promenade deck and illuminated the dark water that rose and fell on the slanting side of the ship . . .

A hatchet was thrust into my hand and I forwarded it to the bow. There was a flash of sparks as it crashed down on the holding pulley. One strand of the rope parted and down plunged the bow, too quick for the stern man. We came to a jerky stop with the stern in the air and the bow down, but the stern managed to lower away until the dangerous angle was eliminated.

Then both tried to lower together. The list of the ship's side became greater, but, instead of our boat sliding down it like a toboggan, the taffrail caught and was held. As the lowering continued, the other side dropped down and we found ourselves clinging on at a new angle and looking straight down on the water.

Many feet and hands pushed the boat from the side of the ship, and we sagged down again, this time smacking squarely on the pillowy top of a rising swell. It felt more solid than mid-air, at least. But we were far from being off. The pulleys stuck twice in their fastenings, bow and stern, and the one ax passed forward and back, and with it my flashlight, as the entangling ropes that held us to the sinking *Laconia* were cut away.

Some shout from that confusion of sound caused me to look up, and I really did so with the fear that one of the nearby boats was being lowered upon us . . .

As we pulled away from the side of the ship, its receding terrace of lights stretched upward. The ship was slowly turning over. We were opposite that part occupied by the engine rooms. There was a tangle of oars, spars, and rigging on the seat and considerable confusion before four of the big sweeps could be manned on either side of the boat . . .

We rested on our oars, with all eyes on the still lighted *Laconia*. The torpedo had struck at 10:30 p.m., according to our ship's time. It was thirty minutes afterward that another dull thud, which was accompanied by a noticeable drop in the hulk, told its story of the second torpedo that the submarine had dispatched through the engine room and the boat's vitals from a distance of two hundred yards.

We watched silently during the next minute, as the tiers of lights dimmed slowly from white to yellow, then to red, and nothing was left but the murky mourning of the night, which hung over all like a pall.

A mean, cheese-colored crescent of a moon revealed one horn above a rag bundle of clouds in the distance. A rim of blackness settled around our little world, relieved only by general leering stars in the zenith, and where the *Laconia*'s lights had shone there remained only the dim outline of a blacker hulk standing out above the water like a jagged headland, silhouetted against overcast sky.

The ship sank rapidly at the stern until at last its nose stood straight up in the air. Then it slid silently down and out of sight like a piece of disappearing scenery in a panorama spectacle.

World War I

HENRY G. WALES

Death Comes to Mata Hari

Mata Hari, born in 1876, was a beautiful double agent. Henry G.
Wales was the Paris staff correspondent for the International News
Service.

International News Service, 19 October 1917

Mata Hari, which is Javanese for Eye-of-the-Morning, is dead.
She was shot as a spy by a firing squad of Zouaves at the Vincennes Barracks. She died facing death literally, for she refused
to be blindfolded.

Gertrud Margarete Zelle, for that was the real name of the
beautiful Dutch-Javanese dancer, did appeal to President Poin-
caré for a reprieve, but he refused to intervene.

The first intimation she received that her plea had been
denied was when she was led at daybreak from her cell in the
Saint-Lazare prison to a waiting automobile and then rushed to
the barracks where the firing squad awaited her.

Never once had the iron will of the beautiful woman failed
her. Father Arbaux, accompanied by two sisters of charity, Captain Bouchardon, and Maître Clunet, her lawyer, entered her
cell, where she was still sleeping – a calm, untroubled sleep, it
was remarked by the turnkeys and trusties.

The sisters gently shook her. She arose and was told that her
hour had come.

"May I write two letters?" was all she asked.

Consent was given immediately by Captain Bouchardon, and pen, ink, paper, and envelopes were given to her.

She seated herself at the edge of the bed and wrote the letters with feverish haste. She handed them over to the custody of her lawyer.

Then she drew on her stockings, black, silken, filmy things, grotesque in the circumstances. She placed her high-heeled slippers on her feet and tied the silken ribbons over her insteps.

She arose and took the long black velvet cloak, edged around the bottom with fur and with a huge square fur collar hanging down the back, from a hook over the head of her bed. She placed this cloak over the heavy silk kimono which she had been wearing over her nightdress.

Her wealth of black hair was still coiled about her head in braids. She put on a large, flapping black felt hat with a black silk ribbon and bow. Slowly and indifferently, it seemed, she pulled on a pair of black kid gloves. Then she said calmly:

"I am ready."

The party slowly filed out of her cell to the waiting automobile.

The car sped through the heart of the sleeping city. It was scarcely half past five in the morning and the sun was not yet fully up.

Clear across Paris the car whirled to the Caserne de Vincennes, the barracks of the old fort which the Germans stormed in 1870.

The troops were already drawn up for the execution. The twelve Zouaves, forming the firing squad, stood in line, their rifles at ease. A subofficer stood behind them, sword drawn.

The automobile stopped, and the party descended, Mata Hari last. The party walked straight to the spot, where a little hummock of earth reared itself seven or eight feet high and afforded a background for such bullets as might miss the human target.

As Father Arbaux spoke with the condemned woman, a French officer approached, carrying a white cloth.

"The blindfold," he whispered to the nuns who stood there and handed it to them.

"Must I wear that?" asked Mata Hari, turning to her lawyer, as her eyes glimpsed the blindfold.

Maître Clunet turned interrogatively to the French officer.

"If Madame prefers not, it makes no difference," replied the officer, hurriedly turning away.

Mata Hari was not bound and she was not blindfolded. She stood gazing steadfastly at her executioners, when the priest, the nuns, and her lawyer stepped away from her.

The officer in command of the firing squad, who had been watching his men like a hawk that none might examine his rifle and try to find out whether he was destined to fire the blank cartridge which was in the breech of one rifle, seemed relieved that the business would soon be over.

A sharp, crackling command, and the file of twelve men assumed rigid positions at attention. Another command, and their rifles were at their shoulders; each man gazed down his barrel at the breast of the woman which was the target.

She did not move a muscle.

The underofficer in charge had moved to a position where from the corners of their eyes they could see him. His sword was extended in the air.

It dropped. The sun – by this time up – flashed on the burnished blade as it described an arc in falling. Simultaneously the sound of the volley rang out. Flame and a tiny puff of greyish smoke issued from the muzzle of each rifle. Automatically the men dropped their arms.

At the report Mata Hari fell. She did not die as actors and moving-picture stars would have us believe that people die when they are shot. She did not throw up her hands nor did she plunge straight forward or straight back.

Instead she seemed to collapse. Slowly, inertly, she settled to her knees, her head up always, and without the slightest change of expression on her face. For the fraction of a second it seemed she tottered there, on her knees, gazing directly at those who had taken her life. Then she fell backward, bending at the waist, with her legs doubled up beneath her. She lay prone, motionless, with her face turned towards the sky.

A non-commissioned officer, who accompanied a lieutenant, drew his revolver from the big, black holster strapped about his waist. Bending over, he placed the muzzle of the revolver almost – but not quite – against the left temple of the spy. He pulled the trigger, and the bullet tore into the brain of the woman.

Mata Hari was surely dead.

The Russian Civil War

MORGAN PHILIPS PRICE

How the Bolsheviks Took
the Winter Palace

Born in 1885, Morgan Philips Price was educated at Harrow and
Trinity College, Cambridge: at the age of twenty-one he inherited a 2,000 acre estate. Unusually for someone from such a
definitively upper-class Edwardian background, he was firmly
Left of the political centre. He opposed World War I, and was
recruited by C.P. Snow as a journalist for the famously liberal
Manchester Guardian. Snow sent Philips Price to report on the
war on the Eastern Front, where he became one of the few Western correspondents to witness the Russian Revolution at close
quarters.

Manchester Guardian, 27 December 1917

When I left the Palace on November 6 I was under the impression that the New Bolshevik rising had completely miscarried.
But the next morning the situation changed almost miraculously. It appeared that all the reports which the generals had
given to Kerensky were misleading. Hardly a single unit in the
Petrograd garrison executed the orders given them on Kerensky's instructions. The troops guarding the arsenal joined hands
with the Bolsheviks, who got possession of all the artillery and
ammunition and enormous stocks of rifles. Every regiment or
company of soldiers in the city had passed a resolution supporting the Bolsheviks, who accused Kerensky's Government of

wishing to "surrender Petrograd to the Germans so as to enable them to exterminate the revolutionary garrison". The Bolsheviks spread the rumours that the government was preparing to move to Moscow. Although a very small minority in each regiment took part in these meetings the effect was to paralyse the Government, because the vast majority of soldiers remained passive. They said they would not interfere in the struggle for fear that "brotherly blood" might be shed. In this way the telegraph and telephone passed into the hands of the Bolsheviks almost without fighting during the night of November 6, and there were no armed forces upon which the Government could rely for its defence. Personally I am under the strong impression that there was a strong element of disloyalty among the military command in Petrograd.

When I arrived at the Palace on the morning of November 7 I found that its food supplies had been stopped, so that the guards had left, being unable to get food. Kerensky had set out on a dangerous mission to bring loyal troops from outside the city.

The new commandants began to organise the defence of the Palace, and for that purpose I, too, went to the wing of the Palace in which the offices of the Palace administration were situated to obtain a plan of the immense building in order to place guards at all possible entrances. But to my great amazement I found the vast offices absolutely deserted by the administration, and the doorkeeper informed me that none of the officials had even put in an appearance that day.

Some of the old servants of the Palace, who had formerly served the Tsar and were well acquainted with the vast building, volunteered to serve as guides.

"You will find no traitors among us," they said to me, and they proved loyal to the end. Fresh units of cadets were called into the Palace. Food was ordered by telephone, but on the way to the Palace it was commandeered by the Bolsheviks.

I was sitting in my study. The next room to mine was that of Konovaloff. The Ministers gathered from time to time in his room or mine, and through the window watched the crowds on the bridges. The situation grew more and more critical. Five thousand sailors arrived from Kronstadt, and the cruiser *Aurora* entered the Neva and lay with guns directed upon the Winter Palace. The Fortress of SS. Peter and Paul was now in the hands of the Bolsheviks, and its guns were also turned upon the Palace. The Government offices on the other side of the square were gradually surrendering to the Bolsheviks, whose troops were little by little surrounding the Palace itself. The palace guards had erected a huge barricade along the principal gates and facades leading to the square from accumulated reserves of timber, and the two opposing forces were awaiting the final onslaught.

Within the Palace the ministers were almost all by now assembled. All our telephone lines were already disconnected except one, through which we occasionally received some disturbing tidings. It began to grow dark. During the day I had several times been obliged to warn the members of the Government from crowding to the windows, as by so doing they were likely to attract unwelcome shots. And now we carefully drew the curtains to hide the few electric lights we were obliged to make use of.

At seven o'clock the Cabinet held its last meeting, which was of a memorable character. It was held in the famous Malachite Hall, where the sittings were usually held. This meeting was held in darkness except for the rays which shone through the open door from a lighted vestibule which had no windows. The Minister of Labour, a Socialist, raised the question whether some of them should not leave the Palace to mix with the populace and try to influence them. Some other Socialists supported him. But after a close debate it was decided that the Ministry should stand and fall together. The welcome news that some food had been scraped together was brought, and at about eight o'clock the Ministers went upstairs to Kerensky's apartments to partake of a scanty meal. By arrangement I was to leave the Palace at eight o'clock. When that time came all the ordinary exits were either besieged or barricaded. My faithful attendant, who was well acquainted with every corner of the Palace, managed to get me through into the central courtyard, which was filled with loyalist guards, and thence I was conducted to the huge iron gate, strongly guarded by loyal sentinels. In front of the gate was a high wooden barricade. A stout female nurse was just being hoisted over this barricade to proceed to her duties in the military hospital situated in one part of the Palace.

I stood for a moment gazing into the darkness. A hand touched me, and somebody said: "Don't stand here. You may be hit by a bullet." I thanked the sentinel and went along by the barricade in the direction of Millionnaya Street, the only passage still kept by the loyalists. They were barring the street, but they allowed me to pass through. When I had proceeded a short distance I heard the order given behind me "Take aim!" I heard the click of the rifles, and two big soldiers who were proceeding some steps in front of me gathered up the skirts of their coats and took to their heels. I looked back and saw the line of loyalist soldiers aiming straight before them in my direction. I realised that the two soldiers in flight were Bolsheviks. Luckily for me they had disappeared in the darkness, and the soldiers did not shoot. I went on and when I reached the next corner I found it guarded by the Bolshevik Red Guard. These were ordinary young workmen, wearing belts and rifles slung across their shoulders. They did not stop me, and I went on in the direction of the Hotel d'Europe, where I was staying. Everywhere at the street corners were stationed Bolshevik soldiers or sailors or detachments of the Red Guard. I reached the hotel unmolested.

Later in the evening, when I was ready to return, I learned that the General Staff had already surrendered to the sailors before I left the Palace, and that the Palace itself had been completely surrounded, so that it was impossible for me to enter it.

I learned that a friend of mine who had gone with Mme. Kerensky in a cab to the Palace had been arrested, with her, by the Bolsheviks and taken to the Smolny Institute. During the night the booming of guns began. I knew they were the guns of the *Aurora* bombarding the Palace. An ultimatum was sent to the Ministers to surrender. They refused. Bolsheviks began to penetrate into the Palace through some unknown entrance, and from the upper floor, where the apartments of Kerensky and of Babushka (Mme. Breshkovsky, the Grandmother of the Russian Revolution) were situated, they began to throw hand grenades into the hall below.

These Bolsheviks were arrested by the loyalists. The *Aurora* discharged a number of shots at the Palace. A violent fusillade of machine-guns and light artillery was also directed against it. A battle ensued, during which there were some hundred casualties on either side. Gradually the Bolsheviks forced an entry and invaded the Palace. On their way they pillaged every room they entered. The Ministers retired from one room to another, until at last they were arrested and conveyed to the fortress.

The Palace was pillaged and devastated from top to bottom by the Bolshevik armed mob, as though by a horde of barbarians. All the State papers were destroyed. Priceless pictures were ripped from their frames by bayonets. Several hundred carefully packed boxes of rare plate and china, which Kerensky had exerted himself to preserve, were broken open and the contents smashed or carried off. The library of Alexander III, the doors of which we had locked and sealed, and which we never entered, was forced open and ransacked, books and manuscripts burnt and destroyed. My study, formerly the Tsaritsa's salon, like all other rooms, was thrown into chaos. The colossal crystal lustre, with its artfully concealed music, was smashed to atoms. Desks, pictures, ornaments – everything was destroyed. I will refrain from describing the hideous scenes which took place in the wine-cellars, and the fate to which some of the captured women soldiers were submitted.

World War I

BEACH THOMAS

German Rout

In the early morning of 8 August 1918, British tanks rolled across the Somme in a surprise offensive that pushed back the German army nearly six miles. "The black day" also shattered the German army's morale; many realized that the end was beginning. The British correspondent Beach Thomas was knighted in 1920 for his services as a war correspondent.

Daily Mail, 9 August 1918

From dawn to midday we watched along the cliff of the Somme one of the greatest single feats of arms in the annals of the British Army, and the arms were of the strangest and most various sorts.

On the ground were our iron horses on caterpillar feet; 300 feet above flew airmen whose impudent audacity has never been excelled.

Seldom did an adventure end more triumphantly or begin in greater strain. A diary of those waiting hours roughly jotted down at the time and place will show how the crisis felt, and incidentally how much had to be overcome to realise that triumph.

It was not yet light when we passed through a village heavily shelled earlier in the night. Two dead horses, a broken ambulance, and the fresh rubble of several houses told some part of the tale. Soon we reached one of the best observation posts ever provided by nature for a battle drama, but darkness and mist clinging like face cloths to the face was over everything and increased the strain felt by the waiting soldiers. Everyone's spirits rose as zero approached. It was now certain as normal signs could make it that the enemy was unaware.

At 4.25 the silence broke into splinters, and even the darkness and mist seemed to open at the clap of our preparatory barrage. A gunner observer who had fought through the Somme and Flanders said as he lifted a telephone in his dug-out, "It is the best I ever saw, and yet not half the guns were registered."

This thunder continued like one protracted clap for just four minutes. As it halted and checked for a moment in order to be lifted farther back on the enemy we knew that the infantry and tanks had charged. But nothing whatever was visible, and the mist now came down thicker than ever and, though it was clear above, one could see scarcely 40 yards along the earth. Aeroplanes nevertheless seemed to hum overhead in about equal numbers with the shells.

At 5.45 appears the first group of prisoners, about two score – a very punctual group. I never before saw prisoners quite like them. They were spick and span, no dirt or heat, no bloody sconces or limp limbs. Only their uniforms and bayonets suggested war. They had apparently surrendered to the barrage itself in sheer admiration without effort to fire.

At 9.30 we all felt that open warfare was beginning, and I could see across Hamel village such movement of men and machines as I never saw before. Not a single German shell fell in their neighbourhood.

At 10 the picture of the battlefield and the sense of triumphant movement were magnificent. The weather is and has been ideal. First the cloaking mist absolved the need for smoke, and as the first enemy lines were won progressive clearness came in time for us but too late for the enemy.

It was hard for me to leave the scene, as the visibility was improving every moment and the panorama was becoming incomparable, but it was time to go farther back and hear the more precise details of the vague but stirring things I had seen.

Later

A general view of the scope and issue of the battle is already possible, though the day is still young. Good news travels faster than bad in battles. The Germans know less than we do . . .

The tanks, which did magnificent work, helped the speed, but the prime credit still belongs to the dash and training of the infantry. They smothered the German infantry as the gunners smothered the German gunners. They showed great ingenuity through the half-open warfare which succeeded the first assault, in manoeuvring round machine-gun nests, and in hiding themselves, octopuslike, in their own smoke. Their movement was so quick and concerted that the enemy had little time to give to removing his guns.

It is reported that all along the line field guns were overrun, and that a particularly large group of them were captured north of the Somme near Chipilly, where escape was impossible, thanks to the sharp bends of the Somme River, of which the reaches thereabouts are a series of S's. I believe more guns, and of course more machine guns, have been captured than can be catalogued in a day or two. A few were used against the enemy quite early in the day.

The feature of the day was the extinction of the German artillery. Its answer to our barrage was rather slow and patchy, though up to standard in some places, notably north of the river, where the concentration and efficiency were both greater; but it lasted a very short time in its first degree of excellence.

Perry Robinson compared the day's events to those of the previous great battles during the last three years of war.

Troubles are multiplying for the Germans to-day; with the French co-operation, we launched the first offensive on a large scale that we have made this year, recalling the great attacks of the Somme battle, of Arras, or of Flanders. It was admirable in its organisation and execution, taking the enemy completely by surprise. Capture both of prisoners and guns will be very large.

In a little more than two hours after the start we had heard of the capture of the whole tier of nearer villages. On the right the French before noon were in possession of villages on the south side of the Avre, while fighting was then in progress on the northern bank. Since then we have continued to advance apparently along the whole front, and more villages are now in our hands.

The Russian Civil War

FRAZIER HUNT

I Capture Vladivostok

A journalist for the Chicago *Tribune*, Hunt reported the civil war
between the Bolsheviks and the White Guard which followed the
Russian Revolution of 1917. The incident recounted below
occurred on 31 December 1919.

We Cover the World, 1937

It isn't every war correspondent who can capture a city. I don't
mean to say that I got one all by myself, but at least I was the first
man in. And, different from the immortal Kipling's tale of how
"Privit Mulvaney tuk the town av Lungtungpen," I had my
trousers on when I took mine.

I've never written the story before, and I doubt if I would do
it now if Frank Martinek, one-time US Naval Intelligence
Officer in Vladivostok, had not told what youthful critics, not
quite dry behind the ears, like to call the *dénouement* of the yarn
in introducing me to a Chicago audience.

I had landed in the colourful and war-weary Siberian port
from a miserable little Japanese tub that had bobbed across the
Sea of Japan like a champagne cork. It was the last day of 1919,
and Vladivostok was being held by a bobtail White Guard army,
supported by Japanese troops. Ten thousand homesick, disgusted
American soldiers were scattered for 1,000 miles up and down
the single line of steel that pointed towards Moscow. About this
time Admiral Kolchak, dictator and White saviour, once head of
the British- and Japanese-supported anti-Bolshevik hopes, had a

rather frightful accident: his own troops mutinied, held a drum-head court-martial, quietly led him out to a convenient wall and filled him full of lead (although I believe it is actually steel bullets they use in such emergencies).

The whole White Guard movement in Siberia was crumbling rapidly, and old Tsarist officials, Japanese generals, Cossack *atamans*, and thick-skinned British advisers did not know what to do about it. The American commander, the incorruptible, wise Major-General Graves, however, did know exactly what to do: simply keep his troops out of mixing in the internal affairs of Russia, and see to it that the 50,000 Japanese soldiers there did not move the hills and the rivers. It was a cinch they were going to try to move everything else.

I was primed for this situation like an Indiana pump in frosty weather. In the previous winter I had spent two months with the North Russian Expedition in the desolate country around Archangel. I had ridden almost 1,000 miles by sledge up frozen rivers and through forests of glistening Christmas-trees, visiting American outposts and snow-bound fronts.

When I left the unsavoury mess I was bitter and resentful. I could not stand the sight of American doughboys being commanded to do British officers' dirty work. A 5,000-word *exposé* cable that I had sneaked out and sent from the transmitting office in Narvik, Norway, had been read in the United States Senate, and, I think, had had a little to do with the promise of the White House to remove the American troops as soon as the ice thawed.

Following this pleasant adventure in the shadow of the Arctic Circle, I had worked my way through the Allied blockade into the heart of the Soviets. For two months I had enjoyed the exclusive privilege of working the greatest news goldmine in history . . . And now I was at the other end of the world in a second intervention mess, and ready for trouble.

It took less than a day for me to see that this American Expeditionary Force was run in quite a different manner from the North Russia fiasco. A Lieutenant-General of the Japanese Army had unanimously elected himself Commander-in-Chief of the Allied Forces, and before General Graves had arrived had sent the two American regiments, rushed up from Manila, westward to pick up a fight with the anti-White peasant outfits called

"Partisans". But the very day General Graves disembarked he called in his troops, and figuratively set the high-ranking little gentleman from Nippon squarely on his west end. So my anticipated story of how American soldiers were a second time doing filthy jobs for someone else evaporated into the cold dry air. And I needed a few good pieces to keep the *Chicago Tribune* contented.

Now, I have always operated on the general theory that the best place to get a story is directly from the people who are mixed up in it. So it was that after I had been a few days in Vladivostok I decided to get out with the fighting Red Siberian moujiks and see for myself how they were feeling about their revolution, their war with the Whites, and their near-war with the Japanese. For my interpreter I found a gentle, old-fashioned Social Democrat named Kolko, who years before had escaped from a Siberian prison, then denned up in New York until the first revolution had broken, and was now a sort of anti-White spy around Vladivostok.

We had a great time for ten days living with the Partisans. As I look back over a long series of "great times" I'm inclined to say this tops my purple list. We rode, slept, drank vodka, and sang with these young peasant soldiers – and I made speeches to bearded old grandfathers on how friendly America really was, and how I wished them luck with their Japanese problem.

I used to do this volunteer lecturing in school-houses, or crowded peasant homes, or anywhere they asked me. At first most of them would be suspicious of me, but when they understood that I'd been in Moscow, and that I was really on their side, they were like eager children. They used to ask all sorts of questions about America, and how people lived and ran their affairs in a free country. Most of the time they would keep the soldiers from coming in, and there would be only Kolko, the interpreter, myself, and the grizzled old fellows in their sheepskin coats and felt boots.

I was surprised too at the depth of the feeling of the youthful Partisan soldiers. They knew what they were fighting for; they were against the return of the ways of the Tsar, and against the interference of the Japanese. They still felt that they wanted some form of assembly and democratic constitution, but the futile efforts of Kerensky, and the coming of Kolchak and the intervention, had shaken their faith in half-way measures.

They were thrilled by the magic of the word "soviet". They thought that possibly that was what they needed too. And somehow or other they knew that Lenin was their true leader . . . When they heard that I had met Lenin and had talked with him for a few minutes they barraged me with a hundred questions. The revolution was vague and shadowy in their minds, but at least it meant land and freedom for them.

Probably it is a bit far-fetched, but time and again I could not help but think how similar this must have been to the mood and dreams of Putnam's men and the Green Mountain boys – when the name of George Washington thrilled the hearts of hungry, beaten soldiers with the same imagery and the same fervour that Lenin's name was doing now, 140 years later, and 10,000 miles to the westward. I'd like to have been a correspondent in those days, too.

Then one day, far back in the snow-covered hills, I joined up with a small Partisan detachment that had five Japanese soldier prisoners, who were eating them out of house and home. They had captured the lads from a *makaka* garrison some twenty miles away. Incidentally, to call a Japanese soldier a *makaka* was like calling him a so-and-so and not smiling when you did it. The Japs had been doing a little village-burning and bayonet practice among the peasant villages, and all the emotional tinder for a nice little war was laid out ready to be lit.

The young Red commander couldn't think of anything to do with his five prisoners except to shoot them humanely. I explained through my interpreter that it would be a fine lesson in hospitality if he'd turn these boys over to me and let me put them in Lieutenant-General Oi's lap, with the word that his troops didn't have to shoot every Partisan soldier they got their hands on. Finally we traded the lot for my watch.

It was all good, clean fun, and in due time I got back to Vladivostok with my Japanese quintuplets. The able little Japanese commander rubbed his bald pate while I gave him a lengthy discourse on the beauty of letting his soldiers have their target practice on something else besides captured Siberians.

Then I heard that down Nikolsk way real fighting was about to start between the Japanese-supported Whites and the Red Partisans. Kolko and I took the twice-a-week train the 100 *versts* or so towards this latest front.

We missed the show by four hours – but it wasn't much of a war to brag about at that. The Whites had quickly surrendered, and, while there was some question as to what to do with the old Tsarist officers, the White troopers themselves had gladly melted into the Partisan forces.

And now they were moving to attack and capture the key city of Vladivostok, still in the hands of the Whites. Two troop trains were being made up directly in front of the station. They would be pulling out very soon.

We hurried back to the Red commander. "Tell him I must go in on that first train," I instructed Kolko.

But the commander shook his head. "There'll be some heavy fighting before we get there," he answered. "The Whites have plenty of artillery, and they'll try to stop us."

But I insisted that I'd like to go along; that I had to go. Then it was that the commander got his brilliant idea. "You might ride in the armoured truck we've just captured," he suggested. "It'll be ahead of the engine on the first train, but it ought to be safe enough in there."

I pumped his hand. I patted his shoulder. It was too good to be true: a war in an armoured truck. Send me there right now!

He called a smiling kid soldier and rolled out a few yards of orders; then we followed the boy down the track to a homemade armoured truck, with steel plates bolted to the sides. In the armour were cut half a dozen oblong slits. I noticed the muzzles of machine-guns sticking out from two or three of these loop-holes.

Behind the armoured truck an ancient wood-burning engine was champing at the bit – or whatever it is engines do. Ahead of the armoured truck there was nothing but snow and two steel rails gleaming in the late afternoon sunlight – and down the track other boys were getting ready to blow this pleasant little armoured truck to kingdom come. It seemed a very silly idea, but it was a bit romantic at that.

Our guide ducked under the truck and disappeared through a trapdoor in the floor. We followed, and pulled ourselves into the car. Two tin lanterns, with candles stuck in them, hung from the ceiling. In the flickering light I could make out six or seven men. A young lad, certainly not over nineteen years old, stepped up, and our guide reeled off his instructions. The truck commander turned to me, welcomed me with a hand-shake and a broad smile. Then one by one I shook hands with the two machine-gun crews. Someone pushed up an ammunition box, and I took off my old furlined trench coat, folded it on top of the box, and sat down. Next I took out a package of cigarettes and passed them round, leaving the remainder of the package on a second ammunition box. I could have had the car after that.

We settled back in the stifling heat. A pot-bellied stove in the centre of the truck was roaring. It was 20 degrees below zero outside, but we were baking here inside our steel oven.

The young commander said something, then slipped down through the trapdoor. Silence settled over the truck. A giant tow-headed boy, astride the seat of a Vickers-Maxim, started humming a Slav song in the inevitable minor chords. Soon we were all dreaming of our worlds outside this hot armoured truck . . . Time drifted by. Then the young chief pushed his head up through the door, popped in, and closed the steel trap behind him. His voice was pitched high with excitement.

"We're starting, comrades!" he announced dramatically. "Let every man do his duty! If anyone falters he knows what to expect!"

Almost immediately we heard the muffled tones of an engine bell and the echoes of men's voices. Then came a violent bump that all but sent us sprawling from our cartridge-box seats. At last we were actually rolling. One of the wheels was a bit flat, and it soured the song the other wheels were singing. I'm sure each of us was making up his own words. Mine were: "This is life! . . . This is life! . . . This is life!"

The young commander pulled up an ammunition case close to mine. It was evident that he was of a little different breed from these square-faced Slav peasants, with their wide cheek-bones and their heavy bodies. Finally Kolko and I got him to talk about himself: he was from Petrograd, and his father had in the Tsar's days been captain of a Russian battleship. He was now a Red Admiral. This boy, Ivan Vasilievitch Trestiakoff, had been a naval cadet for a year; then, when the revolution broke, he had joined up with the Bolshies, and had been swept by one of the strange tides of war to this distant land of Far Eastern Siberia.

I asked him what he wanted to do. He answered straight off. "When we've finished the Whites and driven out the Japs I would like to take my armoured truck to Petrograd and say, 'Here I am, Papa, with my brave machine-gunners.' "

He took a turn round the little truck. Then he came back and went on with his talk. "These Whites thought we were all stupid fools. Well, we were foolish like a fox. You know how they always had trouble getting their engines to run. Our people in the railway shops saw to that. They're running all right now."

As a matter of fact, this particular engine of ours that was pushing us into the night and its black uncertainty wasn't running any too well. Or maybe it was something else that kept us starting and stopping every few miles. We'd get a series of good healthy bumps from both operations. Sometimes we'd pull up, and for what seemed like hours we'd stand dead still. Then there would be that clanking engine bell and the shouting, and we'd get a couple of bumps; then off we'd go again. We were not troubled with any fancy air-brakes on this makeshift troop train.

In one of these long stops our young chief slipped down through the manhole in the bottom of the car. He wore a short curved sword that he'd taken from some dead Cossack, and it would catch on the sides of the narrow trapdoor when he climbed in or out. It was the only side-arm he had, and I thought seriously of giving him my own 45-calibre Colt automatic army pistol which I carried deep in the right-hand pocket of my breeches. But General Graves had presented it to me, and I couldn't get myself around to parting with it.

Our commander was gone for some minutes, and when he finally stuck his head up through the hole he had a broad grin on his face. In his right hand he held a stubby automatic. He announced that we had stopped opposite a station platform, and that he'd just lifted the pistol from an unsuspecting civilian. He dug up a heavy cord, looped it round his neck, tied the ends to the pistol butt, and stuck the gun in his belt. He was a real officer now; he had both a sword and a pistol.

Before long we got our usual bumping, and slowly pushed our way on towards our unknown fate. Kolko and I moved over next to the tow-headed machine-gunner. He'd been fighting with the Partisan troops for almost a year now. He'd had a bad break, and he was disconsolate. "I'm thinking about my wife all the time," he explained. "We'd only been married a month when

I had to join up with the Partisans. I can hardly think of anything else but how I'd like to have her right now."

We offered him our condolences. Maybe he could go home before so very long. If he didn't get there pretty soon some other man might be keeping her warm on these cold nights . . . He only shook his head sadly when we suggested that possibility.

Leaning against the wall was a red-bearded boy who wore his sheepskin jacket despite the incredible heat of this steel baking oven. He was a new recruit; he'd joined up with the Partisans only that morning. "I was afraid to desert from the Whites," he explained to us. "You see, I live in the country near Nikolsk, and they might have punished my family."

A third peasant soldier cut in: "Kolchak and the *makakas* made us all Partisans. While we were fighting for Kolchak the Japs were burning our villages and killing our people. When we finish off the Whites we'll give them something! America understands us. They are men like we are. If America would only help us we could whip the Japs. We never had anything against the Americans. They did a little something against us at the start when they first got here, but that didn't amount to much. They're our friends now."

The blond giant, with the wide mouth and the shining teeth, and the big yearn for his wife, muscled into the conversation. "Did you hear about that American who brought back five Jap prisoners we had and turned them over to the Jap General? He told him that was the way we treated our prisoners, and for him to quit killing ours."

I didn't say anything. It was too hot and stuffy in that truck to be even your own hero. I drifted back to my old seat on the ammunition case.

The boy commander started talking about some mystical thing he called *svoboda* – freedom. He would have made quite a rabble-rouser if he'd put his mind to it.

We jogged along through the interminable hours. The two lanterns, swaying from their hooks, cast weird shadows. The little stove threw off enough heat to barbecue a mule.

We'd talk a few sentences, and then we'd turn to our own dreams. Once in a while the tow-headed homesick lover on the Vickers-Maxim saddle-seat would hum a song. Maybe the others would join in, and, again, maybe they wouldn't.

The young commander would make his rounds and examine the two heavy guns. Their barrels were blanketed, and their water-coolers warm and ready for action. He was a true machine-gunner. He'd pet the guns and call them "Baby". You could get action from the seat of a Vickers-Maxim – especially if you put your heart in your work.

He was a bit of a sentimentalist too. "Wish you could take a picture so you'd remember us," he suggested. Then he began looking around the car again. "I'd like to give you a souvenir of some kind or other, but I can't find any," he went on.

Then he got his inspiration. He hurried to the far end of the truck and pulled the lid off a box.

"Here's something to take home," he said in eager earnestness. Then he rolled a pineapple hand-grenade on the floor straight towards my feet.

I didn't know much about hand-grenades, but I'd seen plenty of men who'd been mangled by them. At least I knew they weren't to play handball with . . . I watched this little package of bad news as it bounced and rolled towards me. I started to count to ten: most grenades were supposed to burst on the fatal ten. Then a sort of sickly grin spread over my face. I was conscious that my comrades were watching me – me, the over-sized American who was supposed to know all the answers.

I casually reached down and picked up the grenade. If it was going to explode it might as well do the job right, and not just mess around. I knew a few Russian words, and, with the steel pineapple cupped in my two hands, I nodded to the young commander and said, "Thanks, comrade!"

I looked it over with feigned professional interest. I saw that the pin was in its proper place and securely bent over. I knew now that we were safe: it couldn't go off as long as that pin was in its place. Then, with just a trace of bravado, I shoved the gift in my trousers-pocket, opposite the one that held my Colt.

I imagine it was an hour later, when we'd got up near Razdolne, that we bumped to another stop. Again there was a long wait. Through the gun slits we could make out, far down the track, what looked to be a bonfire. After a while our commander lifted the trapdoor and slipped down through it.

Within three or four minutes he came back. He was excited, and his dark eyes were snapping. "The White cadets are entrenched 300 yards down the track with three-inch guns!" he shouted. "We'll have a fight now!"

He pushed the tow-headed gunner off the saddle-seat of the gun in the front of the truck, pulled the blankets off the barrel, and squared himself for action. There was tense silence in the car. Any second now we might be pushing forward towards that dull red glow and into those three-inch guns.

I reached behind me and felt the steel sides of the truck. I remembered that the armour-plate was not more than three-eighths of an inch thick. That would be pie for a three-inch high explosive. I'd seen the twisted, pathetic wrecks of dozens of armour-plated tanks that had tried to stop German 77s up in the Soissons area in France. One direct hit on this car of ours and they wouldn't be able to tell which had been me and which the blond gunner with the yearn for his bride.

My throat was parched, and I smacked my dry lips. The heat, the cigarette smoke, and the foul air, smelling of unwashed bodies and sheepskin jackets, were even making my eyes smart. I wanted to get out of here. I didn't want to be blown to bits by some nervous White cadet, pulling a lanyard that would send an unlucky shell, with my number on it, to its unnecessary mission.

The voice of the commander broke the long, hot silence. Kolko whispered that he had said he would slip out and find what was happening. The blond giant took his old seat on the machine-gun, and the boy hurried to the trapdoor and disappeared.

He was gone for what seemed a very long time. Then his Cossack cap popped up from the manhole, and his white teeth showed in the candlelight. He shouted something in Russian.

"What's that? What d'he say?" I demanded of Kolko.

My interpreter did not answer me. He had jumped to his feet and was shouting to the commander. The gunners were talking loudly and excitedly.

"What's doing?" I questioned. But no one paid the slightest attention to me.

"What in hell did he say?" I demanded again, grabbing Kolko's sleeve. But he had no time to answer me.

"God damn it! What d'he say?" I yelled, striking at him.

Kolko came out of his trance. "He said the cadets had surrendered!" he answered, gulping. "The road to Vladivostok is open!"

I joined in the cheering. Two or three of the men were hugging each other. The tow-headed gunner gleefully shouted that maybe he'd get to see his bride again before very long.

Slowly we settled back to our waiting game. Then we got the go-ahead bump and crept on towards what the dough-boys called "Bloodyvostok".

I awoke from sleep with a jerk. We were coming to a stop. The boy commander peered out through a loophole. Kolko translated what he said: "It's getting light . . . Looks as if we're almost in Vladivostok."

I stretched my cramped legs. I drew a deep breath of the foul, dead air and immediately regretted it. I couldn't stand this truck any longer. I'd rather freeze than toast, and I'd rather be shot in the open than smothered to death in a heated vacuum.

Again the commander disappeared through the manhole. I slipped on my fur-lined coat and cap, pulled on my great gloves, and told Kolko I was going to get out of here. He presented arguments and recited pledges. I answered that I didn't give a damn about anything except to leave this steel pigsty. He picked up his coat and started to follow me. But I wouldn't let him come. I explained that I'd only get some fresh air, look round, and report back.

I crawled out between the wheels. We were in a gap in the snow-blanketed hills that surrounded the magnificent "Golden Horn". We couldn't be more than three or four miles from the railway station.

Dawn was just breaking, but here in the Far North it would be a late dawn. It was almost eight o'clock. Several groups of men were evidently conferring by the side of the train, a carriage or two below the engine. I snooped around to see what I could see. A narrow steel ladder on the rear of our armoured truck, that led to the roof, caught my eye. I climbed up and made a quick survey. The truck had a flat wooden roof. I scrambled down, ducked between the wheels, and stuck my head up through the trapdoor. The hot blast and the stench were almost like a smash in the face. I told Kolko not to worry about me, that I was going to stay outside in the clear air. He said he'd join me, but I begged him not to: his clothes were not as warm as mine. Then I slipped out, returned to the ladder, and mounted it to the top of the truck. Carefully I tucked the skirts of my long coat under me, and, with my legs dangling over the front end, sat squarely on the roof. Vladivostok was straight ahead of me.

The engine bell rang, men shouted and scurried to their carriages, and off we started. Suddenly I realized that I was doing a very silly thing. If there was fighting at the station I'd be the first man to be picked off. But the air was champagne to me, and I was intoxicated with this blessed oxygen, the lovely morning, and the whole thrilling business of living gaily and dangerously.

We were getting into town now. A little group of workmen along the track cheered and waved as we went by. Then there was more shouting and waving.

I was taking the salute. I was the man on the white horse at the head of the procession. I chuckled to myself. From my high seat at the front of the No. I truck I sang out "*Tovarish!*" ("Comrade!") to everyone we passed.

Now we were pushing into the station. There was a wild crowd of cheering men here. They had no uniforms, but they were waving rifles and yelling.

I looked down from my box-seat. Two or three officers in American uniforms were in the crowd next to the track. I recognized my friend Frank Martinek, of the Naval Intelligence. The train ground to a stop. Then they saw me and yelled a welcome.

Frank shouted up to me, "We surrender. Will you accept our unconditional surrender?"

"I will!" I shouted back. "And may God have pity on your miserable souls!"

I hurried to the back of the truck and scrambled down the little ladder. Martinek and my tried and true friends, Lieutenant-Colonel Bob Eichelberger and Major Sidney Graves, pounded me on the back.

"Young man," Frank hilariously insisted, "this is the first time in history that a war correspondent ever captured a town!" The others roared and pommelled me.

But a little later, when I sent off my story, I had to admit that the anti-Whites had pulled their *coup d'état* and taken over the town just before dawn, and that even the Japanese had been forced to accept the reverse.

I might have captured only a captured town, but at least I had my trousers on, and, as I have already said, that's something Kipling's Private Mulvaney lacked.

PS I was never able to find out whether or not that tow-headed machine-gunner got him to his wife before it thawed that spring. I've always hoped that he did.

World War I

KIRKE L. SIMPSON

Bugles Sound Taps
for Warrior's Requiem

Two years after the end of the Great War, the United States
dedicated the Tomb of the Unknown Soldier at Arlington Cemetery. Simpson's account of the dedication was the first ever AP
dispatch to earn a byline; it also gained him the 1922 Pulitzer
Prize.

Associated Press, 11 November 1921

Under the wide and starry skies of his own homeland America's
unknown dead from France sleeps tonight, a soldier home from
the wars.

Alone, he lies in the narrow cell of stone that guards his
body; but his soul has entered into the spirit that is America.
Wherever liberty is held close in men's hearts, the honor and
the glory and the pledge of high endeavor poured out over this
nameless one of fame will be told and sung by Americans for
all time.

Scrolled across the marble arch of the memorial raised to
American soldier and sailor dead, everywhere, which stands like
a monument behind his tomb, runs this legend: "We here highly
resolve that these dead shall not have died in vain."

The words were spoken by the martyred Lincoln over the
dead at Gettysburg. And today with voice strong with determination and ringing with deep emotion, another President echoed

that high resolve over the coffin of the soldier who died for the flag in France.

Great men in the world's affairs heard that high purpose reiterated by the man who stands at the head of the American people. Tomorrow they will gather in the city that stands almost in the shadow of the new American shrine of liberty dedicated today. They will talk of peace; of the curbing of the havoc of war.

They will speak of the war in France, that robbed this soldier of life and name and brought death to comrades of all nations by the hundreds of thousands. And in their ears when they meet must ring President Harding's declaration today beside that flag-wrapped, honor-laden bier:

"There must be, there shall be, the commanding voice of a conscious civilization against armed warfare."

Far across the seas, other unknown dead, hallowed in memory by their countrymen, as this American soldier is enshrined in the heart of America, sleep their last. He, in whose veins ran the blood of British forebears, lies beneath a great stone in ancient Westminster Abbey; he of France, beneath the Arc de Triomphe, and he of Italy under the altar of the fatherland in Rome . . .

And it seemed today that they, too, must be here among the Potomac hills to greet an American comrade come to join their glorious company, to testify their approval of the high words of hope spoken by America's President. All day long the nation poured out its heart in pride and glory for the nameless American. Before the first crash of the minute guns roared its knell for the dead from the shadow of Washington Monument, the people who claim him as their own were trooping out to do him honor. They lined the long road from the Capitol to the hillside where he sleeps tonight; they flowed like a tide over the slopes about his burial place; they choked the bridges that lead across the river to the fields of the brave, in which he is the last comer . . .

As he was carried past through the banks of humanity that lined Pennsylvania Avenue a solemn, reverent hush held the living walls. Yet there was not so much of sorrow as of high pride in it all, a pride beyond the reach of shouting and the clamor that marks less sacred moments in life.

Out there in the broad avenue was a simple soldier, dead for honor of the flag. He was nameless. No man knew what part in the great life of the nation he had died as Americans always have been ready to die, for the flag and what it means. They read the message of the pageant clear, these silent thousands along the way. They stood in almost holy awe to take their own part in what was theirs, the glory of the American people, honored here in the honors showered on America's nameless son from France.

Soldiers, sailors, and marines – all played their part in the thrilling spectacles as the cortege rolled along. And just behind the casket, with its faded French flowers on the draped flag, walked the President, the chosen leader of a hundred million, in whose name he was chief mourner at his bier. Beside him strode the man under whom the fallen hero had lived and died in France, General Pershing, wearing only the single medal of Victory that every American soldier might wear as his only decoration.

Then, row on row, came the men who lead the nation today or have guided its destinies before. They were all there, walking proudly, with age and frailties of the flesh forgotten. Judges, Senators, Representatives, highest officers of every military arm of government, and a trudging little group of the nation's most valorous sons, the Medal of Honor men. Some were gray and bent and drooping with old wounds; some trim and erect as the day they won their way to fame. All walked gladly in this nameless comrade's last parade.

Behind these came the carriage in which rode Woodrow Wilson, also stricken down by infirmities as he served in the highest place in the nation, just as the humble private riding in such state ahead had gone down before a shell or bullet. For the dead man's sake, the former President had put aside his dread of seeming to parade his physical weakness and risked health, perhaps life, to appear among the mourners for the fallen.

There was handclapping and a cheer here and there for the man in the carriage, a tribute to the spirit that brought him to honor the nation's nameless hero, whose commander-in-chief he had been.

After President Harding and most of the high dignitaries of the government had turned aside at the White House, the procession, headed by its solid blocks of soldiery and the battalions of sailor comrades, moved on with Pershing, now flanked by secretaries Weeks and Denby, for the long road to the tomb. It marched on, always between the human borders of the way of victory the nation had made for itself of the great avenue; on over the old bridge that spans the Potomac, on up the long hill to Fort Myer, and at last to the great cemetery beyond, where soldier and sailor folk sleep by the thousands. There the lumbering guns of the artillery swung aside, the cavalry drew their horses out of the long line and left to the foot soldiers and the sailors and marines the last stage of the journey.

Ahead, the white marble of the amphitheater gleamed through the trees. It stands crowning the slope of the hills that sweep upward from the river, and just across was Washington, its clustered buildings and monuments to great dead who have gone before, a moving picture in the autumn haze.

People in thousands were moving about the great circle of the amphitheater. The great ones to whom places had been given in the sacred enclosure and the plain folk who had trudged the long way just to glimpse the pageant from afar, were finding their places. Everywhere within the pillared enclosure bright uniforms of foreign soldiers appeared. They were laden with the jeweled order of rank to honor an American private soldier, great in the majesty of his sacrifices, in the tribute his honors paid to all Americans who died.

Down below the platform placed for the casket, in a stone vault, lay wreaths and garlands brought from England's King and guarded by British soldiers. To them came the British Ambassador in the full uniform of his rank to bid them keep safe against that hour.

Above the platform gathered men whose names ring through history – Briand, Foch, Beatty, Balfour, Jacques, Diaz, and others – in a brilliant array of place and power. They were followed by others, Baron Kato from Japan, the Italian statesmen and officers, by the notables from all countries gathered here for tomorrow's conference, and by some of the older figures in American life too old to walk beside the approaching funeral train.

Down around the circling pillars the marbled box filled with distinguished men and women, with a cluster of shattered men from army hospitals, accompanied by uniformed nurses. A surpliced choir took its place to wait the dead.

Faint and distant, the silvery strains of a military band stole into the big white bowl of the amphitheater. The slow cadences and mourning notes of a funeral march grew clearer amid the roll and mutter of the muffled drums.

At the arch where the choir awaited the heroic dead, comrades lifted his casket down and, followed by the generals and the admirals, who had walked beside him from the Capitol, he was carried to the place of honor. Ahead moved the white-robed singers, chanting solemnly. Carefully, the casket was placed above the banked flowers, and the Marine Band played sacred melodies until the moment the President and Mrs Harding stepped to their places beside the casket; then the crashing, triumphant chorus of "The Star Spangled Banner" swept the gathering to its feet again.

A prayer, carried out over the crowd over the amplifiers so that no word was missed, took a moment or two, then the sharp, clear call of the bugle rang "Attention!" and for two minutes the nation stood at pause for the dead, just at high noon. No sound broke the quiet as all stood with bowed heads. It was much as though a mighty hand had checked the world in full course. Then the band sounded, and in a mighty chorus rolled up in the words of America from the hosts within and without the great open hall of valor.

President Harding stepped forward beside the coffin to say for America the thing that today was nearest to the nation's heart, that sacrifices such as this nameless man, fallen in battle, might perhaps be made unnecessary down through the coming years. Every word that President Harding spoke reached every person through the amplifiers and reached other thousands upon thousands in New York and San Francisco.

Mr Harding showed strong emotion as his lips formed the last words of the address. He paused, then with raised hand and head bowed, went on in the measured, rolling periods of the Lord's Prayer. The response that came back to him from the thousands he faced, from the other thousands out over the slopes beyond, perhaps from still other thousands away near the Pacific, or close-packed in the heart of the nation's greatest city, arose like a chant. The marble arches hummed with a solemn sound.

Then the foreign officers who stand highest among the soldiers or sailors of their flags came one by one to the bier to place gold and jeweled emblems for the brave above the breast of the sleeper. Already, as the great prayer ended, the President had set the American seal of admiration for the valiant, the nation's love for brave deeds and the courage that defies death, upon the casket.

Side by side he laid the Medal of Honor and the Distinguished Service Cross. And below, set in place with reverent hands, grew the long line of foreign honors; the Victoria Cross, never before laid on the breast of any but those who had served the British flag; all the highest honors of France and Belgium and Italy and Rumania and Czechoslovakia and Poland.

To General Jacques of Belgium it remained to add his own touch to these honors. He tore from the breast of his own tunic the medal of valor pinned there by the Belgian King, tore it with a sweeping gesture, and tenderly bestowed it on the unknown American warrior.

Through the religious services that followed, and prayers, the swelling crowd sat motionless until it rose to join in the old, consoling Rock of Ages, and the last rite for the dead was at hand. Lifted by his hero-bearers from the stage, the unknown was carried in his flag-wrapped, simple coffin out to the wide sweep of the terrace. The bearers laid the sleeper down above the crypt, on which had been placed a little soil of France. The dust his blood helped redeem from alien hands will mingle with his dust as time marches by.

The simple words of the burial ritual were said by Bishop Brent; flowers from war mothers of America and England were laid in place.

For the Indians of America Chief Plenty Coos came to call upon the Great spirit of the Red Men, with gesture and chant and tribal tongue, that the dead should not have died in vain, that war might end, peace be purchased by such blood as this. Upon the casket he laid the coupstick of his tribal office and the feathered war bonnet from his own head. Then the casket, with its weight of honors, was lowered into the crypt.

A rocking blast of gunfire rang from the woods. The glittering circle of bayonets stiffened to a salute to the dead. Again the guns shouted their message of honor and farewell. Again they boomed out; a loyal comrade was being laid to his last, long rest.

High and clear and true in the echoes of the guns, a bugle lifted the old, old notes of taps, the lullaby for the living soldier, in death his requiem. Long ago some forgotten soldier-poet caught its meaning clear and set it down that soldiers everywhere might know its message as they sink to rest:

> Fades the light;
> And afar
> Goeth day, cometh night,
> And a star,
> Leadeth all, speedeth all,
> To their rest.

The guns roared out again in the national salute. He was home, The Unknown, to sleep forever among his own.

The Spanish Civil War

O.D. GALLAGHER

The Relief of the Alcazar

The civil war between Franco's insurgent Nationalists and Spain's elected leftist Republican government lasted from July 1936 to April 1939. It ended in Nationalist victory. And it would probably have ended in a quicker victory had the Francoist insurgents not gone to the relief of the Toledo Alcazar garrison in September 1936, allowing the Republicans and their International Brigade allies to occupy the capital Madrid in strength.

Daily Express, 30 September 1936

Talavera (Insurgent Headquarters on
the Toledo Front), 29 September

A stockily built man in khaki walked into the dining-room of the Hotel de Española here to-night. He halted between the tables and blinked his eyes as though they were sore. Clutching a military cap in his hand he glanced nervously around at the hundred-odd officers at dinner.

A shout arose over the busy chatter. Knocking over a chair, a Foreign Legion captain rushed forward and clasped the strange figure in his arms. There was silence; all eyes were fixed on the two men.

The captain turned and shouted, "He comes from the Alcazar!"

Dinner was forgotten. All pushed forward to shake the hand and clap the back of the hero in their midst. He swallowed hard, half laughing, half crying.

I cannot tell you his name, as it is forbidden by the insurgent censorship. They fear the Government might seize his relatives in Madrid. But I can describe him for you.

He was about twenty-nine years of age. His skin was the colour of wet wood ashes. His cheeks were sunken, but his brown eyes were bright and his lips were of pink coral. His black hair was tinged with grey.

For nearly two and a half months he had lived underground, on water, on black bread as hard as the stones of the Alcazar itself, and twice a week on the flesh of mules or horses.

Talking quickly, he told his story and answered the questions shot at him by the officers, among whom were some who had led the relief columns.

There were 1,100 people capable of using arms in the Alcazar, he said, and all had signified their willingness to accept the leadership of Colonel Moscado.

It soon became obvious that the fight was going to be a long one. Provisions were rationed. Each had about a pint of water a day. Washing was strictly forbidden.

There were several attempts to undermine the Alcazar. A young officer kept watch on a high point to calculate the effect of each explosion. One day after a heavy mine had been blown he did not return. He was listed among those who had "disappeared", meaning those who had been blown completely to pieces.

To the now silent officers in the dining-room the man from the Alcazar – almost a man back from the dead – told how the besiegers built up a battery of four guns only a few hundred yards from the Alcazar itself. They began to batter the ancient masonry and made great breaches. On some days women arrived to watch.

"I think they were from Madrid. They used to sit and drink wine; sometimes actually fired guns at us. They made it a sort of a holiday."

The imprisoned occupants of the Alcazar were soon driven underground in the dungeons. In one comparatively small cellar beneath the eight-feet-thick walls seventy-five women and children spent four weeks without moving out. The man from the Alcazar told us—

"Constantly moving about were about five pale-faced nuns and three doctors. They performed thirty amputations. There was not one case of infection, despite the tainted air in the dungeon hospital."

The walls of this 400-year-old castle from whose battlements bows and arrows, and arquebuses were used, might have been built for modern warfare. They withstood the most violent bombardments and only crumbled after sustained short-range shelling.

One million cartridges were seized by officers of the Alcazar when the revolt began. Of these, 400,000 rounds were fired.

Normal food soon ran out, but the Alcazar was well stocked with grain. Women baked crude bread in the cellars; enough for one or two weeks at a time.

When the siege began there were ninety-seven horses and twenty-seven mules within the walls. When it ended only one horse and five mules remained. The rest had been eaten.

Several times insurgent airplanes dropped stores to the defenders. At first the defenders feared the provisions had been dropped by Government machines and that they were poisoned. A young chemist in the Alcazar analyzed the food, and declared it wholesome.

Though unable to communicate with the outside world the defenders heard radio war bulletins given out by Lisbon. Sometimes a jazz programme was turned on; then the younger people danced or sang among the ruins.

When the garrison was relieved they had to leave through some second-floor windows and stumble to the ground level over tons of shattered rock.

The Spanish Civil War

GEORGE ORWELL

The Attack on the Fascist Redoubt

Orwell went to Spain in 1936 and joined the militia of the POUM
(United Marxist Workers Party). The following year he was shot
through the neck while fighting on the Ebro Front, and returned to
England where he penned a book of civil war reportage, *Homage
to Catalonia*.

Homage to Catalonia, 1938

One afternoon Benjamin told us that he wanted fifteen volunteers. The attack on the Fascist redoubt which had been called
off on the previous occasion was to be carried out tonight. I
oiled my ten Mexican cartridges, dirtied my bayonet (the things
give your position away if they flash too much), and packed up
a hunk of bread, three inches of red sausage, and a cigar which
my wife had sent from Barcelona and which I had been hoarding for a long time. Bombs were served out, three to a man. The
Spanish Government had at last succeeded in producing a
decent bomb. It was on the principle of a Mills bomb, but with
two pins instead of one. After you had pulled the pins out there
was an interval of seven seconds before the bomb exploded. Its
chief disadvantage was that one pin was very stiff and the other
very loose, so that you had the choice of leaving both pins in
place and being unable to pull the stiff one out in a moment of
emergency, or pulling out the stiff one beforehand and being in
a constant stew lest the thing should explode in your pocket. But
it was a handy little bomb to throw.

A little before midnight Benjamin led the fifteen of us down to Torre Fabian. Ever since evening the rain had been pelting down. The irrigation ditches were brimming over, and every time you stumbled into one you were in water up to your waist. In the pitch darkness and sheeting rain in the farm-yard a dim mass of men was waiting. Kopp addressed us, first in Spanish, then in English, and explained the plan of attack. The Fascist line here made an L-bend and the parapet we were to attack lay on rising ground at the corner of the L. About thirty of us, half English and half Spanish, under the command of Jorge Roca, our battalion commander (a battalion in the militia was about four hundred men), and Benjamin, were to creep up and cut the Fascist wire. Jorge would fling the first bomb as a signal, then the rest of us were to send in a rain of bombs, drive the Fascists out of the parapet and seize it before they could rally. Simultaneously seventy Shock Troopers were to assault the next Fascist "position", which lay two hundred yards to the right of the other, joined to it by a communication-trench. To prevent us from shooting each other in the darkness white armlets would be worn. At this moment a messenger arrived to say that there were no white armlets. Out of the darkness a plaintive voice suggested: "Couldn't we arrange for the Fascists to wear white armlets instead?"

There was an hour or two to put in. The barn over the mule stable was so wrecked by shell-fire that you could not move about in it without a light. Half the floor had been torn away by a plunging shell and there was a twenty-foot drop on to the stones beneath. Someone found a pick and levered a burst plank out of the floor, and in a few minutes we had got a fire alight and our drenched clothes were steaming. Someone else produced a pack of cards. A rumour – one of those mysterious rumours that are endemic in war – flew round that hot coffee with brandy in it was about to be served out. We filed eagerly down the almost-collapsing staircase and wandered round the dark yard, enquiring where the coffee was to be found. Alas! there was no coffee. Instead, they called us together, ranged us into single file, and then Jorge and Benjamin set off rapidly into the darkness, the rest of us following.

It was still raining and intensely dark, but the wind had dropped. The mud was unspeakable. The paths through the beet-fields were simply a succession of lumps, as slippery as a greasy pole, with huge pools everywhere. Long before we got to the place where we were to leave our own parapet everyone had fallen several times and our rifles were coated with mud. At the parapet a small knot of men, our reserves, were waiting, and the doctor and a row of stretchers. We filed through the gap in the parapet and waded through another irrigation ditch. Splash-gurgle! Once again in water up to your waist, with the filthy, slimy mud oozing over your boot-tops. On the grass outside Jorge waited till we were all through. Then, bent almost double, he began creeping slowly forward. The Fascist parapet was about a hundred and fifty yards away. Our one chance of getting there was to move without noise.

I was in front with Jorge and Benjamin. Bent double, but with faces raised, we crept into the almost utter darkness at a pace that grew slower at every step. The rain beat lightly in our faces. When I glanced back I could see the men who were nearest to me, a bunch of humped shapes like huge black mushrooms glid-ing slowly forward. But every time I raised my head Benjamin, close beside me, whispered fiercely in my ear: "To keep ze head down! To keep ze head down!" I could have told him that he needn't worry. I knew by experiment that on a dark night you can never see a man at twenty paces. It was far more important to go quietly. If they once heard us we were done for. They had only to spray the darkness with their machine-gun and there was nothing for it but to run or be massacred.

But on the sodden ground it was almost impossible to move quietly. Do what you would your feet stuck to the mud, and every step you took was slop-slop, slop-slop. And the devil of it was that the wind had dropped, and in spite of the rain it was a very quiet night. Sounds would carry a long way. There was a dreadful moment when I kicked against a tin and thought every Fascist within miles must have heard it. But no, not a sound, no answering shot, no movement in the Fascist lines. We crept onwards, always more slowly. I cannot convey to you the depth of my desire to get there. Just to get within bombing distance before they heard us! At such a time you have not even any fear, only a tremendous hopeless longing to get over the intervening ground. I have felt exactly the same thing when stalking a wild animal; the same agonized desire to get within range, the same dreamlike certainty that it is impossible. And how the distance stretched out! I knew the ground well, it was barely a hundred and fifty yards, and yet it seemed more like a mile. When you are creeping at that pace you are aware as an ant might be of the enormous variations in the ground; the splendid patch of smooth grass here, the evil patch of sticky mud there, the tall rustling reeds that have got to be avoided, the heap of stones that almost makes you give up hope because it seems impossible to get over it without noise.

We had been creeping forward for such an age that I began to think we had gone the wrong way. Then in the darkness thin parallel lines of something blacker were faintly visible. It was the outer wire (the Fascists had two lines of wire). Jorge knelt down, fumbled in his pocket. He had our only pair of wire-cutters. Snip, snip. The trailing stuff was lifted delicately aside. We waited for the men at the back to close up. They seemed to be making a frightful noise. It might be fifty yards to the Fascist parapet now. Still onwards, bent double. A stealthy step, lowering your foot as gently as a cat approaching a mousehole; then a pause to listen; then another step. Once I raised my head; in silence Benjamin put his hand behind my neck and pulled it violently down. I knew that the inner wire was barely twenty yards from the parapet. It seemed to me inconceivable that thirty men could get there unheard. Our breathing was enough to give us away. Yet somehow we did get there. The Fascist parapet was visible now, a dim black mound, looming high above us. Once again Jorge knelt and fumbled. Snip, snip. There was no way of cutting the stuff silently.

So that was the inner wire. We crawled through it on all fours and rather more rapidly. If we had time to deploy now all was well. Jorge and Benjamin crawled across to the right. But the men behind, who were spread out, had to form into single file to get through the narrow gap in the wire, and just at this moment there was a flash and a bang from the Fascist parapet. The sentry had heard us at last. Jorge poised himself on one knee and swung his arm like a bowler. Crash! His bomb burst somewhere over the parapet. At once, far more promptly than one would have thought possible, a roar of fire, ten or twenty rifles, burst out from the Fascist parapet. They had been waiting for us after all. Momentarily you could see every sandbag in the lurid light. Men too far back were flinging their bombs and some of them were falling short of the parapet. Every loophole seemed to be spouting jets of flame. It is always hateful to be shot at in the dark – every rifle-flash seems to be pointed straight at yourself – but it was the bombs that were the worst. You cannot conceive the horror of these things till you have seen one burst close to you and in darkness; in the daytime there is only the crash of explosion, in the darkness there is the blinding red glare as well. I had flung myself down at the first volley. All this while I was lying on my side in the greasy mud, wrestling savagely with the pin of a bomb. The damned thing *would* not come out. Finally I realized that I was twisting it in the wrong direction. I got the pin out, rose to my knees, hurled the bomb, and threw myself down again. The bomb burst over to the right, outside the parapet; fright had spoiled my aim. Just at this moment another bomb burst right in front of me, so close that I could feel the heat of the explosion. I flattened myself out and dug my face into the mud so hard that I hurt my neck and thought that I was wounded. Through the din I heard an English voice behind me say quietly: "I'm hit." The bomb had, in fact, wounded several people round about me without touching myself. I rose to my knees and flung my second bomb. I forget where that one went.

The Fascists were firing, our people behind were firing, and I was very conscious of being in the middle. I felt the blast of a shot and realized that a man was firing from immediately behind me. I stood up and shouted at him: "Don't shoot at me, you bloody fool!" At this moment I saw that Benjamin, ten or fifteen yards to my right, was motioning to me with his arm. I ran across to him. It meant crossing the line of spouting loopholes, and as I went I clapped my left hand over my cheek; an idiotic gesture – as though one's hand could stop a bullet! – but I had a horror of being hit in the face. Benjamin was kneeling on one knee with a pleased, devilish sort of expression on his face and firing carefully at the rifle-flashes with his automatic pistol. Jorge had dropped wounded at the first volley and was somewhere out of sight. I knelt beside Benjamin, pulled the pin out of my third bomb and flung it. Ah! No doubt about it that time. The bomb crashed inside the parapet, at the corner, just by the machine-gun nest.

The Fascist fire seemed to have slackened very suddenly. Benjamin leapt to his feet and shouted: "Forward! Charge!" We dashed up the short steep slope on which the parapet stood. I say "dashed"; "lumbered" would be a better word; the fact is that you can't move fast when you are sodden and muddied from head to foot and weighted down with a heavy rifle and bayonet and a hundred and fifty cartridges. I took it for granted that there would be a Fascist waiting for me at the top. If he fired at that range he could not miss me, and yet somehow I never expected him to fire, only to try for me with his bayonet. I seemed to feel in advance the sensation of our bayonets crossing, and I wondered whether his arm would be stronger than mine. However, there was no Fascist waiting. With a vague feeling of relief I found that it was a low parapet and the sandbags gave a good foothold. As a rule they are difficult to get over. Everything inside was smashed to pieces, beams flung all over the place, and great shards of uralite littered everywhere. Our bombs had wrecked all the huts and dug-outs. And still there was not a soul visible. I thought they would be lurking somewhere underground, and shouted in English (I could not think of any Spanish at the moment): "Come on out of it! Surrender!" No answer. Then a man, a shadowy figure in the half-light, skipped over the roof of one of the ruined huts and dashed away to the left. I started after him, prodding my bayonet ineffectually into the darkness. As I rounded the corner of the hut I saw a man – I don't know whether or not it was the same man as I had seen before – fleeing up the communication-trench that led to the other Fascist position. I must have been very close to him, for I could see him clearly. He was bareheaded and seemed to have nothing on except a blanket which he was clutching round his shoulders. If I had fired I could have blown him to pieces. But for fear of shooting one another we had been ordered to use only bayonets once we were inside the parapet, and in any case I never even thought of firing. Instead, my mind leapt backwards twenty years, to our boxing instructor at school, showing me in vivid pantomime how he had bayoneted a Turk at the Dardanelles. I gripped my rifle by the small of the butt and lunged at the man's back. He was just out of my reach. Another lunge: still out of reach. And for a little distance we proceeded like this, he rushing up the trench and I after him on the ground above, prodding at his shoulder-blades and never quite getting there – a comic memory for me to look back upon, though I suppose it seemed less comic to him.

Of course, he knew the ground better than I and had soon slipped away from me. When I came back the position was full of shouting men. The noise of firing had lessened somewhat. The Fascists were still pouring a heavy fire at us from three sides, but it was coming from a greater distance. We had driven them back for the time being. I remember saying in an oracular manner: "We can hold this place for half an hour, not more." I don't know why I picked on half an hour. Looking over the right-hand parapet you could see innumerable greenish rifle-flashes stabbing the darkness; but they were a long way back, a hundred or two hundred yards. Our job now was to search the position and loot anything that was worth looting. Benjamin and some others were already scrabbling among the ruins of a big hut or dug-out in the middle of the position. Benjamin staggered excitedly through the ruined roof, tugging at the rope handle of an ammunition box.

"Comrades! Ammunition! Plenty ammunition here!"

"We don't want ammunition,' said a voice, "we want rifles."

This was true. Half our rifles were jammed with mud and unusable. They could be cleaned, but it is dangerous to take the bolt out of a rifle in the darkness; you put it down somewhere and then you lose it. I had a tiny electric torch which my wife had managed to buy in Barcelona, otherwise we had no light of any description among us. A few men with good rifles began a desultory fire at the flashes in the distance. No one dared fire too rapidly; even the best of the rifles were liable to jam if they got too hot. There were about sixteen of us inside the parapet, including one or two who were wounded. A number of wounded, English and Spanish, were lying outside. Patrick O'Hara, a Belfast Irishman who had had some training in first-aid, went to and fro with packets of bandages, binding up the wounded men and, of course, being shot at every time he returned to the parapet, in spite of his indignant shouts of "Poum!"

We began searching the position. There were several dead men lying about, but I did not stop to examine them. The thing I was after was the machine-gun. All the while when we were lying outside I had been wondering vaguely why the gun did not fire. I flashed my torch inside the machine-gun nest. A bitter disappointment! The gun was not there. Its tripod was there, and various boxes of ammunition and spare parts, but the gun was gone. They must have unscrewed it and carried it off at the first alarm. No doubt they were acting under orders, but it was a stupid and cowardly thing to do, for if they had kept the gun in place they could have slaughtered the whole lot of us. We were furious. We had set our hearts on capturing a machine-gun.

We poked here and there but did not find anything of much value. There were quantities of Fascist bombs lying about – a rather inferior type of bomb, which you touched off by pulling a string – and I put a couple of them in my pocket as souvenirs. It was impossible not to be struck by the bare misery of the Fascist dug-outs. The litter of spare clothes, books, food, petty personal belongings that you saw in our own dug-outs was completely absent; these poor unpaid conscripts seemed to own nothing except blankets and a few soggy hunks of bread. Up at the far end there was a small dug-out which was partly above ground and had a tiny window. We flashed the torch through the window and instantly raised a cheer. A cylindrical object in a leather case, four feet high and six inches in diameter, was leaning against the wall. Obviously the machine-gun barrel. We dashed round and got in at the doorway, to find that the thing in the leather case was not a machine-gun but something which, in our weapon-starved army, was even more precious. It was an enormous telescope, probably of at least sixty or seventy magnifications, with a folding tripod. Such telescopes simply did not exist on our side of the line and they were desperately needed. We brought it out in triumph and leaned it against the parapet, to be carried off later.

At this moment someone shouted that the Fascists were closing in. Certainly the din of firing had grown very much louder. But it was obvious that the Fascists would not counter-attack from the right, which meant crossing no man's land and assaulting their own parapet. If they had any sense at all they would come at us from inside the line. I went round to the other side of the dug-outs. The position was roughly horseshoe-shaped, with the dug-outs in the middle, so that we had another parapet covering us on the left. A heavy fire was coming from that direction, but it did not matter greatly. The danger-spot was straight in front, where there was no protection at all. A stream of bullets was passing just overhead. They must be coming from the other Fascist position farther up the line; evidently the Shock Troopers had not captured it after all. But this time the noise was deafening. It was the unbroken, drum-like roar of massed rifles which I was used to hearing from a little distance; this was the first time I had been in the middle of it. And by now, of course, the firing had spread along the line for miles around. Douglas Thompson, with a wounded arm dangling useless at his side, was leaning against the parapet and firing one-handed at the flashes. Someone whose rifle had jammed was loading for him.

There were four or five of us round this side. It was obvious what we must do. We must drag the sandbags from the front parapet and make a barricade across the unprotected side. And we had got to be quick. The fire was high at present, but they might lower it at any moment; by the flashes all round I could see that we had a hundred or two hundred men against us. We began wrenching the sandbags loose, carrying them twenty yards forward and dumping them into a rough heap. It was a vile job. They were big sandbags, weighing a hundredweight each and it took every ounce of your strength to prise them loose; and then the rotten sacking split and the damp earth cascaded all over you, down your neck and up your sleeves. I remember feeling a deep horror at everything: the chaos, the darkness, the frightful din, the slithering to and fro in the mud, the struggles with the bursting sandbags – all the time encumbered with my rifle, which I dared not put down for fear of losing it. I even shouted to someone as we staggered along with a bag between us: "This is war! Isn't it bloody?" Suddenly a succession of tall figures came leaping over the front parapet. As they came nearer we saw that they wore the uniform of the Shock Troopers, and we cheered, thinking they were reinforcements. However, there were only four of them, three Germans and a Spaniard. We heard afterwards what had happened to the Shock Troopers. They did not know the ground and in the darkness had been led to the wrong place, where they were caught on the Fascist wire and numbers of them were shot down. These were four who had got lost, luckily for themselves. The Germans did not speak a word of English, French, or Spanish. With difficulty and much gesticulation we explained what we were doing and got them to help us in building the barricade.

The Fascists had brought up a machine-gun now. You could see it spitting like a squib a hundred or two hundred yards away; the bullets came over us with a steady, frosty crackle. Before long we had flung enough sandbags into place to make a low breastwork behind which the few men who were on this side of the position could lie down and fire. I was kneeling behind them. A mortar-shell whizzed over and crashed somewhere in no man's land. That was another danger, but it would take them some minutes to find our range. Now that we had finished wrestling with those beastly sandbags it was not bad fun in a way; the noise, the darkness, the flashes approaching, our own men blazing back at the flashes. One even had time to think a little. I remember wondering whether I was frightened, and deciding that I was not. Outside, where I was probably in less danger, I had been half sick with fright. Suddenly there was another shout that the Fascists were closing in. There was no doubt about it this time, the rifle-flashes were much nearer. I saw a flash hardly twenty yards away. Obviously they were working their way up the communication-trench. At twenty yards they were within easy bombing range; there were eight or nine of us bunched together and a single well-placed bomb would blow us all to fragments. Bob Smillie, the blood running down his face from a small wound, sprang to his knee and flung a bomb. We cowered, waiting for the crash. The fuse fizzled red as it sailed through the air, but the bomb failed to explode. (At least a quarter of these bombs were duds.) I had no bombs left except the Fascist ones and I was not certain how these worked. I shouted to the others to know if anyone had a bomb to spare. Douglas Moyle felt in his pocket and passed one across. I flung it and threw myself on my face. By one of those strokes of luck that happen about once in a year I had managed to drop the bomb almost exactly where the rifle had flashed. There was the roar of the explosion and then, instantly, a diabolical outcry of screams and groans. We had got one of them, anyway; I don't know whether he was killed, but certainly he was badly hurt. Poor wretch, poor wretch! I felt a vague sorrow as I heard him screaming. But at the same instant, in the dim light of the rifle-flashes, I saw or thought I saw a figure standing near the place where the rifle had flashed. I threw up my rifle and let fly. Another scream, but I think it was still the effect of the bomb. Several more bombs were thrown.

The next rifle-flashes we saw were a long way off, a hundred yards or more. So we had driven them back, temporarily at least.

Everyone began cursing and saying why the hell didn't they send us some supports. With a sub-machine-gun or twenty men with clean rifles we could hold this place against a battalion. At this moment Paddy Donovan, who was second-in-command to Benjamin and had been sent back for orders, climbed over the front parapet.

"Hi! Come on out of it! All men to retire at once!"

"What?"

"Retire! Get out of it!"

"Why?"

"Orders. Back to our own lines double-quick."

People were already climbing over the front parapet. Several of them were struggling with a heavy ammunition box. My mind flew to the telescope which I had left leaning against the parapet on the other side of the position. But at this moment I saw that the four Shock Troopers, acting I suppose on some mysterious orders they had received beforehand, had begun running up the communication-trench. It led to the other Fascist position and – if they got there – to certain death. They were disappearing into the darkness. I ran after them, trying to think of the Spanish for "retire"; finally I shouted, "Atrás! Atrás!", which perhaps conveyed the right meaning. The Spaniard understood it and brought the others back. Paddy was waiting at the parapet.

"Come on, hurry up."

"But the telescope!"

"B—— the telescope! Benjamin's waiting outside."

We climbed out. Paddy held the wire aside for me. As soon as we got away from the shelter of the Fascist parapet we were under a devilish fire that seemed to be coming at us from every direction. Part of it, I do not doubt, came from our own side, for everyone was firing all along the line. Whichever way we turned a fresh stream of bullets swept past; we were driven this way and that in the darkness like a flock of sheep. It did not make it any easier that we were dragging a captured box of ammunition – one of those boxes that hold 1,750 rounds and weigh about a hundredweight – besides a box of bombs and several Fascist rifles. In a few minutes, although the distance from parapet to parapet was not two hundred yards and most of us knew the ground, we were completely lost. We found ourselves slithering about in a muddy field, knowing nothing except that bullets were coming from both sides. There was no moon to go by, but the sky was growing a little lighter. Our lines lay east of Huesca; I wanted to stay where we were till the first crack of dawn showed us which was east and which was west; but the others were against it. We slithered onwards, changing our direction several times and taking it in turns to haul at the ammunition-box. At last we saw the low flat line of a parapet looming in front of us. It might be ours or it might be the Fascists'; nobody had the dimmest idea which way we were going. Benjamin crawled on his belly through some tall whitish weed till he was about twenty yards from the parapet and tried a challenge. A shout of "Poum!" answered him. We jumped to our feet, found our way along the parapet, slopped once more through the irrigation ditch – splash-gurgle – and were in safety.

Kopp was waiting inside the parapet with a few Spaniards. The doctor and the stretchers were gone. It appeared that all the wounded had been got in except Jorge and one of our own men, Hiddlestone by name, who were missing. Kopp was pacing up and down, very pale. Even the fat folds at the back of his neck were pale; he was paying no attention to the bullets that streamed over the low parapet and cracked close to his head. Most of us were squatting behind the parapet for cover. Kopp was muttering, "Jorge! Congo! Jorge!" And then in English, "If Jorge is gone it is terreeble, terreeble!" Jorge was his personal friend and one of his best officers. Suddenly he turned to us and asked for five volunteers, two English and three Spanish, to go and look for the missing men. Moyle and I volunteered with three Spaniards.

As we got outside the Spaniards murmured that it was getting dangerously light. This was true enough; the sky was dimly blue. There was a tremendous noise of excited voices coming from the Fascist redoubt. Evidently they had reoccupied the place in much greater force than before. We were sixty or seventy yards from the parapet when they must have seen or heard us, for they sent over a heavy burst of fire which made us drop on our faces. One of them flung a bomb over the parapet – a sure sign of panic. We were lying in the grass, waiting for an opportunity to move on, when we either heard or thought we heard – I have no doubt it was pure imagination, but it seemed real enough at the time – that the Fascist voices were much closer. They had left the parapet and were coming after us. "Run!" I yelled to Moyle, and jumped to my feet. And heavens, how I ran! I had thought earlier in the night that you can't run when you are sodden from head to foot and weighted down with a rifle and cartridges; I learned now you can *always* run when you think you have fifty or a hundred armed men after you. But if I could run fast, others could run faster. In my flight something that might have been a shower of meteors sped past me. It was the three Spaniards, who had been in front. They were back to our own parapet before they stopped and I could catch up with them. The truth was that our nerves were all to pieces. I knew, however, that in a half light one man is invisible where five are clearly visible, so I went back alone. I managed to get to the outer wire and searched the ground as well as I could, which was not very well, for I had to lie on my belly. There was no sign of Jorge or Hiddlestone, so I crept back. We learned afterwards that both Jorge and Hiddlestone had been taken to the dressing-station earlier. Jorge was lightly wounded through the shoulder. Hiddlestone had received a dreadful wound – a bullet which travelled right up his left arm, breaking the bone in several places; as he lay helpless on the ground a bomb had burst near him and torn various other parts of his body. He recovered, I am glad to say. Later he told me that he had worked his way some distance lying on his back, then had clutched hold of a wounded Spaniard and they had helped one another in.

It was getting light now. Along the line for miles around a ragged meaningless fire was thundering, like the rain that goes on raining after a storm. I remember the desolate look of everything, the morasses of mud, the weeping poplar trees, the yellow water in the trench-bottoms; and men's exhausted faces, unshaven, streaked with mud and blackened to the eyes with smoke. When I got back to my dug-out the three men I shared it with were already fast asleep. They had flung themselves down with all their equipment on and their muddy rifles clutched against them. Everything was sodden, inside the dug-out as well as outside. By long searching I managed to collect enough chips of dry wood to make a tiny fire. Then I smoked the cigar which

I had been hoarding and which, surprisingly enough, had not got broken during the night.

Afterwards we learned that the action had been a success, as such things go. It was merely a raid to make the Fascists divert troops from the other side of Huesca, where the Anarchists were attacking again. I had judged that the Fascists had thrown a hundred or two hundred men into the counter-attack, but a deserter told us later on that it was six hundred. I dare say he was lying – deserters, for obvious reasons, often try to curry favour. It was a great pity about the telescope. The thought of losing that beautiful bit of loot worries me even now.

The Spanish Civil War

GEORGE STEER

The Tragedy of Guernica Town Destroyed in an Air Attack: Eyewitness's Account

Steer's account of the bombing of the Basque town Guernica by German aircrew aiding Franco for *The Times* was probably the most significant article to come out of the Spanish Civil War. When Steer's report was reprinted in the French Communist daily, *L'Humanité*, it caused Pablo Picasso to paint his most famous painting; across the Atlantic it was cited in the House of Congress as proof of German complicity in the Spanish Civil War; almost the world over it alerted the public to the nature of fascism. *The Times*, however, proved monumentally ungrateful and sacked him for his sympathy for the Republican side.

With the start of World War II Steer's new employer, the *Daily Telegraph*, sent him to report on the Russo-Finnish War. Soon after, with the world more menaced than ever by bullying totalitarianism of Left and Right, he dropped the pen to take up the sword and joined the British Army. Steer died in a jeep accident in 1944 in the Far East aged thirty-five.

The Times, 27 April 1937

Guernica, the most ancient town of the Basques and the centre of their cultural tradition, was completely destroyed yesterday afternoon by insurgent air raiders. The bombardment of this open town far behind the lines occupied precisely three hours and a quarter, during which a powerful fleet of aeroplanes consisting of three German types, Junkers and Heinkel bombers and Heinkel fighters, did not cease unloading on the town bombs weighing from 1,000lb. downwards and, it is calculated, more than 3,000 two-pounder aluminium incendiary projectiles. The fighters, meanwhile, plunged low from above the centre of the town to machine-gun those of the civilian population who had taken refuge in the fields.

The whole of Guernica was soon in flames except the historic Casa de Jontas with its rich archives of the Basque race, where the ancient Basque Parliament used to sit. The famous oak of Guernica, the dried old stump of 600 years and the young new shoots of this century, was also untouched. Here the kings of Spain used to take the oath to respect the democratic rights (fueros) of Vizcaya and in return received a promise of allegiance as suzerains with the democratic title of Señor, not Rey Vizcaya. The noble parish church of Santa Maria was also undamaged except for the beautiful chapter house, which was struck by an incendiary bomb.

At 2 am today when I visited the town the whole of it was a horrible sight, flaming from end to end. The reflection of the flames could be seen in the clouds of smoke above the mountains from 10 miles away. Throughout the night houses were falling until the streets became long heaps of red impenetrable debris.

Many of the civilian survivors took the long trek from Guernica to Bilbao in antique solid-wheeled Basque farm carts drawn by oxen. Carts piled high with such household possessions as could be saved from the conflagration clogged the roads all night. Other survivors were evacuated in Government lorries, but many were forced to remain round the burning town lying on mattresses or looking for lost relatives and children, while units of the fire brigades and the Basque motorized police under the personal direction of the Minister of the Interior, Señor Monzon, and his wife continued rescue work till dawn.

CHURCH BELL ALARM

In the form of its execution and the scale of the destruction it wrought, no less than in the selection of its objective, the raid on Guernica is unparalleled in military history. Guernica was not a military objective. A factory producing war material lay outside the town and was untouched. So were two barracks some distance from the town. The town lay far behind the lines. The object of the bombardment was seemingly the demoralization of the civil population and the destruction of the cradle of the Basque race. Every fact bears out this appreciation, beginning with the day when the deed was done.

Monday was the customary market day in Guernica for the country round. At 4.30 pm, when the market was full and peasants were still coming in, the church bell rang the alarm for approaching aeroplanes, and the population sought refuge in cellars and in the dugouts prepared following the bombing of the civilian population of Durango on March 31, which opened General Mola's offensive in the north. The people are said to have shown a good spirit. A Catholic priest took charge and perfect order was maintained.

Five minutes later a single German bomber appeared, circled over the town at a low altitude, and then dropped six heavy bombs, apparently aiming for the station. The bombs with a shower of grenades fell on a former institute and on houses and streets surrounding it. The aeroplane then went away. In another five minutes came a second bomber, which threw the same number of bombs into the middle of the town. About a quarter of an hour later three Junkers arrived to continue the work of demolition, and thenceforward the bombing grew in intensity and was continuous, ceasing only with the approach of dusk at 7.45. The whole town of 7,000 inhabitants, plus 3,000 refugees, was slowly and systematically pounded to pieces. Over a radius of five miles round a detail of the raiders' technique was to bomb separate *caserios*, or farmhouses. In the night these burned like little candles in the hills. All the villages around were bombed with the same intensity as the town itself, and at Mugica, a little group of houses at the head of the Guernica inlet, the population was machine-gunned for 15 minutes.

RHYTHM OF DEATH

It is impossible to state yet the number of victims. In the Bilbao
Press this morning they were reported as "fortunately small",
but it is feared that this was an understatement in order not to
alarm the large refugee population of Bilbao. In the hospital of
Josefinas, which was one of the first places bombed, all the 42
wounded militiamen it sheltered were killed outright. In a street
leading downhill from the Casa de Juntas I saw a place where 50
people, nearly all women and children, are said to have been
trapped in an air raid refuge under a mass of burning wreckage.
Many were killed in the fields, and altogether the deaths may
run into hundreds. An elderly priest named Aronategui was
killed by a bomb while rescuing children from a burning house.

The tactics of the bombers, which may be of interest to students of the new military science, were as follows: – First, small
parties of aeroplanes threw heavy bombs and hand grenades all
over the town, choosing area after area in orderly fashion. Next
came fighting machines which swooped low to machine-gun
those who ran in panic from dugouts, some of which had already
been penetrated by 1,000lb bombs, which make a hole 25ft
deep. Many of these people were killed as they ran. A large herd
of sheep being brought in to the market was also wiped out. The
object of this move was apparently to drive the population under
ground again, for next as many as 12 bombers appeared at a
time dropping heavy and incendiary bombs upon the ruins. The
rhythm of this bombing of an open town was, therefore, a logical one: first, hand grenades and heavy bombs to stampede the
population, then machine-gunning to drive them below, next
heavy and incendiary bombs to wreck the houses and burn
them on top of their victims.

The only counter-measures the Basques could employ, for
they do not possess sufficient aeroplanes to face the insurgent
fleet, were those provided by the heroism of the Basque clergy.
These blessed and prayed for the kneeling crowds – Socialists,
Anarchists, and Communists, as well as the declared faithful –
in the crumbling dugouts.

When I entered Guernica after midnight houses were crashing on either side, and it was utterly impossible even for firemen
to enter the centre of the town. The hospitals of Josefinas and

Convento de Santa Clara were glowing heaps of embers, all the churches except that of Santa Maria were destroyed, and the few houses which still stood were doomed. When I revisited Guernica this afternoon most of the town was still burning and new fires had broken out. About 30 dead were laid out in a ruined hospital.

A CALL TO BASQUES

The effect here of the bombardment of Guernica, the Basques' holy city, has been profound and has led President Aguirre to issue the following statement in this morning's Basque Press:–
"The German airmen in the service of the Spanish rebels, have bombarded Guernica, burning the historic town which is held in such veneration by all Basques. They have sought to wound us in the most sensitive of our patriotic sentiments, once more making it entirely clear what Euzkadis may expect of those who do not hesitate to destroy us down to the very sanctuary which records the centuries of our liberty and our democracy.

"Before this outrage all we Basques must react with violence, swearing from the bottom of our hearts to defend the principles' of our people with unheard of stubbornness and heroism if the case requires it. We cannot hide the gravity of the moment; but victory can never be won by the invader if, raising our spirits to heights of strength and determination, we steel ourselves to his defeat.

"The enemy has advanced in many parts elsewhere to be driven out of them afterwards. I do not hesitate to affirm that here the same thing will happen. May to-day's outrage be one spur more to do it with all speed."

The Spanish Civil War

LANGSTON HUGHES

Hughes Bombed in Spain

Poet, novelist and playwright, the black American Langston Hughes also reported on the Spanish Civil War for Carl Murphy's Afro-American.

Baltimore Afro-American, 23 October 1937

Madrid, Spain – I came down from Paris by train. We reached Barcelona at night. The day before there had been a terrific air raid in the city, killing almost a hundred persons in their houses and wounding a great many more. We read about it in the papers at the border: AIR RAID OVER BARCELONA. "Last night!" I thought, "Well, tonight I'll be there."

It was almost midnight when we got to Barcelona. There were no lights in the town, and we came out of the station into pitch darkness. A bus took us to the hotel. It was a large hotel several stories high which, before the Civil War, had been a fashionable stopping place for tourists.

We had rooms on an upper floor. The desk clerk said that in case of air-raids we might come down into the lobby, but that a few floors more or less wouldn't make much difference. The raids were announced by siren, but guests would be warned by telephone as well. That night there was no bombing, so we slept in peace.

At midnight [next day], the public radios began to blare forth the war-news, and people gathered in large groups on corners to hear it. Then the cafe closed and we went to the hotel. I had just barely gotten to my room and had begun to undress when the low extended wail of the siren began, letting us know that the fascist planes were coming. (They come from Mallorca across the sea at terrific speed, drop their bombs, and circle away into the night again.)

Quickly, I put on my shirt, passed Guillén's room, and together we started downstairs. Suddenly all the lights went out in the hotel, but we heard people rushing down the halls and stairways in the dark. A few had flashlights with them to find the way. Some were visibly frightened. In the lobby two candles were burning, casting weird, giantlike shadows on the walls.

In an ever increasing wail the siren sounded louder and louder, droning its deathly warning. Suddenly it stopped. By then the lobby was full of people, men, women, and children, speaking in Spanish, English, and French. In the distance we heard a series of quick explosives.

"Bombs?" I asked.

"No, anti-aircraft gun," a man explained.

Everyone was very quiet. Then we heard the guns go off again.

"Come here," the man called, leading the way. Several of us went out on the balcony where, in the dark, we could see searchlights playing across the sky. Little round puffs of smoke from the anti-aircraft shells floated against the stars. In the street a few women hurried along to public bomb-proof cellars.

Then for a long while nothing happened. After about an hour, the lights suddenly came on in the hotel again as a signal that the danger had passed.

The Spanish Civil War

JOHN DOS PASSOS

Room and Bath at the Hotel Florida

John Dos Passos journeyed to Spain in 1937, partly because of his socialist sympathy with the Republicans, partly because he was paid to observe the war for *Esquire*. The piece below was written during the siege of Madrid in January 1938.

Journeys Between Wars, 1942

I wake up suddenly with my throat stiff. It's not quite day. I am lying in a comfortable bed, in a clean well-arranged hotel room staring at the light indigo oblong of the window opposite. I sit up in bed. Again there's the hasty loudening shriek, the cracking roar, the rattle of tiles and a tinkling shatter of glass and granite fragments. Must have been near because the hotel shook. My room is seven or eight stories up. The hotel is on a hill. From the window I can look out at all the old part of Madrid over the crowded tiled roofs, soot-color flecked with pale yellow and red under the metal blue before dawn gloaming. The packed city stretches out sharp and still as far as I can see, narrow roofs, smokeless chim-ney-pots, buffcolored towers with cupolas and the pointed slate spires of seventeen century Castile. Everything is cut out of metal in the steely brightening light. Again the shriek, the roar, rattle, tinkle of a shell bursting somewhere. Then silence again, cut only by the thin yelps of a hurt dog, and very slowly from one of the roofs below a smudge of dirty yellow smoke forms, rises, thickens and spreads out in the still air under the low indigo sky. The yelping goes weakly on and on.

It's too early to get up. I try going to bed again, fall asleep to wake almost immediately with the same tight throat, the same heavy feeling in my chest. The shells keep coming in. They are small but they are damn close. Better get dressed. The water's running in the bathroom, though the hot's not on yet. A man feels safe shaving, sniffing the little customary odor of the usual shaving soap in the clean bathroom. After a bath and a shave I put on my bathrobe, thinking after all this is what the Madrileños have been having instead of an alarmclock for five months now, and walk downstairs to see what the boys are up to. The shells keep coming in. The hotel, usually so quiet at this time, is full of scamper and confusion.

Everywhere doors fly open onto the balconies round the central glassed-over well. Men and women in various stages of undress are scuttling out of front rooms, dragging suitcases and mattresses into back rooms. There's a curlyhaired waiter from the restaurant who comes out of several different doors in succession each time with his arm round a different giggling or sniveling young woman. Great exhibitions of dishevelment and lingerie.

Downstairs the correspondents are stirring about sleepily. An Englishman is making coffee on an electric coffeepot that speedily blows out the fuse at the same time melting the plug. A Frenchman in pajamas is distributing grapefruit to all and sundry from the door of his room.

The shells keep coming in. Nobody seems to know how to get at the coffee until a completely dressed woman novelist from Iowa takes charge of it and distributes it around in glasses with some scorched toast and halves of the Frenchman's grapefruit. Everybody gets lively and talkative until there's no more coffee left. By that time the shelling has died down a little and I go back to bed to sleep for an hour.

When I woke up again everything was quiet. There was hot water in the bathroom. From somewhere among the close-packed roofs under the window there drifted up a faint taste of sizzling olive oil. Round the balconies in the hotel everything was quiet and normal. The pleasant-faced middle-aged chambermaids were there in their neat aprons, quietly cleaning. On the lower floor the waiters were serving the morning coffee. Outside on the Plaza de Callao there were some new dents in the pavement that hadn't been there the night before. Somebody said an old newsvendor at the corner had been killed. Yesterday the doorman at the hotel got a spent machinegun bullet in the thigh.

The midmorning sunlight was hot on the Gran Via in spite of the frigid dry wind of Castilian springtime. Stepping out of doors into the bustling jangle of the city I couldn't help thinking of other Madrids I'd known, twenty years ago, eighteen years ago, four years ago. The streetcars are the same, the longnose sallow Madrileño faces are the same, with the same mixture of brown bulletheaded countrymen, the women in the dark-colored shawls don't look very different. Of course you don't see the Best People any more. They are in Portugal and Seville or in their graves. Never did see many this early anyway. The shellholes and the scars made by flying fragments and shrapnel have not changed the general look of the street, nor have the political posters pasted up on every bare piece of wall, or the fact that people are so scrappily dressed and that there's a predominance of uniforms in khaki and blue denim. It's the usualness of it that gives it this feeling of nightmare. I happen to look up at the hotel my wife and I stayed in the last time we were here. The entrance on the street looks normal and so does the department store next door, but the upper stories of the building, and the story where our room was, are shot as full of holes as a Swiss cheese.

Nobody hurries so fast along the street, and hardly anybody passes along the Gran Via these days without speeding his pace a little because it's the street where most shells fall, without pausing to glance up at the tall New Yorkish telephone building to look for new shellholes. It's funny how the least Spanish building in Madrid, the baroque tower of Wall Street's International Tel and Tel, the symbol of the colonizing power of the dollar, has become in the minds of the Madrileños the symbol of the defense of the city. Five months of intermittent shellfire have done remarkably little damage. There are a few holes and dents but nothing that couldn't be repaired in two weeks. On the side the shelling comes from, the windows of several stories have been bricked up. The pompous period ornamentation has hardly been chipped.

Inside you feel remarkably safe. The whole apparatus of the telephone service still goes on in the darkened offices. The elevators run. There's a feeling like Sunday in a New York downtown building. In their big quiet office you find the press censors, a cadaverous Spaniard and a plump little pleasant-voiced Austrian woman. They say they are going to move their office to another building. It's too much to ask the newspapermen on the regular services to duck through a barrage every time they have to file a story, and the censors are beginning to feel that Franco's gunners are out after them personally. Only yesterday the Austrian woman came back to find that a shell-fragment had set her room on fire and burned up all her shoes, and the censor had seen a woman made mincemeat of beside him when he stepped out to get a bite of lunch. It's not surprising that the censor is a nervous man; he looks underslept and underfed. He talks as if he understood, without taking too much personal pleasure in it, the importance of his position of guardian of those telephones that are the link with happier countries where the civil war is still being carried on by means of gold credits on bankledgers and munitions contracts and conversations on red plush sofas in diplomatic anterooms instead of with six-inch shells and firing squads. He doesn't give the impression of being complacent about his job. But it's hard for one who is more or less of a free agent from a country at peace to talk about many things with men who are chained to the galley benches of a war.

It's a relief to get away from the switchboards of power and walk out in the sunny streets again. If you follow the Gran Via beyond the Plaza de Callao down the hill towards the North station, stopping for a second in an excellent bookshop that's still open for business, you run into your first defense barricade. It is solidly built of cemented pavingstones laid in regular courses high as your head. That's where men will make a last stand and die if the fascists break through.

I walk on down the street. This used to be the pleasantest and quickest way to walk out into the country, down into the shady avenue along the Manzanares where the little fat church stands that has Goya's frescoes in it, and out through the iron gate into the old royal domain of El Pardo. Now it's the quickest way to the front.

At the next barricade there's a small beady-eyed sentry who smilingly asks to see my pass. He's a Cuban. As Americans we talk. Somehow there's a bond between us as coming from the western world.

There are trenches made with sandbags in the big recently finished Plaza de España. The huge straggling bronze statues of Don Quixote and Sancho Panza look out oddly towards the enemy position in Carabanchel. At a barracks building on the corner a bunch from the International Brigade is waiting for chow. French faces, Belgian faces. North of Italy faces; German exiles, bearded men blackened with the sun, young boys; a feeling of energy and desperation comes from them. The dictators have stolen their world from them; they have lost their homes, their families, their hopes of a living or a career; they are fighting back.

Up another little hill is the burned shell of the Montaña Barracks where the people of Madrid crushed the military revolt last July. Then we're looking down the broad rimedge street of the Paseo de Rusales. It used to be one of the pleasantest places in Madrid to live because the four and fivestory apartmenthouses overlooked the valley of the Manzanares and the green trees of the old royal parks and domains. Now it's no man's land. The lines cross the valley below, but if you step out on the Paseo you're in the full view of the enemy on the hills opposite, and the Moors are uncommonly good riflemen.

With considerable speed the sightseers scuttled into a house on the corner. There's the narrow hall and the row of bells and the rather grimy dark stairs of the regular Madrid apartmenthouse, but instead of the apartment of Señor Fulano de Tal on the third floor you open a ground glass door and find ... the front. The rest of the house has been blown away. The ground glass door opens on air, at your feet a well opens full of broken masonry and smashed furniture, then the empty avenue and beyond across the Manzanares, a magnificent view of the enemy. On the top floor there's a room on that side still intact; looking carefully through the half-shattered shutters we can make out trenches and outposts at the top of the hill, a new government trench halfway up the hill and closing the picture, as always, the great snowy cloud-topped barrier of the Guadarrama. The lines are quiet; not a sound. Through the glasses we can see some militiamen strolling around behind a clump of trees. After all it's lunchtime. They can't be expected to start a battle for the benefit of a couple of sightseers.

Walking back to the hotel through the empty streets of the wrecked quarter back of the Paseo we get a chance to see all the quaint possibilities of shellfire and airbombing among dwelling houses. The dollhouse effect is the commonest, the front or a side of a house sliced off and touchingly revealing parlors, bedrooms, kitchens, dining rooms, twisted iron beds dangling, elaborate chandeliers hanging over void, a piano suspended in the air, a sideboard with dishes still on it, a mirror with a gilt stucco frame glittering high up in a mass of wreckage where everything else has been obliterated.

After lunch I walk out into the northern part of the city to see the mother of an old friend of mine. It's the same apartment where I have been to visit them in various past trips. The same old maid in black with a starched apron opens the door into the dim white rooms with the old oak and walnut furniture that remind me a little of Philip II's rooms in the Escorial. My friend's mother is much older than when I saw her last, but her eyes under the handsomely arched still dark eyebrows are as fine as ever, they have the same black flash when she talks. With her is an older sister from Andalusia, a very old whitehaired woman, old beyond conversation. They have been in Madrid ever since the movement, as they call it, started. Her son has tried to get her to go to Valencia where he has duties but she doesn't like to leave her apartment and she wouldn't like the fascists to think they'd scared her into running away. Of course getting food is a nuisance but they are old now and don't need much, she says. She could even invite me to lunch if I'd come someday and wouldn't expect to get too much to eat. She tells me which of the newspapers she likes; then we fall to talking about the old days when they lived at El Pardo and her husband the doctor was alive and I used to walk out to see them through the beautiful park of liveoaks that always made me feel as if I were walking through the backgrounds of Velasquez's paintings. The park was a royal hunting preserve and was protected, in those days of the Bourbons, by mantraps and royal game keepers in Goya costumes. The deer were tame. Over the tea and the almond paste cakes we talked of walks in the sierra and skiing and visits to forgotten dried-up Castilian villages and the pleasure of looking at the construction of old buildings and pictures and the poems of Antonio Machado.

As I stepped out into the empty street I heard shelling in the distance again. As a precaution I walked over to the metrostation and took the crowded train down to the Gran Via. When I got out of the elevator at the station I found that there weren't so many people as usual walking down towards the Calle de Alcalá. There was a tendency to stand in doorways.

I was thinking how intact this part of the town was when, opposite Molinero's, the pastry shop where we used to go in the intermissions of the symphony concerts at the Price Circus and stuff ourselves with almond paste and egg yolk and whipped cream pastry in the old days, I found myself stepping off the curb into a pool of blood. Water had been sloshed over it but it remained in red puddles among the cobbles. So much blood must have come from a mule, or several people hit at one time. I walked round it. But what everybody was looking at was the division El Campesino in new khaki uniforms parading up the Calle de Alcalá with flags and Italian guns and trucks captured at Brihuega. The bugles blew and the drums rattled and the flags rippled in the afternoon sunlight and the young men and boys in khaki looked healthy and confident walking by tanned from life at the front and with color stung into their faces by the lashing wind off the sierras. I followed them into the Puerta del Sol that, in spite of the two blocks gutted by incendiary bombs, looked remarkably normal in the late afternoon bustle, full of shoeshine boys and newsvendors and people selling shoelaces and briquets and paper-covered books.

On the island in the middle where the metrostation is, an elderly man shined my shoes.

A couple of shells came in behind me far up a street. The dry whacking shocks were followed by yellow smoke and the smell of granite dust that drifted slowly past in the wind. There were no more. Groups of men chatting on the corners went on chatting. Perhaps a few more people decided to take the metro instead of the streetcar. An ambulance passed. The old man went on meticulously shining my shoes.

I began to feel that General Franco's gunner, smoking a cigarette as he looked at the silhouette of the city from the hill at

Carabanchel, was taking aim at me personally. At last the old man was satisfied with his work, and sat down on his box again to wait for another customer while I walked across the half-moonshaped square through the thinning crowd, to the old Café de Lisboa. Going in through the engraved glass swinging doors and sitting down on the faded chartreuse-colored plush and settling down to read the papers over a glass of vermouth was stepping back twenty-one years to the winter when I used to come out from my cold room at the top of a house on the other corner of the Puerta del Sol and warm up with coffee there during the morning. The papers, naturally, were full of victories; this is wartime. When I come out of the café at seven o'clock closing, and head for the Hotel Florida it's already almost dark. For some reason the city seems safer at night.

The correspondents take their meals in the basement of the Hotel Gran Via almost opposite the Telephone Building. You go in through the unlit lobby and through a sort of pantry and down some back stairs past the kitchen into a cavelike place that still has pink lights and an air of night club jippery about it. There at a long table sit the professional foreign correspondents and the young worldsaviours and the members of foreign radical delegations. At the small tables in the alcoves there tend to be militiamen and internationals on sprees and a sprinkling of young ladies of the between the sheets brigade.

This particular night there's a group of British parliamentary bigwigs, including a duchess at a special table. It's been a big day for them, because General Franco's gunners have bagged more civilians than usual. Right outside of the hotel, in fact under the eyes of the duchess, two peaceful Madrileños were reduced to a sudden bloody mess. A splatter of brains had to be wiped off the glassless revolving doors of the hotel. But stuffed with horrors as they were, the British bigwigs had eaten supper.

In fact they'd eaten up everything there was, so that when the American correspondents began to trickle in with nothing in their stomachs but whiskey and were fed each a sliver of rancid ham, there was a sudden explosion of the spirit of Seventy-six. Why should a goddamn lousy etcetera duchess eat three courses when a hardworking American newspaperman has to go hungry.

A slightly punchdrunk little ex-bantamweight prizefighter who was often in the joint wearing a snappy militiaman's uniform, and who had tended in the past to be chummy with the members of the gringo contingent who were generous with their liquor, became our champion and muttered dark threats about closing the place up and having the cooks and waiters sent to the front, lousy profiteers hiding under the skirts of the CNT who were all sons of loose women and saboteurs of the war and worse than fascists, mierda. In the end the management produced a couple of longdead whitings and a plate of spinach which they'd probably been planning to eat themselves, and the fires of revolt died down.

Still in Madrid the easiest thing to get, though it's high in price, is whiskey; so it's on that great national fooddrink that the boys at the other end of the wires tend to subsist. One of the boys who'd been there longest leaned across the table and said plaintively, "Now you won't go home and write about the drunken correspondents, will you?"

Outside the black stone city was grimly flooded with moonlight that cut each street into two oblique sections. Down the Gran Via I could see the flashlight of a patrol and hear them demanding in low voices the password for the night of whoever they met on the sidewalk.

From the west came a scattered hollow popping, soft perforations of the distant horizon. Somewhere not very far away men with every nerve tense were crawling along the dark sides of walls, keeping their heads down in trenches, yanking their right arms back to sling a hand grenade at some creeping shadow opposite. And in all the black houses the children we'd seen playing in the streets were asleep, and the grownups were lying there thinking of lost friends and family and ruins and people they'd loved and of hating the enemy and of hunger and how to get a little more food tomorrow, feeling in the numbness of their blood, in spite of whatever scorn in the face of death, the low unending smoulder of apprehension of a city under siege. And I couldn't help feeling a certain awe, as I took off my clothes in my quiet clean room with electric light and running water and a bathtub, in the face of all these people in this city. I lay down on the bed to read a book but instead stared at the ceiling and thought of the pleasant-faced middle-aged chambermaid who'd cleaned my room that morning and made the bed and put everything in order and who'd been coming regularly every day, doing the job ever since the siege began just as she'd done it in the days of Don Alfonso, and wondered where she slept and what about her family and her kids and her man, and how perhaps tomorrow coming to work there'd be that hasty loudening shriek and the street full of dust and splintered stone and instead of coming to work the woman would be just a mashed-out mess of blood and guts to be scooped into a new pine coffin and hurried away. And they'd slosh some water over the cobbles and the death of Madrid would go on. A city under siege is not a very good place for a sightseer. It's a city without sleep.

World War II

VIRGINIA COWLES

Killed in Finnish Snow

Fearful that Finland might become an "anti-Soviet" centre, Russia determined to occupy the far northern country in November 1939. Yet, as the visiting British correspondent Virginia Cowles discovered, the Finnish under Marshal Mannerheim put up heroic resistance to their giant neighbour. Not until 12 March 1940 did Finland accept the USSR's armistice terms.

Sunday Times, 4 February 1940

Here in the slender waistline of Finland some of the fiercest fighting of the war is taking place. During the last two months more than 100,000 Russian troops have crossed the frontier, in this sector alone, in repeated attempts to cut Finland in two.

The Finns have succeeded in repulsing the onslaught with some of the most spectacular fighting in history. They have annihilated entire divisions and hurled back others thirty and forty miles to the border from whence they came. They have done it not by ordinary methods of trench warfare but by desperate guerilla fighting.

To understand how the Finnish soldiers, hopelessly outnumbered, have stemmed the heavy Russian advance, you must picture a country of thick snow-covered forests and ice-bound roads. You must visualize heavily armed ski patrols sliding ghost-like through the woods, cutting their communications until entire battalions are isolated, then falling on them in furious surprise attacks. This is a war in which skis have outmanœuvred tanks, sleds competed with lorries, and knives even challenged rifles.

I have just returned from a trip to a front-line position on the Finnish-Russian frontier, where I saw the patrols at work and had my first taste of Soviet artillery fire. I left the small town which serves as General Headquarters for the north-central front with four English and American correspondents and a young Finnish Army lieutenant.

We started off with the idea of perhaps accompanying one of the Finnish border patrols on a quick jaunt into Russia and back. Not that any of us imagined that the frozen Russian landscape would prove interesting but we all thought it would be fun to step into the Soviet Union without the formality of getting a visa.

We left at four o'clock in the morning, hoping to arrive at the front before dawn, but the roads were so slippery that our car skidded into the ditch three times, which delayed us considerably but gave us a small idea of what the mechanized Russian units are up against. We arrived near the village of Suomussalmi just as dawn was breaking and here I witnessed the most ghastly spectacle I have ever seen.

It was in this sector that the Finns, a little over a month ago, annihilated two Russian divisions of approximately 30,000 men. The road along which we drove was still littered with frozen Russian corpses, and the forests on either side are now known as "Dead Man's Land". Perhaps it was the beauty of the morning that made the terrible Russian débâcle all the more ghastly when we came upon it. The rising sun had drenched the snow-covered forest, and the trees like lace Valentines, with a strange pink light that seemed to glow for miles. The landscape was marred only by the charred framework of a house; then an overturned truck and two battered tanks.

Then we turned a bend in the road and came upon the full horror of the scene. For four miles the road and forests were strewn with the bodies of men and horses; with wrecked tanks, field kitchens, trucks, gun carriages, maps, books and articles of clothing. The corpses were frozen as hard as petrified wood, and the colour of the skin was mahogany. Some of the bodies were piled on top of each other like a heap of rubbish, covered only by a merciful blanket of snow; others were sprawled against the trees in grotesque attitudes.

All were frozen in the positions in which they huddled. I saw one with his hands clasped to a wound in his stomach; another struggling to open the collar of his coat, and a third pathetically clasping a cheap landscape drawing, done in bright childish colours, which had probably been a prized possession that he had tried to save when he fled into the woods.

What these troops must have suffered in the cold is not difficult to imagine. They were wearing only ordinary knitted hoods with steel helmets over them, and none of them had his gloves on. This is accounted for by the fact that the Russians do not wear "trigger-finger" mittens such as the Finns do; they wear only ordinary mittens which they must take off to fire their rifles.

Some miles further we arrived at our destination. A white-clad sentry stepped out of the forest into the roadway and motioned us to stop. The car was backed into a clearing between the trees and as we followed our guide through the twisting paths, the woods suddenly became alive with stalwart Finnish soldiers with only their black rifles visible against the snow, moving noiselessly in and out among the trees.

The major's hut was built of logs half underground and covered with snow. The camouflage was so clever that the only indication we had was by the skis stacked up against the trees. We crawled in the shelter, which was furnished with two beds, a long desk covered with maps, and a small stove that kept the temperature at thirty degrees.

The major greeted us warmly and told us breakfast was ready; he motioned us towards a table laden with coffee, bread and butter, reindeer meat, cheese and pickled fish. A few minutes later we were interrupted by the whine of an engine, which broke into a loud roar as a Russian plane passed only a few hundred feet above our heads. The major said the Russian planes patrolled the forests for several hours each day and often did a considerable amount of machine-gunning. "That's what we want," he said. "Planes."

Then he asked us if we thought the outside world would send any to Finland and searched our faces eagerly for our replies. "If only," he murmured, "it were possible for some kind old ladies to knit us some aeroplanes and crochet us some anti-tank guns. We should be very happy."

When we asked him if there was any possibility of our sneaking across the frontier into Russia he smiled and said he would send us up to the observation post, where we could have a look at the situation, and if we still wanted to go, it was ours for the asking. He then detailed a captain to look after us.

The captain's hut was some distance away; it was made of beaver-board built around the trunk of a tree so that the smoke from the stove would be diffused by the thick branches. The captain was a gay fellow who showed us with great relish the huge Russian samovar that he had captured in the Suomussalmi battle. He also had a pair of field glasses he had taken from a Russian officer, but his most prized possession was a machine-gun from a Russian tank. He said that every time a plane went by he took a pot shot at it, adding that it wasn't exactly his business but with the gun so handy it was difficult to resist.

The captain led us through the woods to the observation post. It was some distance away and we were accompanied by a ski patrol of eight men equipped with rifles and wicked-looking machine pistols. They slipped in and out through the trees like ghosts, managing their skis with astonishing agility. One moment they slipped behind the trees and we thought they were lost; a few seconds later they were on the path in front of us.

The observation post consisted merely of a shallow pit dug in the snow; in it there was an observer with a pair of field glasses and a telephone. But we did not need glasses to see the Soviet Union. Only three hundred yards away across an icebound lake, lay the frozen landscape of Russia.

We had been in the pit only a few minutes when the Finnish soldiers in our rear opened up artillery fire. A fountain of ice and snow shot up as several shells fell in the lake. The observation officer corrected the range and soon they were disappearing neatly into the trees on the other side. The Russians were not slow to reply, and a few minutes later the air resounded to the nasty whine of three-inch shells, and the pine trees were singing with the moan of grenades and the dull thud of mortars.

Twice, tree branches chipped by grenades fell down on us, and when two shells landed uncomfortably close, wounding two

Finnish soldiers, the captain declared we had better go back to the hut.

Before we left he gave us a cup of tea. While we were drinking it a husky Finnish soldier crawled into the shelter. His cheeks were red with the cold but his blue eyes shone with excitement. He had just come in from a five-hour patrol behind the Russian lines and had penetrated as far back as three miles. He took out a map and explained to the captain the various changes in the enemy positions.

We learned that the boy was a farmer in ordinary life, but had distinguished himself as one of the bravest men in the patrol. The captain said that during the Suomussalmi battle he had destroyed a tank by jumping on top of it, prising the lid open with a crow-bar, and throwing a hand grenade inside.

When the boy departed another Finnish soldier came into the hut to say that a Russian patrol of two hundred men was heading toward the Finnish lines. The captain ordered him to start with a detachment and meet them on the way.

We could see that things were going to be pretty busy soon, so we decided that it was best to leave. Outside the hut a group of soldiers were already strapping on their rifles and adjusting their skis. When we shook hands with the captain he said: "Well, what about Russia? If you want to join the patrol just starting out, you have my permission."

We thanked him very much, but I for one said I was quite happy where I was.

World War II

LELAND STOWE

Too Little, Too Late: War in Norway

Norway sought to remain neutral in the Second World War, but in the morning of 9 April 1940 the Germans launched a full-scale invasion of the country, principally to gain control of the iron-ore port of Kiruna and secure more Atlantic bases for their U-boats. Overwhelmed, the Norwegian government requested military aid from Britain and France.

New York Post, 26 April 1940

Gaeddede, Norwegian-Swedish Frontier, April 25 – Here is the first and only eyewitness report on the opening chapter of the British expeditionary troops' advance in Norway north of Trondheim. It is a bitterly disillusioning and almost unbelievable story.

The British force which was supposed to sweep down from Namsos consisted of one battalion of Territorials and one battalion of the King's Own Royal Light Infantry. These totaled fewer than 1,500 men. They were dumped into Norway's deep snows and quagmires of April slush without a single anti-aircraft gun, without one squadron of supporting airplanes, without a single piece of field artillery.

They were thrown into the snows and mud of 63 degrees north latitude to fight crack German regulars – most of them veterans of the Polish invasion – and to face the most destructive of modern weapons. The great majority of these young Britishers averaged only one year of military service. They have already paid a heavy price for a major military blunder which was not committed by their immediate command, but in London.

Unless they receive large supplies of anti-air guns and adequate reinforcements within a very few days, the remains of these two British battalions will be cut to ribbons.

Here is the astonishing story of what has happened to the gallant little handful of British expeditionaries above Trondheim:

After only four days of fighting, nearly half of this initial BEF contingent has been knocked out – either killed, wounded or captured. On Monday, these comparatively inexperienced and incredibly under-armed British troops were decisively defeated. They were driven back in precipitate disorder from Vist, three miles south of the bomb-ravaged town of Steinkjer.

As I write, it is probable that the British field headquarters has been withdrawn northward and that the British vanguard has been compelled to evacuate one or several villages. Steinkjer was occupied by the Germans Tuesday.

I was in Steinkjer Monday evening just before the British lines were blasted to pieces. I was the only newspaper correspondent to enter the burning town and the only correspondent to visit British advance headquarters and to pass beyond to the edge of the front's heavy firing zone.

A score of buildings were flaming fiercely on the town's waterfront from a bombing two hours earlier. In the midst of the smoky ruins I heard machine-gun cracking at high tempo in the hills just beyond the town. Shell explosions rapped the valley regularly with angry echoes. This was the first sustained battle between German and British troops on Norwegian soil. Already the conflict was snarling hot.

A battalion of 600 territorials was fighting desperately to hold Vist, the point of their farthest southwest advance toward Trondheim. As Monday's twilight closed they were completely done in. For hours they had been torn and broken under the terrible triple onslaught of German infantry, trimotored bombers and naval artillery firing from destroyers at the head of Breitstadfjord.

Within two hours the British troops were in flight. They had no chance whatever of standing off from bombs and three- or six-inch shells with nothing but Bren machine guns and rifles.

Before 11 o'clock that night I talked with the nerve-shattered survivors of the British battalion. We found two truckloads of them several miles above their headquarters and on their way north away from the front.

One of the officers told me that the battalion had lost more than 200 in killed and that one entire company had been captured. He could not estimate the number of missing, but said that perhaps 150 of the battalion's 600 might be rallied later on.

"We have simply been massacred," he declared. "It is the planes. We have no planes to fight back with, and we have no anti-aircraft guns. It is just like the Russians against the Finns, only worse – and we are the Finns."

A subofficer greeted me gratefully when he learned that I was a reporter.

"For God's sake tell them we have got to have airplanes and anti-aircraft guns," he pleaded.

"We were completely at the mercy of the Jerries. Their bombers flew low over us, at 500 feet. They scattered us. We were up to our hips in snow.

"Then they dropped signal flares so their artillery knew our positions. Last night our wounded were crying in the woods, but we couldn't get to them or do anything. We had not even got proper clothes to fight with in the snow. Without white capes the Jerries just spotted us and mowed us down every time the bombers drove us out."

Paul Melander, a Swedish photographer, and I saw these things, together. We were the only newsmen to spend nearly 24 hours in the British sector and to reach the edge of the firing zone on that front.

Although almost exhausted from lack of sleep, the British officers maintained remarkable calm. But this was a small military machine with vital cogs missing. Able to bomb at will, the Germans had seriously disrupted the organization of the little British expeditionary vanguard in their first four days at the front.

Forty British fighting planes at present could probably clear the skies over the entire Allied Norwegian fighting zones and all vital sections of their rear-guard north of Trondheim. The British troops are praying that these fighters will arrive soon before it is too late.

Following the British defeat near Vist, we were told that Norwegian troops had been compelled to take over virtually all the north front above Trondheim. North of Trondheim the military initiative is now held by alert, aggressive and first-class German troops. It is guaranteed by Nazi war planes which are flying constantly at less than 1,000 feet over the Allies' Norwegian sector and which bomb their objectives as easily as a marksman picks off clay pigeons.

Three times in one day German planes roared over my head at only 500 or 600 feet and twice I was in buildings where key Norwegian commands were located. I thought the Nazis' espionage service – with its formidable network throughout Scandinavia – had already betrayed these locations. Providentially, this had not happened and no bombs were dropped. So these two Norwegian control centers escaped. But without the Allies' aircraft and anti-air guns such miracles cannot endure for long.

This is merely an illustration of the tremendous initiative which has been handed to the Germans north of Trondheim by one of the costliest and most inexplicable military bungles in modern British history.

It has been handed to them by those high British authorities who thrust 1,500 young Territorials into the snow and mud below Namsos ten days ago without a single anti-air gun or a single piece of artillery.

World War II

ALEXANDER WERTH

Exodus

The "Phoney War" came to an abrupt end in May 1940, when
Hitler sent his army sweeping into France and the Low Countries.
The Russian-born Werth was the war correspondent of the Manchester *Guardian* during the invasion, his eyewitness accounts of
which were published in book form as *The Last Days of Paris*. He
later covered the Eastern Front for Reuters and the *Sunday Times*.

The Last Days of Paris, 1940

Wednesday, 12th June

The last three days have been crowded with such a mass of
experiences and emotions that I haven't had time to settle
down to write, nor the ability to see the wood for the trees. I
have left Paris – perhaps for ever. This is the *débâcle* of France.
I hope to God England can continue the fight. I am at Tours,
the "provisional capital" of France. I sit in a little open-air café
outside the "Ministry of Information" in the ramshackle old
building of the former post office, in a small, untidy, provincial
side street of Tours. There's a 1918 war memorial – a naked
lady with a helmet – in the middle of the square, and next to it,
a *pissotière*. The square is crowded with cars with Paris number
plates. The sky is dull and grey. Next to me are two Frenchmen
of the *café de commerce* type. One of them has just mentioned
Gambetta – thought it was perhaps only the rue Gambetta.
But – Gambetta and Tours? Only does the situation present
itself in the same way now? Are the French still capable of a

lutte à outrance? I am not blaming the French soldiers, poor devils. There's been some appalling mismanagement of France's whole military policy for years; now the wretched *poilus* have to pay the price for it – for all the luxury of the easy-going Radical-Socialist Republic; though heaven knows, their spirit does not in most cases seem to be what it was in '14; or at Verdun. Then also the Germans had superiority in numbers and equipment; and yet—. There was a patriotic self-sacrificing spirit then which is often lacking to-day. The men think too much of their families, and the women weep too much. War to them is too much of a personal calamity. And their spirit has been weakened by propaganda. Propaganda doesn't work in peaceful surroundings; but it begins to work once you are scared and in grave danger. And then there was, of course, Russia in 1914, and that made a big difference – both materially and morally. But for the Russian advance into East Prussia Paris might well have fallen in 1914.

But never mind about that; I've written it before. What I want to write about is my last day in Paris, and the Exodus.

And so, here I am at Tours – La Touraine, garden of France, land of Rabelais, land of Descartes and all that. And alas! land of Chautemps.

That last day in Paris . . . We had for some days been considering the possibility of the fall of Paris within a very short time. On Saturday there was a wave of optimism at the War Office. On Sunday everything changed. The Boches had crossed the Aisne, were pushing south of Soissons; motorized columns were advancing on Rouen. On Sunday the situation became critical.

There's a Press conference at Prouvost's – the new Minister of Information. I can't be bothered going to it. Gilbert later tells me he talked some platitudes about Anglo-French co-operation. I go instead to see old Peter and Luba. She produces coffee and cherries. I stay half an hour, talk chiefly about my own troubles, though I know that if I have to leave Paris, *their* troubles will be a lot worse than mine. But I leave in the expectation of seeing them again. Poor "Uncle" Peter! I walk into the street – the old street I have known for so many years. I meet Jeanne Lefèvre and Manon at the corner of the Avenue. Jeanne is carrying about a little valise with Anatole France's letters, and with a written and a printed copy of the speech he made at her wedding; she was told these manuscripts were worth a lot of money. She is carrying them about – just in case. They are her only valuable possessions. Even so, she thinks me panicky and says the Germans "certainly won't come to Paris." She tells me, Jules, her son, fighting in the Ardennes has just got the *croix de guerre*. The café with a lot of people sitting about on that golden Sunday afternoon, looks strangely normal. I drive back to the office in a taxi. Have dinner with Gilbert at the rue des Sts-Pères restaurant. Forget what we ate. I decide to move to the flat below the office early next morning; it's no use staying on at the hotel, where the phone has been cut off.

I am very worried, and can't sleep. I get up, and sit at the window, breathing the fresh air from the Seine. There is a starlit sky over the Louvre. I look out to see the dome of the Institute shrouded in darkness. The suitcase is packed. I get up early; and after the *petit déjeuner* I go in search of a taxi. I had stood at the window for some time before that; there was a tremendous rush of cars along the *quai* – and not a single free taxi among them. All the taxis and cars are loaded with luggage and mattresses. I go out and stand on the *quai* for a long time, waving stupidly at the passing traffic. Annette, the little maid with glasses, goes off to the Gare d'Orsay to see what she can find. I go and stand at the rue de Beaune corner. All in vain. In the end I decide to cross the river; and at last I find a taxi on the Pont du Louvre, and come back in it to the hotel. The *patronne* weeps bitterly as I say good-bye. The daughter, with a little baby with violet eyes in her arms, also cries. Oh, not for my sake; but because of the circumstances that make me leave Paris. She is still without news of her husband. What other unhappiness is still in store for these poor women – these noble, sensitive, unhappy women of France?

The bright summer sun shines on the *quais*, which glitter dazzlingly. I go to the office with a Polish officer from the hotel who retains the taxi in order to go on in it. I wait for a long time for Gilbert. Downstairs, in the flat, I play some Chopin preludes – absurd?

Picquart has just come from the Press conference at which Colonel Thomas failed to turn up; no explanation was given. Picquart strongly suspects that the Colonel has buzzed off to Tours. Everybody, everybody is buzzing off. The office manager, I found, had buzzed off at six in the morning, telling his assistant to settle everything – money, wages, etc. He said he would send a car for him at ten. Of course he didn't send any car. I found the wretched assistant frantic with worry about what to do.

Kolya arrives. He is full of projects. He wants to go south but hasn't got a *sauf conduit*. He doesn't see why he shouldn't be all right under the Huns; only he rather hates the thought of it. He talks of going to Périgueux, but he hasn't any money except 1,000 francs. I give him 500 francs more and my portable typewriter which he thinks he may sell; though I really need it myself – but I haven't anything else to give him. He is brave in the face of this appallingly uncertain future. I tell him I probably shan't leave till to-morrow. I wish I could go and see old Peter again; but I think I may still manage it to-night, if we stay till to-morrow. In fact, I don't know whether I mayn't stay on several more days. And yet I feel there isn't long left.

I send a short cable to the paper saying roughly that I know nothing about the war, but that Paris is "away melting". Gilbert arrives at last, and says he may give me "another twenty-four hours grace". We go to Pierre's for lunch in the Place Gaillon. It's a hot day; we sit outside. I tell Gilbert it's an expensive place. "Oh," he says, "it may be your last lunch in Paris." It is terribly hot. We eat *œufs à la gelée*, cold meat and salad and have some Alsace wine and Perrier.

After a morning visit from "Aunt" Sonya, who insists on my taking an ikon which, she says, has miraculous virtues (her father-in-law was preserved by it from a bullet in the Russo-Turkish war of '77 – bullets can't have been very potent in those days!), we decide she'll come again in the morning. She cries, and we say good-bye. What happened after that? I don't remember that crazy day very clearly. Oh, yes, at four Gilbert announced that the censors in the rue Edouard VII had departed. He went off to see Comert to argue – obviously to no purpose. Kerillis in the *Epoque* in the morning said he wasn't as lucky as most papers – he didn't know if he could carry on *en province*. All the other papers have cleared out of Paris – though the *Paris-Soir* is still appearing to-day – for the last time. "We are paying a terrible price for past errors," Kerillis writes, "*mais la France ne peut pas mourir.*"

It is terribly hot. I don't know if we are going to leave to-night or not. Probably not. The censorship has gone; there is nothing to do but to wait. I dump a few possessions into the suitcase – among them three books: *Candide* and Gogol's *Dead Souls*, and Gide's *Journal*; and I put Péguy's *La France* in my pocket. I wrap up the Matisse; but there is no room in the case for the Derain; it'll just have to stay. Pity. At the office I look at my desk; there are papers and letters in the drawers; nothing compromising; so I don't even bother destroying them. I look out of the window, and have a terrible longing to go for another walk through the familiar Paris streets. I wish I could go to the Left bank; but it's too far. I go out and walk down the Boulevard des Italiens, a little beyond the Carrefour Drouot. Pillot's shop is still packed with shoes; there are crowds of people in the street; even a cinema is still open. Strange. Cars, though not as many as in the morning, are rushing past. It is hot and sunny – a perfect summer day in Paris. At the rue Laffitte I stop and look for a long time at the Sacré Cœur in the distance – white and pure against the blue summer sky. I walk back along the Boulevard Haussmann, and sit down outside the *brasserie*. The fat waiter thinks the Boche will be in Paris within forty-eight hours; the *patron* has left Paris, and has left him in charge. "I know how to deal with these *salauds*," he says. "I was in Germany as a war prisoner. *On les aura quand-même*," he adds a trifle doubtfully. I see Kolya pass and call out. He is greatly excited – he has just got 1,000 francs from his employer as a special concession, though the man owes him 8,000. He thinks he will now be able to go to the south of France. Vernetti, the bank manager, arrives; he says the bank is being evacuated to Cognac, but *les caisses* will remain open until—

Back to the office where Gilbert definitely decides to go off tonight. The Germans, he says, are already at Pontoise. We ring up Gaby and Marion to tell them to come to the office at once. Gilbert sends the car for them. They arrive soon after.

A moving good-bye to Kolya; poor devil. I ring up old Mrs MacDonald; she says they were promised a lift in a car; but the people have left without them. They'll have to stay on in Paris. With communications with England cut off, God knows what they'll live on. At seven we learn that Italy has declared war; we take it as a small detail in the general disaster, except that Marion grows indignant and calls them swine.

Also a phone call from Jeanne Lefèvre. She is bewildered.

She was told nobody would be allowed to leave Paris after midnight. She has no car, no conveyance of any kind. "Manon and I will just have to walk," she says with dismal determination. "Only, there's Sam," she adds. "I'll take him to the chemist, and get him to poison him." Sam is my cairn terrier I had passed on to her last year. I had forgotten about him.

Oh, that departure from Paris. To begin with, the car, which Gilbert had sent on some errand to Le Vésinet at 6.30, failed to return. Gilbert stood agitatedly looking out of the office window at all the cars driving into the street. There were many Citroëns, but not ours. Le Vésinet was only fifteen miles away; the car had gone at 6.30 and now it was 8 o'clock, 8.15, 8.30. Had Cosandier been stopped from coming back into Paris? Before leaving he had wondered if something like that mightn't happen to him. At last he arrived. He looked perturbed. The car had got stuck, he said, in a mass of troops – ragged, tired, demoralized-looking, many of them drunk, all of them without rifles, drifting into Paris. A routed army.

Dusk was falling over Paris when we went downstairs to the car with our cases. The concierge, bewildered, distressed-looking, asked if we were *really* going away. What should *she* do, she asked. Her husband was at Poitiers, her child in the Pyrénées. I felt *gené*, guilty, I gave her another 100 francs for no particular reason – it felt such a silly inadequate gesture. I felt a kind of lump in my throat, and wanted to kiss her good-bye, but Gilbert would have thought it ridiculous. It is true I *had* advised her to go south to join her child; and yet – what silly gratuitous advice. It would have been easy for her if she had had a car; and then she said she couldn't leave her *loge*, without giving notice; and her husband's clothes were there, what would she do about *them*? We drove off, Gilbert, Gaby and Marion in the back seat, Cosandier and I in front. It was getting dark and the streets looked deserted. We drove along the Boulevard Haussmann, past the Printemps and St-Augustin and up the Boulevard Malesherbes to a modern block of flats near the Porte Champerret, where Gaby had to collect some things. On the way we passed a crowd of ragged soldiers, many of them drunk, and shouting "*à bas la guerre!*" And then we drove through streets and avenues I did not know, and through the Bois de Boulogne, deserted at that hour, to Auteuil, where in some avenue we tried to refuel. There were queues of cars at the petrol pumps – that is at those which were still open, for most had closed down. At one of the pumps the man refused to serve us because his arm was too sore after all these days of ceaseless work.

There was a red sunset, and an unusual black haze over Paris. And then we drove on through Boulogne, across St-Cloud bridge and up the hill to the block of modern flats where Gilbert lives. At St-Cloud we were going to join the two other cars, both belonging to a Mrs A, a friend of Gilbert's. With her were travelling her son and daughter. She was going to drive one of the cars, Cosandier the other, and Gilbert was going to drive ours. When would the caravan be ready to leave? Gilbert phoned Mrs A and it was agreed we'd leave about midnight. We helped Gilbert to pack his cases, and to wrap up some of his little Chinese jade things of which he is very proud. He has lots of them; but had to leave most of them, and especially all the bigger things behind. When the cases were packed, I said: "Now, let's go and have just another look at our Paris." There is a magnificent view of Paris from Gilbert's St-Cloud terrace up on the hill. Normally you see the Bois de Vincennes, and the Panthéon, and St Sulpice and the Invalides and the Eiffel Tower, and, in the foreground, the capital Bois de Boulogne. But this was the uncanniest moment in all my experience. As we went out on to the terrace and looked down on our Paris for the last time, we saw – nothing. A black fog had hidden it from our view. The smoke screen the Germans had used for crossing the Seine further west had apparently drifted over Paris.

We were all hungry and tired; and proceeded to make supper. There was a strange feeling in that house. I could have stolen anything, and nobody would have cared, least of all the owner. I *did* steal a piece of *port-salut* and wrapped it in a napkin, one of a set. Who cared?

It was pitch black at St-Cloud. One of Mrs A's cars had a faulty tyre, and had to be taken to the garage; which took a lot of time. At last, after midnight, all three cars were downstairs; Mrs A's cars crammed with stuff. Somewhere very near, the guns were going hard. "Big stuff," Gilbert remarked. A panicky man's voice in the neighbouring house shouted about our headlights – "*éteignez les phares, nom de Dieu, mais éteignez donc les phares.*"

At last we drove off. It was 12.40 a.m on Tuesday, 11th June
– Marion's birthday. We drank a gulp of red wine to celebrate.
We drove along a wooded road on to Versailles passing long
rows of French Army lorries on the way. At Versailles the traffic
jam was terrific. Near the statue of Louis XIV outside the Château, we were held up by the military police. Army lorries pass
in endless number – we have to wait. Darkness, a few lights,
shouts of the military police, the rumbling of thousands of
engines; we move on at top gear in jolts of one or two yards at a
time. I have to look back all the time to see if the second car is
following us. With its cycles and mattresses it looks strangely
tank-like in the darkness – the cycle wheels sticking out like
guns. Evacuation is like a funeral. All the bother of the practical
arrangements blunts you during a large part of the time to the
tragedy, to the loss of something you loved. It's worse than any
bother with undertakers. We crawled on slowly, with constant
jolts, to St-Cyr. Near the railway bridge there was a bomb crater
in the road which had just been repaired.

In the midst of all this muddle we lose the last car; we discover its disappearance while we are in a stretch of flat country,
on a road, with a railway viaduct alongside on the left. "Hardly
a very good spot," says Gilbert, looking at the viaduct. It's a still,
misty night. The frogs are croaking their heads off in the marsh
to the right of the road. We have to wait till dawn. Cosandier
wants gulps of red wine, which I give him from an open bottle
of Pommard I took from Gilbert's kitchen. Why leave it to the
Boche? At last dawn comes. The cars driving past become more
numerous, also a lot of lorries evacuating firms from Paris.
Cosandier and Gilbert go a few miles back to look for Mme A;
no sign of her. Then the car in which they went has a puncture.
I am mildly amused – fatalistic. It's all so absurd. Sitting beside
a marsh with croaking frogs at 5 a.m. some twenty miles outside
Paris when we had hoped to get to Tours at 8 a.m. seems as
absurd as the whole situation. We missed the relatively open
roads at night time. Lots of cars begin to pass; also many people
on cycles with wretched little bundles tied to the handlebars. An
empty train rattles along the viaduct towards Paris. At last we
get a move-on. But at Rambouillet there is another appalling
jam. We take over an hour to get through the town. The local
people at the windows look out with a kind of bewildered air at

the endless procession of luggage-laden cars. The bakeries and *bistrots* are opening up. It's about 6 o'clock. The run from Rambouillet to Chartres is a little easier – I take the Péguy out of my pocket. Here it is:

> Cette immense Beauce, grande comme la mer, triste autant et aussi profonde comme la mer; cet océan de blés ... une beauté parfaitement horizontale, sans un défaut, sans une vilenie, sans un manque, sans une petitesse: le pays des véritables couchers du soleil.

It was like that, on that morning when we drove from Rambouillet to Chartres. The roads were, here and there, blocked by gates built of rough stone; as if the tanks couldn't go straight across the *océan de blé*! (which indeed they did a few days later). And in the wood through which we drove, there were soldiers along the road – watching out for parachutists. Had there been any? They didn't know. "*On dit ...*" Most of them looked morose and worried – only one of them looked martial with the rifle pointed towards the wood, as though ready to charge. "*Ça a commencé hier à onze heures du matin*," one of them said about the procession of refugee cars. We passed through wide fields of green wheat. No doubt for the Boche to eat when it's ripe.

At length we reached Chartres. From the road we entered we couldn't see the cathedral: the square where we stopped looked like any square in any second-rate provincial town. The center of the square was crowded with cars. There was an unhealthy bustle in the streets, and a kind of irritably despairing atmosphere in the café. People were coming and going, cursing the waiters and the waiters snapping back. The old red-faced woman behind the counter looked in a hostile kind of way at all new arrivals. She didn't care to see them served. We waited ages for coffee; and then for the *croissants* – good and warm – which had to be fetched from the bakery. We washed at a tap in the yard, and the *patronne* made a row because Mrs A's young son was going to use a table napkin for his hands. "*Quel toupet*," she screamed. In the midst of all this anger, anxiety, irritation, Marion and I walked out and looked from afar at the cathedral of Chartres, so calm, so serene, so eternal – perhaps. The Boches at Chartres – it somehow seemed even more intolerable than in

Paris. We wanted to go up to the cathedral, but there was no time. Only, as we were driving out, we got a full view of it again in all its slightly lopsided beauty. It brought a lump to my throat.

We had tried to get a paper at Chartres, but in vain; there was none to be got. This general ignorance partly accounted for the nervousness; and gave birth to endless rumours – as will be seen from the next bit. The road from Chartres to Tours was much easier. At times Gilbert reached 100 and even 110 km per hour along that long straight road from Chartres to Châteaudun. I wish I could describe Châteaudun, Vendôme and the rest of the towns we passed in this "garden of France" on that lovely summer morning; but I remember them only faintly. What I do remember is the expression on the faces – morose, dejected. Even the children seemed dejected. The soldiers were the worst of all; and it was a pleasant relief to pass a party of British soldiers washing and shaving and having their morning tea out of tin goblets. They looked pink and healthy, and waved cheerfully, and scarcely seemed to realize what was going on. And then we stopped at a village with rose creepers on the walls of the houses; and Cosandier, who was in the front car, came dashing to ours, waving frantically and shouting: "Congratulations! Russia and Turkey have declared war on Germany." He had been told so by a crowd of people chatting in the street. Somebody had heard it on the wireless. (Comert later remarked that the Fifth Column was deliberately spreading optimist rumours so as to create subsequent disappointment and discouragement.) We couldn't believe it, and yet we were desperately anxious to believe it, and Gilbert and I clearly went on day-dreaming, imagining all sorts of combinations. "Even if true it wouldn't save Paris," I said. "No, but it could save the spirit of France," said Gilbert. We watched people's faces – was there any change? No – not really – and yet we imagined there was a *little* change. Only, as we passed a crowd of French soldiers one of them shouted: "*Les Boches sont-ils à Paris?*" How readily they were assuming their defeat! We also stopped – I think it was at Châteaudun – to get some gadget repaired in the first car. We still wanted confirmation about Russia. An old woman said she hadn't heard of that, but she had heard that America had declared war on Italy. "*Mais on ne sait rien au juste. Ah, c'est bien triste, Monsieur.*" When I remarked that there were lots of British troops about, she said bitterly: "*Oh, non, pas assez, pas assez.*" There seemed quite a bit of anti-British feeling in the provinces. In the market place they were still selling cotton goods and other odds and ends.

Before reaching Tours we passed an aerodrome – it had been badly bombed. We crossed the Loire bridge. The streets at Tours were infernally crowded, with cars, buses, lorries and little blue tram-cars. We crawled along the main street – the rue Nationale – and got in the end to the Hotel Metropole. Mme A and her daughter had arrived a few hours earlier by a different road. None of us had slept for a second in the last thirty-six hours, and we were all very tired. Taking the line of least resistance we went to a grocer's shop marked *products coloniaux*, in a side street near the hotel and bought lots of tinned food which we took to the corner café. Gilbert grimly remarked: "Well, I never thought I'd be a refugee." There was no sleeping accommodation anywhere, except that Mme A had got a room for herself at the Metropole. Part of this hotel, as many other hotels, had been commandeered. Later I had a talk with the proprietor of the Metropole, a nice old Frenchman, tall, with a drooping white moustache, and looking like Senator Henri Roy, who admitted that he was ignoring the requisition order as hard as he could – the requisitioned rooms were not paid for in cash, and he didn't know when, if ever, he'd get the official IOUs cashed; so he preferred regular customers. As a result we all got rooms in the end – only not on the first night.

After our lunch at the café, Gilbert and I went in search of the Ministry of Information. What a mess! Nobody knew anything. In a small side street called the rue Gambetta there is a derelict old building, the white stucco walls gone all grey and black with old age. It's the former post office and has still *Postes – Télégraphes – Téléphones* written on the front. Opposite is another decrepit dirty building of the Bourse de Travail. In these two the censorship, the Ministry of Information, the Press rooms, etc., were concentrated. As we arrived, we met André Glarner who informed us that he was arranging a Press workroom on the top floor of the post office building – with school desks for typewriters, etc. We went up the winding stair inside a turret to what looked like a large attic. The place was filthy with paper débris and sawdust. A few packets of typewriting paper and Government circulars were lying about. There was nowhere to sit. A few workmen were scrubbing the floor and the dirty old walls. On the floor below Press Wireless was being set up; the only means of communicating with England was to wire via New York at 8d a word! Next to it were the French censors, among them my friend the captain from the rue Edouard VII, who had said two days before that France would go on fighting even if the capital had to be shifted in stages to Tizi-Ouzou. Sleepy as I was, I wrote a short message to the paper but the censor had been given a new *consigne* – all messages "dealing with the war" must go first to the French and British military censors. These I found downstairs. There was long argument on whether Tours should be called Tours or "somewhere in France". They insisted on the latter. All right – it didn't matter to me; but how ridiculous: the German wireless had already for the last two days been making fun of Tours, "the provisional, the very provisional capital of France".

We hung aimlessly about the street for a while. In the little openair café in the square with the war memorial and the *pissotíre* we ran into Knickerbocker, and Edgar Mowrer, and Eve Curie, and Handler and Heinzen of the UP. We looked for Comert, at the post office building and at the Bourse de Travail. Nobody knew where he was. There was a dreadful *pagaie* everywhere. However, we thought, let's give them a chance. We went back to the hotel in the car through a howling mob of traffic. Fripton of the Ministry of Information was very cordial and obliging – arranged with the hotel proprietor that the chauffeur and I should sleep in the lounge downstairs; while Marion and Gaby got a room to themselves, and Gilbert got a bed in Bob Stockfish's room (Bob's a director of some English firm in Paris). Fripton also let me use his private bathroom, after which I felt much better. We arranged to join him Chez Buré, a famous *tourangeau* restaurant, with one of those wooden *auberge* fronts. It rained like hell; and there was a *bagarre* in the street, a *garde mobile* bullying a soldier about something or other; I don't know what happened, but there was a large excited crowd watching the row and the yelling went on for a long time. We sat at a long table in the *auberge* Buré – good soup and some kind of *bœuf à la mode*, and strawberries, and something else; and a lot of Chinon wine. Fripton, who sat opposite me, was uproariously jovial, parodying my *New Statesman* articles from Paris and calling his predecessors at the Ministry of Information a lot of names. He thought the French were sunk, but that England would carry on. His exuberant joviality was thoroughly distasteful to me; I could not help thinking of Paris; Paris and Chartres cathedral. Stockfish, the fat business man, was in the meantime behaving like somebody out of Fielding – slapping the waitress's behind and insisting on kissing her. And then, all of a sudden, and without any sirens blowing, the lights were put out, and we continued our meal by candlelight – with a solitary candle for the lot of us. Guns were firing. "*C'est la DCA*," somebody said.

I went out into the street. The torrential rain in the square, crowded with cars, was continuing. Nothing could be heard but the booming of guns. After a while, the party departed in their respective cars – the fat bloke yelling *merde* at the police who were ordering him not to put on the headlights. Gilbert, who was with the Fripton crew, later said their joviality soon vanished when they realized that it was a real air-raid. Cosandier, completely exhausted, and I went to sleep on the lounge sofas. The women went upstairs. The firing of guns had ceased by this time. Somebody said that the Boche planes had been looking for the bridge over the Loire but couldn't find it on that rainy night. Were they still bothering to destroy French communications; did they still think the French were going to put up a good fight?

I slept soundly; and had a good breakfast. Then out into the street. I was late for Colonel Thomas's conference on the second floor of the Bourse de Travail, but was told by that Egyptian working on the *Chicago Daily News* what he had said. The Boche were somewhere around Senlis; they had crossed the Seine and also the Marne. The fighting in Champagne was very heavy; they were trying to cut off the Maginot troops from the rest. In other words, to push down into Alsace. Gilbert thought he might run up to Paris in the car. I thought it was crazy; but as a matter of prestige, thought I might go with him. I didn't send the paper anything that morning. Went back to the hotel instead and walked with Marion down the rue Nationale and across the Loire Bridge. We sat on the bridge and recalled the passage about the silver Loire in *St Joan*. We also observed that the Loire wasn't an obstacle of any sort – as shallow as a ditch, with islands and sandbanks in the middle. We walked back along the rue Nationale. The shops were crammed with food of every variety, fancy goods, etc., and the procession of refugee cars was getting thicker and thicker. The cafés were crowded with familiar faces – journalists, politicians, etc. They all looked pleased to be here – out of Paris. They were almost jovial. At first sight, the whole place with its overcrowded hotels and its packed café terraces looked as though a Radical Congress were on at Tours. It was a kind of comic nightmare. To make the frivolous picture complete, even Lop, the village idiot of the République des Camarades, was there, toddling along on his flat feet, and proclaiming that he would still save France. It occurred to me that things couldn't be worse if Lop *had* been Dictator of France these last few years.

Met Lechon of the Polish Embassy. He was full of optimism. "*L'état major est très confiant*," he said. Also ran into that dark chap from *Le Jour* – (a nasty bit of work, like a French screen villain with large hooked nose and little black moustache) – is his name Delpeyrou? "*La guerre sera finie en November – la victoire sera gagnée sur la Loire.*" I looked at him doubtfully. Was he pulling my leg? What was the use of talking such tripe? He added that if only ten British divisions could be sent to Paris at once, even Paris would still be saved.

The meeting place with the Gilbert gang was in the café opposite the hotel. As I was going there I ran into a familiar face, M Jacquin, one of the old *huissiers* of the Chamber of Deputies. No easy optimism about him – "*Quel massacre, quel massacre de la jeunesse française*," he said, with tears in his eyes. "*Ces Allemands, ce ne sont pas des hommes, ce sont des bêtes féroces.*" He seemed convinced of the Germans' invincibility – though he added, not very convincingly: "*Ah, on finira par les avoir quand-même.*" He cursed Daladier and the politicians generally, and the ballyhoo in the Press. He said he was glad his son was only seventeen; but the chief *huissier's* elder son – the fat one – was in the army, and he was very anxious about him. M Jacquin was staying at Vouvray and had come into town for the day to buy some shoes. He did not think Parliament would assemble at tours: "*Tout ça c'est de la foutaise*," he said. "We shan't stay long at Tours." I bought him a Vittel-cassis.

Crawling from one café to another, from one restaurant to another, was an all-day occupation at Tours. There was really little else to do. One just talked and listened to talk. What a life!

We all went to a restaurant in the rue Nationale for lunch. It was very crowded but in the end we got seats; hors d'œuvres, and fish and roast beef and strawberries. There was certainly no shortage of food at Tours. After lunch I went to the Press place; typed a short message to the paper, handed it to the British censor, a small stupid-looking youngster in uniform who promised to pass it on to Press Wireless. Hung about aimlessly at the censorship place and in the café in front of the *pissotière*. Saw Reggie Maynard, who, as usual, looked jovially pessimistic.

There was a full moon over Tours that night when we returned to the hotel. "If there isn't an air-raid to-night I'm a Dutchman," said Gilbert, looking at the sky. And somebody at the hotel said the German wireless had announced that Tours would be bombed to-night. Gaby and Marion and I went out for a stroll. Everything was still. We bumped into a refugee sleeping under a tree. When I went up to my room, Cosandier was already asleep. This luxurious room with a private bath and hot and cold water seemed so incongruous. I felt restless and expected the bombing. However, I got to sleep in the end.

Thursday, 13th June

One of the Americans – I forget who – has just arrived from Paris full of gruesome stories. At the stations people had been trampled to death. Yesterday morning it was pitch black in Paris: one had to go about through the smoke screen with a pocket-torch – one couldn't see even half-way across the Place de la Concorde. In the darkness the sun was a pale-green disc. The shops were closing. It was almost impossible yesterday morning to find a café where they'd serve coffee and *croissants*.

Last night Paul Reynaud made a statement about going on fighting in North Africa, but clearly suggesting that the Battle of France was going to be lost unless France got immediate help. An appeal, he said, had been addressed to Roosevelt. England was not mentioned. We are, apparently, not helping the French any more. Perhaps we are right not throwing good money after bad. The statement was important as an enunciation of the principle of the *lutte à outrance*. But was not Reynaud expressing a purely personal view? And was he not, at the same time, preparing France for a capitulation? Was the way he was placing all the responsibility on America very wise?

After going to Colonel Thomas's conference (now held at the Conservatoire de Musique with a lot of pianos all over the place and with a big garden round it) I ran in the rue Nationale into Coutard and Madame. "*En somm c'est la capitulation pour demain?*" he asked. That's what he thought Reynaud's statement meant. He looked utterly dejected. So did she – her poor fat painted-up face looking so infinitely helpless.

I remembered their studio at Passy – she the daughter of a rich stockbroker; he had obviously married her for her money; and yet he now seemed quite fond of her. I remembered all the old Paris Columbia University gang of 1927 – with whom I had first met them; and all the fun. Mme Coutard wrote abstruse books about the Saracens, or something; probably got them published at her own expense; while he wrote competent Payot octavos on population problems, etc. And now? In his ordinary soldier's uniform he looked so poor and wretched. Who would have thought him a successful Paris barrister? Also met Louis Lévy of the *Populaire*. He was in a state of gloom. "*Mais alors toute la terre devient Nazie?*" He looked pathetic in his War Correspondent's uniform over his fat round body, and the olive beret over his paunchy baby face. "*On ira en Angleterre – je vais m'engager dans l'armée anglaise.*"

Spain declared non-belligerency – in other words pre-belligerency – last night. Picquart thinks Bordeaux will be a lovely spot once the Spaniards have started moving. There is more and more talk of moving from Tours to Bordeaux. In the Press room in the meantime they go on papering the decrepit walls with a dirty-blue paper, and sawing planks.

Major Vautrin, now attached in some capacity to Paul Reynaud's office, invited the Press this afternoon to Comert's office at the back of the ramshackle "Ministry of Information". Vautrin's handsome face seemed lined and had a kind of dead grey colour, but he spoke in a firm voice.

I want to comment to you on the message M Reynaud sent to President Roosevelt, which you have all seen in to-day's paper. Our line (*dispositif*) from the sea to Montmédy is coherent and is still holding out; only our men are being submitted to fearful pressure. Many of the troops have been in the front line for ten days, almost without sleep or respite.

Our losses have been very serious. The Germans opposite have during the same period been changing the front line troops every two or three days. In spite of this the *dispositif* has managed to hold out. There have been local counter-attacks taken on the initiative of small units; but a great counter-offensive has proved impossible. The general picture is one of a Front which still holds, but which is subjected to most terrific pressure. Infantry, scarcely supported by tanks, has to fight against armoured units. There is great German superiority in the air, except in those sectors where we have been able to use the new American bombers. But let us make no mistake; we need a lot more bombers, a lot more tanks *urgently*. Yes, the Front is still holding out; but it is wearing thinner every day, every hour, and is becoming less and less capable of any offensive action. For ten days and nights our men have suffered fearful physical fatigue. Some of our divisions have been attacked, have counter-attacked, have been attacked again, all within twenty-four hours. Some have had to retreat over 100 km in the last few days. There have been heavy losses; in most cases it is impossible to find fresh troops to relieve them; the Front is holding out with rapidly diminishing numbers; while the Germans have thrown 120, perhaps 150 divisions into the battle. We must have more matériel at once.

I asked Vautrin why with five million men mobilized France had only forty-five divisions in the field. He gave me some involved explanation about six or seven men in the rear to every man in the front line; "it's the same in all armies," he said. I couldn't see it; especially why the front-line people always had to be the *same* ones. Vautrin added that Paris was not being evacuated; and that the public services would continue normally.

The papers say Paris has been declared an open town.

I type 200 or 300 words about the extreme gravity of the situation, Reynaud's statement, etc. The damn thing will probably cost the paper about £7; really journalism is becoming impossible. After that I go down to the café in front of the *pissotière*. Talk with Liebling of the *New Yorker*, who's booked a seat for the Clipper on 22nd June. He is not in a funny mood; he says he is ashamed of the isolationist attitude of some of the writers on the

New Yorker. But he is convinced America will come in; very late; but she will. Others sit about – some with typewriters – David Scott, in his green beret and War Correspondent's uniform, André Glarner, Cardozo the bemedalled, Green, Knickerbocker and others; later Reggie Maynard turns up. One of the Embassy chaps appears and reprimands me for "alarmist talk". I ask him whether he thinks the situation is so very pretty? "No, but you mustn't say so publicly in cafés." Gilbert takes me aside, accuses me of indiscreet talk; says I've been reported by *Deuxième Bureau* spies to the French authorities who have passed it on to the British. Damn fools. They had better keep an eye on the Fifth Column chaps – plenty of them. Handler is there; he thinks the Fifth Column are working hard; Laval and Flandin will have a popular argument: "We were *Munichois* because we knew this would happen, and we wanted to spare you this."

Last night, by the way, we met at the hotel an American airman – Mexican-looking or Cuban; we couldn't quite make him out. He reminded me of Del Vaye, the Cuban Franco agent I met in Barcelona. Gilbert thought him fishy. He seemed merely dumb to me with his constant clamour for booze. With his moustache he looked a little like Douglas Fairbanks. He was training somewhere, but was rather vague about that side of things. He said he had been here for three weeks and hadn't done any flying yet.

I go with Gilbert and Reggie to the Univers bar. There are lots of British War Correspondents there talking about nothing in particular. We drink champagne at ten francs a glass. The hotel was commandeered for the Senate, but except for Paul-Boncour, whose white *perruque* I notice in the lounge, most of the Senators seem to have departed. There is going to be no meeting of Parliament at Tours. As we go out I run into Gordon Waterfield, just from Paris, in War Correspondent's uniform, and very dirty and sweaty. I offer him a bath and shave which he gratefully accepts. He thinks journalism is a mug's game from now on, and is frightened of being trapped in France. He wants to get to England to join the army.

Picquart, who had arrived yesterday, said it took him ten hours to travel the first twenty-two miles from Paris. Lots of cars had got stuck on the road for lack of petrol through driving in first gear. Many people on the road were in terrible distress.

Mrs Picquart had tears in her eyes – but she said nothing. One realized only too well how she felt about France.

At lunch I read bits of Péguy's *France*. It made me desperately unhappy – particularly that glorious passage about the "*peuple de Paris, peuple roi . . .*"

Friday, 14*th June*

Go out of the hotel with Cosandier into the crowded Place Jean Jaurès – they *would* call the main square in a town south of the Loire after Jaurès – *de la Nation armée*, blast it. Cars, cars, cars. People sit and stand about in cafés. Lorries with scores of men and women standing on them come into Tours – evacuated workers? Tired-looking people in cafés – they must have slept anywhere – in cars; in the open; or they may not have slept at all.

It rains; it just *would* for the refugees, when it didn't for Hitler's invasion. Cosandier and I have coffee at a counter – with hot *croissants*. There's a kind of dismal look on all faces. Only one young man, unshaven, unwashed, laughs loudly as he orders more *vin blanc*. He's drunk.

I meet Gordon Waterfield who is about to leave for Bordeaux. Havas, he says, are packing up. On to Colonel Thomas's conference at the Conservatoire de Musique. He is no longer there. He must have beaten it as he already did, that last day in Paris. At the Ministry of Information the Havas people are running about with suitcases. *On fout le camp.* I meet old Picot de Pledran of the *Action Française*. "*On s'en va*," he says. "*Où?*" "*A Bordeaux*," says he in a deadly voice. "*Pauvre France, pauvre France, pour en arriver là.*" I want to tell him that his *Action Française* chaps have a good share of responsibility for what has happened; but it isn't a time for polemics; and I am sorry for the old boy. He says that Maurras is at Poitiers, and that they have been publishing the paper there; but he doesn't know what will happen now.

I walk rather aimlessly about the streets, looking for Gilbert. The traffic is getting heavier. Mme Coutard, rouged, fat, pathetic-looking, asks me to sit down at her café table. "*Alors c'est la capitulation demain?*" she asks. I say I don't think so. "*On fera peut-être la lutte à outrance*," I add unconvincingly. "And besides," I add, remembering yesterday's unpleasantness, "I don't like discussing these things in cafés." Coutard, in his soldier's uniform, arrives. He talks about the war. "*On a écrit le Discours de la Méthode en Tourainè,*" he says, "*on l'applique en Prusse. C'est le triomphe de la méthode.*"

Paris, Paris. God knows what's happening there. Are the flowers still growing in the Tuileries? Poor old Uncle Peter. Gaby has just come in; she says Knickerbocker has just heard the Germans have entered Paris. I am in the hotel lounge at Tours, sitting in a red plush arm-chair . . . There are cheap lace curtains on the windows, and the proprietor looks like Senator Henry Roy . . . What a setting for such a wallop over the head.

This morning on the way to the censorship I ran into Albert. He had a kind of leer on his face. "We've lost this war. It's the fault of that disastrous man, Winston Churchill . . ." I didn't want to argue with the swine. "I think we'll go on with the war in England," I said. "Oh, don't be silly," said Albert.

They are all buzzing off; and the hotel is getting empty. What's the hurry? The censorship, I am told, will be open only till 12 o'clock. I hurriedly write a short piece on hotel notepaper – chiefly to tell the paper where I am and where I am going. Outside the censorship I run into Joxe and Dennery of the Centre de Politique Etrangère, the French Chatham House. They look lost; they won't talk; they are dashing off somewhere with their little suitcases in a great hurry. Later I again meet the Coutards. I kiss that fat ugly Betty good-bye; she cries. She looks so pathetic. Then a few minutes later, in front of the Hôtel de Ville (where they were going to hold a meeting of the Chamber of Deputies) I again see Coutard – "*Vous partez maintenant? Il faut partir vite. Ils sont, paraît-il, déjà à Chartres.*" Chartres, Chartres – "*cette Beauce, immense comme la mer*" . . . And tanks, tanks, tanks, rattling over it.

Mrs A, with her absentmindedness, will get us sunk some day. To-day she lost the key of her car. We spent two hours looking for it. In the end, Cosandier had to open the car with a hairpin. The streets are getting emptier. We are packing. I am bad-tempered with Marion; I am fed-up with Mrs A's two dogs, who have piddled all over the place in the bedrooms. I pay the bill. I think of Paris, of the view on to the Seine; of Lyosha and old Peter and the rest. Gilbert thinks it may take two or three days to get to Bordeaux. We may have to camp out. We buy candle lanterns – old-fashioned things, looking as though they belonged to an old cab. The ironmonger can't understand what we want them for. I discover the Matisse has got soaked with the rain pouring down on the luggage last night.

About 6, just as we were going to the ironmonger's to buy more things, the gunfire started and the sirens went off. We scuttled into the hotel, and I escorted the women into an *abri* – deep and vaulted, and pretty well intolerable with heat and lack of air after a few minutes. There are tables and chairs there; but the crowd grows bigger and bigger. There are many old women there. They grumble – *Ah, les salauds, pour en arriver là, quel malheur, quel malheur*. I want to go out and look, but the women insist on coming with me; so I stay. However, I can't stick the heat much longer and get out. There is a kind of garage shed in the yard next to the *abri*. I find Gilbert and Cosandier there looking at the half-dozen Nazi planes flying in circles. A few moments before, the fragment of an AA shell fell in the yard a few feet away from Gilbert. The bombing is heavy, but a good distance away; they are concentrating on the aerodrome. (Later there was a woman in tears at the hotel – her husband, an officer at the aerodrome, was late for dinner. However he turned up in the end; a fine young face and white hair. The damage caused by the raid was very small, he said; an old plane was wrecked and one man was slightly wounded.)

At last the raid is over; though the all-clear hasn't been sounded yet. It has stopped raining; we go to buy oilcloth for the Matisse, and also some candles. The shopkeepers look matter-of-fact. We then go on to a café, where we have coffee and some *tartelettes aux fraises* which Gaby had bought. The *patron* says he had been doing a roaring trade these days; all the apéritifs have been sold out. He doesn't know if he'll get any more.

Back to the hotel. It is now nearly empty. The eyes of the girl at the cash-desk are red with weeping. We have dinner at the hotel. The morose old waiter is in a bad mood. He says he was in the last war; things were managed differently then. He grumbles, especially when Gaby asks in her film-star way for this, that and the next thing. "*Adressez-vous au maître d'hôtel*," is his usual sulky reply. We drink vin de Chinon; it's not good – peppery.

Cardozo and Walter Farr are still at the hotel. Gilbert decides we shall leave early to-morrow morning. We have booked rooms and tell them to waken us at 3.30.

As we all sit in the dark lounge before going to bed, two plebeian Paris women come to the hotel. They say they've got a young woman and a baby in a lorry – they have travelled for three days, all the way from Paris. Are there no rooms? "*Nous sommes de Paris, du 14e.*" We talk about the women to the *patron* who (slightly reluctantly) says they can come and sleep in the lounge till our rooms are empty. One of the women is a pug-dog-faced old thing. We tell her the Boches are in Paris. She and the other woman begin to weep. I feel dreadfully sorry for them as they sob silently, thinking of their Paris, their 14e, behind the Gare Montparnasse. Marion and I accompany them to the station where the lorry is. I offer to carry the pug-dog's suitcase. She won't let me. "*Mais je ne vais donc pas vous la chiper,*" I say jokingly. She gets more *méfiante* than ever. On the way to the station she asks if I'm British. "*Et pourquoi n'êtes-vous pas mobilisé?*" I explain about my leg. She gets still more *méfiante*. When at last we find the lorry, the two women start a long discussion with a soldier and the baby's mother. In the end they say non-committally that they'll come later. A rather frigid "*Merci Madame, merci, Monsieur.*" That's another side of the French character.

Later, another woman with a neat little girl of four arrives. We make the same arrangement for her. She, at least, is grateful.

On the stair I meet a woman who tells a long story of how she was machine-gunned between Dourdan and Etampes. Ten people were killed. She had to abandon her car. A nice story with which to start a new bit of the exodus! *Tant pis*. Dourdan?

> *Nous avons pu coucher dans le calme Dourdan.*
> *C'est un gros bourg très riche et qui sent sa province . . .*

Poor Péguy with his *calme Dourdan*! We all go to bed. Gilbert, Cosandier and I in one room, Marion and Gaby in another, Mrs A and her litter in a third. It's a lot of money for three hours' sleep; but, hell, what does 100 francs one way or the other matter now? Gilbert didn't sleep for more than an hour; I sleep well. Get up, find time to shave. All is ready by 4.30.

The night before, in the hotel hall, I ran into that awful bore, the chap who writes for some Latvian papers. He looks like an old-fashioned German music master and talks every language with a Riga accent. At the Chamber he used to pester the life out of everybody with inane requests for prophecies. There *are* people like that. Yet, poor devil, I felt sorry for him. He looked exhausted. He had walked thirty or forty miles – a panic-stricken person with just nowhere to go. He begs us for a lift. I can't do anything about it. Neither can Gilbert. He's already promised a lift to the *Temps* chap and his wife. Gilbert listens in a bored way to the old bore's lamentations about the egoism of people as he has observed it in the last few days. My last sight of him at 3 the next morning was just this: the old bore lay crumpled up in an arm-chair in the lounge, fast asleep. It is strange, this dreadful ease with which one can say good-bye to people these days, even to people one is fond of, knowing you will never see them again. If you began to dwell on the thing, you'd be a nervous wreck in no time; hence one's automatic resistance to too much emotionalism.

Was it last night, or the night before? There were three soldiers in the hall. Gilbert tells them the British are sending lots of troops to the Seine – "*tenez seulement pendant dix jours.*" Two of them agree; the third, a baldish fellow of about forty, simply says: "*La question ne se pose même pas.*"

Later at Bordeaux Reggie tells me a lovely story about that pompous old bird, Sir Evelyn Cope. He was staying at a château near Tours; most of the official people stayed well *outside* Tours, just in case. When Reggie arrived there he found a letter in Sir Evelyn's writing lying on the desk.

Mon cher Prefet et ami,
    J'ai le plaisir de vous informer que je suis en train d'installer à Tours les services de co-opération Franco-Britannique. Je vous serais bien obligé de . . .

The letter broke off at this point. By this time Sir Evelyn and the rest had already buzzed off to Bordeaux.

And so we leave Tours. It was 4.30 when we left. The streets of Tours were fairly empty at that hour, except for a good number of stationary cars. With us travel the ex-Copenhagen correspondent of the *Temps* and his wife – an insignificant pair. He was attached as Press officer to the French Legation; so after the invasion of Denmark, they were taken by the Germans in the special diplomats' train to Belgium, and were treated with great consideration on the way. The meals on the train were good.

Our caravan of three cars drives through the Touraine country, under a grey morning sky. We pass a town with a large factory, with crowds of workmen outside. There is the same bewildered look on their faces – a look I had already seen all the way from Paris to Tours. The roads are teeming with cyclists going south. We pass through miles of vineyards – who's going to drink the wine? At the Mairie there's a large notice up: *Avis aux Italiens*. Reminds one that we are at war with Italy, too. I had forgotten about it. At Tours they were saying the Italians hadn't started any kind of military operations yet. We reach Poitiers without difficulty. The *Temps* man and his wife leave us at the railway station, where they hope to get a train for Limoges. We drive on to the other end of the town, and decide to stop at a café for breakfast. Opposite is a fruiterer's and grocer's shop. Mountains of strawberries, cherries, peaches, tinned food, sausages; dozens of chickens. How there can still be all this food after hundreds of thousands of refugees have been pouring through the town for days is a wonder to me. We buy strawberries and cherries and settle down to breakfast in the café. The *patron* puts on the table an enormous dish of butter and a gargantuan loaf of bread. As we have our *café au lait* from huge cups, we hear a terrific *engueulade* going on outside the café. An NCO of the French Air Force on a motor-cycle had been stopped by a special constable, who had asked for his papers. The NCO refused to show him any. The special constable, with a blue brassard, flew into a fearful rage. He was an apoplectic elderly man; he screamed and yelled and shook his fists frantically, getting all purple in the face. I thought he'd have a stroke. A large crowd gathered round; some people were shouting that the NCO was a German parachutist. In the end he was taken off to the police station in a car, swearing French obscenities with an unmistakably pure French accent. People are nervous, jumpy and have parachutists on the brain.

*   *   *

We drove on, not along the main Angoulême road to Bordeaux, but by a side-road passing through Saintes. We drove very fast, through lovely wooded country, passing many cars, and other cars passing us at 100 km an hour. The old Citroën was doing her job. This not being the main road, we even managed to refuel in one small town. Further along, at a level crossing, a large number of cars and buses (some of them the old familiar green Paris buses, with their windows blacked out) got stuck. We had to wait for a long time. It was a hot sunny day. We got out of the car, and sat on the grass by the roadside. We gathered a bunch of red poppies. While we were there one or two aeroplanes flew over us; were they friendly?

We stopped at Saintes, a large town with a cathedral and a lot of souvenir shops. It looked like an ideal holiday place; even the hotel where we went to eat was a kind of glorified seaside boarding-house. We weren't exactly on the sea; but the sea wasn't far away – it was only a few miles from here to La Rochelle. The boarding-house was crowded with people, most of them residents – chiefly well-to-do Belgian refugees. The usual *table d'hôte* lunch with hors d'œuvres and things, and sweet white Bordeaux wine *ad lib*.

On to Bordeaux. Black clouds began to gather, and there were thunder and flashes of lightning. It began to rain. The rain battered against the windscreen. It was still raining heavily when we reached the main road. This presented the old familiar sight – buses, Paris cars laden with luggage, all going in one direction. The huge suspension bridge a few miles outside Bordeaux was well guarded by soldiers who examined everybody's papers.

Bordeaux at last. We drove through shoddy, sad-looking streets till at last we reached the Garonne. Cranes, cranes, and more cranes; and many ships on the river. We drove along the Quai du Maréchal Lyautey – what a great name to remember these days! – to the Préfecture. Gilbert and I left Cosandier and the rest in a café and went off. We found the Ministry of Information and the censorship at least nominally established in some large building near the Préfecture – or it may have been the Préfecture itself, I forget. I say "nominally": because the whole place was in an indescribable mess. Nobody knew where anything was. I met Z the Russian Parliamentary reporter from Miliukov's paper, *Poslednia Novosti*. He looked dejected and worried. "*On est très pessimiste ici,*" he said. "There was a semi-official note in last night's *Liberté*: very ominous. It seems to have been handed out by Chautemps. It clearly suggests capitulation." He showed it me; it looked bad. I asked him what he was going to do. He shrugged his shoulders in a hopeless kind of way, and the tears came into his eyes. Clearly in this collapse of France the last remnant of a Free Russia was also going to disappear and what a fine remnant too! What chance could the Russian Liberals under Miliukov have of surviving? They were Liberals, they were anti-Nazis; and their paper carried on a great cultural and literary tradition. They had built up a little highly civilized society of their own on the friendly soil of France, and had kept it up for twenty years. And now –?

The thought that the French might capitulate right away seemed too horrible to take in; and yet – had not events been drifting that way for the last month? With Paris gone, was there any spirit left for a *lutte à outrance*? Reynaud had said at Tours that the French would go on fighting "in one province only, if necessary, in North Africa only, if necessary". But the Chautemps and the Baudouins were there to do their bit; and one never could tell. At Tours already, on the day Churchill came there on his lightning visit, I heard that Ybarnégaray and Baudouin and Chautemps and Prouvost had sounded very doubtful about any possibility of carrying on. We got worried. What if they were going to sign an armistice, and we got trapped at Bordeaux? It wasn't so funny. We went to the Hotel Splendide, a big garish caravanserai where we saw Childs, the Press attaché, and other Embassy people. Childs drew up a list of the journalists present, and promised to let us know if and when there was going to be a ship; "but there mayn't be one," he said, "for a couple of days." Then on to the British Consulate, across the square. We found lots of English people there, making inquiries. The shipping man was very sympathetic; but said he had no information about ships; everything was very uncertain. It was said that German planes had dropped magnetic mines at the mouth of the Gironde. It was therefore very uncertain whether any ships actually at Bordeaux could sail. One was due to sail for Brazil to-morrow, but nothing definite was known.

* * *

After numerous parleys at the Consulate and at the Hotel Splendide we returned to our party on the *quai*. It was 8 o'clock. We looked enviously at the big grey Brazilian liner. There were, of course, no rooms to be got at any hotel at Bordeaux; but one of the Embassy people had given us the address of an Englishman who had gone away to the country for a few days; and if we could get the key from the concierge, we might be able to stay there. We weren't sure whether it was the rue d'Alger, or the rue d'Angers, or the rue d'Anjou. Our caravan of three cars drove through the drab dreary streets of the poorer parts of the town. A kind of petulant hopelessness was written on all faces. At last we found the house – but found it locked. In the houses on the other side of the narrow street people looked out of the windows. An old man, with a white beard and wearing for some reason a red fez, grumbled about this invasion of Bordeaux by "a lot of foreigners". The women were more sympathetic. It transpired that somebody was staying in the house, and would probably be in later. We waited in a small café, where the morose and silent *patron* consented to give us some beer to drink with our sandwiches, but said that he couldn't at this hour be bothered making coffee. Eventually we found that the person occupying Mr J's house had returned. He was a King's Messenger who had just come from Madrid, and was on his way to London – though he was not sure how he would get there. "I believe there is going to be an Embassy plane," he said. "But the Embassy people are not at all pleased at my sudden arrival here." With him was a "gentleman's gentleman", a nice sweet old Londoner; he thought that he, at any rate, would have to go by sea. The King's Messenger and the gentleman's gentleman were very appreciative of our difficulties, and took the intolerable invasion of the tiny flat with good-humoured stoicism. We slept, as best we could, on sofas, arm-chairs and on the floor.

Early next morning – it was Sunday, the 16th – I went to a little *bistrot* with Cosandier, the chauffeur, where we picked up a *Petite Gironde* printed on a single sheet. There was a war communiqué of sorts, showing that the Germans were now advancing wherever they wished to advance:

* * *

In Normandy and south of Paris the situation is unchanged. Further east enemy detachments crossed the Seine in the Romilly region. Enemy pressure became more marked around Troyes and Saint-Dizier, and German advance units reached the Chaumont area. In Alsace the enemy attacked in the Neuf-Brisach area; a number of detachments succeeded in crossing the Rhine, though without breaking through any of our defensive positions.

In short, they were driving right into Burgundy. There was no news in the *Petite Gironde* about the Cabinet meeting which had taken place last night, except that the deliberations had been adjourned until the morning. If Tours with its Radical Congress atmosphere, complete with Lop, was a comic nightmare, that last day at Bordeaux was a tragic nightmare. This lovely, gentle land of France which we had all loved, was, we felt, rapidly disintegrating. This endless sitting about in cafés around the Hotel Splendide with the question hammering at our brains: "Is France capitulating?" was like an intolerable mockery of the past. Here we were, witnessing the end of France in the happy-go-lucky atmosphere of a provincial *café du commerce*.

And the British at Bordeaux were also, not unnaturally, worried by the question whether they could sail in time for England if France were to capitulate. Nor was the danger of a sudden occupation of Bordeaux by German troops landed by planes entirely out of the question. It was, after all, the only large Atlantic port still in French hands. Nantes and Brest had fallen, or were on the point of falling.

Outside the Consulate that morning I met Geoffrey Cox and George Millar who, with *Daily Express* enterprise, were going to do a round of all the sailors' and seamen's hostels at Bordeaux to see if they could get any news of possible sailings. Some newspaper men were talking of hiring a trawler, and Knickerbocker, who greatly disliked the prospect of falling into the hands of the Gestapo, even thought it might be possible to buy one, if the Press stumped up enough money collectively.

The Cabinet was meeting "somewhere in Bordeaux". I discovered where it was, and, going there shortly after noon, I saw the Ministers coming out. Weygand was there, too. He looked extraordinarily unperturbed – almost pleased with himself.

What were they hoping for? Paul Reynaud looked badly harassed. The only man I had a chance to talk to that day was Chautemps. I asked him if there was any likelihood of France continuing the struggle in North Africa. He looked an unhealthy yellow colour, and there was the usual furtive look in his eyes. "*Non*," he said, "*on se dirige plutôt dans l'autre sens*." He said no more, and went. *Dans l'autre sens!* That's to say capitulation. Was Reynaud going to resign?

We spent the rest of the day anxiously, and in idle speculation. The large luxurious restaurant of the Hotel Splendide was packed all day. The waiters were overworked and the service was slow; but we ate good and expensive food. Bordeaux, now the capital of France, was not going to disgrace itself. At the table next to ours sat M Zaleski, the Polish Foreign Minister, with a crowd of Poles. He said he knew very little; the French Cabinet were not keeping him properly informed; but he was fearing the worst. He seemed to distrust Baudouin particularly. Another Pole I knew told me that General Sikorski had sent a long memorandum in November to General Gamelin on Germany's *blitzkrieg* methods in Poland. After Gamelin's dismissal, the document was found among his papers *unopened*. There were no end of familiar faces at and around the Hotel Splendide that day. Reggie, and the charming Mrs Maynard (complete with poodle); she had just arrived at Bordeaux, after driving an ambulance for three weeks "somewhere in France"; Pertinax, looking haggard and in a state of mental distress; also little Geneviève Tabouis, who, with a sad look silently pressed my hand with her frail little fingers. It was like a funeral. Other French anti-Nazi journalists were there, appealing pathetically to the British to be allowed on board – if there was going to be a ship. Pierre Comert was also there: he was still chief of some Press department. But was this Press department still in existence? It didn't seem to matter much, either to him, or to anybody else. Press cables of sorts continued to be accepted by "Press Wireless"; but there was really little to say that was likely to be passed by the censorship.

Later, in the afternoon I went for a walk along the *quais* of the Garonne. It was a hot summer day; I was still in France; why was everybody looking so unhappy? Here were the cranes, and the large ships, all intact; and cars and tram-cars were running along the *quais* and over the wide bridges across the Garonne. Was the war real, or was it only a bad dream? I crossed the large square in front of the Hotel Splendide. It was a large open space, where they held fairs and exhibitions. They must have been preparing for some kind of fair some time ago; for there were several half-built but now abandoned pavilions there: one of them called "Les Vins de France". In the centre of this open space was a dried-up fountain with weird-looking horses, some with frogs', others with tortoises' legs; from the fountain rose a large pillar, with a golden angel of liberty dancing on top. The incongruous thing was the monument to the Girondins. In the square were a number of British troops with their lorries. The French looked at them in a faintly hostile way – though nothing was said. They had come from somewhere farther up the coast.

I returned to the Splendide. The café terraces on either side were packed as before. "*Garçon, un pernod! Garçon, un demi! Garçon, un vittel-cassis!*" Any news of the Cabinet meeting? Rumours, rumours, rumours.

We hung about aimlessly for the rest of the afternoon. The question arose of going to La Rochelle where a small British ship was due in two or three days. The Consulate said there would be accommodation on board for 200 – or 300 at the outside. Was it worth risking? It was said there were about 2,000 British people anxious to get away. At last, about 8, it was announced that the British at Bordeaux should be ready to leave Bordeaux for Le Verdon, the port on the mouth of the Gironde, at 9 the next morning. It was no use going back to our Englishman's flat, at the other end of Bordeaux; we might miss the boat: the instructions might be changed during the night: one never could tell. So we all decided to spend the night in the cars, right in front of the Hotel Splendide. We had a dreary and expensive dinner at the blasted place, and the waiter tried to cheat us out of thirty francs.

At the end of it the news reached us that the French Cabinet meeting – the Cabinet had met four times since yesterday – had this time *really* come to an end; that Reynaud had resigned; and that Pétain was forming a new Cabinet. It was said that fourteen of the Ministers had decided in favour of separate peace talks, and that only ten had opposed this: among them Reynaud, Mandel, Dautry, Marin, Campinchi, Monnet, Delbos. The supporters of capitulation were the Generals, the Fascists and the Radical defeatists – among them Pétain, Baudouin, Ybarné-garay, Prouvost, Chautemps and Pomaret. Old Lebrun threw in his weight on the side of the capitulationists. Weygand, who was present, is said to have declared that the military defeat was complete; and it was no use going on.

It was thought at Bordeaux that night that while the new Government would not capitulate, it would attempt to *negotiate* an armistice. But nobody really knew anything definite; except that it all smelt pretty bad. And for us British it was high time we got out of France. That it should have come to this!

I remember that last night in France so clearly. At the Splendide everything was blacked out about 10. In the dim stone-panelled front hall a few people were still hanging about exchanging the latest information. I ran into William Henry Chamberlin; I had not seen him at Bordeaux before. He thought he and his wife would stay on for a little longer; if necessary, they could always get away to Lisbon and sail for the States. I had not seen him for some time. The last time I had dinner with them in their flat at Neuilly, the American military attaché was there. The Norwegian campaign was in full progress. The battle of Narvik had just been won; but the prospects at Trondhjem looked bad. The attaché thought that we could hold Narvik, but that the adventure in Central Norway was utterly crazy: "You haven't the chance of a snowball in hell," he said. "The obvious thing for the Allies to do when the Germans invaded Denmark," he said, "was to occupy Belgium and Holland. The French have the swellest army in the world – they could have done it easily." That night at Bordeaux I recalled the "swellest army in the world" remark; Lord, how even the experts, especially the experts, had been taken in! And no wonder Bullitt was later blamed for misinforming the United States Government on the real position in France. He knew no more than his military attaché.

In the hall of the Hotel Splendide, the couches and sofas and armchairs were filled with drowsy and sleeping bodies. During the great exodus in France, hotel proprietors were quite decent about that; they let people sleep, free of charge, in their halls and lounges.

We groped our way back into the street. Sleeping in the car seemed the best solution. The whole street in front of the hotel and much of the large open space around the Girondins column was crowded with dark stationary cars – with people sleeping in many of them. The big trees lining the street looked so still on that calm starlit night – my last night in France. An aeroplane was heard, at one moment, flying about somewhere, not far away. But there was no air-raid warning. A nice mess a bomb would have made if it had dropped among all these cars. Except for the cars, the street was empty; there were no lights in the houses; Bordeaux was sleeping. Sleeping? Could people sleep when their country was in its last agony? For things were *happening* all the time. German troops were advancing – and perhaps not so very far from Bordeaux. Paul Reynaud, at this hour, was said to be on his way for Nantes. And here in Bordeaux an old, old man was taking the destinies of his country into his frail hands. As I sat in the car, trying to fall asleep, I thought of Paris, of all these years in France. Was old "Uncle" Peter still going to go out to-morrow morning in his slippers and old coat to the laiterie Hauser across the street to buy the half-litre of milk? Was the proprietor of Paul's at the Pont-Neuf still saying he was going to "*foutre les pessimistes à la Seine*"? Was his *bistrot* with the funny paintings on the walls still open? And if so, who were his customers to-night? The new men – the new masters of France? At length I fell asleep in the car, and dreamed a confused dream about Paris. There were French troops marching across the Place de la Concorde, preparing to storm the Madeleine, a fortress held by the Germans. Ambulances were taking the wounded to the Café Weber – yes, just as they did on the 6th of February. Absurd; or perhaps not so absurd.

It was broad daylight when I woke up. Under a tree, near the car, Gilbert was sleeping on a mattress he had spread out right on the ground. He said he couldn't sleep inside a car, and had to stretch out. At the Hotel Splendide there was already much coming and going. The car-dwellers crowded into the *lavabo* to wash and shave. We then had coffee and *croissants* on the terrace. I bought the *Journal*. Large headlines:

PETAIN A LA TETE DU GOUVERNEMENT.

LE GENERAL WEYGAND PREND LA VICE-PRESIDENCE.

M PAUL REYNAUD A DEMISSIONNE.

That's all. No explanation why. No indication of any sort. Instead, some bits of foreign news:

> La réponse du Président Roosevelt à M Paul Reynaud provoque la colère de Berlin.
> Le Cabinet Tataresco est démissionnaire.
> Les Usines d'Amérique vont travailler à plein pour nous.
> Les sirènes hurlèrent à Marseille et à ce signal 900 Italiens indésirables furent arrêtés.

Also a grotesque piece of news: "The regular air-service between London and France will be re-established within the next few days." Lastly, General Duval's article: a kind of review of why France had lost the war.

> . . . Depuis Montmédy jusqu' à la mer, l'autre moitié de nos forces occupait une ligne d'ouvrages plus ou moins impro-visés, *à peu près inexistants entre Montmédy et Charleville* . . .

After a description of the break-through on the Meuse and the encirclement of the Flanders armies, the General proceeded:

> Privé des *deux-cinquièmes de ses forces* Weygand dut se défen-dre avec ce qui lui restait de Français et deux divisions britanniques sur la ligne Somme-Aisne. Tout l'Armée Alle-mande, 150 divisions, se rua contre cinquante divisions le 5 juin au matin. Nous nous sommes battus, un homme contre trois, un avion contre dix . . .

Regarding Dunkirk, General Duval said that out of 330,000 men rescued, only 90,000 were French. Throughout the article, a faint anti-British undercurrent was unmistakable. The state-ment about the "two-fifths" of the French Army lost in Flanders is, of course, tripe. They had only eight divisions there – though among the best armed.

It's a warm sunny day. A lot of traffic in front of the Splendide. Everybody is packing up; tying up suitcases on top of the cars; many are already leaving. A big trade is going on in second-hand cars. Mme A sells her two cars for 20,000 francs, and goes and reinvests the money in furs and jewellery – which takes her a devil of a time. I don't know if my francs are going to be worth any-thing once we get to England. But one is not in a mood to worry about that. Marion has a five-pound note, which she offers to lend me. In principle, only British subjects are supposed to sail to-night; but a good number of others are admitted too. Several French people, Poles and Czechs are also given passes by Childs, the Press attaché. White slips of paper with "SS *Madura*" written on them. Reggie Maynard and his wife and Lord Kneller, and the Embassy people (except Malet, the Ambassador's Secretary) are not coming on our ship. They, and a few privileged Frenchmen – Pertinax, and Mme Géraud, and Mme Tabouis, and Emile Buré and his wife, are going on board a warship – a cruiser or a destroyer, I forget – right at Bordeaux. Pertinax looks grey with worry. Picquart comes to say good-bye. We urge him to come to England; but he says no, very firmly. "There is too much running away," he says. "This *is* my country; I must stay here whatever happens to it. I've got my little house down in the south; I'll be all right. We are old people." He is calm, and betrays no emotion. But Mme Picquart fails to come: she is probably too upset.

There is great bustle in the streets of Bordeaux. The tram-cars are running as usual; and the shop windows in the Cours de l'Intendance are packed with goods – clothes, and hats, and cakes, and chocolates, and bottles of scent, and bottles of wine and what-not. At the *tabacs* alone many brands of cigarettes are sold out. Looking down one of the side-streets from this shop-ping centre, I can see the cranes and the ships on the river.

Back to where the cars are. At last everything is ready. We leave. We drive through streets, jammed with cars and tram-cars, to the north of Bordeaux, and then out into the open country. I had always wanted to see this sharp long blade-like peninsula between the sea and the mouth of the Gironde; it looks intriguing on the map. It is pleasant, but unexciting coun-try, with vineyards and pine trees, with a road running through it as straight as an arrow. Many of the place names have a famil-iar sound – names often seen on bottles of claret and white bordeaux. We also pass through Lesparre – it occurs to me that this is Mandel's constituency. Mandel – one had heard a lot about him these last few days; he, at any rate, was putting up a good struggle against capitulation.

The country gets more sandy and wooded, and one can smell

the sea air. We pass Le Verdon, and go on to the Pointe de Grave. Out of the pinewood we suddenly emerge into the open. An immense stretch of sand, and the wide mouth of the river, dotted with hundreds of ships, and, far beyond, the other side of the Gironde where one faintly distinguishes a town – it must be Royan. The sky and the river and the sea are a faint pale blue, and the sands a faint pale yellow. There is a light mist over it all; the ships look all the same lilac colour. To the left, on a hillock overlooking the ocean, is a large tower, shaped like a lighthouse – it's the famous Pointe de Grave memorial to the Americans who were the first to land in France in 1917. What a happy moment *that* was for France. What a sad moment *this* is for us – and for France.

The launch will not be ready to take us across to the ship until 4 o'clock. We have time. We have lunch in the little restaurant at the foot of the American memorial. (Awful to think that it was unveiled, shortly before Munich, by Bonnet who made on that occasion a deliberately fatuous speech, which put the American isolationists' backs up.) We feel the bitterness of it all very keenly. Cosandier, the chauffeur, is particularly upset. We have a banal lunch with hors d'œuvres, and roast veal and fruit and cheese, and some sweet white bordeaux *en carafe*. The little restaurant with its wonderful view must have been a favourite place with day trippers from Bordeaux. At the counter, there is a large selection of picture postcards. I'd like to write some; but what's the good, with all communications upset, or cut by the Germans?

We learn that at 12 Pétain made a broadcast saying he was going to "inquire" about an armistice. Bad; but not unexpected. But a pretty effect the announcement is going to have on the troops who in many places are still resisting. Nobody likes the idea of being killed on the *last* day of the war. The announcement is sure to weaken what resistance there still is by ninety per cent. What *are* these people up to?

Somebody who has just come from Bordeaux says that there was this morning an attempted *putsch*, and that Mandel has been arrested. I didn't see any signs of a *putsch*; but the Mandel story seems possible.

At last the launch is ready to take us. We carry the luggage from the cars to the launch. As we say good-bye to Cosandier, he bursts into tears. Nearly everybody is weeping. To leave France, and to leave it like this, is hard.

World War II

WILLIAM L. SHIRER

France Surrenders

Shirer arrived in Berlin in 1934 as the correspondent for Universal News Service (although he later switched to Columbia Broadcasting Service). Most of his broadcasts were heavily censored by the Nazi authorities, but he kept a secret journal containing his true thoughts and observations. This was published as the bestselling *Berlin Diary* shortly after his arrival back in the USA in December 1940. Here is his entry for 21 June 1940, the day France capitulated to Germany and signed a formal surrender. The signing took place in a railway carriage at Compiègne, France.

Berlin Diary, 1941

On the exact spot in the little clearing in the Forest of Compiène where, at five a.m. on 11 November 1918, the armistice which ended the World War was signed, Adolf Hitler today handed *his* armistice terms to France. To make German revenge complete, the meeting of the German and French plenipotentiaries took place in Marshal Foch's private [railway] car, in which Foch laid down the armistice terms to Germany twenty-two years ago. Even the same table in the rickety old *wagon-lit* car was used. And through the windows we saw Hitler occupying the very seat on which Foch had sat at that table when he dictated the other armistice.

The humiliation of France, of the French, was complete. And yet in the preamble to the armistice terms Hitler told the French that he had not chosen this spot at Compiènge out of revenge; merely to right an old wrong. From the demeanour of the French delegates I gathered that they did not appreciate the difference ...

The armistice negotiations began at three fifteen p.m. A warm June sun beat down on the great elm and pine trees, and cast pleasant shadows on the wooded avenues as Hitler, with the German plenipotentiaries at his side, appeared. He alighted from his car in front of the French monument to Alsace-Lorraine which stands at the end of an avenue about 200 yards from the clearing where the armistice car waited on exactly the same spot it occupied twenty-two years ago.

The Alsace-Lorraine statue, I noted, was covered with German war flags so that you could not see its sculptured work nor read its inscription. But I had seen it some years before – the large sword representing the sword of the Allies, and its point sticking into a large, limp eagle, representing the old Empire of the Kaiser. And the inscription underneath in French saying: "TO THE HEROIC SOLDIERS OF FRANCE . . . DEFENDERS OF THE COUNTRY AND OF RIGHT . . . GLORIOUS LIBERATORS OF ALSACE-LORRAINE."

Through my glasses I saw the Führer stop, glance at the monument, observe the Reich flags with their big swastikas in the centre. Then he strode slowly towards us, towards the little clearing in the woods. I observed his face. It was grave, solemn, yet brimming with revenge. There was also in it, as in his springy step, a note of the triumphant conqueror, the defier of the world. There was something else, difficult to describe, in his expression, a sort of scornful, inner joy at being present at this great reversal of fate – a reversal he himself had wrought.

Now he reaches the little opening in the woods. He pauses and looks slowly around. The clearing is in the form of a circle some 200 yards in diameter and laid out like a park. Cypress trees line it all round – and behind them, the great elms and oaks of the forest. This has been one of France's national shrines for twenty-two years. From a discreet position on the perimeter of the circle we watch.

Hitler pauses, and gazes slowly around. In a group just behind him are the other German plenipotentiaries: Göring, grasping his field-marshal's baton in one hand. He wears the sky-blue uniform of the air force. All the Germans are in uniform, Hitler in a double-breasted grey uniform, with the Iron Cross hanging from his left breast pocket. Next to Göring are the two German army chiefs – General Keitel, chief of the Supreme Command, and General von Brauchitsch, commander-in-chief of the German army. Both are just approaching sixty, but look younger, especially Keitel, who had a dapper appearance with his cap slightly cocked on one side.

Then there is Erich Raeder, Grand Admiral of the German Fleet, in his blue naval uniform and the invariable upturned collar which German naval officers usually wear. There are two non-military men in Hitler's suite – his Foreign Minister, Joachim von Ribbentrop, in the field-grey uniform of the Foreign Office; and Rudolf Hess, Hitler's deputy, in a grey party uniform.

The time is now three eighteen p.m. Hitler's personal flag is run up on a small standard in the centre of the opening.

Also in the centre is a great granite block which stands some three feet above the ground. Hitler, followed by the others, walks slowly over to it, steps up, and reads the inscription engraved in great high letters on that block. It says: "HERE ON THE ELEVENTH OF NOVEMBER 1918 SUCCUMBED THE CRIMINAL PRIDE OF THE GERMAN EMPIRE . . . VANQUISHED BY THE FREE PEOPLES WHICH IT TRIED TO ENSLAVE."

Hitler reads it and Göring reads it. They all read it, standing there in the June sun and the silence. I look for the expression on Hitler's face. I am but fifty yards from him and see him through my glasses as though he were directly in front of me. I have seen that face many times at the great moments of his life. But today! It is afire with scorn, anger, hate, revenge, triumph. He steps off the monument and contrives to make even this gesture a masterpiece of contempt. He glances back at it, contemptuous, angry – angry, you almost feel, because he cannot wipe out the awful, provoking lettering with one sweep of his high Prussian boot. He glances slowly around the clearing, and now, as his eyes meet ours, you grasp the depth of his hatred. But there is triumph there too – revengeful, triumphant hate. Suddenly, as though his face were not giving quite complete expression to his feelings, he throws his whole body into harmony with his mood. He swiftly snaps his hands on his hips, arches his shoulders, plants his feet wide apart. It is a magnificent gesture of defiance, of burning contempt for this place now and all that it has stood for in the twenty-two years since it witnessed the humbling of the German Empire . . .

It is now three twenty-three p.m. and the Germans stride over to the armistice car. For a moment or two they stand in the sunlight outside the car, chatting. Then Hitler steps up into the car, followed by the others. We can see nicely through the car windows. Hitler takes the place occupied by Marshal Foch when the 1918 armistice terms were signed. The others spread themselves around him. Four chairs on the opposite side of the table from Hitler remain empty. The French have not yet appeared. But we do not wait long. Exactly at three thirty p.m. they alight from a car. They have flown up from Bordeaux to a nearby landing field. They too glance at the Alsace-Lorraine memorial but it's a swift glance. Then they walk down the avenue flanked by three German officers. We see them now as they come into the sunlight of the clearing.

General Huntziger, wearing a bleached khaki uniform, Air General Bergeret and Vice-Admiral Le Luc, both in dark blue uniforms, and then, almost buried in the uniforms, M Noël, French Ambassador to Poland. The German guard of honour, drawn up at the entrance to the clearing, snaps to attention for the French as they pass, but it does not present arms.

It is a grave hour in the life of France. The Frenchmen keep their eyes straight ahead. Their faces are solemn, drawn. They are the picture of tragic dignity.

They walk stiffly to the car, where they are met by two German officers, Lieutenant-General Tippelskirch, Quartermaster General, and Colonel Thomas, chief of the Führer's headquarters. The Germans salute. The French salute. The atmosphere is what Europeans call "correct". There are salutes, but no handshakes.

Now we get our picture through the dusty windows of that old *wagon-lit* car. Hitler and the other German leaders rise as the French enter the drawing-room. Hitler gives the Nazi salute, the arm raised. Ribbentrop and Hess do the same. I cannot see M Noël to notice whether he salutes or not.

Hitler, as far as we can see through the windows, does not say a word to the French or to anybody else. He nods to General

Keitel at his side. We see General Keitel adjusting his papers. Then he starts to read. He is reading the preamble to the German armistice terms. The French sit there with marble-like faces and listen intently. Hitler and Göring glance at the green table-top.

The reading of the preamble lasts but a few minutes. Hitler, we soon observe, has no intention of remaining very long, of listening to the reading of the armistice terms themselves. At three forty-two p.m., twelve minutes after the French arrive, we see Hitler stand up, salute stiffly, and then stride out of the drawing-room, followed by Göring, Brauchitsch, Raeder, Hess, and Ribbentrop. The French, like figures of stone, remain at the green-topped table. General Keitel remains with them. He starts to read them the detailed conditions of the armistice.

Hitler and his aides stride down the avenue towards the Alsace-Lorraine monument, where their cars are waiting. As they pass the guard of honour, the German band strikes up the two national anthems, *Deutschland, Deutschland über Alles* and the *Horst Wessel* song. The whole ceremony in which Hitler has reached a new pinnacle in his meteoric career and Germany avenged the 1918 defeat is over in a quarter of an hour.

World War II

EDWARD R. MURROW

Fires Were Started

Murrow was the European director for CBS. His radio dispatches during the Battle of Britain and the Blitz (with their trademark "This is London . . ." openings) were particularly resonant, and widely admired alike by his peers and the audience back home in the USA. The report below was broadcast shortly after the Luftwaffe began the Blitz, the mass bombing of London.

CBS Radio, 10 September 1940

All the fires were quickly brought under control. That's a common phrase in the morning communiqués. I've seen how it's done; spent a night with the London fire brigade. For three hours after the night attack got going, I shivered in a sandbag crow's-nest atop a tall building near the Thames. It was one of the many fire-observation posts. There was an old gun barrel mounted above a round table marked off like a compass. A stick of incendiaries bounced off rooftops about three miles away. The observer took a sight on a point where the first one fell, swung his gun-sight along the line of bombs, and took another reading at the end of the line of fire. Then he picked up his telephone and shouted above the half gale that was blowing up there, "Stick of incendiaries, – between 190 and 220 – about three miles away." Five minutes later a German bomber came boring down the river. We could see his exhaust trail like a pale ribbon stretched straight across the sky. Half a mile downstream there were two eruptions and then a third, close together. The first two looked as though some giant had thrown a huge basket of flaming golden oranges high in the air. The third was just a balloon of fire enclosed in black smoke above the house-tops. The observer didn't bother with his gun-sight and indicator for that one. Just reached for his night glasses, took one quick look, picked up his telephone, and said, "Two high explosives and one oil bomb," and named the street where they had fallen.

There was a small fire going off to our left. Suddenly sparks showered up from it as though someone had punched the middle of a huge camp-fire with a tree trunk. Again the gun sight swung around, the bearing was read, and the report went down the telephone lines: "There is something in high explosives on that fire at 59."

There was peace and quiet inside for twenty minutes. Then a shower of incendiaries came down far in the distance. They didn't fall in a line. It looked like flashes from an electric train on a wet night, only the engineer was drunk and driving his train in circles through the streets. One sight at the middle of the flashes and our observer reported laconically, "Breadbasket at 90 – covers a couple of miles." Half an hour later a string of fire bombs fell right beside the Thames. Their white glare was reflected in the black, lazy water near the banks and faded out in midstream where the moon cut a golden swathe broken only by the arches of famous bridges.

We could see little men shovelling those fire bombs into the river. One burned for a few minutes like a beacon right in the middle of a bridge. Finally those white flames all went out. No one bothers about the white light, it's only when it turns yellow that a real fire has started.

I must have seen well over a hundred fire bombs come down and only three small fires were started. The incendiaries aren't so bad if there is someone there to deal with them, but those oil bombs present more difficulties.

As I watched those white fires flame up and die down, watched the yellow blazes grow dull and disappear, I thought, what a puny effort is this to burn a great city.

World War II

CURZIO MALAPARTE

Steel Horses

Curzio Malaparte was the pseudonym of Kurt Erick Suckert, born in Italy in 1898. Like Luigi Barzini he long flirted with Fascism; unlike Barzini Malaparte could be awkwardly independent, several times to the cost of his liberty. Malaparte's dispatches for *Corriere della Sera* from the invasion of Russia in summer 1941 – when he was the only war correspondent of any nation on the front line – so angered Goebbels that he had the reporter removed from the war-zone. Returning to Italy he was placed under house arrest by Mussolini. Ever mercurial, Il Duce then ordered Malaparte back to the Eastern Front; anxious to avoid German reprisals Malaparte chose to report from Finland.

Malaparte's despatches from Finland and Russia were collected as *Il Volga nasce in Europa* in 1943. The book had a luckless birth. An RAF raid destroyed the printing works, sending the entire of the first print run up in smoke; when a new edition finally emerged in Italian bookshops the German authorities, who had recently occupied Italy, ordered its seizure and condemned it to the flames. The 1951 release was happier. The *Times Literary Supplement* concluded of the English translation, *The Volga Rises in Europe*, that it 'convincingly confirms Malaparte's right, whatever his faults, to be one of the most brilliant reporters of our time'. A new edition was published by Birlinn in 2000.

The Volga Rises in Europe, 1951

Cornolena, July 14th

It is not yet dawn when we leave Skuratovoi Farm. The engines cough and splutter. I am reminded of the famous sneeze of the Greek hoplite in Xenophon: "Χαῖρε! Χαῖρε!" The sky to the east has a silvery pallor. The corn makes a faint murmuring sound, as of water flowing between soft banks. Little by little the hills become less steep; they have now the form of breasts, each of those ample undulations is separated from the next by a slight fold in the ground – not a valley, but just a shady hollow, peaceful and somnolent. The slopes are dotted with patrols of infantrymen. They are engaged in mopping-up operations. Slowly they make their way along the furrows, their figures sharply outlined against the pale sky.

Ahead of us the battle rages. The Russians are counterattacking. The counter-offensive of the Soviet troops is developing not only on this front but farther to the south-east, over towards Beltsy, in the sector held by the Rumanian divisions. Patrols of Rumanian light cavalry appear fleetingly away to our right. They form a link between our column and a mixed German-Rumanian column that is advancing obliquely to our line of march.

Above the steady roar of the artillery one hears the sharp bursts of anti-tank shells and the duller sound of the panzers' cannon. Our column advances slowly across the cold, glistening grass. The sky to the east looks like crinkled parchment. Flights of larks burst from the corn. Each of the vehicles has a faint blue aura formed by the smoke from the exhausts. Suddenly, as we make our way down a gentle slope, we are enveloped by a cloud of red dust and the air is filled with the rumble of wheels, the clatter of tank-tracks, and the roar of engines.

An armoured column is like an armoured train. I have climbed on to Oberleutnant Schultz's lorry; I have taken my place beside him, squatting as comfortably as I can on a box of ammunition. I ask him if he has read *Armoured Train No. 1469*, the famous book by the Communist writer Leonov.

"Yes," he says, "you are right – an armoured column is exactly like an armoured train." Woe to the man who gets off the train, who leaves the column. The fields around us are full of hidden perils. Our armoured train runs on invisible rails. The bullets of the Soviet stragglers lying in ambush amid the corn (I was about to say "along the railway-embankment") flatten themselves against the steel sides of our vehicles. "Do you remember the attack on Train No. 1469?" I ask. But it would be impossible to halt the advance of our column, it would be impossible to blow up the invisible track on which our armoured train runs.

We discuss Communist literature.

Oberleutnant Schultz is a *Dozent* in a university. Before the war he concerned himself with social problems, and he has published a number of essays on Soviet Russia. Now he is in command of the anti-aircraft section of our mechanized column. He tells me that in all probability Russia, after her defeat, will live through another period very similar, in a sense, to that described in Pilnyak's *The Naked Year.* "With this difference," he adds: "that the drama described by Pilnyak unfolded, as it were, in an experimental laboratory. Russia will relive the same drama, but this time it will be enacted in the yard of a factory or of a steel-works, against the sordid background of a workers' rising that has been nipped in the bud." Then he looks at me, smiles shyly, and says: "From the social viewpoint, machines are very interesting and very dangerous characters." He confesses to me that he finds this problem extraordinarily fascinating.

The soldiers, standing up in the backs of their lorries, shout, gesticulate, and throw all manner of objects at one another, including combs, brushes, tins of cigarettes, pieces of soap, towels. The order to move has come unexpectedly, and many have not even had time to wash and shave. Now they are smartening themselves up as best they can. Some stand with legs wide apart on the platforms of their anti-aircraft lorries and, stripped to the waist, wash themselves in canvas buckets. Some kneel before mirrors inserted in their rifle-racks or suspended from the tripods of their machine-guns and somehow contrive to shave. Others wash their jackboots with soap and water.

The sun breaks the shell of the horizon, climbs into a sky all streaked with green, timidly illuminates the armour of the vehicles. A light pink down appears on the surface of the grey steel plates. The heavy tanks at the head of the column are enveloped in a pink aura, they emit a delicate yet vivid radiance. And suddenly, far ahead of us, on the distant horizon, amid that vast expanse of waving corn that seems to flow like a golden river – suddenly, in the distance, on the slope of a hill, there is a glint of steel, a glitter of armour.

A cry passes down the column: "The Mongols! The Mongols!" By this time the German soldiers can distinguish the Mongolian units from the other Soviet units by the way they fight, even by their tactical dispositions. As a general rule tanks manned by Asiatic crews fight not in formation but singly, or in groups of two or three at the most. (It is a tactic that recalls, in a sense, that of the cavalry-patrols.) The German soldiers call them *Panzerpferde* – roughly, "armoured horses". Something of the old spirit survives in these Tartar horsemen, whom Soviet industrialization and military Stakanovism have made into specialized workers, mechanics, drivers of tanks.

Some Tartar prisoners, captured last evening and brought to the farm at Skuratovoi, have confirmed that the Soviet troops entrusted with the defence of the Ukraine (and therefore of the industrial and mineral basins of the Dnieper and the Don and of the roads that lead to the Caucasus and to the oil of Baku) are for the most part Asiatics. They comprise Tartars from the Crimea, the remnants of the Golden Horde; Kurds from Turkestan; and Mongols from the banks of the Don and the Volga, from the shores of the Caspian, from the Kirgizian steppes, from the plains of Tashkent and Samarkand. They represent the best that the Five Year Plan of the Mongolian Republic has produced, they are the choicest products of the industrialization of Asiatic Russia, the young recruits of military Stakanovism.

The prisoners, who numbered about fifteen, were assembled in the farmyard. They were a little above medium height, lean, but with sturdy, loose and well-proportioned limbs. At first sight they appeared very young, but their faces gave a false impression. Their ages ranged, I would say, from twenty-five to thirty. They wore a very simple khaki uniform, without any distinguishing mark, not even a number on the collar of the jacket. The forage-caps which partly concealed their glossy black hair were of the same khaki colour. They wore very soft grey leather boots of Tartar design, equally suitable for riding or for crouching inside a tank. They had narrow, slanting eyes and small mouths. About their eyes and extending all along their temples was a fine network of wrinkles, alive and sensitive, which palpi-tated like the nervures in the wings of a dragon-fly.

They were sitting on the ground with their backs resting against that part of the stable-wall which was illuminated by the rays of the setting sun. They were eating sunflower-seeds. They appeared apathetic, and at the same time extremely watchful. Suspicion lurked beneath that air of cold, blank indifference. The patch of sunlight on the wall grew ever smaller, until at last it was no more than a bright spot on the face of one of them.

That yellow mask, brilliantly illuminated by the last fires of sunset, was fixed, immobile: the narrow mouth, the smooth brow, the bright eyes might have been hewn from marble. Only those two fine, delicate networks of wrinkles quivered inces-santly. The prisoner's face reminded me, I know not why, of a dying bird. When the sun finally disappeared the bird folded its wings and lay inert.

They had been captured while trying to make their way back to the headquarters of their unit in two armoured vehicles. The tank that was escorting them had been gutted by a bomb in a field a few miles east of Skuratovoi. They had defended them-selves fiercely against a heavy panzer which had cut off their retreat. But their resistance had been in vain: against panzers machine-gun fire is ineffectual. Some of them had been killed, and the survivors were now sitting in the farmyard, resting their backs against the wall of the stable. Pensively they chewed their sunflower-seeds, screwing up their small, slanting eyes the while.

They seemed to rouse themselves from their lethargy only when one of those miniature tractors equipped with caterpillars and drawn by a kind of motor-cycle, likewise equipped with cat-erpillars, suddenly appeared in the yard. This type of vehicle is something new in the German Army – indeed, it has only made its appearance since this Russian campaign began. It is not, strictly speaking, a motor-cycle with a tractor attached; it is, rather, a tractor guided and at the same time drawn by a sort of powered monocycle which projects from the front of the vehi-cle. The driver sits astride the monocycle with his back resting against the bodywork. Superficially it looks a makeshift sort of vehicle, very light and of no great power. But the Germans speak highly of its exceptional pulling and climbing capacity. It will climb anything. Its inventor intended it for use in mountain-warfare. Employed for the first time on these Russian plains, it has surprised the experts by its remarkable qualities, both mechanical and practical. It serves in the main for the transport of munitions and supplies of petrol. During the actual fighting these strange vehicles follow close behind the tank-formations, moving swiftly from one panzer to another. Some of them are used for the purpose of towing light anti-tank artillery. They are very fast, and as they make their way through the corn they are almost invisible.

The Tartar prisoners looked at this strange machine with intense interest. I observed their hands. They were small and stubby, horny-thumbed and grimy with oil. The skin between thumb and forefinger seemed to be scored with deep black furrows, as is always the case with men who are in the habit of wielding metal implements. They were mechanics' hands. Mongolians, it appears, make excellent mechanics – and by that I mean genuinely skilled craftsmen. Many young Mongolians are employed nowadays in the Russian metallurgical industry, especially in the Kharkov district. They have an extraordinary passion for machines. Among the youth of Soviet Mongolia the traditional passion for horses has given way to an interest in the precise working of engines, gears, manometers, and so forth. They seem naturally suited to this extremely mobile type of warfare, to this technique of offensive thrusts by tanks, which are very similar to the cavalry-thrusts of earlier wars. I would say, indeed, that they use tanks as they once used horses. They employ the same tactics, based on freedom and independence of action. Herein lies the novelty of this war of tanks which the Mongols are waging on the plains of the Ukraine. They come forward not in a body but singly. They advance through the cornfields in a series of broad sweeping movements, like horsemen performing evolutions in some gigantic circus. And their audacity is reminiscent of that for which the old-time cavalry were famous.

"The Mongols! The Mongols!" cry the German soldiers. They have sighted three small tanks swiftly climbing the gentle slope of a hill barely two miles ahead of us. Two large panzers detach themselves from the head of our column. We watch them advance diagonally through the corn, one to the right, the other to the left, gradually widening the distance between them as if they were seeking to check the enemy's advance by means of a pincer movement. The three small Mongolian tanks abruptly disperse. They begin a series of strange evolutions, each describing a broad spiral upon the surface of the plain, whose undulations periodically hide them from view. One has the impression that they are trying to gain time, to engage the German tanks in a kind of gymkhana, so as to give the main body of their formation an opportunity to come to their assistance, or to retreat. Suddenly the two heavy panzers open fire with their cannon.

The bursting shells throw up high fountains of earth around the small Soviet tanks. The battle only lasts ten minutes. The three Russian tanks are far more mobile than the panzers, they evade their fire and disappear behind the hill. "It is a technique of enticement," says Oberleutnant Schultz. "In this war of mobile columns the Mongolian *Panzerpferde* are doing an imaginative and extremely hazardous job of work. One has to be very careful not to swallow the bait – not to allow oneself to be lured on to ground that has been mined or ambushed by large armoured formations concealed in a wood or behind a hill."

After a few hours we reach the village of Cornolenca. It is intact, but deserted. A few hundred yards beyond the village we come upon a group of burning houses. Our column has received orders to take up a position behind a hill, about half a mile outside Cornolenca. We spent a nerve-racking afternoon awaiting developments. One of our medium guns, sited among the houses of a village, fires a shot at intervals of three minutes. Numerous batteries concealed in the woods to our right keep up a continuous bombardment.

Towards evening we see a column of approximately ten German vehicles coming in our direction, escorted by a panzer. Six prisoners dismount from a lorry – four Mongols and two Russians.

After the interrogation, while the prisoners are being locked up in a room of a house situated in the village, Oberleutnant Schultz comes over to me and says: "I have a suspicion that one of those prisoners is a political commissar. Did you notice his uniform?"

It is already dark when I discern a strange coming and going outside the house in which the prisoners are confined. While I am walking towards the house I run into Schultz. He tells me that the "political commissar" has been found dead – strangled. And he shows me a pencilled note, written in Russian. It reads as follows: "I personally gave my men the order to kill me." The signature is clearly legible: "Basil Volinski, political commissar attached to the 15th Armoured Division."

World War II

A.J. LIEBLING

Paddy of the RAF

Joe Liebling covered the Second World War for *The New Yorker*. As
well as a deserving reputation as a war correspondent, he had an
entirely separate one as a champion fighter for the underdog. It
was Liebling who coined the memorable phrase that "Freedom of
the press belongs to the man who owns one."

New Yorker, 6 December 1941

The few British fighting men who have become popular legends
during this war have done so without the connivance of His
Majesty's Government. German and Russian communiqués are
studded with the names of individual heroes, but even the RAF,
although garrulous compared to the British Army and Navy,
believes fliers should be almost anonymous. Whereas the Luftwaffe would announce that the late Werner Mölders had shot
down his ninety-ninth plane – and, incidentally, British airmen
would take no stock in his score – the Air Ministry says merely
that a pilot attached to one of its squadrons scored his eleventh
victory. Weeks later, perhaps when the pilot is due for a decoration, his name will appear in the London *Gazette*, a government
newspaper few civilians read. For this reason, a high score is not
enough in itself to make a fighter pilot a new personality. He has
to have some particularity that the public can remember. Flight
Lieutenant Brendan Finucane – Distinguished Service Order
and Distinguished Flying Cross with two bars – has established
himself in the public mind by being profoundly Irish, so Irish,

that strangers spontaneously address him as Paddy, which is also what his friends call him. He is neither Ulster Irish nor Anglo-Irish, nor public-school-and-Oxford denatured Irish but middle-class Dublin Irish, and so proud of it that he has a big shamrock painted on his Spitfire. It is a shamrock designed by the adoring Yorkshire rigger and Canadian fitter who look after his plane. The shamrock has the initials "B.F." in the center and is surrounded by thorns. The rigger says he knows that thorns belong on a rose, but he feels they are appropriate, and Paddy agrees with him. The same rigger once, after the pilot had shot down his twenty-first plane, thought he would please him by painting twenty-one little swastikas around the periphery of the shamrock. Paddy got angry at this, saying they were an affectation of elegance, and made the rigger remove them. Paddy is twenty-one years and a couple of weeks old, and has a boyish eagerness to avoid any implication of swank. The way he got his most serious war injury fits in almost miraculously with his public personality; he broke his right foot jumping over a wall at a wake.

Being Irish is not itself a rare distinction in the RAF. At least five hundred citizens of Eire wear pilots' wings on their tunics and about fifty have been decorated. What made Paddy identifiable even before the public knew his name was his being both Irish and attached to an Australian squadron. When the Londoner at his breakfast table reads, for example, about a Polish pilot in the RAF shooting down a plane, he has no way of knowing whether or not it is the same Pole he read about last Thursday, but the designation "an Irish pilot officer attached to an Australian squadron," which began to thread its way through the communiqués last June, gave Paddy his public identity. Subsequently the Londoner could follow Paddy's promotions as well as his triumphs, because the communiqués, which early last summer mentioned him as an Irish pilot officer (a pilot officer being the equivalent of an American second lieutenant), later spoke of him as a flying officer and then as a flight lieutenant. The last rank is like our captaincy. Finucane's decorations piled up even faster. He began the summer with a Distinguished Flying Cross left over from 1940, when, as a comparative novice, he had shot down five "certains," as the unquestionably disposed-of planes are called, in the Battle of Britain. As the summer progressed, he added two bars to the cross, and then, just before his birthday, he received the Distinguished Service Order. A couple of days later he broke his foot. By that time he had accumulated twenty-three "certains" and about a dozen "probables". He doesn't try to remember the planes he damages but does not bring down.

There are a good many men in the RAF who think Flight Lieutenant Finucane is the most accomplished fighter pilot of the war, although he has not actually downed the most planes. In support of their argument, they point out that he made almost all his kills last summer and that 1941 was a poorer season for German planes than 1940 had been. Firth, Paddy's Yorkshire rigger, holds this point of view. In 1940, he says, there were "oondreds of jerries – all you'd to do was fly oop in air and poosh booton. But this year, when Paddy wants one, he has to go to France for it." Also, the technique of air fighting has been much refined since 1940. As there has been no general mêlée this year, German and British veterans alike have had time to teach the new pilots their tricks. None of the other pilots in Paddy's outfit, Squadron 452, had fought before last June, though they were the pick of the first lot to enter training in Australia. They had continued their training in Canada and Scotland. Paddy, who had been in the RAF since 1938, joined them last spring at their first fighter station, which was in England, with the assignment of teaching them by example. They were the highest-scoring squadron in England in August and September. They were nosed out by the American Eagle Squadron in October, while Paddy was nursing his foot, as he still is.

The wake at which Paddy broke this foot was expressly an Australian fliers' variant of the rite. All squadron members leave a couple of extra shillings in a kitty each time they settle their mess bills; then, when a pilot goes missing, the survivors drink up what he has left. The day before this particular observance, a sergeant pilot had been shot down over France. He had left two pounds ten, which was enough to finance only a modest wake. That, Paddy says, is why it was emotion and not drink which was responsible for his accident. The sergeant had been a close pal of his, and when, at the party, Paddy came upon a wall, he decided to jump over it, as a gesture of respect. There was a blackout, he says, and the wall looked like any other wall in the same circumstances. However, there happened to be a twenty-foot drop into an areaway on the other side, so he broke his foot. He was consoled a couple of days later by the news that the sergeant was safe in a prison camp. "In a way, the whole party was a waste," he says, "but I don't bear him any hard feeling." The hospital ward to which he was immediately afterward assigned was devoted entirely to RAF leg injuries, and every pilot present, except himself, had been hurt either in a motorbike accident or a Rugby match. This excess of animal spirits may result in the loss of some flying hours, but it is also a sign that the men are in prime condition.

Paddy Finucane is an unusually serious young fighting man except when he is actually in the midst of the Australians, which is perhaps why he likes them so much. One Australian flight lieutenant, called Blue because he has such red hair, says, "We had to teach Paddy to play the fool when he came to us. The poor man had been with an English squadron so long he was trying to act dignified." The Australians, though few of them are older than Paddy – one pilot officer with a magnificent drooping mustache is nineteen – are relatively worldly types. One, upon returning recently from what the fliers call a sweep, remarked that he had shot a German into the Channel and that after the plane had struck, a bright green stain had appeared on the surface of the water, something he had never seen before. "Heavy crème-de-menthe drinker, no doubt," he concluded. Most of them, before joining the Force, were university undergraduates or students in Australian public schools, whereas Paddy, right before he enlisted in the RAF, was an assistant book-keeper in an office in London. Yet today, on all questions pertaining to air fighting, the Australians defer to Paddy's advice and obey his instructions. When he is flying with them, he sometimes, by radio-telephone, directs four dogfights simultaneously. "Has one of those beautifully efficient minds that work along just one line," a disciple of his says. "He can remember the positions of a dozen planes at once, although they change by the split second. And he has phenomenal eyes. Some fellows say Paddy smells Messerschmitts, but what really happens is that he sees them before anybody else can."

This exceptional vision may be the one quality all great pilots have in common. Once Paddy's mates saw him going after two Messerschmitt 109 Fs, of which he downed one. The second plane flew into a cloud and was lost to view. Finucane flew in after it, opened fire while in the cloud, and a moment later flew out of the other side as the German fell out of it, trailing flames. Another time, when the Australians and a New Zealand squadron were taking part in a sweep, Paddy, three miles away, saw some Messerschmitts flying near the New Zealanders and warned them before they were aware of their own danger. He isn't a "suicide fighter," his comrades say. He will sometimes maneuver his section for five or ten minutes before he sends it in to the kill, but when he does, every Spitfire is apt to be on a German plane's tail. "The idea isn't just to get a plane for yourself," Finucane himself says. "You want to see the other fellows get some shooting, too." He derives more pleasure from helping a new pilot to his first certain than out of increasing his own bag. Paddy thinks his squadron is perfect. "All the Australians are mad," he says in a tone of heartiest approbation. "Waggle your wings, and they'll follow you through hell and high."

Paddy is of almost exactly medium weight and height; he is probably an inch too short for the New York police force. He boxed as a welterweight on the RAF team in a match against the combined Scottish universities just before the war began, which means he weighed a hundred and forty-seven pounds, or ten stone seven in the national jargon. He is a few pounds heavier when he isn't in boxing trim, and he has the strong neck, the wide cheekbones, and the broad jaw of a good Irish ring type. He has wavy dark-brown hair, blue eyes, and a pink-and-white complexion that looks like a soap ad; he reddens to his ears when flustered. He was wild about boxing until he turned to air fighting, which he thinks a more exhilarating form of competition, and constantly draws analogies between the two. "Some pilots roll better to their right than to their left," he may say, "the way some boxers move better to one side." Or he says, "You have to take the play from the other fellow, just like boxing. I don't let them dither around." It isn't that Paddy is frivolous or brutal; in his direct way, he has made a mental adjustment that he couldn't have bought from a psychoanalyst for under a million dollars. "The personality never enters my mind," he says. "I always think to myself, 'I'm just shooting down a machine.' Some things get you rather angry, though," he adds. "For instance, if they shoot at our chaps after they've bailed out. That's like hitting a man when he's down." He has never seen this happen, he explains, but he has talked to fellows who say they have. He used to like Rugby almost as well as boxing. When the Army beat the RAF at Rugby this fall, 30–3, Paddy took it as hard as missing three Germans. He watched the game on crutches.

He has never been shot down or wounded or forced to bail out, although during the 1940 hurly-burly he got a number of bullets through various Spitfires he was piloting. All last summer his planes were unscathed, a proof of his skill at maneuvering. Pilots like to find a couple of bullet holes in their planes after they get safely back to the airdromes, because it gives them something to talk about at mess. Once this year Paddy landed with holes in the tail fin of his plane, but they proved to have been made by the branches of a tree he had scraped. His rigger and fitter say he was much disappointed. He has never fought in anything but Spitfires, and has had them in all their editions. During the summer he ran through five planes – three early Spits and two of the latest Spit fives. He cracked up two machines on his own airdromes, stunting near the ground. Stunting is an officially discouraged but universal custom among fighting pilots. He is very careful about selecting a plane; he not only puts it through all the tricks he knows but he fires several trial bursts with its cannon and machine guns. If a cannon jams, he gets out instantly and walks away from the machine. Once he has picked a Spit, he leaves it in the care of his rigger and fitter, who work with an armorer, an electrican, and a radio man. Aircraftsmen in the last three categories take care of three planes apiece, so they are not identified with one pilot as a rigger and a fitter are. Finucane does not fancy himself an engineering shark. When he comes in from a sweep, he may say to his retainers, "She's flying left wing down," or "right wing down," but he leaves the remedy to the ground crew. This delights them. Firth, the rigger, who is dark, solid, and snaggle-toothed, says, "When Spit's been in dogfight, she's oopsey." His tone implies that the ordeal is rather like a childbirth for a delicate woman. Moore, the fitter, who is small and blond, says, "Some officers get a big head when they down one or two planes, but not Paddy." They both carry decks of snapshots of Finucane in their pockets.

After Paddy has chosen a plane, his shamrock and the letter "W" are painted on it. Each plane in a squadron is identified by a letter, as moviegoers who saw *Target for Tonight* know. Senior pilots usually get low letters, but Finucane insists on his "W", for sentimental reasons. It stands for Wheezy Anna, a nickname he gave his first Spit because its engine made such strange sounds. In those days the RAF was short of planes and young pilots took what they could get. "Wheezy was a good old girl," Paddy says. "I cracked her up so hard I had the mark of the stick on my chest for a month."

When Paddy is on leave, as he is now on account of his foot, he lives with his parents, a small brother named Joseph, and two sisters, Monica and Claire, aged eleven and seven, in Richmond, the London suburb south of Kew. He has another brother, Raymond Patrick, who is nineteen and a sergeant air gunner in the Bomber Command. The house looks like several thousand others in suburban London and America. It is Tudor of a recent vintage, complete with the path of irregular concrete flagstones from gate to front door. Paddy's father is a night office manager at an airplane-parts factory that works the clock around. He is black-haired, energetic, witty, and a firm teetotaller. He looks a good deal younger than his forty-nine years and used to be an amateur soccer star in Ireland. Mr Finucane pronounces his surname "Finewcan", but Paddy says "Finoocan". Paddy, who admires his father, has never developed a taste for beer or whiskey. Recently, in an effort to keep up with the Australians, he has learned to order a bottled drink called Pimm's No. 1, which is like a sweet Tom Collins. Mrs Finucane is good-natured and hospitable. When Joe, the small brother, gets home from school, his favorite reading is a monthly publication called *Rockfist Rogan of the RAF*, the adventures of a British Superman with a war slant. Rockfist, typically, will jump from his flying plane into that of a wounded brother pilot, drag him from the cockpit, and make a double parachute jump to safety, perhaps lassoing the propeller of a Heinkel on the way down and hauling the crew into captivity. This serial greatly increased Joe's respect for his older brothers. Paddy himself prefers more realistic books about flying. There is a recently published one called *Fighter Pilot*, which he describes as wizard, his favorite adjective of praise. He uses it, too, to describe the two Australian flight lieutenants who roomed with him at the airdrome up to the time of his jumping over the wall. One, the red-haired fellow called Blue, is addicted to mystery stories and the other reads poetry, forms of composition that Paddy runs down at every opportunity, out of a spirit of contradiction. The poetical Australian says he knows Paddy has a poetic soul, a suggestion that drives Paddy into a picturesque fury. The mystery-story Australian, who has downed ten German planes, wears the jacks of spades, hearts, clubs, and diamonds inked on his "Mae West", as the fliers call their bulbous yellow inflatable life-saving jackets, because these cards are the sign of a fictional detective he admires.

The mantelpiece in the Finucanes' dining-sitting room is decorated with cutouts of Snow White and the Seven Dwarfs made by Monica, a large square clock with an inscription saying it was presented to Flight Lieutenant Brendan Finucane by the night staff at the factory where his father works, and a bronze cigarette lighter in the form of an aircraftsman spinning a propeller. This last is a gift to Paddy from his girl friend. He doesn't think it a good idea to get married during the war, he says, because "someday I might be going on a sweep and I would have it in the back of my head that I wanted to get back that night and that would distract me." Even now, he acknowledges, he sometimes has "a funny feeling in my tummy" just before he takes off, and he is afraid that marriage might make it funnier. He is a devout Catholic and attends Mass whenever he gets a chance. The Australians, he says regretfully, are "free and easy" about spiritual matters. He gives you a feeling that this worries him a little. He is always worrying about the fellows he flies with. Blue says that Paddy once woke him at four in the morning by shouting "Break, Blue! There's a Messerschmitt on your tail!" "I guess he dreams about air fighting all night," Blue says.

The Finucanes' move from Dublin to Richmond took place early in 1938. In Dublin, Paddy had attended a wonderful institution of learning called the O'Connell School, where the headmaster was a retired Army officer who had held a service boxing title. Like headmasters the world over, this one believed in his own favorite sport as a character builder. Every morning at eight thirty, according to Paddy, the boys were turned out under a large shed in the schoolyard and told to whack each other. Paddy developed such a taste for whacking that the future pattern of his life lay clear before him when he came to England; he was destined to be a fighter pilot. He was too young to enlist in the RAF immediately, so he worked without pleasure at an office job until May, 1938. Then, on the precise day that he became seventeen years and six months old, the minimum age allowed, he enrolled for a course leading to a short-term commission. Richmond had seemed somewhat humdrum after the O'Connell School, and the Finucane brothers, during their first few months there, found the English rather "standoffish". After Paddy joined the RAF, things went much better. He is still, however, a vocally patriotic Dubliner. Being an RAF officer, he does not go in for political arguments, he explains, but occasionally somebody says something about Eire which betrays a lack of understanding, and then Paddy puts him right.

Men accepted for the course Paddy took were supposed to put in four years of active service and then pass to the volunteer reserve for six more. That was considered the expedient way to raise a body of fliers for what some people thought might be an emergency. The British did not sufficiently hurry the training of their pilots even after the war began to give Paddy an opportunity to fly in France with the expeditionary squadrons. He did not get into action until June, 1940, a couple of weeks after Dunkirk. He was first posted to the East India Squadron at an airdrome in the south of England. The squadron got its name from the fact that people in India had contributed money for its Spitfires. Most of the pilots were British. That is a fine Squadron, Paddy says; he had a good deal of fun there. "First the Germans started pushing over high-flying fighters, and then bombers with fighter escort," he reminisces happily. "There was something doing all the time." On his first flight with a formation in combat, he says, he was so preoccupied with keeping his place in the formation that he "could not see a sausage". The squadron broke up an incursion of eighty German fighters, but Paddy says he wasn't much help. Afterward formation flying became automatic, and then he began to enjoy himself.

In the East India Squadron days, the pilots slept with their flying suits on when the weather was clear, and their planes were kept warmed up constantly. One time, Paddy remembers, the squadron was just taking off when some Heinkels started bombing the field. A number of Spitfires bumped over fresh bomb craters as they got into the air. A bomb dropped directly in front of a pilot named Kenny Hart, and the blast stopped his propeller. He scrambled out and ran for a shelter trench, with bombs continuing to drop about him, while his mates, gaining height, took after the Heinkels. "We shot down a couple of them," Paddy says, "but seeing Kenny run was the cream of it." On another occasion the boys were gathered around a table in the middle of the field, having afternoon tea before taking off for a sweep. Unexpectedly, some Messerschmitts dived on the field and started plunking cannon shells into the tea service. The pilots, conspicuous targets in their yellow Mae Wests, dashed for shelter while the ground defenses had a go at the Germans, who got away intact. "Things like that amuse us when we think of them," Finucane says. He shot down five certains while he was with the East Indias and contributed to the destruction of other enemy planes, and the Fighter Command tabbed him a coming man.

There is nothing unorthodox about Finucane's methods. The secret seems to be that he does everything exactly right, and a fraction of a second before his opponent. A fighter pilot aims at his adversary by means of a small, electrically operated arrangement called a reflector. When the enemy shows in the reflector he is in line with the guns, although, of course, he may be at a quite impractical range. There are two ideal shooting positions: one close behind the other plane, the other head on. Paddy prefers the first. The inconvenience of the second is that you are at the same time in line with the other fellow's guns. Polish pilots like this position. Even if you are hit, they say, you can ram the German before it is possible for him to pull out. You are therefore certain of your German. Paddy has a high regard for Polish pilots, but his mind does not run in the same channel.

The most difficult style of attack is called deflection shooting. This means firing as an enemy plane flies across your path. The angles of approach, rates of climb or descent, and speeds of the two planes all enter into the instantaneous guess the pilot must make as he pushes the button which operates the cannon and machine guns. Inexperienced pilots usually fire behind the other plane. Old hands have a tendency to fire in front of it. Paddy is a wizard shot, but he does not consider that deflection shooting pays. "Sometimes you take a long squirt at something that way and see bits fly off it, but you don't see it crash," he says. "What you want to do is get on their tail, close in. I give them a squirt in the tank and if they break up, I'm quite happy." A squirt is the burst of cannon and machine-gun fire that results from pressing the button and holding it down a couple of seconds. Paddy gets on the other fellow's tail in various ways: by pouncing, if he has an initial advantage in height; by waiting for the German to dive and then getting him as he pulls out; or by facing him at a safe distance and then circling him, as a mongoose goes around a cobra, finishing up at the back of his neck. A Spitfire can out-turn a Messerschmitt, although it cannot out-climb one. By practicing rigid economy in shooting, which is usual with him, Paddy once was able to down three German fighters in a single trip and arrive back at his airdrome with a quarter of his ammunition. It was his best afternoon's work. The squadron, collectively, got eight. The Australians had been "squatting on top of the bombers" that afternoon; that is, flying just above some Blenheims that were going to France for a daylight raid. A big formation of German fighters had dived from a great altitude, ignoring the Spitfires and going straight for the bombers. They dived right past the bombers without getting any. Then, as the Messerschmitts pulled out of their dives, Paddy, who was commanding the whole squadron that day, led the Spits above and at them.

Paddy has no personal feeling against Germans. His contacts with them have been limited. He remembers once seeing a couple at the Dublin Horse Show, and last August, after the East Indias shot down a Dornier near their airdrome, he and some other pilots went over to a hospital to visit the wounded German pilot and observer. "They had never flown together before," he says. Crews in the British Bomber Command rehearse their teamwork many times before they go out on a serious job.

Paddy's assignment to the Australian squadron was a masterpiece of psychology, as well as a good technical selection, because the Australians might have taken less kindly to a more formalized version of the British officer. At almost any time five

314 A.J. Liebling

or six of them are likely to be found around a table in one of the squadron's huts playing poker and saying, on any provocation, "Ectualleh." One boy will say "Two cards," and the dealer will say "Ectualleh?" The next will say "I'll have three," and the dealer will say "Ectualleh?" again. Then another will say "I'll stand" and the dealer will shout "Ectualleh!" and they will all roll on the floor with laughter because they believe that a certain type of Englishman never says anything but "ectualleh". Their own favorite interjection is "bloody oath", which they consider more spirited and democratic. They also say "very *crook*" when they mean put-out, and "fair dinkum" to indicate good faith. By this time Paddy is so steeped in their patois that it is sometimes hard to tell whether he is talking Irish or Australian. All the Australians are given to puns, and Paddy, who affects to be above them, used to run around punching the punsters on their biceps. One night some Australians went out and painted kangaroos all over his Spit's shamrock, an outrage that excited him for days. The Australians love to tell Finucane stories, and they think he is wonderful.

When Paddy is to go on a sweep, he usually sleeps late in the morning and then takes an extremely hot bath. Most athletic trainers say hot baths are enervating, but Paddy says they just make him feel relaxed. He then has tea and goes to receive the day's orders from the commanding officer. Last year RAF fighter squadrons generally had the mission of intercepting German bombers. This year they escort British bombers to France and protect them from enemy fighters. In a sweep, which may involve a dozen squadrons, each has a special role. Sometimes the Australians fly closely above the bombers, sometimes they fly beneath or among them ("on the deck"), and sometimes they go very high, looking for Messerschmitts in ambush in the sub-stratosphere. The last is the assignment that Paddy likes best. The conventional order that goes with it is "Seek out and destroy." The only mission he really dislikes is a Balbo, which is an RAF term for a reconnaissance in formation without any particular object. It is named after the late Italian aviator, who always flew high and never hurt anybody.

There are days when no large general operation is planned and the planes go off in pairs, flying very high, looking for some object of innocent merriment, like a little train on a *chemin de fer départmental* that may be carrying German Army supplies, or a lorry loaded with middle-aged Landsturm men on a road. Coastal steamers are particularly agreeable sights to them. When they fix on a target, they come plummeting down as straight as a stalk and squirt twenty-millimetre cannon shells just to see what will happen. Paddy remembers that one time he hit a steamer and it flew to pieces with a report that was heard on both sides of the Channel. "It must have been full of ammo," he says. The best day's sport he ever had resulted from another patrol. He and a pal were flying high and got into a cloud bank. Suddenly the cloud dissolved and they saw that they were sitting in among twenty Messerschmitts. "Twenty was a wee bit too many," Paddy says, "because we had the height and the sun against us, so I said to my mate, 'Come on along and beat up some gun positions,' and we left. We got down to about ten thousand feet and ran into another forty Messerschmitts, so we gave them a squirt to help them on their way and continued. Then, way down below us, just over the Channel, we could see two Messerschmitts attacking a lone Spitfire. We went along down and each shot one of them into the water. That brought me pretty low, and I was just above the surface when I saw cannon shells splashing into the water in a steady stream, so I could figure that one of the big bunch of Jerries had followed me on down and was in back of me. It is a very good position to be in in a fight, because you can judge the angle of fire by the splashes, and then you know where your man is. As the angle gets smaller, you can figure he's getting in line with you. Just before that happens, you give a quick turn. If he tries to follow, he goes in the drink, because he won't be able to pull out quick enough. If he doesn't follow, you whip up behind him, and there you are. I got him and went home quite happy, with the other lad."

Paddy doesn't know what he will do after he goes back to active duty, or rather what the Fighter Command will tell him to do. He may get a new outfit to whip into shape next spring, by which time, other RAF officers say, he is fairly sure to be a squadron leader. What he would like most is to travel to the Middle East, or anywhere else, even if it's only by bomber. "My brother Raymond Patrick has all the luck," he says. "He goes to

Bremen and other fascinating places every week, but I hardly
get out of the country." His pet scheme, which the Fighter Command probably won't endorse, is to get to the United States as
the pilot of a Catafighter. A Catafighter is a land plane carried
on a merchant ship and launched from a catapult whenever one
of the big German flying boats appears. The pilot shoots down
the flying boat and then tries to get to the nearest land on the
petrol he has left. If he can't make it, he lands in the water and
hopes for the best.

"That would be wizard," Paddy says. "Free passage and all.
Besides, I have an aunt and uncle and three cousins in Detroit,
all named O'Callahan."

World War II

O.D. GALLAGHER

The Loss of *Repulse*

The principal cause of war in the Far East was Japan's decision to acquire a Pacific empire. She had invaded China in the 1930s but the jewels she truly coveted were the colonial possessions of the British, the French and the Dutch. This imperial desire also led directly to hostilities with the USA, which was zealously protective of her influence in the region. By 7 December 1941 the Pacific was aflame as Japanese units simultaneously attacked Pearl Harbor, Hong Kong, Wake Island, Guam and Midway. To protect the great naval base of Singapore, the British dispatched a surface fleet to intercept Japanese invasion forces while they were still at sea, but in the event the British were spotted first, and attacked by swarms of Japanese fighter-bombers. The British fleet had no fighter protection. The battleships HMS *Repulse* and HMS *Prince of Wales* were sunk within a single hour on 10 December. Two months later Singapore fell to the army of Nippon.

Daily Express, 12 December 1941

This is the simple story of a naval force which went into north-eastern Malayan waters on Monday. *Prince of Wales* and *Repulse* were the backbone of this force. I was in *Repulse*. The aim of the force was, in the words of the signal C-in-C Admiral Sir Tom Phillips sent to all ships: "The enemy has made several landings on the north coast of Malaya and has made local progress. Meanwhile fast transports lie off the coast. This is our opportunity before the enemy can establish himself.

"We have made a wide circuit to avoid air reconnaissance and hope to surprise the enemy shortly after sunrise to-morrow (Wednesday). We may have the luck to try our metal against the old Jap battle cruiser *Kongo* or against some Jap cruisers or destroyers in the Gulf of Siam.

"We are sure to get some useful practices with our high-angle armament, but whatever we meet I want to finish quickly and get well clear to eastward before the Japanese can mass a too formidable scale of air attack against us. So shoot to sink."

But at 5.20 that same evening a bugle sounded throughout my ship *Repulse* over the ship's loud-speakers, giving immediate orders to the whole ship's company and filling every space of engine room and wardroom with its urgent bugle notes, followed by the order: "Action stations. Enemy aircraft!"

I rushed on to the flag deck which was my action station. It was a single Nakajama Naka 93 twin-floated Jap reconnaissance plane. She kept almost on the horizon, too far for engagement, for a couple of hours.

A voice from the bridge came out of the loud-speakers: "We are being shadowed by enemy aircraft. Keep ready for immediate action to repel aircraft."

Two more Nakajama Naka 93s appeared. They kept a long relay watch on us. What an admiral most wishes to avoid has happened.

His ships were out at sea, sufficiently distant from shore to prevent him receiving air support before dawn the following morning, when a mass enemy air attack now seemed certain. We had not yet sighted any enemy naval force or received reports of an enemy transport convoy.

For dinner in our wardroom that night we had hot soup, cold beef, ham, meat pie, oranges, bananas, pineapples, and coffee. We discussed this unfortunate happening. We had travelled all day in good visibility without being spotted. Now, as the last hour of darkness fell, a lucky Jap had found us.

One of the *Repulse*'s Fleet Air Arm pilots who fly the ship's aircraft – this one a young New Zealander with a ginger beard – came in cursing: "My God! Someone's blacked the right eye of my air-gunner – the one he shoots with." The laughter ended. Everyone was fitted with a tight-fitting asbestos helmet which makes you look like a Disney drawing. We were all expecting action at dawn to-morrow, hoping to meet a Jap cruiser. At 9.5 p.m. came a voice from the loudspeakers: "Stand by for the Captain to speak to you."

Captain: "A signal has just been received from the Commander-in-Chief. We were shadowed by three planes. We were spotted after dodging them all day. Their troop convoy will now have dispersed. We will find enemy aircraft waiting for us now. We are now returning to Singapore."

Then followed a babble of voices and groans. A voice said: "This ship will never get into action. It's too lucky."

So it was. In the message from the Captain the previous day, in which he said: "We're going looking for trouble and I expect we shall find it," he noted that *Repulse* had travelled 53,000 miles in this war without action, although it trailed the *Bismarck* and was off northern Norway and has convoyed throughout the war.

I slept in the wardroom fully clothed that night and awoke to the call "Action stations" at 5 a.m. on Wednesday. It was a thin oriental dawn, when a cool breeze swept through the fuggy ship, which had been battened down all night as a result of the order to "darken ship".

The sky was luminous as pearl. We saw from the flag deck a string of black objects on the port bow. They turned out to be a line of landing barges, "like railway trucks", as a young signaller said. At 6.30 a.m. the loud-speaker voice announced: "Just received message saying enemy is making landing north of Singapore. We're going in."

We all rushed off to breakfast, which consisted of coffee, cold ham, bread, and marmalade. Back at action stations all the ship's company kept a look-out. We cruised in line-ahead formation, *Prince of Wales* leading, the *Repulse* second, and with our destroyer screen out.

Down the Malayan coast, examining with the help of terrier-like destroyers all coves for enemy landing parties.

At 7.55 a.m. *Prince of Wales* catapulted one of her planes on reconnaissance, with instructions not to return to the ship, but to land ashore after making a report to us on what she found.

We watched her become midget-size and drop out of sight behind two hummock-back islands, behind which was a beach invisible to us. We all thought that was where the enemy lay. But it reappeared and went on, still searching.

Meanwhile all the ship's company on deck had put on anti-flash helmets, elbow-length asbestos gloves, goggles and tin hats.

Prince of Wales looked magnificent. White-tipped waves rippled over her plunging bows. The waves shrouded them with watery lace, then they rose high again and once again dipped. She rose and fell so methodically that the effect of staring at her was hypnotic. The fresh breeze blew her White Ensign out stiff as a board.

I felt a surge of excited anticipation rise within me at the prospect of her and the rest of the force sailing into enemy landing parties and their escorting warships.

A young Royal Marines lieutenant who was my escort when first I went aboard the *Repulse* told me: "We've not had any action but we're a perfect team – the whole twelve hundred and sixty of us. We've been working together so long. We claim to have the Navy's best gunners."

My anticipatory reverie was broken by the voice from the loudspeakers again: "Hello, there. Well, we've sighted nothing yet, but we'll go down the coast having a look for them."

More exclamations of disappointment. The yeoman of signals said: "Don't say this one's off, too."

As we sped down Malaya's changing coastline the wag of the flag-deck said travel-talkwise: "On the starboard beam, dear listeners, you see the beauty spots of Malaya, land of the orang-outang."

Again the loud-speaker announces: "Nothing sighted."

The *Repulse* sends off one of her aircraft. The pilot is not the ginger-bearded New Zealander, as he tossed a coin with another pilot and lost the toss, which means that he stays behind.

We drift to the wardroom again until 10.20 a.m. We are spotted again by a twin-engined snooper of the same type as attacked Singapore the first night of this new war.

We can do nothing about it, as she keeps well beyond range while her crew presumably studies our outlines and compares them with silhouettes in the Jap equivalent of *Jane's Fighting Ships*.

At 11 a.m. a twin-masted single funnel ship is sighted on the starboard bow. The force goes to investigate her. She carries no flag.

I was looking at her through my telescope when the shock of an explosion made me jump so that I nearly poked my right eye out. It was 11.15 a.m. The explosion came from the *Prince of Wales*'s portside secondary armament. She was firing at a single aircraft.

We open fire. There are about six aircraft.

A three-quarter-inch screw falls on my tin hat from the bridge deck above from the shock of explosion of the guns. "The old tub's falling to bits," observes the yeoman of signals.

That was the beginning of a superb air attack by the Japanese, whose air force was an unknown quantity.

Officers in the *Prince of Wales* whom I met in their wardroom when she arrived here last week said they expected some unorthodox flying from the Japs. "The great danger will be the possibility of these chaps flying their whole aircraft into a ship and committing hara-kiri."

It was nothing like that. It was most orthodox. They even came at us in formation, flying low and close.

Aboard the *Repulse*, I found observers as qualified as anyone to estimate Jap flying abilities. They know from first-hand experience what the RAF and the Luftwaffe are like. Their verdict was: "The Germans have never done anything like this in the North Sea, Atlantic or anywhere else we have been."

They concentrated on the two capital ships, taking the *Prince of Wales* first and the *Repulse* second. The destroyer screen they left completely alone except for damaged planes forced to fly low over them when they dropped bombs defensively.

At 11.18 the *Prince of Wales* opened a shattering barrage with all her multiple pom-poms, or Chicago Pianos as they call them. Red and blue flames poured from the eight-gun muzzles of each battery. I saw glowing tracer shells describe shallow curves as they went soaring skyward surrounding the enemy planes. Our Chicago Pianos opened fire; also our triple-gun four-inch high-angle turrets. The uproar was so tremendous I seemed to feel it.

From the starboard side of the flag-deck I could see two torpedo planes. No, they were bombers. Flying straight at us.

All our guns pour high-explosives at them, including shells so delicately fused that they explode if they merely graze cloth fabric.

But they swing away, carrying out a high-powered evasive action without dropping anything at all. I realize now what the purpose of the action was. It was a diversion to occupy all our guns and observers on the air defence platform at the summit of the mainmast.

There is a heavy explosion and the *Repulse* rocks. Great patches of paint fall from the funnel on to the flag-deck. We all gaze above our heads to see planes which during the action against the low fliers were unnoticed.

They are high-level bombers. Seventeen thousand feet. The first bomb, the one that rocked us a moment ago, scored a direct hit on the catapult deck through the one hangar on the port side.

I am standing behind a multiple Vickers gun, one which fires 2,000 half-inch bullets per minute. It is at the after end of the flag-deck.

I see a cloud of smoke rising from the place where the final bomb hit. Another comes down bang again from 17,000 feet. It explodes in the sea, making a creamy blue and green patch ten feet across. The *Repulse* rocks again. It was three fathoms from the port side. It was a miss, so no one bothers.

Cooling fluid is spouting from one of the barrels of a Chicago Piano. I can see black paint on the funnel-shaped covers at the muzzles of the eight barrels actually rising in blisters big as fists.

The boys manning them – there are ten to each – are sweating, saturating their asbestos anti-flash helmets. The whole gun swings this way and that as spotters pick planes to be fired at.

Two planes can be seen coming at us. A spotter sees another at a different angle, but much closer.

He leans forward, his face tight with excitement, urgently pounding the back of the gun swiveller in front of him. He hits that back with his right hand and points with the left a stabbing forefinger at a single sneaker plane. Still blazing two-pounders the whole gun platform turns in a hail of death at the single plane. It is some 1,000 yards away.

I saw tracers rip into its fuselage dead in the centre. Its fabric opened up like a rapidly spreading sore with red edges. Fire . . .

It swept to the tail, and in a moment stabilizer and rudder

became a framework skeleton. Her nose dipped down and she went waterward.

We cheered like madmen. I felt my larynx tearing in the effort to make myself heard above the hellish uproar of guns.

A plane smacked the sea on its belly and was immediately transformed into a gigantic shapeless mass of fire which shot over the waves fast as a snake's tongue. The *Repulse* had got the first raider.

For the first time since the action began we can hear a sound from the loud-speakers, which are on every deck at every action station. It is the sound of a bugle.

Its first notes are somewhat tortured. The young bugler's lips and throat are obviously dry with excitement. It is that most sinister alarm of all for seamen: "Fire!"

Smoke from our catapult deck is thick now. Men in overalls, their faces hidden by a coat of soot, man-handle hoses along decks. Water fountains delicately from a rough patch made in one section by binding it with a white shirt.

It sprays on the Vickers gunners, who, in a momentary lull, lift faces, open mouths and put out tongues to catch the cooling jets. They quickly avert faces to spit – the water is salt and it is warm. It is sea water.

The Chicago Piano opens up again with a suddenness that I am unable to refrain from flinching at, though once they get going with their erratic shell-pumping it is most reassuring.

All aboard have said the safest place in any battleship or cruiser or destroyer is behind a Chicago Piano. I believe them.

Empty brass cordite cases are tumbling out of the gun's scuttle-like exit so fast and so excitedly it reminds me of the forbidden fruit machine in Gibraltar on which I once played. It went amok on one occasion and ejected £8 in shillings in a frantic rush.

The cases bounce off the steel C deck, roll and dance down the sloping base into a channel for easy picking up later.

At 11.25 we see an enormous splash on the very edge of the horizon. The splash vanishes and a whitish cloud takes its place.

A damaged enemy plane jettisoning its bombs or another enemy destroyed? A rapid Gallup poll on the flag deck says: "Another duck down." Duck is a word they have rapidly taken from the Aussie Navy. It means enemy plane.

Hopping about the flag-deck from port to starboard, which-ever side is being attacked, is the plump figure of the naval photographer named Tubby Abrahams.

He was a Fleet Street agency pictureman now in the Navy. But all his pictures are lost. He had to throw them into the sea with his camera. He was saved. So was United States broad-caster Cecil Brown, of Columbia System.

Fire parties are still fighting the hangar outbreak, oblivious of any air attack used so far. Bomb splinters have torn three holes in the starboard side of the funnel on our flag-deck.

Gazing impotently with no more than fountain pen and note-book in my hands while gunners, signallers, surgeons and range-finders worked, I found emotional release in shouting rather stupidly, I suppose, at the Japanese.

I discovered depths of obscenity previously unknown, even to me.

One young signaller keeps passing me pieces of information in between running up flats. He has just said: "A couple of blokes are caught in the lift from galley to servery. They're trying to get them out."

The yeoman of signals interjected: "How the bloody hell they got there, God knows."

There is a short lull. The boys dig inside their overalls and pull out cigarettes. Then the loud-speaker voice: "Enemy air-craft ahead." Lighted ends are nipped off cigarettes. The ship's company goes into action again. "Twelve of them." The flag-deck boys whistle. Someone counts them aloud: "One, two, three, four, five, six, seven, eight, nine – yes, nine." The flag-deck wag, as he levels a signalling lamp at the *Prince of Wales*: "Any advance on nine? Anybody? No? Well, here they come."

It is 12.10 p.m. They are all concentrating on the *Prince of Wales*. They are after the big ships all right. A mass of water and smoke rises in a tree-like column from the *Prince of Wales*'s stern. They've got her with a torpedo.

A ragged-edged mass of flame from her Chicago Piano does not stop them, nor the heavy instant flashes from her high-angle secondary armament.

She is listing to port – a bad list. We are about six cables from her.

A snottie, or midshipman, runs past, calls as he goes: "*Prince of Wales*'s steering gear gone." It doesn't seem possible that those slight-looking planes could do that to her.

The planes leave us, having apparently dropped all their bombs and torpedoes. I don't believe it is over, though. "Look, look!" shouts someone, "there's a line in the water right under our bows, growing longer on the starboard side. A torpedo that missed us. Wonder where it'll stop."

The *Prince of Wales* signals us again asking if we've been torpedoed. Our Captain Tennant replies: "Not yet. We've dodged nineteen."

Six stokers arrive on the flag-deck. They are black with smoke and oil and are in need of first aid. They are ushered down to the armoured citadel at the base of the mainmast.

The *Prince of Wales*'s list is increasing. There is a great rattle of empty two-pounder cordite cases as Chicago Piano boys gather up the empties and stow them away and clear for further action.

12.20 p.m . . . The end is near, although I didn't know it.

A new wave of planes appears, flying around us in formation and gradually coming nearer. The *Prince of Wales* lies about ten cables astern of our port side. She is helpless.

They are making for her. I don't know how many. They are splitting up our guns as they realize they are after her, knowing she can't dodge their torpedoes. So we fire at them to defend the *Prince of Wales* rather than attend to our own safety.

The only analogy I can think of to give an impression of the *Prince of Wales* in those last moments is of a mortally wounded tiger trying to beat off the *coup de grâce*.

Her outline is hardly distinguishable in smoke and flame from all her guns except the fourteen-inchers. I can see one plane release a torpedo. It drops nose heavy into the sea and churns up a small wake as it drives straight at the *Prince of Wales*. It explodes against her bows.

A couple of seconds later another explodes amidships and another astern. Gazing at her turning over on the port side with her stern going under and with dots of men leaping from her, I was thrown against the bulkhead by a tremendous shock as the *Repulse* takes a torpedo on her portside stern.

With all others on the flag-deck I am wondering where it

came from, when the *Repulse* shudders gigantically. Another torpedo.

Now men cheering with more abandon than at a Cup Final. What the heck is this? I wonder. Then see it is another plane down. It hits the sea in flames also. There have been six so far as I know.

My notebook, which I have got before me, is stained with oil and is ink-blurred. It says: "Third torp."

The *Repulse* now listing badly to starboard. The loud-speakers speak for the last time: "Everybody on main deck."

We all troop down ladders, most orderly except for one lad who climbs the rail and is about to jump when an officer says: "Now then – come back – we are all going your way." The boy came back and joined the line.

It seemed slow going. Like all the others I suppose I was tempted to leap to the lower deck, but the calmness was catching. When we got to the main deck the list was so bad our shoes and feet could not grip the steel deck. I kicked off mine, and my damp stockinged feet made for sure movement.

Nervously opening my cigarette case I found I hadn't a match. I offered a cigarette to a man beside me. He said: "Ta. Want a match?" We both lit up and puffed once or twice. He said: "I'll be seeing you, mate." To which I replied: "Hope so, cheerio."

We were all able to walk down the ship's starboard side, she lay so much over to port.

We all formed a line along a big protruding anti-torpedo blister, from where we had to jump some twelve feet into a sea which was black – I discovered it was oil.

I remember jamming my cap on my head, drawing a breath and leaping.

Oh, I forgot – the last entry in my notebook was: "Sank about 12.20 p.m." I made it before leaving the flag-deck. In the water I glimpsed the *Prince of Wales*'s bows disappearing.

Kicking with all my strength, I with hundreds of others tried to get away from the *Repulse* before she went under, being afraid of getting drawn under in the whirlpool.

I went in the wrong direction, straight into the still spreading oil patch, which felt almost as thick as velvet. A wave hit me and swung me round so that I saw the last of the *Repulse*.

Her underwater plates were painted a bright, light red. Her bows rose high as the air trapped inside tried to escape from underwater forward regions, and there she hung for a second or two and easily slid out of sight.

I had a tremendous feeling of loneliness, and could see nothing capable of carrying me. I kicked, lying on my back, and felt my eyes burning as the oil crept over me, in mouth, nostrils, and hair.

When swamped by the waves, I remember seeing the water I spurted from my mouth was black. I came across two men hanging on to a round lifebelt. They were black, and I told them they looked like a couple of Al Jolsons. They said: "Well, we must be a trio, 'cos you're the same."

We were joined by another, so we had an Al Jolson quartet on one lifebelt. It was too much for it and in the struggle to keep it lying flat on the sea we lost it.

We broke up, with the possibility of meeting again, but none of us would know the other, owing to the complete mask of oil.

I kicked, I must confess somewhat panicky, to escape from the oil, but all I achieved was a bumping into a floating paravane. Once again there were four black faces with red eyes gathered together in the sea.

Then we saw a small motor boat with two men in it. The engine was broken. I tried to organize our individual strength into a concerted drive to reach the idly floating boat. We tried to push or pull ourselves by hanging on the paravane, kicking our legs, but it was too awkward, and it overturned.

I lost my grip and went under. My underwater struggles happily took me nearer to the boat.

After about two hours in the water, two hours of oil-fuel poisoning, I reached a thin wire rope which hung from the boat's bows.

My fingers were numb and I was generally weak as the result of the poisoning, but I managed to hold on to the wire by clamping my arms around it. I called to the men aboard to help me climb the four feet to the deck.

They tried with a boat hook, but finally said: "You know, we are pretty done in, too. You've got to try to help yourself. We can't do it alone."

I said I could not hold anything. They put the boathook in my shirt collar, but it tore and finally they said: "Sorry pal, we can't lift you. Have you got that wire?"

"Yes," I said. They let me go and there I hung. Another man arrived and caught the wire. He was smaller than I was. I am thirteen stone. The men aboard said they would try to get him up. "He's lighter than you," they said.

They got him aboard during which operation I went under again when he put his foot on my shoulder. The mouth of one black face aboard opened and showed black-slimed teeth, red gums and tongue. It said: "To hell with this."

He dived through the oil into the sea, popped up beside me with a round lifebelt which he put over my head, saying: "Okay. Now let go the wire."

But I'm sorry to say I couldn't. I couldn't bear to part with it. It had kept me on the surface about fifteen minutes.

They separated us, however, and the next thing I was draped through the lifebelt like a dummy being hauled aboard at a rope's end, which they could grip as it was not oily or shiny.

Another oil casualty was dragged aboard, and later thirty of us were lifted aboard a destroyer. We were stripped, bathed and left naked on the fo'c'sle benches and tables to sweat the oil out of the pores in the great heat.

World War II

HOMER BIGART

Reporter Rides Fortress in Wilhelmshaven Raid

Bigart was one of eight correspondents selected to fly with the USAAF on bombing missions over Germany. The eight – dubbed the "Flying Typewriters" and "the Writing 69th" – were given a week's high-altitude aircrew training in England and flew their first mission on 26 February 1943. It was also their last; the death of the *New York Times*'s Bob Post on the raid was such bad publicity that the idea was dropped. Below is Bigart's story of the mission, which he dispatched to the *Herald Tribune* by telephone.

New York *Herald Tribune*, 27 February 1943

An American bomber station, somewhere in England, Feb. 26, 1943 – Our target was Wilhelmshaven. We struck at Fuehrer Adolf Hitler's North Sea base from the southwest after stoogeing around over a particularly hot corner of the Third Reich for what seemed like a small eternity.

I could not quite make out our specific target for obliteration, the submarine pens, because at our altitude the installations along the Jade Busen (Jade Bay) seemed no larger than a pinhead. But the street pattern of the Prussian town stood out in perfect visibility and so did the large suburb of Rustringen, down the bay.

Our Fortress, "Old Soljer", piloted by Captain Lewis Elton

Lyle of Pine Bluff, Ark., led the squadron. I was up in the nose with the bombardier, Second Lieutenant Reinaldo J. Saiz of Segundo, Colo., and the navigator, First Lieutenant Otis Allen Hoyt of Dawn, Mo. We were lucky. Just before our arrival a heavy cloud formation cleared the northwest tip of Germany, drifting east and disclosing Wilhelmshaven to our bombsight.

And there was no Focke-Wulf on our tail when we started our bomb run. We had a good run and we were squarely over the town. I watched Saiz crouch lower over his sight. I heard him call "Bombs away."

Our salvo of 500-pounders plunged through the open bomb bay. From where I stood I could not see them land, but our ball turret gunner, Staff Sergeant Howard L. Nardine of Los Angeles, took a quick look back and saw fires and smoke.

Frankly, I wasn't so much interested in the target. What intrigued me was the action upstairs. Flak was bursting all around the squadron just ahead and to our left. The shells were exploding in nasty black puffs, leaving curious smoke trails of hour-glass shape.

Enemy fighters were darting in all directions. "Hoss" Lyle said there must have been 35. They were out for stragglers and they let us alone. There was a flak burst about 200 yards off our starboard wing, but that was the nearest we came to the casualty list.

Once our bombs were dropped Hoss Lyle pulled some evasive action. He had us shifting like the Notre Dame varsity, changing course so often that the Focke-Wulfs sitting there against the horizon never had a chance to set us up for a frontal attack. That's the way they like to come in on a Fortress – from 11 o'clock or 1 o'clock position. They seem to like the big glass nose of a B-17.

[In air-force parlance, "o'clocks" are used for compass points.]

You see them far ahead, mere specks in the sky, and they are on to you in a minute. He's doing about 400 miles an hour and you are not exactly standing still, so you have only a few seconds to put the bead on him and press the trigger.

Our squadron is back without loss, but the other formations had a few casualties.

The Liberators took a nasty going over. Coming home we saw a Liberator trying to shake off a whole swarm of fighters.

He was racing for a cloud bank over the North Sea, with Messerschmitts hot on his trail. He disappeared in the cloud; and that was the last we saw of him.

Initiation for Reporters

It was a fairly easy initiation for the six newspaper correspondents who got themselves assigned to the 8th Bomber Squadron in the fervent hope of seeing Berlin by daylight from American bombers.

The worst moment came early in the attack. I saw a ship ahead of us go down in a dizzy spin, with two parachutes opening in its wake. For an instant I almost wished I was back in Brooklyn.

Yet the whole trip was so theatrical that you forgot to be scared. The Technicolor was excellent, the action fairly gripping and the casting superb. Only the scenario needed cutting. I got awfully tired of looking at the North Sea, a disagreeable piece of scenery in February.

Our first view of the Continent was a low and desolate sand strip, which I identified as one of the Frisian Islands. The Frisians are heavily defended, but the flak was surprisingly light and inaccurate. We were close to the Dutch border, and far to the south I thought I saw the broad mouth of the Zuyder Zee shining in the sun.

Before we reached the mainland, the enemy was upstairs waiting with a reception committee of Focke-Wulfs and Messerschmitts. For about an hour thereafter I heard the gunners drone, "Fighters at 6 o'clock; fighters at 3 o'clock; fighters at 9 o'clock."

All our gunners were shooting at one time or another but the enemy stayed just out of range of our .50-caliber guns.

Peeling off after an attack on another ship, a fighter dove in front of us. Our bombardier gave him a spray, but he was going so fast I couldn't tell whether he was a Focke-Wulf or a Messerschmitt.

With Wilhelmshaven behind us we followed the Jade Busen down to the sea. There appeared to be a lot of flak ships in the roadstead and further up we passed over an island that fairly bristled with guns directly below. We were over that island for what seemed like an intolerable spell.

The Focke-Wulfs didn't follow us far. They were replaced by heavier twin-engined jobs, Messerschmitt-110s, which hung around like vultures until we were halfway to England, waiting to pounce on a cripple. The pink tip of Helgoland was far to the northeast when the Messerschmitts finally decided to go home.

This was "Hoss" Lyle's 13th operation, and he told me it was "a piece of cake" compared with jobs on Lorient and St Nazaire, for Reich Marshal Hermann Wilhelm Goering has his best fighters around Abbeville and on the Brest peninsula.

"Hoss" is 26 years old and one of the smartest pilots in the air force. He intends to stay with the army after the war.

"Old Soljer" has an able crew. Our co-pilot, Captain Jacob Wayne Frederick of Wakarusa, Ind., Purdue '38, is a veteran of equal experience with Lyle. Frederick was 26 years old today and the crew serenaded him all the way home.

The rest of the cast were: Third gunner, Technical Sergeant Michael ("Big Stoop") Hlastala, 23, who is 6½ feet tall and comes from Uniontown, Pa.; waist gunners, Sergeant Henry George ("Hank") Schneiderman of Freeport, Ill., who was celebrating his 25th birthday, and Sergeant Harvie Cecil Collins of Hoxie, Ark.; tail gunner Staff Sergeant Gilbert Agnew Murray, 24, of Oakland, Calif; radio operator, Technical Sergeant Richard J. ("Snuffy") Smith of Boston.

I did not tell the crew that during our training course a few weeks ago I was chosen as the man least likely to return from a mission.

World War II

ERNIE PYLE

German Supermen Up Close

Ernie Pyle was probably the best-known, certainly the best-loved
American war correspondent of the 1939–45 conflict. More so than
anybody else, the balding, unassuming Pyle was the real interpreter
– and voice – of ordinary GI experience.

Washington *Daily News*, 10 May 1943

Northern Tunisia, *May 8, 1943* – Before the first day of the
great surrender on the Bizerte-Tunis front was over, I believe
half the Americans in the area had German souvenirs of some
sort.

There was very little of what one would call looting of
German supply dumps. The Germans gave away helmets, goggles and map cases, which they will not be needing anymore.
The spoils of war which the average doughboy has on him are
legitimate, and little enough recompense for his fighting.

Practically every American truck has a German or Italian
helmet fastened to its radiator. Our motorcycles are decorated
like a carnival, with French flags and the colorful little black-
and-yellow death's-head pennants the Germans use for marking
their own mine fields.

Many soldiers have new Lugers in their holsters. Lots of our
men clowningly wear German field caps. German goggles are
frequently seen on American heads. I got in on the souvenirs,
too. I got one memento that is a little gem. It's an automobile –
yep, a real automobile that runs.

I drove back to camp the first evening in my German "Volkswagen", the bantam car the Nazis use as we use our jeep. It is a topless two-seater with a rear motor, camouflaged a dirty brown.

Mine was given me by our 1st Armored Division for – as they said – "sweating it out with us at Faïd Pass all winter". As I drove back from the lines, Americans in the rear would stare, startled-like and belligerent; then, seeing an American at the wheel they would laugh and wave. I have owned half a dozen autos in my life, but I've never been so proud of one as of my clattering little Volkswagen.

On the first day of surrender the Germans sat in groups of hundreds in the fields, just waiting. They lay on their overcoats, resting. They took off their shirts to sun themselves. They took off their shoes to rest their feet.

They were a tired army but not a nondescript one. All were extremely well equipped. Their uniforms were good. They had plenty in the way of little personal things, money, cigarettes, and food. Their equipment was of the best materials.

One English-appearing soldier had a Gem nailclipper. He said he paid twenty-five cents for it in New York in 1939.

Some were cleanly shaven, some had three- or four-day beards, just like our soldiers. Lots of them had red-rimmed eyes from lack of sleep.

As a whole, they seemed younger than our men, and I was surprised that on the average they didn't seem as big. But they did appear well fed and in excellent health.

They think Americans are fine fighters. They express only good-natured contempt for their allies, the Italians. As one of them said:

"It isn't just that Italians don't fight well. It's simply that Germans don't like Italians very much in the first place."

Wherever any American correspondents stopped, prisoners immediately gathered around. They all seemed in good spirits. Even those who couldn't speak a word of English would try hard to tell you something.

The main impression I got, seeing German prisoners, was that they were human like anybody else, fundamentally friendly, a little vain. Certainly they are not supermen. Whenever a group of them would form, some American soldier would pop up with a camera to get a souvenir picture. And every time, all the prisoners in the vicinity would crowd into the picture like kids.

One German boy had found a broken armchair leaning against a barn, and was sitting in it. When I passed he grinned, pointed to his feet and then to the chair arms, and put back his head in the international sign language for "Boy, does this chair feel good!"

This colossal German surrender has done more for American morale here than anything that could possibly have happened. Winning in battle is like winning at poker or catching lots of fish – it's damned pleasant and it sets a man up. As a result, the hundreds of thousands of Americans in North Africa now are happy men, laughing and working with new spirits that bubble.

World War II

MARGARET BOURKE-WHITE

Over the Lines

The photographer Margaret Bourke-White joined *Life* magazine in 1935. She photographed the Second World War from Russia to North Africa, from Italy to Germany, as well as penning several volumes of war memoirs. Here she recalls an assignment over the Cassino Valley, Italy, in 1943.

Purple Heart Valley, 1944

"This strip is really a nerve jerker," Lieutenant Mike Strok called to me over his shoulder.

We were circling above the tiniest airfield I had ever seen. The landing strip was so pocked with shell craters that I did not see how my Grasshopper pilot was going to slip in among them. It was nothing more than the beaten edge of a plowed field, but for the Air OP's, the "Eyes of the Artillery" as they are called in heavy-gun circles, this strip was their most forward operating base.

Lieutenant Strok had to divide his attention between the shell pits below and the sky above. This was because we were landing in the region airmen called Messerschmitt Alley. If an unarmed, unarmored observation plane such as our Cub is attacked, the pilot's means of escape is to outmaneuver the enemy.

"Good idea to make sure there's no Jerry fighter hanging about," said Lieutenant Strok. "If you can see him first, then he doesn't get the chance to blast the daylights out of you."

A final inspection confirmed that the sky was clear, and he brought our tiny Cub to a standstill on a piece of earth as big as a back yard in Brooklyn.

The commanding officer of the field and his ground crew of one ran up to greet us.

The ground crew spoke first. "If that ain't an American girl, then I'm seeing things!" he exclaimed.

The young officer laughed. "Sorry we're out of red carpet," he said. "We live like gypsies up here."

The CO of the Grasshoppers was twenty-six-year-old Captain Jack Marinelli of Ottumwa, Iowa. He was chief pilot and supervisor for a group of artillery liaison pilots who hedge-hopped along the front lines in their Cubs, acting as flying observation posts to spot enemy targets and adjust fire for Fifth Army artillery. I had seldom seen a flier who bore less resemblance to Hollywood's idea of a pilot than Captain Marinelli. He looked more like the tractor and hay-machine demonstrator which I learned he had been back in Iowa before the war. He was plump, pleasant, and easygoing. This last characteristic, I was to find, faded as soon as the enemy was in sight. He had the reputation of being the coolest and most resourceful artillery pilot on the Fifth Army front.

Mike Strok explained that I wanted to take airplane pictures of the front, and Captain Marinelli said, "Well, I've just had a call to go out on a mission. There's a *Nebelwerfer* holding up an infantry division and they asked me to go out and try to spot it. She can come along if she wants to."

"Jees, you don't want to take a girl on a mission," said the ground crew of one.

"She'll go if you'll take her," stated Lieutenant Strok.

"What's a *Nebelwerfer*?" I inquired.

"You've heard of a screaming meemie, haven't you? Wicked weapon! It's a multiple mortar: eight-barreled rocket gun."

By the time the screaming meemie was explained to me, I had been strapped into the observer's seat, and the ground crew was adjusting a parachute to my back and shoulders.

Knowing that one of the functions of observer is to watch all quadrants of the sky for enemy planes, I said to the Captain, "I'm not going to make a very good observer for you. Most of the time I'll have my face buried in my camera, and even when

I haven't, I'm not sure I'll know the difference between an enemy fighter and one of ours."

"Don't worry about that," Captain Marinelli said. "If you see anything that looks like an airplane, you tell me and I'll decide whether it's a bandit or an angel."

I placed my airplane camera on my knees and arranged additional equipment and a couple of spare cameras, telephoto lenses, and some aerial filters on the low shelf behind my shoulders. The space was so cramped, and any extra movement so pinched, with the parachute crowded on my back, that I wanted to be sure I had everything near at hand where I could reach it in a hurry. There was no room in the Cub to wear helmets, as our heads touched the roof. Someone had lent me one of the fur caps used by our Alaska troops, and I tucked my hair back under it and tied it firmly around my chin. When you lean out into the slipstream with an airplane camera, any escaping strand of hair will lash into your eyes and sometimes blind you during just that vital second when you are trying to catch a picture. The Captain lowered the whole right side of the airplane, folding it completely out of the way so I would have an unobstructed area in which to lean out and work. Then he spoke into his microphone. "Mike-Uncle-Charlie! This is Mike-Uncle-Charlie five-zero. I'm taking off on a mission. Stand by!"

"Who is Mike-Uncle-Charlie?" I asked.

"That's our brigade HQ's code word for today," replied the Captain. "Just our phonetic alphabet for MUC – today's call letters. When I find something that radio guy will be sitting up there with his ear phones on, listening."

The ground crew spun the props. "We'll be back in time for lunch," shouted Captain Marinelli to Lieutenant Strok as we started to taxi between the shell craters. I glanced at my watch. which registered quarter after eleven, and couldn't help wondering if we really would be back for lunch. I was trying hard not to wonder whether we would be back at all.

As we headed toward the front I was impressed with how regular the pattern of war, seemingly so chaotic from the ground, appears from the air. The tracks of pattern bombing on an airfield were as regular as though drawn with ruler and compass. In some olive groves the traffic patterns made by trucks and jeeps which had parked there looked as if a school child had drawn circles in a penmanship exercise, his pen filled not with ink but with a silvery mud-and-water mixture which held the light of the sun. Each bridge had been demolished with a Teutonic precision. The delicate arches of the small bridges were broken through the crest; larger bridges were buckled like giant accordions. Paralleling these were bypasses and emergency bridges which our engineers had thrown up. Most regular of all was German railroad demolition. Between the rails an endless succession of Vs marched into the distance, an effect produced by the giant plow which the retreating Germans had dragged from their last railroad train, cracking each tie in two so neatly that it seemed as if someone had unrolled a narrow length of English tweed, flinging this herringbone strip over the hills and valleys of Italy.

The irregularities were furnished by the smashed towns, so wrecked that seldom did two walls stand together, and never was a roof intact. Flying low, sometimes we could see Italian civilians picking through the sickening rubble that once had been their homes.

As we flew over the ghastly wreckage of Mignano and headed toward the still more thoroughly wrecked town of San Pietro, suddenly our plane was jarred so violently that it bounced over on its side, and we heard what sounded like a thunderclap just below.

"That's a shell leaving one of our big hows," Marinelli said as he righted the plane.

"Sounded close," I said.

"I'd hate to tell you how close," Captain Marinelli replied.

"How are you going to know when you get to the front?" I asked.

"Oh, that's easy," he explained. "When you stop seeing stars on things you know you've left your own side behind."

I looked down and saw our jeeps, trucks, and half-tracks crawling along Highway Six below us, each plainly marked with its white star.

"But the best way to tell is by the bridges," he continued. "As long as you see trestle bridges below you know we're over friendly territory, because those are bridges our engineers have built. When you begin spotting blown-out bridges you know we're approaching no man's land. The last thing the Germans do when they pull out is to blow up their bridges, and if they haven't been repaired it's because it's been too hot for our men to get in and mend them.

"When you see a stretch of road with no traffic at all, that's no man's land. And when you see the first bridge intact on the other side, you know you're crossing into Jerry territory."

We were flying over the crest of hills which surrounded Cassino valley like the rim of a cup. Highway Six wound between bald, rocky mountains here, and we almost scraped their razor-back edges as we flew over. I could look down and see entrenchments and gun emplacements set in layers of rock. Then the land dropped away sharply, and all at once we were high over Cassino corridor.

As I looked down, the earth seemed to be covered with glistening polka dots – almost as though someone had taken a bolt of gray coin-spotted satin and unrolled it over the landscape. I knew these were shell holes, thousands of them, and made by the guns of both sides, first when we shelled the Germans here, and now by their guns shelling us. As we rose higher I could look down and see hundreds of thousands of these holes filled with rain and glistening in the sun.

"It's been so rough down there," said Captain Marinelli, "that the boys are calling it Purple Heart Valley."

I could hardly believe that so many shells could have fallen in a single valley. It was cruelly contradictory that with all this evidence of bloodshed and destruction, the valley seemed to clothe itself in a sequin-dotted gown.

As we flew on, we glanced back toward our own territory and could see the muzzle flashes from our guns winking on and off as though people were lighting matches over the hillsides. Each gun flash left a smoke trail until our Allied-held hills appeared to be covered with the smoke of countless campfires.

"The worst of that smoke is from our howitzers," Marinelli said.

And then he added, "Usually we don't fly across the lines unless the mission absolutely requires it. But it looks to me as though we're going to have to today, to find that *Nebelwerfer*. OK with you?"

"I'm right with you, Captain."

We circled lower over a loop of Highway Six where wrecked tanks were tumbled, around the curve of road. "First day they've brought tanks out into the open," said Marinelli. "I want to radio back a report." The tanks seemed to have been picked off one by one as they tried to round the bend, but I could see one tank charging bravely ahead. Then as we bobbed over it, I could see a giant retriever coming in with a derrick to evacuate one of the blasted tanks.

Just beyond we began seeing demolished bridges, and we circled above these also, because the Captain's secondary mission was to report on any bridges that had been blown up. He was just phoning back his observations, and I was taking pictures, when suddenly our plane was rocked sharply back and forth and we heard a sound like freight trains rumbling under us.

"Jerry shells," said Marinelli. "High explosives! You know, they've been missing that road junction by a hundred yards every day this week."

We were tossing around violently now, and dark whorls and spirals of greasy smoke were blanketing the ground beneath.

"We've got infantry troops down there," the Captain said. The realization was almost more than I could bear – that our own boys were trying to slog through that fatal square of earth being chewed up by high-explosive shells.

An instant later we were flying over a desolate stretch of road with no traffic at all. This, then, was no man's land. At the farther end we saw a beautifully, arched ancient bridge, its masonry quite intact.

"Jerry territory," said the Captain, and took the plane sharply upward.

Over our own side the Cubs make a practice of flying low, because this makes an attack by enemy fighters more difficult, as they cannot come in under, but when the observation planes cross the lines, they must increase altitude, for without armor they are very vulnerable to small-arms fire.

In search of the German rocket gun, we flew four miles over enemy territory and Captain Marinelli began hunting for the *Nebelwerfer* in the region of San Angelo.

"That's the 'Gargling River'," he pointed out. "GI for Garigliano. And there's the Rapido." The road to Rome stretched forward into the distance, with a railroad running parallel some distance to the left. A hairpin turn branched upward toward the Benedictine monastery, at that time still intact. The ruins of Cassino lay in white smudges at the foot of snowcapped Mt Cairo.

Cassino corridor presented an extraordinary appearance, with white plumes rising up at intervals from the valley floor. These were phosphorus shells from our own Long Toms, falling on the enemy. Whenever one landed close below us we could see it opening out into a pointed splash of fire, which quickly became transformed into a rising chunk of smoke.

Suddenly I spotted a tiny silhouette in the sky, behind us. "There's a plane," I yelled.

"Just another Cub out on a mission," said Marinelli. "But you did the right thing. Tell me anything you see."

Just then he picked up the flash of the German *Nebelwerfer* – too quick for my untrained eye – and caught sight of the shrubbery blowing back on the ground from the gun blast.

"Mike-Uncle-Charlie," he spoke into his microphone. "This is Mike-Uncle-Charlie Five-zero. Enemy gun battery located at co-ordinate 86–16–2. I can observe. Over."

Then to me, over his shoulder, "It's going to take them a little time now, because they've got to compute their data and consult their fire-direction chart to see which guns can reach the target. They'll let me know when they've assigned a battery. We'll be hanging right around here, so speak up if you want to be put into position for anything special."

There were many things that I wanted to be put into position for. Below us it looked as though someone were shaking an enormous popcorn shaker with white grains of popcorn bursting all over the valley floor. These were thickest in front of Cassino. The Captain maneuvered the plane so that I was practically lying on my side over the valley, and – strapped in safely – I could get an unobstructed view of the battleground below.

In a few minutes a message came through that Xray-King-Item would fire. While I took pictures of the popcorn-sprinkled valley, Marinelli carried on his radio conversation with Xray-King-Item, the battery assigned to knock out the *Nebelwerfer*.

I was overwhelmed to learn that it would be my pilot, up in our little Cub, who would actually give the command to fire. The next message he received was, "Mike-Uncle-Charlie five-zero, this is Xray-King-Item. Will fire on your command. Over."

"Fire," said Marinelli, and the reply came back, "Seventy-two seconds. On the way."

It seemed amazing that the shell travelling from the Long Tom battery several miles back of us would take almost a minute and a quarter to reach the enemy gun target below. The Captain was checking with his watch. "Don't want to sense the wrong round," he explained.

He had to make this precise time check because with other guns peppering the valley it was easy to make an error, and it would have caused great confusion had he started correcting the aim of some other gun.

On the seventy-second second, a white geyser began rising toward us from below, and we knew that this was Xray-King-Item's smoke shell. Marinelli spoke into his microphone: "Xray-King-Item; this is Mike-Uncle-Charlie five-zero; five hundred yards right, one hundred yards short. Over."

Then he explained, "We've got to give them a little time again to make their correction. They're laying number-one gun on it now. When they get it adjusted they'll tie in the whole battery."

Soon another message came from Xray-King-Item: seventy-two seconds on the way. Again at the end of the seventy-two seconds a feather of smoke rose from below. The aim was closer now: "Five-zero right; seven-zero short," Captain Marinelli radioed.

I realized that the Captain was handling a great many tasks at once. Not only was he checking his watch during each seventy-two-second intervals, radioing his sensings in terms of deflection and elevation data, but he was keeping an eye on the sky for enemy planes. And taking care of me, too! Every time I saw a fresh shell burst I would yell to be put in position, and he would maneuver the Cub so that I could photograph while he observed.

Suddenly he exclaimed, "We're being shot at." We could hear faint sounds as though twigs were snapping against the plane – a little like hot grease spitting in a frying pan just beyond us. "It's a Spandau," said Marinelli, and he knew exactly what to do. Since the Spandau, a German machine gun, has an effective range up to 2400 feet, he simply circled up to 3200 feet, where he went on making his observations and I went on taking photographs.

"Hands cold?" he called.

They were almost numb. At our higher altitude the air was colder and I had been leaning out into the windstream with the camera. The Captain, more protected by the nose of the Cub, stripped off his gloves and gave them to me.

The whole process of adjusting fire had gone on for about fourteen minutes when Captain Marinelli finally radioed, "Deflection correct, range correct. Fire for effect."

"They're bringing in several batteries this time," said the Captain. "And this time it will be HE shells."

At the end of seventy-two seconds we could see that whole area being blanketed, not with white smoke bursts as before, but with the deadlier high-explosive shells. Curls and twists of black smoke spurted over the ground and billowed upward, and we knew that the *Nebelwerfer* was being chewed to bits.

"This is Mike-Uncle-Charlie five-zero," called Captain Marinelli. "Target area completely covered. Fire effective. Enemy battery neutralized."

Less than a minute later he exclaimed, "I see a fighter." Then, "I see two fighters."

Coming around Mt Cevaro I could see them too: a black speck growing larger and behind it another smaller speck. In less time than it takes to tell, they had taken on the size and shape of airplanes.

We were in such a steep dive by that time that I was practically standing on my head, when I heard Marinelli say, "I see four fighters."

Sure enough, there were four shapes coming toward us, looking unmistakably like Focke-Wulf 190s.

This was the steepest dive I had ever been in in my life. I tried to take a picture, a plan I very quickly had to abandon because, with the whole side of the plane completely open, and the shelf behind me full of cameras and lenses, it was all I could do to hold back my equipment with my elbow and shoulders, to keep it from sailing into space.

I was bracing myself with the back of my neck when Captain Marinelli exclaimed, "I've lost my mike. Can you find my mike for me?" I knew he needed his microphone so he could report the fighters as a warning to all the other Cubs in the air. Groping with my left hand, and holding back my cameras with my right below, I retrieved his mike and handed it to him. We were still gliding down at a terrific angle when he reported, "Four enemy fighters sighted."

We were within fifteen feet of the ground when he pulled out of that dive. I have never seen such flying. He ducked into a gully and began snaking along a stream bed. Soon we were behind a small hill and over our own territory, where the fighters could not follow us in so low. In another instant we were behind a mountain and blocked from sight of the enemy planes.

We flew back to our field in time for mess, and when we rolled into the tiny landing strip, the ground crew came running up, bursting with news. To Captain Marinelli this news was much more exciting than being chased by four Focke-Wulfs: there was steak for lunch.

World War II

JOHN STEINBECK

It Was Dark as Hell

Famous for his Pulitzer Prize-winning novel *The Grapes of Wrath*, Steinbeck took a turn as a war reporter in Italy, covering the grim American landings at Salerno (thirty miles south of Naples) on 9 September 1943.

New York *Herald Tribune*, 4 October 1943

There are little bushes on the sand dunes at Red Beach south of the Sele River, and in a hole in the sand buttressed by sand bags a soldier sat with a leather-covered steel telephone beside him. His shirt was off and his back was dark with sunburn. His helmet lay in the bottom of the hole and his rifle was on a little pile of brush to keep the sand out of it. He had staked a shelter half on a pole to shade him from the sun, and he had spread bushes on top of that to camouflage it. Beside him was a water can and an empty "C" ration can to drink out of.

The soldier said, "Sure you can have a drink. Here, I'll pour it for you." He tilted the water can over the tin cup. "I hate to tell you what it tastes like," he said. I took a drink. "Well, doesn't it?" he said. "It sure does," I said. Up in the hills the 88s were popping and the little bursts threw sand about where they hit, and off to the seaward our cruisers were popping away at the 88s in the hills.

The soldier slapped at a sand fly on his shoulder and then scratched the place where it had bitten him. His face was dirty and streaked where the sweat had run down through the dirt, and his hair and his eyebrows were sunburned almost white. But there was a kind of gayety about him. His telephone buzzed and he answered it, and said, "Hasn't come through yet. Sir, no sir. I'll tell him." He clicked off the phone.

"When'd you come ashore?" he asked. And then without waiting for an answer he went on. "I came in just before dawn yesterday. I wasn't with the very first, but right in the second." He seemed to be very glad about it. "It was hell," he said, "it was bloody hell." He seemed to be gratified at the hell it was, and that was right. The great question had been solved for him. He had been under fire. He knew now what he would do under fire. He would never have to go through that uncertainty again. "I got pretty near up to there," he said, and pointed to two beautiful Greek temples about a mile away. "And then I got sent back here for beach communications. When did you say you got ashore?" and again he didn't wait for an answer.

"It was dark as hell," he said, "and we were just waiting out there." He pointed to the sea where the mass of the invasion fleet rested. "If we thought we were going to sneak ashore we were nuts," he said. "They were waiting for us all fixed up. Why, I heard they had been here two weeks waiting for us. They knew just where we were going to land. They had machine guns in the sand dunes and 88s on the hills.

"We were out there all packed in an LCI and then the hell broke loose. The sky was full of it and the star shells lighted it up and the tracers crisscrossed and the noise – we saw the assault go in, and then one of them hit a surf mine and went up, and in the light you could see them go flying about. I could see the boats land and the guys go wiggling and running, and then maybe there'd be a lot of white lines and some of them would waddle about and collapse and some would hit the beach.

"It didn't seem like men getting killed, more like a picture, like a moving picture. We were pretty crowded up in there though, and then all of a sudden it came on me that this wasn't a moving picture. Those were guys getting the hell shot out of them, and then I got kind of scared, but what I wanted to do mostly was move around. I didn't like being cooped up there where you couldn't get away or get down close to the ground.

"Well the firing would stop and then it would get pitch black even then, and it was just beginning to get light too but the 88s sort of winked on the hills like messages, and the shells were bursting all around us. They had lots of 88s and they shot at everything. I was just getting real scared when we got the order to move in, and I swear that is the longest trip I ever took, that mile to the beach. I thought we'd never get there. I figured that if I was only on the beach I could dig down and get out of the way. There was too damn many of us there in that LCI. I wanted to spread out. That one that hit the mine was still burning when we went on by it. Then we bumped the beach and the ramps went down and I hit the water up to my waist.

"The minute I was on the beach I felt better. It didn't seem like everybody was shooting at me, and I got up to that line of brush and flopped down and some other guys flopped down beside me and then we got feeling a little foolish. We stood up and moved on. Didn't say anything to each other, we just moved on. It was coming daylight then and the flashes of the guns weren't so bright. I felt a little like I was drunk. The ground heaved around under my feet and I was dull. I guess that was because of the firing. My ears aren't so good yet. I guess we moved up too far because I got sent back here." He laughed openly. "I might have gone on right into Rome if some one hadn't sent me back. I guess I might have walked right up that hill here."

World War II

ERNIE PYLE

The Death of Captain Waskow

Although Pyle despaired of the following column on the death of Captain Waskow ("This stuff stinks"), when the editors at the *Daily News* received it, they recognized its true value and devoted the day's entire front page to it. He won the Pulitzer Prize later in the same year.

Washington *Daily News*, 10 January 1944

At the front lines in Italy. Jan. 10 (By Wireless) – In this war I have known a lot of officers who were loved and respected by the soldiers under them. But never have I crossed the trail of any man as beloved as Capt. Henry T. Waskow of Belton. Tex.

Capt. Waskow was a company commander in the 36th Division. He had been in this company since long before he left the States. He was very young, only in his middle twenties, but he carried in him a sincerity and gentleness that made people want to be guided by him.

"After my own father, he comes next," a sergeant told me.

"He always looked after us," a soldier said. "He'd go to bat for us every time."

"I've never known him to do anything unkind," another one said.

I was at the foot of the mule trail the night they brought Capt. Waskow down. The moon was nearly full, and you could see far up the trail, and even part way across the valley. Soldiers made shadows as they walked.

Dead men had been coming down the mountain all evening, lashed onto the backs of mules. They came lying belly down across the wooden packsaddle, their heads hanging down on the left side of the mule, their stiffened legs sticking awkwardly from the other side, bobbing up and down as the mule walked.

The Italian mule skinners were afraid to walk beside dead men, so Americans had to lead the mules down that night. Even the Americans were reluctant to unlash and lift off the bodies, when they got to the bottom, so an officer had to do it himself and ask others to help.

The first one came early in the morning. They slid him down from the mule, and stood him on his feet for a moment. In the half light he might have been merely a sick man standing there leaning on the other. Then they laid him on the ground in the shadow of the stone wall alongside the road.

I don't know who that first one was. You feel small in the presence of dead men, and you don't ask silly questions . . .

We left him there beside the road, that first one, and we all went back into the cowshed and sat on watercans or lay on the straw, waiting for the next batch of mules.

Somebody said the dead soldier had been dead for four days, and then nobody said anything more about him. We talked for an hour or more: the dead man lay all alone, outside in the shadow of the wall.

Then a soldier came into the cowshed and said there were some more bodies outside. We went out into the road. Four mules stood there in the moonlight, in the road where the trail came down off the mountain. The soldiers who led them stood there waiting.

"This one is Capt. Waskow," one of them said quickly.

Two men unlashed his body from the mule and lifted it off and laid it in the shadow beside the stone wall. Other men took the other bodies off. Finally, there were five lying end to end in a long row. You don't cover up dead men in the combat zones. They just lie there in the shadows until somebody else comes after them.

The uncertain mules moved off to their olive groves. The men in the road seemed reluctant to leave. They stood around, and gradually I could sense them moving, one by one, close to Capt. Waskow's body. Not so much to look, I think, as to say something in finality to him and to themselves. I stood close by and I could hear.

One soldier came and looked down, and he said out loud:

"God damn it!"

Another one came, and he said. "God damn it to hell anyway!" He looked down for a few last moments and then turned and left.

Another man came. I think he was an officer. It was hard to tell officers from men in the dim light, for everybody was grimy and dirty. The man looked down into the dead captain's face and then spoke directly to him, as tho he were alive:

"I'm sorry, old man."

Then a soldier came and stood beside the officer and bent over, and he too spoke to his dead captain, not in a whisper but awfully tender, and he said:

"I sure am sorry, sir."

Then the first man squatted down, and he reached down and took the Captain's hand, and he sat there a full five minutes holding the dead hand in his own and looking intently into the dead face. And he never uttered a sound all the time he sat there.

Finally he put the hand down. He reached up and gently straightened the points of the Captain's shirt collar, and then he sort of rearranged the tattered edges of his uniform around the wound, and then he got up and walked away down the road in the moonlight, all alone.

The rest of us went back into the cowshed, leaving the five dead men lying in a line, end to end, in the shadow of the low stone wall. We lay down on the straw in the cowshed, and pretty soon we were all asleep.

World War II

GUY REMINGTON

Second Man Out

The Allied invasion of Normandy began on 6 June 1944. Remington parachuted into France in the early hours of D-Day.

New Yorker, 19 August 1944

The parachute infantry regiment to which I was attached spent the eight days before D Day confined in a marshalling area in England, where we stored up food and sleep and so much knowledge of Normandy that we began to feel as though we knew the country at first hand. On Monday, June 5th, D Day-minus-one, after several hours spent in sharpening knives, cleaning guns, being issued grenades, and adjusting our equipment, we had an early supper and heard a final lecture. Then we blackened our faces, collected our gear, and marched off to our planes. As we passed a railroad crossing, the watchwoman on duty caught my arm and squeezed it impulsively. "Give it to them, Lieutenant," she said. There were tears in her eyes, and, for all I know, in mine.

At the airfield, we were directed to the planes that were to carry us over the Channel. I had seen some action before, so I had at least an idea of what to expect. Not many of the other men were so fortunate. The only thing that worried me, as we sat in the dark waiting for the takeoff, was the thought that I might break a leg in my jump. I tried not to think about that. We took off at ten thirty, just as the moon was coming up. There appeared to be very little ground wind, and the weather seemed ideal for a night jump. Through the open door of my plane, I watched the other transports lifting heavily off the ground. They looked like huge, black bats as they skimmed slowly over the treetops and fell into formation. Before long, we took off too. Presently, near the coast of England, a squadron of fighters appeared below us. They flashed their lights on and off, and then wheeled away. That was *adiós*.

We had a two-hour run ahead of us, so I settled down in my seat. A major, sitting directly across from me, smiled, his teeth startlingly white in the dark. I smiled back. The noise of the plane made it impossible to talk. Suddenly the jump master shouted, "Stand up and hook up!" I realized that I had been asleep, hard as it was to believe. The plane was rocking and bucking, trying to dodge the occasional bursts of flak from the dark, anonymous countryside below. A small red light gleamed in the panel by the door. We hooked up our parachutes, lined up close together, and waited. Then we stood there, waiting, for twelve and a half minutes. It seemed a long and terrible time.

The green light flashed on at seven minutes past midnight. The jump master shouted, "Go!" I was the second man out. The black Normandy pastures tilted and turned far beneath me. The first German flare came arching up, and instantly machine guns and forty-millimeter guns began firing from the corners of the fields, striping the night with yellow, green, blue, and red tracers. I pitched down through a wild Fourth of July. Fire licked through the sky and blazed around the transports heaving high overhead. I saw some of them go plunging down in flames. One of them came down with a trooper, whose parachute had become caught on the tailpiece, streaming out behind. I heard a loud gush of air: a man went hurtling past, only a few yards away, his parachute collapsed and burning. Other parachutes, with men whose legs had been shot off slumped in the harness, floated gently toward the earth.

I was caught in a machine-gun crossfire as I approached the ground. It seemed impossible that they could miss me. One of the guns, hidden in a building, was firing at my parachute, which was already badly torn; the other aimed at my body. I reached up, caught the left risers of my parachute, and pulled on them. I went into a fast slip, but the tracers followed me down. I held the slip until I was about twenty-five feet from the ground and then let go the risers. I landed up against a hedge in a little garden at the rear of a German barracks. There were four tracer holes through one of my pants legs, two through the other, and another bullet had ripped off both my breast pockets, but I hadn't a scratch.

I fought behind the German lines for eight days before I was relieved by our seaborne troops.

World War II

ERNEST HEMINGWAY

Voyage to Victory

Hemingway took his first taste of war as an ambulance driver on the Italian Front in the First World War, and found it hard to give up. He reported the Civil War in Spain and would not be dissuaded from covering the Second World War, by the time of which he was among the globe's most famous writers. "Voyage to Victory" is Hemingway's account of D-Day 1944, as witnessed from a US landing craft.

Collier's, 22 July 1944

. . . As we came roaring in on the beach, I sat high on the stern to see what we were up against. I had the glasses dry now and I took a good look at the shore. The shore was coming toward us awfully fast, and in the glasses it was coming even faster.

On the beach on the left where there was no sheltering overhang of shingled bank, the first, second, third, fourth and fifth waves lay where they had fallen, looking like so many heavily laden bundles on the flat pebbly stretch between the sea and the first cover. To the right, there was an open stretch where the beach exit led up a wooded valley from the sea. It was here that the Germans hoped to get something very good, and later we saw them get it.

To the right of this, two tanks were burning on the crest of the beach, the smoke now grey after the first violent black and yellow billows. Coming in I had spotted two machine-gun nests. One was firing intermittently from the ruins of the smashed house on the right of the small valley. The other was 200 yards to the right and possibly 400 yards in front of the beach.

The officer commanding the troops we were carrying had asked us to head directly for the beach opposite the ruined house.

"Right in there," he said. "That's where."

"Andy," I said, "that whole sector is enfiladed by machine-gun fire. I just saw them open twice on that stranded boat."

An LCV (P) was slanted drunkenly in the stakes like a lost grey steel bathtub. They were firing at the water line, and the fire was kicking up sharp spurts of water.

"That's where he says he wants to go," Andy said. "So that's where we'll take him."

"It isn't any good," I said. "I've seen both those guns open up."

"That's where he wants to go," Andy said. "Put her ahead straight in." He turned astern and signalled to the other boats, jerking his arm, with its upraised finger, up and down.

"Come on, you guys," he said, inaudible in the roar of the motor that sounded like a plane taking off. "Close up! Close up! What's the matter with you? Close up, can't you? Take her straight in, coxswain!"

At this point, we entered the beaten zone from the two machine-gun points, and I ducked my head under the sharp cracking that was going overhead. Then I dropped into the well in the stern sheets where the gunner would have been if we had any guns. The machine-gun fire was throwing water all around the boat, and an anti-tank shell tossed up a jet of water over us.

The lieutenant was talking, but I couldn't hear what he said. Andy could hear him. He had his head down close to his lips.

"Get her the hell around and out of here, coxswain!" Andy called. "*Get her out of here!*"

As we swung round on our stern in a pivot and pulled out, the machine-gun fire stopped. But individual sniping shots kept cracking over or spitting into the water around us. I'd got my head up again with some difficulty and was watching the shore.

"It wasn't cleared, either," Andy said. "You could see the mines on all those stakes."

"Let's coast along and find a good place to put them ashore,"

I said. "If we stay outside of the machine-gun fire, I don't think they'll shoot at us with anything big because we're just an LCV(P), and they've got better targets than us."

"We'll look for a place," Andy said.

"What's he want now?" I said to Andy.

The lieutenant's lips were moving again. They moved very slowly and as though they had no connection with him or with his face.

Andy got down to listen to him. He came back into the stern. "He wants to go out to an LCI we passed that has his commanding officer on it."

"We can get him ashore farther up toward Easy Red," I said.

"He wants to see his commanding officer," Andy said. "Those people in that black boat were from his outfit."

Out a way, rolling in the sea, was a Landing Craft Infantry, and as we came alongside of her I saw a ragged shell hole through the steel plates forward of her pilot-house where an 88-mm. German shell had punched through. Blood was dripping from the shiny edges of the hole into the sea with each roll of the LCI. Her rails and hull had been befouled by seasick men, and her dead were laid forward of her pilot-house. Our lieutenant had some conversation with another officer while we rose and fell in the surge alongside the black iron hull, and then we pulled away.

Andy went forward and talked to him, then came aft again, and we sat up on the stern and watched two destroyers coming along towards us from the eastern beaches, their guns pounding away at targets on the headlands and sloping fields behind the beaches.

"He says they don't want him to go in yet; to wait," Andy said. "Let's get out of the way of this destroyer."

"How long is he going to wait?"

"He says they have no business in there now. People that should have been ahead of them haven't gone in yet. They told him to wait."

"Let's get in where we can keep track of it," I said. "Take the glasses and look at that beach, but don't tell them forward what you see."

Andy looked. He handed the glasses back to me and shook his head.

"Let's cruise along it to the right and see how it is up at that end," I said. "I'm pretty sure we can get in there when he wants to get in. You're sure they told him he shouldn't go in?"

"That's what he says."

"Talk to him and get it straight."

Andy came back. "He says they shouldn't go in now. They're supposed to clear the mines away, so the tanks can go, and he says nothing is in there to go yet. He says they told him it is all fouled up and to stay out yet awhile."

The destroyer was firing point blank at the concrete pillbox that had fired at us on the first trip into the beach, and as the guns fired you heard the bursts and saw the earth jump almost at the same time as the empty brass cases clanged back on to the steel deck. The five-inch guns of the destroyer were smashing at the ruined house at the edge of the little valley where the other machine-gun had fired from.

"Let's move in now that the can has gone by and see if we can't find a good place," Andy said.

"That can punched out what was holding them up there, and you can see some infantry working up that draw now," I said to Andy. "Here, take the glasses."

Slowly, laboriously, as though they were Atlas carrying the world on their shoulders, men were working up the valley on our right. They were not firing. They were just moving slowly up the valley like a tired pack train at the end of the day, going the other way from home.

"The infantry has pushed up to the top of the ridge at the end of the valley," I shouted to the lieutenant.

"They don't want us yet," he said. "'They told me clear they didn't want us yet.'"

"Let me take the glasses – or Hemingway," Andy said. Then he handed them back. "In there, there's somebody signalling with a yellow flag, and there's a boat in there in trouble, it looks like. Coxswain, take her straight in."

We moved in toward the beach at full speed, and Ed Banker looked around and said, "Mr Anderson, the other boats are coming, too."

"Get them back!" Andy said. "*Get them back!*"

Banker turned around and waved the boats away. He had difficulty making them understand, but finally the wide waves they were throwing subsided and they dropped astern.

"Did you get them back?" Andy asked, without looking away from the beach where we could see a half-sunken LCV(P) foundered in the mined stakes.

"Yes, sir," Ed Banker said.

An LCI was headed straight toward us, pulling away from the beach after having circled to go in. As it passed, a man shouted with a megaphone, "There are wounded on that boat and she is sinking."

"Can you get in to her?"

The only words we heard clearly from the megaphone as the wind snatched the voice away were "machine-gun nest".

"Did they say there was or there wasn't a machine-gun nest?" Andy said.

"I couldn't hear."

"Run alongside of her again, coxswain,' he said. 'Run close alongside."

"*Did you say there was a machine-gun nest?*" he shouted.

An officer leaned over with the megaphone. "A machine-gun nest has been firing on them. They are sinking."

"Take her straight in, coxswain," Andy said.

It was difficult to make our way through the stakes that had been sunk as obstructions, because there were contact mines fastened to them that looked like large double pie plates fastened face to face. They looked as though they had been spiked to the pilings and then assembled. They were the ugly, neutral grey-yellow colour that almost everything is in war.

We did not know what other stakes with mines were under us, but the ones that we could see we fended off by hand and worked our way to the sinking boat.

It was not easy to bring on board the man who had been shot through the lower abdomen, because there was no room to let the ramp down the way we were jammed in the stakes with the cross sea.

I do not know why the Germans did not fire on us unless the destroyer had knocked the machine-gun pillbox out. Or maybe they were waiting for us to blow up with the mines. Certainly the mines had been a great amount of trouble to lay and the Germans might well have wanted to see them work. We were in the range of the anti-tank gun that had fired on us before, and all the time we were manoeuvring and working in the stakes I was waiting for it to fire.

As we lowered the ramp the first time, while we were crowded in against the other LCV(P), but before she sank, I saw three tanks coming along the beach, barely moving, they were advancing so slowly. The Germans let them cross the open space where the valley opened on to the beach, and it was absolutely flat with a perfect field of fire. Then I saw a little fountain of water jut up, just over and beyond the lead tank. Then smoke broke out of the leading tank on the side away from us, and I saw two men dive out of the turret and land on their hands and knees on the stones of the beach. They were close enough so that I could see their faces, but no more men came out as the tank started to blaze up and burn fiercely.

By then, we had the wounded man and the survivors on board, the ramp back up, and were feeling our way out through the stakes. As we cleared the last of the stakes, and Currier opened up the engine wide as we pulled out to sea, another tank was beginning to burn.

We took the wounded boy out to the destroyer. They hoisted him aboard it in one of those metal baskets and took on the survivors. Meantime, the destroyers had run in almost to the beach and were blowing every pillbox out of the ground with their five-inch guns. I saw a piece of German about three feet long with an arm on it sail high up into the air in the fountaining of one shell burst. It reminded me of a scene in *Petrushka*.

The infantry had now worked up the valley on our left and had gone on over that ridge. There was no reason for anyone to stay out now. We ran in to a good spot we had picked on the beach and put our troops and their TNT and their bazookas and their lieutenant ashore, and that was that.

The Germans were still shooting with their anti-tank guns, shifting them around in the valley, holding their fire until they had a target they wanted. Their mortars were still laying a plunging fire along the beaches. They had left people behind to snipe at the beaches, and when we left, finally, all these people who were firing were evidently going to stay until dark at least.

The heavily loaded ducks that had formerly sunk in the waves on their way in were now making the beach steadily. The famous thirty-minute clearing of the channels through the mined obstacles was still a myth, and now, with the high tide, it was a tough trip in with the stakes submerged.

We had six craft missing, finally, out of the twenty-four LCV(P)s that went in from the *Dix*, but many of the crews could have been picked up and might be on other vessels. It had been a frontal assault in broad daylight, against a mined beach defended by all the obstacles military ingenuity could devise. The beach had been defended as stubbornly and as intelligently as any troops could defend it. But every boat from the *Dix* had landed her troops and cargo. No boat was lost through bad seamanship. All that were lost were lost by enemy action. And we had taken the beach.

There is much that I have not written. You could write for a week and not give everyone credit for what he did on a front of 1,135 yards. Real war is never like paper war, nor do accounts of it read much the way it looks. But if you want to know how it was in an LCV(P) on D-Day when we took Fox Green beach and Easy Red beach on 6 June 1944, then this is as near as I can come to it.

World War II

JOHN HERSEY

Survival

John Hersey reported the Second World War for *Time*, *Life* and the *New Yorker*. He also penned one of the war's most popular novels, *A Bell for Adano*, the Pulitzer Prize-winner of 1944. During his Pacific beat he covered the sinking of an American Motor Torpedo Boat and the subsequent survival of her crew. The crew was led by one John F. Kennedy, destined to become the President of the USA.

New Yorker, 17 June 1944

Our men in the South Pacific fight nature, when they are pitted against her, with a greater fierceness than they could ever expend on a human enemy. Lieutenant John F. Kennedy, the ex-Ambassador's son and lately a PT skipper in the Solomons, came through town the other day and told me the story of his survival in the South Pacific. I asked Kennedy if I might write the story down. He asked me if I wouldn't talk first with some of his crew, so I went up to the Motor Torpedo Boat Training Center at Melville, Rhode Island, and there, under the curving iron of a Quonset hut, three enlisted men named Johnston, McMahon, and McGuire filled in the gaps.

It seems that Kennedy's PT, the 109, was out one night with a squadron patrolling Blackett Strait, in mid-Solomons. Blackett Strait is a patch of water bounded on the northeast by the volcano called Kolombangara, on the west by the island of Vella Lavella, on the south by the island of Gizo and a string of coral-fringed islets, and on the east by the bulk of New Georgia. The boats were working about forty miles away from their base on the island of Rendova, on the south side of New Georgia. They had entered Blackett Strait, as was their habit, through Ferguson Passage, between the coral islets and New Georgia.

The night was a starless black and Japanese destroyers were around. It was about two thirty. The 109, with three officers and ten enlisted men aboard, was leading three boats on a sweep for a target. An officer named George Ross was up on the bow, magnifying the void with binoculars. Kennedy was at the wheel and he saw Ross turn and point into the darkness. The man in the forward machine-gun turret shouted, "Ship at two o'clock!" Kennedy saw a shape and spun the wheel to turn for an attack, but the 109 answered sluggishly. She was running slowly on only one of her three engines, so as to make a minimum wake and avoid detection from the air. The shape became a Japanese destroyer, cutting through the night at forty knots and heading straight for the 109. The thirteen men on the PT hardly had time to brace themselves. Those who saw the Japanese ship coming were paralyzed by fear in a curious way: they could move their hands but not their feet. Kennedy whirled the wheel to the left, but again the 109 did not respond. Ross went through the gallant but futile motions of slamming a shell into the breach of the 37-millimetre anti-tank gun which had been temporarily mounted that very day, wheels and all, on the foredeck. The urge to bolt and dive over the side was terribly strong, but still no one was able to move; all hands froze to their battle stations. Then the Japanese crashed into the 109 and cut her right in two. The sharp enemy forefoot struck the PT on the starboard side about fifteen feet from the bow and crunched diagonally across with a racking noise. The PT's wooden hull hardly even delayed the destroyer. Kennedy was thrown hard to the left in the cockpit, and he thought, "This is how it feels to be killed." In a moment he found himself on his back on the deck, looking up at the destroyer as it passed through his boat. There was another loud noise and a huge flash of yellow-red light, and the destroyer glowed. Its peculiar, raked, inverted-Y stack stood out in the brilliant light and, later, in Kennedy's memory.

There was only one man below decks at the moment of collision. That was McMahon, engineer. He had no idea what was up. He was just reaching forward to slam the starboard engine into gear when a ship came into his engine room. He was lifted from the narrow passage between two of the engines and thrown painfully against the starboard bulkhead aft of the boat's auxiliary generator. He landed in a sitting position. A tremendous burst of flame came back at him from the day room, where some of the gas tanks were. He put his hands over his face, drew his legs up tight, and waited to die. But he felt water hit him after the fire, and he was sucked far downward as his half of the PT sank. He began to struggle upward through the water. He had held his breath since the impact, so his lungs were tight and they hurt. He looked up through the water. Over his head he saw a yellow glow – gasoline burning on the water. He broke the surface and was in fire again. He splashed hard to keep a little island of water around him.

Johnston, another engineer, had been asleep on deck when the collision came. It lifted him and dropped him overboard. He saw the flame and the destroyer for a moment. Then a huge propeller pounded by near him and the awful turbulence of the destroyer's wake took him down, turned him over and over, held him down, shook him, and drubbed on his ribs. He hung on and came up in water that was like a river rapids. The next day his body turned black and blue from the beating.

Kennedy's half of the PT stayed afloat. The bulkheads were sealed, so the undamaged watertight compartments up forward kept the half hull floating. The destroyer rushed off into the dark. There was an awful quiet: only the sound of gasoline burning.

Kennedy shouted. "Who's aboard?"

Feeble answers came from three of the enlisted men, McGuire, Mauer, and Albert: and from one of the officers, Thom.

Kennedy saw the fire only ten feet from the boat. He thought it might reach her and explode the remaining gas tanks, so he shouted, "Over the side!"

The five men slid into the water. But the wake of the destroyer swept the fire away from the PT, so after a few minutes, Kennedy and the others crawled back aboard. Kennedy shouted for survivors in the water. One by one they answered: Ross, the third officer; Harris, McMahon, Johnston, Zinsser, Starkey, enlisted men. Two did not answer: Kirksey and Marney, enlisted men. Since the last bombing at base, Kirksey had been sure he would die. He had huddled at his battle station by the fantail gun, with his kapok life jacket tied tight up to his cheeks. No one knows what happened to him or to Marney.

Harris shouted from the darkness, "Mr Kennedy! Mr Kennedy! McMahon is badly hurt." Kennedy took his shoes, his shirt, and his sidearms off, told Mauer to blink a light so that the men in the water would know where the half hull was, then dived in and swam toward the voice. The survivors were widely scattered. McMahon and Harris were a hundred yards away.

When Kennedy reached McMahon, he asked, "How are you, Mac?"

McMahon said, "I'm all right. I'm kind of burnt."

Kennedy shouted out, "How are the others?"

Harris said softly, "I hurt my leg."

Kennedy, who had been on the Harvard swimming team five years before, took McMahon in tow and headed for the PT. A gentle breeze kept blowing the boat away from the swimmers. It took forty-five minutes to make what had been an easy hundred yards. On the way in, Harris said, "I can't go any farther." Kennedy, of the Boston Kennedys, said to Harris, of the same home town, "For a guy from Boston, you're certainly putting up a great exhibition out here, Harris." Harris made it all right and didn't complain any more. Then Kennedy swam from man to man, to see how they were doing. All who had survived the crash were able to stay afloat, since they were wearing life preservers – kapok jackets shaped like overstuffed vests, aviators' yellow Mae Wests, or air-filled belts like small inner tubes. But those who couldn't swim had to be towed back to the wreckage by those who could. One of the men screamed for help. When Ross reached him, he found that the screaming man had two life jackets on. Johnston was treading water in a film of gasoline which did not catch fire. The fumes filled his lungs and he fainted. Thom towed him in. The others got in under their own power. It was now after 5 a.m., but still dark. It had taken nearly three hours to get everyone aboard.

The men stretched out on the tilted deck of the PT. Johnston, McMahon, and Ross collapsed into sleep. The men talked about how wonderful it was to be alive and speculated on when the other PTs would come back to rescue them. Mauer kept blinking the light to point their way. But the other boats had no idea of coming back. They had seen a collision, a sheet of flame, and a slow burning on the water. When the skipper of one of the boats saw the sight, he put his hands over his face and sobbed, "My God! My God!" He and the others turned away. Back at the base, after a couple of days, the squadron held services for the souls of the thirteen men, and one of the officers wrote his mother, "George Ross lost his life for a cause that he believed in stronger than any one of us, because he was an idealist in the purest sense. Jack Kennedy, the Ambassador's son, was on the same boat and also lost his life. The man that said the cream of a nation is lost in war can never be accused of making an overstatement of a very cruel fact . . ."

When day broke, the men on the remains of the 109 stirred and looked around. To the northeast, three miles off, they saw the monumental cone of Kolombangara; there, the men knew, ten thousand Japanese swarmed. To the west, five miles away, they saw Vella Lavella; more Japs. To the south, only a mile or so away, they actually could see a Japanese camp on Gizo. Kennedy ordered his men to keep as low as possible, so that no moving silhouettes would show against the sky. The listing hulk was gurgling and gradually settling. Kennedy said, "What do you want to do if the Japs come out? Fight or surrender?" One said, "Fight with what?" So they took an inventory of their armament. The 37-millimetre gun had flopped over the side and was hanging there by a chain. They had one tommy gun, six 45-calibre automatics, and one .38. Not much.

"Well," Kennedy said, "what do you want to do?"

One said, "Anything you say, Mr Kennedy. You're the boss."

Kennedy said, "There's nothing in the book about a situation like this. Seems to me we're not a military organization any more. Let's just talk this over."

They talked it over, and pretty soon they argued, and Kennedy could see that they would never survive in anarchy. So he took command again.

It was vital that McMahon and Johnston should have room to lie down. McMahon's face, neck, hands, wrists, and feet were horribly burned. Johnston was pale and he coughed continually. There was scarcely space for everyone, so Kennedy ordered the other men into the water to make room, and went in himself. All morning they clung to the hulk and talked about how incredible it was that no one had come to rescue them. All morning they watched for the plane which they thought would be looking for them. They cursed war in general and PTs in particular. At about ten o'clock the hulk heaved a moist sigh and turned turtle. McMahon and Johnston had to hang on as best they could. It was clear that the remains of the 109 would soon sink. When the sun had passed the meridian, Kennedy said, "We will swim to that small island," pointing to one of a group three miles to the southeast. "We have less chance of making it than some of these other islands here, but there'll be less chance of Japs, too." Those who could not swim well grouped themselves around a long two-by-six timber with which carpenters had braced the 37-millimetre cannon on deck and which had been knocked overboard by the force of the collision. They tied several pairs of shoes to the timber, as well as the ship's lantern, wrapped in a life jacket to keep it afloat. Thom took charge of this unwieldy group. Kennedy took McMahon in tow again. He cut loose one end of a long strap on McMahon's Mae West and took the end in his teeth. He swam breast stroke, pulling the helpless McMahon along on his back. It took over five hours to reach the island. Water lapped into Kennedy's mouth through his clenched teeth, and he swallowed a lot. The salt water cut into McMahon's awful burns, but he did not complain. Every few minutes, when Kennedy stopped to rest, taking the strap out of his mouth and holding it in his hand, McMahon would simply say, "How far do we have to go?"

Kennedy would reply, "We're going good." Then he would ask, "How do you feel, Mac?"

McMahon always answered, "I'm OK, Mr Kennedy. How about you?"

In spite of his burden, Kennedy beat the other men to the reef that surrounded the island. He left McMahon on the reef and told him to keep low, so as not to be spotted by Japs. Kennedy went ahead and explored the island. It was only a hundred yards in diameter; coconuts on the trees but none on the ground; no visible Japs. Just as the others reached the island, one of them spotted a Japanese barge chugging along close to shore. They all lay low. The barge went on. Johnston, who was very pale and weak and who was still coughing a lot, said, "They wouldn't come here. What'd they be walking around here for? It's too small." Kennedy lay in some bushes, exhausted by his effort, his stomach heavy with the water he had swallowed. He had been in the sea, except for short intervals on the hulk, for fifteen and a half hours. Now he started thinking. Every night for several nights the PTs had cut through Ferguson Passage on their way to action. Ferguson Passage was just beyond the next little island. Maybe . . .

He stood up. He took one of the pairs of shoes. He put one of the rubber life belts around his waist. He hung the .38 around his neck on a lanyard. He took his pants off. He picked up the ship's lantern, a heavy battery affair ten inches by ten inches, still wrapped in the kapok jacket. He said, "If I find a boat, I'll flash the lantern twice. The password will be 'Roger,' the answer will be 'Wilco.' " He walked toward the water. After fifteen paces he was dizzy, but in the water he felt all right.

It was early evening. It took half an hour to swim to the reef around the next island. Just as he planted his feet on the reef, which lay about four feet under the surface, he saw the shape of a very big fish in the clear water. He flashed the light at it and splashed hard. The fish went away. Kennedy remembered what one of his men had said a few days before, "These barracuda will come up under a swimming man and eat his testicles." He had many occasions to think of that remark in the next few hours.

Now it was dark. Kennedy blundered along the uneven reef in water up to his waist. Sometimes he would reach forward with his leg and cut one of his shins or ankles on sharp coral. Other times he would step forward onto emptiness. He made his way like a slow-motion drunk, hugging the lantern. At about nine o'clock he came to the end of the reef, alongside Ferguson Passage. He took his shoes off and tied them to the life jacket, then struck out into open water. He swam about an hour, until he felt he was far enough out to intercept the PTs. Treading water, he listened for the muffled roar of motors, getting chilled, waiting, holding the lamp. Once he looked west and saw flares and the false gaiety of an action. The lights were far beyond the little islands, even beyond Gizo, ten miles away. Kennedy realized that the PT boats had chosen, for the first night in many, to go around Gizo instead of through Ferguson Passage. There was no hope. He started back. He made the same painful promenade of the reef and struck out for the tiny island where his friends were. But this swim was different. He was very tired and now the current was running fast, carrying him to the right. He saw that he could not make the island, so he flashed the light once and shouted "Roger! Roger!" to identify himself.

On the beach the men were hopefully vigilant. They saw the light and heard the shouts. They were very happy, because they thought that Kennedy had found a PT. They walked out onto the reef, sometimes up to their waists in water, and waited. It was very painful for those who had no shoes. The men shouted, but not much, because they were afraid of Japanese.

One said, "There's another flash."

A few minutes later a second said, "There's a light over there."

A third said, "We're seeing things in this dark."

They waited a long time, but they saw nothing except phosphorescence and heard nothing but the sound of waves. They went back, very discouraged.

One said despairingly, "We're going to die."

Johnston said, "Aw, shut up. You can't die. Only the good die young."

Kennedy had drifted right by the little island. He thought he had never known such deep trouble, but something he did shows that unconsciously he had not given up hope. He dropped his shoes, but he held onto the heavy lantern, his symbol of contact with his fellows. He stopped trying to swim. He seemed to stop caring. His body drifted through the wet hours, and he was very cold. His mind was a jumble. A few hours before, he had wanted desperately to get to the base at Rendova. Now he only wanted to get back to the little island he had left that night, but he didn't try to get there; he just wanted to. His mind seemed to float away from his body. Darkness and time took the place of a mind in his skull. For a long time he slept, or was crazy, or floated in a chill trance.

* * *

The currents of the Solomon Islands are queer. The tide shoves and sucks through the islands and makes the currents curl in odd patterns. It was a fateful pattern into which Jack Kennedy drifted. He drifted in it all night. His mind was blank, but his fist was tightly clenched on the kapok around the lantern. The current moved in a huge circle – west past Gizo, then north and east past Kolombangara, then south into Ferguson Passage. Early in the morning the sky turned from black to gray, and so did Kennedy's mind. Light came to both at about six. Kennedy looked around and saw that he was exactly where he had been the night before when he saw the flares beyond Gizo. For a second time, he started home. He thought for a while that he had lost his mind and that he only imagined that he was repeating his attempt to reach the island. But the chill of the water was real enough, the lantern was real, his progress was measurable. He made the reef, crossed the lagoon, and got to the first island. He lay on the beach awhile. He found that his lantern did not work any more, so he left it and started back to the next island, where his men were. This time the trip along the reef was awful. He had discarded his shoes, and every step on the coral was painful. This time the swim across the gap where the current had caught him the night before seemed endless. But the current had changed; he made the island. He crawled up on the beach. He was vomiting when his men came up to him. He said, "Ross, you try it tonight." Then he passed out.

Ross, seeing Kennedy so sick, did not look forward to the execution of the order. He distracted himself by complaining about his hunger. There were a few coconuts on the trees, but the men were too weak to climb up for them. One of the men thought of sea food, stirred his tired body, and found a snail on the beach. He said, "If we were desperate, we could eat these." Ross said. "Desperate, hell. Give me that. I"ll eat that.' He took it in his hand and looked at it. The snail put its head out and looked at him. Ross was startled, but he shelled the snail and ate it, making faces because it was bitter.

In the afternoon, Ross swam across to the next island. He took a pistol to signal with, and he spent the night watching Ferguson Passage from the reef around the island. Nothing came through. Kennedy slept badly that night; he was cold and sick.

*   *   *

The next morning everyone felt wretched. Planes that the men were unable to identify flew overhead and there were dogfights. That meant Japs as well as friends, so the men dragged themselves into the bushes and lay low. Some prayed. Johnston said, "You guys make me sore. You didn't spend ten cents in church in ten years, then all of a sudden you're in trouble and you see the light." Kennedy felt a little better now. When Ross came back, Kennedy decided that the group should move to another, larger island to the southeast, where there seemed to be more coconut trees and where the party would be nearer Ferguson Passage. Again Kennedy took McMahon in tow with the strap in his teeth, and the nine others grouped themselves around the timber.

This swim took three hours. The nine around the timber were caught by the current and barely made the far tip of the island. Kennedy found walking the quarter mile across to them much harder than the three-hour swim. The cuts on his bare feet were festered and looked like small balloons. The men were suffering most from thirst, and they broke open some coconuts lying on the ground and avidly drank the milk. Kennedy and McMahon, the first to drink, were sickened, and Thom told the others to drink sparingly. In the middle of the night it rained, and someone suggested moving into the underbrush and licking water off the leaves. Ross and McMahon kept contact at first by touching feet as they licked. Somehow they got separated, and, being uncertain whether there were any Japs on the island, they became frightened. McMahon, trying to make his way back to the beach, bumped into someone and froze. It turned out to be Johnston, licking leaves on his own. In the morning the group saw that all the leaves were covered with droppings. Bitterly, they named the place Bird Island.

On this fourth day, the men were low. Even Johnston was low. He had changed his mind about praying. McGuire had a rosary around his neck, and Johnston said, "McGuire, give that necklace a working over." McGuire said quietly, "Yes, I'll take care of all you fellows." Kennedy was still unwilling to admit that things were hopeless. He asked Ross if he would swim with him to an island called Nauru, to the southeast and even nearer Ferguson Passage. They were very weak indeed by now, but after an hour's swim they made it.

They walked painfully across Nauru to the Ferguson Passage
side, where they saw a Japanese barge aground on the reef.
There were two men by the barge – possibly Japs. They apparently spotted Kennedy and Ross, for they got into a dugout
canoe and hurriedly paddled to the other side of the island.
Kennedy and Ross moved up the beach. They came upon an
unopened ropebound box and, back in the trees, a little shelter
containing a keg of water, a Japanese gas mask, and a crude
wooden fetish shaped like a fish. There were Japanese hardtack
and candy in the box and the two had a wary feast. Down by the
water they found a one-man canoe. They hid from imagined
Japs all day. When night fell, Kennedy left Ross and took the
canoe, with some hardtack and a can of water from the keg, out
into Ferguson Passage. But no PTs came, so he paddled to Bird
Island. The men there told him that the two men he had spotted
by the barge that morning were natives, who had paddled to
Bird Island. The natives had said that there were Japs on Nauru
and the men had given Kennedy and Ross up for lost. Then the
natives had gone away. Kennedy gave out small rations of crackers and water, and the men went to sleep. During the night, one
man, who kept himself awake until the rest were asleep, drank all
the water in the can Kennedy had brought back. In the morning
the others figured out that he was the guilty one. They swore at
him and found it hard to forgive him.

Before dawn, Kennedy started out in the canoe to rejoin Ross
on Nauru, but when day broke a wind arose and the canoe was
swamped. Some natives appeared from nowhere in a canoe, rescued Kennedy, and took him to Nauru. There they showed him
where a two-man canoe was cached. Kennedy picked up a
coconut with a smooth shell and scratched a message on it with
a jackknife: "ELEVEN ALIVE NATIVE KNOWS POSIT
AND REEFS NAURU ISLAND KENNEDY." Then he said to
the natives, "Rendova, Rendova."

One of the natives seemed to understand. They took the
coconut and paddled off.

Ross and Kennedy lay in a sickly daze all day. Toward evening
it rained and they crawled under a bush. When it got dark, conscience took hold of Kennedy and he persuaded Ross to go out
into Ferguson Passage with him in the two-man canoe. Ross

argued against it. Kennedy insisted. The two started out in the canoe. They had shaped paddles from the boards of the Japanese box, and they took a coconut shell to bail with. As they got out into the Passage, the wind rose again and the water became choppy. The canoe began to fill. Ross bailed and Kennedy kept the bow into the wind. The waves grew until they were five or six feet high. Kennedy shouted, "Better turn around and go back!" As soon as the canoe was broadside to the waves, the water poured in and the dugout was swamped. The two clung to it, Kennedy at the bow, Ross at the stern. The tide carried them southward toward the open sea, so they kicked and tugged the canoe, aiming northwest. They struggled that way for two hours, not knowing whether they would hit the small island or drift into the endless open.

The weather got worse; rain poured down and they couldn't see more than ten feet. Kennedy shouted, "Sorry I got you out here, Barney!" Ross shouted back, "This would be a great time to say I told you so, but I won't!"

Soon the two could see a white line ahead and could hear a frightening roar – waves crashing on a reef. They had got out of the tidal current and were approaching the island all right, but now they realized that the wind and the waves were carrying them toward the reef. But it was too late to do anything, now that their canoe was swamped, except hang on and wait.

When they were near the reef, a wave broke Kennedy's hold, ripped him away from the canoe, turned him head over heels, and spun him in a violent rush. His ears roared and his eyes pinwheeled, and for the third time since the collision he thought he was dying. Somehow he was not thrown against the coral but floated into a kind of eddy. Suddenly he felt the reef under his feet. Steadying himself so that he would not be swept off it, he shouted, "Barney!" There was no reply. Kennedy thought of how he had insisted on going out in the canoe, and he screamed, "Barney!" This time Ross answered. He, too, had been thrown on the reef. He had not been as lucky as Kennedy; his right arm and shoulder had been cruelly lacerated by the coral, and his feet, which were already infected from earlier wounds, were cut some more.

The procession of Kennedy and Ross from reef to beach was a crazy one. Ross's feet hurt so much that Kennedy would hold one paddle on the bottom while Ross put a foot on it, then the other paddle forward for another step, then the first paddle forward again, until they reached sand. They fell on the beach and slept.

Kennedy and Ross were wakened early in the morning by a noise. They looked up and saw four husky natives. One walked up to them and said in an excellent English accent, "I have a letter for you, sir." Kennedy tore the note open. It said, "On His Majesty's Service. To the Senior Officer, Nauru Island. I have just learned of your presence on Nauru Is. I am in command of a New Zealand infantry patrol operating in conjunction with US. Army troops on New Georgia. I strongly advise that you come with these natives to me. Meanwhile I shall be in radio communication with your authorities at Rendova, and we can finalize plans to collect balance of your party. Lt. Wincote. PS Will warn aviation of your crossing Ferguson Passage."

Everyone shook hands and the four natives took Ross and Kennedy in their war canoe across to Bird Island to tell the others the good news. There the natives broke out a spirit stove and cooked a feast of yams and C ration. Then they built a leanto for McMahon, whose burns had begun to rot and stink, and for Ross, whose arm had swelled to the size of a thigh because of the coral cuts. The natives put Kennedy in the bottom of their canoe and covered him with sacking and palm fronds, in case Japanese planes should buzz them. The long trip was fun for the natives. They stopped once to try to grab a turtle, and laughed at the sport they were having. Thirty Japanese planes went over low toward Rendova, and the natives waved and shouted gaily. They rowed with a strange rhythm, pounding paddles on the gunwales between strokes. At last they reached a censored place. Lieutenant Wincote came to the water's edge and said formally, "How do you do. Leftenant Wincote."

Kennedy said, "Hello. I'm Kennedy."

Wincote said, "Come up to my tent and have a cup of tea."

In the middle of the night, after several radio conversations between Wincote's outfit and the PT base, Kennedy sat in the war canoe waiting at an arranged rendezvous for a PT. The moon went down at eleven twenty. Shortly afterward, Kennedy heard the signal he was waiting for – four shots. Kennedy fired four answering shots.

A voice shouted to him, "Hey, Jack!"

Kennedy said, "Where the hell you been?"

The voice said, "We got some food for you."

Kennedy said bitterly, "No, thanks, I just had a coconut."

A moment later a PT came alongside. Kennedy jumped onto it and hugged the men aboard – his friends. In the American tradition, Kennedy held under his arm a couple of souvenirs: one of the improvised paddles and the Japanese gas mask.

With the help of the natives, the PT made its way to Bird Island. A skiff went in and picked up the men. In the deep of the night, the PT and its happy cargo roared back toward base. The squadron medic had sent some brandy along to revive the weakened men. Johnston felt the need of a little revival. In fact, he felt he needed quite a bit of revival. After taking care of that, he retired topside and sat with his arms around a couple of roly-poly, mission-trained natives. And in the fresh breeze on the way home they sang together a hymn all three happened to know:

> *Jesus loves me, this I know,*
> *For the Bible tells me so;*
> *Little ones to Him belong,*
> *They are weak, but He is strong.*
> *Yes, Jesus loves me; yes, Jesus loves me . . .*

World War II

HELEN KIRKPATRICK

Helen Kirkpatrick Reports Sniper Attacks on French Leaders at Notre Dame Cathedral

Helen Kirkpatrick, a former Macy shopgirl, joined the Chicago *Daily News* as European correspondent in 1939. When war broke out she was told that front-line reporting was no suitable job for a woman, but overcame such chauvinism to produce some of the best reportage of the Second World War. The *Daily News*, in something of a *volte face*, made her reports the centrepieces of their circulation promotions under the slogan "Read Helen Kirkpatrick". Kirkpatrick was in Paris for the liberation, where she was persuaded to lunch at the Ritz by Ernest Hemingway. Despite Hemingway's pleas that their lunch was of historic importance, she refused to dawdle over coffee and went off to cover the victory parade. The result was a scoop, an eyewitness report on fascist sympathisers sniping at De Gaulle.

Chicago *Daily News*, *27 August 1944*

Paris' celebration of its liberation was very nearly converted into a massacre by the Fascist militia's attempt to eliminate French leaders and to start riots during the afternoon's ceremonies.

All Paris streamed into the center of the town – to the Arc de

Triomphe, the Place de la Concorde, along the Champs Elysees, at the Hotel de Ville and to Notre Dame Cathedral.

Gens De Gaulle, Koenig, Leclerc and Juin led the procession from the Etoile to Notre Dame amid scenes of tremendous enthusiasm.

Lt John Reinhart, USN, and I could not get near enough to the Arc de Triomphe to see the parade, so we turned back to Notre Dame where a Te Deum service was to be held . . .

The generals' car arrived on the dot of 4:15. As they stepped from the car, we stood at salute and at that very moment a revolver shot rang out. It seemed to come from behind one of Notre Dame's gargoyles. Within a split second a machine gun opened from a nearby room . . . It sprayed the pavement at my feet. The generals entered the church with 40-odd people pressing from behind to find shelter.

I found myself inside in the main aisle, a few feet behind the generals. People were cowering behind pillars. Someone tried to pull me down.

The generals marched slowly down the main aisle, their hats in their hands. People in the main body were pressed back near the pillars . . .

Suddenly an automatic opened up from behind us – it came from behind the pipes of Notre Dame's organ. From the clerestory above other shots rang out and I saw a man ducking behind a pillar above. Beside me FFI men and the police were shooting.

For one flashing instant it seemed that a great massacre was bound to take place as the cathedral reverberated with the sound of guns . . .

It seemed hours but it was only a few minutes, perhaps ten, when the procession came back down the aisle. I think the shooting was still going on but, like those around me, I could only stand amazed at the coolness, imperturbability and apparent unconcern of French generals and civilians alike who walked as though nothing had happened. Gen. Koenig, smiling, leaned across and shook my hand.

I fell in behind them and watched them walk deliberately out and into their cars. A machine gun was still blazing from a nearby roof.

Once outside, one could hear shooting all along the Seine . . . I learned later that shooting at the Hotel de Ville, the Tuileries, the Arc de Triomphe and along the Elysees had started at exactly the same moment . . .

It was a clearly planned attempt probably designed to kill as many of the French authorities as possible, to create panic and to start riots after which probably the mad brains of the militia, instigated by the Germans, hoped to retake Paris.

World War II

ROBERT SHAPLEN

Lovely Americans

Bob Shaplen was the Pacific War correspondent for *Newsweek*.
During the 1950s and 1960s he worked the Asia beat for *Collier's*
and the *New Yorker*.

New Yorker, 18 November 1944

For nearly two and a half years the American troops in General
Douglas MacArthur's Southwest Pacific Command fought in
some of the world's most uncivilized territory. As they made
their way along the New Guinea coast and invaded New Britain, the Admiralty Islands, Biak, Morotai, and other places with
strange names, they experienced none of the satisfaction of the
Allied troops in Europe, who have been marching through town
after town on triumphant crusades of liberation. The only towns
the men in the Pacific saw were the native *kampongs* and the
only welcome they received from the not visibly overjoyed
inhabitants was an unintelligible chatter. With the invasion of
the Philippines, MacArthur's men finally got their reward. Ever
since Bataan, as the world knew, MacArthur had had one aspir-
ation: to return to the Islands. For him the invasion of Leyte was
a personal triumph, the end of a long, complicated battle. But
for the men, weary of jungles, it was something more; it was like
coming out of darkness into the light.

I landed on Leyte the morning of October 20th as a correspondent attached to the Seventh Regiment of the First Cavalry
Division, which was dismounted when it left the United States,

soon after Pearl Harbor, with the objective, even then, of helping recapture the Philippines. Under cover of violent naval gunfire, capped by a cascade of rockets that literally tore our landing beach apart, we got ashore successfully, with less opposition than we had expected. A few bomb-happy Japanese snipers were still in the trees and a few others were still in the concrete pillboxes along the shore, but these were quickly disposed of. The snipers were picked off their perches by sharpshooters with carbines and Garands and the pillboxes were dynamited. Three divisions to the south of us, particularly the Twenty-fourth Division, on our left flank, ran into much heavier opposition. We were able to push rapidly north toward the town of Tacloban, four miles from our landing point. It turned out that the troops of the notorious Sixteenth Imperial Japanese Division, whom our division had expected to encounter in the Tacloban area, had been moved south just before the invasion. In the village of San José, some four hundred yards from where we landed, we found several Japanese automobiles, a large quantity of Japanese beer (bottled in Manila), and some new guns the enemy had not taken the time to destroy in his flight. San José was deserted. All but a few of the houses, which had been bombed for days from the air before the landing and shelled for hours from the sea that morning, were rubble, and even those that were standing looked as if they were ready to fall down. The cavalrymen didn't stay in San José very long. They pushed on toward the Barayan River, a narrow stream a little less than a mile ahead. Here the Japs had, conveniently, left a bridge intact, so the cavalry kept moving. By dusk we had reached what was supposed to be our second-day objective, a road junction a mile or so from Tacloban. Here we established a perimeter defense for the night, and here began the magnificent reception we got in the Philippines. This, it seemed to me, was what all the men had been waiting for during the long, malarial months in the jungles.

Hundreds of soldiers will always remember the white-clad figure of the Filipino who came walking toward us (running was more like it), wheeling a bicycle, at four o'clock that afternoon. It had been raining and the road was too slippery to ride on. The advance troops spied him several hundred yards ahead through the trees and held their fire when they saw him waving frantically, taking off and putting on his broad-brimmed hat again and again. As he approached, his face appeared to be composed entirely of smile. It was impossible to understand what he was saying, but it was easy to see that he was filled with an almost hysterical happiness. He grabbed the hand of every soldier he could reach and shook it ecstatically. When he had quieted down, we were able, with the help of one of the Filipino soldiers with us, to learn that his name was Isaios Budlong and that he had formerly been a telegraph operator in Tacloban. To him went the honor of being the first liberated Filipino. He had left the town that morning and made his way through whatever was left of the Japanese lines to reach us.

Having liberated Budlong, the troops began digging foxholes and setting up mortars and machine guns in preparation for a possible Jap counterattack. As they dug in, more Filipinos came running down the two roads leading to the junction. In half an hour there were a hundred of them milling around us. There were men, one of whom brought a large box of Japanese hard crackers and gave it to Lieutenant Colonel Robert P. Kirk, our squadron commander; and there were young girls, mothers carrying crying infants in their arms, and old women, their faces wrinkled, their skin hanging loosely. One old woman stood at the side of the road, her hands outstretched. Like Budlong, she reached out at the soldiers near her, but whereas his hands had darted eagerly, hers moved through the air with a gentle, swinging motion, touching a man only now and then, as a woman would fondle a piece of silk. She looked as if she were dreaming and couldn't believe her dream, and she had as beatific a smile on her worn, brown face as I have ever seen.

Most of the men and women who came toward us were in rags. After a few minutes, those of them that lived nearby ran home to change into the clothes they had been saving for the day of liberation. Before it was dark, they were back again, the girls in bright cotton dresses, the men in white or blue trousers and shirts. The young men were exuberant. They wanted, even before food – which they obviously needed badly – guns, so that they could join in the fight against the Japs. Most of them spoke English, but haltingly. A twenty-one-year-old lad named Guillermo Peñaranda asked us, "Where is our president?" We were glad to be able to tell him that President Sergio Osmeña was with General MacArthur and would be in Tacloban in a day or two. Restituta Jarohohon, a pretty twenty-year-old girl with her first child in her arms, shook hands with everyone and said, "We are very glad to meet you." The Filipinos told us that the Japanese had fled into the hills beyond Tacloban. Despite the artillery and mortar fire from the beach behind us, and the mosquitoes that swarmed into our fox-holes, we slept peacefully that night.

In the morning, we went on north toward Tacloban. On the out-skirts, we ran into some opposition. Two hundred Japs were well entrenched on a low hill on the southeast side. It took us three hours to clean them out with artillery and mortar fire. While we were stalled, the Filipinos once again came to us before we could get to them. A long-legged, loosely put-together figure who looked as if he had been drawn by Thomas Benton came run-ning up the road to Colonel Walter E. Finnegan, our regimental commander, and said that he was Governor Bernardo Torres. He wore lavender pants, a yellow shirt, and a broad yellow hat. He told us that he had been the Governor of Leyte Province before the Japs came to Tacloban, in May, 1942, and that the Japs had kept him on as Governor until they had become dis-satisfied with him in that job. Then they had appointed him Director of Agriculture for the Philippines and put him in charge of food production for the Visayan island group, of which Leyte is one. Torres seemed more than eager to tell us what he could about the Japs – where they were and what they had done to the civilians of the town. He said that the hated Kempeitai, the Jap military police, had had a large force in Tacloban and had maltreated the natives.

The case of Torres is a queer one and a good example of the ticklish question: when is a collaborationist not a collaboration-ist? Torres was so eager to tell everything he knew that he was suspect. Three days later, when Colonel Ruperto Kangleon, the guerrilla chief on Leyte, was made military governor of the island, one of his first actions was to have Torres put in jail, together with about two hundred other suspected collaboration-ists. Kangleon had for nearly three years led an armed revolt in the hills, and his forces had killed thirty-eight hundred Japanese soldiers since February. This was a case of a bitter, fighting opponent of the Japs showing his contempt for a man who had stayed behind and tried to compromise. Yet there may well be something to be said for Torres, and if there is, it will be said at the trial that he and others like him will get before the Philippine and American authorities. Townspeople whose loyalty to the Americans cannot be doubted thought highly of Torres and trusted him. He got for them what little food the Japs did not steal and maintained as amicable relations as possible with an entrenched enemy through the difficult months. He was no Pétain, like the Japanese puppet Governor Pastor Salazar, but he was not a Tito, like Kangleon, either.

While we were talking to Torres in front of the command post, we could hear shots in the center of the town. From the windows of the houses, Jap sharpshooters were trying to pick off the Americans in the streets. Before the war, Tacloban was a town of eighteen thousand. It had a movie theater, an ice plant, an athletic field, several restaurants, and a sizable business district near the wharves. The Japs had occupied practically all the business buildings and the best dwellings, and when several other correspondents and I reached the town, the remains of their paraphernalia of war were scattered everywhere.

We correspondents walked into town behind the troops and were directed to the two-story house of Mayor Vicente Quintero, a small, bespectacled man, who was looking very happy. He set up some Jap beer for us and also brought out a bottle of whiskey he said he had been saving for the great day. His home had beautiful, polished floors of narra and molave, Philippine hardwoods. Quintero has been Mayor for twelve years. "We are very glad to see you," he said. "It has been a long time. Things have been very hard under the Japanese." Until three months before, he said, most families had managed to get enough rice and *camotes*, or yams. Since then, the Japanese had pressed more and more Filipinos into the labor battalions, and there had been few left to work the fields. The Japanese had needed the additional forced labor for a series of airstrips they were feverishly building on the island. Children as young as ten, as well as old men and women, had been conscripted, Quintero told us. As we left his house, toward evening, we encountered fifty Formosans, used by the Japs as laborers, who had been taken prisoner by our forces and were being brought through town to division headquarters. They looked scared and frazzled as they stumbled by, their thin arms upraised.

*   *   *

Robert Shaplen

That night I slept, along with many of the cavalrymen, on the floor of the Leyte Intermediate School for Girls. In the morning I walked to the market place, where there was to be a meeting of the citizens at ten o'clock. There I met young Bob Price, the son of Tacloban's most celebrated citizen, Walter Price, an American. The elder Price went to the Philippines as an infantry captain in the Spanish-American War and stayed there when the war was over, married a Filipina, and raised a family of seventeen. Price was the founder and owner of the Leyte Transportation Company, and probably the wealthiest man on the island, and he and his family lived in a luxurious concrete house that has six bathrooms. He is now a prisoner of the Japanese in Manila. Bob and his brother Joe, who were beaten and imprisoned three times – once for seventy-seven days, on a charge of working with the guerrillas – were allowed to remain in Tacloban. They both look more like Filipinos than Americans.

The ten o'clock meeting was the principal event of the liberation of Tacloban. One purpose of the gathering was to welcome the American troops and another was to recruit native labor to work for the Philippine Civil Affairs Unit, an organization set up in Australia a year ago to control civilian affairs on the Islands when we got there. The meeting was opened by Caesar Sotto, a former Davao assemblyman and Labor Commissioner of Leyte Province, who had been forced by the Japs to recruit the workers for the airstrips. Sotto was dressed in an immaculate white suit. He mounted a platform that had been set up in the center of the market place and, in a brief speech in Visayan, introduced Saturino Gonzales, a member of the Provincial Board, who spoke in English. "The Americans have arrived to redeem us from slavery," Gonzales said. "We had to obey the Japanese to save our necks, but there was never any doubt, as you know, what our feelings were beneath. I ask you to consider now what the policies of the American government were like before the Japanese came and how they are to be compared to the Japanese administration. You will now understand the famous democratic ways of the United States."

Sotto spoke again, and a man next to me in the crowd explained that he was comparing the food policies of the Japanese and Americans as an argument to round up labor volunteers. As Sotto waved a K-ration container to emphasize his point, the crowd roared, in English, "Long live the Americans! Lovely Americans!" Mr Sotto went on to say that ten thousand tons of rice would be brought in shortly by the Americans and that President Osmeña was already on Leyte. The rice and their president being the two things the Filipinos most wanted, this statement brought forth further cries of "Lovely Americans!"

The next speaker was Captain Abner Pickering, one of the American Civil Affairs officers. Pickering has been in the Philippines off and on for twenty-five years and before the war was in business in Manila. "My friends," he said, in English, after the applause died down, "when I landed in Leyte the day before yesterday, it was the first time in three years that I had been in the Philippines. The Japanese will never come back to Tacloban. It took us several years to get organized, to get the ships, to get the bases for us to return, but now we're here to stay. The Philippines are yours. Your Commonwealth Government will be set up under your own president, President Osmeña. We are going to see that you get food and clothing. We want you to be patient. We need labor. You will get paid for the work you do in Philippine currency and with it you will be able to buy the rice and the other products we will bring. But, by God, you'll do it as free men!" It is doubtful whether most of the audience understood everything Captain Pickering said. Whether they did or not, the important fact to them was that here, on the platform in front of them, an American was talking; that was enough. When he finished, the applause lasted several minutes.

Vicente Delacruz, ex-Governor of Leyte Province and the last speaker, touched upon more spiritual matters. "We all need to be rebaptized in our churches," he said. "The first sin was committed by Adam and Eve. The second sin was committed by Germany and Japan. When the Japanese were here, our mouths were talking for them but our hearts were one-hundred-percent American. For the Americans we will work not three, not four days a week but three hundred and sixty-five days a year, and we will work for nothing." Captain Pickering waved a hand in protest, but the gesture was ignored. "Lovely Americans!" the crowd shouted. "We will work, we will work!"

World War II

MARTHA GELLHORN

The Battle of the Bulge

The sometime wife of Ernest Hemingway, Gellhorn began her
career as war correspondent in 1937 with the Spanish Civil War
and ended it in 1990 with the invasion of Panama. She was then
aged eighty-two. Below is her report of the Battle of the Bulge,
fought in December 1944 when Hitler tried the desperate gamble
of an offensive on the Western Front. The dispatch was originally
published in January 1945.

The Face of War, 1959

They all said it was wonderful Kraut-killing country. What it
looked like was scenery for a Christmas card: smooth white
snow hills and bands of dark forest and villages that actually
nestled. The snow made everything serene, from a distance.
At sunrise and sunset the snow was pink and the forests grew
smoky and soft. During the day the sky was covered with ski
tracks, the vapor trails of planes, and the roads were dangerous iced strips, crowded with all the usual vehicles of war,
and the artillery made a great deal of noise, as did the bombs
from the Thunderbolts. The nestling villages, upon closer
view, were mainly rubble and there were indeed plenty of
dead Krauts. This was during the German counteroffensive
which drove through Luxembourg and Belgium and is now
driven back. At this time the Germans were being "contained", as the communiqué said. The situation was "fluid"
– again the communiqué. For the sake of the record, here is a

little of what containing a fluid situation in Kraut-killing country looks like.

The road to Bastogne had been worked over by the Ninth Air Force Thunderbolts before the Third Army tanks finally cleared the way. A narrow alley was free now, and two or three secondary roads leading from Bastogne back to our lines. "Lines" is a most inaccurate word and one should really say "leading back through where the Germans weren't to where the Americans were scattered about the snowscape." The Germans remained on both sides of this alley and from time to time attempted to push inward and again cut off Bastogne.

A colleague and I drove up to Bastogne on a secondary road through breath-taking scenery. The Thunderbolts had created this scenery. You can say the words "death and destruction" and they don't mean anything. But they are awful words when you are looking at what they mean. There were some German staff cars along the side of the road; they had not merely been hit by machine-gun bullets, they had been mashed into the ground. There were half-tracks and tanks literally wrenched apart, and a gun position directly hit by bombs. All around these lacerated or flattened objects of steel there was the usual riffraff: papers, tin cans, cartridge belts, helmets, an odd shoe, clothing. There were also, ignored and completely inhuman, the hard-frozen corpses of Germans. Then there was a clump of houses, burned and gutted, with only a few walls standing, and around them the enormous bloated bodies of cattle.

The road passed through a curtain of pine forest and came out on a flat, rolling snow field. In this field the sprawled or bunched bodies of Germans lay thick, like some dark shapeless vegetable.

We had watched the Thunderbolts working for several days. They flew in small packs and streaked in to the attack in single file. They passed quickly through the sky and when they dived you held your breath and waited; it seemed impossible that the plane would be able to pull itself up to safety. They were diving to within sixty feet of the ground. The snub-nosed Thunderbolt is more feared by the German troops than any other plane.

You have seen Bastogne and a thousand other Bastognes in the newsreels. These dead towns and villages spread over Europe and one forgets the human misery and fear and despair that the cracked and caved-in buildings represent. Bastogne was a German job of death and destruction and it was beautifully thorough. The 101st Airborne Division, which held Bastogne, was still there, though the day before the wounded had been taken out as soon as the first road was open. The survivors of the 101st Airborne Division, after being entirely surrounded, uninterruptedly shelled and bombed, after having fought off four times their strength in Germans, look – for some unknown reason – cheerful and lively. A young lieutenant remarked, "The tactical situation was always good." He was very surprised when we shouted with laughter. The front, north of Bastogne, was just up the road and the peril was far from past.

At Warnach, on the other side of the main Bastogne road, some soldiers who had taken, lost and retaken this miserable village were now sightseeing the battlefield. They were also inspecting the blown-out equipment of two German tanks and a German self-propelled gun which had been destroyed here. Warnach smelled of the dead; in subzero weather the smell of death has an acrid burning odor. The soldiers poked through the German equipment to see if there was anything useful or desirable. They unearthed a pair of good bedroom slippers alongside the tank, but as no one in the infantry has any chance to wear bedroom slippers these were left. There was a German Bible but no one could read German. Someone had found a German machine pistol in working order and rapidly salted it away; they hoped to find other equally valuable loot.

The American dead had been moved inside the smashed houses and covered over; the dead horses and cows lay where they were, as did a few dead Germans. An old civilian was hopelessly shovelling grain from some burned and burst sacks into a wheelbarrow; and farther down the ruined street a woman was talking French in a high angry voice to the chaplain, who was trying to pacify her. We moved down this way to watch the goings-on. Her house was in fairly good shape; that is to say, it had no windows or door and there was a shell hole through the second-floor wall, but it was standing and the roof looked rain-proof. Outside her parlor window were some German mines, marked with a white tape. She stood in her front hall and said bitterly that it was a terrible thing, she had left her house for a few moments that morning, and upon returning she found her sheets had been stolen.

"What's she saying?" asked an enormous soldier with red-rimmed blue eyes and a stubble of red beard. Everyone seems about the same age, as if weariness and strain and the unceasing cold leveled all life. I translated the woman's complaint.

Another soldier said, "What does a sheet look like?"

The huge red-bearded man drawled out, "My goodness," a delicious expression coming from that face in that street. "If she'd of been here when the fighting was going on, she'd act different."

Farther down the street a command car dragged a trailer; the bodies of Germans were piled on the trailer like so much ghastly firewood.

We had come up this main road two days before. First there had been a quick tempestuous scene in a battalion headquarters when two planes strafed us, roaring in to attack three times and putting machine-gun bullets neatly through the second-story windows of the house. The official attitude has always been that no Germans were flying reclaimed Thunderbolts, so that is that. No one was wounded or killed during this brief muck-up. One of the battalion machine-gunners, who had been firing at the Thunderbolts, said, "For God's sake, which side are those guys fighting on?" We jumped into our jeep and drove up nearer the front, feeling that the front was probably safer.

A solitary tank was parked close to a bombed house near the main road. The crew sat on top of the tank, watching a village just over the hill which was being shelled, as well as bombed by the Thunderbolts. The village was burning and the smoke made a close package of fog around it, but the flames shot up and reddened the snow in the foreground. The armed forces on this piece of front consisted, at the moment, of this tank, and out ahead a few more tanks, and somewhere invisibly to the left a squadron of tanks. We did not know where our infantry was. (This is what a fluid situation means.) The attacked village would soon be entered by the tanks, including the solitary watchdog now guarding this road.

We inquired of the tank crew how everything went. "The war's over," said one of the soldiers, sitting on the turret. "Don't you know that? I heard it on the radio, a week ago. The Germans haven't any gasoline. They haven't any planes. Their tanks are no good. They haven't any shells for their guns. Hell, it's all over. I ask myself what I'm doing here," the tankist went on. "I say to myself, boy, you're crazy, sitting out here in the snow. Those ain't Germans, I say to myself, didn't they tell you on the radio the Germans are finished?"

As for the situation, someone else on the tank said that they would gratefully appreciate it if we could tell them what was going on.

"The wood's full of dead Krauts," said another, pointing across the road. "We came up here and sprayed it just in case there was any around and seems the place was full of them, so it's a good thing we sprayed it all right. But where they are right now, I wouldn't know."

"How's your hen?" asked the Captain, who had come from Battalion HQ to show us the way. "He's got a hen," the Captain explained. "He's been sweating that hen out for three days, running around after it with his helmet."

"My hen's worthless," said a soldier. "Finished, no good, got no fight in her."

"Just like the Germans," said the one who listened to the radio.

Now two days later the road was open much farther and there was even a rumor that it was open all the way to Bastogne. That would mean avoiding the secondary roads, a quicker journey, but it seemed a good idea to inquire at a blasted German gun position. At this spot there were ten Americans, two sergeants and eight enlisted men; also two smashed German bodies, two dead cows and a gutted house.

"I wouldn't go up that road if I was you," one of the sergeants said. "It's cut with small-arms fire about a quarter of a mile farther on. We took about seventeen Heinies out of there just a while back, but some others must of got in."

That seemed to settle the road.

"Anyhow," the sergeant went on, "they're making a counter-attack. They got about thirty tanks, we heard, coming this way."

The situation was getting very fluid again.

"What are you going to do?" I said.

"Stay here," said one of the soldiers.

"We got a gun," said another.

War is lonely and individual work; it is hard to realize how small it can get. Finally it can boil down to ten unshaven gaunt-looking young men, from anywhere in America, stationed on a vital road with German tanks coming in.

"You better take that side road if you're going to Bastogne," the second sergeant said.

It seemed shameful to leave them. "Good luck," I said, not knowing what to say.

"Sure, sure," they said soothingly. And later on they got a tank and the road was never cut and now if they are still alive they are somewhere in Germany doing the same work, as undramatically and casually – just any ten young men from anywhere in America.

About a mile from this place, and therefore about a mile and a half from the oncoming German tanks, the general in command of this tank outfit had his headquarters in a farmhouse. You could not easily enter his office through the front door, because a dead horse with spattered entrails blocked the way. A shell had landed in the farmyard a few minutes before and killed one cow and wounded a second, which was making sad sounds in a passageway between the house and the barn.

The air-ground-support officer was here with his van, checking up on the Thunderbolts who were attacking the oncoming German tanks. "Argue Leader," he said, calling on the radio-phone to the flight leader. "Beagle here. Did you do any good on that one?"

"Can't say yet," answered the voice from the air.

Then over the loud-speaker a new voice came from the air, talking clearly and loudly and calmly. "Three Tigers down there with people around them."

Also from the air the voice of Argue Leader replied rather peevishly, "Go in and get them. Don't stand there talking about it." They were both moving at an approximate speed of three hundred miles an hour.

From the radio in another van came the voice of the colonel commanding the forward tank unit, which was stopping this counterattack on the ground. "We got ten and two more coming," said the colonel's voice. "Just wanted to keep you posted on the German tanks burning up here. It's a beautiful sight, a beautiful sight, over."

"What a lovely headquarters," said a soldier who was making

himself a toasted cheese sandwich over a small fire that served everyone for warmth and cookstove. He had opened the cheese can in his K ration and was doing an excellent job, using a German bayonet as a kitchen utensil.

"Furthermore," said a lieutenant, "they're attacking on the other side. They got about thirty tanks coming in from the west too."

"See if I care," remarked the soldier, turning his bread carefully so as to toast it both ways. A shell landed, but it was farther up the road. There had been a vaguely sketched general ducking, a quick reflex action, but no one of course remarked it.

Then Argue Leader's voice came exultantly from the air. "Got those three. Going home now. Over."

"Good boys," said the ground officer. "Best there is. My squadron."

"Listen to him," said an artillery officer who had come over to report. "You'd think the Thunderbolts did everything. Well, I got to get back to work."

The cow went on moaning softly in the passageway. Our driver, who had made no previous comment during the day, said bitterly, "What I hate to see is a bunch of livestock all beat up this way. Goddammit, what they got to do with it? It's not their fault."

Christmas had passed almost unnoticed. All those who could, and that would mean no farther forward than Battalion Headquarters, had shaved and eaten turkey. The others did not shave and ate cold K rations. That was Christmas. There was little celebration on New Year's Eve, because everyone was occupied, and there was nothing to drink. Now on New Year's Day we were going up to visit the front, east of Luxembourg City. The front was quiet in the early afternoon, except for artillery, and a beautiful fat-flaked snowstorm had started. We decided, like millions of other people, that we were most heartily sick of war; what we really wanted to do was borrow a sled and go coasting. We borrowed a homemade wooden sled from an obliging little boy and found a steep slick hill near an abandoned stone quarry. It was evidently a well-known hill, because a dozen Luxembourg children were already there, with unsteerable sleds like ours. The sky had cleared and the ever present Thunderbolts returned and were working over the front less than four kilometers away. They made a lot of noise, and the artillery was pounding away too. The children paid no attention to this; they did not watch the Thunderbolts, or listen to the artillery. Screaming with joy, fear, and good spirits, they continued to slide down the hill.

Our soldier driver stood with me at the top of the hill and watched the children. "Children aren't so dumb," he said. I said nothing. "Children are pretty smart," he said. I said nothing again. "What I mean is, children got the right idea. What people ought to do is go coasting."

When he dropped us that night he said, "I sure got to thank you folks. I haven't had so much fun since I left home."

On the night of New Year's Day, I thought of a wonderful New Year's resolution for the men who run the world: get to know the people who only live in it.

There were many dead and many wounded, but the survivors contained the fluid situation and slowly turned it into a retreat, and finally, as the communiqué said, the bulge was ironed out. This was not done fast or easily; and it was not done by those anonymous things, armies, divisions, regiments. It was done by men, one by one – your men.

World War II

IRIS CARPENTER

First Girl War Correspondent to Cross Rhine at Remagen

Born in England, Carpenter's initial foray into journalism was as film critic for the London *Daily Express*. With the outbreak of war in 1939, she transferred to 'domestic' war reportage, covering the Home Front and the Blitz; when it became apparent that the Allies would invade France, she applied for accreditation with the British Expeditionary Force but, like other women correspondents, was turned down. Determined to bypass the no-women rule, Carpenter signed with America's *Boston Globe* and was promptly accredited as correspondent to the US First Army. And secured one of the scoops of the war.

Boston Globe, 10 March 1945

March 8 – Read that wonderful dateline again, please – "with the American 1st Army Troops across the Rhine." We are over. And in strength. At long last that last great river we had to cross flows behind us! Our first troops were on the eastern Rhine bank at 3:50 yesterday afternoon. Ever since, strong forces of infantry have been surging over to establish a bridgehead which is extending every hour.

One of Greatest Stories of All Time

Once in every journalist's life there is a story that is such a thrill and privilege to tell that anything and everything the getting costs is more than worthwhile. Such a story is today's.

Though it meant getting up at 4 a.m. to jeep through driving rain and spewing mud for 13 hours, getting pinned down under .88 fire, having the wind screen of my jeep splintered by shell-fire, getting sniped at, and finally, having crossed the Rhine I am unable to tell you anything but the barest bones of narrative until the security blackout is lifted somewhat.

I can only promise that when detail is possible, it will be one of the greatest stories of all time, not just of this war.

It began yesterday when, driving through toward the Rhine River south of Cologne, we reached the banks to find the situation was not as we had expected to find it.

Resistance was not the type we expected – it was such, in fact, that the troops called upon their commanding officer for a discussion. He heard what they had to tell him. He put his field telephone back in its leather case with a terse: "I'll be right down, boys."

The conference – in the street of as picturesque a Rhine village as ever decorated a wine label – lasted a matter of minutes. Then the first Allied soldiers to set foot on the far banks of the blue river, which is anything but blue in March, whatever it may be at other times of the year, were on their way to take the first German village on the eastern shore.

Infantry First Over

The first men over were the infantry with a few engineers. They were led by 1st Lt. Carl Timmeran, of Nebraska, and they met comparatively little resistance in the first phase of the operation.

There were small-arms fire, but such enemy as we were mainly concerned about were themselves too busy getting across the river to do anything else. They were all Nazis trying to make their way out across the Rhine from Schnee Eifel, where our converging 1st and 3d armies have them practically surrounded.

In fact, the prisoners we took this afternoon on our side of the river were just being waved on by Doughboys to wander alone into their cages, past the tide of Allied vehicles that flowed along the last roads in Europe over which the enemy expected them to come. They were roads much too narrow, seemingly, much too shelled, much too bad for the weight, the power and material needed for such an attack as ours.

Fast bulldozers, cranes and engineering equipment, with various other vehicles looking like lumbering prehistoric monsters rather than a supply train of modern war were weaving their way today through road blocks, burned-out tanks and trucks, over shell craters and towns so recently taken that we had not yet had time to pick up our dead or bulldoze more than mud tracks through the rubble.

We got jammed. We got ditched. Yet somehow or other our material got through to the other side.

World War II

RICHARD DIMBLEBY

The Cess Pit Beneath

Dimbleby visited Belsen extermination camp shortly after its liberation. Some six million Jews were killed by the SS, many of them
gassed at Belsen.

BBC Radio, 19 April 1945

I picked my way over corpse after corpse in the gloom, until I
heard one voice raised above the gentle undulating moaning. I
found a girl, she was a living skeleton, impossible to gauge her
age for she had practically no hair left, and her face was only a
yellow parchment sheet with two holes in it for eyes. She was
stretching out her stick of an arm and gasping something, it was
"English, English, medicine, medicine", and she was trying to
cry but she hadn't enough strength. And beyond her down the
passage and in the hut there were the convulsive movements of
dying people too weak to raise themselves from the floor.

In the shade of some trees lay a great collection of bodies. I
walked about them trying to count, there were perhaps 150 of
them flung down on each other, all naked, all so thin that their
yellow skin glistened like stretched rubber on their bones. Some
of the poor starved creatures whose bodies were there looked so
utterly unreal and inhuman that I could have imagined that they
had never lived at all. They were like polished skeletons, the skeletons that medical students like to play practical jokes with.

At one end of the pile a cluster of men and women were gathered round a fire; they were using rags and old shoes taken from

the bodies to keep it alight, and they were heating soup over it. And close by was the enclosure where 500 children between the ages of five and twelve had been kept. They were not so hungry as the rest, for the women had sacrificed themselves to keep them alive. Babies were born at Belsen, some of them shrunken, wizened little things that could not live, because their mothers could not feed them.

One woman, distraught to the point of madness, flung herself at a British soldier who was on guard at the camp on the night that it was reached by the 11th Armoured Division; she begged him to give her some milk for the tiny baby she held in her arms. She laid the mite on the ground and threw herself at the sentry's feet and kissed his boots. And when, in his distress, he asked her to get up, she put the baby in his arms and ran off crying that she would find milk for it because there was no milk in her breast. And when the soldier opened the bundle of rags to look at the child, he found that it had been dead for days.

There was no privacy of any kind. Women stood naked at the side of the track, washing in cupfuls of water taken from British Army trucks. Others squatted while they searched themselves for lice, and examined each other's hair. Sufferers from dysentery leaned against the huts, straining helplessly, and all around and about them was this awful drifting tide of exhausted people, neither caring nor watching. Just a few held out their withered hands to us as we passed by, and blessed the doctor, whom they knew had become the camp commander in place of the brutal Kramer.

I have never seen British soldiers so moved to cold fury as the men who opened the Belsen camp this week.

World War II

DON WHITEHEAD

Linkup: US and Russian Troops Meet

Don Whitehead reported on World War II for Associated Press, during which time he gained the nickname "Beachhead Don" in honour of his unsurpassed record as witness to Allied invasions, landing with US troops at Sicily, Anzio and Normandy. He later earned two Pulitzer Prizes for his reporting of the Korean conflict.

Associated Press, 25 April 1945

With the U.S. Sixty-ninth Division, April 25 (12 midnight) – An American infantry officer and a Russian private squirmed across a girder of a blown bridge in the Elbe River today, pounded each other on the back and shook hands to seal a historic meeting of Gen. Hodges' First Army with Marshal Ivan S. Konev's First Ukrainian Army group.

"Put it there," were the first words Second Lt. William D. Robertson, Los Angeles, called to his Red Army friend in the bizarre meeting at 4:40 p.m. over the waters of the Elbe at Torgau, twenty-eight miles northeast of Leipzig.

It was one of at least three contacts with the Russians made by men of the Sixty-ninth Division.

The union of the two great armies climaxed sensational drives from the west and east and ended intense suspense along the front over which unit would be the first to make the junction.

The Sixty-ninth Division is commanded by Maj. Gen. Emil

F. Reinhardt, Detroit, Mich. It won the historic honor of making the first contact with patrols.

Just who was the first individual to meet the Russians was not entirely clear at this writing, but Robertson got a big share of the credit because he was the first to bring back proof to his division headquarters. The proof was a Russian major, captain, lieutenant and private.

One of the first to meet the Russians – if not the first – was Lt. Albert L. Kotzebue of Houston, Texas. (A.P. Correspondent Hal Boyle said Kotzebue was the first.)

The happy Russians, beaming at everyone, were brought into the crowded command post of the division for a celebration of the event.

Each of them made a speech which was interpreted for the throng.

"This is a great day on the meeting of two nations," said Maj. Anaphim Larionov of Konev's Fifty-eighth Guards Division. "We extend warmest greetings and congratulations on the destruction of Nazism. We hope this meeting will be the basis for peace in the world to come."

Capt. Vassili Petrov Nedov added:

"We have wanted to meet you for a long time. This is a great holiday for the whole world."

This linkup with the Russians was one of the strangest stories of the entire war and was not even anticipated when a group of Americans set out in a jeep at 10 a.m.

Among the Americans in the jeep were Cpl. James J. McDonnell of Peabody, Miss., Pfc. Frank P. Huff, Washington, Va., and Pfc. Paul Staub of the Bronx, New York.

This was the story as told by Lt. William Robertson of Los Angeles, Calif.:

"Our company commander sent us out this morning to chase civilians off the roads. They were piling into Wurtzen in droves, running away from the Russians.

"You have no idea of the number of people on the roads. There were thousands of them and among them were many Allied prisoners of war who escaped from prison camps.

"German troops had thrown their weapons into ditches and were standing waiting to be taken prisoner.

"We kept on the move, now and then getting off the

congested roads. We met about thirty British boys who were headed for Wurtzen. We told them where they could get food.

"The British told us they had seen some wounded Americans up the road at Torgau.

"We went on east to Torgau and found these Americans who had been held by the Germans to be shot, because they were accused of espionage. They had been in Bavaria quite a while. We got some German guns for them and they guarded German prisoners who had thrown down their arms.

"We could hear small arms fire very close and they told us the Russians were just across the river.

"We left our jeep and went down on foot toward the river. We rigged up a big white flag so they wouldn't shoot at us.

"We didn't know what the Russian uniform looked like and I wasn't sure the Russians would recognize our uniform.

"Near the Elbe was a very large castle with a high tower.

"We broke into a drugstore and got some paint. I painted four red stripes on our white flag and a field of blue, because I figured the Russians would recognize the American flag better than anything else.

"I climbed into the tower and stuck my head out and waved the flag. They stopped firing for a while.

"I yelled, 'American, Tovarish, Kamerad.'

"They were yelling at me from across the river and fired two flares but I didn't see any flares to fire back.

"I left the flag flying and went down and found a Russian who had been a prisoner of the Germans. He shouted at the Russians to stop firing and I saw one Russian start across the bridge which was partly blown."

World War II

MOLLIE PANTER-DOWNES

The Big Day

The Second World War in Europe ended on May 7 1945, with complete German surrender. The Victory in Europe celebrations began the next day.

New Yorker, 19 May 1945

The big day started off here with a coincidence. In the last hours of peace, in September, 1939, a violent thunderstorm broke over the city, making a lot of people think for a moment that the first air raid had begun. Early Tuesday morning, VE Day, nature tidily brought the war to an end with an imitation of a blitz so realistic that many Londoners started awake and reached blurrily for the bedside torch. Then they remembered, and, sighing with relief, fell asleep again as the thunder rolled over the capital, already waiting with its flags. The decorations had blossomed on the streets Monday afternoon. By six that night, Piccadilly Circus and all the city's other focal points were jammed with a cheerful, expectant crowd waiting for an official statement from Downing Street. Movie cameramen crouched patiently on the rooftops. When a brewer's van rattled by and the driver leaned out and yelled "It's all over", the crowd cheered, then went on waiting. Presently word spread that the announcement would be delayed, and the day, which had started off like a rocket, began to fizzle slowly and damply out. Later in the evening, however, thousands of Londoners suddenly decided that even if it was not yet VE Day, it was victory, all right, and something to celebrate. Thousands of others just went home quietly to wait some more.

When the day finally came, it was like no other day that anyone can remember. It had a flavour of its own, an extemporaneousness which gave it something of the quality of a vast, happy village fete as people wandered about, sat, sang, and slept against a summer background of trees, grass, flowers, and water. It was not, people said, like the 1918 Armistice Day, for at no time was the reaction hysterical. It was not like the Coronation, for the crowds were larger and their gaiety, which held up all through the night, was obviously not picked up in a pub. The day also surprised the prophets who had said that only the young would be resilient enough to celebrate in a big way. Apparently the desire to assist in London's celebration combusted spontaneously in the bosom of every member of every family, from the smallest babies, with their hair done up in red-white-and-blue ribbons, to beaming elderly couples who, utterly without self-consciousness, strolled up and down the streets arm in arm in red-white-and-blue paper hats. Even the dogs wore immense tricoloured bows. Rosettes sprouted from the slabs of pork in the butcher shops, which, like other food stores, were open for a couple of hours in the morning. With their customary practicality, housewives put bread before circuses. They waited in the long bakery queues, the string bags of the common round in one hand and the Union Jack of the glad occasion in the other. Even queues seemed tolerable that morning. The bells had begun to peal and, after the night's storm, London was having that perfect, hot, English summer's day which, one sometimes feels, is to be found only in the imaginations of the lyric poets.

The girls in their thin, bright dresses heightened the impression that the city had been taken over by an enormous family picnic. The number of extraordinarily pretty young girls, who presumably are hidden on working days inside the factories and government offices, was astonishing. They streamed out into the parks and streets like flocks of twittering, gaily plumaged cockney birds. In their freshly curled hair were cornflowers and poppies, and they wore red-white-and-blue ribbons around their narrow waists. Some of them even tied ribbons around their bare ankles. Strolling with their uniformed boys, arms candidly about each other, they provided a constant, gay, simple marginal decoration to the big, solemn moments of the day. The crowds milled back and forth between the Palace, Westminster, Trafalgar Square, and Piccadilly Circus, and when they got tired they simply sat down wherever they happened to be – on the grass, on doorsteps, or on the kerb – and watched the other people or spread handkerchiefs over their faces and took a nap. Everybody appeared determined to see the King and Queen and Mr Churchill at least once, and few could have been disappointed. One small boy, holding on to his father's hand, wanted to see the trench shelters in Green Park too. "You don't want to see shelters today," his father said. "You'll never have to use them again, son." "Never?" the child asked doubtfully. "Never!" the man cried, almost angrily. "*Never*! Understand?" In the open space before the Palace, one of the places where the Prime Minister's speech was to be relayed by loudspeaker at three o'clock, the crowds seemed a little intimidated by the nearness of that symbolic block of grey stone. The people who chose to open their lunch baskets and munch sandwiches there among the flower beds of tulips were rather subdued. Piccadilly Circus attracted the more demonstrative spirits.

By lunchtime, in the Circus, the buses had to slow to a crawl in order to get through the tightly packed, laughing people. A lad in the black beret of the Tank Corps was the first to climb the little pyramidal Angkor Wat of scaffolding and sandbags which was erected early in the war to protect the pedestal of the Eros statue after the figure had been removed to safekeeping. The boy shinnied up to the top and took a tiptoe Eros pose, aiming an imaginary bow, while the crowd roared. He was followed by a paratrooper in a maroon beret, who, after getting up to the top, reached down and hauled up a blonde young woman in a very tight pair of green slacks. When she got to the top, the Tank Corps soldier promptly grabbed her in his arms and, encouraged by ecstatic cheers from the whole Circus, seemed about to enact the classic role of Eros right on the top of the monument. Nothing came of it, because a moment later a couple of GIs joined them and before long the pyramid was covered with boys and girls. They sat jammed together in an affectionate mass, swinging their legs over the sides, wearing each other's uniform caps, and calling down wisecracks to the crowd. "My God," someone said, "think of a flying bomb coming down on this!" When a firecracker went off, a hawker with a tray of tin brooches of Monty's head happily yelled that comforting, sometimes fallacious phrase of the blitz nights. "All right, mates, it's one of ours!"

All day long, the deadly past was for most people only just under the surface of the beautiful, safe present, so much so that the Government decided against sounding the sirens in a triumphant "all clear" for fear that the noise would revive too many painful memories. For the same reason, there were no salutes of guns – only the pealing of the bells, and the whistles of tugs on the Thames sounding the doot, doot, doot, dooooot of the "V", and the roar of the planes, which swooped back and forth over the city, dropping red and green signals toward the blur of smiling, upturned faces.

It was without any doubt Churchill's day. Thousands of King George's subjects wedged themselves in front of the Palace throughout the day, chanting ceaselessly "We want the King" and cheering themselves hoarse when he and the Queen and their daughters appeared, but when the crowd saw Churchill there was a deep, full-throated, almost reverent roar. He was at the head of a procession of Members of Parliament, walking back to the House of Commons from the traditional St Margaret's Thanksgiving Service. Instantly, he was surrounded by people – people running, standing on tiptoe, holding up babies so that they could be told later they had seen him, and shouting affectionately the absurd little nurserymaid name, "Winnie, Winnie!" One of two happily sozzled, very old, and incredibly dirty cockneys who had been engaged in a slow, shuffling dance, like a couple of Shakespearean clowns, bellowed, "That's 'im, that's 'is little old lovely bald 'ead!" The crowds saw Churchill again later, when he emerged from the Commons and was driven off in the back of a small open car, rosy, smiling, and looking immensely happy. Ernest Bevin, following in another car, got a cheer too. One of the throng, an excited East Ender, in a dress with a bodice concocted of a Union Jack, shouted, "Gawd, fancy me cheering Bevin, the chap who makes us work!" Herbert Morrison, sitting unobtrusively in a corner of a third car, was hardly recognized, and the other Cabinet Ministers did no better. The crowd had ears, eyes, and throats for no one but Churchill, and for him everyone in it seemed to have the hearing, sight, and lungs of fifty men. His slightly formal official broadcast, which was followed by buglers sounding the "cease firing" call, did not strike the emotional note that had been expected, but he hit it perfectly in his subsequent informal speech ("My dear friends, this is your victory . . .") from a Whitehall balcony.

All day long, little extra celebrations started up. In the Mall, a model of a Gallic cock waltzed on a pole over the heads of the singing people. "It's the Free French," said someone. The Belgians in the crowed tagged along after a Belgian flag that marched by, its bearer invisible. A procession of students raced through Green Park, among exploding squibs, clashing dustbin lids like cymbals and waving an immense Jeyes Disinfectant poster as a banner. American sailors and laughing girls formed a conga line down the middle of Piccadilly and cockneys linked arms in the Lambeth Walk. It was a day and night of no fixed plan and no organized merriment. Each group danced its own dance, sang its own song, and went its own way as the spirit moved it. The most tolerant, self-effacing people in London on VE Day were the police, who simply stood by, smiling benignly, while soldiers swung by one arm from lamp standards and laughing groups tore down hoardings to build the evening's bonfires. Actually, the police were not unduly strained. The extraordinary thing about the crowds was that they were almost all sober. The number of drunks one saw in that whole day and night could have been counted on two hands – possibly because the pubs were sold out so early. The young service men and women who swung arm in arm down the middle of every street, singing and swarming over the few cars rash enough to come out, were simply happy with an immense holiday happiness. They were the liberated people who, like their counterparts in every celebrating capital that night, were young enough to out-live the past and to look forward to an unspoilt future. Their gaiety was very moving.

Just before the King's speech, at nine Tuesday night, the big lamps outside the Palace came on and there were cheers and obs from children who had never seen anything of that kind in their short, blacked-out lives. As the evening wore on, most of the public buildings were floodlighted. The night was as warm as midsummer, and London, its shabbiness now hidden and its domes and remaining Wren spires warmed by lights and bonfires, was suddenly magnificent. The handsomest building of all was the National Gallery, standing out honey-coloured near a ghostly, blue-shadowed St Martin's and the Charles I bit of Whitehall. The illuminated and floodlighted face of Big Ben loomed like a kind moon. Red and blue lights strung in the bushes around the lake in St James's Park glimmered on the sleepy, bewildered pelicans that live there.

By midnight the crowds had thinned out some, but those who remained were as merry as ever. They went on calling for the King outside the Palace and watching the searchlights, which for once could be observed with pleasure . . .

World War II

WILLIAM L. LAURENCE

A Mushroom Cloud

Nicknamed "Atomic Bill" for his interest in the development of the A-bomb, Laurence missed the Hiroshima mission but was aboard a B-29 on 9 August 1945 to see the destruction of Nagasaki. His account of the bombing won him his second Pulitzer Prize.

New York Times, 3 September 1945

We flew southward down the channel and at 11:33 crossed the coastline and headed straight for Nagasaki, about one hundred miles to the west. Here we again circled until we found an opening in the clouds. It was 12:01 and the goal of our mission had arrived.

We heard the prearranged signal on our radio, put on our arc welder's glasses, and watched tensely the maneuverings of the strike ship about half a mile in front of us.

"There she goes!" someone said.

Out of the belly of *The Great Artiste* what looked like a black object went downward.

Captain Bock swung around to get out of range; but even though we were turning away in the opposite direction, and despite the fact that it was broad daylight in our cabin, all of us became aware of a giant flash that broke through the dark barrier of our arc welder's lenses and flooded our cabin with intense light.

We removed our glasses after the first flash, but the light still lingered on, a bluish-green light that illuminated the entire sky all around. A tremendous blast wave struck our ship and made it tremble from nose to tail. This was followed by four more blasts in rapid succession, each resounding like the boom of cannon fire hitting our plane from all directions.

Observers in the tail of our ship saw a giant ball of fire rise as though from the bowels of the earth, belching forth enormous white smoke rings. Next, they saw a giant pillar of purple fire, ten thousand feet high, shooting skyward with enormous speed.

By the time our ship had made another turn in the direction of the atomic explosion the pillar of purple fire had reached the level of our altitude. Only about forty-five seconds had passed. Awe-struck, we watched it shoot upward like a meteor coming from the earth instead of from outer space, becoming ever more alive as it climbed skyward through the white clouds. It was no longer smoke, or dust, or even a cloud of fire. It was a living thing, a new species of being, born right before our incredulous eyes.

At one stage of its evolution, covering millions of years in terms of seconds, the entity assumed the form of a giant square totem pole, with its base about three miles long, tapering off to about a mile at the top. Its bottom was brown, its center was amber, its top white. But it was a living totem pole, carved with many grotesque masks grimacing at the earth.

Then, just when it appeared as though the thing had settled down into a state of permanence, there came shooting out of the top a giant mushroom that increased the height of the pillar to a total of forty-five thousand feet. The mushroom top was even more alive than the pillar, seething and boiling in a white fury of creamy foam, sizzling upward and then descending earthward, a thousand Old Faithful geysers rolled into one.

It kept struggling in an elemental fury, like a creature in the act of breaking the bonds that held it down. In a few seconds it had freed itself from its gigantic stem and floated upward with tremendous speed, its momentum carrying it into the strato-sphere to a height of about sixty thousand feet.

But no sooner did this happen when another mushroom, smaller in size than the first one, began emerging out of the pillar. It was as though the decapitated monster was growing a new head.

As the first mushroom floated off into the blue it changed its shape into a flowerlike form, its giant petals curving downward, creamy white outside, rose-colored inside. It still retained that shape when we last gazed at it from a distance of about two hundred miles. The boiling pillar of many colors could also be seen at that distance, a giant mountain of jumbled rainbows, in travail. Much living substance had gone into those rainbows. The quivering top of the pillar was protruding to a great height through the white clouds, giving the appearance of a monstrous prehistoric creature with a ruff around its neck, a fleecy ruff extending in all directions, as far as the eye could see.

World War II

HOMER BIGART

Hope This is the Last One, Baby

Japan agreed an unconditional surrender on 14 August. When the surrender came through a B-29 bombing mission was in mid-air, and it was too late to recall it. It was the last combat run of the Second World War. Aboard one of the B-29s was the *Herald Tribune*'s war correspondent, Homer Bigart, who was no stranger to bomber life and death, having ridden with the USAAF over Germany (see pages 329–332).

New York *Herald Tribune*, 16 August 1945

In a B-29 over Japan, Aug. 15

The radio tells us that the war is over but from where I sit it looks suspiciously like a rumor. A few minutes ago – at 1:32 a.m. – we fire-bombed Kumagaya, a small industrial city behind Tokyo near the northern edge of Kanto Plain. Peace was not official for the Japanese either, for they shot right back at us.

Other fires are raging at Isesaki, another city on the plain, and as we skirt the eastern base of Fujiyama Lieutenant General James Doolittle's B-29s, flying their first mission from the 8th Air Force base on Okinawa, arrive to put the finishing touches on Kumagaya.

I rode in the *City of Saco* (Maine), piloted by First Lieutenant Theodore J. Lamb, twenty-eight, of 103–21 Lefferts Blvd, Richmond Hill, Queens, NY. Like all the rest, Lamb's crew showed the strain of the last five days of the uneasy "truce" that kept Superforts grounded.

They had thought the war was over. They had passed most of the time around radios, hoping the President would make it official. They did not see that it made much difference whether Emperor Hirohito stayed in power. Had our propaganda not portrayed him as a puppet? Well, then, we could use him just as the war lords had done.

The 314th Bombardment Wing was alerted yesterday morning. At 2:20 p.m., pilots, bombardiers, navigators, radio men, and gunners trooped into the briefing shack to learn that the war was still on. Their target was to be a pathetically small city of little obvious importance, and their commanding officer, Colonel Carl R. Storrie, of Denton, Texas, was at pains to convince them why Kumagaya, with a population of 49,000, had to be burned to the ground.

There were component parts factories of the Nakajima aircraft industry in the town, he said. Moreover, it was an important railway center.

No one wants to die in the closing moments of a war. The wing chaplain, Captain Benjamin Schmidke, of Springfield, Mo., asked the men to pray, and then the group commander jumped on the platform and cried: "This is the last mission. Make it the best we ever ran."

Colonel Storrie was to ride in one of the lead planes, dropping four 1,000-pound high explosives in the hope that the defenders of the town would take cover in buildings or underground and then be trapped by a box pattern of fire bombs to be dumped by eighty planes directly behind.

"We've got 'em on the one yard line. Let's push the ball over," the colonel exhorted his men. "This should be the final knockout blow of the war. Put your bombs on the target so that tomorrow the world will have peace."

Even after they were briefed, most of the crewmen hoped and expected that an official armistice would come before the scheduled 5:30 take-off. They looked at their watches. Two and a half hours to go.

You might expect that the men would be in a sullen, almost mutinous, frame of mind. But morale was surprisingly high.

"Look at the sweat pour off me," cried Major William Marchesi, of 458 Baltic Street, Brooklyn. "I've never sweated out a mission like this one."

A few minutes earlier the Guam radio had interrupted its program with a flash and quoted the Japanese Domei Agency announcement that Emperor Hirohito had accepted the peace terms.

Instantly the whole camp was in an uproar. But then a voice snapped angrily over the squawk box: "What are you trying to do? Smash morale? It's only a rumor."

So the crews drew their equipment – parachutes, Mae Wests, and flak suits – and got on trucks to go out to the line. We reached the *City of Saco* at about 4:30 p.m., and there was still nearly an hour to go before our plane, which was to serve as a pathfinder for the raiders, would depart.

We were all very jittery. Radios were blaring in the camp area but they were half a mile from us and all we could catch were the words "Hirohito" and "Truman". For all we knew, the war was over.

Then a headquarters officer came by and told Lieutenant Lamb that the take-off had been postponed thirty minutes in expectation of some announcement from Washington.

By that time none of us expected to reach Japan, but we knew that unless confirmation came soon the mission would have to take off, and then very likely salvo its bombs and come home when the signal "Utah, Utah, Utah," came through. That was the code agreed upon for calling off operations in the event of an announcement of peace by President Truman.

Lamb's crew began turning the plane's props at 5:45, and we got aboard. "Boy, we're going to kill a lot of fish today," said Sergeant Karl L. Braley, of Saco, Maine.

To salvo the bombs at sea is an expensive method of killing fish.

We got San Francisco on the radio. "I hope all you boys out there are as happy as we are at this moment," an announcer was saying. "People are yelling and screaming and whistles are blowing."

"Yeah," said one of the crewmen disgustedly, "they're screaming and we're flying."

We took off at 6:07.

We saw no white flags when we reached Japanese territory. Back of the cockpit Radioman Staff Sergeant Rosendo D. Del Valle Jr., of El Paso, Texas, strained his ears for the message,

"Utah, Utah, Utah." If it came on time, it might save a crew or two, and perhaps thousands of civilians at Kumagaya.

The message never came. Each hour brought us nearer the enemy coast. We caught every news broadcast, listening to hours of intolerable rot in the hope that the announcer would break in with the news that would send us home.

The empire coast was as dark and repellent as ever. Japan was still at war, and not one light showed in the thickly populated Tokyo plain.

Lamb's course was due north to the Kasumiga Lake, then a right angle, turning west for little Kumagaya. It was too late now. There would be bombs on Kumagaya in a few minutes.

Kumagaya is on featureless flats five miles south of the Tone River. It is terribly hard to pick up by radar. There were only two cues to Kumagaya. Directly north of the town was a wide span across the Tone, and a quarter of a mile south of it was a long bridge across the Ara River.

The radar observer, Lieutenant Harold W. Zeisler, of Kankakee, Ill, picked up both bridges in good time and we started the bomb run.

An undercast hid the city almost completely but through occasional rifts I could see a few small fires catching on from the bombs dropped by the two preceding pathfinders.

The Japanese were alert. Searchlights lit the clouds beneath us and two ack-ack guns sent up weak sporadic fire. Thirty miles to the north we saw Japanese searchlights and ack-ack groping for the bombers of another wing attacking Isesaki.

Leaving our target at the mercy of the eighty Superforts following us, we swerved sharply southward along the eastern base of Fujiyama and reached the sea. At one point we were within ten miles of Tokyo. The capital was dark.

Every one relaxed. We tried to pick up San Francisco on the radio but couldn't. The gunners took out photos of their wives and girl friends and said: "Hope this is the last, baby."

This postscript is written at Guam. It was the last raid of the war. We did not know it until we landed at North Field.

The results of the raid we learned from the pilots who followed us over the target. General conflagrations were devouring both Kumagaya and Isesaki. Japan's tardiness in replying to the peace terms cost her two cities.

World War II

SERGEANT DALE KRAMER

The Japanese Drink Bitter Tea Aboard the USS *Missouri*

Kramer was a staff writer for *Yank*, the weekly magazine published by the US military during World War II. He was aboard the *Missouri* when the Japanese signed the instrument of surrender – the stroke of the pen that ended World War II.

Yank, 5 October 1945

For a while it looked as though the proceedings would go off with almost unreasonable smoothness. Cameramen assigned to the formal surrender ceremonies aboard the battleship *Missouri* arrived on time and although every inch of the turrets and housings and life rafts above the veranda deck where the signing was to take place was crowded, no one fell off and broke a collarbone.

The ceremonies themselves even started and were carried on according to schedule. It took a Canadian colonel to bring things back to normal by signing the surrender document on the wrong line.

No one had the heart to blame the colonel, though. A mere colonel was bound to get nervous around so much higher brass.

The other minor flaw in the ceremonial circus was that it was something of an anticlimax. Great historic events probably are always somewhat that way, and this one, to those of us who had taken off three weeks before with the Eleventh Airborne

Division from the Philippines, was even more so. We had started out thinking in terms of a sensational dash to the Emperor's palace in Tokyo, only to sweat it out on Okinawa and later off Yokohama.

When it did come, the signing aboard the *Missouri* was a show which lacked nothing in its staging. A cluster of microphones and a long table covered with a green cloth had been placed in the center of the deck. On the table lay the big ledger-size white documents of surrender; bound in brown folders.

The assembly of brass and braid was a thing to see – a lake of gold and silver sparkling with rainbows of decorations and ribbons. British and Australian Army officers had scarlet stripes on their garrison caps and on their collars. The French were more conservative, except for the acres of vivid decorations on their breasts. The stocky leader of the Russian delegation wore gold shoulder boards and red-striped trousers. The Dutch had gold-looped shoulder emblems. The British admirals wore snow-white summer uniforms with shorts and knee-length white stockings. The olive-drab of the Chinese was plain except for ribbons. The least decked-out of all were the Americans. Their hats, except for Admiral Halsey's go-to-hell cap, were gold-braided, but their uniforms were plain suntan. Navy regulations do not permit wearing ribbons or decorations on a shirt.

Lack of time prevented piping anyone over the side, and when General MacArthur, Supreme Commander for the Allied powers, came aboard he strode quickly across the veranda deck and disappeared inside the ship. Like the other American officers, he wore plain suntans. A few minutes later, a gig flying the American flag and operated by white-clad American sailors putted around the bow of the ship. In the gig, wearing formal diplomatic morning attire, consisting of black cut-away coat, and striped pants and stove-pipe hat, sat Foreign Minister Mamoru Shigemitsu, leader of the Japanese delegation.

Coming up the gangway, Shigemitsu climbed very slowly because of a stiff left leg, and he limped onto the veranda deck with the aid of a heavy, light-colored cane. Behind him came ten other Japs. One wore a white suit, two more wore formal morning attire, the rest were dressed in pieced-out uniforms of the Jap Army and Navy. They gathered into three rows on the forward side of the green-covered table. The representatives of the Allied powers formed on the other side. When they were arranged, General MacArthur entered and stepped to the microphone.

His words rolled sonorously: "We are gathered here, representatives of the major warring powers, to conclude a solemn agreement whereby peace may be restored." He emphasized the necessity that both victors and vanquished rise to a greater dignity in order that the world may emerge forever from blood and carnage. He declared his firm intention as Supreme Commander to "discharge my responsibility with justice and tolerance while taking all necessary dispositions to insure that the terms of surrender are fully, promptly, and faithfully complied with."

The Japanese stood at attention during the short address, their faces grave, but otherwise showing little emotion. When the representatives of the Emperor were invited to sign, Foreign Minister Shigemitsu hobbled forward, laid aside his silk hat and cane, and lowered himself slowly into a chair. The wind whipped his thin, dark hair as he reached into his pocket for a pen, tested it, then affixed three large Japanese characters to the first of the documents. He had to rise and bend over the table for the others.

The audience was conscious of the historic importance of the pen strokes, but it watched for something else, too. General MacArthur had promised to present General Wainwright, who had surrendered the American forces at Corregidor and until only a few days before had been a prisoner of war, with the first pen to sign the surrender. Shigemitsu finished and closed his pen and replaced it in his pocket. There could be no objection. He had needed a brush-pen for the Japanese letters.

When the big surrender folders were turned around on the table, General MacArthur came forward to affix his signature as Supreme Commander. He asked General Wainwright and General Percival, who had surrendered the British forces at Singapore, to accompany him. General MacArthur signed the first document and handed the pen to General Wainwright. He used five pens in all, ending up with one from his own pocket.

Sailors have been as avid souvenir collectors in this war as anyone else, but when Admiral Nimitz sat down to sign for the U.S. he used only two pens. After that the representatives of

China, the United Kingdom, Russia, Australia, Canada, France, the Netherlands, and New Zealand put down their signatures.

As the big leather document folders were gathered, a GI member of a sound unit recorded a few historic remarks of his own. "Brother," he said, "I hope those are my discharge papers."

World War II

KINGSBURY SMITH

Execution of Nazi War Criminals

The trials held by the International Military Tribunal at Nuremberg found twelve of the surviving members of the Nazi Party guilty of crimes against humanity. The twelve, who included Martin Bormann, tried *in absentia*, were sentenced to hang on 16 October 1946. Kingsbury Smith was chosen by lot to represent the American press at the hangings.

It Happened in 1946, 1947

Hermann Wilhelm Göring cheated the gallows of Allied justice by committing suicide in his prison cell shortly before the ten other condemned Nazi leaders were hanged in Nuremberg gaol. He swallowed cyanide he had concealed in a copper cartridge shell, while lying on a cot in his cell.

The one-time Number Two man in the Nazi hierarchy was dead two hours before he was scheduled to have been dropped through the trapdoor of a gallows erected in a small, brightly lighted gymnasium in the gaol yard, thirty-five yards from the cell block where he spent his last days of ignominy.

Joachim von Ribbentrop, foreign minister in the ill-starred regime of Adolf Hitler, took Göring's place as first to the scaffold.

Last to depart this life in a total span of just about two hours was Arthur Seyss-Inquart, former *Gauleiter* of Holland and Austria.

In between these two once-powerful leaders, the gallows

claimed, in the order named, Field Marshal Wilhelm Keitel; Ernst Kaltenbrunner, once head of the Nazis' security police; Alfred Rosenberg, arch-priest of Nazi culture in foreign lands; Hans Frank, *Gauleiter* of Poland; Wilhelm Frick, Nazi minister of the interior; Fritz Sauckel, boss of slave labour; Colonel General Alfred Jodl; and Julius Streicher, who bossed the anti-Semitism drive of the Hitler Reich.

As they went to the gallows, most of the ten endeavored to show bravery. Some were defiant and some were resigned and some begged the Almighty for mercy.

All except Rosenberg made brief, last-minute statements on the scaffold. But the only one to make any reference to Hitler or the Nazi ideology in his final moments was Julius Streicher.

Three black-painted wooden scaffolds stood inside the gymnasium, a room approximately thirty-three feet wide by eighty feet long with plaster walls in which cracks showed. The gymnasium had been used only three days before by the American security guards for a basketball game. Two gallows were used alternately. The third was a spare for use if needed. The men were hanged one at a time, but to get the executions over with quickly, the military police would bring in a man while the prisoner who preceded him still was dangling at the end of the rope.

The ten once great men in Hitler's Reich that was to have lasted for a thousand years walked up thirteen wooden steps to a platform eight feet high which also was eight feet square.

Ropes were suspended from a crossbeam supported on two posts. A new one was used for each man.

When the trap was sprung, the victim dropped from sight in the interior of the scaffolding. The bottom of it was boarded up with wood on three sides and shielded by a dark canvas curtain on the fourth, so that no one saw the death struggles of the men dangling with broken necks.

Von Ribbentrop entered the execution chamber at 1.11 a.m. Nuremberg time. He was stopped immediately inside the door by two Army sergeants who closed in on each side of him and held his arms, while another sergeant who had followed him in removed manacles from his hands and replaced them with a leather strap.

It was planned originally to permit the condemned men to walk from their cells to the execution chamber with their hands free, but all were manacled immediately following Göring's suicide.

Von Ribbentrop was able to maintain his apparent stoicism to the last. He walked steadily toward the scaffold between his two guards, but he did not answer at first when an officer standing at the foot of the gallows went through the formality of asking his name. When the query was repeated he almost shouted, "Joachim von Ribbentrop!" and then mounted the steps without any sign of hesitation.

When he was turned around on the platform to face the witnesses, he seemed to clench his teeth and raise his head with the old arrogance. When asked whether he had any final message he said, "God protect Germany," in German, and then added, "May I say something else?"

The interpreter nodded and the former diplomatic wizard of Nazidom spoke his last words in loud, firm tones: "My last wish is that Germany realize its entity and that an understanding be reached between the East and the West. I wish peace to the world."

As the black hood was placed in position on his head, von Ribbentrop looked straight ahead.

Then the hangman adjusted the rope, pulled the lever, and von Ribbentrop slipped away to his fate.

Field Marshal Keitel, who was immediately behind von Ribbentrop in the order of executions, was the first military leader to be executed under the new concept of international law – the principle that professional soldiers cannot escape punishment for waging aggressive wars and permitting crimes against humanity with the claim they were dutifully carrying out orders of superiors.

Keitel entered the chamber two minutes after the trap had dropped beneath von Ribbentrop, while the latter still was at the end of his rope. But von Ribbentrop's body was concealed inside the first scaffold; all that could be seen was the taut rope.

Keitel did not appear as tense as von Ribbentrop. He held his head high while his hands were being tied and walked erect toward the gallows with a military bearing. When asked his name he responded loudly and mounted the gallows as he might have mounted a reviewing stand to take a salute from German armies.

He certainly did not appear to need the help of guards who walked alongside, holding his arms. When he turned around atop the platform he looked over the crowd with the iron-jawed haughtiness of a proud Purssian officer. His last words, uttered in a full, clear voice, were translated as "I call on God Almighty to have mercy on the German people. More than 2 million German soldiers went to their death for the fatherland before me. I follow now my sons – all for Germany."

After his black-booted, uniformed body plunged through the trap, witnesses agreed Keitel had showed more courage on the scaffold than in the courtroom, where he had tried to shift his guilt upon the ghost of Hitler, claiming that all was the Führer's fault and that he merely carried out orders and had no responsibility.

With both von Ribbentrop and Keitel hanging at the end of their ropes there was a pause in the proceedings. The American colonel directing the executions asked the American general representing the United States on the Allied Control Commission if those present could smoke. An affirmative answer brought cigarettes into the hands of almost every one of the thirty-odd persons present. Officers and GIs walked around nervously or spoke a few words to one another in hushed voices while Allied correspondents scribbled furiously their notes on this historic though ghastly event.

In a few minutes an American Army doctor accompanied by a Russian Army doctor and both carrying stethoscopes walked to the first scaffold, lifted the curtain and disappeared within.

They emerged at 1.30 a.m. and spoke to an American colonel. The colonel swung around and facing official witnesses snapped to attention to say, "The man is dead."

Two GIs quickly appeared with a stretcher which was carried up and lifted into the interior of the scaffold. The hangman mounted the gallows steps, took a large commando-type knife out of a sheath strapped to his side and cut the rope.

Von Ribbentrop's limp body with the black hood still over his head was removed to the far end of the room and placed behind a black canvas curtain. This all had taken less than ten minutes.

The directing colonel turned to the witnesses and said, "Cigarettes out, please, gentlemen." Another colonel went out the door and over to the condemned block to fetch the next man. This was Ernst Kaltenbrunner. He entered the execution chamber at 1.36 a.m., wearing a sweater beneath his blue double-breasted coat. With his lean haggard face furrowed by old duelling scars, this terrible successor to Reinhard Heydrich had a frightening look as he glanced around the room.

He wet his lips apparently in nervousness as he turned to mount the gallows, but he walked steadily. He answered his name in a calm, low voice. When he turned around on the gallows platform he first faced a United States Army Roman Catholic chaplain wearing a Franciscan habit. When Kaltenbrunner was invited to make a last statement, he said, "I have loved my German people and my fatherland with a warm heart. I have done my duty by the laws of my people and I am sorry my people were led this time by men who were not soldiers and that crimes were committed of which I had no knowledge."

This was the man, one of whose agents – a man named Rudolf Hoess – confessed at a trial that under Kaltenbrunner's orders he gassed 3 million human beings at the Auschwitz concentration camp!

As the black hood was raised over his head Kaltenbrunner, still speaking in a low voice, used a German phrase which translated means, "Germany, good luck."

His trap was sprung at 1.39 a.m.

Field Marshal Keitel was pronounced dead at 1.44 a.m. and three minutes later guards had removed his body. The scaffold was made ready for Alfred Rosenberg.

Rosenberg was dull and sunken-checked as he looked around the court. His complexion was pasty-brown, but he did not appear nervous and walked with a steady step to and up the gallows.

Apart from giving his name and replying "no" to a question as to whether he had anything to say, he did not utter a word. Despite his avowed atheism he was accompanied by a Protestant chaplain who followed him to the gallows and stood beside him praying.

Rosenberg looked at the chaplain once, expressionless. Ninety seconds after he was swinging from the end of a hangman's rope. His was the swiftest execution of the ten.

There was a brief lull in the proceedings until Kaltenbrunner was pronounced dead at 1.52 a.m.

Hans Frank was next in the parade of death. He was the only one of the condemned to enter the chamber with a smile on his countenance.

Although nervous and swallowing frequently, this man, who was converted to Roman Catholicism after his arrest, gave the appearance of being relieved at the prospect of atoning for his evil deeds.

He answered to his name quietly and when asked for any last statement, he replied in a low voice that was almost a whisper, "I am thankful for the kind treatment during my captivity and I ask God to accept me with mercy."

Frank closed his eyes and swallowed as the black hood went over his head.

The sixth man to leave his prison cell and walk with hand-cuffed wrists to the death house was sixty-nine-year-old Wilhelm Frick. He entered the execution chamber at 2.05 a.m., six minutes after Rosenberg had been pronounced dead. He seemed the least steady of any so far and stumbled on the thirteenth step of the gallows. His only words were, "Long live eternal Germany," before he was hooded and dropped through the trap.

Julius Streicher made his melodramatic appearance at 2.12 a.m.

While his manacles were being removed and his hands bound, this ugly, dwarfish little man, wearing a threadbare suit and a well-worn bluish shirt buttoned to the neck but without a tie (he was notorious during his days of power for his flashy dress), glanced at the three wooden scaffolds rising up menacingly in front of him. Then he glared around the room, his eyes resting momentarily upon the small group of witnesses. By this time, his hands were tied securely behind his back. Two guards, one on each arm, directed him to Number One gallows on the left of the entrance. He walked steadily the six feet to the first wooden step but his face was twitching.

As the guards stopped him at the bottom of the steps for identification formality he uttered his piercing scream: "Heil Hitler!"

The shriek sent a shiver down my back.

As its echo died away an American colonel standing by the

steps said sharply, "Ask the man his name." In response to the interpreter's query Streicher shouted, "You know my name well."

The interpreter repeated his request and the condemned man yelled, "Julius Streicher."

As he reached the platform, Streicher cried out, "Now it goes to God." He was pushed the last two steps to the mortal spot beneath the hangman's rope. The rope was being held back against a wooden rail by the hangman.

Streicher was swung around to face the witnesses and glared at them. Suddenly he screamed, "*Purim Fest 1946.*" (Purim is a Jewish holiday celebrated in the spring, commemorating the execution of Haman, ancient persecutor of the Jews described in the Old Testament.)

The American officer standing at the scaffold said, "Ask the man if he has any last words."

When the interpreter had translated, Streicher shouted, "The Bolsheviks will hang you one day."

When the black hood was raised over his head, Streicher said, "I am with God."

As it was being adjusted, Streicher's muffled voice could be heard to say, "Adele, my dear wife."

At that instant the trap opened with a loud bang. He went down kicking. When the rope snapped taut with the body swinging wildly, groans could be heard from within the concealed interior of the scaffold. Finally, the hangman, who had descended from the gallows platform, lifted the black canvas curtain and went inside. Something happened that put a stop to the groans and brought the rope to a standstill. After it was over I was not in a mood to ask what he did, but I assume that he grabbed the swinging body and pulled down on it. We were all of the opinion that Streicher had strangled.

Then, following removal of the corpse of Frick, who had been pronounced dead at 2.20 a.m., Fritz Sauckel was brought face to face with his doom.

Wearing a sweater with no coat and looking wild-eyed, Sauckel proved to be the most defiant of any except Streicher.

Here was the man who put millions into bondage on a scale unknown since the pre-Christian era. Gazing around the room from the gallows platform he suddenly screamed, "I am dying innocent. The sentence is wrong. God protect Germany and make Germany great again. Long live Germany! God protect my family."

The trap was sprung at 2.26 a.m. and, as in the case of Streicher, there was a loud groan from the gallows pit as the noose snapped tightly under the weight of his body.

Ninth in the procession of death was Alfred Jodl. With the black coat-collar of his *Wehrmacht* uniform half turned up at the back as though hurriedly put on, Jodl entered the dismal death house with obvious signs of nervousness. He wet his lips constantly and his features were drawn and haggard as he walked, not nearly so steady as Keitel, up the gallows steps. Yet his voice was calm when he uttered his last six words on earth: "My greetings to you, my Germany."

At 2.34 a.m. Jodl plunged into the black hole of the scaffold. He and Sauckel hung together until the latter was pronounced dead six minutes later and removed.

The Czechoslovak-born Seyss-Inquart, whom Hitler had made ruler of Holland and Austria, was the last actor to make his appearance in this unparalleled scene. He entered the chamber at 2.38 ½ a.m., wearing glasses which made his face an easily remembered caricature.

He looked around with noticeable signs of unsteadiness as he limped on his left clubfoot to the gallows. He mounted the steps slowly, with guards helping him.

When he spoke his last words his voice was low but intense. He said, "I hope that this execution is the last act of the tragedy of the Second World War and that the lesson taken from this world war will be that peace and understanding should exist between peoples. I believe in Germany."

He dropped to death at 2.45 a.m.

With the bodies of Jodl and Seyss-Inquart still hanging, awaiting formal pronouncement of death, the gymnasium doors opened again and guards entered carrying Göring's body on a stretcher.

He had succeeded in wrecking plans of the Allied Control Council to have him lead the parade of condemned Nazi chieftains to their death. But the council's representatives were determined that Göring at least would take his place as a dead man beneath the shadow of the scaffold.

The guards carrying the stretcher set it down between the first and second gallows. Göring's big bare feet stuck out from under the bottom end of a khaki-coloured United States Army blanket. One blue-silk-clad arm was hanging over the side.

The colonel in charge of the proceedings ordered the blanket removed so that witnesses and Allied correspondents could see for themselves that Göring was definitely dead. The Army did not want any legend to develop that Göring had managed to escape.

As the blanket came off it revealed Göring clad in black silk pyjamas with a blue jacket shirt over them, and this was soaking wet, apparently the result of efforts by prison doctors to revive him.

The face of this twentieth-century freebooting political racketeer was still contorted with the pain of his last agonizing moments and his final gesture of defiance.

They covered him up quickly and this Nazi warlord, who like a character out of the days of the Borgias, had wallowed in blood and beauty, passed behind a canvas curtain into the black pages of history.

Part III

The Savage Little Wars of Peace, 1950–2006

The Korean War

MARGUERITE HIGGINS

The Report of a Woman Combat Correspondent

Determined to unify Korea under communist rule, North Korean forces invaded South Korea in June 1950. The United Nations came to the aid of the South, and sixteen member nations – but principally the US and Great Britain – sent troops. And war reporters. By the time of Korea, Higgins was a veteran combat correspondent, having covered the liberation of Europe during the Second World War for both the New York *Herald Tribune* and *Mademoiselle*. Her dispatches from Korea secured her a Pulitzer Prize.

War in Korea, 1951

I met the Eighth Army commander, Lieutenant General Walton H. Walker, for the first time when I returned to the front in mid-July after MacArthur had lifted the ban on women correspondents in Korea. General Walker was a short, stubby man of bulldog expression and defiant stance. I wondered if he were trying to imitate the late General George Patton, under whom he served in World War II as a corps commander.

He was very much of a spit-and-polish general, his lacquered helmet gleaming and the convoy of jeeps that escorted him always trim and shiny. I shall never forget the expression on the faces of two United States marine lieutenants who, on driving

up to the Eighth Army compound at Seoul, were told by the
military policeman at the gate: "You can't drive that vehicle in
here. It's too dusty. No dusty jeeps in here. General Walker's
orders!"

"Well, I'll be damned," breathed the marine lieutenant with
deliberately exaggerated astonishment. "Everything we've been
saying about the United States Army *is* true."

General Walker was very correct and absolutely frank with
me.

He said he still felt that the front was no place for a woman,
but that orders were orders and that from now on I could be
assured of absolutely equal treatment.

"If something had happened to you, an American woman,"
the general explained, "I would have gotten a terrible press. The
American public might never have forgiven me. So please be
careful and don't get yourself killed or captured."

General Walker kept his promise of equal treatment, and
from then on, so far as the United States Army was concerned,
I went about my job with no more hindrance than the men.

Despite large-scale reinforcements, our troops were still falling back fast. Our lines made a large semicircle around the city
of Taegu. The main pressure at that time was from the northwest down the Taejon–Taegu road. But a new menace was
developing with frightening rapidity way to the southwest. For
the Reds, making a huge arc around our outnumbered troops,
were sending spearheads to the south coast of Korea hundreds
of miles to our rear. They hoped to strike along the coast at
Pusan, the vital port through which most of our supplies funneled.

It was at this time that General Walker issued his famous
"stand or die" order. The 1st Cavalry 25th Division were freshly
arrived. Like 24th Division before them, the new outfits had to
learn for themselves how to cope with this Indian-style warfare
for which they were so unprepared. Their soldiers were not yet
battle-toughened. Taking into account the overwhelming odds,
some front-line generals worried about the performance of their
men and told us so privately.

General Walker put his worries on the record and at the
same time issued his "no retreat" order. In a visit to the 25th
Division front at Sangju in the north, he told assembled

headquarters and field officers, "I am tired of hearing about lines being straightened. There will be no more retreating. Reinforcements are coming, but our soldiers have to be impressed that they must stand or die. If they fall back they will be responsible for the lives of hundreds of Americans. A Dunkerque in Korea would be a terrible blow from which it would be hard to recover."

Immediately General Walker, in a massive straightening operation of his own, took the entire 25th Division out of the line there north of Taegu. He sent them barreling to the southwest front to bear the brunt of the enemy's attempt to break through to Pusan. The operation was skillfully done and the reshuffled troops arrived just in time.

To fill the gap vacated by the 25th Division, the 1st Cavalry and the South Koreans were pulled back in a tightening operation in which we relinquished about fifty miles, but we attained a smaller, better-integrated defense arc.

It is certainly a tribute to General Walker that in the period when he had so few troops on hand and no reserve at all he was able to juggle his forces geographically so as to hold that great semicircle from the coast down the Naktong River valley to Masan on the southern coast.

I reached the southwest front in time for the 25th's first big battle after the "stand or die" order. By luck, I happened to be the only daily newspaperman on the scene. The rest of the correspondents were at Pusan covering the debarkation of the United States Marines. My colleague on the *Herald Tribune* had selected the marine landing for his own. So I left Pusan and hitchhiked my way west.

At Masan, I borrowed a jeep from the 724th Ordnance and drove in the dusk over the beautiful mountains that wind west and overlook the deep blue waters of Masan Bay. The jewel-bright rice paddies in the long, steep-sided valley held a soft sheen and the war seemed far away. But only a few nights later the sharp blue and orange tracer bullets were flicking across the valley's mouth until dawn.

The valley leads to Chindongni, where the 27th (Wolfhound) Infantry Regiment had established its headquarters in a battered schoolhouse under the brow of a high hill. Windows of the schoolhouse were jagged fragments, and glass powdered the floor. For our big 155-millimeter artillery guns were emplaced in the schoolhouse yard, and each blast shivered the frail wooden building and its windows. The terrific effect of these guns is rivaled only by the infernal explosions of aerial rockets and napalm bombs, which seem to make the sky quake and shudder.

I had been looking forward with great interest to seeing the 27th in action. Other correspondents had praised both the regiment's commander, Colonel John ("Mike") Michaelis, Eisenhower's onetime aide, and the professional hard-fighting spirit of his officers and men.

The spirit of the 27th impressed me most in the anxious "bowling-alley" days when the regiment fended off platoon after platoon of Soviet Red tanks bowled at them in the valley north of Taegu. I will never forget the message that bleated through on a walkie-talkie radio to the regiment from Major Murch's hard-pressed forward battalion. Sent close to midnight, the message said: "Five tanks within our position. Situation vague. No sweat. We are holding."

On that first night at Chindongni, I found Colonel Michaelis in a state of tension. Mike Michaelis is a high-strung, good-looking officer with much of the cockiness of an ex-paratrooper. His ambition and drive have not yet been broken by the army system.

He has inherited from his onetime boss, "Ike" – or perhaps he just had it naturally – the key to the art of good public relations: complete honesty, even about his mistakes.

That night Mike Michaelis felt he had made a bad one. His very presence in Chindongni was technically against orders. He had turned his troops around and rushed them away from assigned positions when he heard the Reds had seized the road junction pointing along the southern coast straight at Masan and Pusan. There was nothing in their path to stop them. But, reaching Chindongni, his patrols could find no enemy. There were only swarms of refugees pumping down the road. And at the very point Michaelis had left, heavy enemy attacks were reported.

Miserably, Michaelis had told his officers: "I gambled and lost. I brought you to the wrong place."

But depression could not subdue him for long. He decided he would find the enemy by attacking in battalion strength. If the road really was empty, his men might recapture the critical road junction some twenty miles to the east.

Michaelis asked the 35th Regiment to the north to send a spearhead to link up with his troops approaching the junction on the coastal route, and ordered Colonel Gilbert Check to push forward the twenty miles. The advance turned into the first major counterattack of the Korean campaign.

Michaelis told me about it in the lamplit headquarters room where conversation was punctuated by roars from the 155 guns. Again he was unhappily belaboring himself for having made a bad gamble.

It appeared that the Reds had been on the coastal road after all. Disguised in the broad white hats and white linen garb of the Korean farmer, they had filtered unhindered in the refugee surge toward Chindongni. Then, singly or in small groups, they had streamed to collecting points in the hills, some to change into uniform and others simply to get weapons.

From their mountainous hiding places they had watched Colonel Check's battalion plunge down the road. Then they had struck from the rear. Mortars and machine guns were brought down to ridges dominating the road. This screen of fire – sometimes called a roadblock – cut the road at half a dozen points between Michaelis's headquarters and Colonel Check's attacking battalion. Rescue engineer combat teams had battered all day at the hills and roads to sweep them clean of enemy, but had failed. The worst had seemingly happened. The regiment was split in two; the line of supply cut. The 35th Regiment to the north had been unable to fight its way to the road junction.

The fate of Colonel Check's battalion showed that the enemy was here in force and proved that Michaelis had been right to wheel his forces south to block this vital pathway to Pusan. But he felt he had bungled in ordering the battalion to advance so far.

"I overcommitted myself," Michaelis said miserably. "Now Check's men are stranded eighteen miles deep in enemy territory. From early reports, they've got a lot of wounded. But we've lost all contact. I sent a liaison plane to drop them a message to beat their way back here. I'm afraid we've lost the tanks."

Colonel Check's tanks took a pummeling, all right, from

enemy antitank guns. But the tanks got back. Colonel Check himself told us the remarkable story as his weary battalion funneled into Chindongni at one o'clock in the morning.

"Antitank guns caught us on a curve several miles short of our objective," Check said. "Troops riding on the tanks yelled when they saw the flash, but they were too late. The tanks caught partially afire and the crews were wounded. But three of the tanks were still operable. I was damned if I was going to let several hundred thousand dollars' worth of American equipment sit back there on the road. I yelled, 'Who around here thinks he can drive a tank?' A couple of ex-bulldozer operators and an ex-mason volunteered. They got about three minutes' checking out and off they went."

One of the ex-bulldozer operators was Private Ray Roberts. His partly disabled tank led Check's column through ambush after ambush back to safety. Men were piled all over the tanks, and the gunners – also volunteers – had plenty of practice shooting back at Reds harassing them from ridges. Once the tank-led column was halted by a washout in the road. Another time Colonel Check ordered a halt of the whole column so that a medic could administer plasma.

"It might have been a damn-fool thing to do," Colonel Check said, "and the kids at the back of the column kept yelling they were under fire and to hurry up. But – well, we had some good men killed today. I didn't want to lose any more."

That might I found ex-bulldozer operator Roberts in the darkness still sitting on the tank. He was very pleased to show me every dent and hole in it. But he dismissed his feat with, "I fiddled around with the tank a few minutes. It's really easier to drive than a bulldozer. You just feel sort of funny lookin' in that darn periscope all the time."

I was amused after the roadside interview when Roberts and several of the other volunteers came up and said, "Ma'am, if you happen to think of it, you might tell the colonel that we're hoping he won't take that tank away from us. We're plannin' to git ordnance to help us fix it up in the mornin'." Private Roberts and company graduated from dogfeet to tank-men that night, but no special pleas were necessary. There were no other replacements for the wounded crews.

The battalion at final count had lost thirty men. In their

biggest scrap, just two miles short of the road junction, the battalion artillery had killed two hundred and fifty enemy soldiers.

"We counted them when we fought our way up to the high ground where they had been dug in," Colonel Check said. "And earlier we caught a whole platoon napping by the roadside. We killed them all."

As Check concluded, Michaelis, with a mock grimace on his face, sent for his duffel bag, reached deep into it, and produced a bottle of scotch whisky, probably the only bona fide hard liquor in southwest Korea at the time.

"Here, you old bum," he said. "Well done."

When Check had gone, Michaelis turned to Harold Martin of the *Saturday Evening Post* and myself. We had been scribbling steadily as the colonel told of the breakout from the trap.

"Well, is it a story?" Michaelis asked. "You've seen how it is. You've seen how an officer has to make a decision on the spur of the moment and without knowing whether it's right or wrong. You've seen how something that looks wrong at first proves to be right. F'rinstance, coming down here against orders. And you've seen how a decision that seems right proves to be wrong – like sending Check's column up that road without knowing for sure what it would face. And then you've seen how a bunch of men with skill and brains and guts, like Check and the kids who drove the tanks, can turn a wrong decision into a right one. But is it a story?"

I said it was a honey and that I'd head back to Pusan first thing the next morning to file it.

With an entire battalion swarming in and around the schoolhouse, regimental headquarters was in an uproar. Colonel Michaelis had been planning to move his command post farther forward. But due to the lateness of the hour and the exhaustion of the headquarters staff and the troops, he postponed the transfer.

It was another of those chance decisions on which victories are sometimes balanced. We found out the next morning how close we had shaved our luck – again.

Half a dozen regimental staff officers, myself, and Martin were finishing a comparatively de luxe breakfast in the schoolhouse (powdered eggs and hot coffee) when suddenly bullets exploded from all directions. They crackled through the windows, splintered through the flimsy walls. A machine-gun burst slammed the coffeepot off the table. A grenade exploded on the wooden grill on which I had been sleeping, and another grenade sent fragments flying off the roof.

"Where is the little beauty who threw that?" muttered Captain William Hawkes, an intelligence officer, as he grabbed at his bleeding right hand, torn by a grenade splinter.

We tried to race down the hall, but we had to hit the floor fast and stay there. We were all bewildered and caught utterly by surprise. It was impossible to judge what to do. Bullets were spattering at us from the hill rising directly behind us and from the courtyard on the other side.

Thoughts tumbled jerkily through my mind . . . "This can't be enemy fire . . . we're miles behind the front lines . . . that grenade must have been thrown from fifteen or twenty yards . . . how could they possibly get that close . . . My God, if they are that close, they are right behind the schoolhouse . . . they can be through those windows and on top of us in a matter of seconds . . . dammit, nobody in here even has a carbine . . . well, it would be too late anyway . . . why did I ever get myself into this . . . I don't understand the fire coming from the courtyard . . . what has happened to our perimeter defense . . . could it possibly be that some trigger-happy GI started all this . . ."

There was soon no doubt, however, that it was enemy fire. We were surrounded. During the night the Reds had sneaked past our front lines, avoiding the main roads and traveling through the mountain trails in the undefended gap between us and the 35th Regiment to the north. In camouflaged uniforms, they crept onto the hillside behind the schoolhouse, while others, circling around, set up machine guns in a rice paddy on the other side of the schoolyard. This accounted for the vicious cross fire.

They had managed to infiltrate our defenses for several reasons. The GIs forming the perimeter defense were utterly exhausted from their eighteen-mile foray into enemy territory and some of the guards fell asleep. And at least one column of the enemy was mistaken, by those officers awake and on duty, as South Korean Police.

We had been warned the night before that South Koreans were helping us guard our exposed right flank. This was only one of the hundreds of cases in which confusion in identifying the enemy lost us lives. It is, of course, part of the difficulty of being involved in a civil war.

The Communist attack against the sleeping GIs wounded many before they could even reach for their weapons.

I learned all of this, of course, much later. On the schoolhouse floor, with our noses scraping the dust, the only thought was how to get out of the bullet-riddled building without getting killed in the process. A whimpering noise distracted my attention. In the opposite corner of the room I saw the three scrawny, dirty North Koreans who had been taken prisoner the night before. They began to crawl about aimlessly on their stomachs. They made strange moaning sounds like injured puppies. One pulled the blindfold from his eyes. On his hands and knees he inched toward the door. But the fire was too thick. The bullets of his Communist comrades cut off escape. When next I saw the three of them they were dead, lying in an oozing pool of their own blood that trickled out the room and down the hall.

The bullets cutting through the cardboard-thin walls ripped the floor boards around us, and we all kept wondering why one of us didn't get hit. I mumbled to Harold that it looked as if we would have a very intimate blow-by-blow account of battle to convey to the American public. But he didn't hear me because one of the officers suddenly said, "I'm getting out of here," and dove out the window into the courtyard in the direction away from the hill. We all leaped after him and found a stone wall which at least protected us from the rain of fire from the high ground.

In the courtyard we found a melee of officers and non-coms attempting to dodge the incoming fire and at the same time trying to find their men and produce some order out of the chaos. Some of the soldiers in the courtyard, in their confusion, were firing, without aiming, dangerously close to the GIs racing in retreat down the hill. Many of them were shoeless, but others came rushing by with rifles in one hand and boots held determinedly in the other.

Michaelis, his executive officer, Colonel Farthing, and company commanders were booting reluctant GIs out from under jeeps and trucks and telling them to get the hell to their units up the hill.

A ruckus of yelling was raised in the opposite corner of the courtyard. I poked my head around in time to see an officer taking careful aim at one of our own machine gunners. He winged him. It was a good shot, and an unfortunate necessity. The machine gunner had gone berserk in the terror of the surprise attack and had started raking our own vehicles and troops with machine-gun fire.

By now the regimental phones had been pulled out of the town schoolhouse and were located between the stone wall and the radio truck. Division called, and the general himself was on the phone. I heard Colonel Farthing excusing himself for not being able to hear too well. "It's a little noisy," he told the general.

Almost immediately Lieutenant Carter Clarke of the reconnaissance platoon rushed up to report he had spotted a new group of enemy massing for attack in a gulch to the north. Another officer came up with the gloomy information that several hundred Koreans had landed on the coast a thousand yards beyond.

I started to say something to Martin as he crouched by the telephone methodically recording the battle in his notebook. My teeth were chattering uncontrollably, I discovered, and in shame I broke off after the first disgraceful squeak of words.

Then suddenly, for the first time in the war, I experienced the cold, awful certainty that there was no escape. My reactions were trite. As with most people who suddenly accept death as inevitable and imminent, I was simply filled with surprise that this was finally going to happen to me. Then, as the conviction grew, I became hard inside and comparatively calm. I ceased worrying. Physically the result was that my teeth stopped chattering and my hands ceased shaking. This was a relief, as I would have been acutely embarrassed had anyone caught me in that state.

Fortunately, by the time Michaelis came around the corner and said. "How you doin', kid?" I was able to answer in a respectably self-contained tone of voice, "Just fine, sir."

A few minutes later Michaelis, ignoring the bullets, wheeled suddenly into the middle of the courtyard. He yelled for a cease-fire.

"Let's get organized and find out what we're shooting at," he shouted.

Gradually the fluid scramble in the courtyard jelled into a pattern of resistance. Two heavy-machine-gun squads crept up to the hill under cover of protecting rifle fire and fixed aim on the enemy trying to swarm down. Platoons and then companies followed. Light mortars were dragged up. The huge artillery guns lowered and fired point-blank at targets only a few hundred yards away.

Finally a reconnaissance officer came to the improvised command post and reported that the soldiers landing on the coast were not a new enemy force to overwhelm us, but South Korean allies. On the hill, soldiers were silencing some of the enemy fire. It was now seven forty-five. It did not seem possible that so much could have happened since the enemy had struck three quarters of an hour before.

As the intensity of fire slackened slightly, soldiers started bringing in the wounded from the hills, carrying them on their backs. I walked over to the aid station. The mortars had been set up right next to the medics' end of the schoolhouse. The guns provided a nerve-racking accompaniment for the doctors and first-aid men as they ministered to the wounded. Bullets were still striking this end of the building, and both doctors and wounded had to keep low to avoid being hit. Because of the sudden rush of casualties, all hands were frantically busy.

One medic was running short of plasma but did not dare leave his patients long enough to try to round up some more. I offered to administer the remaining plasma and passed about an hour there, helping out as best I could.

My most vivid memory of the hour is Captain Logan Weston limping into the station with a wound in his leg. He was patched up and promptly turned around and headed for the hills again. Half an hour later he was back with bullets in his shoulder and chest. Sitting on the floor smoking a cigarette, the captain calmly remarked, "I guess I'd better get a shot of morphine now. These last two are beginning to hurt."

In describing the sudden rush of casualties to my newspaper, I mentioned that "one correspondent learned to administer blood plasma." When Michaelis saw the story he took exception, saying that it was an understatement. Subsequently the colonel wrote a letter to my editors praising my activities in a fashion that, I'm afraid, overstated the case as much as I perhaps originally understated it. But that Mike Michaelis should take time out from a war to write that letter was deeply moving to me. I treasure that letter beyond anything that has happened to me in Korea or anywhere. And, wittingly or unwittingly, Michaelis did me a big favor. After the publication of that letter it was hard for headquarters generals to label me a nuisance and use the "nuisance" argument as an excuse for restricting my activities.

It was at the aid station that I realized we were going to win after all. Injured after injured came in with reports that the gooks were "being murdered" and that they were falling back. There was a brief lull in the fighting. Then the enemy, strengthened with fresh reinforcements, struck again. But Michaelis was ready for them this time. At one thirty in the afternoon, when the last onslaught had been repulsed, more than six hundred dead North Koreans were counted littering the hills behind the schoolhouse.

We really had been lucky. The enemy had attacked the first time thinking to find only an artillery unit. We had been saved by Michaelis's last-minute decision of the night before to postpone the transfer of the command post and bed down Colonel Check's battle-weary battalion at the schoolhouse. Without the presence of these extra thousand men, the Reds would easily have slaughtered the artillerymen, repeating a highly successful guerrilla tactic.

The North Koreans didn't go in much for counter-battery fire. They preferred to sneak through the lines and bayonet the artillerymen in the back.

Michaelis's self-doubts were not echoed by his bosses. The series of decisions – some of them seemingly wrong at the time – that led to the battle of the schoolhouse resulted in a spectacular victory for the 27th Regiment. For Michaelis it meant a battlefield promotion to full colonel, and for Colonel Check a silver star "for conspicuous gallantry".

After the schoolhouse battle I usually took a carbine along in our jeep. Keyes, an ex-marine, instructed me in its use. I'm a lousy shot, but I know I duck when bullets start flying my way, even if they are considerably off course. I reasoned that the enemy had the same reaction and that my bullets, however wild, might at least scare him into keeping his head down or might throw his aim off. Since Keyes usually drove our jeep, I, by default, had to "ride shotgun".

Most correspondents carried arms of some kind. The enemy had no qualms about shooting unarmed civilians. And the fighting line was so fluid that no place near the front lines was safe from sudden enemy attack.

In those days the main difference between a newsman and a soldier in Korea was that the soldier in combat had to get out of his hole and go after the enemy, whereas the correspondent had the privilege of keeping his head down. It was commonplace for correspondents to be at company and platoon level, and many of us frequently went out on patrol. We felt it was the only honest way of covering the war. The large number of correspondents killed or captured in Korea is testimony of the dangers to which scores willingly subjected themselves.

Fred Sparks of the Chicago *Daily News*, pondering about the vulnerability of correspondents, once observed: "I was lying there in my foxhole one day after a battle in which the regimental command post itself had been overrun. I started thinking to myself, 'Suppose a Gook suddenly jumps into this foxhole. What do I do then? Say to him, "Chicago *Daily News*"!' " After that Sparks announced he, too, was going to tote "an instrument of defense".

At Chindongni, when the battle was finally over, I went up to Michaelis and asked if he had any message for the division commander.

"Tell him," said Mike, "that we will damn well hold."

And they did, in this and in many subsequent battles. So did the Marines, who replaced the 27th in that area, and the 5th Regimental Combat Team, who came after the Marines. Thousands of Americans "stood and died" to hold Chindongni and the emerald valley behind it.

In battles of varying intensity, the "stand or die" order was carried out all along the Taegu perimeter. The defense arc was ominously dented on many occasions, with the most critical period being the Red offensive early in September. But it never broke. And because the line held despite the great numbers of the enemy, the fabulous amphibious landing at Inchon was made possible.

The Korean War

JAMES CAMERON

The Inchon Landings

Eager to take the war to the enemy, US marines hit the beach at
Inchon – behind North Korean lines – on 15 September 1950.
Riding with them was the British *Picture Post* correspondent James
Cameron. The landings were a military success, but the cost in
North Korean civilian lives concerned Cameron greatly, so did the
atrocities committed by the South Korean militia. His reports on
these atrocities were censored by the *Post*'s owner, and a disen-
chanted Cameron eventually beat a path to the rival *News
Chronicle*.

Point of Departure, 1986

They told us we should be going in for the landing at seventeen
thirty.

We lay in a channel between long flat bands of grey silt that
were slowly being engulfed by the tide; very soon the tide would
be full and then we could go in. If we failed to go in then we
should not go in at all; if some of us got ashore and the others
did not we could be neither reinforced nor rescued. The coast
lay ahead with the sun still on it: low hills, and the roofs of the
town, a drift of smoke; enemy country. Over to the left was
Wolmi-do, a little island linked to Inchon by half a mile of cause-
way; the Marines had taken it already and it burned sulkily.

In the wardroom they were serving coffee and cakes, of all
things to start an invasion on; the stomach contracted at the
thought, but we drank the coffee because there was nothing else

to do. We had learned the drill, or hoped we had; the Marine had said: "When you gentlemen hit the beach you better run diagonally for one-fifty yards and then get your goddam heads down behind a tussock, and wait till somebody does something."

"Till who does what?"

"Till anybody does anything, for Christ sake. What am I, a fortune-teller?"

"Roger."

We had checked our gear and put two sets of laces in our boots and tested our lifejackets; there was no conceivable thing to do until we had to get over the side down the scaling nets and into the boat. Where was the boat? We were not to fuss about that; it would be there. For the thirtieth time we went up and peered over the rail at the crowded walls of the fleet. It was an extraordinary sight: the ships lay now assembled offshore along the channel more densely than ever before; Inchon had surely never seen any such concentration of vessels, of all types and of all sizes, for all purposes, swinging round to the incoming tide as though for some strange review, with the sun sinking gently and beautifully on our port bow, and the enemy shore ahead.

Then the challenge, when it came, was really too loud, the effect too abrupt; it was not reasonable to fight a war so noisily. We had waited too long – however you anticipate the stage revolver shot it always makes you wince; so I suppose invasions are always more startling and uproarious than you expect. The guns began erratically: a few heavy thuds from the cruisers, an occasional bark of five-inch fire, a tuning-up among the harsh orchestra. At what point the laying of the guns merged into the final and awful barrage I do not know; so many things began to take place, a scattered pattern of related happenings gradually coalescing and building up for the blow.

All around among the fleet the landing-craft multiplied imperceptibly, took to the water from one could not see exactly where, because the light was failing now – circled and wheeled and marked time and milled about, filling the air with engines. There seemed to be no special hurry. We could not go in until the tide was right; meanwhile we lay offshore in a strange, insolent, businesslike serenity, under whatever guns the North Koreans had, building up the force item by item, squaring the sledgehammer. The big ships swung gently in the tideway, from time to time coughing heaving gusts of iron towards the town. It began to burn, quite gently at first. What seemed to be a tank or a self-propelled gun sent back some quick resentful fire, but it soon stopped. Later we found that one ship had thrown a hundred and sixty-five rounds of five-inch ammunition at the one gun: the economics of plenty.

Then we saw the floating tanks, and the Amptracks, the grotesque sea-going masses of amphibious ironmongery; they crawled out of the hull of the mother-ship; she spawned them out in growling droves, a grotesque mechanical parturition. They were surrealistic and terrifying – ludicrous and dreadful at once; like a flock of rattling tortoises they lurched out of the womb of the ship and began to crawl over the surface of the water, their treads spinning, with the heads of their little men growing from their carapaces.

As the light faded the noise rose in key, soared in volume; the intervals shortened between the explosions; from over to the south the aircraft came in – steady formations, everything very neat: the approach, the dive; the plane pulled out of the dive but the rockets continued. The din was hypnotic, something out of a laboratory.

It was time to get into our landing-craft – and even dread of shellfire made it no easier, scuffling and dangling down the vertical net in the rising sea, awkward and fumbling among the rolls of lifejacket, the helmet swinging and bumping on the nose; the final uncertain drop into a crowded heaving steel box full of edged things. When the diesels shouted and ground, and we were leaping over the waves towards the shore, the concussion of shells and bombs was no longer a noise but a fierce sensation, a thudding jar on the atmosphere, on the hull of the boat, on the body itself.

The waterfront of Inchon began to disappear behind a red-shot screen of smoke; it seemed somehow to vibrate. Staring at it, as every minute a new volcano of smoke and scarlet gushed upwards, one felt that it *must* be too much, that by now life must have ceased to exist there – and yet it hadn't; in that shuddering blazing place people were somehow sheltering, surviving, hiding, and waiting – for silence, for respite, and for us.

Staring at it, too, we did not notice the long low ships under whose lee we were passing, until they – the Rocket Ships – let go, and then we knew that everything else had been endurable, and possible, but that this was too much. This was the most appalling uproar of all – the rocket-squadron burst at our ears into extravagant pyrotechnics, with a new and ghastly sound, the sound of a tremendous escape of gas, the roar of a subway, a demoniac thing that sent its groups of projectiles arcing into the beaches, grinding a solid groove of noise through the air, and when one prayed for it to stop just for a moment it howled out again.

At last, as the hundreds of troops began to surge towards Inchon, row after row of craft in line abreast, like a cavalry formation, with what seemed to be powerful express trains roaring overhead, there came the stage when individual sounds ceased and the thuds and crashes united in a continuous roll of intolerable drums. The town, and what remained of its quarter-million inhabitants, was gaudy with flame, and with more explosions leaping out of the flames – one more inconsiderable little city, one more trifling habitation involved by its betters in the disastrous process of liberation.

Now the twilight was alive with landing-craft, tank landers, marshal craft, swimming tanks, things full of guns and bulldozers and Marines – US Marines and ROK Marines, and X Army Corps – forty thousand men in Operation Inchon, twenty-five hundred to be put ashore with the tide. Tall boats and squat boats and bad-dream amphibious inventions – and in the middle of it all, if such a thing be faintly conceivable, a wandering boat marked in great letters: "PRESS", full of agitated and contending correspondents, all of us trying to give an impression of determination to land in Wave One, while seeking desperately to contrive some reputable method of being found in Wave Fifty.

We headed into a heavy bank of smoke, and there we were.

No beach, no diagonal run, no tussocks – just a sea wall. By some extravagant miscalculation our Press boat reached it just ahead of the Marine assault-party; they were there remorselessly behind us, making retreat quite out of the question. The wall was a sixty-degree incline of masonry, rising seven or eight feet up above highwater mark, with a concrete parapet. My feet were numb; I lost my grip on the slippery wall and slid down to my waist in the sea – for a moment there was much more terror from the roaring LCIs that were slamming into the wall than from anything on the other side. I scrambled ingloriously up the stones and over the parapet and instantly fell flat on my face into a North Korean defence trench, most happily empty of North Koreans.

There seemed to be a field ahead, and a tidal basin, and beyond that the town still surging with smoke and jarring to the bombs; a place – it must have been – of stark despair. We were ashore. The fact that in our flurry we had reached an unscheduled area, that we had in fact hit entirely the wrong beach, were considerations that moved us only when we were made aware of them some time later.

That was the landing. There were many mysteries about it, the greatest of which was that we had been allowed to do it at all. We would know more later. Then, and for some time, there was no debate about our survival, and the rest of the evening surged past in a confusion of thankfulness, doubt, speculation, pity, and relief.

Later, in the real darkness, I was being ferried back to the fleet; I was among the big ships again; I was groping and sprawling over a swaying staircase up the side of the command-ship, and my helmet lost at last over the rail.

It was the USS *Mount McKinley*. It was the *McKinley*, and I knew her. Once upon a time I had been in her company before – four years back in another sea and another age: outside the Pacific atoll called Bikini, and inside that coral circus had been an Atom Bomb. I had seen the Atom Bomb, and *Mount McKinley* had seen it, and now we had seen Inchon, and somewhere – in the racket of that night, in the fatigue and emptiness and emotion and endlessness of everything – there seemed to be the edge of a wheel that had come full circle.

When I realized that I was in *Mount McKinley* I had remembered that I was in the wrong ship, since I had come in *Seminole*, and that all my luggage was aboard her, and there was no way of knowing where she was or of getting there if I did. I never saw the *Seminole* again.

That day, then, the biggest landing force ever assembled since the last war – bigger than North Africa, bigger than the biggest amphibious force of the Pacific war – was at Inchon. There were two hundred and sixty-two ships – a hundred and ninety-four American, twelve British, three Canadian, two

Australian, two New Zealand, one French and one Dutch; thirty-two were US ships leased to Japan, and fifteen were South Korean.

Why the North Koreans did not resist more effectively we did not know, unless the obvious reason were true: they had too few troops there and could not disengage forces quickly enough from the south. That they did not mine the channel, that they did not scrape together even a squadron of planes, however decrepit, to sprinkle bombs on that crowded roadstead, that they did not send fireboats or saboteurs down that dense lane of shipping on the rushing ebb – that in fact they behaved with a helplessness and irresolution they had never shown before: those were matters that no one at the time could explain.

But that was the landing, the hammer-blow to the heart, the opening of the gate to Seoul. The rest was to come at next day's light – the consolidation, the flattening of ruins, concealment of corpses, tending of wounds, the sifting of friends from enemies, the quick from the dead, the simple from the suspects.

We went in again at dawn; it was like motoring through a regatta, and the silence was like a blanket of lead.

Up the road from Red Beach the bulldozers had swept a swathe through the debris, the collapsed walls; here and there some fires still burned. Cables and power-lines drooped all over the ruins.

There was quite a lot of Inchon still standing; one wondered how. There were quite a number of citizens still alive. They came stumbling from the ruins – some of them sound, some of them smashed, numbers of them quite clearly driven into a sort of numbed dementia by the night of destruction. They ran about, capering crazily or shambling blankly, with a repeated automatic gesture of surrender. Some of them called out as we passed them their one English phrase, as a kind of password: "Sank you!" "Sank you!"; and the irony of that transcended the grotesque into the macabre.

The pacification and securing of the town was the task of the South Korean militia; this they undertook with violent and furious zeal.

The lines of bemused people were driven from place to place; old men and ancient crones, baby toddlers were lined against the remaining walls and threatened with the butts of guns; every now and again a ROK patrol would see a straggler groping help-lessly down the street and cut him down with a quick volley. We passed the open door of what must the previous day have been a small laundry; ten minutes later we re-passed, and three bodies lay sprawled in the corner, two men and an old woman.

Outside the town there was still some desultory fighting. Here and there prisoners waited crouched on the ground with their hands round their necks; they were naked. The dead were arranged by the roadside, the wounded lay in groups beside them, and American medical corpsmen were moving methodi-cally among them. One of them moaned quietly, like a dog; he was a collander of bullet holes; once again a Korean mutilated to a degree that would have meant death to a European – yet con-tinued to live. The doctor came over to give him morphia; he crushed the needle of the omnopon capsule three or four times against the Korean's arm without making a puncture.

"It sure is the damnedest thing," he said. "The Gook has genuinely got a thicker skin than any other guy, in a strictly physical sense."

The soldier suddenly sat up briskly and began to explain something rapidly to the doctor. He spoke urgently, shaking his head. "Let's have the interpreter," said the doctor, but the Korean attempted one gesture too many with his shattered arm, and died in mid-sentence.

I got a lift back to Red Beach in an Amptrack; it was like riding in some gigantic clockwork toy. Down through the town; the queues of civilians still stood against the walls, and in one corner a ROK sentry stood guard over a dozen little children; they were four and five years old, their hands above their heads, gaping in bewilderment.

The Beach had indeed been a beach once – a day ago? – and now it was a churned-up, tormented quagmire, a lunar land-scape of mud ground into pits and gullies by the tracks of the machines. From far away to the east there was a little rifle fire, and occasionally an aircraft whined low overhead, above the smoke and the dying fires. Inchon itself was silent. By and by an LCI came splashing into the shore and slipped its ramp down in the mud.

The seaman in charge said: "Where to, Mac?" and we looked out at the concourse of ships a mile or two away, standing by the silhouette of a castellated city. We didn't know. Any one of them would do. I remember *Mount McKinley* was officially the communications ship, but I had nothing to communicate. Nothing that could be said in three hundred words of efficient cablese, that would tell anything or explain anything. I remembered that the wardroom there was warm, with chairs to sleep on and copies of *Time* and *Collier's* and *Life* and the *Saturday Evening Post*, all the sources of solid certainty and conviction, the firm omniscient dogma unclouded by moral doubt or fear.

"To the *Mount McKinley*, please."

"Roger."

It was like taking a taxi, taking a launch from Southend – that, with two hundred and sixty-two ships of eight nations ahead, and the broken smouldering town behind, the old men clapping and the little boys with their hands up.

The Korean War

RELMAN MORIN

Hatred to Stay

Morin won the first of two Pulitzer Prizes for war correspondence for the following dispatch detailing strife between communist and non-communist villagers near Inchon.

Associated Press, 25 September 1950

Long after the last shot is fired, the weeds of hatred will be flourishing in Korea, nourished by blood and bitter memories.

This is the heritage of the short weeks during which most of South Korea was learning Communism.

Only weeks ago in the region around Seoul and Inchon, people were being killed, dispossessed of land and homes, left to starve, or driven away from all they held dear – because they were not Communists and refused to act like Communists.

Expect to remain red

Today, in that same region, the same things are still happening – because some Koreans are Communists and propose to remain so.

Hidden in the hills a mile off the road to Seoul, there is a village of twenty-four mud-stone huts with thatched roots. The people raise rice and corn. Once they had a few cattle.

There were no rich here and, by Koreans standards, no poor either.

Even before the North Korean military invasion last June, nine of the men in the village were Communists.

The headman didn't know why. He simply said they belonged to a Red organization, and frequently went to meetings in Inchon at night.

They talked of the division of land and goods.

"It made trouble," the headman told an American intelligence officer through an interpreter.

The interpreter says the lectures talked about life in Russia, how things are done there, and how good everything is. She says it was convincing, and people believed what they heard . . .

Beat the communists

As a result, the headman said, some of the other villages banded together and beat the Communists.

"There was always trouble and fighting," said the headman, "and we talked of driving the Reds away."

Then the North Korean army swept southward over this little village. The nine Communists suddenly appeared in uniforms.

They killed some of their neighbors and caused others to be put in jail at Inchon. The headman himself fled to safety in the south. One of the villagers went with him.

"He did not want to go," said the headman. "He was to be married. The girl stayed here. She is eighteen and a grown woman, but she did not know what to do."

Back in the village the nine Communists began putting theory into practice. First they confiscated all land. Then they summoned landless tenant farmers from nearby villages and told them the land would be given to them if they became Communists.

Conformed to get land

"The farmers are ignorant of these things," the headman said. "They were very glad, and they accepted the land and said they were Communists."

Next the nine Reds went to the homes of all the men who had fought with them before.

"They took away all the furniture, even the pots and kettles, and put all these things into one house," the headman related. "Then they said the people who were Communists could come and take whatever they wanted.

"Even the people who were robbed in this way were permitted to come. If they agreed to be Communists they could take back some of their things. Most of them did that."

The parents of the engaged girl were among those who fled. She stayed. Maybe she was waiting for the man who escaped to the south with the headman.

Promised food by reds

"She was hungry most of the time," the headman said. "The Communists told her that if she would attend some cultural classes they would give her food." So she went to the school.

Then, ten days ago, the Americans attacked Inchon. Before the Communists left they herded thirty-three men into a large cell in the Inchon jail and locked the doors. Then the thirty-three were shot to death.

As soon as possible the headman came back to his village. Soon the man who had fled with him came back too.

The landowners took back their own fields and furniture. Some of the newly made "Communists" were bewildered, and tried to resist. Some were injured.

The American officer asked: "What would you do if the nine Communists came back?"

The headman and the others listening burst into hearty laughter.

"Kill them, naturally," the headman said.

The Korean War

JIM LUCAS

Our Town's Business is War

Lucas was a former army officer turned war reporter. By the time
of his dispatch below the Korean War had staggered into a stale-
mate astride the 38th parallel.

Scripps Howard, 3 January 1953

Pork Chop Hill, Korea

Our town atop pork chop hill is in a world of its own.

Its contacts with the outside world are few – but imperative.
Its immediate concern is the enemy on the next ridge. That's
"His Town." Our Town gives grudging respect. But, if possible,
"His Town" is going to be wiped out.

Our Town's business is war. It produces nothing but death.
To exist, therefore, it must rely on others. Food, mail, clothing
– even the weapons of destruction – are shipped in.

These items are sent in from that part of the outside world
which the men of Our Town call "rear". As often – and far more
passionately – they are at war with "rear" as they are with the
enemy. "Rear", which includes anything beyond the foot of
Pork Chop, is populated, Our Town is convinced, by idiots and
stumblebums.

Physically, Our Town – while hardly attractive – is not uncomfortable. Much municipal planning went into it.

The streets are six to eight feet deep. At times after dark, Our
Town's streets are invaded by men from His Town. The citizens

of Our Town invariably expel these interlopers. To assist in maintaining law and order on such occasions, the shelves along the streets of Our Town are liberally stocked with hand grenades.

There are thirty to fifty houses in Our Town. They are referred to as bunkers. Each street and each bunker is numbered. After a few days it's comparatively easy to find one's way.

Half of Our Town's bunkers are living quarters. The others are stores – storage bunkers, that is. From these you can obtain a wide assortment of ammunition, sandbags, candles, charcoal, or canned rations.

Our Town's buildings are sturdy. The typical building is at least six feet underground. It is made of four-by-ten-inch logs to which are added many sandbags. It's almost impervious to enemy shelling.

Our Town is not without its social life.

I went visiting this morning at 19 Third Street in Our Town. Entering No. 19, one gets down on his hands and knees. The front door is low.

My hosts were First Lieutenant Pat Smith of Hollywood, California, Corporal Joe Siena of Portland, Connecticut, Private First Class Eddie Williams of Brooklyn, New York, and Private Don Coan of Anadarko, Oklahoma.

Don had coffee brewing in an old ration can. He opened a can of sardines. Eddie was heading for the rear on a shopping trip. His list included candles, a coffeepot (which he's had on order for a month already), and a reel of communications wire. He also was taking a field telephone for repairs.

Our Town, like others, enjoys small talk. Over coffee, the group discussed what a man should do if a grenade-wielding Chinese suddenly appeared at the door. There was no unanimous decision.

Our Town has its own banker – Warrant Officer James W. Cherry of Jackson, Tennessee. He came up the other afternoon. Within three hundred yards of the enemy, he distributed $23,411.

Many men didn't want their money, really. Money is an almost valueless commodity up here. Three days from now, the postal officer will come up the hill, selling money orders.

If money has no value, other things do. Things like candles, fuel, toilet tissue. There's never enough charcoal for the stoves which heat the bunkers. To stay warm you can climb into your sleeping bag – if you're a fool. The men refer to sleeping bags as "coffins". Too many soldiers have been killed before they could unzip their sleeping bags.

Our Town's Mayor is a tall, gangling Texan – Captain Jack Conn of Houston. He's company commander. The Vice Mayor is his executive officer – First Lieutenant Bill Gerald, also of Houston. Bill Gerald is a Negro.

The battalion commander, Lieutenant Colonel Seymour Goldberg of Washington, DC, is convinced Our Town's residents think Colonel Goldberg is a martinet.

Colonel Goldberg always arrives in a foul mood, to be expected, since high-up officials usually are blind to local problems. The Colonel expects miracles overnight. (Privately, he concedes this is an act – "If I didn't raise hell, they wouldn't take me seriously.")

Our Town endures this outsider stoically. The Colonel says the men need haircuts. "When would they have time to get haircuts?" say Our Town's citizens. He says the bunkers need cleaning. "They look all right to us," fume Our Towners. "We live here." He says ammunition isn't stored properly. "Let up on these all-night patrols and we'll store it right," retorts Our Town – not to the Colonel's face, of course.

Invariably the Colonel corrals a hapless private and demands he be court-martialed for one thing or another. Our Town's Mayor dutifully notes the boy's name and then throws away the notes when the Colonel leaves.

But the Colonel expects this.

There was much glee the other day when the Colonel issued an order that any man found outside a bunker without a bulletproof vest be punished. A moment later, the Colonel left the bunker – and forgot his vest.

There's method in the Colonel's madness. He deliberately sets out to make Our Town hate him. "If I didn't,' he says, 'it would go to pot."

You see, the Colonel once was a company commander who hated "rear". He knows he must prod the men up front, so that their outfit will remain – despite the presence of death itself – a proud, disciplined, organized Army fighting unit.

The Suez Crisis

DONALD EDGAR

The Suez Invasion

President Nasser's nationalization of the Suez Canal led to military intervention in Egypt by Britain and France, as both countries sought to ensure passage of their ships through the zone. Airborne troops landed at Port Said on 5 November 1956; Donald Edgar, a journalist with the London *Daily Express*, accompanied the sea-borne forces, who landed at Port Said on the following day. The expedition was quickly called off after joint pressure from Washington and Moscow, and marked a humiliating climbdown for the British. Many date 6 November 1956 as the day when Britain ceased to be a world power.

Express '56, 1957

It was a sunny morning with a blue sky and our ship was in the centre of a great array of warships and transports which covered a great arc of sea from Port Fuad to the left of the Canal to Port Said in the centre and Gamil airfield on the right. Our ship was nearly stationary about three miles off shore, distant enough to reduce the scene to the size of a coloured picture postcard and the warships to toys on the Round Pond in Kensington Gardens.

It was only with an effort of will I could grasp that it was all for real, not a sequence from a film. It was really happening.

To the left of the Canal entrance a great cloud of black smoke from burning oil tanks was drifting over the city forming a sinister cloud. Along the sea-front puffs of white smoke were rising from shell-fire and red flames were taking hold on the right where the shanty town lay. Just off shore a line of elegant destroyers were moving along the beach firing into the city. As they had guns of only small calibre the reports at this distance were no more disturbing than the muffled woofs of a sleeping dog.

But to the extreme left, off Port Fuad, the French sector, lay a great battleship, the *Jean Bart*, and from time to time it fired a heavy shell from its great guns which made the air tremble a little where I stood.

Around us and further out to sea were cruisers and an aircraft carrier or two, waiting in ominous silence. Helicopters were ferrying back and forth from the beach. I learned later they had carried the 45 Royal Marine Commando in to support 40 and 42 Commandos which had earlier landed in their Buffalos together with C Sqdn of the 6 Royal Tank Regiment. I watched one helicopter fall into the sea and a ship nearby suddenly leaped forward to the rescue with the speed of a greyhound. I learned it was HMS *Manxman*, the fastest ship in the Royal Navy at the time.

I took in everything I could and asked questions of the Captain, who tried to be helpful within his limits. He told us with a wry smile that there had been trouble with the American Sixth Fleet which was in the area, escorting a shipload of American refugees from Alexandria. In fact, I gathered the Anglo-French convoy was being closely shadowed by the Americans and the air had been filled with tough, rude radio exchanges. Hanson Baldwin smiled – but in somewhat wintry fashion. I did not really believe that Eisenhower would give orders to the Sixth Fleet to blow us out of the water, but I knew the political situation was so tense that even the impossible might happen.

I was busy making notes, drawing rough sketch-maps and then began to feel somewhat dispirited as the first excitement wore off.

I kept telling myself how lucky I was – standing on the bridge watching the most impressive military operation the British had put on for many a year, with parachutists, Marine Commandos, tanks, aircraft and a naval bombardment. What is more I was looking at it all in safety. In the cussed way of the English I think this last factor was beginning to have its effect on me. I was beginning to feel sorry for the people of Port Said who were on the receiving end.

I remembered only too well what it felt like. In 1940 in France it was the Germans who had the tanks, the aircraft and the overwhelming force and I was at the receiving end, taking shelter in ditches and cellars.

However, I fought these feelings back. A few miles away British troops were fighting their way through a city, perhaps against heavy opposition, suffering casualties. What is more in a few hours I could well be in danger myself.

The captain went to the radio room and came back to say that as it was taking longer than expected to clear the area round the jetties of the Canal we should not be landing until the afternoon. He suggested we had lunch.

It was a lunch to remember. A steward served us imperturbably with a drink while we studied the menu. Another took our order with the same solicitude as a head-waiter in the Savoy Grill. A wine-waiter suggested an excellent Burgundy. Outside, not far away, the Marine Commandos with the Centurion tanks were fighting their way through the wrecked buildings of Port Said. No doubt men, women and children were dying in fear and anguish. Yet here was I sitting down to an excellent lunch as if I was a first-class passenger on a luxury Mediterranean cruise.

But I ate the lunch and drank the wine with enjoyment. All my instincts as an old soldier came to my aid – eat and drink whilst you can, you never know where the next meal is coming from. Whilst we were finishing our coffee and brandy the ship started to move gently towards the Canal.

We went up again to the bridge. The ship was easing its way towards the jetty on the right-hand of the entrance to the Canal and the scene of destruction along the water-front cleared through the smoke. Crumbled masonry, blackened walls still standing with nothing behind, burnt-out vehicles, debris scattered over the road. A few soldiers hurried to and fro, but the firing – rifle and machine-gun and mortar – seemed to be concentrated a few hundred yards down the Canal. The captain had a radio set on the bridge tuned to the BBC and we heard a bland voice announcing that all resistance had ceased in Port Said. It was just then when with a great scream that froze me in terror, a section of naval fighter-bombers dived down over us dropping their rockets and firing their cannon just ahead of us. Almost quicker than sight they wheeled away into the sky while clouds of grey smoke rose into the air. We were all silent on the bridge for a minute or two. This was the attack by Sea Furies on Navy House where 40 Commando had encountered tough resistance from a hundred-odd Egyptians who had barricaded themselves in. Even the tanks, firing at point-blank range, had been unable to dislodge them so the Navy was called in to help with an airstrike. The Navy complied, but with some regret for the building had become over the years part of the Royal Navy's heritage. Even after this devastating attack, however, the Egyptians fought on and a Marine officer told me they had to clear them out room by room. "They didn't know how to fight professionally," he said to me. "But by God they fought to the end."

It was not until the next day that twenty survivors gave themselves up. Their bravery was another proof that the Egyptians, often abandoned by their officers, can fight magnificently.

By now it was late afternoon. In front of us a transport was unloading more tanks and paratroops who moved off down the Canal road. There were two barges from the *Jean Bart* filled with French paratroops lying down philosophically in the open holds. I noticed with a certain surprise, some female contours among the camouflage uniforms. I had not known till then that the French paratroops had women in their ranks among whose duties were cooking and first-aid. It was an imaginative re-creation of the traditional *vivandières*!

As I was looking at the quayside I saw a group of senior officers who seemed to be waiting for transport while snipers' bullets seemed to me to be getting uncomfortably close. Campbell recognized the leader – Lt General Sir Hugh Stockwell, the Allied Commander, who cheerily waved his swagger-stick at the passing troops. He had been spending a few hours looking at the situation and was trying to get back to the headquarters ship, HMS *Tyne*. I was not to know then that he had a hazardous journey back in a landing-craft which was nearly swamped and when he finally got aboard was greeted with the fateful order to cease-fire at midnight (two a.m. local time).

It grew dark and we were told that no one would be allowed to disembark until the morning to avoid confusion. Then Baldwin and I had a stroke of luck. The Brigadier in charge of

Medical Services was a passenger and brusquely said he was
going ashore whatever anyone said. He was determined to contact the airborne medical team which had landed the day before.
He had seen stretchers going into the damaged Casino Palace
Hotel about fifty yards away from us by the side of the Canal.
Baldwin and I asked him if we could go along. He nodded and
we picked up our bags and followed him ashore.

There were fires enough around to light our way across
ropes, hose-pipes and debris to the hotel. The entrance-hall was
filled with stretcher-cases. A big reception-room on the right
had been cleared for the medical team. In another room along a
passage an operating-room had been fixed up with emergency
lighting and surgeons stripped to the waist wearing leather
aprons were at their tasks. The British casualties had for the
most part been flown back by helicopter to an aircraft carrier.
This team was dealing now with Egyptian casualties – some
military, most civilian – men, women and children.

The dead were being carried out to the garden in the back to
be buried in a shallow grave temporarily.

It was a sombre scene with few words spoken. The surgeons
looked to me very young and very tired. They were working in
relays, coming back to the main room to sit down and drink a
glass of whisky in between operating.

Baldwin had dumped his bag and disappeared. He knew
exactly where he was going – to the American consulate whose
position further along the Canal he had pin-pointed on a street
map before he had landed.

I went out to the road. Night had fallen and the fires had
dimmed. Sentries had been posted. Out at sea there was not a
light to give a hint of the great convoy and its accompanying
warships. A few shots sounded in the distance, but silence was
enveloping the stricken city.

The Cuban Civil War

EDWIN TETLOW

Revolution in Havana

After two years of guerrilla warfare, Fidel Castro's rebels reached the Cuban capital on the last day of 1958. Edwin Tetlow, foreign correspondent for the London *Daily Mail*, happened to be in the right place at the right time.

As It Happened, 1990

The approaches to the city from the airport seemed normal enough as viewed from a big old Buick taxi which I shared with the young American, who confided to me that he expected to find "a lovely young thing" among those welcoming him to Cuba. The dark-complexioned driver hummed softly to the music from his radio as he piloted us skilfully through the turbulent traffic. The Hotel Nacional, a great oblong block of a place, had a few rooms available, at a hefty rate for those days. I settled in and had a leisurely dinner from an expansive menu in the hotel restaurant, which was filled with well-dressed, and obviously well-heeled, Cubans and a minority of foreigners. Feeling comfortable, I set out to stroll in the warm evening air, dropping in on some of the tourist haunts of suburban Vedado and upper midtown Havana, amassing material for the feature article I should be writing the following morning.

Eventually, around 11 p.m. [31 December 1958], I strolled into the casino at the Hotel Nacional to await midnight. I noted that the bar was being heavily patronized. A four-piece band was playing in one corner of the ornate salon, accompanying a lusty and busty Cuban contralto who was singing at full strength to make herself heard above the band and the hubbub from the bar, and the softer, sleeker noises from the casino itself, so different from the rattle, slap and clap made by dice-players as they thumped down their leathern cups on tables in the humbler haunts of the city. As the time passed towards midnight the noise became unbelievably piercing. How Cubans love noise! Eventually neither band nor contralto could be heard as separate entities.

Around the gaming tables, under glittering chandeliers bigger and more fanciful than any I had seen for years, guests both Cuban and foreign gambled with deep concentration. Only occasionally did heads turn and envious smiles appear round tight-lipped mouths when somebody shrieked in ecstasy after hitting the jackpot at one of the fruit machines lining the walls of the casino. Also along the walls were several armed policemen stationed like sentries. I asked once or twice of seemingly knowledgeable guests why they were there. One man just shrugged and said languidly: "Who knows?" One other man told me they had appeared for the first time only a few evenings earlier.

At midnight there came a token acknowledgement that 1959 had arrived. The intense proceedings at the gaming tables and the fruit machines were halted for but a few moments. A few men and women kissed and some people shook hands and smiled at each other before resuming the serious business of the night. At about 12.30 a.m. the members of the band quietly packed their instruments, the singer folded up her microphone stand, and she and the musicians walked off into the night. Only the bar and the gaming tables continued operations, the former being sustained mainly by a party of American and other foreigners, who, growing more disarrayed almost by the minute, still managed to keep the tiring bartenders busy. At that hour I decided I had seen enough. I wanted to go to bed. Once there, I spent a few minutes jotting down facts and reminders for the writing I expected to be doing next morning. Satisfied that I had my assignment under control, I settled down and went to sleep.

I was awakened before 8 a.m. by an excited phone call from

Robert Perez, my local correspondent, an energetic Puerto Rican who had lived for some years in Havana. "He's gone," he spluttered into the phone. "Who's gone?" I asked, still half-asleep. "Batista! Batista!" came the galvanizing answer from Perez. "He went in the night."

So he had. At about the time I was settling down to sleep he and a party of about forty, including many members of his family, had motored over to a military airfield at Camp Columbia, on the fringe of Havana, and – excessively heavily laden with baggage – had boarded an Army plane for a short hop eastwards across the water to the Dominican Republic, then still in the grip of Batista's fellow-dictator, Generalissimo Rafael Trujillo, later assassinated.

Pure luck had landed me in the very centre of a revolution while it was happening and being won. No hasty packing of a suitcase this time, no mad rush to catch the first plane to the scene of action, no hectic chase after news which was already growing old! This was a foreign correspondent's dream come true, and I was determined to make the most of it. First, on the sound recommendation of Robert Perez, I moved out of the lordly but isolated Hotel Nacional and into the Hotel Colina, a small and well-placed observation-post giving a view from my third-floor window of the approaches to the University of Havana, where Fidel Castro had been educated and where he was said to have substantial secret support.

The city was eerily quiet at about 8.45 a.m. as Perez and I made our cautious way to the Colina, not at all sure what might happen as we did so. Weren't revolutions affairs of wild shooting and melodramatic action? Not this one – yet. I felt as if I were in the eye of a hurricane, the centre where everything is still while furious winds whirl all around. Hardly anybody was moving. Perez told me as we inched our way towards the Colina that Cubans in the capital had done exactly what people in most countries of the Caribbean did when, as happens all too often in that steamy region, trouble threatened. They closed and locked their shutters, bolted all their doors, and holed up.

Once installed in my new strategic headquarters I implemented my plan of campaign. I despatched Perez on a mission of news-gathering in the city, asking him to phone me as often

as seemed necessary with any information he had. I calculated
that because of his intimate knowledge of the city, contacts he
had, plus his command of his native Spanish, he would have no
trouble about keeping me in touch with what was happening.
And he did so with great efficiency. As for myself, I stayed as a
willing prisoner in my hotel room. I put in a telephone call to my
newspaper after having been told by the local exchange that
there was, predictably, "long delay" in calls to the outside world,
including distant London. While I waited I began assembling
the story I would telephone as soon as the call came through. I
listened to Radio Havana as it broadcast messages from Fidel
Castro telling the populace to keep calm while it waited for him
to take control of the nation. "Don't worry, I shall come to you,"
he said. I took messages from the assiduous Perez and as best I
could I kept an eye on what was happening in the streets leading
to the University.

In fact, very little happened all that morning. Only a very few
people were to be seen hurrying along in order to carry out missions which presumably could not be put off. I noticed that
almost all these scurrying pedestrians kept as close as possible
to any nearby wall or other cover they were afforded. However,
my heaven-sent story was shaping up well. It was helped greatly
by word from Robert Perez that Fidel Castro had sent an ampli-
fied message to the people of Havana. Speaking from his field
camp near Santa Clara, the last sizeable city between him and
the capital, he said he did not accept as a bargaining agent a
three-man junta of "so-called neutrals" whom Batista had left
behind to represent him. "I shall be coming into Havana soon,"
Castro promised. "Keep the peace until then. I am sending a
company of Barbudos [bearded ones] to administer Havana
until I get there. They will preserve Havana – and you."

This message galvanized the nervous population of the city.
Reassured, thousands of them opened their shutters and doors
and got into their cars, to celebrate their unexpected liberation.
They staged a fantastic crawl-around of the city streets. They
draped their vehicles, almost all of them American-made, with
Cuban flags. If the car was a convertible, they wound down the
top and then joined the follow-my-leader procession of their
neighbourhood. As they did so, more and more people climbed
up on and into the cars until, as I counted from my

observation-point in the Hotel Colina, there were often as many as ten persons in one car. As each individual procession made its slow progress along the old, narrow streets, the ecstatic celebrants chanted the word *Li-ber-tad* and most of them added emphasis by pounding with their fists their car's side or roof in rhythm with the three syllables of the word for liberty. Very soon the din became hard to stand. I was staggered by the intensity, emotion and, I must add, childlike character of the manifestation of happy relief. Nobody could possibly foresee the tribulations in store for Cuba for the next forty years . . .

My telephone call to London came through at last in the early afternoon, in time for me to dictate over fifteen hundred words, many of them forming impromptu sentences, as thoughts occurred to me, across the bed of the Atlantic Ocean. Even my vigil the previous evening in the casino of the Hotel Nacional was not wasted; indeed, the languid scene around the gaming tables and the jollity in the bar on the eve of one of the most startling and profound revolutionary upheavals of the century in Latin America added to the impact of the story I was able to tell. This was by far the most vivid first-hand report I had written in fifty years, during war as well as peace; and now that it was safely in the hands of my editors in Fleet Street, I was free to leave my bedroom at the Hotel Colina. I could spend the next couple of hours before my second phone call seeing for myself what was going on in the liberated city.

I permitted myself one substantial tot of Bacardi rum before I set out on the long walk from Vedado to midtown Havana. I had to thrust my way through the thick ranks of people watching, some with tears of joy coursing down their faces, the motorized crawl-around. But just as I was making the last turn into the Prado, which roughly marks the boundary between respectable bourgeois Havana and the livelier but sleazy downtown, I saw that something had happened to cut short the touching celebration. Panic was spreading among both Cubans in their cars and the onlookers who had been cheering them on. Vehicles were peeling off from the processions, screeching away into side-streets, and the crowds were scurrying for cover as quickly as their feet would race. In a matter of minutes I found myself uncomfortably alone in the mid-section of the broad Prado. What had happened?

The answer was forthcoming almost as soon as I asked myself the question. The underworld was taking over. One by one a party of dirty and ruffianly looking young Cubans emerged from Calle Neptuno and other side-streets. Each was carrying a rifle or shotgun across his chest. They walked warily along the street, their gaze darting everywhere as they made sure that nobody was going to challenge them. Nobody did. Batista's hated armed policemen had fled into hiding once they heard that their protector had gone. (It transpired that by no means all of them escaped vengeance. Stories of beatings and murders of these men abounded during the next twenty-four hours.) The small-time gangsters now taking over central Havana were organized and ingenious. Some took up positions as watchdogs at strategic points, ordering away at gunpoint people such as myself, while their comrades went on a rampage of looting. Their first targets were parking-meters. These were smashed apart so that their contents could be rattled out and pocketed. Then came the turn of pinball machines and other gaming devices in arcades and deserted casinos which could easily be entered, including an especially lucrative one close to the Sevilla Biltmore Hotel. Here, from a discreet distance, I watched one gang of looters drag a slot-machine into the street and batter it open with jagged pieces of metal from a destroyed parking-meter. It struck me as a remarkable and possibly unique confirmation of the validity of the old saying that money makes money.

The physical hazards of remaining outdoors grew as the bandits got their hands on rum. They started shooting. Mostly it was the wildest kind of exhibitionism, but even so it claimed victims. Ambulances soon began making screaming runs through the streets on journeys to and from hospitals – and mortuaries. Late in the afternoon I went into one hospital and found it in chaos, overflowing with wounded persons and roughly bandaged out-patients. "Some have been in street accidents, but mostly they seem to have been hit by flying bullets," said one nurse to me.

There appeared to be no reason for most of the shooting. Indeed, one series of incidents which I ran into on my way back to the Colina tended to show that Cubans just weren't to be trusted with weapons. A man's rifle would go off either because it was defective or because he had forgotten his finger was on the trigger, or even because of a need – common in Latin America – to show off. The trouble was that very often a haphazard shot would start a chain reaction. Men who heard the shot would start firing their own weapons, with the result that shotgun pellets and bullets began flying around an area, ricocheting off walls, smashing windows and occasionally hitting an unlucky pedestrian. Rarely did there seem to be a justifiable target. Alas, this kind of irresponsibility seemed to be occurring mostly near the University, and I was disturbed to deduce that the perpetrators were not underworld bandits of the kind I had met in the Prado but students who were supporters of Fidel Castro and were apparently obeying his broadcast admonitions to preserve the peace in Havana until he arrived. They were probably earnest enough in their devotion to his cause, but they wouldn't be much use if Batista's police and troops rallied. I reasoned that Fidel Castro would be well advised to get his trained Barbudos into Havana as quickly as he could. If they didn't come soon, there would probably be a confrontation between his amateur followers and the downtown bandits, and if the latter won, which seemed likely, unimaginable bloody chaos would follow.

The most senseless shooting spree of all happened on the afternoon of 2 January, the second day of the revolution. I was standing in the shelter of a shopping arcade near the Parque Centrale, in the centre of Havana, and was looking at the debris of splintered windows and doors and ransacked shelves left by yesterday's looters when I became aware of a noisy commotion on a street corner close to the Sevilla Biltmore. The cracks made by ragged rounds of gunshots were coming from somewhere close at hand. I crept cautiously forward to investigate. A squad of about half a dozen young men wearing armbands to show that they were members of a pro-Castro group which had come out of hiding during the past forty-eight hours were firing rifles and automatic pistols from the west side of the Prado at an upper window of a building on the opposite side of the wide thoroughfare. Their collective aim was atrocious. I could see bullets squelching into stonework far above, below and around the window, and only one or two were flying through it into the room beyond. The attack lasted at least half an hour, without, as I noted most carefully, a single shot coming back in reply. This one-sided "battle" was happening so close to the Sevilla Biltmore that a party of American tourists, wisely obeying a recommendation from the US Embassy not to venture outdoors, could hear all the shooting but had no more idea of what it all meant than, it emerged, did the men involved.

The facts came to me eventually. Word had reached a volunteer unit of Castro supporters that some fugitives of the Batista regime were hiding in a room on the top floor of the building now being attacked. There were said to be at least a dozen armed followers of Rolando Masferrer, a notorious henchman of Batista, locked inside the room. When the shooting ended, one militiaman said gloatingly to me: "We got the lot." In truth, as I was able to confirm for myself a little later, there had been nobody at all in the whole building.

As taxis had vanished from the streets, we were walking on foot when we ran into trouble. A voice called out suddenly in grating Spanish from somewhere in the darkness a few feet ahead of us: "Halt. Hands up!" Peering ahead, I could see three men with rifles pointed straight at us. Two of them were kneeling side by side on the pavement while the third, their leader, stood barring the way directly ahead. He had a revolver in his right hand – and an armed Cuban was not a man to be trifled with. His gun might very well go off by chance.

But I have never had much time for amateur warriors anywhere. Tonight, also, I was tired, hungry and consequently bad-tempered and of fallible judgement. I was tempted to bluff my way through and I was slow to comply with the orders of our interceptors. My American companions were perhaps wiser. They all raised their hands and one of them muttered impatiently to me as he did so: "Come on, man. You'll get us all shot!" Unwillingly, I complied.

Our captors motioned us into the passageway of an apartment house. There, blocking the way, sat an unshaven young fellow at a desk. We were in the unit's rough-and-ready headquarters. The man at the desk started questioning the two Americans nearest to him. I was very hot indeed in that passageway. I sidled back into the street, leaving it to others who spoke far better Spanish than I to argue and protest against this unwarranted interference with the free movement of foreign civilians pursuing their daily task in extremely difficult circumstances, and so on. As I breathed the welcome fresh air I mentally assessed the odds about being able to make a dash for it and go up the hill to my hotel. I decided against trying to do so. Several of these amateur gunmen were still around, for I could hear them talking close to me. Even though there was a good chance that if they fired after me as I ran away they might very well miss me, I considered the risk not worth taking. If I were wounded or killed, my newspaper would be the innocent loser.

Meanwhile our negotiators were making no impression whatever on the man at the desk. He told them he was chief of one of the paramilitary units which had been ordered by Fidel Castro to keep the city peaceful, and he couldn't in good conscience let us go on our way. "My authority doesn't extend very far," he confessed. "There are a lot of bandits still roaming around out there. You might get robbed – or worse – if I let you go off into the night." It availed nothing that our spokesman told him we were well able to take care of ourselves and anyway intended to hole up in our hotels as soon as we got there. "Sorry, you'll have to spend tonight under our protection," the man insisted.

We were bundled into two cars and driven to a dingy-looking house in one of the streets running diagonally off the Malecon boulevard on the sea front. It turned out to have been a "safe" house used by revolutionary agents and couriers as well as by fugitives from Batista's police. I was shown to a small and none-too-savoury bedroom immediately underneath a rooftop water cistern. Dumping my typewriter, my only luggage, resignedly in a corner of the room, I obeyed my captors' order to go down to the desk, sign my name in a register and claim a key.

As I did so, the good fortune which had sent me to Havana in the first place and had attended me for forty-eight hours thereafter worked again. I was walking away from the hotel desk when I noticed a big utility truck standing in the street outside the hotel entrance. Half a dozen laughing soldiers – real soldiers this time – were unloading their kit and other baggage from it. I was astonished to observe that two of them standing with their backs facing me had black hair hanging down so long below their shoulders that I should have said they were girls if they obviously had not been blessed with thick black beards. I walked forward and began talking with them. They were, they said, the very first detachment of Barbudos which Castro had promised to send into Havana.

So the seeming ill-luck that had landed me into being arrested had also brought me another lively segment for the morrow's story. This is yet another example of how compensations have so frequently offset what seemed initially to be setbacks in my profession as a journalist. A missed train or plane, failure to establish contact by phone or cable with London, somebody's refusal to tell me something, were irritating when encountered, but so often were followed by a piece of unexpected good fortune. Perhaps this helps to explain my perennial optimism.

The Barbudos were among the fittest and happiest young warriors I have ever seen. They had good reason for being so. They had had very little serious fighting and, as the never-robust morale had seeped away from Batista's conscripts during the past few months in the Sierra Maestra, an astonishingly easy victory had fallen to them. They told me that they had enjoyed a leisurely, unchallenged, advance upon the capital from the eastern province of Oriente, through Camagüey and Las Villas. The peasants in these mostly rural areas had welcomed them with increasing ardour as the reality of Castro's total victory had become manifest. People had been eager to give them anything they wanted. One Barbudo told me he couldn't remember when he had been last paid. "The one thing we didn't need was money," he said. "People couldn't do enough for us. They lavished everything, especially food, on us."

Proof of this was forthcoming as some of the contents of the truck were arrayed on the counter of the hotel reception desk. There were hams, strings of sausages, cottage-made bread, butter, beer and many other such good provender. We were all invited to tuck into a midnight feast – rebel soldiers, our captors, American reporters, including one lone Englishman, and anybody else who happened to be about. Good fellowship bloomed with every mouthful. There was much hearty back-slapping, joking, talk and toasting of international understanding, and some glowing forecasts from the Barbudos of the future Cuba once Fidel Castro took charge.

The Vietnam War

MALCOLM W. BROWNE

Death in the Rice Fields

America became fatally embroiled in Vietnam in 1960, when "advisors" were sent to Saigon to aid the anti-communist South Vietnamese against Viet Cong guerrillas, controlled and armed by Red North Vietnam. At first the "advisors" instructed at training bases, then they guided field operations . . . and then they were fighting the war themselves. By 1968 US troops – no longer euphemistically called "advisors" – in Vietnam had swollen to half a million. Malcolm W. Browne covered Vietnam for AP and later ABC, winning a Pulitzer Prize in the process, his experiences there melted and melded into the book *The New Face of War*. Here he accompanies South Vietnamese forces on an anti-VC sweep in the Mekong Delta in 1961.

The New Face of War, 1965

A drenching, predawn dew had settled over the sloping steel deck of the landing craft, and I slipped several times climbing aboard in the inky darkness.

Soldiers cursed sleepily as they heaved heavy mortar base plates and machine guns from the pier onto their field packs on the deck.

The night was still and moonless, and the air would have been warm except for that unpleasant dew, sometimes laced with raindrops. The French used to call it "spitting rain".

This was December, 1961, and I was going out for my first look at an operation against the Viet Cong. There were no American field advisors in those days (and no helicopters and almost no communications), and I tried to stay close to soldiers or officers who could speak French. Most of them could.

The place was a town called Ben Tre in the heart of the flat, fertile Mekong River Delta, about fifty miles south of Saigon. Ben Tre, the capital of Kien Hoa Province, still takes pride in the fact that it has produced some of Viet Nam's top Communists. Ung Van Khiem, former Foreign Minister of the Hanoi government, came from here. Kien Hoa is also famous for its pretty girls.

It was about 4 a.m., and I was dead tired. I had been up late with the province chief, Colonel Pham Ngoc Thao, a cat-like man with short-cropped hair and a disconcerting walleye.

Thao had been an intelligence officer in the Viet Minh during the Indochina War, and had gone over to Diem after independence in 1954.

The night before, Thao had invited me to the opening of a theater he had had built in Ben Tre, and the curious town residents had turned out in their holiday best. The bill of fare was a traditional Vietnamese drama and some comedians, jugglers and singers. It lacked the glamour of a Broadway opening night, but it was about the fanciest thing Ben Tre had ever seen.

Two masked actors in ornate classical costume were intoning verses about a murder they were planning and the audience was murmuring expectantly when Thao leaned toward me.

"My troops are going out in the morning. We have intelligence that a battalion of Viet Cong is moving through one of my districts. I'm not going, but would you be interested?"

Just then, the action on stage reached a high point. Several actors in stilted, oriental poses were supposed to portray violence, their brilliantly colored robes swishing. Applause rushed through the theater, and children put down their pop bottles to chatter. Thao, obviously pleased, warmly joined the applause.

He always liked the theater. A year or so later, when Diem sent him on a special mission to the States, he made a special point of visiting Hollywood, where he was photographed with actress Sandra Dee. The picture was sent back to Viet Nam by news agencies, but Diem's censors prohibited its publication, presumably because they felt it would be detrimental to fighting spirit.

The three hundred or so troops on the pier that morning were an odd-looking bunch, a mixture of civil guards and self-defense corpsmen. Some were in neat fatigue uniforms with helmets, others in the loose, black garb of the Vietnamese peasant, topped with old French bush hats. There were no troops from the regular army on this operation. The commander was a crusty, French-trained captain with several rows of combat ribbons on his faded olive drab uniform.

The diesel engines of the three landing craft carrying our makeshift task force belched oily smoke and we were moving, the black silhouettes of palm trees sliding past along the edges of the narrow canal. Here and there a dot of light glimmered through the trees from some concealed cluster of huts.

For a few minutes, the commander studied a map with a neat plastic overlay, making marks with red and black grease pencils, under the light of a pocket flashlight.

One of the few things Western military men have taught Vietnamese officers to do really well is mark up maps. The Vietnamese officer studies his sector map like a chessboard. Even if he has only a squad or two of men under his command, he uses all the ornate symbols of the field commander in marking his deployment on maps. This love of maps has often infuriated American advisors, who feel more time should be spent acting and less on planning.

After a while the light flicked out. A few of the troops were smoking silently, but most had arranged their field packs as pillows and had gone to sleep amid the clutter of weapons. We were not scheduled to reach our objective until several hours after sunrise.

I finally dropped off to sleep, and must have been asleep about an hour when a grinding lurch and the sound of splintering wood roused me.

It was still pitch dark, but people were screaming, and on the deck of the landing craft, troops were rushing around. In the darkness, we had somehow collided with and sunk a large, crowded sampan. Twenty or thirty sleeping occupants had been thrown into the canal, with all their worldly possessions. A few of them apparently were hurt.

The two other landing craft were chugging on down the canal, but we had stopped. Troops holding ropes were helping swing the people in the water over to the shore. When everyone had reached safety, we started up again, people still yelling at us in the distance. We must have destituted several large families at a blow, but there was no thought of getting their names so that they could be compensated by the government. I couldn't help feeling that their feelings for the government must be less than cordial.

The sky began to turn gray, and at last we left the maze of narrow canals and turned into a branch of the great Mekong itself.

The sun rose hot and red, its reflection glaring from the sluggish expanse of muddy water. We were moving slowly ("We don't want to make too much engine noise or the Viet Cong will hear us coming," the commander told me), and the dense wall of palm trees on both banks scarcely seemed to move at all.

It was nearly 9 a.m. when our little flotilla abruptly turned at right angles to the left, each vessel gunning its engines. We had reached the objective and were charging in for the beach. As we neared the shore we could see that the beach actually was a mud flat leading back about fifty yards to the palm trees, and it would be arduous hiking getting ashore.

The other two landing craft were going ashore about one mile farther up the river. The idea of this exercise, it was explained to me, was to seize two sets of hamlets running back from the river front, trapping the reported Viet Cong battalion in the wide expanse of rice fields in between.

We slammed into the mud, and the prow of our clumsy ship clanked down to form a ramp. We leapt into waist-deep water and mud and began the charge toward higher ground.

If the Viet Cong had even one machine gun somewhere in the tree line, they certainly could have killed most of us with no danger of encountering serious fire from us. Each step in that smelly ooze was agonizingly slow, and at times both feet would get mired. Little soldiers carrying heavy mortars and machine guns sank nearly to their necks. It happened that no one was shooting at us that day.

The first squads clambered up to high ground and began firing. Two light machine guns began thumping tracers across the open rice field, and mortars began lobbing shells at random. Individual soldiers with Tommy guns (I was surprised how many of our group were equipped with submachine guns) were emptying their magazines into a string of huts or into the field. Off a mile or so to our right, noises told us that our companion party was similarly employed. It really sounded like a war.

I was standing on a high path running parallel to the river near a machine-gun position, looking out over the field where our Viet Cong battalion was supposed to be trapped. The green rice was nearly waist high, and there might easily be a battalion concealed in this field for all anyone knew.

Suddenly, a man leapt up about fifty yards away and began to run. This was it!

Every machine gun, Tommy gun, rifle and pistol in our sector poured fire at that man, and I was amazed at how long he continued to run. But finally he went down, silently, without a scream.

Our little army continued to pour intense fire into the field and several huts until it occurred to someone that no one was shooting back, and it might be safe to move forward a little.

Some of the troops began to move into the huts, shooting as they went.

Near me was a cluster of five Dan Ve (local Self-Defense Corpsmen) dressed in ragged black uniforms with American pistol belts and rusty French rifles. The group was detailed to go into the field to look for the man we had seen go down, and I went with them.

We found him on his back in the mud, four bullet holes stitched across the top of his naked chest. He was wearing only black shorts. He was alive and conscious, moving his legs and arms, his head lolling back and forth. There was blood on his lips.

The Dan Ve squad, all young peasant boys, looked down at the man and laughed, perhaps in embarrassment. Laughter in Viet Nam does not always signify amusement.

Perhaps as an act of mercy, perhaps as sheer cruelty, one of the men picked up a heavy stake lying in the mud and rammed one end of it into the ground next to the wounded man's throat. Then he forced the stake down over the throat, trying to throttle the man. The man continued to move. Someone stamped on the free end of the stake to break the wounded man's neck, but the stake broke instead. Then another man tried stamping on the man's throat, but somehow the spark of life still was too strong. Finally, the whole group laughed, and walked back to the path.

The firing had stopped altogether, and several old peasant men were talking to the officers of our party. Two of the old men had a pole and a large fish net.

The peasants – I think they were hamlet elders – walked out to the wounded man, rolled him into the fish net, and with the net slung between them on the pole, carried him back to the path. As they laid him out on the ground, two women, both dressed in baggy black trousers and blouses, ran up from one of the huts. One of them put a hand to her mouth as she saw the wounded man, whom she recognized as her husband.

She dashed back to her hut and returned in a moment carrying a bucket, which she filled with black water from the rice field. Sitting down with her husband's head cradled in her lap, she poured paddy water over his wounds to clean off the clotting blood. Occasionally she would stroke his forehead, muttering something.

He died about ten minutes later. The woman remained seated, one hand over her husband's eyes. Slowly, she looked around at the troops, and then she spotted me. Her eyes fixed on me in an expression that still haunts me sometimes. She was not weeping, and her face showed neither grief nor fury; it was unfathomably blank.

I moved away some distance to where the operation commander was jabbering into a field telephone. When his conversation ended, I handed him a 500-piastre note (worth about $5.00), asking him to give it to the widow as some small compensation.

"Monsieur Browne, please do not be sentimental. That man undoubtedly was a Viet Cong agent, since these hamlets have been Viet Cong strongholds for years. This is war. However, I will give her the money, if you like."

I don't know what happened to that money, and I didn't go near the place where the woman was sitting, but I walked into the hut I had seen her leave.

It was typical of thousands of Mekong Delta huts I have seen.

The framework was bamboo, and the sides and roof were made of dried, interlaced palm fronds with a layer of rice straw thatch on top. The floor was hardened earth. A large, highly polished wooden table stood near the door. Peasants eat their meals on these tables, sleep on them and work on them. There were four austerely simple chairs. In a corner were several knee-high earthen crocks filled with drinking water. Just inside the door was the family altar, extending all the way to the ceiling. Pinned to it were yellowed photographs and some fancy Chinese calligraphy. On a little shelf a sand pot containing incense sticks smoldered fragrant fumes.

To the right, from behind a woven bamboo curtain, two children were peering with wide eyes. The eyes were the only expressive elements in their blank, silent little faces. Incongruously, one of them was standing next to a gaily painted yellow rocking horse, one rocker of which was freshly splintered by a bullet hole.

I walked out of the hut and down the path. By now, troops were strung all along the path between the two hamlets about a mile apart, and were stringing telephone wire and performing other military chores.

Snaking through the palm trees, a water-filled ditch about twenty feet across obstructed my progress. But a few yards away, a soldier had commandeered a small sampan from an old woman and was ferrying troops back and forth. I went across with him. As I continued down the path, scores of mud walls about five feet high obstructed progress. All were obviously freshly built, and most had gun slots. It was strange that no one had decided to defend these good emplacements against us.

I came to a small hut straddling the path, consisting only of upright bamboo spars and a roof. The little building was festooned with painted banners, the largest of which read "*Da Dao My-Diem*" ("Down with US-Diem"). A group of young women were dismantling the hut as soldiers trained rifles at them. I was told that this was a Viet Cong "information center".

Finally, the troops began moving out from the tree line into the field itself, converging from three sides: the two hamlets and the path itself. The battle would come now, if ever.

We moved single file along the tops of the dykes that

divided the field into an immense checkerboard. The thought struck me that if there were guerrillas hiding in the tall rice we would make fine targets as we moved along, but no one seemed worried.

Progress was slow. The mud dykes were slippery as grease, and every time a soldier toppled into the muddy paddy, the whole column halted as he was pulled out. I was reminded somehow of the White Knight in Lewis Carroll's *Through the Looking Glass*. Superficially, we combed the field from one end to the other, our various forces finally meeting in the middle.

A little L19 spotter plane droned overhead, radioing what was no doubt useful information to the ground commander.

It would be difficult to search that field more completely than we did, and we found not the slightest trace of a human being. Of course, the rice could easily have concealed a thousand or even ten thousand guerrillas, without our knowing.

Viet Cong guerrillas have developed the art of camouflage to an incredible degree. In rice fields, they often remain completely submerged under the muddy water for hours, breathing through straws.

But by now the sun stood like a blast furnace in the sky, and the troops were tired. A few had tied to their packs live ducks and chickens they had pilfered from the hamlets, and were looking around for level ground on which to prepare lunch.

"It looks as though the Viet Cong got away again," the commander told me. "It's time to go. It's not a good idea to be moving around out here when the sun starts going down."

By noon, three hundred mud-drenched, tired troops were boarding the landing craft, and silence had settled over the hamlets again. We had suffered one wounded – a Civil Guard who had stepped on a spike trap, which had pierced his foot.

The three landing craft churned their way out into deep water, and the tension disappeared. Soldiers lighted cigarettes, talked and laughed, and spread their sopping clothing on the deck to dry.

All of them had a warm feeling of accomplishment, of having done a hard day's work under the cruel sun. The irregularity in the palm-lined shore that marked our hamlet receded into the distance.

And I couldn't help thinking of the old travelogues that end, "And so we leave the picturesque Mekong River Delta, palm trees glimmering under a tropic sun, and happy natives on the shore bidding us 'aloha.' "

The Vietnam War

NICHOLAS TOMALIN

The General Goes Zapping Charlie Cong

Tomalin's article "The General Goes Zapping Charlie Cong" was one of the sources for Coppola's *Apocalypse Now*; the character of Lt-Col Bill "Charlie Don't Surf" Kilgore is, in large part, General James F. Hollingsworth as refracted through Tomalin's eyes.

The article has yet another claim to fame: it is one of the earliest British examples of New Journalism. (Tomalin, indeed, was the only Briton collected in Tom Wolfe's definitive manifesto-cum-anthology, *The New Journalism*.) In the same year that *The New Journalism* was published, 1973, Tomalin was killed by a missile on the Golan Heights reporting the Yom Kippur War. He was forty-one. *Press Gazette* later ranked him in the top forty journalists of modern times.

Sunday Times, 5 June 1966

After a light lunch last Wednesday, General James F. Hollingsworth, of Big Red One, took off in his personal helicopter and killed more Vietnamese than all the troops he commanded.

The story of the General's feat begins in the divisional office, at Ki-Na, twenty miles north of Saigon, where a Medical Corps colonel is telling me that when they collect enemy casualties they find themselves with more than four injured civilians for every wounded Viet Cong – unavoidable in this kind of war.

The General strides in and pins two medals for outstanding gallantry to the chest of one of the colonel's combat doctors. Then he strides off again to his helicopter, and spreads out a polythene-covered map to explain our afternoon's trip.

The General has a big, real American face, reminiscent of every movie general you have seen. He comes from Texas, and is forty-eight. His present rank is Brigadier General, Assistant Division Commander, 1st Infantry Division, United States Army (which is what the big red figure one on his shoulder flash means).

"Our mission today," says the General, "is to push those goddam VCs right off Routes Thirteen and Sixteen. Now you see Routes Thirteen and Sixteen running north from Saigon toward the town of Phuoc Vinh, where we keep our artillery. When we got here first we prettied up those roads, and cleared Charlie Cong right out so we could run supplies up.

"I guess we've been hither and thither with all our operations since, an' the ol' VC he's reckoned he could creep back. He's been puttin' out propaganda he's goin' to interdict our right of passage along those routes. So this day we aim to zapp him, and zapp him, and zapp him again till we've zapped him right back where he came from. Yes, sir. Let's go."

The General's UH 18 helicopter carries two pilots, two 60-calibre machine-gunners, and his aide, Dennis Gillman, an apple-cheeked subaltern from California. It also carries the General's own M-16 carbine (hanging on a strut), two dozen smoke-bombs, and a couple of CS anti-personnel gas-bombs, each as big as a small dustbin. Just beside the General is a radio console where he can tune in on orders issued by battalion commanders flying helicopters just beneath him, and company commanders in helicopters just below them.

Under this interlacing of helicopters lies the apparently peaceful landscape beside Routes Thirteen and Sixteen, filled with farmhouses and peasants hoeing rice and paddy fields.

So far today things haven't gone too well. Companies Alpha, Bravo and Charlie have assaulted a suspected Viet Cong HQ, found a few tunnels but no enemy.

The General sits at the helicopter's open door, knees apart, his shiny black toecaps jutting out into space, rolls a filtertip cigarette to-and-fro in his teeth, and thinks.

"Put me down at Battalion HQ," he calls to the pilot.

"There's sniper fire reported on choppers in that area, General."

"Goddam the snipers, just put me down."

Battalion HQ at the moment is a defoliated area of four acres packed with tents, personnel carriers, helicopters and milling GIs. We settle into the smell of crushed grass. The General leaps out and strides through his troops.

"Why, General, excuse us, we didn't expect you here," says a sweating major.

"You killed any 'Cong yet?"

"Well no, General, I guess he's just too scared of us today. Down the road a piece we've hit trouble, a bulldozer's fallen through a bridge, and trucks coming through a village knocked the canopy off a Buddhist pagoda. Saigon radioed us to repair that temple before proceeding – in the way of civic action, General. That put us back an hour . . ."

"Yeah. Well, Major, you spread out your perimeter here a bit, then get to killin' VCs, will you?"

Back through the crushed grass to the helicopter.

"I don't know how you think about war. The way I see it, I'm just like any other company boss, gingering up the boys all the time, except I don't make money. I just kill people, and save lives."

In the air the General chews two more filtertips and looks increasingly forlorn. No action on Route Sixteen, and another Big Red One general has got his helicopter in to inspect the collapsed bridge before ours.

"Swing us back along again," says the General.

"Reports of fire on choppers ahead, sir. Smoke flare near spot. Strike coming in."

"Go find that smoke."

A plume of white rises in the midst of dense tropical forest, with a Bird Dog spotter plane in attendance. Route Sixteen is to the right, beyond it a large settlement of red-tiled houses.

"Strike coming in, sir."

Two F-105 jets appear over the horizon in formation, split, then one passes over the smoke, dropping a trail of silver, fish-shaped canisters. After four seconds' silence, light orange fire explodes in patches along an area fifty yards wide by three-quarters of a mile long. Napalm.

The trees and bushes burn, pouring dark oily smoke into the sky. The second plane dives and fire covers the entire strip of dense forest.

"Aaaaah," cries the General. "Nice. Nice. Very neat. Come on low, let's see who's left down there."

"How do you know for sure the Viet Cong snipers were in that strip you burned?"

"We don't. The smoke position was a guess. That's why we zapp the whole forest."

"But what if there was someone, a civilian, walking through there?"

"Aw come on, you think there's folks just sniffing flowers in tropical vegetation like that? With a big operation on hereabouts? Anyone left down there, he's Charlie Cong all right."

I point at a paddy field full of peasants less than half a mile away.

"That's different, son. We know they're genuine."

The pilot shouts, "General, half right, two running for that bush."

"I see them. Down, down, goddam you."

In one movement he yanks his M-16 off the hanger, slams in a clip of cartridges and leans right out of the door, hanging on his seatbelt to fire one long burst in the general direction of the bush.

"General, there's a hole, maybe a bunker, down there."

"Smoke-bomb, circle, shift it."

"But General, how do you know those aren't just frightened peasants?"

"Running? Like that? Don't give me a pain. The clips, the clips, where in hell are the cartridges in this ship?"

The aide drops a smoke canister, the General finds his ammunition and the starboard machine-gunner fires rapid bursts into the bush, his tracers bouncing up off the ground round it.

We turn clockwise in ever tighter, lower circles, everyone firing. A shower of spent cartridge cases leaps from the General's carbine to drop, lukewarm, on my arm.

"I . . . WANT . . . YOU . . . TO . . . SHOOT . . . RIGHT . . . UP . . . THE . . . ASS . . . OF . . . THAT . . . HOLE . . . GUNNER."

Fourth time round the tracers flow right inside the tiny sand-bagged opening, tearing the bags, filling it with sand and smoke.

The General falls back off his seatbelt into his chair, suddenly relaxed, and lets out an oddly feminine, gentle laugh. "That's it," he says, and turns to me, squeezing his thumb and finger into the sign of a French chef's ecstasy.

We circle now above a single-storey building made of dried reeds. The first burst of fire tears the roof open, shatters one wall into fragments of scattered straw, and blasts the farmyard full of chickens into dismembered feathers.

"Zapp, zapp, zapp," cries the General. He is now using semi-automatic fire, the carbine bucking in his hands.

Pow, pow, pow, sounds the gun. All the noises of this war have an unaccountably Texan ring.

"Gas bomb."

Lieutenant Gillman leans his canister out of the door. As the pilot calls, he drops it. An explosion of white vapour spreads across the wood a full hundred yards downwind.

"Jesus wept, lootenant, that's no good."

Lieutenant Gillman immediately clambers across me to get the second gas bomb, pushing me sideways into his own port-side seat. In considerable panic I fumble with an unfamiliar seatbelt as the helicopter banks round at an angle of fifty degrees. The second gas bomb explodes perfectly, beside the house, covering it with vapour.

"There's nothing alive in there," says the General. "Or they'd be skedaddling. Yes there is, by golly."

For the first time I see the running figure, bobbing and sprinting across the farmyards towards a clump of trees dressed in black pyjamas. No hat. No shoes.

"Now hit the tree."

We circle five times. Branches drop off the tree, leaves fly, its trunk is enveloped with dust and tracer flares. Gillman and the General are now firing carbines side by side in the doorway. Gillman offers me his gun: No thanks.

Then a man runs from the tree, in each hand a bright red flag which he waves desperately above his head.

"Stop, stop, he's quit," shouts the General, knocking the machine-gun so tracers erupt into the sky.

"I'm going to take him. Now watch it everyone, keep firing round-about, this may be an ambush."

We sink swiftly into the field beside the tree, each gunner

firing cautionary bursts into the bushes. The figure walks towards us.

"That's a Cong for sure," cries the General in triumph and with one deft movement grabs the man's short black hair and yanks him off his feet, inboard. The prisoner falls across Lieutenant Gillman and into the seat beside me.

The red flags I spotted from the air are his hands, bathed solidly in blood. Further blood is pouring from under his shirt, over his trousers.

Now we are safely in the air again. Our captive cannot be more than sixteen years old, his head comes just about up to the white name patch – Hollingsworth – on the General's chest. He is dazed, in shock. His eyes calmly look first at the General, then at the Lieutenant, then at me. He resembles a tiny, fine-boned wild animal. I have to keep my hand firmly pressed against his shoulder to hold him upright. He is quivering. Sometimes his left foot, from some nervous impulse, bangs hard against the helicopter wall. The Lieutenant applies a tourniquet to his right arm.

"Radio base for an ambulance. Get the information officer with a camera. I want this Commie bastard alive till we get back . . . just stay with us till we talk to you, baby."

The General pokes with his carbine first at the prisoner's cheek to keep his head upright, then at the base of his shirt.

"Look at that now," he says, turning to me. "You still thinking about innocent peasants? Look at the weaponry."

Around the prisoner's waist is a webbing belt, with four clips of ammunition, a water bottle (without stopper), a tiny roll of bandages, and a propaganda leaflet which later turns out to be a set of Viet Cong songs, with a twenty piastre note (about one shilling and six pence) folded in it.

Lieutenant Gillman looks concerned. "It's OK, you're OK," he mouths at the prisoner, who at that moment turns to me and with a surprisingly vigorous gesture waves his arm at my seat. He wants to lie down.

By the time I have fastened myself into yet another seat we are back at the landing pad. Ambulance orderlies come board, administer morphine, and rip open his shirt. Obviously a burst of fire has shattered his right arm up at the shoulder. The cut shirt now allows a large bulge of blue-red tissue to fall forward, its surface streaked with white nerve fibres and chips of bone (how did he ever manage to wave that arm in surrender?).

When the ambulance has driven off the General gets us all posed round the nose of the chopper for a group photograph like a gang of successful fishermen, then clambers up into the cabin again, at my request, for a picture to show just how he zapped those VCs. He is euphoric.

"Jeez I'm so glad you was along, that worked out just dandy. I've been written up time and time again back in the States for shootin' up VCs, but no one's been along with me like you before."

We even find a bullet hole in one of the helicopter rotor blades. "That's proof positive they was firin' at us all the time. An' firin' on us first, boy. So much for your fellers smellin' flowers."

He gives me the Viet Cong's water bottle as souvenir and proof. "That's a Chicom bottle, that one. All the way from Peking."

Later that evening the General calls me to his office to tell me the prisoner had to have his arm amputated, and is now in the hands of the Vietnamese authorities, as regulations dictate. Before he went under, he told the General's interpreters that he was part of a hardcore regular VC company whose mission was to mine Route Sixteen, cut it up, and fire at helicopters.

The General is magnanimous in his victory over my squeamish civilian worries.

"You see, son, I saw rifles on that first pair of running men. Didn't tell you at the time. And, by the way you mustn't imagine there could have been ordinary farm folk in that house, when you're as old a veteran as I am you get to know about those things by instinct. I agree there was chickens for food with them, strung up on a pole. You didn't see anything bigger, like a pig or a cow, did yuh? Well then."

The General wasn't certain whether further troops would go to the farmhouse that night to check who died, although patrols would be near there.

It wasn't safe moving along Route Sixteen at night, there was another big operation elsewhere the next day. Big Red One is always on the move.

"But when them VC come back harassin' that Route Sixteen why, we'll zapp them again. And when they come back after that we'll zapp them again."

"Wouldn't it be easier just to stay there all the time?"

"Why, son, we haven't enough troops as it is."

"The Koreans manage it."

"Yeah, but they've got a smaller area to protect. Why, Big Red One ranges right over – I mean up to the Cambodian Border. There ain't no place on that map we ain't been.

"I'll say perhaps your English generals wouldn't think my way of war is all that conventional, would they? Well, this is a new kind of war, flexible, quick moving. Us generals must be on the spot to direct our troops. The helicopter adds a new dimension to battle.

"There's no better way to fight than goin' out to shoot VCs. An' there's nothing I love better than killin' 'Cong. No, sir."

The Six Day War

JAMES CAMERON

What a Way to Run the Tribe

On 5 June 1967 Israel pre-empted an attack by her Arab neighbours by striking simultaneously at Egypt, Syria and Jordan. Within a week the Arab nations sued for peace, leaving Israeli soldiers in charge of Sinai, the Gaza Strip and the west bank of the Jordan. Among the journalists covering 'The Six Day War' was the veteran British reporter James Cameron.

Evening Standard, 11 June 1967

The war has etched its picture over the face of the desert like a surrealist drawing. From the air over Sinai the whole conduct of campaign is physically imprinted on the sand by the tank-tracks – a fantastically elaborate pattern of whorls and loops and intensely meaningful straight lines and sudden stops. It is the most extraordinarily effective record of an engagement I have ever seen, perhaps anyone has ever seen.

Yesterday I went on the first survey of the whole peninsula, perhaps one of the biggest single battlefields ever known, the place where the Egyptian Army died. In a lifetime not too unfamiliar with such things I have never seen anything like this. I believe that only now we and the Israeli people are beginning to realize just how immense this action was, and how complete the conquest. Figures do not really mean very much, even if there were any accurate figures, which naturally there aren't.

An Egyptian force of five infantry and two armoured divisions abruptly eliminated; an army of some 90,000 or more men disintegrated, with some tens of thousands killed or captured, or left, ignored, to wander and struggle somehow or other in the general direction of anywhere. Several million pounds' worth of extremely expensive and sophisticated military ironmongery now reduced to booty or to crushed and blackened scrap. The tanks and vehicles litter the desert like the nursery floor of an angry child. Nothing I have ever experienced so illustrates the extravagance, the mercilessness, the wastefulness of war.

It is somehow imperative to see it physically. From the air one sees the hundreds and hundreds of tanks strewn across the miles of wilderness like broken toys. Some are hideously burned and mangled lumps of complicated metal, some are totally untouched. The Israelis found concentrations of up to forty tanks unmanned, abandoned, their crews fled without firing a shot. Some of these costly new Soviet T 51s are still coloured in the Russian forest grey; the Egyptians had no time to repaint them in the desert ochre camouflage.

This is how statistics come to life. The almost incredible figures of the destruction of the Arab air-force in that lightning pre-emptive strike becomes comprehensible now. Wandering over a captured Sinai airstrip, seeing the neatly arranged jet aircraft, each taken out with a pitiless precision that has left them little black heaps of debris in the middle of almost untouched ground, one only concludes that the Israeli marksmanship must be extraordinary, or they are using projectiles of a very unusual kind. They seem to have wasted hardly one cannon-shell or rocket. The whole thing has the appearance of an exact and clinically brutal surgery.

As I flew on south, the Canal looming on the starboard horizon, it became, if possible, harsher yet. Here the roads crawl through the red mountains whose razorback ridges make an unearthly foreground to the searing sun. And here they caught the convoys. A couple of miles of road suddenly looks like a thin strip of hell. Anything up to a couple of hundred vehicles, caught in the Mitla Pass, are trapped, burned, exploded, demolished; they are strung along in a caterpillar of ruination, upside-down, inside out, fragmented, terrible. Some – desperately leaving the road altogether – have been delicately picked out on the desert. They were heading home, but it was just that much too far away.

So down to Sharm-el-Sheikh, the remote pinhead of a place at the entrance of the Gulf of Eilat, which has a meaning for history only because this is effectively where it all began, when Egypt seized it from the United Nations – when? Last month? A generation ago? – and blocked Israel's traffic through the narrow straits, her only exit to the south and east.

I was here, on this very arid, austere and baking spot, some ten and a half years ago, when once before Israel had taken it from the Egyptians – and with me now, by the usual wild Israeli coincidence, was the man who had taken it then: Colonel Asher Levi, whom I know because until last week he was Military Attaché round the corner from me in London, until he flew back here, to become like apparently everyone else in this country, a soldier.

The place has little changed; it is still one of the most unattractive and disagreeable locations in a campaign not noted for its easeful amenities. There was no battle here. The Egyptians had it manned by an infantry brigade and a squadron of tanks and auxiliaries, perhaps 5,000 men. They evacuated Sharm-el-Sheikh on Wednesday morning; the Israelis came in that afternoon. Sharm-el-Sheikh was taken by two torpedo-boats and a handful of parachutists, who didn't even have a parachute, somewhat to their annoyance, since they get a bonus for a drop.

The Egyptians took their artillery, but they left the hills around stored with ammunition and food – but of course no water; that has to be brought in by sea, and very precious stuff it is.

The new occupiers found the place commanded by no guns, the narrow turquoise waters un-mined. I wonder what, after all, it was all about? And then the most wry irony of all: the first ship that came knocking on the door of the Gulf for Israeli permission to enter was a Soviet freighter bound for Aqaba. The Israelis challenged it, noted it, and politely waved it on. The next day Russia broke off relations with Israel. It really needed only that.

Bolivia

RICHARD GOTT

The Last Journey of Che Guevara

After playing a leading role in the Cuban Revolution, the Argen-
tine-born Guevara departed Cuba in 1965 to foment guerrilla
warfare in Bolivia. Within months he was captured and executed
by Bolivian troops and the CIA.

Guardian, 11 October 1967

The body of Che Guevara was flown into this small hill town in
south-eastern Bolivia at five o'clock last night.

From the moment the helicopter landed bearing the small
figure strapped in a stretcher to the landing rails, the succeeding operation was to a large extent left in the hands of a man in
battledress, who, all the correspondents here agree, was
unquestionably a representative of one of the United States
intelligence agencies.

He was probably a Cuban exile and so Che Guevara, who in
life had declared war almost singlehanded on the United States,
found himself in death face to face with his major enemy.

The helicopter purposely landed far from where a crowd had
gathered and the body of the dead guerrilla leader was hastily
transferred to a van. We commandeered a jeep to follow it and
the driver managed to get through the gates of the hospital
grounds where the body was taken to a small colour-washed hut
that served as a mortuary.

The doors of the van burst open and the American agent
leapt out, emitting a war cry of "Let's get the hell out of here."

One of the correspondents asked him where he came from. "Nowhere," was the surly response.

The body, dressed in olive green fatigues with a zippered jacket, was carried into the hut. It was undoubtedly that of Che Guevara. Ever since I first reported in January that Che was probably in Bolivia I have not shared the general scepticism about his whereabouts.

I am probably one of the few people here who have seen him alive. I saw him in Cuba at an Embassy reception in 1963 and there is no doubt in my mind that this body was that of Che. It had a black wispy beard, long matted hair, and the shadow of a scar on the right temple, probably the result of an accident in July when he was grazed by a rifle shot.

On his feet he wore moccasins as though he had been shot down while running fleet-footed through the jungle. He had two wounds in the lower part of the neck and possibly one in the stomach. It is believed that he was captured when seriously wounded, but died before a helicopter could arrive to take him out of the battle zone.

My only doubts about the identity arose because Che was much thinner and smaller than I had recalled, but it is hardly surprising that after months in the jungle he had lost his former heavy appearance.

As soon as the body reached the mortuary the doctors began to pump preservative into it, and the American agent made desperate efforts to keep off the crowds. He was a very nervous man and looked furious whenever cameras were pointed in his direction. He knew that I knew who he was and he also knew that I knew that he should not be there, for this is a war in which the Americans are not supposed to be taking part. Yet here was this man, who has been with the troops in Vallegrande, talking to the senior officers on familiar terms.

One can hardly say that this was the factor with which Che failed to reckon, for it was his very purpose to provoke United States intervention in Latin America as a way of bringing help and succour to the embattled Vietnamese. But he certainly did fail to estimate correctly the strength and pervasiveness of the US intelligence agencies in this continent, and this more than anything else has been the cause of his downfall and that of the Bolivian guerrillas.

And so he is dead. As they pumped preservative into his half-naked, dirty body and as the crowd shouted to be allowed to see, it was difficult to recall that this man had once been one of the great figures of Latin America.

It was not just that he was a great guerrilla leader, he had been a friend of Presidents as well as revolutionaries. His voice had been heard and appreciated in inter-American councils as well as in the jungle. He was a doctor, an amateur economist, once Minister of Industries in revolutionary Cuba, and Fidel Castro's right-hand man. He may well go down in history as the greatest continental figure since Bolivar. Legends will be created around his name.

He was a Marxist but impatient of the doctrinal struggles between the Russians and the Chinese. He was perhaps the last person who tried to find a middle way between the two and attempted to unite radical forces everywhere in a concerted campaign against the US. He is now dead, but it is difficult to feel that his ideas will die with him.

The Vietnam War

PETER ARNETT

Hill 875

Born in New Zealand, Arnett served as the AP's Vietnam correspondent from 1962 through to the fall of Saigon, winning the
Pulitzer Prize in 1966. He later covered El Salvador, Iran, Lebanon and the Gulf War for Cable News Network.

Associated Press, 22 November 1967

Hill 875, Vietnam AP – Hour after hour of battle gave the living
and the dead the same gray pallor on Hill 875. At times the only
way to tell them apart was to watch when the enemy mortars
crashed in on the exhausted American paratroopers.

The living rushed unashamedly to the tiny bunkers dug into
the red clay.

The wounded squirmed toward the shelter of trees blasted to
the ground.

The dead – propped up in bunkers or face down in the dust
– didn't move.

Since Sunday the most brutal fighting of the Vietnam war has
ebbed and flowed across this remote hill in the western sector of
the Dak To battleground. The 2nd Battalion of the 173rd Airborne Brigade went up 875 first. It nearly died.

Of the 16 officers who led the men across the ridgeline
Sunday, eight were killed and the other eight wounded. Eleven
of the 13 medics died.

The battalion took its first casualties at midday Sunday as it
crested Hill 875, one of the hundreds of knolls that dot the

ridges in the Dak To fighting region near the Cambodian-Laotian border.

All weekend as the paratroopers moved along the jungle hills enemy base camps were uncovered. The biggest was on 875 and D Company lost several men in the first encounter with the bunkers.

A Company moved back down the hill to cut a landing zone and was chopped to pieces by a North Vietnamese flanking attack.

The remnants fled back to the crest of the hill while a paratrooper propped his gun on the trail and kept firing at the advancing enemy, ignoring orders to retreat with the others.

"You can keep gunning them down, but sooner or later when there is enough of them they'll get to you," said Pfc. James Kelly of Fort Myers, Fla, who saw the machine gunner go down after killing about 17 North Vietnamese.

D Company, hearing the roar of battle below it, returned to the crest of the hill and established a 50-yard perimeter "because we figure we were surrounded by a regiment", one officer said.

As the battalion was regrouping late in the afternoon for another crack at the bunker system, one of the American planes striking at the nearby enemy dropped a 500-pound bomb too soon. About 30 of the paratroopers were killed.

"A foul play of war," said one survivor bitterly.

From then until a reinforcing battalion arrived the following night, the paratroopers on the hill dug in desperately. Only one medic was able to work on the many wounded, and the enemy kept driving off the rescue helicopters.

The relief battalion made it into the tiny perimeter on 875 Monday night. In the moonlight bodies of the dead lay spread-eagled across the ground. The wounded whimpered.

The survivors, hungry and thirsty, rushed up eagerly to get food and water, only to learn that the relief battalion had brought enough supplies for one day only and had already consumed them.

Monday night was sleepless but uneventful. On Tuesday the North Vietnamese struck with renewed fury.

From positions just 100 yards away, they pounded the American perimeter with 82mm mortars. The first rounds slapped in at daybreak, killing three paratroopers in a foxhole and wounding 17 others on the line.

For the rest of the day, the Communists methodically worked over the hill, pumping rounds in five or six at a time, giving new wounds to those who lay bleeding in the open and tearing through bunkers. The plop of the rounds as they left the enemy tubes gave the paratroopers a second or two to dash for cover.

The foxholes got deeper as the day wore on. Foxhole after foxhole took hits. A dog handler and his German shepherd died together. Men joking with you and offering cigarettes writhed on the ground wounded and pleading for water minutes later. There was no water for anyone.

Crouched in one bunker, Pfc. Angel Flores, 20, of New York City said: "If we were dead like those out there we wouldn't have to worry about this stuff coming in."

He fingered a plastic rosary around his neck and kissed it reverently as the rounds blasted on the ground outside.

"Does that do you any good?" a buddy asked him.

"Well, I'm still alive," Flores replied.

"Don't you know that the chaplain who gave you that was killed on Sunday?" said his buddy.

The day's pounding steadily reduced the platoon commanded by 1st Lt. Bryan Macdonough, 25, of Fort Lee, Va. He had started out Sunday with 27 men. He had nine left by noon Tuesday.

"If the Viets keep this up, there'll be none left by evening," he said.

The enemy positions seemed impervious to constant American air strikes. Napalm fireballs exploded on the bunkers 30 yards away. The earth shook with heavy bombs.

"We've tried 750 pounders, napalm and everything else, but air can't do it. It's going to take manpower to get those positions," Macdonough said.

By late afternoon a new landing zone was cut below the hill. The enemy mortars searched for it but the helicopters came in anyway. A line of wounded trudged down the hill and by evening 140 of them had been evacuated.

The arrival of the helicopters with food, water and ammunition seemed to put new life into the paratroopers. They talked eagerly of a final assault on the enemy bunkers.

As darkness fell flame throwers were brought up. The first stubborn bunker yielded, and the paratroopers were at last started on their way to gain the ridgeline which they had set out to take three days earlier.

The Vietnam War

MICHAEL HERR

Khe Sanh Nights

Herr covered the war in Vietnam for *Esquire* magazine and *Rolling Stone* in 1967 and 1968. The screenplay for *Apocalypse Now* relied heavily on the 'Nam reports Herr had collected together as *Dispatches*.

Dispatches, 1977

Sometimes you'd step from the bunker, all sense of time passing having left you, and find it dark out. The far side of the hills around the bowl of the base was glimmering, but you could never see the source of the light, and it had the look of a city at night approached from a great distance. Flares were dropping everywhere around the fringes of the perimeter, laying a dead white light on the high ground rising from the piedmont. There would be dozens of them at once sometimes, trailing an intense smoke, dropping white-hot sparks, and it seemed as though anything caught in their range would be made still, like figures in a game of living statues. There would be the muted rush of illumination rounds, fired from 60-mm mortars inside the wire, dropping magnesium-brilliant above the NVA trenches for a few seconds, outlining the gaunt, flat spread of the mahogany trees, giving the landscape a ghastly clarity and dying out. You could watch mortar bursts, orange and grey-smoking, over the tops of trees three and four kilometres away, and the heavier shelling from support bases farther east along the DMZ, from Camp Carrol and the Rockpile, directed against suspected troop movements or NVA rocket and mortar positions. Once in a while – I guess I saw it happen three or four times in all – there would be a secondary explosion, a direct hit on a supply of NVA ammunition. And at night it was beautiful. Even the incoming was beautiful at night, beautiful and deeply dreadful.

I remembered the way a Phantom pilot had talked about how beautiful the surface-to-air missiles looked as they drifted up towards his plane to kill him, and remembered myself how lovely 50-calibre tracers could be, coming at you as you flew at night in a helicopter, how slow and graceful, arching up easily, a dream, so remote from anything that could harm you. It could make you feel a total serenity, an elevation that put you above death, but that never lasted very long. One hit anywhere in the chopper would bring you back, bitten lips, white knuckles and all, and then you knew where you were. It was different with the incoming at Khe Sanh. You didn't get to watch the shells very often. You knew if you heard one, the first one, that you were safe, or at least saved. If you were still standing up and looking after that, you deserved anything that happened to you.

Nights were when the air and artillery strikes were heaviest, because that was when we knew that the NVA was above ground and moving. At night you could lie out on some sandbags and watch the C-47s mounted with Vulcans doing their work. The C-47 was a standard prop flareship, but many of them carried .20- and .762-mm guns on their doors, Mike-Mikes that could fire out 300 rounds per second, Gatling style, "a round in every square inch of a football field in less than a minute", as the handouts said. They used to call it Puff the Magic Dragon, but the Marines knew better: they named it Spooky. Every fifth round fired was a tracer, and when Spooky was working, everything stopped while that solid stream of violent red poured down out of the black sky. If you watched from a great distance, the stream would seem to dry up between bursts, vanishing slowly from air to ground like a comet tail, the sound of the guns disappearing too, a few seconds later. If you watched at a close range, you couldn't believe that anyone would have the courage to deal with that night after night, week after week, and you cultivated a respect for the Viet Cong and NVA who had crouched under it every night now for months. It was awesome, worse than anything the Lord had ever put down on Egypt, and at night, you'd hear the Marines talking, watching it, yelling, "Get some!" until they grew quiet and someone would say, "Spooky understands." The nights were very beautiful. Night was when you really had the least to fear and feared the most. You could go through some very bad numbers at night.

Because, really, what a choice there was; what a prodigy of things to be afraid of! The moment that you understood this, really understood it, you lost your anxiety instantly. Anxiety was a luxury, a joke you had no room for once you knew the variety of deaths and mutilations the war offered. Some feared head wounds, some dreaded chest wounds or stomach wounds, everyone feared the wound of wounds, the Wound. Guys would pray and pray – Just you and me, God. Right? – offer anything, if only they could be spared that: Take my legs, take my hands, take my eyes, take my fucking *life*, You Bastard, but please, please, please, don't take *those*. Whenever a shell landed in a group, everyone forgot about the next rounds and skipped back to rip their pants away, to check, laughing hysterically with relief even though their legs might be shattered, their kneecaps torn away, kept upright by their relief and shock, gratitude and adrenaline.

There were choices everywhere, but they were never choices that you could hope to make. There was even some small chance for personal style in your recognition of the one thing you feared more than any other. You could die in a sudden bloodburning crunch as your chopper hit the ground like dead weight, you could fly apart so that your pieces would never be gathered, you could take one neat round in the lung and go out hearing only the bubble of the last few breaths, you could die in the last stage of malaria with that faint tapping in your ears, and that could happen to you after months of firefights and rockets and machine guns. Enough, too many, were saved for that, and you always hoped that no irony would attend your passing. You could end in a pit somewhere with a spike through you, everything stopped forever except for the one or two motions, purely involuntary, as though you could kick it all away and come back. You could fall down dead so that the medics would have to spend half an hour looking for the hole that killed you, getting

more and more spooked as the search went on. You could be
shot, mined, grenaded, rocketed, mortared, sniped at, blown up
and away so that your leavings had to be dropped into a sagging
poncho and carried to Graves Registration, that's all she wrote.
It was almost marvellous.

And at night, all of it seemed more possible. At night in Khe
Sanh, waiting there, thinking about all of them (40,000, some
said), thinking that they might really try it, could keep you up. If
they did, when they did, it might not matter that you were in the
best bunker in the DMZ, wouldn't matter that you were young
and had plans, that you were loved, that you were a non-combatant, an observer. Because if it came, it would be in a
bloodswarm of killing, and credentials would not be examined.
(The only Vietnamese many of us knew was the words "Bao
Chi! Bao Chi!" – Journalist! Journalist! or even "Bao Chi Fap!"
– French journalist!, which was the same as crying, Don't shoot!
Don't shoot!) You came to love your life, to love and respect the
mere fact of it, but often you became heedless of it in the way
that somnambulists are heedless. Being "good" meant staying
alive, and sometimes that was only a matter of caring enough at
any given moment. No wonder everyone became a luck freak,
no wonder you could wake at four in the morning some mornings and *know* that tomorrow it would finally happen, you could
stop worrying about it now and just lie there, sweating in the
dampest chill you ever felt.

But once it was actually going on, things were different. You
were just like everyone else, you could no more blink than spit.
It came back the same way every time, dreaded and welcome,
balls and bowels turning over together, your senses working like
strobes, free-falling all the way down to the essences and then
flying out again in a rush to focus, like the first strong twinge of
tripping after an infusion of psilocybin, reaching in at the point
of calm and springing all the joy and all the dread ever known,
ever known by *everyone* who *ever* lived, unutterable in its speeding brilliance, touching all the edges and then passing, as though
it had all been controlled from outside, by a god or by the moon.
And every time, you were so weary afterwards, so empty of
everything but being alive that you couldn't recall any of it,
except to know that it was like something else you had felt once
before. It remained obscure for a long time, but after enough

times the memory took shape and substance and finally revealed itself one afternoon during the breaking off of a firefight. It was the feeling you'd had when you were much, much younger and undressing a girl for the first time.

The Vietnam War

JOHN T. WHEELER

Life in the V Ring

Wheeler worked for Associated Press in Vietnam from 1965 through to 1969. Here he reports on Khe Sanh during the North Vietnamese Tet offensive.

Associated Press, 12 February 1968

Khe Sanh, Vietnam (AP) – The first shell burst caught the Marines outside the bunkers filling sandbags. More exploding rockets sent showers of hot fragments zinging. The Americans dove for cover.

"Corpsman! Corpsman!"

The shout came from off to the right.

"We've got wounded here!"

"Corpsman! Corpsman!" The shouts now came from the distance. You could see the men dragging a bleeding buddy toward cover.

Inside the bunkers the Marines hugged their legs and bowed their heads, unconsciously trying to make themselves as small as possible. The tempo of the shelling increased and the small opening to the bunker seemed in their minds to grow to the size of a barn door. The 5,000 sandbags around and over the bunker seemed wafer thin.

Although it could increase their chances of survival only minutely, men shifted their positions to get closer to the ground.

Some measured the angle to the doorway and tried to wiggle a bit more behind those next to them.

There were no prayers uttered aloud. Two men growled a stream of profanity at the North Vietnamese gunners who might snuff out their lives at any moment.

Near misses rocked the bunker and sent dirt cascading down everyone's neck.

Outside the random explosions sent thousands of pounds of shrapnel tearing into sandbags and battering already damaged messhalls and tent areas long ago destroyed and abandoned for a life of fear and filth underground.

This is the life in the V Ring, a sharpshooter's term for the inner part of the bull's eye. At Khe Sanh the V Ring for the North Vietnamese gunners neatly covers the bunkers of Bravo Company, 3rd Reconnaissance Battalion. In three weeks, more than half the company had been killed or wounded. It was recon's bad luck to live in an area bordered by an ammunition dump, a flightline loading area, and the 26th Marine Regiment's command post.

Shrapnel and shell holes cover the area. The incoming rounds could hardly be noticed once the barrage stopped, such is the desolation.

And then the shells did stop. Silent men turned their faces from one to the other. Several men scrambled out of the bunker to see if more dead or wounded men from their unit were outside. Medics scurried through the area, crouching low.

Inside one bunker a Marine returned to his paperback book, a tale of Wild West adventure. Another man whose hand had stopped in the midst of strumming a guitar resumed playing. Two men in a card game began flipping the soggy pasteboards again.

The shelling wasn't worth discussing. It was too commonplace and none from Bravo Company had been hit this time. Like jungle rot, snipers and rats, artillery fire was something to be hated and accepted at the same time.

But the shellfire had taken its toll. Minutes before the barrage opened, Army Spec. 4 William Hankinson had drifted off from the other members of his communications team assigned to this Marine base.

When the first shell hit, he dived into a Marine bunker. After the explosions stopped, he talked with the Marines awhile before starting back to his bunker.

A white-faced Leatherneck joined the group.

"You look kind of sick," a Marine buddy said. "What happened?"

"The whole Army bunker got wiped out," he replied. "Jesus, what a mess."

Hankinson started to run toward the smashed bunker where his friends' shattered bodies lay. Marines caught and blocked him. Then with a tenderness not at all out of place for hardened fighting men, they began to console the Army specialist, a man most had never spoken to before that day.

One dud mortar round was half-buried in the runway of the airstrip. Planes carrying priority supplies had to be waved off until the round could be removed.

Two demolition experts raced from shelter with fire axes and chopped it out of the aluminum sheet runway. Neither would give his name. Both had told their families they were safely out of the war zone.

"An awful lot of Marines are big liars on that point," one said.

The men of No. 2 gun, Charlie Battery, didn't think of cover when the shelling began. After what they had been through when the main ammunition dump 200 yards away exploded during an earlier barrage, "This is coasting," one gunner said.

And alone of the Marines at Khe Sanh, the artillery could fire back at the enemy. No. 2 gun, commanded by Cpl Anthony Albo, kept pouring out 105mm rounds even though a shell splinter had started a fire in the gun's ready ammo bunker.

At Charlie Med, the main casualty clearing station, wounded were coming in. Some were on stretchers, some hobbled by themselves, some were hauled in across the shoulder of a comrade.

One prayed, a few cried, some were unconscious. Many showed shock on their faces.

In between shellings, Lance Cpl Richard Noyes, 19, of Cincinnati, Ohio, roughhoused on the dirt floor of his bunker with a friend. Noyes lives with five buddies in the center of the V Ring. The war was pushed far into the background for a moment as ripples of laughter broke from the tangled, wrestling forms.

Then the first shell of a new barrage hit.

Both men recoiled as if a scorpion had been dropped between them. Even though they were underground in a bunker, everyone put on helmets. Across the front of his "brain pot", Noyes long ago had written in ink, "God walks with me."

A blank stare in the eyes of some is not uncommon at Khe Sanh where the Communists have fired up to 1,500 rounds of rockets, artillery and mortar shells in a single day.

It is called the 1,000-yard stare. It can be the sign of the beginning of combat fatigue.

For Noyes and thousands of others at this surrounded combat base, the anguish is bottled up within tolerable limits.

Noyes had had luck, lots of it. A rocket once drove through the bunker's sandbags and exploded, killing 4 and wounding 14 of the 20 men inside. Noyes was slightly wounded.

It was Noyes' second Purple Heart. One more and he automatically would be sent out of Vietnam under Marine regulations. Noyes doesn't want the third medal.

Despite heavy casualties, the survivors of the recon company are frightened but uncowed. When the call for stretcher bearers comes, the young Marines unhesitatingly begin wriggling through the opening in their bunker to help.

At night the men in Noyes' bunker sit and talk, sing, play cards, almost anything to keep from being alone with their thoughts. During a night when more than 1,000 rounds hit Khe Sanh, Noyes turned to a buddy and said:

"Man, it'll be really decent to go home and never hear words like incoming shells, mortars, rifles, and all that stuff. And the first guy who asks me how it feels to kill, I'll . . ." A pause. Then: "You know, my brother wants me to go duck hunting when I get home. Man, I don't want to even see a slingshot when I get out of here."

Lt C.J. Slack of Carlsbad, Calif., said: "When I get back to California, I'm going to open a bar especially for the survivors of Khe Sanh. And any time it gets two deep at that bar, I'll know someone is lying."

Noyes smokes heavily and his hands never seem to be entirely still. Looking at the side of a cigarette pack, Noyes said with a wry smile, "Caution, Khe Sanh may be hazardous to your health. Oh, man, yeah."

Still later, he called out, "Okay, we're going to sing now.

Anyone who can't sing has to hum. Because I said so. Okay, let's hear it."

Lance Cpl Richard Morris, 24, of North Hollywood, Calif., began playing a guitar. Two favorites that night were "Five Hundred Miles" and "Where Have All the Flowers Gone?"

A hard emphasis accompanied the verse that went: "Where have all the soldiers gone? To the graveyard every one. When will they ever learn? When will they ever learn?"

Finally the two small naked light bulbs were turned out and the Marines struggled toward sleep.

The Vietnam War

MARY MCCARTHY

An American in Hanoi

The radical American writer McCarthy was one of the few Americans allowed to visit North Vietnam during hostilities. She visited in March 1968.

Hanoi, 1968

"*Attachez vos ceintures, s'il vous plaît.*" "Fasten your seat belts." The hostess, plump, blonde, French, brown-eyed, in a light-blue smock, passed through, checking. It was funny to find a hostess on a military plane. Like the plane itself, loaded with mail, canned goods, cases of beer, she was a sort of last beep from the "other" world behind the mountains in Vientiane. Born in Hanoi, she had been making the run from Saigon with the ICC – Poles, Indians, Canadians, of the inspection team – six times a month, weather permitting, for thirteen years, practically since the Geneva Accords.

As the ICC plane, an obsolete non-pressurized Convair, circled in the dark above Hanoi, waiting to get the OK to land, out the window, by stretching against our seat belts, we could see tiny headlights of cars moving on the highways below and then the city all lit up like a big glowworm. In Phnom Penh, at the North Vietnamese Delegation, where they issued our visas, they had prepared us for this surprise, but it remained a surprise nonetheless. I thought of the Atlantic coast during World War II and the blackout curtains we had had to buy on the Cape – a Coast Guard order designed to foil enemy submarines. When the Convair taxied to a stop, it instantly doused its lights, though, and the hostess held a flashlight for the boarding officials to examine our papers. But then the airport, brilliant white and blazing with electricity. "You really don't have a blackout!" I exclaimed to the delegation from the Vietnamese Peace Committee who had come to meet us, with bouquets of snapdragons, pink sweet peas, pale-pink roses, larkspur, and little African daisies. A Japanese author and a journalist from a Tokyo paper were receiving bouquets, too. The Vietnamese did not know the word "blackout", and I tried *couvre-feu*. They dismissed the term "curfew" with laughter. "Passive defense!" In fact, there was no curfew of any sort in Hanoi – except the bell that rang at eleven o'clock nightly, closing the hotel bar – though there was one in Saigon. It was only when the sirens blew that the lights of the city went out and the cars and trucks halted and waited for the All Clear.

On the way from Gia Lam Airport into the city, we had our first alert – a pre-alert, really, given by loud-speakers; the pre-alert usually means the planes are sixty kilometers away; it is not till they are within thirty kilometers of the center that the sirens scream. Suddenly, still deep in the countryside, the driver braked the car; he had heard the pre-alert on his radio. He turned off the engine. I sat in the back seat, holding my bouquet in my lap and feeling quite apprehensive. On March 17, two days before, the much-feared swing-wing F-IIIAs had appeared in Thailand; there had been pictures of them in the Bangkok papers. The driver got out of the car. "He is looking for the shelter," one of my companions explained. "He has found the shelter," they announced a few minutes later, and we all climbed out of the car. In the moonlight, we could see the remains of a brick house, with its roof torn off; up the lane, there had been a hamlet, but now there were only indistinct masses of debris and, somewhere in the dark, the shelter, which I never actually saw. It was enough to know that it was there.

Outside Hanoi, the driver's first job, I discovered, was to look for a shelter for the passengers whenever the alert or the pre-alert sounded. Every hamlet, sometimes every house, is equipped with a loud-speaker, and the alarm is rung out by the hamlet bell – the same bell that calls the peasants to work in the fields. When there is no hamlet nearby, a band of young soldiers, tramping along with a transistor radio, may warn you that the planes are coming. Once, in Hoa Binh Province, out in the west, I sat huddled in the car with the thin, large-eyed young woman interpreter while the driver conducted the search; he came back, and there was a quick conference in Vietnamese. "Here there is no shelter," she whispered, gravely touching my arm, as we listened to the bombs, fortunately some miles off. Though the shelter may be only a hole in the ground, the assurance that there is such a burrow handy gives a sort of animal comfort – possibly not unlike the ostrich's. Or maybe it is a grateful sense that somebody, an unknown friend, has thought about your safety; even if the uncovered earth shelter cannot protect you from a direct hit, the thought, as they say of small presents, is what counts.

In the city, there are individual cement cylinders, resembling manholes, every few feet, with round fitted covers of cement or of plaited reeds – good against fragmentation bombs. In a pinch, they will accommodate two small Vietnamese. But what happened, I wondered, if there were more people on a given street when the alarm sounded than there were shelters to hold them? As in a game of going to Jerusalem or musical chairs, who would be left outside? It is a schoolmen's problem, that of the outsider, which is posed in the scramble of extreme situations, and I was curious – anxious, even – about the socialist solution. But I never was able to observe for myself what did in fact occur: in my two and a half weeks in North Vietnam, it chanced that only once was I in the city streets during an alert and then only long enough to see the people scattering as our driver raced toward the hotel and its communal shelter. And I felt that it would be somehow impolite to express my curiosity in the form of a point-blank question; there are many questions one does not want to ask in Hanoi.

In any case, the target of the Hanoi government is one shelter per person within the city limits – I am not sure whether this ratio takes into account the communal shelters attached to institutions. During my stay, hundreds of brand-new cylinders were lying along the sidewalks, waiting for the pavement to be dug up and holes sunk to contain them, and every day trucks kept dumping more. Production and delivery were ahead of the picks and shovels. "Manufacturing shelters is one of our principal industries now," people remark, rather ruefully, watching the gray cylinders being put into place. What can be done with these grim manholes, war memorials, when and if peace comes? The only answer I could think of was to plant flowers in them.

Johnson's speech of March 31 – and the subsequent eerie absence of alerts – did not cause even a momentary flagging in the shelter program. Yet, so far as I could tell, the shelters were more a symbol of determination than places to scuttle to when the planes approached. The city population had a certain disdain for using them. "There are toads in them," a pretty girl said, making a face. Like the white-gowned surgeon I met, a Hero of Labor, who had calculated the statistical probabilities of being killed by a bomb in the night and decided that he preferred to stay in bed, to be fresh for operating the next morning, many people in Hanoi decline to leave their beds or their offices when the peremptory siren shrills; it is a matter of individual decision. Only foreign visitors are hustled to safety by their guides and interpreters and told to put on their steel helmets or their pellet-absorbent hats of woven reeds or straw. A pellet in the brain is the thing most dreaded by the Vietnamese – a dread that as a brain-worker I more than shared; unfortunately the hat they gave me was too small for my large Western head, and I had to trust to my helmet, hurriedly strapping it on as I trotted down the hotel stairs to the communal shelter and glad of the excuse of social duty to do what private fear was urging.

Your guides are held responsible by the authorities if anything happens to you while you are in their care. This applies particularly to guests invited by North Vietnamese organizations (which we were); accredited journalists are allowed more rein. I was asked not to go out into the street alone, even for a short walk, though the rule was relaxed when the bombing of Hanoi stopped on April I – Hanoi time. This of course limited one's bodily freedom, but I accepted it, being a law-abiding person. Our hosts of the Peace Committee told us that they had been severely reprimanded because some frisky young South Americans had eluded their control last summer and roved unsupervised about the country; one got a pellet in the brain and had to be sent by plane to Moscow to be operated on; he lived. Whenever we traveled, one of the comrades of the Peace

Committee made sure I had my helmet by personally carrying it for me. I was never alone, except in bed or writing in my room. In the provinces, when we stayed at a guest house or came to inspect a village, each time I went to the outlying toilet, the young woman interpreter went with me as far as the door, bearing my helmet, some sheets of tan toilet paper she had brought from Hanoi, and, at night, the trusty flashlight. She waited outside till I was through and then softly led me back.

That first night, driving in from the airport, everything was novel. The driver had left the radio turned on in the car when he switched off the lights. We could hear it talking, as if to itself, as we paced up and down, and I had the foolish notion that the planes, wherever they were, might hear it, too. Other shadowy sedans and passengers were grouped by the roadside; there had been a great influx at the airport that night because for over three weeks, four times running, the ICC flight had not been able to make it down the narrow air corridor from Vientiane to Hanoi. On the road we had passed several cars with diplomatic license plates, one, surely, containing the Indonesian ambassador, who had boarded the plane with his golf clubs; he used them to exercise on his lawn. Now abruptly all the headlights went on again; motors started. "They are going away. They are going away," the radio voice had said in Vietnamese; the pre-alert was over.

Activity resumed. A chattering stream of people, mostly young, was flowing along the highway from the city, walking or riding bicycles and motor bikes: boys in work clothes or uniforms, with camouflage leaves in their helmets, girls and women, some riding pillion, carrying baskets of salad greens and other provisions; now and then a wrinkled old peasant, in black, with balance-pole on shoulder or pushing a cart. A cow raised its head from a field. All that nocturnal movement and chatter gave an impression of revelry, as if a night ball game or a theater had just let out; probably a work shift had ended in the factories. Along the road's edge cases of supplies were stashed, covered with jute or tarpaulin. Jeeps and military trucks, some heavily camouflaged, were moving steadily in the opposite direction.

We were passing pretty rows of small, compact trees – perhaps pruned fruit trees; it was too dark to tell – a pre-alert to the fact that Hanoi is a shady, leafy city, like Minneapolis or Warsaw;

like Minneapolis, too, it has lakes, treated as a municipal feature, with parks and promenades. The people are proud of the trees, particularly of the giant camphor, wreathed in a strange parasite with dangling coinlike leaves. Near the bombed brick house where we waited during the alert, there was a big bare blasted trunk, maybe an oak, which was putting out a few new leaves; my companions eagerly pointed them out, making sure I did not miss the symbol of resistance and rebirth. To the North Vietnamese, I soon became aware, everything is now a symbol, an ideogram, expressing the national resolve to overcome. All of Nature is with them, not just the "brother socialist countries". Nodding their heads in time with a vast patriotic orchestra, they are hearing tongues in trees, terrible sermons in stones and the twisted metal of downed aircraft. In Hung Yen Province, you eat a fresh-caught carp under a red-and-white-nylon canopy, like a billowing circus tent enclosing the whole room; it is the giant parachute of the pilotless reconnaissance plane they have shot down. Near Hanoi, in a village co-operative, raising model pigs and making handicrafts, they show you a small mute cluster bomb, olive drab, and, beside it, the mute rusty primitive soil-scratching implement the young peasant was using in the co-operative fields when pellets from the cluster bomb killed him. Visual education, they feel, for the people, and they are not afraid of hammering the lesson in. But it is Johnson, finally, they wish to give food for thought.

Growth statistics, offered everywhere, on bicycle ownership, irrigation, rice harvests, maternity clinics, literacy are the answer to "the war of destruction", which began February 7, 1965; a bombed oak putting out new leaves is a "reply" to the air pirates of the Air Force and the Seventh Fleet. All Communist countries are bent on furnishing growth statistics (it is their form of advertising), but with Hanoi this is something special, carrying a secondary meaning – defiance. On a big billboard in the city center, the number of US planes shot down is revised forward almost daily in red paint – 2,818, they claimed when I left, and the number keeps growing. In villages, the score is kept on a blackboard. Everything they build is dated, down to the family wells in a hamlet – a means of visibly recording progress, like penciling the heights of children, with the dates opposite, on a door. And each date has a clear significance in the story of resistance: 1965 or 1966, stamped on a well, proclaims that it was built *in spite of* the air pirates.

Hanoi, it is whispered, is going underground, digging shelters, factories, offices, operating theaters, preparing for "the worst", i.e., for saturation bombing by the B-52s or even – draw a deep breath – for atom bombs, although if you mention those to one of the leaders, he tersely answers that Johnson is not crazy. This feverish digging, while dictated no doubt by a very practical mistrust of the Pentagon, seems to have a secondary meaning, too – mythic, as though the city were an allegorical character. Hanoi appears to be telling its people that it is ready to go underground, harrow hell, to rise again like the rice plants from the buried seed. To a Westerner, this sounds fantastic so much so that I hesitate to bring it up; after all, you can tell me, Hanoi's leaders are Marxists, and Marxists do not believe in resurrection stories.

Yet the Vietnamese folk beliefs are highly animistic; they venerate (or did) the souls of their ancestors, resting in the rice fields, and the souls of rocks and trees. Their classic relief sculpture surprises you with delicate, naturalistic representations of plants, birds, animals, and flowers – much more typical of Vietnamese art than grotesque images of gods and the Buddha. The love of Nature is strong in their literature, too, and is found even in the "captured enemy documents" the US is fond of distributing for publication. This helps explain their root-attachment to the fatherland, as every observer has noticed, going deeper than politics, into some sphere of immanence the foreigner is almost embarrassed to name – "spiritual", "religious"? Much is made in the North of the fatherland's sacred, indivisible unity, and, despite or because of a history of partitions like Poland's, the sentiment of being one country seems to be authentic and shared, incidentally, by the South Vietnamese firebrands who would like to "march on Hanoi". As a symbol of that unity, the North has planted the coconut palm; the visitor may be slow to grasp the significance of this. "Coconut trees." "Yes, I see them." "Before, here in the North, we did not have the coconut tree. It is a native of Saigon."

In Hanoi you find cabbages and tomato plants growing in the ornamental garden of a museum, in parks, around an anti-aircraft unit; the anti-aircraft battery has planted a large flower garden as well and it has chickens running around the gun-emplacements. Today the abundant use of camouflage – exuberant sprigs of plants, fronds, branches, leaves of coconut and banana on helmets, anti-aircraft, military vehicles, even tied to the backs of school children – cannot be meant entirely to fool the enemy overhead. For one thing, the foliage on the anti-aircraft artillery does not begin to conceal the guns' muzzles. This camouflage, snatched from Nature, must be partly a ritual decoration, a "palm" or "laurel" of prowess and connected with ancient notions of metamorphosis – pursued by a powerful enemy, you could "survive" in the verdant form of a tree. In Hanoi, the innocent protective mimicry of coconut leaves "disguising" military hardware always made me think of Palm Sunday in a Catholic country and the devout coming out of church with palm leaves or olive branches – a pre-Easter mood. In the country, a column of army trucks and half-tracks proceeding under its thatch of greenery made me feel that Birnam Wood was rolling on to Dunsinane: "Your leavy screens throw down, And show like those you are."

The determination of Hanoi appears at first incredible – legendary and bizarre; also disturbing. We came eventually to the pontoon bridge, floating on bamboo, the replacement, for automobiles, of the Paul Doumer Bridge that still hangs, half bombed, like a groping tentacle, over the Red River. On the bridge, the traffic goes single file, and you wait for the oncoming cars to finish their turn before a policeman gives you the signal to advance. This waiting in line by the river's edge is scary – there has been a lot of bombing in the area, as you can see by looking around – and it is even scarier when you start across the frail, wavy bridge; traffic moves very slowly, with many halts, and if the bombers should come while you are there, suspended over the water, there would be no escape; useless to look for shelters on the insubstantial bridge, obviously, and you could not jump into the dark, quite swift river. You just have to put your mind on something else, make conversation; I always dreaded this crossing, the sense of being imprisoned in a metal box, a helpless, all-but-motionless target, and I had the impression that the Vietnamese did not care for it either; each time, there was a general easing of tension when the bridge was finally negotiated.

In the hotel, to my stupefaction, there was hot water, plenty of it. During nearly a month spent in South Vietnam the year before, I had had *one* hot bath – on the USS *Enterprise*. In my room at the Continental in Saigon, there was only cold water, and when I was once offered a bath in the room of a New York *Times* correspondent, the water ran dark red, too rusty to get into. In theory, they had hot water in the Marine Press Base at Da Nang, but in practice they didn't. Other luxuries I found at the Thong Nhat Hotel were sheets of toilet paper laid out on a box in a fan pattern (keys at the desk were laid out in a fan pattern, too), a thermos of hot water for making tea, a package of tea, a teapot, cups and saucers, candies, cigarettes, and a mosquito net draped over the bed and tucked in; in Saigon, I had been tortured by mosquitoes.

It was obvious that the foreigners at the Thong Nhat lived better than the general population, but this could be said, too, of the foreigners at the Continental, who moreover had to pay for what they got, whereas in Hanoi a guest of a Vietnamese organization was not allowed to pay for anything – I never had to change so much as a dollar bill into dongs. The knowledge of living much better than others (the meals were very good) and at the expense of an impecunious government whose food-production areas were being pounded every day by my government produced a certain amount of uneasiness, which, however, wore off. There was nothing to be done about it anyway, and I soon was able to verify that outside no families were sleeping in the streets, as they had been in Saigon, nobody was begging or in rags, and the people appeared healthy, though tired in some cases, particularly those who were old and had doubtless been hungry a good part of their lives.

On opening the window, I found that there was an extraordinary amount of traffic, extremely noisy traffic, though nobody in Hanoi owns a private car – only bicycles and motor bikes. The honking of horns and screeching of brakes went on all night. To someone who lives in a European city where it is against the law to honk your horn, the constant deafening noise seems very old-fashioned. My ears had forgotten those sounds, as they had forgotten the clanging of streetcars and the crowing of cocks at 4:00 A.M. Hanoi still has both cocks and streetcars, and you can hear the whistle of trains, as well as the more up-to-date noise of MIGs overhead and the almost continuous voice of the loud-speakers, invariably feminine and soothing, sugared, in tone. Unless you know Vietnamese, you cannot guess whether they are announcing an air raid or telling you the planes have left or simply giving a news broadcast or a political diatribe.

There is a good deal in North Vietnam that unexpectedly recalls the past. Waiting to cross the Red River recalled my first trip to Italy, just after World War II, when most of the bridges were down ("Bombed by the Liberators," in Italian, was scrawled all over the devastated cities and towns) and our bus crossed the Po or the Adda on a tremulous pontoon bridge; the loud-speaker outside the hotel window ("Attention, citizens, attention") recalled the loud-speakers in Florence during a spring election campaign (*"Attenzione, cittadini, attenzione"*). Jouncing along a highway deeply pitted by pellets from cluster bombs made me think of my childhood: bumpy trips in northern Minnesota; Grandma in a motoring hat and duster; and how each time we struck a pothole her immense white head, preceded by the hat, would bounce up and hit the car's canvas top. North Vietnam is still pioneer country, where streams have to be forded; the ethnic minorities, Meos, Muongs, and Thais, in the mountains of the wild west, though they do not wear feathers, recall American Indians. The old-fashioned school desks and the geometry lesson on the blackboard in an evacuated school, the kerosene lamps in the villages, the basins of water filled from a well to use to wash up before meals on an open porch, the one- or two-seater toilets with a cow ruminating outside brought back buried fragments of my personal history. I was aware of a psychic upheaval, a sort of identity crisis, as when a bomb lays bare the medieval foundations of a house thought to be modern.

The Vietnam War

JOHN FETTERMAN

P.F.C. Gibson Comes Home

Fetterman's story on the return home of the body of "Little Duck"
Gibson won a Pulitzer Prize for local news reporting.

Louisville *Times*, July 1968

It was late on a Wednesday night and most of the people were
asleep in Hindman, the county seat of Knott County, when the
body of Private First Class James Thurman (Little Duck)
Gibson came home from Vietnam.

It was hot. But as the gray hearse arrived bearing the gray
Army coffin, a summer rain began to fall. The fat raindrops
glistened on the polished hearse and steamed on the street.
Hindman was dark and silent. In the distance down the town's
main street the red sign on the Square Deal Motor Co. flashed
on and off.

Private Gibson's body had been flown from Oakland, California, to Cincinnati and was accompanied by Army Staff Sgt
Raymond A. Ritter, assigned to escort it home. The body was
picked up in Cincinnati by John Everage, a partner in the local
funeral home, and from that point on it was in the care of people
who had known the 24-year-old soldier all his life.

At Hindman, the coffin was lifted out while Sgt Ritter, who
wore a black mourning band on his arm, snapped a salute. One
funeral home employee whispered to another: "It's Little Duck.
They brought him back."

Most of his life he had been called Little Duck – for so long that many people who knew him well had to pause and reflect to recall his full name.

By Thursday morning there were few people who did not know that Little Duck was home – or almost home. During the morning the family came; his older brother, Herschel, whom they call Big Duck; his sister Betty Jo; and his wife Carolyn.

They stood over the glass-shielded body and let their tears fall upon the glass, and people spoke softly in the filling station next door and on the street outside.

The soldier's parents, Mr and Mrs Norman Gibson, waited at home, a neat white house up the hollow which shelters Flax Patch Creek, several miles away. Mrs Gibson had been ill for months, and the family did not let her take the trip to Hindman. Later in the morning, they took Little Duck home.

Sweltering heat choked the hills and valleys as Little Duck was placed back in the hearse and taken home. The cortege had been joined by Maj. Lyle Haldeman, a survival assistance officer, sent, like Sgt Ritter, to assist the family. It was a long, slow trip – over a high ridge to the south, along Irishman Creek and past the small community of Amburgey.

At Amburgey, the people stood in the sun, women wept and men removed their hats as the hearse went past. Mrs Nora Amburgey, the postmistress, lowered the flag of the tiny fourth-class post office to half-mast and said, "We all thought a lot of Little Duck."

At the point where Flax Patch Creek empties into Irishman Creek, the hearse turned, crossed a small wooden bridge and drove the final mile up Flax Patch Creek to the Gibson home. The parents and other relatives waited in a darkened, silent home.

As the coffin was lifted upon the front porch and through the door into the front living room, the silence was broken by cries of grief. The sounds of anguish swelled and rolled along the hollow. Little Duck was home.

All afternoon and all night they came, some walking, some driving up the dusty road in cars and trucks. They brought flowers and food until the living room was filled with floral tributes and the kitchen was crammed with food. The people filled the house and yard. They talked in small groups, and members of the family clasped to each other in grief.

They went, time and time again, to look down into the coffin and weep.

The mother, a sweet-faced mountain woman, her gray hair brushed back and fastened behind her head, forced back the pangs of her illness and moved, as in a trance, among the crowd as she said:

"His will will be done no matter what we say or do."

The father, a tall, tanned man, his eyes wide and red from weeping, said:

"He didn't want to go to the Army, but he knew it was the right thing to do; so he did his best. He gave all he had. I'm as proud of him as I can be. Now they bring him home like this."

Around midnight the rain returned and the mourners gathered in the house, on the porch and backed against the side of the house under the eaves.

The father talked softly of his son.

"I suppose you wonder why we called him Little Duck. Well, when the boys were little they would go over and play in the creek every chance they got. Somebody said they were like ducks.

"Ever since then Herschel was "Big Duck" and James was 'Little Duck'.

"You worked hard all your life to raise your family. I worked in 32-inch seam of coal, on my hands and knees, loading coal to give my family what I could.

'There was never a closer family. Little Duck was born here in this house and never wanted to leave."

Other mourners stepped up to volunteer tributes to Little Duck.

"He never was one to drink and run up and down the road at night."

"He took care of his family. He was a good boy."

Little Duck was a big boy. He was 6 feet 5½ inches tall and weighed 205 pounds. His size led him to the basketball team at Combs High School where he met and courted the girl he married last January.

Little Duck was home recently on furlough. Within a month after he went down Flax Patch Creek to return to the Army, he was back home to be buried. He had been married six months, a soldier for seven.

The Army said he was hit by mortar fragments near Saigon, but there were few details of his death.

The father, there in the stillness of the early morning, was remembering the day his son went back to the Army.

"He had walked around the place, looking at everything. He told me, 'Lord, it's good to be home.'"

"Then he went down the road. He said, 'Daddy, take care of yourself and don' work too hard.'"

"He said, 'I'll be seeing you.' But he can't see me now."

An elderly man, walking with great dignity, approached and said, "Nobody can ever say anything against Little Duck. He was as good a boy as you'll ever see."

Inside the living room, the air heavy with the scent of flowers, Little Duck's mother sat with her son and her grief.

Her hand went out gently, as to comfort a stranger, and she talked as though to herself:

"Why my boy? Why my baby?"

She looked toward the casket, draped in an American flag, and when she turned back she said:

"You'll never know what a flag means until you see one on your own boy."

Then she went back to weep over the casket.

On Friday afternoon Little Duck was taken over to the Providence Regular Baptist Church and placed behind the pulpit. All that night the church lights burned and the people stayed and prayed. The parents spent the night at the church.

"This is his last night," Little Duck's mother explained.

The funeral was at 10 o'clock Saturday morning, and the people began to arrive early. They came from the dozens of hollows and small communities in Letcher, Knot, and Perry counties. Some came back from other states. They filled the pews and then filled the aisle with folding chairs. Those who could not crowd inside gathered outside the door or listened beneath the windows.

The sermon was delivered by the Rev. Archie Everage, pastor at Montgomery Baptist Church, which is on Montgomery Creek near Hindman. On the last Sunday that he was home alive, Little Duck attended services there.

The service began with a solo, "Beneath the Sunset," sung by a young girl with a clear bell-like voice; then there were hymns from the church choir.

Mr Everage, who had been a friend of Little Duck, had difficulty in keeping his voice from breaking as he got into his final tribute. He spoke of the honor Little Duck had brought to his family, his courage and his dedication. He spoke of Little Duck "following the colors of his country". He said Little Duck died "for a cause for which many of our forefathers fought and died". *Rubbish, He died for politicians Ambitions*

The phrase touched off a fresh wail of sobs to fill the church. Many mountain people take great pride in their men who "follow the colors". It is a tradition that goes back to October 1780, when a lightly regarded band of mountaineers handed disciplined British troops a historic defeat at Kings Mountain in South Carolina and turned the tide of the Revolutionary war.

Shortly before Little Duck was hit in Vietnam, he had written two letters intended for his wife. Actually the soldier was writing a part of his own funeral. Mr Everage read from one letter:

"Honey, they put me in a company right down on the Delta. From what everybody says that is a rough place, but I've been praying hard for the Lord to help me and take care of me so really I'm not too scared or worried. I think if He wants it to be my time to go that I'm prepared for it. Honey, you don't know really when you are going to face something like this, but I want you to be a good girl and try to live a good life. For if I had things to do over I would have already been prepared for something like this. I guess you are wondering why I'm telling you this, but you don't know how hard it's been on me in just a short time. But listen here, if anything happens to me, all I want is for you to live right, and then I'll get to see you again."

And from another letter:

"Honey, listen, if anything happens to me I want you to know that I love you very very much and I want you to keep seeing my family the rest of their lives and I want you to know you are a wonderful wife and that I'm very proud of you. If anything happens I want Big Duck and Betty Jo to know I loved them very much. If anything happens also tell them not to worry, that I'm prepared for it."

The service lasted two hours and ended only after scores of people, of all ages, filed past the coffin.

Then they took Little Duck to Resthaven Cemetery up on a hill in Perry County. The Army provided six pallbearers, five of whom had served in Vietnam. There was a seven-man firing squad to fire the traditional three volleys over the grave and bugle to sound taps.

The pallbearers, crisp and polished in summer tans, folded the flag from the coffin and Sgt Ritter handed it to the young widow, who had wept so much, but spoken so little, during the past three days.

Then the soldier's widow knelt beside the casket and said softly, "Oh, Little Duck."

Then they buried Little Duck beneath a bit of the land he died for.

The Vietnam War

SEYMOUR M. HERSH

My Lai: Lieutenant Accused of Murdering 109 Civilians

Hersh's investigation of the My Lai atrocity, and its subsequent cover-up by the US military, won him a Pulitzer Prize. His book *My Lai 4* was published in 1970.

St Louis Dispatch, 13 November 1969

Fort Benning, Ga., Nov. 13 – Lt William L. Calley Jr, 26 years old, is a mild-mannered, boyish-looking Vietnam combat veteran with the nickname "Rusty". The Army is completing an investigation of charges that he deliberately murdered at least 109 Vietnamese civilians in a search-and-destroy mission in March 1968 in a Viet Cong stronghold known as "Pinkville".

Calley has formally been charged with six specifications of mass murder. Each specification cites a number of dead, adding up to the 109 total, and charges that Calley did "with premeditation murder ... Oriental human beings, whose names and sex are unknown, by shooting them with a rifle".

The Army calls it murder; Calley, his counsel and others associated with the incident describe it as a case of carrying out orders.

"Pinkville" has become a widely known code word among the military in a case that many officers and some Congressmen believe will become far more controversial than the recent murder charges against eight Green Berets.

Army investigation teams spent nearly one year studying the incident before filing charges against Calley, a platoon leader of the Eleventh Brigade of the American Division at the time of the killings.

Calley was formally charged on or about Sept. 6, 1969, in the multiple deaths, just a few days before he was due to be released from active service.

Calley has since hired a prominent civilian attorney, former Judge George W. Latimer of the US Court of Military Appeals, and is now awaiting a military determination of whether the evidence justifies a general court-martial. Pentagon officials describe the present stage of the case as the equivalent of a civilian grand jury proceeding.

Calley, meanwhile, is being detained at Fort Benning, where his movements are sharply restricted. Even his exact location on the base is a secret; neither the provost marshal, nor the Army's Criminal Investigation Division knows where he is being held.

The Army has refused to comment on the case, "in order not to prejudice the continuing investigation and rights of the accused". Similarly, Calley – although agreeing to an interview – refused to discuss in detail what happened on March 16, 1968.

However, many other officers and civilian officials, some angered by Calley's action and others angry that charges of murder were filed in the case, talked freely in interviews at Fort Benning and Washington.

These factors are not in dispute:

The Pinkville area, about six miles northeast of Quang Ngai, had been a Viet Cong fortress since the Vietnam war began. In early February 1968, a company of the Eleventh Brigade, as part of Task Force Barker, pushed through the area and was severely shot up.

Calley's platoon suffered casualties. After the Communist Tet offensive in February 1968, a larger assault was mounted, again with high casualties and little success. A third attack was quickly mounted and it was successful.

The Army claimed 128 Viet Cong were killed. Many civilians also were killed in the operation. The area was a free fire zone from which all non-Viet Cong residents had been urged, by leaflet, to flee. Such zones are common throughout Vietnam.

One man who took part in the mission with Calley said that in the earlier two attacks "we were really shot up."

"Every time we got hit it was from the rear," he said. "So the third time in there the order came down to go in and make sure no one was behind.

"We were told to just clear the area. It was a typical combat assault formation. We came in hot, with a cover of artillery in front of us, came down the line and destroyed the village.

"There are always some civilian casualties in a combat operation. He isn't guilty of murder."

The order to clear the area was relayed from the battalion commander to the company commander to Calley, the source said.

Calley's attorney said in an interview: "This is one case that should never have been brought. Whatever killing there was was in a firefight in connection with the operation.

"You can't afford to guess whether a civilian is a Viet Cong or not. Either they shoot you or you shoot them.

"This case is going to be important – to what standard do you hold a combat officer in carrying out a mission?

"There are two instances where murder is acceptable to anybody: where it is excusable and where it is justified; If Calley did shoot anybody because of the tactical situation or while in a firefight, it was either excusable or justifiable."

Adding to the complexity of the case is the fact that investigators from the Army inspector general's office, which conducted the bulk of the investigation, considered filing charges against at least six other men involved in the action March 16.

A Fort Benning infantry officer has found that the facts of the case justify Calley's trial by general court-martial on charges of premeditated murder.

Pentagon officials said that the next steps are for the case to go to Calley's brigade commander and finally to the Fort Benning post commander for findings on whether there should be a court-martial. If they so hold, final charges and specifications will be drawn up and made public at that time, the officials said.

Calley's friends in the officer corps at Fort Benning, many of them West Point graduates, are indignant. However, knowing the high stakes of the case, they express their outrage in private.

"They're using this as a Goddamned example," one officer complained. "He's a good soldier. He followed orders.

"There weren't any friendlies in the village. The orders were to shoot anything that moved."

Another officer said: "It could happen to any of us. He has killed and has seen a lot of killing . . . Killing becomes nothing in Vietnam. He knew that there were civilians there, but he also knew that there were VC among them."

A third officer, also familiar with the case, said: "There's this question – I think anyone who goes to [Viet] Nam asks it. What's a civilian? Someone who works for us at day and puts on Viet Cong pajamas at night?"

There is another side of the Calley case – one that the Army cannot yet disclose. Interviews have brought out the fact that the investigation into the Pinkville affair was initiated six months after the incident, only after some of the men who served under Calley complained.

The Army has photographs purported to be of the incident, although these have not been introduced as evidence in the case, and may not be.

"They simply shot up this village and [Calley] was the leader of it," said one Washington source. "When one guy refused to do it, Calley took the rifle away and did the shooting himself."

Asked about this, Calley refused to comment.

One Pentagon officer discussing the case tapped his knee with his hand and remarked, "Some of those kids he shot were this high. I don't think they were Viet Cong. Do you?"

None of the men interviewed about the incident denied that women and children were shot.

A source of amazement among all those interviewed was that the story had yet to reach the press.

"Pinkville has been a word among GIs for a year," one official said. "I'll never cease to be amazed that it hasn't been written about before."

A high-ranking officer commented that he first heard talk of the Pinkville incident soon after it happened; the officer was on duty in Saigon at the time.

Why did the Army choose to prosecute this case? On what is it basing the charge that Calley acted with premeditation before killing? The court-martial should supply the answers to these questions, but some of the men already have their opinions.

"The Army knew it was going to get clobbered on this at some point," one military source commented. "If they don't prosecute somebody, if this stuff comes out without the Army taking some action, it could be even worse."

Another view that many held was that the top level of the military was concerned about possible war crime tribunals after the Vietnam war.

As for Calley – he is smoking four packs of cigarettes daily and getting out of shape. He is 5-foot-3, slender, with expressionless gray eyes and thinning brown hair. He seems slightly bewildered and hurt by the charges against him. He says he wants nothing more than to be cleared and return to the Army.

"I know this sounds funny," he said in an interview, "but I like the Army . . . and I don't want to do anything to hurt it."

Friends described Calley as a "gung-ho Army, man . . . Army all the way". Ironically, even his stanchest supporters admit, his enthusiasm may be somewhat to blame.

"Maybe he did take some order to clear out the village a little bit too literally," one friend said, "but he's a fine boy."

Calley had been shipped home early from Vietnam, after the Army refused his request to extend his tour of duty. Until the incident at Pinkville, he had received nothing but high ratings from his superior officers. He was scheduled to be awarded the Bronze and Silver Stars for his combat efforts, he said. He has heard nothing about the medals since arriving at Fort Benning.

Calley was born in Miami, Fla, and flunked out of the Palm Beach Junior College before enlisting in the Army. He became a second lieutenant in September 1967, shortly after going to Vietnam. The Army lists his home of record as Waynesville, NC.

An information sheet put out by the public affairs officer of the American Division the day after the March 16 engagement contained this terse mention of the incident: "The swiftness with which the units moved into the area surprised the enemy. After the battle the Eleventh Brigade moved into the village searching each hut and tunnel."

Cambodia

DONALD KIRK

I Watched Them Saw Him Three Days

Political instability in Vietnam spilled over the country's borders into neighbouring Cambodia, where left-wing guerrillas – the Khmer Rouge – under Pol Pot eventually toppled the pro-American government of President Lon Nol.

Chicago *Tribune*, 14 July 1974

Tuol Sampeou, Cambodia – Twenty-five-year-old Sanguon Preap had been serving in the Khmer Rouge for only three months when he witnessed a display of ruthlessness that led him to flee to the sanctuary of this refugee village some eight miles southwest of Phnom Penh.

"I was very frightened when I saw the Khmer Rouge saw off the neck of a civilian with the sharp edge of sugar palm leaves," said Preap, standing amid a cluster of refugees beside a row of flimsy huts.

"They spent three days cutting his head off," said Preap. "They sawed a little one morning, and then in the evening, and finally the following day in the morning and then in the evening, and finally the following day in the morning and night.

"They made the victim stand up while they were cutting in front of hundreds of people living in the Khmer Rouge area. Then they held him up when he could stand no longer."

The episode was not just an isolated case but one of many I heard during visits to refugee camps. Khmer Rouge soldiers also have used the knife-like edges of sugar palm leaves to lop off the heads of Cambodian officers captured while overrunning nearby towns and military installations.

"They want the victims to suffer more and to serve as examples for people," said one informant. "They denounce them as traitors before the crowd."

"I had to join the Khmer Rouge army or they would have killed me," said Preap. "Those who refuse to serve they send to their deaths. They walk thru villages telling the people to follow them, and the people must obey."

Another refugee, who fled here with his wife and nine children from an area some 50 miles to the east, said that he had never personally witnessed any executions.

"They tied up people by putting both hands behind their backs and telling them they were sending them to the high command," said the refugee Lach Pech. "Whenever they did that, then we knew the man would be sent to his death in the forests. It was a secret why they killed people, and nobody dared ask why."

Lach Pech said that in his village Buddhist monks were forced to dig up the roots of large trees – and then throw bodies into the ground where roots had been.

"There is no real security around here," said one village leader. "There are government soldiers somewhere, but there are not enough of them. We worry the enemy will come back again, and we will be in danger. They are only a mile away."

The Vietnam War

PAUL VOGLE

Flight into Hell

Paul Vogle was the United Press International's stringer in Vietnam from 1968 to the fall of Saigon.

UPI, 29 March 1975

Da Nang, March 29 (UPI) – Only the fastest, the strongest, and the meanest of a huge mob got a ride on the last plane from Da Nang Saturday.

People died trying to get aboard and others died when they fell thousands of feet into the sea because even desperation could no longer keep their fingers welded to the undercarriage.

It was a flight into hell, and only a good tough American pilot and a lot of prayers got us back to Tan Son Nhut air base alive – with the Boeing 727 flaps jammed and the wheels fully extended.

It all started simply enough. I asked World Airways Vice-President, Charles Patterson, if he had anything going to Da Nang. He said, "Get on that truck and you've got yourself a ride."

It was a ride I'll never forget.

World Airways President Ed Daly was aboard. He was angry and tired. Daly said he had been up all night arguing with American and Vietnamese officials for permission to fly into besieged Da Nang to get some more refugees out.

Daly finally said to hell with paperwork, clearances, and caution, and we were on our way.

It seemed peaceful enough as we touched down at the airport 370 miles northeast of Saigon.

Over a thousand people had been waiting around a quonset hut several hundred yards away from where we touched down.

Suddenly it was a mob in motion. They roared across the tarmac on motorbikes, jeeps, Lambretta scooters, and on legs speeded by sheer desperation and panic.

Ed Daly and I stood near the bottom of the 727's tail ramp. Daly held out his arms while I shouted in Vietnamese, "One at a time, one at a time. There's room for everybody."

There wasn't room for everybody and everybody knew damn well there wasn't.

Daly and I were knocked aside and backward.

If Ed Daly thought he'd get some women and children out of Da Nang, he was wrong. The plane was jammed in an instant with troops of the 1st Division's meanest unit, the Hac Bao (Black Panthers).

They literally ripped the clothes right off Daly along with some of his skin. I saw one of them kick an old woman in the face to get aboard.

In the movies somebody would have shot the bastard and helped the old lady on the plane. This was no movie. The bastard flew and the old lady was tumbling down the tarmac, her fingers clawing toward a plane that was already rolling.

A British television cameraman who flew up with us made the mistake of getting off the plane when we landed, to shoot the loading.

He could not get back aboard in the pandemonium. In the very best tradition of the business he threw his camera with its precious film into the closing door and stood there and watched the plane take off.

We heard later that an Air America helicopter picked him up and carried him to safety.

As we started rolling, insanity gripped those who had missed the last chance. Government troops opened fire on us. Somebody lobbed a hand grenade towards the wing. The explosion jammed the flaps full open and the undercarriage in full extension.

Communist rockets began exploding at a distance.

Our pilot, Ken Healy, 52, of Oakland, Calif., slammed the

throttles open and lurched into the air from the taxiway. There was no way we could have survived the gunfire and got onto the main runway.

A backup 727 had flown behind us but had been ordered not to land when the panic broke out. He radioed that he could see the legs of people hanging down from the undercarriage of our plane.

UPI photographer Lien Huong, who was in the cockpit of that backup plane, saw at least one person lose his grip on life and plummet into the South China Sea below.

There were 268 or more people jammed into the cabin of the little 727 limping down the coast.

Only two women and one baby among them. The rest were soldiers, toughest of the tough, meanest of the mean. They proved it today. They were out. They said nothing. They didn't talk to each other or us. They looked at the floor.

I saw one of them had a clip of ammunition and asked him to give it to me. He handed it over. As I walked up the aisle with the clip, other soldiers started loading my arms with clips of ammunition, pistols, hand grenades. They didn't need them anymore. In the cockpit we wrapped the weapons and ammo in electrical tape.

There was no more fight left in the Black Panthers this day.

They had gone from humans to animals and now they were vegetables.

We flew down the coast, the backup plane behind us all the way. Healy circled Phan Rang air base 165 miles northeast of Saigon, hoping to put down for an emergency landing.

On the backup plane Lien Huong served as interpreter, radioing Phan Rang control tower that the Boeing had to land there in an emergency. The reply came back that there was no fire-fighting equipment at Phan Rang so Healy aimed the plane for Tan Son Nhut.

I heard Healy on the radio, telling Tan Son Nhut, "I've got control problems." The backup plane was shepherding us in.

Huong, in the cockpit of the backup plane, told me later when we touched down safe the pilot and cabin crew on his plane pulled off their headphones, some of them crossed themselves, and all thanked God for a small miracle delivered this Easter weekend.

When we touched down the troops who had stormed us were offloaded and put under arrest. They deserved it.

A mangled body of one soldier, M16 rifle still strapped to his shoulder, was retrieved from the undercarriage. He got his ride to Saigon, but being dead in Saigon is just the same as being dead in Da Nang.

Over a score of others came out of the baggage compartment, cold but alive. Somebody told me that four others crawled out of the wheel wells alive. One died.

The last plane from Da Nang was one hell of a ride. For me. For Ed Daly. For Ken Healy. For the Black Panthers. And for two women and a baby.

But the face that remains is that of the old woman lying flat on the tarmac seeing hope, seeing life itself, just off the end of her fingertips and rolling the other way.

The Vietnam War

PHILIP CAPUTO

Running Again on the "Street without Joy"

Caputo's first tour of duty in Vietnam was as an officer with the USMC. He joined the staff of the Chicago *Tribune* in 1968, working as their correspondent in Vietnam in the early 1970s.

Chicago *Tribune*, 28 April 1975

Long Binh, South Viet Nam – This is a personal account of what must be one of the great tragedies of modern times.

What is happening here is an exodus of humanity of staggering magnitude, so staggering that no words of mine can capture anything but the smallest fraction of it.

I am writing this in a thatch hut on Highway I, the long Vietnamese road which the French soldiers who fought in Indochina dubbed la rue sans joie, the street without joy.

Today, Sunday, it is living up to that name. A hundred yards away, North Vietnamese mortar shells and rockets are slamming into government positions guarding the bridge over the Dong Hai River, whose brown waters meander with mocking indifference thru green rice fields and murky swamps.

[The Associated Press reported that early Monday Communist sappers had seized a section of Highway I, cutting the refugee flow into the capital from the east.]

I am writing under the pressure of those bursting shells.

Pouring over the river bridge is another kind of stream, a stream of flesh and blood and bone, of exhausted, frightened faces, of crushed hopes and loss. The long, relentless column reaches forward and backward as far as the eye can see, for miles and miles and in places 50 feet across.

These are thousands upon thousands of Vietnamese refugees fleeing the fighting in Trang Bom, east of here, the shellings in Long Thanh, south of here, the attacks near Bien Hoa, north of here. They are jammed on the blacktop in crowds as thick as those pouring out of a football stadium, but this crowd is at least 20 miles long.

They are running from what looks like the Communist drive on Saigon and that's where they're trying to go. Many of them are refugees two and three times over – people who ran from Xuan Loc, from Da Nang and Ham Tan and Qui Nhon.

Now they are running again, but this is their last retreat. This is the end of the road, for them, for South Viet Nam, and for a war that's gone on for over a generation.

They are filing past me on foot, their sandals scraping mournfully against the pavement, their heads hunched down against the driving monsoon rain that lashes them.

They are riding on motor scooters, in cars, in trucks, buses, oxcarts all piled up with crates and suitcases and ragged bundles of clothes. Sometimes the noise of the vehicles is deafening, but not so deafening as to drown out the wind-rushing sound of an incoming rocket that whips over their heads to burst in the paddylands beyond the river.

At other times, all you hear is that solemn, processional shuffling of sandalled feet, bare feet, bloodied feet against the rainslick asphalt. You hear that and the chorusing of crying children.

A three-year-old boy, his face and hands covered with sores and insect bites, a toy-like sun helmet on his toy-like head, toddles thru the crowd, whimpering for his lost parents.

They find him finally and his whimpering stops as they prop him on their motor scooter.

Two enemy mortars have just exploded near the South Vietnamese bunkers and earthworks guarding the bridge. White and gray smoke is billowing upward, dissipating, wafting over the multitudes like some noxious cloud.

Some of the scenes here are almost Goyaesque in their horror. Vietnamese soldiers are picking thru slabs of meat which they will eat for supper. In the middle of the road a few yards away is the lower half of a man's leg swollen and rotting in the rain. The upper half is a mass of rended flesh indistinguishable from the meat the soldiers are preparing to cook.

An old woman with teeth turned blackish-red from chewing betel-nuts screams at a truck that seems to be slowing down to pick her up. She grabs her bundle of clothes, but it is almost as heavy as she is, and it breaks open, and as she tries to gather it up, the truck presses on.

A company of South Vietnamese soldiers and sailors stationed at the naval base on the river stumbles across the paddies into the village where the North Vietnamese mortars are emplaced.

They vanish into the trees. Soon shells are thudding in on top of them. Small arms fire crackles in between the punctuating thumps of the mortars. Then the soldiers come running out, fanning thru the sea of green rice like flushed rabbits.

A heavy shell whines in, explodes on the river bank with an ear-splitting crash.

"Ya, ya, eeyah," a farmer shouts at his herd of water buffalo as they plod across the bridge, fouling up the traffic even more, the great gray beasts tossing their horned heads and bellowing at the sound of man at war.

Mixed into the column are scores of retreating soldiers, some with their weapons, some without, all beaten.

The endless river of people flows on, part of it coming from further east on Highway I, part from Highway 15 to the south, both parts meeting in a sorrowful confluence at this bridge.

A flight of South Vietnamese fighters screams overhead. Within minutes comes the hollow rumbling of bombs. A pillar of smoke, as if rising from an enormous funeral pyre, swirls into the leaden, sagging sky. The planes are strafing Communist tank columns rumbling up Route 15. They are only a few miles away.

A teenage boy, behind the wheel of a rickety truck in which his parents and family sit amidst piles of belongings, looks at me and says:

"We come from Long Thanh. Many shells fall on us last night. Many VC [Viet Cong] in Long Thanh. Much fighting. Many die."

Meanwhile, all up and down the column, South Vietnamese soldiers are firing their rifles into the air in an attempt to stem the tide.

It is futile. The crowd seems to have a momentum all its own, and the sharp cracks of the soldiers' M-16s is not half as frightening as the Communist tanks that growl like armored monsters somewhere behind this procession.

A few have stopped to rest at the entrance to the National Military Cemetery. They flop down in the shadow of a statue of a South Vietnamese soldier.

He is sitting, his jaw slack with exhaustion, his helmet pushed back on his head, his rifle lying across his knees. He is a symbol of the weariness and the pity of war.

At the base of the monument, mingled with refugees, a few living soldiers are sitting in almost the same position.

Like the statue, their pose seems to say that it is over. This is the end of the road, the end of a war. And the nearness of an end is all there is to mitigate the incalculable suffering of the Vietnamese who are making their last march down the street without joy.

Cambodia

SYDNEY H. SCHANBERG

An American Reporter's Brief Brush with Arrest and Death

The Cambodian capital, Phnom Penh, fell to the Khmer Rouge on 17 April 1975. Schanberg served as South-East Asia correspondent for the *New York Times* for the last two years of Cambodia's civil war. His articles about Dith Pran, a Cambodian employed by the *New York Times*, formed the basis for the 1984 film *The Killing Fields*.

New York Times, 9 May 1975

Bangkok, Thailand, May 8 – Some of the foreigners who stayed behind after the American evacuation of Phnom Penh learned quickly and at first hand that the Communist-led forces were not the happy-go-lucky troops we had seen in the initial stage of the Communist take-over.

I had my first experience with the tough Khmer Rouge troops early in the afternoon of the first day of the take-over.

With Dith Pran, a local employee of the *New York Times*, Jon Swain of the *Sunday Times* of London, Alan Rockoff, a freelance American photographer, and our driver, Sarun, we had gone to look at conditions in the largest civilian hospital, Preah Keth Mealea. Doctors and surgeons, out of fear, had failed to come to work and the wounded were bleeding to death in the corridors.

As we emerged from the operating block at 1 p.m. and started driving toward the front gate, we were confronted by a band of heavily armed troops just then coming into the grounds. They put guns to our heads and, shouting angrily, threatened us with execution. They took everything – cameras, radio, money, typewriters, the car – and ordered us into an armored personnel carrier, slamming the hatch and rear door shut. We thought we were finished.

But Mr Dith Pran saved our lives, first by getting into the personnel carrier with us and then by talking soothingly to our captors for two and a half hours and finally convincing them that we were not their enemy but merely foreign newsmen covering their victory.

We are still not clear why they were so angry, but we believe it might have been because they were entering the hospital at that time to remove the patients and were startled to find us, for they wanted no foreign witnesses.

At one point they asked if any of us were Americans, and we said no, speaking French all the time and letting Mr Dith Pran translate into Khmer. But if they had looked into the bags they had confiscated, which they did not, they would have found my passport and Mr Rockoff's.

We spent a very frightened half-hour sweating in the baking personnel carrier, during a journey on which two more prisoners were picked up – Cambodians in civilian clothes who were high military officers and who were, if that is possible, even more frightened than we.

Then followed two hours in the open under guard at the northern edge of town while Mr Dith Pran pulled off his miracle negotiation with our captors as we watched giddy soldiers passing with truckloads of looted cloth, wine, liquor, cigarettes and soft drinks, scattering some of the booty to soldiers along the roadside.

We were finally released at 3:30 p.m., but the two Cambodian military men were held. One was praying softly.

The Falklands/Malvinas War

BRIAN HANRAHAN

Argentine Air Attacks

On Friday, 2 April 1982 the Argentines occupied the Falkland Islands, an archipelago in the South Atlantic which was formally part of the dwindled British Empire but to which Buenos Aires had long claimed sovereignty. The British determined on reoccupation, and within days a Task Force had set sail from British ports for the South Atlantic. The British landings on the Falklands, which came in mid May, were severely harassed by Argentine jets armed with French-built Exocet missiles. Brian Hanrahan was one of the BBC's TV/Radio correspondents accompanying the Task Force.

BBC News, Saturday, 22 May 1982

It was a brilliantly clear dawn. A beautiful day – a clear one. Clear enough to see the troops climbing up the hillside as they secured the beachhead. Clear enough to see the first settlement to fall back under British control. Thirty-one people, six children now back under the British umbrella; their white cottages tucked into the rolling pastures, where the sheep were grazing. But it was clear, too, for the enemy aircraft that came to find the fleet and attack it.

The air attack started an hour after dawn, and has continued right through the day until now. First came the small Pucara bombers' ground attack. Low and surprising. One of them got right into the bay to drop its bombs, but without success. For a few moments the air was full of missiles, as the defending ships fired back. I saw one Pucara making off over a hill with a missile chasing it. The Captain saw a flash in the sky and debris tumbling down. That set the pattern for the rest of the day. Wave after wave of air attacks came against the fleet. First they had to fight or outwit the Harriers which were between them and the islands. Then they had to go through the Task Force frigates and destroyers, which were deployed to put up a missile stream, but still some of the attacking planes got through to where we were anchored.

This morning, for example, two Mirages came sweeping down across the bay. We didn't see them at first. We saw the red wake of the anti-aircraft missiles rushing out to meet them. Then there was a roar of their engines, the explosion of bombs, missiles, everybody firing together. One stray missile went off in the air about 100 yards away. Two bombs exploded harmlessly in the hilltops as the planes curved away, diving back where they'd come from.

But much of the fighting didn't take place in the bay where we were. It was out in the channel outside. We could see the smoke rising over the hills that cut us off. Three of the ships out there were hit by guns or bombs. Two suffered serious damage. But it's not yet clear what the casualties were. The Argentine forces too were suffering losses. The garrison here was cut off. Some we think were killed, the others surrendered. Then we heard of two Mirages which had been shot down. Then another two, a Pucara, a Skyhawk. Another Skyhawk.

As the day went on, more of the attacks came from the Skyhawk fighter-bombers. In one short period ten or a dozen of them dived down on the ships at anchor, producing the same barrage of fire and counterfire. This time there was a new element. The anti-aircraft batteries on the shore joined in. Slowly a defensive screen was being built over the bay, and the worst period of our vulnerability was over. Throughout the day, beneath the air attacks, the helicopters kept on flying. They stayed below radar range. They left the air above clear for the missiles. But they went on, ferrying in men and machinery and all the equipment that the troops need to build a secure beachhead. They also brought in, most urgently of all, the anti-aircraft batteries that are being built on the shores alongside us to secure the beachhead and make it safe for all the troops to move through in their bid to recapture the Falkland Islands.

The Falklands/Malvinas War

ROBERT FOX

The Liberation of Goose Green

At the end of May 1982 British forces broke out of their bridgehead in West Falkland, and achieved one of the most famous victories of the Falklands/Malvinas War, when 2 Para took Goose Green. Robert Fox, already a "wireless" veteran at thirty-seven, was the BBC's Radio correspondent for the Falklands conflict.

BBC Radio News, Sunday, 30 May 1982

At one end of the Goose Green settlement a Union Jack now flies above a school; and at the other end the flag of the Second Battalion, the Parachute Regiment. After a whole day's bitter fighting and a morning's delicate surrender negotiations, the cheer of liberation came in the early afternoon. Women handed round cups of tea in Royal Wedding mugs; children carried round tins of cakes and biscuits to the young Paras, their faces still camouflaged and their eyes bleary with exhaustion.

For nearly a month, the 114 people had been shut into the community hall by the Argentines. Their houses had been raided, with furniture smashed and excrement on the floor. The store had been looted, the Argentine troops were underfed, and in one house used by pilots it seemed the officers were hoarding tinned food. The Argentines committed acts of petty meanness, smashing and stealing radios and shooting up a shepherd from a helicopter as he tended his sheep. Now the prisoners are being made to clear up the mess they made in the settlements.

The surrender came after a fourteen-hour battle the previous day. It began before dawn – a full battalion assault on an enemy twice as numerous as expected, almost 1500 in all and very well dug in. The attack began under naval gunfire, and shells lit the sky as the Paras moved forward. But in the daylight they were on their own, covered only by guns and mortars. The enemy were falling back slowly to prepared positions. At each post their own mortars had been ranged perfectly. Time and again we were pinned down by fire from mortars and anti-aircraft guns. I was with the battalion headquarters, and if we were within ten feet of death from shrapnel and shells once, we were there forty times.

Around mid-morning we were pinned down in a fold in the land by mortar fire when the first prisoners and casualties came in. The prisoners made a pathetic sight, looking for their own dead and preparing them for burial. This was interrupted by an air attack from Pucara aircraft. As they swung across the sky every firearm available opened up to no effect, and the two planes shot down a Scout helicopter just beyond our ridge. In mid-afternoon we were again pinned down by mortar fire among some gorse bushes.

We were told that the commanding officer, Lt-Col. H. Jones, always known as "H", had been shot by machine-gunners as he led an attack against machine-gun nests which had held up the battalion for over half an hour. A generous, extrovert man, he died in the manner in which he led his battalion, in peace and war. Before the operation he confided to me that, while he was eager to get on with the attack, he was worried about achieving one hundred per cent success with such a complex plan of attack. The victory is entirely his. "It was his plan that worked," said the Second-in-Command, Major Chris Keeble. "He was the best, the very best," said Staff Sergeant Collins. In the evening they brought his body down from the hillside, a soldier walking in front, his weapon pointed to the ground. The silhouette of this silent ceremony the most indelible image of the day.

The architect of the surrender was acting CO, Major Keeble. At midday we walked across the Goose Green airfield. My colleague David Norris of the *Daily Mail* and I were asked to be civilian witnesses. Within two hours the senior Argentine officer, Air Vice-Commodore Wilson Doser Pedroza, had agreed surrender terms. He paraded his airmen and gave a political speech. And after singing the national anthem, they threw their guns and helmets to the ground. There were whoops of joy from one group as they threw their weapons down. They were glad to be going home, they said. Senior British officers, watching, were amazed at the numbers, nearly three times the strength of the ground forces they had been led to expect in the area. There were two lessons for the future: first, the tenacity with which the Argentines held well-prepared defensive positions; second, there were rivalries between their services and between conscripts, officers and NCOs.

But the liberation of Goose Green was due above all to the courage of the Second Battalion of the Parachute Regiment. They carried out a type of attack not seen since the last war, and its success was due to the dash and heroism of their commander and of the men who fought and died with him.

On a wintry sunny evening, the men who died freeing Port Darwin and Goose Green were buried together in a mass grave on a bare hillside above the anchorage at San Carlos Water. The funeral lasted a few minutes. As the dead were carried to the grave by company commanders and soldiers of the Second Battalion, Parachute Regiment, there was no oration or firing party over the grave. The battalion padre, the Reverend David Cooper, read the roll of the dead from No. 2 Para, the Army Air Corps and 59 Field Squadron, Royal Engineers. First was the name of the CO, Lieutenant-Colonel H. Jones, who died assaulting a machine-gun post. Then there was the adjutant, Captain David Wood, who died alongside the colonel. Then their fellow officers and men, a helicopter pilot and a sapper. At the end, the RSM threw a handful of earth into the grave and the Marines and Paras saluted in silence. In the bay a frigate quietly trained her guns skyward against a possible air-raid. The Paras are anxious that their dead comrades should not remain in an anonymous mass-grave here at Ajax Bay. "They must be taken back to England." one company commander said. An RSM told me, "The lads want the dead to go home. It's tradition. People will want to visit the graves."

The Falklands/Malvinas War

MAX HASTINGS

Max Hastings Leads the Way: The First Man into Port Stanley

The war between Britain and Argentina for the Falklands/Malvinas ended on 14 June 1982, with the surrender of the Argentine forces under General Menendez. It had been a "good war" for the *Standard*'s astute and athletic Max Hastings, who put the cherry on his reputation by becoming the first Briton to enter Port Stanley, the Falklands' capital.

London *Standard*, 15 June 1982

British forces are in Port Stanley. At 2.45 p.m. British time today [14 June], men of the 2nd Parachute Regiment halted on the outskirts at the end of their magnificent drive on the capital pending negotiations.

There, we sat on the racecourse until, after about twenty minutes I was looking at the road ahead and there seemed to be no movement. I thought, well I'm a civilian so why shouldn't I go and see what's going on because there didn't seem to be much resistance.

So I stripped off all my combat clothes and walked into Stanley in a blue civilian anorak with my hands in the air and my handkerchief in my hand.

The Argentinians made no hostile movement as I went by the apparently undamaged but heavily bunkered Government House.

I sort of grinned at them in the hope that if there were any Argentinian soldiers manning the position they wouldn't shoot at me.

Nobody took any notice so I walked on and after a few minutes I saw a group of people all looking like civilians a hundred yards ahead and I shouted at them.

I shouted: "Are you British?" and they shouted back: "Yes, are you?" I said "Yes."

They were a group of civilians who had just come out of the civil administration building where they had been told that it looked as if there was going to be a ceasefire.

We chatted for a few moments and then I walked up to the building and I talked to the senior Argentinian colonel who was standing on the steps. He didn't show any evident hostility.

They were obviously pretty depressed. They looked like men who had just lost a war but I talked to them for a few moments and I said: "Are you prepared to surrender West Falkland as well as East?"

The colonel said: "Well, maybe, but you must wait until four o'clock when General Menendez meets your general."

I said: "May I go into the town and talk to civilians?" He said: "Yes," so I started to walk down the main street past Falklanders who were all standing outside their houses.

They all shouted and cheered and the first person I ran into was the Catholic priest, Monsignor Daniel Spraggon, who said: "My God, it's marvellous to see you."

That wasn't directed at me personally but it was the first communication he had had with the British forces.

I walked on and there were hundreds, maybe thousands, of Argentinian troops milling around, marching in columns through the streets, some of them clutching very badly wounded men and looking completely like an army in defeat with blankets wrapped around themselves.

There were bits of weapons and equipment all over the place and they were all moving to central collection points before the surrender or ceasefire.

Eventually I reached the famous Falklands hotel, the Upland Goose. We had been dreaming for about three months about walking into the Upland Goose and having a drink, and I walked in and again it was marvellous that they all clapped and cheered.

They offered me gin on the assumption that this is the traditional drink of British journalists, but I asked if they could make it whisky instead and I gratefully raised my glass to them all.

Owner of the Upland Goose, Desmond King said: "We never doubted for a moment that the British would turn up. We have just been waiting for the moment for everybody to come."

The last few days had been the worst, he said, because Argentinian guns had been operating from among the houses of Stanley and they had heard this terrific, continuous battle going on in the hills.

They were afraid that it was going to end up with a house-to-house fight in Stanley itself. The previous night when I had been with the Paras we were getting a lot of shell fire coming in on us and eventually we sorted out the coordinates from which it was firing. Our observation officer tried to call down fire on the enemy batteries and the word came back that you could not fire on them because they are in the middle of Stanley.

So the battalion simply had to take it and suffer some casualties.

Anyway, there we were in the middle of the Upland Goose with about twenty or thirty delighted civilians who said that the Argentinians hadn't done anything appalling. It depends what one means by appalling, but they hadn't shot anybody or hung anybody up by their thumbs or whatever.

They had looted a lot of houses that they had taken over. At times they got very nervous and started pushing people around with submachine guns in their backs and the atmosphere had been pretty unpleasant.

Robin Pitaleyn described how he had been under house arrest in the hotel for six weeks, since he made contact by radio with the *Hermes*. He dismissed criticism of the Falkland Island Company representatives who had sold goods to the occupiers.

"We were all selling stuff," he said. "You had a simple choice – either you sold it or they took it. I rented my house to their air force people. They said – either you take rent or we take the house. What would you have done?"

Adrian Monk described how he had been compulsorily evicted from his own house to make way for Argentinian soldiers who had then totally looted it. There appears to have been widespread looting in all the houses of Stanley to which the Argentinians had access.

The houses on the outskirts of the town in which the Argentinians had been living were an appalling mess full of everything from human excrement all over the place to just property lying all over the place where soldiers had ransacked through it. But they were all alive and they all had plenty of food and plenty to drink and they were all in tremendous spirits.

It wasn't in the least like being abroad. One talks about the Falklanders and yet it was as if one had liberated a hotel in the middle of Surrey or Kent or somewhere.

It was an extraordinary feeling just sitting there with all these girls and cheerful middle-age men and everybody chatting in the way they might chat at a suburban golf club after something like this had happened.

I think everybody did feel a tremendous sense of exhilaration and achievement. I think the Paras through all their tiredness knew they had won a tremendous battle.

It was the Paras' hour and, after their heavy losses at Goose Green and some of the fierce battles they had fought, they had made it all the way to Stanley and they were enjoying every moment of their triumph.

A question that has to be answered is how the Argentinian troops managed to maintain their supplies of food and ammunition.

I think it's one of the most remarkable things. I think intelligence hasn't been one of our strong points throughout the campaign.

Even our commanders and people in London agree that we have misjudged the Argentinians at several critical points in the campaign.

Our soldiers have been saying in the last couple of days how astonished they were when they overran enemy positions. We have been hearing a great deal about how short of food and ammunition they were supposed to be but whatever else they lacked it certainly was not either of those.

They had hundreds of rounds of ammunition, masses of weapons and plenty of food.

The civilians told me they had been running Hercules on to the runway at Port Stanley despite all our efforts with Naval gunnery, with Vulcans, with Harriers up to and including last night and, above all, at the beginning of May they ran a very big container ship called the *Formosa* through the blockade and got her back to Buenos Aires again afterwards. She delivered an enormous consignment of ammunition which really relieved the Argentinians' serious problems on that front for the rest of the campaign.

I think in that sense we have been incredibly lucky. The British forces have been incredibly lucky.

Considering the amount of stuff the Argentinians got in, we have done incredibly well in being able to smash them when they certainly had the ammunition and equipment left to keep fighting for a long time.

So why did they surrender? I think their soldiers had simply decided that they had had enough. Nobody likes being shelled and even well-trained troops find it an ordeal.

Even the Paras freely admit that it's very, very unpleasant being heavily shelled.

The last two nights, the Argentinian positions had been enormously heavily shelled by our guns. They gave them a tremendous pounding and when an Army starts to crumble and collapse it's very, very difficult to stop it.

I think that the Argentinian generals simply had to recognize that their men no longer had the will to carry on the fight.

This story of the fall of Port Stanley begins last night, when men of the Guards and the Gurkhas and the Parachute Regiment launched a major attack supported by an overwhelming British bombardment on the last line of enemy positions on the high ground above the capital.

Three civilians died in British counter-battery fire the night before last, as far as we know the only civilian casualties of the war. Mrs Doreen Burns, Mrs Sue Whitney and 82-year-old Mrs Mary Godwin were all sheltering together in a house hit by a single shell. Altogether only four or five houses in Stanley have been seriously damaged in the battle.

At first light the Paras were preparing to renew their attack in a few hours after seizing all their objectives on Wireless Ridge under fierce shell and mortar fire. Suddenly, word came that enemy troops could be seen fleeing for their lives in all directions around Port Stanley. They had evidently had enough. The decision was taken to press on immediately to complete their collapse.

Spearheaded by a company of the Parachute Regiment commanded by Major Dair Farrar-Hockley, son of the regiment's colonel, British forces began a headlong dash down the rocky hills for the honour of being first into Stanley.

I marched at breakneck speed with Major Farrar-Hockley through the ruins of the former Royal Marine base at Moody Brook, then past the smoking remains of buildings and strongpoints destroyed by our shelling and bombing.

Our route was littered with the debris of the enemy's utter defeat.

We were already past the first houses of the town, indeed up to the War Memorial beside the sea, when the order came through to halt pending negotiations and to fire only in self-defence.

The men, desperately tired after three nights without sleep, exulted like schoolboys in this great moment of victory.

The Parachute Regiment officer with whom I was walking had been delighted with the prospect that his men who had fought so hard all through this campaign were going to be the first British troops into Stanley. But they were heart-broken when, just as we reached the racecourse, the order came to halt.

Major Farrar-Hockley ordered off helmets, on red berets. Some men showed their sadness for those who hadn't made it all the way, who had died even during the last night of bitter fighting.

The Regiment moved on to the racecourse and they tore down the Argentinian flag flying from the flagpole. Afterwards they posed for a group photograph . . . exhausted, unshaven but exhilarated at being alive and having survived a very, very bitter struggle.

After half an hour with the civilians I began to walk back to the British lines. Scores of enemy were still moving through the town, many assisting badly wounded comrades, all looking at the end of their tether.

Damaged enemy helicopters were parked everywhere among the houses and on the racecourse. Argentine officers still looked clean and soldierly, but they made no pretence of having any interest in continuing the struggle.

Each one spoke only of "four o'clock", the magic moment at which General Moore was scheduled to meet General Menendez and the war presumably came to a halt.

Back in the British lines, Union Jacks had been hoisted and Brigadier Julian Thompson and many of his senior officers had hastened to the scene to be on hand for the entry into the capital.

Men asked eagerly about the centre of Stanley as if it was on the other side of the moon.

By tomorrow, I imagine, when everyone has seen what little there is of this little provincial town to be seen, we shall all be asking ourselves why so many brave men had to die because a whimsical dictator, in a land of which we knew so little, determined that his nation had at all costs to possess it.

The Israeli Invasion of Lebanon

ROBERT FISK

Massacre at Chatila Camp

Following the Israeli invasion of South Lebanon in June 1982, PLO (Palestinian Liberation Organization) fighters were evacuated to Syria. Many non-combatant Palestinians, however, remained behind in refugee camps in the Lebanon; in late August control of these camps passed from Israel to the Lebanese Christian militia.

Pity the Nation, 1990.

What we found inside the Palestinian Chatila camp at ten o'clock on the morning of 18 September 1982 did not quite beggar description, although it would have been easier to retell in the cold prose of a medical examination. There had been massacres before in Lebanon, but rarely on this scale and never overlooked by a regular, supposedly disciplined army. In the panic and hatred of battle, tens of thousands had been killed in this country. But these people, hundreds of them, had been shot down unarmed. This was a mass killing, an incident – how easily we used the word "incident" in Lebanon – that was also an atrocity. It went beyond even what the Israelis would have in other circumstances called a *terrorist* atrocity. It was a war crime.

Jenkins and Tveit and I were so overwhelmed by what we found in Chatila that at first we were unable to register our own shock. Bill Foley of AP had come with us. All he could say as he walked round was "Jesus Christ!" over and over again. We might have accepted evidence of a few murders; even dozens of bodies, killed in the heat of combat. But there were women lying in houses with their skirts torn up to their waists and their legs wide apart, children with their throats cut, rows of young men shot in the back after being lined up at an execution wall. There were babies – blackened babies because they had been slaughtered more than twenty-four hours earlier and their small bodies were already in a state of decomposition – tossed into rubbish heaps alongside discarded US army ration tins, Israeli army medical equipment and empty bottles of whisky.

Where were the murderers? Or, to use the Israelis' vocabulary, where were the "terrorists"? When we drove down to Chatila, we had seen the Israelis on the top of the apartments in the Avenue Camille Chamoun but they made no attempt to stop us. In fact, we had first driven to the Bourj al-Barajneh camp because someone told us that there was a massacre there. All we saw was a Lebanese soldier chasing a car thief down a street. It was only when we were driving back past the entrance to Chatila that Jenkins decided to stop the car. "I don't like this," he said. "Where is everyone? What the fuck is that smell?"

Just inside the southern entrance to the camp, there used to be a number of single-storey concrete-walled houses. I had conducted many interviews inside these hovels in the late 1970s. When we walked across the muddy entrance of Chatila, we found that these buildings had all been dynamited to the ground. There were cartridge cases across the main road. I saw several Israeli flare canisters, still attached to their tiny parachutes. Clouds of flies moved across the rubble, raiding parties with a nose for victory.

Down a laneway to our right, no more than fifty yards from the entrance, there lay a pile of corpses. There were more than a dozen of them, young men whose arms and legs had been wrapped around each other in the agony of death. All had been shot at point-blank range through the cheek, the bullet tearing away a line of flesh up to the ear and entering the brain. Some had vivid crimson or black scars down the left side of their throats. One had been castrated, his trousers torn open and a settlement of flies throbbing over his torn intestines.

The eyes of these young men were all open. The youngest was only twelve or thirteen years old. They were dressed in jeans and coloured shirts, the material absurdly tight over their flesh now that their bodies had begun to bloat in the heat. They had not been robbed. On one blackened wrist, a Swiss watch recorded the correct time, the second hand still ticking round uselessly, expending the last energies of its dead owner.

On the other side of the main road, up a track through the debris, we found the bodies of five women and several children. The women were middle-aged and their corpses lay draped over a pile of rubble. One lay on her back, her dress torn open and the head of a little girl emerging from behind her. The girl had short, dark curly hair, her eyes were staring at us and there was a frown on her face. She was dead.

Another child lay on the roadway like a discarded doll, her white dress stained with mud and dust. She could have been no more than three years old. The back of her head had been blown away by a bullet fired into her brain. One of the women also held a tiny baby to her body. The bullet that had passed through her breast had killed the baby too. Someone had slit open the woman's stomach, cutting sideways and then upwards, perhaps trying to kill her unborn child. Her eyes were wide open, her dark face frozen in horror.

Tveit tried to record all this on tape, speaking slowly and unemotionally in Norwegian. "I have come to another body, that of a woman and her baby. They are dead. There are three other women. They are dead . . ." From time to time, he would snap the "pause" button and lean over to be sick, retching over the muck on the road. Foley and Jenkins and I explored one narrow avenue and heard the sound of a tracked vehicle. "They're still here," Jenkins said and looked hard at me. They were still there. The murderers were still there, in the camp. Foley's first concern was that the Christian militiamen might take his film, the only evidence – so far as he knew – of what had happened. He ran off down the laneway.

Jenkins and I had darker fears. If the murderers were still in the camp, it was the witnesses rather than the photographic evidence that they would wish to destroy. We saw a brown metal gate ajar; we pushed it open and ran into the yard, closing it quickly behind us. We heard the vehicle approaching down a neighbouring road, its tracks clanking against pieces of concrete. Jenkins and I looked at each other in fear and then knew that we were not alone. We *felt* the presence of another human. She lay just beside us, a young, pretty woman lying on her back.

She lay there as if she was sunbathing in the heat, and the blood running from her back was still wet. The murderers had just left. She just lay there, feet together, arms outspread, as if she had seen her saviour. Her face was peaceful, eyes closed, a beautiful woman whose head was now granted a strange halo. For a clothes line hung above her and there were children's trousers and some socks pegged to the line. Other clothes lay scattered on the ground. She must have been hanging out her family's clothes when the murderers came. As she fell, the clothes pegs in her hand sprayed over the yard and formed a small wooden circle round her head.

Only the insignificant hole in her breast and the growing stain across the yard told of her death. Even the flies had not yet found her. I thought Jenkins was praying but he was just cursing again and muttering "Dear God" in between the curses. I felt so sorry for this woman. Perhaps it was easier to feel pity for someone so young, so innocent, someone whose body had not yet begun to rot. I kept looking at her face, the neat way she lay beneath the clothes line, almost expecting her to open her eyes.

She must have hidden in her home when she heard the shooting in the camp. She must have escaped the attention of the Israeli-backed gunmen until that very morning. She had walked into her yard, heard no shooting, assumed the trouble was over and gone about her daily chores. She could not have known what had happened. Then the yard door must have opened, as quickly as we had just opened it, and the murderers would have walked in and killed her. Just like that. They had left and we had arrived, perhaps only a minute or two later.

We stayed in the yard for several more minutes. Jenkins and I were very frightened. Like Tveit, who had temporarily disappeared, he was a survivor. I felt safe with Jenkins. The militiamen – the murderers of this girl – had raped and knifed the women in Chatila and shot the men but I rather suspected they would hesitate to kill Jenkins, an American who would try to talk them down. "Let's get out of here," he said, and we left. He peered into the street first, I followed, closing the door very slowly because I did not want to disturb the sleeping, dead woman with her halo of clothes pegs.

Foley was back in the street near the entrance to the camp. The tracked vehicle had gone, although I could still hear it moving on the main road outside, moving up towards the Israelis who were still watching us. Jenkins heard Tveit calling from behind a pile of bodies and I lost sight of him. We kept losing sight of each other behind piles of corpses. At one moment I would be talking to Jenkins, at the next I would turn to find that I was addressing a young man, bent backwards over the pillar of a house, his arms hanging behind his head.

I could hear Jenkins and Tveit perhaps a hundred yards away, on the other side of a high barricade covered with earth and sand that had been newly erected by a bulldozer. It was perhaps twelve feet high and I climbed with difficulty up one side of it, my feet slipping in the muck. Near the top, I lost my balance and for support grabbed a hunk of dark red stone that protruded from the earth. But it was no stone. It was clammy and hot and it stuck to my hand and when I looked down I saw that I was holding a human elbow that protruded, a triangle of flesh and bone, from the earth.

I let go of it in horror, wiping the dead flesh on my trousers, and staggered the last few feet to the top of the barricade. But the smell was appalling and at my feet a face was looking at me with half its mouth missing. A bullet or a knife had torn it away and what was left of the mouth was a nest of flies. I tried not to look at it. I could see, in the distance, Jenkins and Tveit standing by some more corpses in front of a wall but I could not shout to them for help because I knew I would be sick if I opened my mouth.

I walked on the top of the barricade, looking desperately for a place from which to jump all the way to the ground on the other side. But each time I took a step, the earth moved up towards me. The whole embankment of muck shifted and vibrated with my weight in a dreadful, springy way and, when I looked down again, I saw that the sand was only a light covering over more limbs and faces. A large stone turned out to be a stomach. I could see a man's head, a woman's naked breast, the feet of a child. I was walking on dozens of corpses which were moving beneath my feet.

The bodies had been buried by someone in panic. They had been bulldozed to the side of the laneway. Indeed, when I looked up, I could see a bulldozer – its driver's seat empty – standing guiltily just down the road.

I tried hard but vainly not to tread on the faces beneath me. We all of us felt a traditional respect for the dead, even here, now. I kept telling myself that these monstrous cadavers were not enemies, that these dead people would approve of my being here, would want Tveit and Jenkins and me to see all this and that therefore I should not be frightened. But I had never seen so many corpses before.

I jumped to the ground and ran towards Jenkins and Tveit. I think I was whimpering in a silly way because Jenkins looked around, surprised. But the moment I opened my mouth to speak, flies entered it. I spat them out. Tveit was being sick. He had been staring at what might have been sacks in front of a low stone wall. They formed a line, young men and boys, lying prostrate. They had been executed, shot in the back against the wall and they lay, at once pathetic and terrible, where they had fallen.

This wall and its huddle of corpses were reminiscent of something we had all seen before. Only afterwards did we realize how similar it was to those old photographs of executions in occupied Europe during the Second World War. There may have been twelve or twenty bodies there. Some lay beneath others. When I leaned down to look at them closely, I noticed the same dark scar on the left side of their throats. The murderers must have marked their prisoners for execution in this way. Cut a throat with a knife and it meant the man was doomed, a "terrorist" to be executed at once.

As we stood there, we heard a shout in Arabic from across the ruins. "They are coming back," a man was screaming. So we ran in fear towards the road. I think, in retrospect, that it was probably anger that stopped us leaving, for we now waited near the entrance to the camp to glimpse the faces of the men who were responsible for all this. They must have been sent in here with Israeli permission. They must have been armed by the Israelis. Their handiwork had clearly been watched – closely observed – by the Israelis, by those same Israelis who were still watching us through their field-glasses.

Another armoured vehicle could be heard moving behind a wall to the west – perhaps it was Phalangist, perhaps Israeli – but no one appeared. So we walked on. It was always the same.

Inside the ruins of the Chatila hovels, families had retreated to their bedrooms when the militiamen came through the front door and there they lay, slumped over the beds, pushed beneath chairs, hurled over cooking pots. Many of the women here had been raped, their clothes lying across the floor, their naked bodies thrown on top of their husbands or brothers, all now dark with death.

The Gulf War

JOHN SIMPSON

The Bombing of Baghdad

Operation Desert Storm, the Allied attempt to drive Iraq from its illegal occupation of Kuwait, began with an aerial armageddon comprising 110,000 air sorties in two weeks. Targets included the Iraqi capital city of Baghdad, first bombed in the early morning of 17 January 1991. John Simpson, the Foreign Affairs Editor of the BBC, was among the Western journalists in Baghdad when the heavens opened with bombs.

Observer, 20 January 1991

It had taken us much too long to get our gear together. I was angry with myself as we ran across the marble floor of the hotel lobby, scattering the security men and Ministry of Information minders.

A voice wailed after us in the darkness: "But where are you going?" "There's a driver here somewhere," said Anthony Wood, the freelance cameraman we had just hired. When I saw which driver it was, I swore. He was the most cowardly of them all. The calmer, more rational voice of Eamonn Matthews, our producer, cut in: "We'll have to use him. There's no one else." It was true. The other drivers knew there was going to be an attack, and had vanished.

We had no idea where we wanted to go. There was no high ground, to give us a good shot of the city. We argued as the car screeched out of the hotel gate and down into the underpass. "No bridges," I said. "He's heading for 14 July Bridge. If they bomb that we'll never get back."

The driver swerved alarmingly, tyres squealing. At that moment, all round us, the anti-aircraft guns started up. Brilliant red and white tracers arched into the sky, then died and fell away. There was the ugly rumble of bombs. I looked at my watch: 2.37 a.m. The bombing of Baghdad had begun twenty-three minutes earlier than we had been told to expect. For us, those minutes would have made all the difference.

The sweat shone on the driver's face in the light of the flashes. "Where's he going now?" He did a wild U-turn, just as the sirens started their belated wailing. Anthony wrestled with the unaccustomed camera. "I'm getting this," he grunted. The lens was pointing at a ludicrous angle into the sky as another immense burst of fireworks went off beside us. It was hard not to flinch at the noise.

"The bloody idiot – he's heading straight back to the hotel." The driver had had enough. He shot in through the gates and stopped. We had failed ignominiously in our effort to escape the control of the authorities and now we were back.

I had become obsessed with getting out of the Al Rasheed Hotel. It smelled of decay, and it lay between five major targets: the presidential palace, the television station, an airfield, several Ministries. I had no desire to be trapped with 300 people in the underground shelters there, and I wanted to get away from the government watchers. Television requires freedom of action, and yet we were trapped again.

In the darkness of the lobby angry hands grabbed us and pushed us downstairs into the shelter. The smell of frightened people in a confined space was already starting to take over. Anthony held the camera over his head to get past the sobbing women who ran against us in the corridor. Children cried. Then the lights went out, and there was more screaming until the emergency power took over. Most of the Western journalists were hanging round the big shelter. I was surprised to see one of the cameramen there: he had a reputation for courage and independence, but now he was just looking at the waves of frightened people with empty red eyes. Anthony, by contrast was neither worried nor elated. He was mostly worried about getting his equipment together.

Not that it *was* his equipment. Anthony had stepped in to help us because our own cameramen had to leave. It had been a difficult evening. As more and more warnings came in from New York, Paris and London, about the likelihood of an attack, almost every news organization with people in Baghdad was instructing them to leave. The personal warnings President Bush had given to American editors suggested that the coming onslaught would be the worst since the Second World War.

I remembered my grandfather's stories of men going mad under the bombardment at the Somme and Passchendaele. This would be the first high-tech war in history and most newspapers and television companies were reluctant to expose their employees to it. The BBC, too, had ordered us out. Some wanted to; others didn't. In the end it came to a four-three split: Bob Simpson, the radio correspondent and a good friend of mine for years, decided to stay; so did Eamonn Matthews. I was the third. In our cases the BBC, that most civilized of British institutions, came up with a sensible formula: it was instructing us to leave, but promised to take no action against us if we refused.

We still needed a cameraman. But by now there were several people whose colleagues had decided to move out, but who were determined to stay themselves. We found two who were prepared to work with us: Nick Della Casa and Anthony Wood.

There seemed to be no getting out of the shelter. Guards, some of them armed with Kalashnikovs, stood at each of the exits from the basement. They had orders to stop anyone leaving. The main shelter was now almost too full to sit or lie down. Some people seemed cheerful enough, and clapped and sang or watched Iraqi television. Children were crying, and guests and hotel staff were still arriving all the time from the upper floors.

In the general panic, the normal patterns of behaviour were forgotten. A woman in her thirties arrived in a coat and bath towel, and slowly undressed and put on more clothes in front of everyone. Nobody paid her the slightest attention. The heavy metal doors with their rubber linings and the wheel for opening and closing them, as in a submarine, stayed open.

Even so, I felt pretty bad. From time to time it seemed to me that the structure of the hotel swayed a little as if bombs were landing around us. Perhaps it was my imagination. To be stuck here, unable to film anything except a group of anxious people, was the worst thing I could imagine. Anthony and I got through the submarine door and tried to work our way up the staircase that led to the outside world. A guard tried to stop us, but I waited till the next latecomer arrived and forced my way through. Anthony followed.

The upper floors were in darkness. We laboured along the corridor, trying to work out by feel which was our office. Listening at one door, I heard the murmur of voices and we were let in. The sky was lit up by red, yellow and white flashes, and there was no need for us to light torches or candles. Every explosion had us cowering and ducking. I wandered round a little and asked a friendly cameraman to film what's called in the trade "a piece to camera" for me.

Despite the crash and the whine of bombs and artillery outside we whispered to each other. By now, though, I was acclimatizing to the conditions, and sorted out the words in my head before I started. You are not popular with cameramen if you need too many takes under such circumstances.

Back in the corridor there was a flash from a torch, and an Iraqi called out my name. A security man had followed me up from the shelter. In order to protect the others I walked down towards him in the yellow torchlight. I had no idea what I was going to do, but I saw a partly open door to my left and slipped inside. I was lucky. The vivid flashes through the window showed I was in a suite of rooms which someone was using as an office.

I worked my way past the furniture and locked myself in the bedroom at the end. Lying on the floor, I could see the handle turning slowly in the light from the battle outside. When the security man found the door was locked he started banging on it and calling out my name, but these doors were built to withstand rocket attacks; a mere security man had no chance.

Close by, a 2,000-pound penetration bomb landed, but contrary to the gossip in the hotel neither my eyeballs nor the fillings in my teeth came out. I switched on the radio I found by the bed and listened to President Bush explaining what was going on. It was 5.45, and I was soon asleep.

At nine o'clock there was more banging on the door, and more calling of my name. It was Eamonn, who had tracked me down to tell me he had got our satellite telephone to work. Smuggling the equipment through the airport two weeks before had been a smart piece of work, and in a city without power and without communications we now had both a generator and the means to broadcast to the outside world.

Eamonn moved the delicate white parasol of the dish around until it locked on to the satellite. It was hard to think that something so complex could be achieved so easily. We dialled up the BBC and spoke to the pleasant, cool voice of the traffic manager. It was just as if we were somewhere sensible, and not sheltering against a brick wall from the air raids. I gave a brief account to the interviewer at the other end about the damage that the raids had caused in the night: the telecommunications tower damaged, power stations destroyed. I had less idea what was happening on the streets. Directly the broadcast was over, I headed out with Anthony for a drive around. "Not good take picture now, Mr John," said the driver. He was an elderly crook but I had an affection for him all the same. "Got to work, I'm afraid, Ali." He groaned.

It was extraordinary: the city was in the process of being deprived of power and communications, and yet the only sign of damage I could see was a broken window at the Ministry of Trade. The streets were almost empty, except for soldiers trying to hitch a lift. "Going Kuwait, Basra," said Ali. Some were slightly wounded, and their faces seemed completely empty.

Iraqis are normally animated and sociable, but there was no talking now, even in the bigger groups. A woman dragged her child along by its arm. A few old men squatted with a pile of oranges or a few boxes of cigarettes in front of them. An occasional food shop or a tea-house was open; that was all.

"Allah." A white car was following us. "He see you take picture." I told Ali to take a sudden right turn, but he lacked the courage. The security policeman waved us down. "Just looking round," I said, as disarmingly as I could. "He say you come with him." "Maybe," said Anthony.

We got back into the car, and followed the white car for a little. The Al Rasheed Hotel was in the distance. "Go there," I said loudly, and Ali for once obeyed. The policeman waved and shouted, but by now the sirens were wailing again and the Ministry of Defence, on the left bank of the river, went up in a column of brown and grey smoke.

Ali put his foot down, and made it to the hotel. The policeman in his white car arrived thirty seconds after us, but obediently searched for a place in the public car park while the three of us ran into the hotel and lost ourselves in the crowd which filled the lobby.

In a windowless side office, where our minders sat for safety, I spotted a face I knew: Jana Schneider, an American war photographer, completely fearless. Throughout the night she had wandered through Baghdad filming the falling missiles. Near the Sheraton she had watched a "smart" bomb take out a Security Ministry building while leaving the houses on either side of it undamaged.

I found it hard to believe, and yet it tied in with my own observation. This extraordinary precision was something new in warfare. As the day wore on, Baghdad seemed to me to be suffering from an arteriosclerosis – it appeared unchanged, and yet its vital functions were atrophying with each new air raid. It was without water, power and communication.

I was putting together an edited report for our departing colleagues to smuggle out when someone shouted that a cruise missile had just passed the window. Following the line of the main road beside the hotel and travelling from south-west to north-east, it flashed across at 500 miles an hour, making little noise and leaving no exhaust. It was twenty feet long, and was a good hundred yards from our window. It undulated a little as it went, following the contours of the road. It was like the sighting of a UFO.

Another air raid began, and I ran down the darkened corridor to report over our satellite phone. Lacking the navigational sophistication of the cruise missile, I slammed into a heavy mahogany desk where the hotel security staff sometimes stationed themselves. I took the corner in the lower ribs and lay there for a little.

When I reported soon after that I was the only known casualty of the day's attacks among the Al Rasheed's population and explained that I had cracked a couple of ribs, this was taken in London to be a coded message that I had been beaten up.

I was deeply embarrassed. Having long disliked the journalist-as-hero school of reporting, I found myself a mild celebrity for something which emphatically hadn't taken place. An entire country's economic and military power was being dismantled, its people were dying, and I was broadcasting about cracked ribs. Each time they hurt I felt it was a punishment for breaking the basic rule: don't talk about yourself.

In the coffee shop, a neat but exhausted figure was reading from a thick sheaf of papers. Naji Al-Hadithi was a figure of power for the foreign journalists in Baghdad, since he was Director-General of the Information Ministry. Some found him sinister: a *New York Times* reporter took refuge in the US embassy for four nights after talking to him. I thought he was splendid company, a considerable Anglophile, and possessed of an excellent sense of humour. Once I took a colleague of mine to see him, and he asked where we'd been. "We went to Babylon, to see what the whole country will look like in a fortnight's time," I said. For a moment I thought I'd gone much too far, then I saw Al-Hadithi was rocking with silent laughter.

Now he looked close to exhaustion, and his clothes were rumpled. He read out some communiques and a long, scarcely coherent letter from Saddam Hussein to President Bush. Afterwards we talked about the censorship the Ministry planned to impose. In the darkened lobby of the hotel, with the candlelight glinting on glasses and rings and the buttons of jackets, we argued amicably about the new rules. It seemed to me that it was the Security Ministry, not his own, that was insisting on them.

That evening Brent Sadler, the ITN correspondent, rang me. CNN had warned him that our hotel was to be a target that evening. I told the others. No one wanted to go down to the shelter. We decided instead to do what Jana Schneider had done the previous night, and roam the streets.

I cleared out my safety deposit box, and gathered the necessities of my new life: identification in case of arrest, money for bribes, a hairbrush in case I had to appear on television, a notebook and pen. No razor, since without water shaving was impossible. But we were unlucky again. The sirens wailed early, at eight o'clock, and the automatic doors of the hotel were jammed shut. Once again, we were taken down into the shelter.

The whole cast of characters who inhabited our strange new world was there: Sadoun Jenabi, Al-Hadithi's deputy, a large, easy-going man who had spent years in Britain and stayed in the shelter most of the time now; an English peace campaigner, Edward Poore, who was a genuine eccentric, carried a cricket bat everywhere and had knotted a Romanian flag round his neck to remind himself of the time he spent there in the revolution; most of our minders and security men; just about all the journalists; and a large number of the hotel staff and their families, settling down nervously for the night. It was cold. I put a flak-jacket over me for warmth and used my bag as a pillow.

The Gulf War

EDWARD BARNES

When Freedom Came

Barnes was the first newspaper reporter to arrive in Kuwait City after its liberation.

Life, 11 March 1991

Thirty miles from Kuwait City, the roads were empty, eerily empty, and the only evidence that the Iraqis had ever been there was the acrid smoke from hundreds of oil well fires, so thick it stung the eyes and cast a pall of perpetual twilight across the sky. Photographer Tony O'Brien and I had been traveling with a Marine scout battalion, part of the lead element of the allied offensive into Kuwait, and we had broken off to head straight for the capital. We'd be safest driving across the expanse of sand using a string of power lines for bearings, a Marine captain had told us: it was the best way, he'd said, to avoid the minefields spread throughout the desert.

There was nothing to guide us but a compass, the six months of experience we'd had in the desert and the simple urge to avoid danger. We were afraid of the mines. We were afraid of the ambushes. Most of all, we feared we might be coming into the city on the same roads that the Iraqis were using to leave it. We scrambled across the barren sand until we connected with an advance column of Kuwaiti tanks rumbling toward town. If they were safe, so were we.

As the Kuwaiti unit got closer to the city, we passed a row of squat houses set back from the road, and their residents emerged

– tentatively at first, then with growing boldness – to wave Kuwaiti flags. And that's when I realized exactly what was happening: This was the liberation of Kuwait City.

We sped ahead of the Kuwaitis and arrived in a deserted downtown. The sidewalks were empty, as were the roads; there weren't even any cars parked on the streets, since most Kuwaitis had long since hidden them from their occupiers. But as soon as we pulled into the city center, a great flood of Kuwaitis began to appear – by car and foot, laughing, crying, waving flags, hugging one another, hugging us, shooting into the air and honking their horns in manic jubilation.

Some of those early moments seemed like replays of the liberation of Paris. Others had a logic all their own. At the outskirts of town, a white Chevy with two Kuwaitis had pulled alongside us. The driver rolled down his window. "Thank you for coming," he said politely. "Is there anything I can do for you?" Then he handed me a gin and tonic.

Everywhere, the first question we were asked was the same: "American?" Then the Kuwaitis would touch us, to make sure we weren't some surreal apparition brought on by despair. An old man, blinded by cataracts, ran his hands across my face; a woman thrust her baby into my arms. One man – an obvious CNN watcher – grabbed me by the neck and kissed me. "God bless George Bush!" he cried. "God bless James Baker, God bless Dick Cheney, God bless Margaret Tutwiler!"

The displays of affection were almost overwhelming, and at times I felt close to tears. Remaining an observer seemed an impossible task just then, but I did notice one thing in the crush of a thousand people pressing against me as if I were the embodiment of their liberation. Through the thick black clouds, a thin sun began to emerge, and amid the devastation of this nearly ruined country, that in itself seemed a miracle.

Rwanda

MARK FRITZ

No Hard Feelings

Mark Fritz won the 1995 Pulitzer Prize for International Reporting for his stories covering the ethnic conflict between the minority Tutsi tribe and majority Hutus in the African state of Rwanda.

Associated Press, 13 May 1994

Musha, Rwanda (AP) – Juliana Mukankwaya is the mother of six children and the murderer of two, the son and daughter of people she knew since she herself was a child.

Last week, Mukankwaya said, she and other women rounded up the children of fellow villagers they perceived as enemies. With gruesome resolve, she said, they bludgeoned the stunned youngsters to death with large sticks.

"They didn't cry because they knew us," said the woman. "They just made big eyes. We killed too many to count."

Wearing a black shawl and a blank expression, the slightly built 35 year old said she was doing the children a favor, since they were now orphans who faced a hard life. Their fathers had been butchered with machetes and their mothers had been taken away to be raped and killed, she said.

Mukankwaya is a member of the Interahamwe, the name for the innumerable Hutu tribal militias that have been blamed for slaughtering an estimated 100,000 to 200,000 people since April 6, when a mysterious plane crash killed the Hutu presidents of Rwanda and neighboring Burundi.

Most of the victims have been members of the minority Tutsi tribe and Hutus perceived as opponents of the government.

Mukankwaya was among 30 peasants from around Kigali, the capital, rounded up in recent days by the Rwandan Patriotic Front, the Tutsi-dominated rebel army that has captured large chunks of the country since the carnage began.

The people are being held in a former village community center at a small rebel base in Musha, 20 miles northeast of Kigali, the site of fierce artillery battles between the rebels and the government army backed by the Hutu militias.

The rebel commander of this strategic outpost north of Kigali agreed to let The Associated Press interview the militia members. All appeared healthy and there was no evidence of mistreatment.

Lt. Vincent Anyakarundi, a rebel officer, said the captives were being "re-educated" rather than punished because they were exhorted and coerced into killing their neighbors. The instigators, he said, were the government, local officials and army soldiers, who the prisoners said supplied them with weapons ranging from clubs to grenades.

"They are peasants" he said. "They are just puppets of the government."

In areas where rebels have seized control, they have appointed political officers to urge people not to listen to exhortations of violence against Tutsis or Hutu foes of the government. The "re-educators" have been preaching national unity and the official party line is no reprisals, no revenge and no punishment.

"People who would carry out such massacres, especially against children, are less than animals," said Tito Rutaremara, 49, a former party coordinator and leading political influence in the rebel movement. "You have to teach people to forgive and forget. It's like the Nazis. Most people were behind the Nazis, but you can't punish all the people.'"

Although individual acts of revenge likely have taken place, there have been no independently confirmed instances of mass reprisals.

In Musha, captives gave detailed accounts of the horrors they helped to carry out in their villages, when one part of the community suddenly rose up and destroyed another part.

Virtually all of the prisoners recounted their horrific deeds in dull, emotionless voices, their faces a collection of impassive masks.

Mukankwaya blithely mentioned the names of the parents of the two children she killed during the killing spree that she said left hundreds dead in her village of Nyatovu, just north of Kigali.

Potato and sorghum farmer Alfred Kirukura, 29, said he joined in the murderous orgy in his village of Muhazi, 30 miles north of Kigali, on May 9. He said he took a machete to three childhood pals – one a Tutsi and the others Hutus branded by the locals as anti-government agitators.

As he killed them, "They said, 'We are friends! We shared the same classroom!' " he said.

Maria-Devota Mukazitoni, 24, said she didn't kill anybody in her village of Rutonde, just north of Kigali, but organized the looting of homes after hundreds of people in her town were massacred.

Sixteen-year-old Kitazigurwa – who said he had no first name – said his job was to spy on people saying bad things about the government. People he named were killed.

Joseph Rukwavu, 74, said he was too old to kill anybody but acted as the key authority in his village of Mwuma on people who claimed to be Hutu but whose parents or grandparents were, in fact, Tutsi.

"Two hundred were killed in my sector, even my wife, because she would not join Interahamwe," he said in a dull monotone, his face unmoving even as he mentioned his wife's death.

"The militia gathered everybody up near a big hole," he said. "They were weeping, even the men. Even the week before we killed them they were weeping in fear."

He said the army supplied the villagers with the necessary killing tools and oversaw the slaughter.

"They [the victims] said, 'Oh, we are the same people, we are your neighbors. Instead of hiding us you are killing us.' "

Boniface Gasana, 52, said he invited 15 people on the local hit list into his home on the pretense of hiding them, then tipped the village killers of their whereabouts when the massacre began. A woman near him shouted that he also took part.

Even as they spoke, the evening air brought the stench of rotting corpses from the gentle hills around Musha, a common odor throughout the country.

At Kiramuruz, 60 miles northeast of Kigali, 20 bodies lay in a neat row in the woods just outside the seemingly sedate and bustling village.

Resident Vitali Rudasingwa said the people were killed by Hutu militias two weeks ago, even though rebels were in control of the town.

"These militias are still killing people," he said. "But now they are hiding in the corners."

The Bosnian War

DAVID ROHDE

How a Serb Massacre Was Exposed

In 1991, Bosnia and Herzegovina declared independence from the former Socialist Federal Republic of Yugoslavia, which triggered an ugly and complicated civil war between Bosnia's Muslims, Orthodox Serbs and Catholic Croats. Ethnic cleansing and systematic rape became the hallmarks of the war; the genocide of Bosnian Muslims at Srebrenica had been called the worst crime on European soil since World War II. David Rohde won the Pulitzer Prize for his exposure of the massacre.

Christian Science Monitor, 25 August 1995

Nearing the Serb-held village of Nova Kasaba in Bosnia, I stared at a blurry, faxed copy of a US spy satellite photo. Were there really mass graves in the fields near this road, as US officials alleged from the photo?

Another photo, taken earlier, reportedly showed a soccer field half mile away where Muslim prisoners had been held, just before the alleged graves showed up in the later photos.

I had reached this spot somewhat by happenstance. I was allowed to enter Bosnian Serb territory, but only to travel to Pale and Banja Luka to cover Serbian refugees who had fled Croatia.

Because Serb officials somehow failed to provide me with a military escort and gave me wrong directions, I ended up on the road to the towns of Nova Kasaba and Bratunac. Suddenly, I realized I was near the area shown in the photos.

The soccer field, now filled with grazing cows and horses, rolled by on my right. Bosnian Serb soldiers at a military command post eyed my car warily. I turned back and parked my car on a dirt road where it could not be seen. I left my Serb driver and interpreter in the car.

But something seemed wrong. The Jadran River snaked through the valley of fields and bombed-out houses where the alleged mass graves should be.

But the photo showed no river. Convinced I was in the wrong place, I walked toward the soccer field. As cars passed by, I spotted a 10-foot-by-20-foot hole just off the road. It was empty, but a piece of paper filled with scribbled Muslim names lay in the grass nearby.

A series of Muslim names, the date of March 15, 1995, and the name "Potocari" – a village located inside Srebrenica – were legible. I put it in my pocket.

Cars and trucks, some carrying soldiers, whizzed by as I walked the half mile to the soccer field. Three villagers shepherding cows were greeted with hellos and good mornings. They looked at me strangely, but moved on. In the soft early morning light, surrounded by peaceful green fields and wildflowers, massacres seemed impossible

The soccer field, where two survivors of the alleged massacre say that Bosnian Serb military commander Ratko Mladic gave a speech promising the prisoners they would not be harmed, contained nothing but grazing cows and horses. I spent a half hour crisscrossing the field, but found only one pair of abandoned sneakers.

The Search

Discouraged and nervous, I headed back toward the car.

The number of villagers on the road was slowly increasing. I saw faint truck tracks heading through a field toward the river, but three to four villagers were walking in the area. A truck pulled up and stopped directly in front of me. The door opened, and an elderly couple, to my relief, got out. We greeted each other, and I moved on.

Seeing another set of faint truck tracks, I followed them. They dead-ended at the river, and appeared to be used by a truck harvesting corn from the surrounding fields. As I headed back to the road, a half-dozen Bosnian Serb soldiers riding in a horse-drawn cart passed by. They stared intently at me and started speaking to each other.

I turned my back and pretended to go to the bathroom. Slowly, the sound of the horse's hoofs disappeared into the distance.

Ignoring Land Mines

I walked back to where I had found the paper and noticed another faint set of truck tracks leading toward the river. Ignoring the possibility of land mines, I followed the tracks down a slight slope to the river.

A large empty green ammunition box, which appeared relatively new, sat about 50 feet off the road, and a second empty box was found later nearer the road. Closer to the river, a 200 foot-by-200 foot area recently had been dug up. A smooth, earthen ramp leading into the water had recently been bulldozed. Another earthen ramp and fresh truck tracks led up the opposite bank.

The graves must be on the other side of the river, I thought. But the 100-foot-wide river appeared too deep to wade through. I turned back and noticed some papers in the grass.

It was a primary school diploma that had been awarded to a Muslim boy in a village near Srebrenica in 1982. And photos, rendered unrecognizable by rain, were also scattered in the grass. Muslim names were written on the back.

I stuck the diploma in my pocket and crisscrossed the area of fresh dirt. I saw nothing but grass that had begun to spring from some parts of the rich brown soil. A shot rang out from a nearby hill, and I froze. I waited, heard nothing more, then hurried back up to the main road.

Convinced the mass graves were on the other side of the river, I walked away from the center of the village hoping to find a bridge. Traffic had increased, and some men cut hay on a hillside.

Piles of Fresh Dirt

About a mile up the road, I crossed over a bridge and followed a dirt track back toward the earthen truck crossing. About a mile farther, two 25-foot-high piles of fresh dirt had been dumped near a stream.

The dirt track narrowed, and I crossed into a field. Shots rang out again from a nearby hill and whizzed overhead. I froze. Crouching in the wide open field, I decided to walk slowly. If I ran, I could be mistaken for one of the hundreds of Muslim men from Srebrenica that Bosnian Serb soldiers said were still hiding in the area. The Muslims were being shot on sight, they said.

As I neared the truck crossing, despair began to set in. I saw no indication of digging in any of the fields; only a relatively new pitch fork lay in my path.

More shots. The sound of a truck passing and men shouting came from the road. A machine gun fired, but this time farther away. Another burst. I realized a group of Bosnian Serb soldiers were driving by celebrating by shooting their guns in the air.

I crossed another field. Nothing. I reached the truck crossing. Nothing. I looked through two abandoned houses. Nothing. Truck tracks crossed the fields, but I thought it was probably hay harvesters. I again looked at the blurry fax of the satellite photo. Again, no river.

Dejected and nervous, I turned back, amazed and embarrassed that I was unable to find the alleged graves. I had ventured into the surrounding fields and spent two hours in the area, something I swore I would not do.

I started back across the field. Three to four shots rang out from hills to my left. Two shots were fired back from my right. I panicked and crouched. Move or stay still. Run or walk. I waited. Silence.

Pitchfork Gone

Slowly, I rose and walked across the open field. The right side of my face tingled. No shots. Nothing. But as I retraced my steps, the pitchfork was gone.

I reached the dirt path and saw what looked like some clothes in the distance. The clothes, an empty cloth bag, some papers, a bullet, and Muslim prayer beads lay scattered across the grass. Dozens of the papers had "Srebrenica" stamped on them. I grabbed the prayer beads, bullet, and papers and headed back to the car. Along the path I briefly saw the silhouette of a man on a nearby footpath. No shots rang out.

Bones Discovered

Back at the car, I headed down the steep embankment to check the small field next to the river where earlier I had spotted an area of fresh digging. I finally realized that if the satellite photo only covered a few hundred square yards, then it was possible the river was just outside the frame of the picture.

I walked toward the dirt. To my left, something white jutted from a 20 foot by 20 foot plot of freshly dug earth. Two long, thin bones, one the size and shape of a human femur, the other of a human tibia, stared up at me.

Pictures from friends' medical books and X-rays of my own once-broken femur raced through my mind. I later visited the Belgrade University veterinarian school, staring at the femurs and tibias of cows, horses, pigs, bears, dogs, deer, and other animals. What I saw was too long, too thin for an animal. Traces of blue cloth surrounded the femur as it entered the ground.

Fresh Dig

I turned and crisscrossed the larger area of fresh digging and found nothing. A car passed by. I again stared at the bone. Animals and insects appeared to have eaten away all the flesh. When I heard no cars, I scrambled up the embankment.

With one last field to check, I walked nervously down the main road. A truck rounded the corner. A dozen Bosnian Serb soldiers, armed with assault rifles, stood in the back. An area of fresh digging was clearly visible a few hundred yards to my right. The truck sped toward me.

Soldiers Watch

I waved. The soldiers stared. The truck slowed, and I stopped breathing. After what seemed an eternity, the driver – apparently slowing for the turn in the road – hit the accelerator and sped off.

I checked the last field, looked at the bones one last time, picked up some shell casings from the side of the road, and got in the car.

As I sped north toward the border, despair washed over me.

He must have been tall, I thought, and he must have died horribly.

It was a diploma awarded to a Muslim boy in a village near Srebrenica. And photos, with Muslim names on the backs, were scattered in the grass.

The Taliban Insurrection

JOHN F. BURNS

An Afghan Village, Destroyed at the Hands of Men Who Vowed Peace

John F. Burns won the 1997 Pulitzer Prize for his dispatches recounting the fundamentalist Taliban insurrection in Afghanistan.

New York Times, 27 October 1997

Sar Cheshma, Afghanistan – In a country where at least 10,000 villages have been bombed, shelled and burned into rubble, the razing of one more hamlet can pass almost unnoticed. For hundreds of thousands of Afghan families who have lost their homes, the anonymity of the loss only adds to the pain.

So when a battered Kabul taxi arrived here Thursday morning, smoke still rising and the smell of torched ruins heavy in the air, villagers clamored to tell outsiders how Sar Cheshma had died.

Hastening down narrow lanes between fire-blackened houses, the handful of people remaining in the village abandoned for a moment their rush to board trucks waiting to carry them away as refugees.

The villagers' story has been a familiar one in the 18 years that Afghanistan has been at war. The twist this time was that the men who destroyed Sar Cheshma were the turbaned warriors of the Taliban, the ultra-conservative Muslims who have imposed a medieval social order across much of Afghanistan.

Two years ago, the Taliban sprang from religious schools with a promise to suppress the carnage that has killed an estimated 1.5 million Afghans and driven millions of others from their homes.

The villagers of Sar Cheshma say 30 Taliban fighters swept in at dawn on Tuesday, then spent several hours pouring canisters of gasoline into the 120 courtyard houses and setting them on fire.

Sar Cheshma lies barely five miles from the northern outskirts of Kabul, the capital, where the Taliban forces are fighting a village-by-village battle with the forces of Ahmad Shah Massoud, a less conservative Muslim leader whose troops used Sar Cheshma briefly on Monday as a base to fire on the Taliban.

A young mother and her three sons were killed by a Taliban rocket fired when the Massound forces were in the village.

There were no further deaths in the torching that nearly obliterated the village. But in one mud-walled courtyard after another, where hundreds of people lived, little remains but buckled bed frames, melted kitchen utensils and charred piles of grain.

"Are we not humans?" sobbed a 45-year-old woman named Narwaz, rushing forward with others to greet visitors who had slipped past Taliban checkpoints posted to keep outsiders away.

Beside her, a villager named Khairuddin, 55, waved a bloodied burqa, the head-to-toe shroud that the Taliban force all women to wear outside their homes. The garment was all that remained of his daughter, the woman killed with her sons in the Taliban rocket attack.

In a home up one of the village's dusty pathways, another man, Najmuddin, 30, broke away from sifting through his blackened grain supply, hoping to find enough uncharred bits to carry away.

Suddenly, the grain forgotten, his face contorted, he rushed to fetch a metal bowl piled high with ashes that had been balanced on a section of broken wall. It was all that remained of a copy of the Koran that he said had been in his family for generations.

"Tyrants! Tyrants!" he shouted, referring to the Taliban. "This is the book of God. Kill us if you must, but don't burn our holy book!"

Their attention attracted by his cries, several neighbors rushed forward, one with a large metal plate sitting among the utensils that Najmuddin had saved from the fire. Reverentially, Najmuddin placed the bowl with the ashes onto the plate and carried it away.

"We honor these ashes," he said, weeping. "The Koran is the book of God."

The shock of what happened here appeared to be all the greater among the villagers because the perpetrators were the Taliban.

When they emerged as a fighting force in 1994, the Taliban presented themselves as the harbingers of a new Afghanistan, modeled on the teachings of the Koran and inspired by a burning zeal to reunify the country.

From their original base in the southern city of Kandahar, they swept east and west, suppressing local militias that had reduced much of the country to anarchy. The Muslim clerics who led the Taliban promised that their forces would set new standards of decency in the fighting.

Taliban units appear to have avoided raping and pillaging in the manner of most of the other Afghan forces that have fought in the civil war. But they have become widely hated for the draconian social order laid down by the Taliban leaders, which bans women from working outside the home and girls from going to school, requires men to grow beards and forbids children to fly kites or play soccer.

Since Kabul fell to the Taliban four weeks ago, there has been a series of uprisings against them in towns and villages north of the capital. Now the Taliban have gone a step further, using tactics indistinguishable from those of other forces that have contributed to the country's destruction.

Today, two days after the attack on Sar Cheshma, Taliban jets bombed Kalakan, a village under the control of the Massoud forces about 10 miles further north.

According to an account by a reporter for the BBC who visited the village, the bombing killed 20 civilians.

Scene of Fighting Against Russians

In the case of Sar Cheshma, the Taliban attack was the latest in a series of disasters. The residents have repeatedly found themselves in the middle of the fighting because of the village's strategic position, hard up against the Ghoza mountain range, which runs like a shield across the northwestern flank of Kabul.

In the decade that Soviet forces were here, Sar Cheshma became a stronghold for the Muslim guerrillas who ultimately drove out the Soviet troops.

Soviet bombers pounded the village more than once, leaving jagged ruins where mudwalled homes once stood and forcing many villagers to flee to Pakistan and Iran as refugees. Some returned after the Russians left, but barely a third of the village's 300 homes were occupied this week.

In the atmosphere of panic that gripped Sar Cheshma Thursday, many villagers said the Taliban were worse than the Russians.

"We killed more than 40 Russian soldiers in this village, but they never burned our houses," said Nizamuddin, 35, who like most others here had supported his family by raising livestock and working a small plot of land.

Again and again the villagers voiced special loathing for the Taliban because of the religious movement's claim to be the true upholders of the Koran.

"Didn't they do a wonderful job here, these Muslims?" said Nizamuddin, leading the visitors on a house-by-house tour. "Wasn't this burning of our village a true act of faith? We should applaud them – they are surely the best Muslims in the world."

If razing the village showed how none of the armies fighting for control of Afghanistan shows much mercy for civilians, it also demonstrated that the war has gone beyond a competition between faiths and ideologies and become little more than an ethnic struggle.

One reason the Taliban have been driven back so quickly from the northward advances they made after overrunning Kabul is that many villages dotting the dusty plain between Kabul and the Hindu Kush mountains 60 miles to the north are inhabited by ethnic Tajiks, the second-largest population group in Afghanistan.

All but a tiny minority of Taliban fighters are from the Pathan ethnic group, which is the largest in Afghanistan, accounting for about half the country's 16 million people.

As a Tajik village, Sar Cheshma was a natural attraction for Massoud's forces, and a natural target for Taliban suspicion. The villagers say Taliban fighters arrived last weekend, summoned them and ordered them to surrender all of their weapons. This done, the Taliban departed with a warning that any attempt by Massoud forces to enter the village should be reported immediately to a nearby Taliban post.

"We gave them our Kalashnikovs, and they said they would protect us," said the villager named Khairuddin.

On Monday, the villagers said, they awoke to find that a group of Massoud fighters under the command of a Muslim cleric from the village, Mullah Taj Mohammed, had slipped into Sar Cheshma overnight.

The Massoud fighters ordered the villagers to stay in their homes, making any warning to the Taliban impossible, the villagers said. A brief battle followed, they said, in which Khairuddin's family members were killed, then the Massoud fighters slipped away to the mountains, leaving the villagers to face the Taliban's wrath at first light on Tuesday.

For most of the villagers, the immediate future appears to lie in joining hundreds of thousands of refugees in Kabul, many of them so destitute that they wander the streets begging.

But one Sar Cheshma resident said she was finished with fleeing. Sajida, 40, a widow, clutched her son, Abdullah, 12, and said she would stay amid the ruins of her home.

Six years ago, her husband, an officer in the Communist army that disintegrated in 1992, was killed by a guerrilla rocket in Kabul. "I left Kabul to escape from the fighting," she said, "but the fighting has followed me wherever I have gone. Now, if I must, I will stay and die here."

The Kosovo Crisis

MATTHEW MCALLESTER

Crisis in Yugoslavia: Eyewitness to the Flames

As part of the crack-up of the former Socialist Federal Republic of Yugoslavia, fierce fighting broke out in March 1998
between separatist Albanians and Serbs in the province of
Kosovo. A truce brokered by the United Nations failed as units
of the Yugoslav army, together with Serbian paramilitaries,
began an offensive against the Kosovo Liberation Army in
spring 1999, causing tens of thousands of ethnic Albanians to
flee the region.

Newsday, 2 February 1999

Mountains of the Damned, Kosovo – Gray smoke billowed
from the charred rafters of the house in Jablanica. From behind
the blazing home appeared a small red car. Apparently having
finished their job, two Serbian paramilitaries drove away.

It was late Wednesday afternoon and around the village
nothing else moved except the narrow river running alongside
the road, dozens of stray cows grazing in the flat fields and the
smoke that floated over the village. Jablanica, a village of
roughly 1,500 residents, was deserted except for the paramilitaries carrying rifles across their chests and wearing telltale
dark uniforms as they moved through the abandoned village to
their base.

Fifteen minutes later they re-emerged from that building and drove to another house in the village. Soon white smoke was pouring from its windows.

Crossing the brutally rugged Prokletijes, or "Mountains of the Damned", which border Kosovo on the west, provided a view last week into the hell that now is Kosovo. It was the first independent eyewitness corroboration of accounts of the torchings in western Kosovo given by refugees fleeing into Montenegro and Albania in the past five weeks.

At times more than 20 separate fires could be seen blazing across the western Kosovo plain, a fertile stretch of land that is home to farms, a luxury spa resort, a tree nursery and the numerous villages that seem to have been prosperous and well tended but are now deserted. On both Tuesday and Wednesday, new fires appeared with greater frequency toward the evening, the orange blaze of the initial flames turning to thick black and gray plumes of smoke that rolled silently into the sky above the red-tiled roofs of the villages.

Living in a kind of purgatory in a tent city in the mountains just above Jablanica, amid isolated shepherds' huts high in the snow are those few ethnic Albanian Kosovars who are too old, too sick, or too defiant to leave.

"They got what they wanted, they got our houses and they burnt our houses," said Emrush Zekaj, a former resident of Jablanica and one of the roughly 50 people who remain in the tent city. Other members of his family, including his wife, live in one of the huts.

Once in the past two weeks he visited his still-standing house, crawling across fields at night and then creeping through the village. "If they burn what I have made here, I'll go up the mountain and dig out a cave. I am 52 years old and I have lived here all those years. I may have left my home but I'll never leave my land. Never."

Much of that land, however, is burning. Pec, the first major town in Kosovo to be ethnically cleansed when the NATO bombings began, continued to burn last week, a full five weeks after refugees reported the attack on the city had begun. Several miles south of Jablanica, Pec was too far away to confirm whether it has been almost completely burned out as many refugees have said, but smoke from the fires hung over the city for two days without a break and fresh flames glowed Wednesday night.

The last remaining residents of the region are defiant and sickly.

In the tent city nestled in the mountains, Sali Demaj lives under a roof of plastic sheeting. He is 75, has no teeth and wanders around near his tent in slippers. His family all fled Jablanica when the shelling started. He said he is staying partly because he has "nowhere else to go" and partly because "I was born in Jablanica and I don't want to leave." But although none of the people looking after him said so, it was obvious that the old man could never make it up the precipice that surrounds him.

There are people in worse condition than Demaj.

His legs outlined under his knit pants like raw bones, Selman Sabani, 82, lay motionless against a tractor. His skin was tight against his skull, but hung like worn leather from his arms.

Nearby, Ahmet Smatij, 83, bent over and, helped by his granddaughter, slowly walked over to a bench. Once a political prisoner under Tito's Communist regime of Yugoslavia, he spent several years in the infamously brutal Goli Otok prison. "I was in Goli Otok," he said slowly, "and this is worse than that."

Further down the valley, Rabe Hasanaj burst into tears as soon as she started talking about her husband, Zek, 85, who lay inside one of the only huts in the valley. She had no medication for her husband she said. Inside, Zek lay on a mattress and looked close to death.

The ethnic Albanians live off dwindling food supplies and often sleep seven to a tiny hut or tent.

"If this lasts any longer there will be no need for anyone to kill them," said Besnik Ibraj, 22, a medical student from nearby Novo Selo, who carries a handgun but no stethoscope. "They'll be dead anyway."

From a hill above the misery of the tent city, those villagers strong enough to make the climb and brave enough to risk the Serb snipers that keep their binoculars pinned on the mountains, can look down on their abandoned homes.

Jeton Zekaj, Emrush's son, gazed down at Jablanica and pointed out his house. It sits next to the village mosque. He has visited the house several times, always at night, always watching the village for two hours beforehand to make sure there are no paramilitaries there.

"I went last night to get some flour we have stored there," he said on Wednesday morning. He held a large plastic bottle of milk which he had fetched from his father, who milks a cow every day. Jeton, 30, and his wife Merita, 18, are living in a hut above the snowline with his mother and other elderly relatives. He makes the journey down the steep hillside at least once a day to collect the milk and visit his stubborn father. "All the food in the refrigerator is rotten now," he said.

Jeton and Emrush seem to make their desperately dangerous nighttime visits to the house in Jablanica simply because it is their home as much as from a need to bring back the last stores of food. On his trip back, Emrush spent his time creeping around the house fixing the doors that the Serb paramilitaries had broken. "I was there an hour, or an hour and a half," he said. "I tried to use wire to fix the doors."

Both men know that being caught would mean certain death. Jablanica and its surrounding villages, where they lived, loved and worked in freedom, are now firmly Serb-controlled territory.

With no wind blowing across the area, the smoke hung in flat opaque clouds over large parts of the Dugadjin plain, as this region of Kosovo is called. At night, the fires dotted the plain. Only a handful of electric lights shone, presumably from Serb generators. Refugees have long reported that the region's supply of electricity has been cut.

The burnings show no discernible pattern. The fires did not appear to be set in blocks of houses, but were more randomly spread out, although often two or three nearby buildings burned.

In Jablanica, for example, most houses remained untouched but some were gutted by fire. The walls of two three-storey houses next to each other still stood but their roofs were gone, their interiors burned black and their windows just dark holes. Piles of charred wood and rubble were all that remained of two other houses, which also had stood side by side.

A yellow bulldozer sat idle next to the burned and flattened buildings. And in the roofs and walls of others, large holes gaped where, villagers said, shells had landed when the Serbs attacked two weeks ago.

It was at that point that even the most defiant of Jablanica's residents fled for the mountains. Most took the Savina Voda road up to Kula Pass and down to the Montenegrin border town of Rozaje. Others drove their tractors and cars straight into the mountains, abandoned them in the bushes and trees when the terrain became too steep and rocky. These foothills of the Prokletije Mountains are now littered with red tractors and cars. One new Volkswagen Passat had been carefully parked and its doors locked before being abandoned.

The makeshift tents in the valley are also nearly all empty now. Two weeks ago, its remaining residents said, about 300 people drove or walked into the gorge. They tore or sawed branches off the trees, bending them over into semi-circles that they lined up and strapped together with twine. Over these frames they laid plastic sheeting, weighed down by heavier branches that lay across the outside of the tents. Inside they slept on mattresses and blankets they brought with them. Some managed to pack their tractors' trailers with pans and utensils and food. Some even brought their wood-burning stoves. Soon, however, the Serbs started shelling the valley. No one was hit but the attack was enough to make most people flee to Montenegro.

The detritus of their temporary lives in the valley remains. Children's T-shirts lie in the mud. Pots still sit on stoves, half full of food. Mattresses and comforters and pillows cover the ground in the tents.

Overhead, NATO planes fly by, heard but not seen. On the other side of a mountain the sound of Serb shelling, anti-aircraft artillery and machine-gun fire echoes across the valley. No one pays attention unless the boom is a particularly loud one.

On Tuesday, Zejnepe, Jeton Zekaj's aunt, had a visitor in the one-room mountainside shack that now houses six people.

Concerned about his mother, Zejnepe's son Haki, 35, made the trip from outside Kosovo that he has been making every few days for the past three weeks. Passing through thigh-deep snow-banks that bore the footprints of wolves and bears, Haki trudged over the punishing peaks and through the backways of a forest, known to be the temporary home of a group of notoriously aggressive Yugoslav army reservists. In recent days, several ethnic Albanian men making the journey have gone missing and one reportedly had his throat slit by the reservists.

Haki, his wife and their three children fled Kosovo but his mother refuses to leave. So he risks his life to check up on her.

Zejnepe has more reason than most to fear the Serbs. They killed her husband a few weeks ago.

She and her family lived mainly in Pec, although they owned half of the large building in Jablanica that the Zekaj family lived in. When the NATO bombing started and the Serbs started to shell Pec and clear out its residents, Zejnepe's son Naim, 30, and her husband Musa, 68, took turns standing on guard at the front door of their four-bedroomed two-storey house.

At about 1 a.m. on Friday, March 26, Musa replaced Naim on guard.

"My son went to sleep and my husband went out a couple of times but there was nothing there," said Zejnepe, her eyes narrowing with tears. "Then we heard two shots."

Zejnepe found her husband's body in the doorway. Two cars sped away into the night.

Later in the day the family fled Pec for Jablanica, where they buried Musa in the afternoon. "He never did any evil to anyone," Zejnepe said. "He never did any wrong."

Like everyone else in Jablanica, she and the family left the village two weeks ago when the Serbs started shelling. But she's gone as far as she's going to go, she said.

"I hope to see Pec again,' she said. 'I will not leave unless I see them burning this house."

East Timor

JANINE DI GIOVANNI

In This Well There Are An Estimated Thirty Rotting Bodies

In August 1999 East Timor voted in favour of full independence from Indonesia. In response, pro-Jakarta militias, with the connivance of the occupying Indonesian army, began a rampage against pro-independence East Timorese.

The Times, 23 September 1999

You smell death before you see it. Inside the overrun garden of the independence leader Manuel Carrascalao, the sick, sweet smell leads to a corner where the well is full of bodies. The corpse at the top is covered with live worms. The body is bloated and discoloured, the skin leathery and burnt. The dead man's arms jut in front as though he had tried to prevent himself from falling farther down the well. He is not there alone. The Australian soldier guarding the destroyed villa reckons that there are nearly 30 bodies thrown inside; to judge by the discoloration of the corpse I saw, they have been there about two weeks.

All over Dili there are bodies. In a sewage tunnel in a remote and burnt-out shopping complex, a man in blue shorts, dead maybe two weeks, lies face up. You can see his ribs. His guts are ripped out of his torso and swim alongside him. His head is nearly skeletal. He floats among debris, sweet wrappers and moss. Pigs sniff the ground nearby.

Near the sea, overlooking the mountains, is a small river called Kampung Alor. In another time or place it might be idyllic; now it is contaminated. Floating among tin pots and long green weeds is a man of indistinguishable age, size and weight. He's wearing brown jeans. A crowd of children stand on the banks and stare.

Nearby there is more. Next to what once was the Prigondani restaurant in Hudi Laran district there is a vacant field. The corpse lying there for two weeks was buried yesterday by local people, who couldn't bear the dead man's indignity. "He has no name," one man says. "Maybe he comes from Sami, a nearby village, but nobody knows for sure."

This is day three of a liberated Dili but the militia who killed these men are still on the streets. Major-General Peter Cosgrove, the Australian head of the peacekeeping mission, called it "a dangerous 24 hours". Sander Thoenes, the *Financial Times* Jakarta correspondent, was killed on Tuesday night by soldiers who were possibly militia, possibly Indonesian Army. Early yesterday morning United Nations soldiers go to inspect the body. In the distance is a column of heavy black smoke coming from the vicinity of the Santa Cruz cemetery, where in 1991 an estimated 200 people died, protesting against Indonesian occupation.

Driving through ghostly streets, empty of people, it is clear that the militia has been at work. The houses are burning with freshly lit fires. Through the thickness of the smoke small groups of Indonesian soldiers getting ready to return to Jakarta are standing on corners smoking. Their barracks, as well as houses, are burning. It is clearly a scorched-earth policy designed to leave behind nothing that Indonesia built. The soldiers are not friendly. Who started these fires? "No comment!" they scream. One puts up a middle finger. Are they going back to Jakarta? "No!" another one shouts.

In Aituri Laran, near Kuluhun, a pro-independence village and scene of numerous clashes before and after the referendum on independence, the town is on fire. Either the militia or the military started throwing grenades into houses at 9 am and burning them in a last-ditch attempt to destroy. Thick columns of smoke rise from the houses, loud explosions come from within. Soldiers with the Indonesian Army Battalion 744, which is based there, stand and watch. They say they didn't do it; the villagers say they did.

"It's difficult for us to control the militias," says one soldier weakly. "We tell them to stop but they don't."

Truckloads of Kopassus, special forces wearing red berets, drive by jeering at the flames. An old farmer emerges from his house: "It was the army, not the militia, who started it," he whispers. "I saw them. They had red berets."

"Today they're burning Julio Varres's house," says Fernando da Cruz, a teacher who was shot in the hip by militia ten days ago. "Even though the UN troops are here, the militias are still in control."

The Falantil, the armed force of the East Timorese resistance, have been living in the mountains protecting the people who fled the fighting during the militia rampage. Although they have launched guerrilla attacks before, the Falantil were given specific orders by their leader, Xanana Gusmão, that they were not to engage in fighting with the militia.

Since the UN has arrived, the refugees have been returning slowly to their villages to try to find food. Then, still fearful of the militias, they climb back to the mountains clutching coconuts, sacks of rice or mangos.

Reaching the Falantil involves a trip across a dried-out riverbed, driven by a local supporter of the National Council of Timorese Resistance. Approaching a steep hill where the camp is clearly visible, the driver beeps his horn until he is waved forward into the camp where the Falantil have temporarily located.

Now they seem intent on launching their own vigilante attempt to find militia members and bring them to justice. "We will not kill them, we will just bring them back to the mountains and try to get the bad out of them," says Comandante Agosto. His camp is in a compound formerly used by the Brimob, the Indonesian special mobile police force.

His men carry spears and small knives, and today they have captured a hostage: an Aitarak militiaman who sits barefoot on a bench. He is Lorenzo Dotal, and the Falantil captured him as he was trying to escape town.

What does a killer look like? Completely innocuous, which demonstrates that while many of the militiamen were bent on destruction and killing, others might have been coerced into joining by intimidation or the promise of money. Lorenzo is middle-aged and slight, with two tattoos on his left arm. He looks harmless until you see his eyes. He joined the militia four months ago when he was offered the equivalent of $3 a month and given explicit orders to "go and kill pro-independence people". He says he killed only two people but that he burnt down many, many houses. He threw grenades and sometimes followed them with petrol. He says: "I feel bad now but I needed the money."

He adds ominously that Aitarak are still in town operating under the noses of the UN, and that his leader, Eurico Guterres, instructed all his men to keep on killing until there were no proindependence people left. "If we saw them in the street we were supposed to kill them," he says.

He claims the Indonesian Army was "directly involved" with supplying the militia with training and weapons. He does not think Aitarak will die. Guterres, who now operates out of West Timor, has said the Australians should be prepared to take home a thousand body-bags.

Many of the former militia leaders – including the notorious EMP (Red White and Iron), who recruited with a policy of terror, death threats and intimidation from ordinary peasants, old people and young boys – are now re-establishing themselves in West Timor.

The Aitarak are still in evidence in Dili, but yesterday, at the former headquarters, conveniently located next door to Carrascalao's well, Australian troops arrested several members and confiscated a cache of home-made weapons: crude grenades, spears, knives, handmade rifles with stickers reading "I fought for autonomy". One soldier says: "They left these behind because they've got better ones now."

Also left behind on the floor is a computerised list detailing 550 names of members, their professions and the amount they were paid. It is a chilling record of the militia: most are students, unemployed or government workers, and the highest figure they were paid was around $15 a month.

The militia list is a terrible indictment. Whether the men on it were tortured and forced to join or whether they genuinely wanted to fight for autonomy with Indonesia, there is now a computerised list showing each and every one of their names and the amount of money that each received. Should there ever be a war crimes tribunal established, it is an important document that the Aitarak, in their haste to leave, failed to destroy.

Comandante Agosto is stunned when he sees the list. "I know this family – I know this man," he says. "I had no idea this many people had joined." Maybe, like Lorenzo, they were coerced into joining – or maybe they simply like to kill.

Nobody is sure when the corpses in Carrascalao's gardens will be removed, but the house is already haunted. In April Carrascalao had 143 refugees and members of his family hiding inside when militia charged the house. They killed 12 people, including his 18-year-old son.

One of his cousins also died at the hands of the militias. The people had taken refuge in Carrascalao's house following the arrival of a heavy influx of paramilitary forces trained by the Indonesian Army arriving from Jakarta. On April 17 there was a pro-autonomy rally in Dili in front of the Governor's office attended by a number of the militia groups. It was there that Guterres urged his followers to "conduct a cleansing of all those who had betrayed integration."

Carrascalao's personal tragedy in a sense mirrors the tragedy of East Timor – it could have been prevented. Earlier he had gone to the Indonesian Army and begged them to send guards to protect the unarmed refugees. Colonel Tono Suratman refused to guard the house. "The military must remain neutral," he told Carrascalao.

After the massacre a distraught Carrascalao barged into a meeting between Bishop Carlos Belo and the Irish Foreign Minister, David Andrews. Incoherent with grief, he sobbed: "My son is dead!"

Last week I met Carrascalao shortly before he boarded a flight for Lisbon. He told me that he did not feel safe in Jakarta. The death of his 18-year-old son, Manuelito, at the hands of the militia has clearly affected the independence leader. As his family sat around a table cheering and clapping a television reporter who said the Indonesian Army had clearly worked with the militias, he called East Timor the "killing fields". In the same breath he said, without much conviction, that he was optimistic that "East Timor will rebuild itself". But even as he said it he sounded doubtful.

Wandering through the ruins of his ransacked villa is eerie. There is the usual rubbish and debris, the aftermath of a militia gone wild.

But it is hard to describe the emotional impact of finding a family photograph lying in shards of glass. It is a photograph of Carrascalao surrounded by his children.

Now his house is destroyed, his family diminished, and there are faceless, nameless bodies floating in his garden well. They may never be identified, their families may never know what happened to them or how they met their gruesome end.

Although Carrascalao insists that East Timor will heal, it is difficult to imagine that he – or anyone else who lived through the terror here – can ever heal themselves.

The War in Afghanistan

ROBERT FISK

My Beating by Refugees
Is a Symbol of the Hatred
and Fury of this Filthy War

A month after the terrorist attacks of 11 September 2001, the US
and British began military action against al-Qaeda and the extrem-
ist Islamic Taliban government in Afghanistan which succoured
the group. Robert Fisk is the veteran war correspondent for the
London-based *Independent*.

Independent, 10 December 2001

They started by shaking hands. We said "Salaam aleikum" –
peace be upon you – then the first pebbles flew past my face. A
small boy tried to grab my bag. Then another. Then someone
punched me in the back. Then young men broke my glasses,
began smashing stones into my face and head. I couldn't see for
the blood pouring down my forehead and swamping my eyes.
And even then, I understood. I couldn't blame them for what
they were doing. In fact, if I were the Afghan refugees of Kila
Abdullah, close to the Afghan-Pakistan border, I would have
done just the same to Robert Fisk. Or any other Westerner I
could find.

So why record my few minutes of terror and self-disgust
under assault near the Afghan border, bleeding and crying like
an animal, when hundreds – let us be frank and say thousands

– of innocent civilians are dying under American air strikes in Afghanistan, when the "War of Civilisation" is burning and maiming the Pashtuns of Kandahar and destroying their homes because "good" must triumph over "evil"?

Some of the Afghans in the little village had been there for years, others had arrived – desperate and angry and mourning their slaughtered loved ones – over the past two weeks. It was a bad place for a car to break down. A bad time, just before the Iftar, the end of the daily fast of Ramadan. But what happened to us was symbolic of the hatred and fury and hypocrisy of this filthy war, a growing band of destitute Afghan men, young and old, who saw foreigners – enemies – in their midst and tried to destroy at least one of them.

Many of these Afghans, so we were to learn, were outraged by what they had seen on television of the Mazar-i-Sharif massacres, of the prisoners killed with their hands tied behind their backs. A villager later told one of our drivers that they had seen the videotape of CIA officers "Mike" and "Dave" threatening death to a kneeling prisoner at Mazar. They were uneducated – I doubt if many could read – but you don't have to have a schooling to respond to the death of loved ones under a B-52's bombs. At one point a screaming teenager had turned to my driver and asked, in all sincerity: "Is that Mr Bush?"

It must have been about 4.30pm that we reached Kila Abdullah, halfway between the Pakistani city of Quetta and the border town of Chaman; Amanullah, our driver, Fayyaz Ahmed, our translator, Justin Huggler of the *Independent* – fresh from covering the Mazar massacre – and myself.

The first we knew that something was wrong was when the car stopped in the middle of the narrow, crowded street. A film of white steam was rising from the bonnet of our jeep, a constant shriek of car horns and buses and trucks and rickshaws protesting at the road-block we had created. All four of us got out of the car and pushed it to the side of the road. I muttered something to Justin about this being "a bad place to break down". Kila Abdullah was home to thousands of Afghan refugees, the poor and huddled masses that the war has produced in Pakistan.

Amanullah went off to find another car – there is only one thing worse than a crowd of angry men and that's a crowd of angry men after dark – and Justin and I smiled at the initially friendly crowd that had already gathered round our steaming vehicle. I shook a lot of hands – perhaps I should have thought of Mr Bush – and uttered a lot of "Salaam aleikums". I knew what could happen if the smiling stopped.

The crowd grew larger and I suggested to Justin that we move away from the jeep, walk into the open road. A child had flicked his finger hard against my wrist and I persuaded myself that it was an accident, a childish moment of contempt. Then a pebble whisked past my head and bounced off Justin's shoulder. Justin turned round. His eyes spoke of concern and I remember how I breathed in. Please, I thought, it was just a prank. Then another kid tried to grab my bag. It contained my passport, credit cards, money, diary, contacts book, mobile phone. I yanked it back and put the strap round my shoulder. Justin and I crossed the road and someone punched me in the back.

How do you walk out of a dream when the characters suddenly turn hostile? I saw one of the men who had been all smiles when we shook hands. He wasn't smiling now. Some of the smaller boys were still laughing but their grins were transforming into something else. The respected foreigner – the man who had been all "salaam aleikum" a few minutes ago – was upset, frightened, on the run. The West was being brought low. Justin was being pushed around and, in the middle of the road, we noticed a bus driver waving us to his vehicle. Fayyaz, still by the car, unable to understand why we had walked away, could no longer see us. Justin reached the bus and climbed aboard. As I put my foot on the step three men grabbed the strap of my bag and wrenched me back on to the road. Justin's hand shot out. "Hold on," he shouted. I did.

That's when the first mighty crack descended on my head. I almost fell down under the blow, my ears singing with the impact. I had expected this, though not so painful or hard, not so immediate. Its message was awful. Someone hated me enough to hurt me. There were two more blows, one on the back of my shoulder, a powerful fist that sent me crashing against the side of the bus while still clutching Justin's hand. The passengers were looking out at me and then at Justin. But they did not move. No one wanted to help.

I cried out "Help me Justin", and Justin – who was doing more than any human could do by clinging to my ever loosening grip asked me – over the screams of the crowd – what I wanted him to do. Then I realised. I could only just hear him. Yes, they were shouting. Did I catch the word "kaffir" – infidel? Perhaps I was wrong. That's when I was dragged away from Justin.

There were two more cracks on my head, one on each side and for some odd reason, part of my memory – some small crack in my brain – registered a moment at school, at a primary school called the Cedars in Maidstone more than 50 years ago when a tall boy building sandcastles in the playground had hit me on the head. I had a memory of the blow *smelling*, as if it had affected my nose. The next blow came from a man I saw carrying a big stone in his right hand. He brought it down on my forehead with tremendous force and something hot and liquid splashed down my face and lips and chin. I was kicked. On the back, on the shins, on my right thigh. Another teenager grabbed my bag yet again and I was left clinging to the strap, looking up suddenly and realising there must have been 60 men in front of me, howling. Oddly, it wasn't fear I felt but a kind of wonderment. So this is how it happens. I knew that I had to respond. Or, so I reasoned in my stunned state, I had to die.

The only thing that shocked me was my own physical sense of collapse, my growing awareness of the liquid beginning to cover me. I don't think I've ever seen so much blood before. For a second, I caught a glimpse of something terrible, a nightmare face – my own – reflected in the window of the bus, streaked in blood, my hands drenched in the stuff like Lady Macbeth, slopping down my pullover and the collar of my shirt until my back was wet and my bag dripping with crimson and vague splashes suddenly appearing on my trousers.

The more I bled, the more the crowd gathered and beat me with their fists. Pebbles and small stones began to bounce off my head and shoulders. How long, I remembered thinking, could this go on? My head was suddenly struck by stones on both sides at the same time – not thrown stones but stones in the palms of men who were using them to try and crack my skull. Then a fist punched me in the face, splintering my glasses on my nose, another hand grabbed at the spare pair of spectacles round my neck and ripped the leather container from the cord.

I guess at this point I should thank Lebanon. For 25 years, I have covered Lebanon's wars and the Lebanese used to teach me, over and over again, how to stay alive: take a decision – any decision – but don't do nothing.

So I wrenched the bag back from the hands of the young man who was holding it. He stepped back. Then I turned on the man on my right, the one holding the bloody stone in his hand and I bashed my fist into his mouth. I couldn't see very much – my eyes were not only short-sighted without my glasses but were misting over with a red haze – but I saw the man sort of cough and a tooth fall from his lip and then he fell back on the road. For a second the crowd stopped. Then I went for the other man, clutching my bag under my arm and banging my fist into his nose. He roared in anger and it suddenly turned all red. I missed another man with a punch, hit one more in the face, and ran.

I was back in the middle of the road but could not see. I brought my hands to my eyes and they were full of blood and with my fingers I tried to scrape the gooey stuff out. It made a kind of sucking sound but I began to see again and realised that I was crying and weeping and that the tears were cleaning my eyes of blood. What had I done, I kept asking myself? I had been punching and attacking Afghan refugees, the very people I had been writing about for so long, the very dispossessed, mutilated people whom my own country – among others – was killing along, with the Taliban, just across the border. God spare me, I thought. I think I actually said it. The men whose families our bombers were killing were now my enemies too.

Then something quite remarkable happened. A man walked up to me, very calmly, and took me by the arm. I couldn't see him very well for all the blood that was running into my eyes but he was dressed in a kind of robe and wore a turban and had a white-grey beard. And he led me away from the crowd. I looked over my shoulder. There were now a hundred men behind me and a few stones skittered along the road, but they were not aimed at me – presumably to avoid hitting the stranger. He was like an Old Testament figure of some Bible story, the Good Samaritan, a Muslim man – perhaps a mullah in the village – who was trying to save my life.

He pushed me into the back of a police truck. But the policemen didn't move. They were terrified. "Help me," I kept shouting through the tiny window at the back of their cab, my hands leaving streams of blood down the glass. They drove a few metres and stopped until the tall man spoke to them again. Then they drove another 300 metres.

And there, beside the road, was a Red Cross-Red Crescent convoy. The crowd was still behind us. But two of the medical attendants pulled me behind one of their vehicles, poured water over my hands and face and began pushing bandages on to my head and face and the back of my head. "Lie down and we'll cover you with a blanket so they can't see you," one of them said. They were both Muslims, Bangladeshis and their names should be recorded because they were good men and true: Mohamed Abdul Halim and Sikder Mokaddes Ahmed. I lay on the floor, groaning, aware that I might live.

Within minutes, Justin arrived. He had been protected by a massive soldier from the Baluchistan Levies – true ghost of the British Empire who, with a single rifle, kept the crowds away from the car in which Justin was now sitting. I fumbled with my bag. They never got the bag, I kept saying to myself, as if my passport and my credit cards were a kind of Holy Grail. But they had seized my final pair of spare glasses – I was blind without all three – and my mobile telephone was missing and so was my contacts book, containing 25 years of telephone numbers throughout the Middle East. What was I supposed to do? Ask everyone who ever knew me to re-send their telephone numbers?

Goddamit, I said and tried to bang my fist on my side until I realised it was bleeding from a big gash on the wrist – the mark of the tooth I had just knocked out of a man's jaw, a man who was truly innocent of any crime except that of being the victim of the world.

I had spent more than two and a half decades reporting the humiliation and misery of the Muslim world and now their anger had embraced me too. Or had it? There were Mohamed and Sikder of the Red Crescent and Fayyaz who came panting back to the car incandescent at our treatment and Amanullah who invited us to his home for medical treatment. And there was the Muslim saint who had taken me by the arm.

And – I realised – there were all the Afghan men and boys who had attacked me who should never have done so but whose brutality was entirely the product of others, of us – of we who had armed their struggle against the Russians and ignored their pain and laughed at their civil war and then armed and paid them again for the "War for Civilisation" just a few miles away and then bombed their homes and ripped up their families and called them "collateral damage".

So I thought I should write about what happened to us in this fearful, silly, bloody, tiny incident. I feared other versions would produce a different narrative, of how a British journalist was "beaten up by a mob of Afghan refugees".

And of course, that's the point. The people who were assaulted were the Afghans, the scars inflicted by us – by B-52s, not by them. And I'll say it again. If I was an Afghan refugee in Kila Abdullah, I would have done just what they did. I would have attacked Robert Fisk. Or any other Westerner I could find.

The Iraq War

ANTHONY SHADID

A Boy Who Was "Like a Flower"

Having worked for the *Boston Globe*, Associated Press and the *Washington Post*, Anthony Shadid was, at the time of his death from an asthma attack in Syria in February 2012, foreign correspondent for the *New York Times*. The many awards accorded his journalism include the Pulitzer Prize for International Reporting in 2004 (for his coverage of the Iraq War) and 2010, and the George Polk Award for Foreign Reporting in 2003 and 2012.

Washington Post Foreign Service, 31 March 2003

Baghdad, March 30 – On a cold, concrete slab, a mosque caretaker washed the body of 14-year-old Arkan Daif for the last time.

With a cotton swab dipped in water, he ran his hand across Daif's olive corpse, dead for three hours but still glowing with life. He blotted the rose-red shrapnel wounds on the soft skin of Daif's right arm and right ankle with the poise of practice. Then he scrubbed his face scabbed with blood, left by a cavity torn in the back of Daif's skull.

The men in the Imam Ali mosque stood somberly waiting to bury a boy who, in the words of his father, was "like a flower." Haider Kathim, the caretaker, asked: "What's the sin of the children? What have they done?"

In the rituals of burial, the men and their families tried, futilely, to escape the questions that have enveloped so many lives here in fear and uncertainty. Beyond some neighbors, family, and a visitor, there were no witnesses; the funeral went unnoticed by a government that has eagerly escorted journalists to other wartime tragedies. Instead, Daif and two cousins were buried in the solitude of a dirt-poor, Shiite Muslim neighborhood near the city limits.

The boys were killed at 11 a.m. today when, as another relative recalled, "the sky exploded." Daif had been digging a trench in front of the family's concrete shack that could serve as a shelter during the bombing campaign that continues day and night. He had been working with Sabah Hassan, 16, and Jalal Talib, 14. The white-hot shrapnel cut down all three. Seven other boys were wounded.

The explosion left no crater, and residents of the Rahmaniya neighborhood struggled to pinpoint the source of the destruction. Many insisted they saw an airplane. Some suggested Iraqi antiaircraft fire had detonated a cruise missile in the air. Others suggested rounds from antiaircraft guns had fallen back to earth and onto their homes.

Whoever caused the explosion, the residents assigned blame to the United States, insisting that without a war, they would be safe. "Who else could be responsible except the Americans?" asked Mohsin Hattab, a 32-year-old uncle of Daif.

"This war is evil. It's an unjust war," said Imad Hussein, a driver and uncle of Hassan. "They have no right to make war against us. Until now, we were sitting in our homes, comfortable and safe."

As he spoke, the wails of mourners pouring forth from homes drowned out his words. He winced, turning his head to the side. Then he continued. "God will save us," he said softly.

At the mosque, hours after the blast, Kadhim and another caretaker prepared Daif's body for burial – before sundown, as is Islamic custom.

Bathed in the soft colors of turquoise tiles, the room was hushed, as the caretakers finished the washing. They wrapped his head, his gaze fixed, with red and yellow plastic. They rolled the corpse in plastic sheeting, fastening it with four pieces of white gauze – one at each end, one around his knees and one around his chest.

Kadhim worked delicately, his gestures an attempt to bring

dignity to the corpse. He turned Daif's body to the side and wrapped it in a white sheet, secured with four more pieces of gauze. Under their breaths, men muttered prayers, breaking the suffocating silence that had descended. They then moved toward the concrete slab and hoisted the limp body into a wood coffin.

"It's very difficult," said Kadhim, as the men closed the coffin.

On Friday, he had gone to another mosque, Imam Moussa Kadhim, to help bury dozens killed when a blast ripped through a teeming market in the nearby neighborhood of Shuala. The memories haunted him. He remembered the severed hands and heads that arrived at the Shiite mosque. He recalled bodies, even that of an infant, with gaping holes.

"It was awful and ugly," he said. "This is the first time I've ever seen anything like this."

In an open-air courtyard, the men set the coffin down on the stone floor of a mosque still under construction. In two rows, they lined up behind it, their shoes removed before them. Their lips moved in prayers practiced thousands of times.

"God is greatest," they repeated, their palms facing upward in supplication.

In the background, men discussed the war. In the repression and isolation that reigns in Iraq, rumors often serve as news, and the talk today was of carnage unleashed on a convoy taking the body of an 80-year-old woman to be buried in the southern city of Najaf, where U.S. forces are confronting Iraqi irregulars and soldiers.

For Shiite Muslims, Najaf is among their most sacred cities, housing the tomb of Ali, the son-in-law of the prophet Muhammad, whom Shiites regard as his rightful heir. Tradition has it that the dying Ali asked his followers to place his body on a camel and bury him wherever it first knelt; Najaf was the site. Millions of pilgrims visit each year, and devout Shiites will spend their life's savings for the blessings of being buried in the vast cemeteries that gird the city.

The woman from Rahmaniya never made it. Residents said U.S. forces attacked three cars, one carrying her body. It was another ignominy visited on the city, the men agreed. They insisted that infidels would never enter the city by force of arms.

The U.S. siege of the city – its severity accentuated as rumors circulated – was an act of humiliation.

"It's a disgrace," said Hattab, one of Daif's uncles.

Hussein, another relative, echoed the words of others. "They didn't come to liberate Iraq," he said, "they came to occupy it."

In his words was a fear that strikes deep into the Iraqi psyche. Many worry that the U.S. invasion is a threat to their culture and traditions. They wonder if an occupation would obliterate what they hold dear, imposing an alien culture by force on a society that, in large part, remains deeply conservative and insulated.

"We don't want the Americans or British here. Our food is better than their food, our water is better than their water," he said.

With the prayers over, the men hoisted Daif's coffin over their heads. They left through the mosque's gray, steel gates and ventured into the desolate, dirt streets awash in trash. Some were barefoot and others wore sandals.

"There is no god but God," one man chanted. "There is no god but God," the pallbearers answered. Bombing on the horizon provided a refrain. The men crossed the street, past concrete and brick hovels, the Shiite flags of solid black, green, red and white flying overhead.

As they approached Daif's house, its door emblazoned with the names Muhammad and Ali, they were greeted with wails of women covered by black chadors. They screamed, waving their hands and shaking their heads. The cries drowned out the chants, as the coffin disappeared indoors. The despair poured out of the home, its windows shattered by the blast that killed Daif.

"My son! My son!" his mother, Zeineb Hussein, cried out. "Where are you now? I want to see your face!"

The men in Daif's family embraced each other, sobbing uncontrollably on their shoulders. Others cried into their hands. From within the house came the sounds of women methodically beating their chests in grief.

In the houses along the street, neighbors and relatives spoke of injustice – a resonant theme in the lives of Shiites Muslims, whose saints and centuries of theology are infused with examples of suffering and martyrdom.

"We're poor. We can't go anywhere else. What is the fault of the families here? Where's the humanity?" asked Abu Ahmed, a 53-year-old neighbor sitting in a home with three pictures of Ali and a painting of his son, Hussein. "I swear to God, we're scared."

Their talk was angry, and they were baffled.

If the Americans are intent on liberation, why are innocent people dying? If they want to attack the government, why do bombs fall on civilians? How can they have such formidable technology and make such tragic mistakes?

In Hussein's Iraq, with a 30-year-political culture built on brutality, some were convinced the Americans were intent on vengeance for the setbacks they believed their forces were delivered in Basra and other southern Iraqi cities. Others, in moments of striking candor, pleaded for the United States and Britain to wage war against their government, but spare the people.

"If they want to liberate people, they can kick out the government, not kill innocent civilians," one relative said. "The innocent civilians are not in business with the government. We're living in our houses."

Before dusk, Daif's coffin was carried from his house. It was set on the back of a white pickup truck headed for the cemetery. As it drove away, kicking up clouds of dirt, some of the neighbors and relatives shouted, "God be with you." Other men waved, a gesture so casual that it suggested the strength of their faith, that they would eventually be reunited with Daif.

Hattab, the uncle, looked on at the departing coffin. His eyes were red, and his face was drawn.

"He has returned to God," he said. "It's God's wish."

The Iraq War

DAVID ZUCCHINO

US Troops Find Lions and Luxury in Palace

A foreign correspondent for the *Los Angeles Times*, David Zucchino
has covered wars in Libya, Afghanistan and Iraq. He won a Pulitzer
Prize in 1989, and has four times been a Pulitzer finalist, including
for his reporting from Iraq in 2003. His books include *Thunder
Run: The Armored Strike to Capture Baghdad*.

Los Angeles Times, 11 April 2003

For the record, Saddam Hussein prefers Italian suits, double-
breasted, by Canali and Luca's. He favors silk ties in solids or
subtle patterns and brushes with Colgate.

The dictator's clothes were hanging Thursday in the ward-
robe of a luxurious upstairs bedroom in one of the dozens of
compounds within a palace complex that stretches 2 miles along
the west bank of the Tigris River here.

On a coffee table lay a wedding album containing photos of
Hussein cutting a wedding cake, and on a bureau were snapshots of his sons.

Lt. Col. Philip deCamp, commander of a tank battalion that
pounded its way onto the palace grounds Monday, rifled through
the photos. He let out a soft whistle, amazed to be standing in the
room where Hussein apparently had slept, perhaps very recently.

"Hey," deCamp said, pointing to three packed suitcases in an
anteroom. "It looks like he left in a pretty big hurry."

Thursday was a day of revelations for the armored crews and commanders camped at the palace – one of dozens built by Hussein, who is known for changing his location almost nightly – as the battle for Baghdad wore on. They discovered a pen of emaciated lions, cheetahs and bears on the palace grounds, and a stroll through the rose gardens revealed the corpses of Iraqi soldiers blown up by U.S. tank shells.

Scouts from the U.S. Army's 3rd Infantry Division found a live sheep and fed it to a cheetah, which was joined in the feast by three lions. Across the pen, a thin brown bear cub bounded through the grass, dragging the entrails of a sheep provided earlier by the same scouts. The soldiers laughed in approval.

On the other side of the palace, an engineer battalion tore into the dry earth with backhoes to dig graves. Local Iraqis were recruited to ensure that the bodies were properly washed in the Muslim tradition and buried facing Mecca. They had buried 15 by mid afternoon, with scores more waiting in the gardens and in bunkers carved into the riverbank.

The palace was so large deCamp had his men count the rooms and wrote down the numbers: 142 offices, 64 bathrooms, 19 meeting rooms, 22 kitchens, countless bedrooms, one movie theater, five "huge ballrooms" and one "football-field sized monster ballroom."

In Hussein's bedroom, deCamp thumbed through a *Newsweek* magazine on a nightstand. The cover story was "Inside America's new way of war," an examination of high-tech U.S. weaponry.

"Guess he was trying to get ready for us," said deCamp, who commands the 4th Battalion in the 3rd Infantry Division's 2nd Brigade – the brigade that took central Baghdad.

DeCamp later climbed into his Humvee, and the sergeant behind the wheel cruised past more palace compounds. There were swimming pools, exercise rooms with treadmills and bikes, movie theaters, palm trees and pruned pink rose bushes.

In the parks lay Iraqi corpses not yet recovered by the engineers. At the base of a bridge, deCamp spotted two bloated forms – believed to be the remains of drivers who had tried to ram their vehicles into U.S. tanks.

Afghanistan

CHRISTINA LAMB

Have You Ever Used a Pistol?

Christina Lamb is the Foreign Correspondent of the *Sunday Times* and the author of *Small Wars Permitting: Dispatches from Foreign Lands*, 2008.

Sunday Times, 2 July 2006

"Have you ever used a pistol?" yelled Sergeant-Major Mick Bolton amid the Kalashnikov fire and bursts from a machine-gun as we ran across a baked-mud field and dived for cover. "If it comes down to it, everyone's going to have to fight."

Round after round fizzed past our ears, sending up clouds of dust. My heart was thudding crazily against my flak jacket, my breath coming in short, rasping pants.

The whoosh of a rocket-propelled grenade (RPG) close enough to lift the hairs on the back of my neck was followed by an orange blaze of flame as it landed nearby.

I hurled myself into an irrigation ditch and crouched amid the tall reeds, the soil just above me flying up as bullets landed all around. Then firing started coming from behind too. The Taliban had us from three sides.

It was late last Tuesday afternoon. Justin Sutcliffe, the photographer, and I were with the elite of the British Army, 48 men of C company, the 3rd Battalion the Parachute Regiment – with an attachment of airborne troops of the Royal Irish Regiment – facing a bunch of Afghans in rubber sandals.

We could not see them, but we knew they were less than 100 yards away.

The silver-haired sergeant-major had kept us amused for days with his wisecracks, behind which was a touching concern for his soldiers and adoration for the girlfriend he was due to marry in November, whose photo he had shown me.

Now this veteran of two tours in Iraq and six in Northern Ireland was telling us we were the closest he had ever come to being "rolled up".

"If we get overrun I'll save the last bullet for myself," said Private Kyle Deerans, a handsome South African of 23. With his black floppy hair, I was sure he had broken a string of hearts.

In horror, it dawned on me what had been wrong about Zumbelay, the village we had just visited on a hearts and minds mission with soft hats and offers of development projects. I should have noticed there were no children around.

There was no more time to think about that as a mortar landed nearby. "Get out of the ditch!" screamed someone.

I wanted to stay in hiding. "No, no, it's not safe," said Lee, a military policeman attached to the unit, tugging me away.

I clawed my way up the slippery bank, oblivious to the thorns ripping my hands. I felt terrifyingly exposed as I climbed over the mound and rolled down the other side. "Keep down! Keep down!" came another shout. As I flattened myself, a mortar landed just where I had been crouching.

For the next two hours we were trapped under such relentless fire we thought we would be killed. The ambush of our lightly armed patrol not only was unexpected but also brought into question the entire strategy being pursued by the British in Helmand, the huge province they have taken on.

The paras had been in lively mood earlier that day when we left Camp Price, the British base at Gereshk, a sprawling town of walled compounds, two bridges and a bazaar. C company is a close-knit group and the trip was the furthest east they had ventured since arriving in Gereshk two months ago.

The plan was to go to Zumbelay, meet villagers, then camp before stopping at another village on the way back.

Some of the soldiers had not been out of the camp before and none had experienced a "contact" with Taliban, unlike their fellow paras in A company who have had what they describe as a "fruity" time and were engaged alongside British special forces further north.

To keep the men occupied, Major Paul Blair, C company's wiry Irish commander, had organised an "iron man" contest the day before involving ordeals such as flipping a giant tyre and sprinting round the camp carrying boxes of ammunition.

As we set off with cold drinks and Pringles, we joked about going on a picnic.

"Aggressive camping is what I call it," said Colour Sergeant Michael Whordley.

They laughed at me in my local dress of shalwar kameez worn with desert boots and a flak jacket.

We were in a convoy of 15 vehicles, an assortment of Snatches – the lightly armoured Land Rovers that have caused such controversy over their vulnerability to roadside bombs in Iraq – open troop-carriers and Wmiks, open Land Rovers that look a bit like safari vehicles except for the machine-gun on the front and heavy guns mounted on top. Their firepower would save us.

As we drove out of Gereshk we noticed a man in a black turban pull out on a motorbike and follow alongside for a while. But we could hardly hide our intentions, sending up clouds of dust visible for miles as we travelled east through the desert.

Long ago, when the Russians occupied Afghanistan, I travelled around on the backs of motorbikes of anti-Soviet mujaheddin who went on to become Taliban. Even back in 1989 they regarded them as the best transport against a fixed army.

The journey east took about 90 minutes through a landscape of undulating sand and gullies in temperatures close to 55°C.

We were close to Zumbelay by late afternoon – that special time of day when fingers of fading sunlight trap the dust being churned up by men returning to the village with herds of goats.

Most of Helmand is desert but Zumbelay seemed a small oasis. Bedouin tents and mud-walled houses, some with courtyards of flowers, were scattered amid a patchwork of fields of tall green grass and dried poppy stalks. A wide canal ran through one side, with deep irrigation ditches leading off between fields.

The convoy stopped about a mile from Zumbelay. A fire support group (FSG) drove off in the Wmiks with a mortar team to take up a secure position beyond a ridge to protect us in the event of trouble.

The rest of us downed helmets and walked in, crossing a field where a few scrawny camels gazed at us. I caused hilarity by falling into a ditch.

Everyone commented how quiet and bucolic the village seemed. "All it needs is a nice pub where we could enjoy a cold pint," joked Major Blair as we watched a kingfisher swoop low over the water in a flash of bright green.

Even the name had a nice ring to it: Zumbelay made me think of Manderley from Daphne du Maurier's *Rebecca*. Of course Manderley had a sinister secret and in retrospect the quiet of Zumbelay was suspicious. The one thing we should have noticed was the lack of children, who usually come running up demanding pens or baksheesh.

We sat on a raised bank at the edge of the field under a mulberry tree along with a few other men, one of whom seemed to be glaring at us from under his sparkly prayer cap.

"We are British not Americans," explained the major through an interpreter. "We come at the invitation of your government as friends and brothers to help you and find out what you need."

An old man with a white beard said the other elders were at the mosque for prayers. (Later we would realise it was not prayer time.) He said the village had no problems and suggested we come back for tea two days later on Thursday at 10am when everyone would be around.

As we took our leave, he pointed in the opposite direction to the way we had come.

"If you go that way there is a bridge," he said.

Afghans are the most hospitable people on earth, offering everything when they have nothing. I was thinking it was unlike them not to offer tea to visitors; but Major Blair seemed happy. "I think that went well – they seemed quite friendly," he said to me as we walked away.

Almost immediately a burst of gunfire rang out from the ridge to the left where the FSG was deployed.

"We've had a contact," came the message over the radio.

They had spotted a gathering of 12–14 men dressed in black and armed. Two of the support group's vehicles had peeled off to try to intercept them; but as they did so RPGs started to rain in on the support base – followed by small arms fire.

For a moment we stood staring up at the ridge listening to the gunfire and explosions. Then we started walking again through a field, looking for the bridge.

Within seconds we heard the staccato crack of Kalashnikovs. I threw myself into a ditch as bullets whizzed overhead. "Helmets on!" shouted someone. "Put your f****** helmets on!"

I followed the paratroopers, running for our lives across the fields. The ground had been ploughed weeks before and had baked hard into dry, treacherous ridges. We stumbled over the furrows, with bullets and loud explosions all around us. I wished I was wearing camouflage instead of the blue press flak jacket and helmet that made me so visible.

I did not see Justin fall as we ran. "I lost my footing and managed to turn onto my back as I ploughed into the ground, my body armour taking the impact of the fall," he said later.

"Looking up, a rocket-propelled grenade flew over our heads about 10ft above, bursting in the field near a group of paras who had made the sprint in better time.

"I struggled back to my knees in time to see the first mortar round land exactly where we had been only half a minute earlier. The troops returned fire. A prolonged burst of rapid machine-gun and rifle fire. Then, using white phosphorus grenades as cover, they moved left to take up firing positions behind the ridge.

"Again we were diving to the ground to avoid incoming fire, but this time it was to our left flank as well as the original direction. Feeling very exposed, we returned fire and ran back to a ridge along the field at right angles to our position.

"Once again we took incoming fire, this time from behind us. Their mortars seemed mercifully slow at retargeting and they fell where we had just left."

All around me was shouting and screaming. The two platoons had been scattered by the ferocity of the ambush. In the deep ditches their radios were not working. The soldiers were releasing canisters of red or green smoke to show each other their positions, even though this would reveal them to the Taliban too.

The firing came again and again, with hardly any break in between. The 8ft deep irrigation ditches which crisscrossed the fields had turned into trenches. In and out of them we climbed, slipping in the muddy water as the paras tried to regroup, yelling instructions I did not understand, such as "Go firm!", which means stay still.

"When we shout 'rapid fire', run!" yelled Corporal Matt D'Arcy as we crouched in yet another ditch. "Rapid fire!" he screamed and, ears ringing amid a clatter of heavy fire that I could not identify as ours or theirs, I forced myself to climb out of the trench.

One of the Afghan interpreters stayed praying and moaning in the ditch until Private Deerans, the handsome South African, grabbed him by the collar and kicked him out.

I thought about my husband Paulo and our six-year-old son Lourenco back home in East Sheen, southwest London; of the World Cup birthday party Lourenco was due to have this afternoon; and how stupid it would be to die in this Helmand field from a Taliban bullet.

In my belt purse were some of Lourenco's toy cars and pens he had given me for the "poor children of Afghanistan". I had taken them to the village but never got a chance to give them out. I had to survive and the image of my son's face kept me running and jumping into yet another trench.

Frantically, I looked around for Justin. We have worked together on and off for years, surviving everything from arrest in west Africa to abduction in Pakistan and regard each other as a kind of talisman. In the confusion we had split up and I had no idea if he was all right.

In fact he was with Major Blair, a usually charming man, who was very angry indeed.

"Where's the f****** air support?" the major was yelling on the radio to British headquarters at Camp Bastion, reading off a GPS position.

"Two A10s 10 minutes away can be with you for 20 minutes," came the reply. Nothing arrived.

"We need air support. Where's the air support?" Major Blair radioed again after sliding on his back in another trench, pulled down by the weight of the kit on the mud.

The message came back that the A10s had been called off to Sangin, a village to the north where two British special forces had been killed. No other planes were available because fighting was still going on.

Why they were more important than us was unclear.

"We're going to have to get out of this alone," Blair said. He checked the grenades on his belt. Later he explained: "I was counting them because I thought the fight would get down to 25 yards."

I was in a group led by Corporal D'Arcy. At one point we ran one way back towards the village only to be fired on from that direction.

"They're playing with us like chess pieces," shouted the corporal. The Taliban clearly had someone on the ridge to the right of us directing movements, for they were constantly changing position.

I ran again and found myself in a trench with the platoon snipers, including Private Deerans. Some used .338 Magnum rifles, which sounded like a cannon. Others were armed with Minimi 5.56s, the army's lightweight machine-gun.

"Look, two over there behind that white mound!" shouted Sergeant Whordley, who at 39 is in his last year in the army.

Known as the Buzzard, the sergeant usually controls the helicopters in and out of camp, but he had begged to go along on the patrol. "In 22 years of service I've never been in anything like that," he said later.

"Got him!" shouted Private Deerans as a man in a blue shalwar kameez and short beard popped out from behind the mound and straight into his sights to be hit in the chest. "I f****** killed him!"

The day before I had learnt that a private like him earns just over Pounds 1,000 a month, and that the British Army is the only one in the world whose soldiers pay tax while overseas.

"Happy days!" shouted someone back. I looked at him incredulously. This was the worst day of my life by an awfully long way.

In the 19th century thousands of Englishmen spilt their blood on fields like this and I didn't want to join them. I thought about John Reid, the former defence secretary, glibly saying he hoped to complete the three-year British mission to Helmand without a shot being fired.

Why were we there? Why had we thought the Afghans would not fight – they defeated the Russians after all. And why did everyone in Kabul and London keep insisting nobody in

Helmand really wanted to support the Taliban but were being forced to?

What if they were wrong? After all, almost everyone in the province now depends on growing poppies. Whatever the British commanders might say, villagers must see the presence of British troops as threatening the opium trade.

I thought back to a conversation with Captain Alex McKenzie, commander of the FSG, before the patrol began. "We've never been out to these villages and want to see what kind of reaction we get," he had said, adding that, according to US intelligence, there were between six and eight medium-level Taliban commanders in the valley less than a mile to the north.

"If you ask me, what we get is a Taliban attack," I had said to Justin.

"How much ammo have you got left?" Corporal D'Arcy called to his snipers. Were we running out? And where was the promised air support? What about Britain's new Apache helicopters that we had all heard so much about?

"Targets at 10 o'clock! Targets at 10 o'clock!" shouted someone.

"No, don't shoot, they're civvies!" yelled Corporal D'Arcy.

"How can we f****** tell?" screamed someone else.

The firing had been going on for almost two hours and I was finding it harder and harder to run. I had thrown off everything, even dropping my notebook – something I have never done in 19 years as a foreign reporter – and, less wisely in Helmand's infernal heat, my water bottle.

I was gasping from thirst. Lee, the military policeman, saw my plight, thrusting the straw from his camel pack into my mouth and urging "Drink!" before pushing me to run again.

My helmet was almost falling off because of the broken strap I had never got round to fixing.

I have been in some hairy situations, not least in Afghanistan, a country that I love, where at the age of 22 I was trapped in trenches by Russian tanks with a group of mujaheddin. But this was the first time in my life that I thought I would not survive.

Worse, I looked at the taut faces around me and could see the soldiers thought that too.

I thought about all the things left undone in my life, words left unsaid or unwritten, but most of all, my little boy's big blue eyes and curly hair, and I just wanted it to stop.

We were under relentless fire from AK-47s, RPGs, mortars and a Dushka, a Russian-made heavy machine-gun.

Justin – separated in a trench with a group led by Major Blair – was under attack from all sides, but witnessed the turning of the battle.

"We were ordered out of the ditch and, under heavy covering fire, scrambled up the sides. Breaking towards the river, we came under fire again. This time there was a massive burst of fire from the FSG on the ridge directed at the Taliban."

The paras had managed to regroup impressively. The men of the FSG beat off their own ambushers, drove their vehicles to the south where they were more secure and then moved back along the ridge to our aid – with devastating effect.

"We could see the group of 10 to 15 men who engaged us moving towards the houses down below," said Captain McKenzie later, "so we let rip with the four 50-cal heavy guns.

"The force of the blast from those guns is so powerful it can rip off your arm without even hitting you. All that was left of those guys was a pink mist."

Down below we managed to get away from the fields of trenches and onto open ground, where I felt even less secure but the paras were much happier because they could see. They assured me it was all right to run across the exposed hillside.

"Single file with good spaces between! Single file!" barked Sergeant-Major Bolton.

"This is not Club Med!"

By that time it was 8.30pm and light was fading. Only then came the reassuring sound of the Apaches, almost two hours after they had been requested. With those overhead, we reached the vehicles and withdrew.

The battle was not over. There was only one way back to Camp Price and only one bridge back over the Helmand river. Major Blair was convinced the Taliban would lay an improvised explosive device (IED) or ambush us there. We could not go back to Zumbelay.

Instead we drove south through the desert. At last we had air support. I was in Major Blair's Land Rover and all the time his radio operator was in touch with the planes overhead.

On and on we drove through the bumpy sand until the pilots assured us there were no ACMs (anti-coalition militia) within a mile or so and we pulled the vehicles into a herringbone formation, where we would stay for the next few hours.

We all tumbled out of the vehicles and started talking, pumped up with adrenaline at having survived. Veterans of conflicts all over the world said they had never experienced such a battle, and none of us could believe we had survived unscathed.

"I've never been in anything as intense as that," said Major Blair. "That was a 360-degree battle."

Everyone was stunned at how quickly the Taliban had organised themselves and how co-ordinated they had been. From the time we had walked into the village to the start of the ambush was less than an hour and they had been undeterred by our array of hardware.

"That's as bold as it comes," said Captain McKenzie, shaking his head in awe. "The Taliban are quite ingenious but they've probably got 25 dead blokes and we've got none, and that speaks volumes."

Private Deerans said: "We don't tend to think the Taliban can fight as well as us, but they're fighting for something they really believe in and they have the advantage of local terrain. They're world class at getting rounds down but fortunately their shooting was crap.

"Still, it was close enough for me. They had the advantage from the beginning and I don't know how none of us got shot." Some of the men realised they had forgotten to wear their wedding rings that day.

"I have my fiancee's ring on a string and it's the first time I've gone on an operation without it," said Sergeant-Major Bolton.

I looked at my own bare finger, remembering how while checking in for my flight at Heathrow 20 days earlier I had realised the two rings I always wear were in an oyster shell by the side of my bed.

The big question was whether the villagers were in on the ambush. It seemed clear to me they had directed us straight into it, and there must have been locals fighting for them to organise so quickly.

"Maybe they were coerced by the Taliban," said Major Blair. The official British line is that 80% of the population of

Helmand are "floating voters" stuck between a rock and a hard place of an evil Taliban and a government in Kabul that does nothing for them.

It seemed more likely to me that they feared the British had come to take away their source of income, the poppy.

While we were discussing this, another burst of gunfire rang out. Surely we were not under attack again? "Hush," warned the sergeant-major. "Everyone still and quiet. It's not over yet."

We still had to get back across the bridge into Gereshk, and we needed air support.

I lay on the warm sand staring up at the stars that covered the sky. In the distance were flashes I first thought were shooting stars until someone told me it was from the fighting at Sangin.

I looked at my watch. It was after midnight Afghan time, mid-evening in Britain. I realised that had I been in England I would have been at a summer party on the roof of New Zealand House in Haymarket, central London.

For the next two hours Camp Bastion kept telling us that "all assets" were tied up in Sangin where the snatch raid on four Taliban commanders had succeeded in getting two of them before descending into a bloody firefight where Harriers, Apaches and A10s had all been called in.

Surely they weren't going to leave us to go back on our own?

In between his radio pleas for air support, Captain McKenzie and I discovered we grew up near each other, although I had done so a good 10 years before him, and knew the same pubs.

It was after 1.30am when we finally got the nod for air support – only to find three of our Snatches had got bogged down in the sand. Amid all the stars we could just see the lights of two American A10s, anti-tank aircraft of awesome firepower.

"How long have we got air for?" asked Major Blair as spades were used to dig the vehicles out. "Forty more minutes," came back the pilot's American accent. After that they would have to refuel.

Major Blair checked his watch. It was going to take a good half an hour to get to the bridge and some of the Snatches were still stuck.

I remembered Corporal Robert Jones, an American Humvee driver I had met, who had expressed horror at how exposed the British vehicles were. He had told me that if any American vehicles got bogged down for more than five minutes in Helmand they abandoned them.

"We just hate going west from Kandahar," he said. "It's all IEDs, RPGS, Taliban, Al-Qaeda. We call it Hell-man."

Eventually the vehicles were pulled out and we were on the road to the bridge. We reached it just before the planes had to refuel.

"Please don't let there be an IED," I prayed.

"Do you want me to give a show of force?" came the pilot's drawl over the radio.

"Could drop to 5,000ft and drop some flares."

"Many thanks," replied our controller and we laughed in relief at his very British reply as we crossed the bridge safely, white flares dropping all around.

It was first light as we drove into Camp Price to be met by those who had been left behind, half-anxious and half-envious. It was clear there was now a big question mark over the British hearts and minds operation.

"I'm going to have to review our approach to villages," said Major Blair. "We're going to have to go in with far more security. It's very annoying to think we were sitting there offering things and having a laugh and a joke with villagers who knew that five minutes later we'd be attacked."

More and more senior military officers are saying it has been an enormous mistake for British troops to move out of the main urban centres of Lashkar Gah and Gereshk and into outlying areas.

They blame the Americans – and some over-enthusiastic British generals – for dragging British forces into Operation Mountain Thrust, a large offensive against the Taliban in which some 500 people have died across the south, creating much local resentment.

What some have described as "military and developmental anarchy" may change when Lieutenant-General David Richards, Nato commander in Afghanistan, takes control of the Helmand operation on July 31.

On the military front, the general wants more fixed-wing aircraft and helicopters, and the British government is seeking more military support from its European allies. But General Richards has also been bashing heads together on the need to make some improvements in the lives of the Afghans.

Five years after the fall of the Taliban, Afghanistan still remains bottom of the list for almost every significant indicator from infant mortality to lack of access to water or electricity.

"We've got to stop talking and start doing," he said last week. "Otherwise we're in danger of losing this."

It may be just too late. Disillusion with the government of President Hamid Karzai has never been so high. The Taliban have reorganised, possibly with the help of both the Pakistani military intelligence and Al-Qaeda, to use the sophisticated tactics I experienced first hand in Zumbelay.

No longer are they just a few dozen ragtag fighters here and there. Now groups often include hundreds of heavily armed men equipped with motorbikes, cars and radios.

All over the south they have set up shadow administrations and kill any Afghan who is even indirectly associated with the government, such as teachers. About 1,500 Afghan security guards and civilians were killed by the Taliban last year and some 900 already this year.

The Taliban are also winning the propaganda game. Within hours of our return to Camp Price, the Afghan Islamic Press in Peshawar had put out a statement claiming the Taliban had killed seven British soldiers in Zumbelay.

Far from losing any men, the brave paras from C company had killed about 20 Taliban. Yet the Ministry of Defence put out nothing. If Justin and I had not been there, you would probably never have read about it.

Acknowledgements

Personal thanks go to: Michele Harrison for her knowledge and expertise in tracking down a copy of Langston Hughes' dispatch from Spain; my editor at Constable and Robinson, Duncan Proudfoot; the staff of the Brotherton Library, Leeds; and, as ever, my wife, Penny Lewis-Stempel.

The editor has made every effort to locate all persons having any rights in the selections appearing in this anthology and to secure permission from the holders of such rights. Any queries regarding the use of material should be addressed to the editor c/o the publishers.

Arnett, Peter, "Hill 875": Associated Press wire copy, 22 November 1967. Copyright © 1967 Associated Press. Reprinted by permission of Associated Press

Barnes, Edward, "When Freedom Came": *Weekly LIFE In The Times of War*, 11 March 1991. Copyright © 1991 LIFE

Barzini, Luigi, "The Battle in the Snows": *War Illustrated*, 9 August 1916

Bigart, Homer, "Reporter Rides Fortress in Wilhelmshaven Raid": Reprinted from *Forward Positions: The War Correspondence of Homer Bigart*, ed Betsy Wade, University of Arkansas Press, 1992

Bigart, Homer, "Hope This is the Last One, Baby": New York *Herald Tribune*, August 1945. Copyright © 1945 New York *Herald Tribune*

Bourke-White, Margaret, extract from *Taste of War*: Century, 1985. Copyright © 1944 Margaret Bourke-White. Renewed 1972 by the author/her estate

Browne, Malcolm W., extract from *The New Face of War*: Bobbs-Merrill, 1965. Copyright © 1965, 1968 Malcolm W. Browne. Reprinted by permission of Simon & Schuster Inc.

Burns, John F., "An Afghan Village, Destroyed at the Hands of Men Who Vowed Peace": *New York Times*, 27 October 1997

Cameron, James, extract from *Point of Departure*: Arthur Barker, 1967. Copyright © 1967 James Cameron

Cameron, James, "What a Way to Run the Tribe": *Evening Standard*, 11 June 1967. Copyright (C) 1967 ES London Limited

Caputo, Philip, "Running Again on the 'Street Without Joy' ": Chicago *Tribune*, 28 April 1975. Copyright © Chicago Tribune Company

Carpenter, Iris, "The First Girl Correspondent to Cross Rhine at Remagen": extracted from *Women War Correspondents of World War II*, Lilya Wagner, Greenwood Press, 1989

Cowles, Virginia, "Killed in Finnish Snow": *Sunday Times*, February 1940. Copyright © 1940 *Sunday Times*

Crane, Stephen, "Stephen Crane at the Front for the *World*": *World*, 7 July 1898

di Giovanni, Janine, "In This Well There are an Estimated Thirty Rotting Bodies": *The Times*, 23 September 1999. Copyright © 1999 *The Times*. Reprinted by permission of News International Syndication

Dimbleby, Richard, extract from *Richard Dimbleby: Broadcaster*: ed. Leonard Miall, BBC Books, 1966. Copyright © 1966 British Broadcasting Corporation

Dos Passos, John, extract from *Journeys Between Wars*: Constable & Co, 1938

Fetterman, John, "P.F.C. Gibson Comes Home": Louisville *Times*, July 1968. Copyright © Louisville *Times* 1968

Fisk, Robert, extract from *Pity the Nation*: André Deutsch, 1990. Copyright © 1990

Fisk, Robert, "My Beating by Refugees Is a Symbol of the Hatred and Fury of this Filthy War": *Independent*, 10 December 2001. Copyright (C) 2001 The *Independent*

Fox, Robert, "The Liberation of Goose Green": BBC News, 30 May 1982. Copyright © 1982 British Broadcasting Corporation

Fritz, Mark, "No Hard Feelings": Associated Press, 13 May 1994. Copyright (C) 1994 AP

Gallagher, O. D., "The Relief of the Alcazar": *Daily Express*, 30 September 1936. Copyright © 1936 Express Newspapers Ltd

Gallagher, O.D., "The Loss of *Repulse*": *Daily Express*, 1941. Copyright © 1941 Express Newspapers Ltd

Gellhorn, Martha, extract from *The Face of War*: Hart Davis, 1959. Copyright © 1945 Martha Gellhorn. Copyright renewed 1993.

Gott, Richard, "The Last Journey of Che Guevara": *Guardian*, 11 October 1967

Hanrahan, Brian, "Argentine Air Attacks": BBC News, 22 May 1982. Copyright © 1982 British Broadcasting Corporation

Hastings, Max, "Max Hastings Leads the Way: The First Man into Port Stanley": *Evening Standard*, 1982. Copyright © 1982 Max Hastings and the *Evening Standard*. Reprinted by permission of Solo Syndication

Hemingway, Ernest, extract from "Voyage to Victory": *Collier's*, July 1944. Reprinted from *By-Line Ernest Hemingway*, ed. William White, Collins, 1968. Copyright © 1944 Crowell-Collier Publishing Company, Mary Hemingway, Ernest Hemingway By-Line Company. Reprinted by permission of Charles Scribner's Sons, an imprint of Macmillan

Herr, Michael, extract from *Dispatches*: Alfred Knopf, 1977. Copyright © 1968, 1970, 1977 Michael Herr

Hersey, John, "Survival": *New Yorker*, 17 June 1944. Copyright © 1944 F-R Publishing Corporation (New Yorker Magazine Inc.)

Hersh, Seymour M., "My Lai: Lieutenant Accused of Murdering 109 Civilians": *St Louis Post-Dispatch*, 13 November 1969. Copyright © 1969 St Louis-Dispatch

Higgins, Marguerite, extract from *War in Korea*: Doubleday, 1951. Copyright © 1951 Marguerite Higgins

Hughes, Langston, "Hughes Bombed in Spain": *Baltimore Afro-American*, 23 October 1937. Copyright (C) 1937 Afro American News & Information Consortium

Kipling, Rudyard, extract from *Something of Myself*: Macmillan & Co, 1937. Reprinted by permission of Macmillan

Kirk, Donald, "I Watched Them Saw Him Three Days": Chicago *Tribune*, 14 July 1974 copyright © Chicago Tribune Company

Kirkpatrick, Helen, "Helen Kirkpatrick Reports Sniper Attacks on French Leaders at Notre Dame Cathedral": Chicago *Daily News*, 26 August 1944. Copyright © 1944 Chicago *Daily News*

Kramer, Dale, "The Japanese Drink Bitter Tea Aboard the USS *Missouri*": *Yank*, 5 October 1945

Lamb, Christina, "Have You Ever Used a Pistol?": *Sunday Times*, 2 July 2006. Copyright (C) Times Newspapers/New International

Liebling, A.J., "Paddy of the RAF": *New Yorker*, 6 December 1941. Copyright © 1940 F-R Publishing Corporation (New Yorker Magazine Inc.)

London, Jack, "Beware the Monkey Cage": reprinted from *Jack London Reports: War Correspondence, Sports Articles, and Miscellaneous Writings*, ed. Hendricks *et al.*, Doubleday, 1970

Lucas, Jim, "Our Town's Business is War": Scripps Howard, 3 January 1953. Copyright © 1953 Scripps Howard. Reprinted by permission

Malaparte, Curzio, "Steel Horses": extracted from *The Volga Rises in Europe*, Birlinn, 2000. Reprinted by permission of Birlinn Limited

McAllester, Matthew, "Crisis in Yugoslavia". *Newsday*, 2 February 1999. Copyright © 1999 Matthew McAllester. Reprinted by permission of Newsday Inc.

McCarthy, Mary, extract from *Hanoi*: Harcourt, Brace & World, 1968. Copyright © 1968 Mary McCarthy, renewed 1996 by James West. Reprinted by permission of Harcourt, Inc.

Morin, Relman, "Hatred to Stay". Associated Press wire copy, 25 September 1950. Copyright © 1950 Associated Press

Murrow, Edward R., extract from *This is London*: Cassell, 1941

Orwell, George, extract from *Homage to Catalonia*: Martin Secker & Warburg, 1938. Copyright © 1938, 1953 the Estate of Eric Blair. Reprinted by permission of the Estate of the late Sonia Brownell Orwell, Martin Secker & Warburg, Harcourt Inc. and A.M. Heath Ltd.

Panter-Downes, Mollie, "The Big Day" (originally published as "Letter from London"): *New Yorker*, 12 May 1945. Copyright © 1945 Mollie Panter-Downes

Philips Price, Morgan, "How the Bolsheviks Took the Winter Palace": *Manchester Guardian*, 27 December 1917. Copyright (C) Guardian Media

Pyle, Ernie, "German Supermen Up Close": Washington *Daily News*, 19 May 1943. Copyright © 1944 Scripps Howard Foundation. Reprinted by permission of the Scripps Howard News Alliance

Pyle, Ernie, "The Death of Captain Waskow": Washington *Daily News*, 1 January 1944. Copyright © 1944 Scripps Howard Foundation. Reprinted by permission of the Scripps Howard News Alliance

Ransome, Arthur, "War and Revolution": telegrams and *Daily News* article: Leeds University Library Special Collections, MS20C Ransome. Telegrams reprinted by permission of Leeds University Library

Reed, John, "The Coming of the Colorados": extracted from *Insurgent Mexico*, D. Appleton & Co., 1914

Remington, Guy, "Second Man Out": *New Yorker*, 19 August 1944. Copyright © 1945 F-R Publishing Corporation (New Yorker Magazine Inc.)

Rohde, David, "How a Serb Massacre Was Exposed": *Christian Science Monitor*, 25 August 1995. Copyright (C) 1995 Christian Science Monitor

Schanberg, Sidney H., "American Reporter's Brief Brush with Arrest and Death": *New York Times*, 9 May 1975. Copyright © 1975 New York Times Company

Shadid, Anthony, "A Boy Who was 'Like a Flower' ": *Washington Post* Foreign Service, 31 March 2003. Copyright (C) 2003 *The Washington Post*

Shaplen, Robert, "Lovely Americans": *New Yorker*, 19 November 1944. Copyright © 1944 F-R Publishing Corporation (New Yorker Magazine Inc.)

Shirer, William L., extract from *Berlin Diary*: Alfred A. Knopf Inc., 1939. Copyright © 1939 Alfred A. Knopf. Reprinted by permission of Don Congdon Associates and Alfred A. Knopf

Simpson, John, "The Bombing of Baghdad": *The Observer*, January 1991. Copyright © 1991 *The Observer*

Simpson, Kirke L., "Bugles Sound Taps for Warrior's Requiem": Associated Press wire copy, 11 November 1921. Copyright © 1921 Associated Press

Steinbeck, John, "It Was Dark as Hell": New York *Herald Tribune*, 4 October 1943. Copyright © 1943 New York *Herald Tribune*

Steer, George, "The Tragedy of Guernica Town Destroyed in Air Attack: Eyewitness's Account": *The Times*, 27 April 1937. Copyright (C) 1937 Times Newspapers/News International

Stowe, Leland, "Too Little, Too Late": *New York Post*, 25 April 1940. Copyright © 1943 *New York Post* and Chicago *Daily News*

Tomalin, Nicholas, "The General Goes Zapping Charlie Cong": *Sunday Times*, 5 June 1966. Copyright (C) 1966 Times Newspapers/News International

Trotsky, Leon, extract from *The Balkan Wars 1912–1913*. Trans. Brian Pearce, Monaad Press, 1980. Translation Copyright © 1980 the Anchor Foundation Inc.

Vogle, Paul, "Flight into Hell": UPI wire copy, 29 March, 1975. Reprinted from *55 Days: The Fall of South Vietnam*, Prentice-Hall, 1977

Werth, Alexander, extract from *The Last Days of Paris*: Hamish Hamilton, 1940. Copyright © 1940 Alexander Werth

Wheeler, John T., "Life in the V Ring": Associated Press wire copy, 12 February 1968

Whitehead, Don, "Linkup: US and Russian Troops Meet": extracted from *Beachhead Don: Reporting the War from the European Theater 1942–45*, ed. John B. Romeiser, Fordham University Press, 2004

Whitman, Walt, "The Great Army of the Sick": reprinted from *The Complete Writings of Walt Whitman*, New York, 1902

Zucchino, David, "US Troops Find Lions and Luxury in Palace": *Los Angeles Times*, 11 April 2003. Copyright (C) 2003 Tribune Company